The Dent
CONCERTGOER'S
COMPANION

The Dent
CONCERTGOER'S
COMPANION

Antony Hopkins

J. M. Dent, London

First published in two volumes
1: Bach to Haydn (1984)
2: Holst to Webern (1986)
First published in one volume 1993

Music examples set by Tabitha Collingbourne

Made and printed in Great Britain by
Butler & Tanner Ltd, Frome and London
for
J. M. Dent
The Orion Publishing Group
Orion House
5 Upper St Martin's Lane
London WC2H 9EA

British Library Cataloguing-in-Publication Data

A catalogue record for this book is available from
The British Library

ISBN hardback: 0 460 86109 3
ISBN paperback: 0 460 86112 3

Dedicated to the Malcolm who asked for it
but doesn't need it and to the Malcolm
who didn't ask for it but does.

CONTENTS

FOREWORD

Analytical notes in programmes can often cause more confusion than illumination since of necessity they are so concentrated that two or three sentences may have to cover music taking a substantial time to perform. All the same, major symphonic works are not always easy to understand fully, unless the listener has an educated ear. This book is an attempt to offer guidance to the musically uninitiated by the use of descriptive analysis which is (so far as possible) free from technical jargon. Such musical examples as there are are virtually all confined to a single line, omitting the additional complexity of supporting harmony which the average reader finds difficult to imagine in terms of sound; any musical terms that may be unfamiliar are explained at the time. Ideally the book should be read while listening to the chosen work on tape or disc since all the significant events are described in the manner of a running commentary.

The many omissions need more justification than the inclusions – for instance, why no Bruckner? It seemed to me impossible to give an adequate description of a symphony on Bruckner's scale without a very considerable number of music examples. Furthermore to have included him with Bach, Bartók, Beethoven, Berg, Berlioz, Brahms and Britten would have sufficed to fill an entire book without ever escaping from the Bs. I have tried to include a representative collection of the standard works in the orchestral repertoire. Composers as prolific as Haydn presented the biggest problem since I could hardly allow him space for 104 symphonies; I have therefore chosen a small selection of what are generally considered to be his finest.

The brief biographical essays are intended to make the composers themselves seem less remote, for I feel that the ability to identify oneself with the composer is often the way to enhance one's appreciation of his music. To take an obvious example, which of us can listen to late Beethoven without being affected by a knowledge of his deafness? While it is not always true that 'to know is to love', the prime purpose of this book is not to add to the sum of knowledge but rather to enhance affection and understanding. If it succeeds in doing that, I shall feel that my function of 'guide' will have been adequately fulfilled.

A.H.

INTRODUCTION
The Need for Form

Music is not like a picture. We cannot look at it in a single glance and then take in all the detail at our leisure. It exists in motion; it passes by, affecting us in one way or another, thrilling us with its climaxes, soothing us with its soft passages, puzzling us with its complexities, sometimes boring us or even rousing our antagonism. Within the span of a large-scale movement many events will happen, events that may be closely related or deliberately contrasted. If we are to understand music rather than merely to feel its emotional stimulus, we need to be aware of such relationships, to appreciate the contrasts, to understand the way a movement is planned. To do this we need to know the *form* of a piece, for listening to a Nocturne is a different experience from listening to a Fugue; listening to a Prelude by Bach is not the same as listening to a Prelude by Chopin or Debussy.

Most of the works described in this volume are symphonies or concertos. Many readers may already have a fairly clear idea of the ground-plan of such works; all the same it may be worth while to give a brief description of basic forms so as to avoid having to make the same points over and over again. At once we are confronted with a paradox; not one work in this book is called a sonata and yet nearly every work has at least one movement (usually the first) in 'Sonata form'. The word Sonata literally means a 'sounding' piece as opposed to Cantata, a 'singing' piece. Symphonies are really large-scale Sonatas for orchestra; Concertos are Sonatas for soloist and orchestra. Therefore although we are not concerned with Sonatas as a *genre*, we certainly need to have some understanding of the conventions of Sonata form, even if only to appreciate the way in which composers use form to create a sense of expectation and then to deny it. Surprise is the frustration of expectation; you cannot have a surprise unless you are expecting something to behave in a normal or orthodox manner and it then deviates from normality. Composers take much delight in this since to surprise us is to keep our interest alive. The reason why we need an understanding of form, then, is not so that we can apply the chilling hand of analysis but rather so that we can better appreciate inspired *departures* from it. It is these that help to give a work its vitality and originality.

Science fiction has given us an instinctive dread of clones; we value what is individual to each of us though we share a common mould of physical similarity. Sonata-form movements are not clones and it is a fundamental mistake to expect them all to conform to a pattern; but just as most people have the same number of eyes, arms, legs and ears and yet are all different, we can expect sonata-form movements to have some common factors. What they are I shall endeavour to explain.

The simplest analogy is to think of a play in three scenes. In Scene I we meet the characters; naturally there will be a contrast between them – masculine/feminine, aggressive/soothing, cheerful/sad – as the playwright chooses. Some link needs to be established between them to justify their being in the same scene.

In musical terms Scene I is the Exposition in which we meet two contrasting groups of ideas, the First Subject (seldom a single theme) and the Second Subject, usually more lyrical in character. The link that joins them is called a Bridge Passage. It has another function, though, and that is to 'modulate', to shift the music into a different key, or 'family' of notes. The 'home' key is called the Tonic and the Bridge Passage will most probably modulate to its nearest relative, the Dominant, the key whose 'home' is a fifth higher. If a symphony or sonata is 'in' C, the First Subject will be in that key; the Bridge Passage will modulate to G, a fifth higher, and the Exposition (Scene I) will end in that key.

In Scene II of our play we learn a lot we didn't know before about the characters; their relationships towards each other change; the aggressive man may show unsuspected tenderness, the unhappy girl may become more cheerful.

This in music is the Development in which the composer manipulates the material, effecting such changes as he wishes and even introducing new ideas if it suits his purpose. (This is especially likely to happen in a concerto where the soloist is liable to be permitted to roam free.) The music will probably modulate to more 'distant' keys – ones whose notes differ markedly from those of the 'home' key – while themes may change in mood or be disguised in numerous ways.

Scene III of our play appears to start exactly as Scene I did; the same characters appear in the same surroundings, but we now know much more about them and view them in a different light. To conclude there must be a denouement, a summing-up.

Musically this third section is known as the Recapitulation. It usually begins with a reprise of the First Subject followed by a modified Bridge Passage that does *not* modulate, allowing the Second Subject to appear in the 'home' key for the first time. To round the movement off we have a Coda, usually brief but sometimes very substantial.

This, with many subtle variations, is the basic form of the first movements of most symphonies, concertos, quartets and sonatas written between approximately 1750 and 1880. Many such movements have an Introduction, but it is by no means essential. Sonata form may also be used in finales or even, more rarely, in slow movements. What I have omitted to mention, because it departs from my theatrical analogy, is that the Exposition was normally repeated. This was to enable the listener to absorb the material and in particular to take in the relative proportions of the various ideas so that the changes carried out in the Development could be better appreciated. In this respect Concertos have an advantage over Symphonies since the first Exposition was usually given to the orchestra alone while the repeat featured the soloist.

The four-movement Symphony derives partly from the orchestral Suite of dances from an earlier period, partly from a type of Overture that was divided into contrasting sections. Essentially it was designed to satisfy the need for contrast but also to show that the composer could write music to appeal to the intellect (first movements), the sentiments (slow movements), wit (minuets or scherzos) and aspirations to glory (finales). But many finales are pure entertainment, in which case a likely form is the Rondo. As its name suggests a Rondo is a circular form in which one theme returns a number of times with intervening and contrasting episodes.

Slow movements are often in the form of Theme and Variations, a self-explanatory title, while the Minuet and Trio – later to become Scherzo and Trio – falls into several sections. The traditional Minuet form begins with two matching sections, each of which is repeated. There follows a central section called a Trio which is also usually in two parts, both repeated. The players then return to the beginning of the movement and play the first two sections without repeats. This movement is normally omitted from Concertos, the custom being to have three movements rather than four.

Forms are not rigid, and during the nineteenth and twentieth centuries many changes have taken place. We find the order of movements being changed, we find extra movements being added, we find symphonies in one movement, concertos without soloists, choral symphonies, symphonies for organ and so on. But only the most eccentric of composers will attempt to dispense with form entirely since it is not merely a framework for his ideas but an invaluable prop to the listener in his search for points of reference.

There are many books that devote far more space to the subject of Form than I have allocated here, but this brief survey should clarify the subject sufficiently for us to be able to embark on the voyages ahead with some of the necessary aids to navigation.

BACH

1685–1750

To pass a talent from father to son is common enough; but for that same talent to pass from generation to generation for a span of more than two centuries is altogether remarkable. Such was the case with the Bach family in the German province of Thuringia, for the first acknowledged musician to bear the name Bach was born around 1578 while the last died in 1846. Thus the musical inheritance continued unbroken for upwards of 250 years so that there was always at least one Bach – usually more – to carry on the tradition; yet for the concertgoer of today the name Bach needs no further identification, even the initials J.S. being superfluous. The eldest son, Carl Philipp Emanuel, may interest us for his historical importance in the development of a truly pianistic style of composition; Johann Christian, another son, may charm us with his anticipations of Mozart, on whom he had some influence when that prodigious child visited London; but among the multitude of musical Bachs Johann Sebastian stands a giant supreme, to be ranked amongst the greatest masters of all time.

As with most great and prolific composers, Bach's output falls into several categories, each of which makes different demands on the listener and which therefore should be approached in a frame of mind suitable to its purpose. First place must be given to the great religious works, the Passions, Masses, Oratorios and Cantatas, not only for their exceptional scale but also for their spiritual profundity. Secondly we find a number of orchestral compositions, the magnificent set of six Brandenburg concertos, the four orchestral suites, and a substantial group of concertos for one or more solo instruments of which some are admittedly transcriptions of compositions by Vivaldi while others are re-arrangements of his own work, as, for instance, the D minor keyboard concerto which is certainly a transcription of a violin concerto whose original version has been irrevocably lost. Thirdly comes the wealth of organ works, still unsurpassed by any later hand, to which, as a subsidiary if even larger category, we must add the repertoire for solo keyboard, the '48' Preludes and Fugues, the French and English Suites, the

Partitas, the Fantasias, Toccatas, the Inventions in two and three parts, the 'Italian' Concerto and the elaborate 'Goldberg' variations. Fourth would come the works for solo violin or cello, while a fifth category might be termed 'learned', and would include 'The Musical Offering' and 'The Art of Fugue'.

This last work, which the composer left incomplete, demonstrates his absolute mastery of the fugue as a musical form, a mastery which however brought him an undeserved reputation as a 'mathematical' and, by implication, an unfeeling composer. While it is true that certain works of his do presuppose an intellectual interest on the part of the listener, they represent a relatively small proportion of the total. Indeed if one were to search for a common factor in all the five categories I have suggested, it would be not the fugue but the dance. Even in such profoundly spiritual works as the *St. Matthew Passion* many arias are essentially dances in character, while far the larger proportion of the purely instrumental music is conceived in dance forms. The Allemande, the Gavotte, the Minuet, Sarabande or Gigue (Jig) came as naturally to Bach's pen as the Fugue, a fact which, once realised, instantly makes him far more accessible. The problem for the layman's ear lies in the multi-layered textures that Bach delighted in. Although he knew perfectly well how to write a long sustained melody over a simple accompaniment, he clearly preferred to give himself (and us) a greater challenge by weaving together a number of strands of more or less equal importance. It is the performer's duty to clarify the web of counterpoint, the listener's duty to accept that Bach is not a 'top-line' composer. However there are many works which are neither melodic nor contrapuntal, consisting as they do of harmonies broken up into undulating and, for the most part, unvarying patterns. A classic instance is the first prelude from Book I of the '48', which has no tune and no counterpoint, but whose repetitive patterns weave a hypnotic spell. Clearly we need to listen to such 'pattern' preludes in a wholly different way from a richly harmonised chorale, a festive chorus, or an elegiac sarabande for solo cello. More than with most composers we need to learn to accept Bach on the terms he offers us in his immensely varied compositions, for his textures may range from the huge complexity of a double chorus and orchestra to a single unaccompanied line, while his time-scale may vary from the immense span of the B minor Mass to a tiny minuet written for a beloved wife or child.

The Brandenburg Concertos

To his Royal Highness, Monseigneur Crêtien Louis, Margrave of Brandenburg.

Monseigneur,

As I had the honour of playing before Your Royal Highness a couple of years ago, and as I observed that You took some pleasure in the small talent that heaven has given me for music, and in taking leave of Your Royal Highness You honoured me with a command to send You some pieces of my composition, I now, according to Your gracious orders, take the liberty of presenting my very humble respect to Your Royal Highness, with the present concertos, which I have written for several instruments, humbly praying You not to judge their imperfection by the severity of the fine and delicate taste that every one knows You to have for music, but rather to consider benignly the profound respect and the very humble obedience to which they are meant to testify. For the rest, Monseigneur, I very humbly beg Your Royal Highness to have the goodness to continue Your good graces towards me, and to be convinced that I have nothing so much at heart as the wish to be employed in matters more worthy of You and Your service, for with zeal unequalled Monseigneur,

I am
Your Royal Highness's most humble and most obedient servant

Jean Sebastian Bach.[1]

So wrote Bach in unaccustomed French to the Margrave of Brandenburg in the spring of 1721. At the time he was at Cöthen where, since 1717, he had been in the service of the young Prince Leopold. It was one of the happiest periods of his life for the Prince had a genuine enthusiasm for music as well as a resident orchestra of eighteen musicians. Thus it was circumstance as much as inclination that caused him during the Cöthen period to devote his talents more to instrumental music than he had previously done. We do not know precisely how Bach came to meet the Margrave of Brandenburg – it was either in Meiningen or Karlsbad some time in 1719; what is certain, as the letter above reveals, is that Bach had played for him and in doing so had found another musical enthusiast among the aristocracy. Although it would be nice to believe that the so-called Brandenburg concertos were made to measure for the Margrave's own household orchestra, modern scholarship has established that this was not so; nor does the necessarily sycophantic dedication mention a specific commission. Perhaps the Margrave provided the incentive to write some of the concertos, but it seems that the set of six was a collection of varied works whose very different instrumentation would almost preclude their performance by one relatively small orchestra. Had they been written specifically for the Margrave's band, Bach would surely

[1]Albert Schweitzer, *J.S. Bach*, Vol. I, p. 404 (A.&C. Black, London, 1945).

have ascertained its composition and used a more or less comparable orchestration for all six works.

Although Bach himself called them concertos, they represent an evolutionary stage between the *concerto grosso* and the true solo concerto. The standard form in a *concerto grosso* was to establish a contrast between the main body of less skilled players (the *ripieno*) and a small group of more gifted performers capable of playing music that was technically more demanding (the *concertino*). The composer would control the performance from the harpsichord at his own discretion above a left-hand part that exactly corresponded with the orchestral bass (the *continuo*). The composition of the concertino group was largely dependent on a realistic assessment of the technical ability of the players available at the time; it might consist of three string players, or two oboes and a bassoon or even a mixture of wind and strings. What seems extremely unlikely is that if Bach was writing for the Margrave's resident orchestra he would have demanded so varied a range of potential soloists and yet employed them in such an inconsistent manner. Thus we find two horns, three oboes and a bassoon in the first concerto, of whom only one oboist is required further; the second concerto has an exceptionally demanding trumpet part, but the player is never used again; the third concerto is for strings alone, divided, uniquely, into three string trios of equal calibre; concerto no. 4 introduces two recorders, also for the only time, while the fifth concerto has an enormously important solo keyboard part in addition to a single flute and violin. As for the sixth concerto, it employs nothing but two violas, two *viole da gamba*, cello, double bass and continuo harpsichord, an exploitation of the lower string tones that surely has no parallel until Villa-Lobos wrote his *Bachiana Brasileira* for soprano and eight cellos.

In the conventional nineteenth-century use of the word Bach had little feeling for orchestration since, as we shall see, the blending of tone colours was not his prime concern. He seldom uses sustained chords on wind or brass to establish focal points of harmony as later composers did. For the most part his music is conceived in horizontal strands rather than vertical blocks; musical values were more important than mere colour; consequently we often find passages woven into a complex web of sound that is difficult for the untrained ear to disentangle. The harmonic framework of the music is perfectly clear but there is something of an excess of decoration strung across it. Whether he uses flutes or oboes or strings, they will all play the same material even if at different times, so much so that some parts are extraordinarily difficult to play since they pay little heed to the idiosyncrasies of the instrument concerned. For him a theme was a theme; its musical value would be unaffected whether it was played on a violin, a flute, an oboe or a trumpet. This is an attitude no nineteenth-century composer would have accepted. Even in Purcell's day instruments were seen to have a clearly defined character – the 'martial' trumpet, the 'tender, soothing' flute. While

Bach was certainly not indifferent to these characteristics, as his masterly choice of obbligato instruments in the Passions and cantatas shows, he seems to have felt that in purely instrumental compositions it might be entertaining for each instrument to bring its individual timbre to the same theme in turn, rather than to devise music appropriate to its inborn characteristics. To amplify the point a little, the choice of an obbligato instrument in a cantata will relate to the mood indicated by the text; a meditation on death might suitably be accompanied by an oboe d'amore, whereas the joyful news of the resurrection would call for a trumpet or, if it was a choral work, three trumpets. Such type-casting simply does not occur in the Brandenburgs.

Concerto No. 1 (in F major)

The first concerto of the set is enterprisingly scored for two horns, three oboes, bassoon and strings. There is an additional part for a *violino piccolo*, not, as is sometimes thought, the little dancing-master's fiddle, but a three-quarter size violin tuned a fourth higher than the normal instrument. The keyboard part is assumed though not written out. Although the bass line is usually shared by all those instruments capable of playing it — bassoon, cello, *violone grosso* (predecessor to the double-bass) and the harpsichordist's left hand — in this work Bach occasionally allocates passages specifically to the cello or bassoon alone.

The concerto begins with an exceptionally complex texture consisting of three distinct ideas: the horns have a fanfare whose occasional triplet rhythms are at odds with everything surrounding them, the oboes have a chattering semiquaver figure divided into three distinct parts; the bass instruments give characteristically sturdy support, albeit with a quite independent pattern. As for the violins, they quickly transfer their allegiance from the horns in bar 1 to the oboes in bar 2. Further complication is added by the viola and the third oboe, both of whom go their separate ways. Thus in bar 2 alone, where the horns are divided, there are in all seven different strands of music, none of which can be regarded as mere supporting harmony. After this initial free-for-all, lasting some eighteen bars, Bach begins to take his small orchestra apart so that we find a bar for strings, a bar for oboes, a bar for horns, then a brief *tutti*. The principle of blocks of sound is very evident here, but notice in this game of 'pass-the-parcel' it is not the identity of the instruments but the identity of the material that is preserved. Horns are no longer given the concession of conventional fanfares; they are expected to be as nimble as oboes or violins.

The movement continues with occasional though not substantial variations of material and it is here that we realise the huge difference between this and, say, a movement by Mozart or Haydn. There are no breaks, no half-bar silences before the presentation of a new idea, no double-bars with repeats, no cadenzas, no positive cadences to establish the dominant key (in this case C major). The music is woven into a continuous tapestry of sound but the rapid changes of sharply differentiated tone-colours, horns—oboes—strings, ensure that the ear is kept continually alert.

In the second movement we find something nearer to the conventional concept of orchestration, a melody at the top with a discreet accompaniment. The tune is given to the first oboe, the accompanying chords are on the strings with just the first beat underlined by the other two oboes. But in the fifth bar we find a swap round which would have been inconceivable to Mozart or Haydn: he gives the tune to the violino piccolo and transfers the accompanying chords to the three oboes. Oboes in those days were not unduly refined and although Bach marks them *p* and the violin *f* I cannot believe that the balance would ever have been satisfactory; it is hard enough to manage even with modern skills. In a third stage the tune is shifted down to the bass accompanied by sighing chords that alternate tenderly between oboes and strings. The musical content is sublime; the tone-colours are certainly crystal clear. However, the subtleties of balance are put firmly into the performers' court; Bach could not have been so unrealistic as to expect oboes to play as softly as violins; it seems therefore that the discrepancies in tone and volume between them did not perturb him, an attitude which a nineteenth century-composer would have found amateurish and inept. It is revealing that when he begins a long and elaborate canon between the first oboe and the violino piccolo (who follows a beat behind) the accompaniment is stripped bare so as not to obscure the contrapuntal interweaving of the two solo lines.

The movement ends with an intriguing dissolution of the orchestra, individual chords from the continuo group, the three oboes, the violins and viola in turn. This sudden fragmentation of sound is a striking effect, making a feature of the essentially differing tone-colours with an almost Webern-like economy.

The third movement, which surprisingly is not the finale, begins with the horns re-establishing their existence after their silence during the preceding adagio. However the first oboe and first violins are soon left in the clear, and the whole texture of this movement shows Bach letting in a good deal more air to the score than he did in the first movement. All the same, some combinations of sound are distinctly unusual as, for instance, when a solo horn, a solo violin and the bass line (without bassoon) play a trio that is distinctly uneasy in balance. The music is gloriously tuneful, though, and we are easily swept along by its rhythm, taking such oddities in our stride.

The two movements that follow, a Menuet and a Polacca, were probably added as an afterthought, a concession to the French taste which the Margrave was known to prefer. In some ways they are the most intriguing from the point of view of orchestration, in that Bach uses a genuinely full orchestral sound in the minuet without so much concern for counterpoint and using the horns far more conventionally. Certainly the virtuoso element so noticeable in the first three movements has been completely abandoned. As for the central Trio in the Menuet, it really is one, for two oboes and one bassoon.

Strangest of all is the second Trio (in the Polacca) where he puts three oboes in unison against two separate horn parts, presumably with the idea that three oboes equal one trumpet. It is a curious sound, certainly not to be found anywhere in Haydn, Mozart or Beethoven. Nor is the rhythmical structure of this Trio at all conventional, consisting as it does of a pair of three-bar phrases followed by a two-bar phrase. The horn parts throughout the concerto are frighteningly difficult, and Bach may well have learned from experience that they were too demanding since nothing like them occurs again.

Concerto No. 2 (in F major)

Although it is in the same key, the Second Concerto is surprisingly different from the first. The solo group, or concertino, is an oddly assorted mixture: trumpet, flute, oboe and violin. Such a selection brings home forcibly Bach's conception that even instruments so palpably different from each other could be regarded not merely as equals but as interchangeable. As in the first concerto, the opening bars (properly called a *ritornello* since they return a number of times) consist of a blend of several clearly differentiated themes. The trumpet spells out a straightforward if somewhat martial version of the notes of the common chord of F major, ending with a running ascent to the first of many high C's. (The trill on this sustained high note is sheer exuberance.) Meanwhile flute, oboe, solo violin and the first orchestral violins combine in unison to give rugged strength to the most important theme in the movement, a rustic dance tune with an irresistible bounce to it. As for the bass, it circles round in a surprisingly agile fashion for two bars, infecting the upper parts with a comparable rash of semiquavers in bars 3–4. With F major well and truly established, the solo violin breaks ranks and offers a cheerful little theme of rather more aristocratic breeding. After all, it is only right that the conversation of skilled soloists should be at a more elevated level than that of the common mob. But the common mob will have none of it and immediately return to their rustic cavorting. 'That was rather interesting – what you said just now . . .' says the oboe taking over the violinist's theme, while the violin has an accompanying figure that nods in agreement. But their conversation is again interrupted by the initial dance, bouncy as ever and given additional spice by a rush of semiquavers to the trumpeter's head. Flute and oboe now pick up the conversation where the oboe and violin had left it off, followed, after yet another rustic interjection, by the trumpet and flute. And so this marvellously logical construction is built up:

```
                                                                    ⎧ trumpet
                                                                    ⎨
                                              ⎧ flute               ⎩ flute
                                              ⎨
                      ⎧ oboe                  ⎩ oboe
                      ⎨
        violin        ⎩ violin

        2 bars        2 bars                  2 bars                2 bars

Tutti 8 bars │ · · · · · │ 2 bars │ · · · · · │ 2 bars │ · · · · · │ 2 bars │ · · · · ·
```

Ever present, of course, is the continuo — hence its name — providing the necessary bass and supporting harmonies via cello and harpsichord.

Up to this point each two-bar interpolation from the tutti or ripieno has been based on bars 1–2 of the movement, but now, the quartet of soloists all having had a say, Bach allows the ripieno a longer section based on bars 3–8 of the opening. From here on the tendency is for the solo parts to become more elaborate, introducing several new developments, while the ripieno, no longer content to sit back and listen for even two bars at a time, takes a continuously active part, even though it may not always be of great musical import. In due course, after some fifty-nine bars, a miniature fugue emerges, based on the elegant phrase introduced by the solo violin as far back as bar 9. The order of entries is flute, violin, oboe, trumpet; but no sooner has the trumpet finished its phrase than all four soloists are caught up once again in the general dance, this time in the unexpected key of C minor. Another extended section of some thirty-four bars ensues with the soloists showing off prettily while the ripieno either reminds us of the main theme or introduces interesting new elements ranging from organ-like sustained harmonies to mischievous syncopations. At last, in bar 103, there is a united agreement that it is time to restate the initial theme unadorned save for a cheerful variant on the trumpet. A brief and hushed excursion into a few foreign keys provides a moment or two of mystery before we emerge once more into the clear daylight of F major and the expected triumphant conclusion.

Not surprisingly the trumpet is omitted from the slow movement, partly for the practical reason that the player's lip will need a rest, but also because the instrument would be out of place in what is essentially a piece of chamber music since the main body of strings is also silent. Flute, oboe and violin share an exquisite trio, mostly in canon (exact imitation) while two cellos and harpsichord provide a constantly moving bass as well as such harmony as may be needed. This is minimal since the three solo lines are so interwoven as to provide both elegant counterpoint and expressive harmony.

The third movement has a truly arresting opening as the solo trumpet presents a brilliant fugue subject, pivoting around high C and even leaping daringly to a top F. Oboe, violin and flute pick up the ensuing entries but with no real hope of matching the exciting impact of the trumpet's clarion tones. A composer from a later period would surely have saved the trumpet for the fourth entry rather than the first so that it would provide a climax; as it is, Bach leads with his ace. The ripieno strings, awe-struck by the display of virtuosity from the concertino, delay their entry till the forty-seventh bar; even then it is a surprisingly tentative one and within ten bars they drop out again leaving the soloists to continue developing the fugue. In comparison to the bustling complexity of the first movement the ripieno has a relatively small contribution to make, Bach preferring to focus our attention on the brilliance of the quartet of soloists.

Before we leave this concerto a word should be said about the trumpet part which makes demands that find no parallel in Mozart, Haydn or Beethoven. It seems that there was a guild of trumpet players who had mastered the secret of playing very high and rapid passages on the valveless instruments of the day; for some inexplicable reason the secret was not passed on to succeeding generations. By comparison even Beethoven's trumpet parts are very unadventurous; in fact, even as recently as the 1930s Bach's writing was regarded as impractical and the part was often performed on a clarinet — not really an adequate substitute. The current preoccupation with authenticity in the preformance of Baroque music has produced a crop of players who have mastered the ancient skills and it would be surprising nowadays not to hear this exceptional piece played as Bach intended.

Concerto No. 3 (in G major)

At first glance the Third Concerto would seem to be the least interesting in orchestral colour even if the best blended since it is scored for a group of strings with no wind or brass to provide variety. A more careful look at the score shows that Bach devised a completely original, possibly unique disposition of his forces — three violin parts, three viola parts, three cello parts, plus the usual violone (double bass) and harpsichord to give support to the bottom line. While the work is often played by a string orchestra, eleven players would seem to be the ideal — even ten if the harpsichord is omitted as it frequently is in this work. The three-note figure with which the movement begins proves to be astonishingly fruitful, its passage from one group to another being like a sonic game which Bach plays with the greatest dexterity.

The first eight bars present the main theme in three-part counterpoint, violins, violas and cellos each grouped in unison as 'families' with the violas having a marginally less interesting part than their colleagues. The end of this brief exposition is made clear by a general agreement to converge on a descending scale of G major. No sooner is this done than the parties split up; a fragment of the initial theme (two beats' worth) is offered by the violins, accepted by the violas and then commented on by the cellos. It is a game that will be played a number of times in the movement though at this point it is cut short by a return to the second part of the theme which is agreed by all. Once more that fragment is passed from group to group but this time it leads to new developments culminating in a sturdy tune easily recognised by the three-fold repetition of its highest (and then its second highest) note. Suddenly the tone is reduced to *p* to allow us to hear a witty exchange between the lower and upper sections, tossing the tiny three-note pattern with which the work began between them like a ball. Other notable exchanges follow; for instance in bar 32 we find the opening theme in the bass in a new tonality — C major. The three violins greet this event with a chortle of delight, a bustling phrase all in semiquavers; but when the cellos restore their theme to G major it is the violas' turn to laugh. It is these constant interchanges that hold our attention since the thematic interest is continuously on the move. For instance, at one point (bar 47) the first violin decides to show off a bit with a miniature cadenza, causing the violas to mark time in admiration; but at bar 51 the second violin says 'I can do that as well, and what's more in a more awkward key'. In due course, after some further discussion of the three-note fragment, the third violin takes a turn at a similar passage, again causing the violas to stop in their tracks. The whole movement is full of such pleasantries. Three-quarters of the way through Bach has a joke at our expense; we have reached the point where we might legitimately expect a convincing return to the opening material (bar 78). Unsupported by anyone save the three viola players, the second violinist bravely sets out on theme 1 in its original form. Without warning the *first* violinist simultaneously embarks on a completely new idea whose first three notes (*doh-mi-soh*) remind us of the opening of the violin concerto in E major. The idea proves sufficiently attractive to divert the second violin off course, following his leader in fugal style. After a few bars of animated discussion they are joined by the third violin, supported by the third viola, and it looks as though the fugue is really going to develop. But it is not to be, and in one of the most memorable passages in the whole movement the fugue dissolves in a cloud of oscillating harmonies which descend to the alien world of B flat major. Here the first violin again embarks on a cadenza, reducing his colleagues to mere onlookers. More and more emphasis on the three-note fragment leads to an increasing desire to return to theme 1, which, after a murky passage through the underground, finally surfaces in triumph. 'Did you think "finally"?' says Bach and begins to tease us with the swiftest and most extensive juggling so far. One phrase, a single bar taken from the cadenza passages, appears on six different instruments in turn — Violin II, Violin I, Violin III, Viola I, Viola II, Viola III — all in the space of six bars. And then, for the first time, the cellos are allowed to gratify any ambitions they may have as soloists with an athletic cadenza five bars long which is finally released in a scattering of three-note fragments. At last the pieces converge and, after 125 bars, there is a genuine reprise of the opening theme to bring the movement to a close.

What follows has been the subject of much debate; can a single bar, marked *Adagio* and consisting of two chords, be regarded as a slow movement? Nothing has been lost, for this unique curiosity appears in mid-page in the manuscript. Was Bach really content to have this strange A-men and nothing more? Various solutions have been suggested, ranging from the interpolation of a slow movement from a trio sonata to the Draconian gesture of removing the bar completely. Majority opinion favours a cadenza either from the first violinist or from the unnoticed keyboard player, but one which would set out from the first chord and come to rest on the second. Bach, who it should not be forgotten was nearly as accomplished on the violin as the harpsichord, could easily have filled in with a spontaneous improvisation on either instrument.

The finale is a lively dance in which we initially get the impression that four couples take the floor in rapid succession, the circling semiquaver runs suggesting the girls' skirts swirling round while the strutting quavers evoke images of the proud male dancers. There are no pauses for breath and the two sections into which it is divided are both repeated, the first part being a mere twelve bars long, the second part three times as lengthy. The impetus never flags for a moment, though, while the basic figuration is maintained throughout, there are occasional moments of exhibitionism as there would be in any high-spirited folk-dance. Thus in bars 15–16 the first violin has a series of upward flips which have more than a suggestion of the excited squeals which girls traditionally give in folk-dancing when their partners lift them in the air. In bars 35–6 we find an exactly comparable display in the first viola part, the deeper timbre suggests that this time it is a male dancer who indulges in the high kicks while the others watch with bated breath. If the idea seems too fanciful, I would quote no less an authority than Professor Arnold Schering who in his introductory note to the Eulenberg score says without apology that the movement is a German *Ländler*, a peasant dance that has endured to this day.

Concerto No. 4 (in G major)

This concerto exists in two forms, either for violin solo, two recorders and the normal string ripieno or, in a less familiar version transposed down a tone to F major, with a keyboard replacing the violin. The idea of transcribing violin concertos onto the harpsichord did not seem at all strange to Bach and one could say with some degree of confidence that all the so-called solo keyboard concertos are transcriptions of violin works. Such an idea would have been virtually unthinkable in the nineteenth century even though Beethoven did make a piano version of his violin concerto at his publisher's request. It is also said that the scherzo of the Brahms B flat piano concerto originated from a sketch for a second violin concerto; even so one cannot imagine the music having anything like the same impact if it were to be transferred to the violin.

Bach specifies recorders (*flutes à bec*) rather than the normal flute (*flauto traverso*), a decision which dictates a marked difference of approach to the scoring. Compare the density of the opening pages of the First Concerto to the start of this work. In No. 1 we find two horns, three oboes and strings all playing at once in a complex web of sounds in varied rhythms; here the scoring is transparent, with the ripieno supplying soft dabs of harmony on each first beat to allow the recorders every chance of being heard. The music is light and airy, and the delicate tracery of the recorders (even when joined by the solo violin) stands out with wonderful clarity. As the movement develops we find long passages for solo violin, virtually unaccompanied, and it may well be that Bach found that he had taken economy too far here, prompting him to transfer the music to the harpsichord. However, despite its apparent light weight the first movement is very substantial in content, 427 bars in all as opposed to the mere eighty-three bars of the much more solidly orchestrated No. 1. The solo violin part is of true concerto dimensions with long passages demanding the utmost agility as well as an episode involving extensive use of double-stopping (pairs of notes played simultaneously a sixth apart.) Indeed this is as much on the way to being a violin concerto as the Fifth Concerto is to a harpsichord concerto. It is in such ways that these two works in particular may be seen as a transitional stage between the concerto grosso and the true solo concerto.

The second movement is a stately minuet in character if not in name. A notable feature is the way in which the quavers throughout are phrased in pairs. Knowing the Margrave's taste for French music this suggests that Bach was indicating that the players should observe a French style of playing known as *notes inégales* or unequal notes. It was an affectation designed to give extra grace to the music as much as to save the composer trouble in writing down a rhythm whose exact notation was anyway hard to indicate. (The written figure ♫♫ would be played somewhere between ♪♪♪ and ♫♫♫). Musically the most remarkable passages are to be found in the recorder parts, where a series of chromatic descents presents a severe test of intonation. Four bars from the end there is a brief cadenza for solo recorder which any player worth his salt would almost certainly have embellished. The movement ends interestingly enough with the identical two harmonies which constituted the enigmatic 'slow movement' of the Third Concerto.

The third movement is a vigorous fugue whose subject is presented boldly by the violas over a running bass. The order of entries is viola, second violins, first violins, cellos and lastly recorders, whose high D makes a thrilling effect. After some forty bars the solo violin and the two recorders are left on their own to delight us with a little fugue-within-a-fugue into which, after twenty-two bars, the violas trip decorously to usher in the supporting players. Before long the solo violin once again attempts to transform the work into a solo concerto with a lengthy display of virtuosity which reduces the recorders to silence. (One senses the strong influence of Vivaldi, whom Bach greatly admired.) Subsequently, when all the players have rejoined the fray, Bach begins to use his recorders and solo violin in an almost organ-like way, sustaining relatively slow-moving harmonies against a much more energetic contribution from the ripieno. Towards the very end of the work there is a dramatic piece of writing in which pairs of strong chords are followed by brief silences, as though the sheer effort of playing so forcefully demands a breathing space. The whole movement is a brilliant demonstration of Bach's contrapuntal skill, and although the display passages for solo violin may remind us of Vivaldi, there is nothing Vivaldi-like in the working-out of the fugue.

Concerto No. 5 (in D major)

If it seems probable that Bach would have played the solo violin part in the Fourth Concerto, it is virtually certain that he wrote the elaborate harpsichord part in this concerto with the intention of performing it himself. Not even in the solo keyboard concertos do we find so demanding a part, and the massive cadenza towards the end of the movement is conceived on a far grander scale than had hitherto been known. Bach had acquired a new and splendid harpsichord from Berlin in 1719 and he presumably wanted to exploit its capabilities to the full. The other two soloists involved, a flute and a violin, are inevitably overshadowed by the harpsichord, their most significant contribution being made in the slow movement, a genuine trio in which the main body of strings plays no part.

The work begins with a rousing tune built on first the arpeggio and then the descending scale of D major. It is a stirring ritornello which, though it recurs many times in truncated forms, the soloists completely disregard once its first statement has been made. As in the Second Concerto we gain a distinct impression that there are two levels of music here, commoners and aristocracy. The utterances of the soloists have a refinement and elegance that is denied to the ripieno as the frequent use of a playful triplet figure indicates; it is never given to the 'orchestral' strings.

The three soloists make their entrance in the ninth bar, violin and flute bland and suave while the harpsichord tends to chatter rather more busily. Twice the strings try to reintroduce the opening ritornello but their efforts are abortive. An elegant conversation between flute and violin makes much of the playful triplet figure already mentioned until, in bar 19, the strings make another attempt to bring back the ritornello, this time in the dominant key. (A major.) Once more they are interrupted by the soloists who skilfully transform the character of the theme by smoothing it out and removing the most recognisable feature of repeated notes. At bar 29 the ripieno strings try to make a more positive impression by producing the second part of their main theme though with little greater success. As before they are quickly reduced to a supporting role although mutterings of discontent can be heard in various interwoven fragments of the theme now transposed into B minor (bars 35–7.) Bach stays for a while in this key (known as the 'relative' minor since it shares the same key signature as D major), but soon the harpsichordist embarks on some dazzling runs that virtually silence the opposition. Although it is devoid of malice or of the heroic rhetoric we find in nineteenth-century piano concertos, there is an element of competition here and it is worth mentioning that the derivation of the word 'concerto' is from the Italian *certare*, to combat or strive and *con*, with. There are therefore implications of a struggle for supremacy even though a *concerted* effort implies a unity of purpose.

Towards the middle of the movement there is a passage of some thirty bars which provides a complete contrast, an almost static period which is devoid of the forward thrust so evident in previous sections. The music settles quietly into the key of F sharp minor, easily recognizable since the strings play smooth sequences of repeated notes, emphasising the static nature of the harmony. Meanwhile the flute and violin exchange time after time a somewhat melancholy phrase lasting only a single bar. For a long period the mood is curiously veiled until some weirdly dissonant trills usher a return to bright daylight and a triumphant reappearance of the opening ritornello. Once again it is cut off in mid-flight by the soloists who, having regained the home key of D major by a slightly devious route, do begin a virtually exact recapitulation of their opening material without even allowing the ritornello to take its proper place.

In due course the harpsichordist begins once again to demonstrate his agility in swift scale-passages until his increasingly brilliant playing demands our total attention. So begins the massive cadenza, over sixty bars in length and, apart from the final fireworks, largely relevant to thematic material already presented at the keyboard. After such a display there is little to be said and all the orchestra can do is to round off the movement with a reprise of the opening ritornello, only the second time in the whole movement that it is heard in its entirety.

The slow movement is pure chamber music without even a supporting cello or gamba to duplicate the harpsichordist's left-hand part. Bach gives the indication *Affetuoso*, affectionately, implying a tender and expressive style of playing. Although each individual phrase is emotional in content, the texture is subjected to the contrapuntal discipline that came naturally to Bach, with the initial entry of any phrase invariably being copied by a second instrument. Thus the first main theme is presented by the violin and copied (though not pedantically) by the flute two beats later. In bar 5 the harpsichord leads off with the same theme, echoed in turn by the flute and violin in that order. In bar 10 the flute leads off, shedding new light on the theme by putting it into the major, a suggestion which the violin happily accepts two beats later and which is even briefly shadowed in the left hand part of the keyboard. There is no drama, no climactic point leading to a cadenza; the music is an eminently civilized discussion between three equals, too good-mannered to become involved in argumentative dispute.

The last movement is an unashamed dance based on a theme that (to English ears at least) bears a close resemblance to 'A frog he would a-wooing go'. The music is initially presented as a four-part not-to-be-taken-too-seriously fugue, by which I mean that its academic pretensions are soon abandoned. The solo violin leads the dance, the flute is next to take the floor, while the harpsichordist provides the next two entries, first with the left hand then the right. The three soloists continue in playful mood for twenty-eight bars before the accompanying strings are persuaded to join in. (Again the image of royalty leading off before the commoners dare participate comes to mind.) Bach briefly reverts to a fugal style with the ripieno entry but it is soon dispelled by some nimble runs in the harpsichord part. Shortly after, in bar 79, the flute introduces a substantially modified version of the original fugue subject; only the first four notes are clearly related and even they are given a new slant by being in a minor key. Although the tempo remains as lively, there is an undeniable change of mood which duly spreads to the other two soloists when they, in turn, take over the same idea. It is not long before once again they are left on their own, flute and violin providing a more sustained line than has been offered so far while the harpsichord continues its busy triplets. They are called to order by the ripieno strings with a reminder of the original subject, but an exciting ascending passage leads not to the expected reprise but to an orchestral take-over of the modification described above. The music bustles along happily for a considerable time, toying with fragments of the opening theme. At last, in bar 233 a genuine recapitulation of the initial fugue begins, the music pursuing an identical course for no less than seveny-eight bars before coming to a gloriously satisfying end. Some idea of the perfect proportions of the movement is revealed when we find that the exposition and recapitulation combined come to 155 bars while the central section consists of 153. It is extremely unlikely that Bach planned so close a correlation but it does show his intuitive feeling for a balanced form in music.

Concerto No. 6 (in B flat major)

Political revolutions may be accomplished overnight; musical ones take rather longer. New and improved instruments may be devised and made but it takes time for them to become generally available. Harpsichord and fortepiano existed side by side for some time before the former came to be regarded as obsolete; Haydn's trumpet concerto was written for a player who had acquired a new, more versatile instrument equipped with pistons; Mozart re-scored his late G minor symphony (No. 40) to include clarinets once they became available; Beethoven, in his Ninth Symphony, wrote a special part for the fourth horn-player, the only member of the orchestra to be the proud possessor of one of the first two-valved horns. Such developments are not irrelevant to a discussion of the Sixth Brandenburg Concerto since its most notable feature is the employment of instruments that were already obsolescent but which were still being played alongside their ultimate replacements. Purists will argue that the viola and cello are as different from the viola da braccio ('arm' viol) and viola da gamba ('leg' viol) as the harpsichord and spinet are different from the piano; they have substantially different body shapes, different numbers of strings, different types of bow and different techniques of playing. Yet in a historical and evolutionary sense they can be said to be related since, as with the harpsichord and fortepiano, they co-existed for some time before the greater tonal power of the viola and cello led to the virtual extinction of the earlier instruments. Blend also proved to be a factor since a 'consort of viols' consists of one family of like-sounding instruments whereas a viola da gamba is less satisfactory than a cello when it comes to mixing in with violins.

The historical interest of the Sixth Concerto lies in its use of instruments which were shortly to disappear from normal concert-giving, even though Bach might still use them in a solo capacity or as obbligato instruments in vocal music. (See St. Matthew Passion No. 66.) The viola da braccio is also known as the 'tenor' viol, the viola da gamba the 'bass' viol, yet Bach also specifies a cello, violone and harpsichord. Notice that he employs neither treble viols nor violins so that the music becomes the string equivalent of a male-voice choir. Naturally enough the somewhat archaic instrumentation has led scholars to assume that this, though numbered six, was the first of the set to be written. The case is not proven although the relative simplicity of the bass viol parts has led to the interesting suggestion that one of them was designed for Bach's patron and employer Prince Leopold to play.

The concerto begins with a stirring version of the arpeggio of B flat major with the second violas following the first in close canon a mere quaver behind. The extreme proximity of the two lines suggests argument rather than agreement, lending an intriguing tension to what might otherwise be a rather conventional statement, especially as the bass remains unusually static. After sixteen bars of this closely knitted texture the music breaks free and a more varied discussion ensues, still imitative, but involving the cello and gambas in what is essentially a four-part contrapuntal structure. However, after a mere eight bars of this, the first motif returns in the dominant key (F major) albeit in a substantially abbreviated version. In fact, despite its very different tone-colour the form is not dissimilar to that of the Third Concerto — an opening ritornello to which frequent partial references are made, punctuated by a number of excursions into new but congruent material.

Deeper musical values are to be discovered in the second movement, a serenely beautiful fugue in E major treated in such a way that there are usually three different metric units continuing at the same time, minims, crotchets and quavers. Particularly effective are the final entries of the fugue subject in the bass, above which the two tenor viols weave a decorative web of two-part counterpoint. The movement comes to rest on a less than final cadence (D major, the dominant of G minor), only to plunge us without warning into the third movement, a jig that shows Bach in his most bucolic mood. As in the first movement, he makes considerable use of syncopated rhythms which give a nice rustic bounce to the music. There are a number of more athletic passages, usually circling runs in semiquavers. Bach shows an obvious concern for balance here, ensuring clarity by thinning out a texture that by being confined to the lower register runs the risk of muddiness. This is particularly evident when some dashing arpeggios appear in a swift interchange between the two tenor viols; the sole accompaniment is a series of separated notes from the cello, implying that even the harpsichord should be silent.

It is certain that Bach never visualised all six concertos as a single concert programme; it is a mistake therefore to regard this work as something of an anticlimax after the more overtly brilliant Fifth. Each of the Brandenburgs has a markedly individual quality, showing Bach ever ready to experiment with different combinations of sound. Orchestration as we interpret the word today was an art that had to be learned once orchestras as such emerged. Bach never had what Beethoven would have called an orchestra, but he did marvels with what resources he could command.

St. Matthew Passion

This monumental work is unequalled as a musical testament to the Christian faith and even the most hardened agnostic must be moved by its profound beauty and the intense feeling with which Bach unfolds the story of Christ's betrayal and suffering. Although the forces called for seem on paper to be large — two choruses, two orchestras and a number of soloists — it seems that the performances Bach directed himself were not overwhelming in sheer numbers. It is unlikely that he had more than three or four singers to each part since for the whole work, including the double choruses, he copied out only eight voice parts. While it is true that further copies might have been made by members of the family or pupils, it seems unlikely; after all, if Bach knew that such help was to be forthcoming, why did he not content himself with one master-copy instead of going through the labour of making the eight? As for the soloists, they would have been drawn from the choir; not for Bach the highly-paid international stars of the concert-platform that we have grown accustomed to in modern performances.

It seems that Bach made several versions of the Passion but the only two to survive are the *St. John* and the *St. Matthew*. The *St. John* is shorter, more concentrated, but, despite its many qualities, it has been relegated to second place in public affection. Even so, it provided one of the greatest choruses in the *St. Matthew*, for Bach had originally ended Part I with an unadorned chorale; second thoughts (some twenty years later) led him to lift in its entirety the richly complex setting of 'O Man bewail thy grievous sin' and transfer it from the *St. John* to the later work. In fact the composition of the *St. Matthew Passion* appears to have come in two stages, an original but substantially shorter version having been performed in 1727, followed two years later by the more expansive treatment we are familiar with today. The text was provided by Picander, but Bach made a number of alterations to it to satisfy his musical requirements. The chorales make use of hymn tunes by earlier composers such as Hassler (1562–1612) and Isaac (*c.* 1450–1517), tunes that would have been familiar favourites to Bach's congregation in Leipzig.

Although there are seventy-eight 'numbers' in all in the vocal score, some are extremely short — a few bars of recitative to move the story forward or a chorale of a mere twelve or sixteen bars. The overall plan becomes clearer if we regard it as two 'Acts' containing twenty-four 'scenes', the twelve subsidiary ones being marked by chorales, the twelve more substantial ones indicated by arias. These arias are scored in such a way that a specially prominent part is given to one instrument (sometimes a pair) whose function is partly to provide the orchestra with a 'solo voice', partly to lend an individual tone-colour suited to the sentiment expressed. Such a part is called an 'obbligato'. Musically we can divide the work into four clearly defined styles; first, the simple telling of the narrative which is either recounted by a solo tenor (the Evangelist) or acted out by a few soloists such as Jesus, Peter, Judas or Pilate; second, the arias of contemplation in which it seems as though Bach himself pauses to reflect upon the full implications of any particular event for humanity at large; third we find the choir's reaction to the story, whether withdrawn from the drama (as in the chorales) or actually involved in it as the crowd or *turba*; fourth, and on quite a different scale from the rest, we find three monumental choruses, one at the beginning, one to end 'Act I' (and therefore serving as a centre point), and one at the conclusion. Of these, the first chorus is not only the most magnificent but also the most complex. In it Bach makes clear the function of his two choirs, one representing those who are actually involved in the story, the other standing for the questioning observer, unfamiliar with the events. In all probability they were placed at opposite ends of the nave, hence the need for two orchestras; it must be said though that at times Bach combines his forces rather than using them alternately.

Part One[1]

1   Prologue. Unlike Handel, Bach was never drawn towards opera; nevertheless the opening bars of this massive chorus, climbing step by gradual step through the span of an octave, give the impression of an immense curtain rising to reveal the scene we have come to witness; the impression is confirmed when in the sixth bar cellos and basses at last leave the key-note of E with a marvellous ascent covering an octave and a half. Although the tempo is not fast, Choir I suggests a milling crowd converging from all directions to see some momentous event, though one that fills them with anguish in anticipation of tragedy. Like recent arrivals unaware of the situation Chorus II interpolate monosyllabic queries — 'How? Whom? When?'. The music is restless and uneasy, but suddenly a new strand appears, serenely confident in faith, the treble voices Bach would surely have used suggesting purity and innocence.

> O Lamb of God most holy
> Who on the cross didst languish
> O saviour meek and lowly
> Who suffered bitter anguish.

The measured tones of this great Lutheran hymn symbolise unswerving faith; it may even be that Bach, visualising the crowd of spectators thronging the narrow streets, saw in his mind's eye the figure of Christ walking, heedless of the mob, and used this sturdy tune to convey that image. The idea is not too far-fetched since his religious music is filled with vivid symbols, as we shall discover.

2   The first huge chorus having ended, Bach immediately establishes two important conventions — that the Evangelist as narrator should set the scene virtually unaccompanied so that every word shall be clear, and that the utterances of Jesus shall be accompanied by soft string chords, a musical 'halo'. Note also the extended distortion of the word 'Crucified', already suggesting the agony of the cross.

---

[1]The translations of the text are taken from the Novello edition edited by Ivor Atkins and Edward Elgar, as are the numberings of individual sections.

3   The first chorale, sung by both choruses expressing incredulity that such a fate can lie in store for the Saviour.

4–5   The Evangelist tells of the conspiracy of the priests to kill Jesus. With almost cinematic brevity we 'cut' to the gathering of the priests who in a confusion of voices argue 'Not upon the feast lest haply there be an uproar.'

6–7   The scene changes to Bethany where the woman anoints Jesus with a precious ointment; now it is the disciples' turn to protest and we hear them ask indignantly 'To what purpose is this waste?' After the huge span of the opening chorus these interpolations, whether of priests or disciples, are notable for their dramatic timing, concise and to the point.

8   Jesus rebukes the disciples and commends the action of the woman.

9–10   The first aria of contemplation, sung by a contralto so as to identify with (though not portray) the woman. The preceding recitative 'My Master and my Lord' is accompanied by two flutes who, throughout, repeat a pattern that is a symbol of lamentation much used by Bach and his contemporaries. The ensuing aria, also accompanied by the flutes, is the first example of Bach's remarkable use of dance forms in a profoundly spiritual context. An initial reaction may be to feel that there is something almost pagan about this, for did not priestesses dance in the temples of Delphi or Luxor? It is impossible to believe that Bach had such an analogy in mind. To him, as to all Baroque composers, Faith was a cause for rejoicing. (Pergolesi's *Stabat Mater* is a remarkable example of joyous music married to an essentially harrowing text.) Therefore, even though the contralto sings of grief rending the guilty heart, belief in ultimate salvation defeats despair. Even the tears depicted by a delicate arpeggio figure in the flute part sound more like a scatter of droplets from a fountain; the music would not be out of place in a gentle pastoral scene.

11–12   The mood darkens as Judas names the price of treachery. The ensuing soprano aria 'Break in grief' is a true lament, the paired notes in the orchestral part eloquent of sighs. The middle section has some vivid examples of musical word-painting, circling phrases for 'around' and a sinuous writhing figure for a 'serpent'.

4–15   The Preparation of the Passover.
Jesus prophesies that one of the disciples will betray him. Incredulously they ask 'Lord, is it I?' With a dramatic subtlety that might easily pass unnoticed Bach poses the question eleven times in all. The twelfth disciple, the betrayer, has no need to ask.

16   A marvellously harmonised chorale in which both choruses identify themselves with Judas. ' 'Tis I whose sin now binds Thee.' Should they not share Christ's suffering in atonement?

17   The first Communion at the Last Supper, the most openly lyrical music given to Jesus in the whole work.

18–19   A recitative and aria of contemplation for soprano that perfectly balances 9–10 for contralto. In place of flutes we find two *oboi d'amore* but in other respects the match is remarkable in its similarity. Both recitatives are accompanied by constantly repeated patterns symbolising lamentation; both arias are essentially dances. Here the soprano seems to step forward eagerly to offer her total commitment to Jesus. 'Jesus, Saviour, I am thine; come and dwell within my heart.'

21–4   At the Mount of Olives Jesus foretells Peter's denial of Him. The action moves at an almost operatic pace but is interrupted by two deeply moving chorales. Jesus comes to Gethsemane and bids the disciples to watch with Him.

25   For the first time Bach combines a soloist with the chorus. There is a wonderful contrast between the anguished phrases of the solo tenor and the restrained grief of the choir. Their music is a decorated version of the chorale first associated with the crucifixion (No. 3), here transposed down from B minor to the much darker-sounding F minor. One has the impression that they are stunned by their impotence to intervene whereas the tenor is filled with a passionate desire to go to Jesus' aid.

26   In one of the most beautiful arias in the whole work the tenor expresses the wish that he might be a member of that watching group surrounding Jesus in Gethsemane. Meanwhile the chorus sings a slumber song that might be said to lull the disciples to sleep. Here again soloist and chorus have markedly different kinds of music.

27   Christ prays in the garden: . . . 'Let this cup pass from Me: yet not as I will, but as Thou wilt.'

28–9   The first bass recitative and aria. As before we find a 'pattern' recitative followed by a dance aria. Note the drooping phrases in the strings to symbolise 'the Saviour low before His Father *bending* . . .' The voice in the aria is, we feel, Bach's own:

> Gladly would I take upon me
> Cross and cup and all His burden
> Could I follow Christ my Lord.

Time and again in this work we have an impression of Bach turning his eyes away from the drama unfolding before him, unable to look any more until he has had time to meditate upon its full implications for humanity and in particular for the devout Christian.

30   Jesus finds the disciples asleep and gently rebukes them, an action that prompts the ensuing chorale (31).

32   The Betrayal and Arrest of Jesus: one of the longest sections of pure action, the Evangelist sustaining the narrative with occasional interpolations from Jesus or Judas. Notice the restraint with which Bach refrains from introducing the chorus when Judas arrives with 'a great multitude with swords and staves.' A set-piece here would be out of place.

33   Christ is bound and led into the city. Here we find a wonderful example of Bach's ability to combine two completely opposing types of music. Flute and oboe begin with a forlorn descending scale, gently syncopated so as to intensify the impact of the dissonant notes, while beneath them the violins have a restless uneasy figure betokening agitation. Soprano and contralto soloists bewail in turn 'My Saviour now is taken'. This is a duet of contemplation; in their imagination they see Christ being led bound through the streets but they are helpless to intervene. However, every now and then their lament is almost swamped by furious shouts from the chorus: 'Loose Him! Leave Him! Bind Him not!' These abrupt interjections seem to belong to a different time dimension, as if part of the actual event, whereas the two soloists disclose Bach's own distress at the contemplation of the scene across the centuries. At the words 'They lead Him hence, with cords they bind Him' notice the two descending scales in measured and weighty crotchets, symbolising the guards leading Jesus down into the prison cell. Without pause we are launched into a chorus of extraordinary violence:

Have lightnings and thunders their fury forgotten?

The fugal entries in the order bass, tenor, alto, soprano give an impression of accumulated anger that the elements themselves do not intervene; a rapidly circling figure in the bass gives a graphic depiction of the continuous rumble of thunder, while pairs of sharply accented chords, always descending, suggest lightning spitting from the clouds. A dramatic silence in the middle — the eye of the hurricane? — is broken by a dramatic change of key (G major to B major). The whole chorus is operatic in conception, a strikingly graphic example of Bach's descriptive sense.

34 After the tumult and turbulence a scene of calm, the serene string chords surrounding the words of Jesus serving as a point of repose before the great chorus that concludes 'Act' I.

35 This truly monumental piece was added to the St. Matthew Passion some twenty years after the original performances. It was taken from the earlier St. John Passion, either because Bach felt that it was on too large a scale for the earlier work or perhaps because he felt that the St. Matthew would inevitably supplant the St. John in public esteem. (Composers of the day had little thought for posterity and were eminently pragmatic when it came to transplanting and re-using material.)

The orchestral introduction is based almost entirely on paired semiquavers, played in such a way that the second note is slightly shortened. They appear in flutes, oboi d'amore and violins, or in cellos and basses, who move either in parallel with the upper parts or alternating with them. This figure continues virtually unbroken for ninety-eight majestic bars; it is completely independent of the voice parts who pursue their own course with a richly contrapuntal treatment of one of the greatest of all chorale tunes, 'O Man bewail thy grievious sin'. (*O Mensch bewein' dein Sünde gross.*) It is easy enough in hindsight to understand that Bach felt that this masterly movement made a more fitting end to the First Part than the simple thirteen-bar chorale he had originally used; but it should be remembered that the Passion was intended to be performed as a church service on Good Friday with an inevitably lengthy sermon given between the two parts. Incidentally, on the same Good Friday which saw the first performance of this supreme religious masterpiece, at the same hour, a Passion by Gottlieb Frober was performed. He was candidate for the vacant post of cantor at the New Church, and for the Leipzig public this event was the more novel and therefore the more important.

Part Two

36   Prologue. Here we find not, as we might expect, another large-scale chorus but a contralto solo whose sentiments are reflected and shared by the second chorus. Once again the music is basically a dance with a light first beat and a stressed second beat (3/8). 'Whither is thy beloved [Saviour] gone?' asks the chorus, and the introductory music suggests not only anxiety but also the actual motion of searching through a crowd, looking from side to side and occasionally turning to hurry in a new direction. The initial contralto note, sustained for more than four bars, may well be intended to depict the searcher standing still at some vantage point before mingling with the throng. The search is in vain for Jesus has been taken to the house of Caiaphas the high priest, as we are told in the ensuing recitative (37). A chorale condemning the injustice of the accusations laid against Him (38) leads to the depositions of the false witnesses (39) and Christ's refusal to answer their allegations. Unusually this is described not by the Evangelist but by a tenor from Chorus II, as though he himself had been present at the interrogation (40).

41   The same voice embarks on a tortuous aria, notable for its important cello obbligato. The first bar of the instrumental part consists of eight quavers, smoothly paired, symbolising the word 'Endure!'. The following three bars exploit jagged intervals and a sharply dotted rhythm, clearly designed to suggest the vicious malice of 'lying tongues and taunting'. (Handel uses the identical rhythm, albeit less adventurously, in his '*Messiah*' beneath the words 'All they that see Him laugh Him to scorn'.) The word-painting in the voice-part is especially vivid with the jerky elongations of the word 'taunting' suggesting sardonic laughter.

42   The high priest questions Jesus and denounces His reply as blasphemous. Five aggressive bars suffice for the chorus's shout of agreement — 'He is worthy of death'.

43   A brief recitative describes the wrath of the crowd as Jesus is buffeted to and fro. The writing is deliberately chaotic with terse phrases tossed rapidly from one choir to another as the unfortunate victim is cuffed from side to side.

44   Bach turns his eyes from the scene in horror and anger in the chorale 'O Lord who dares to smite Thee?' There is a tradition amongst English choirs that this should be sung in hushed tones, but it seems

more proper dramatically to begin it as an outraged protest. There is always a danger that the chorales may be treated too sentimentally.

45–6 Peter is discovered in a courtyard and is accused, first by a couple of girls and then by a group of curious bystanders, of being a disciple of Jesus. He denies it angrily . . . 'And immediately the cock crew . . .' Ordinarily, the Evangelist should sing with a certain detachment, as though reading from the Bible. Here though he is allowed a deeply expressive phrase as Peter 'wept bitterly'. The peak of this cry of agony (A-G♯–F♯) is transformed in rhythm and pitch into the opening phrase of the ensuing aria. (D–C♯–B).

47 Here for the first time, as though to emphasise the expressive quality of the music, the obbligato instrument is a solo violin. The instrumental introduction could easily be mistaken for the slow movement of a violin concerto in the style of a Siciliano. So graceful a dance seems scarcely in keeping with the contralto's plea, 'Have mercy Lord on me', yet the apparent incongruity is justified as soon as we realise that its purpose is to reassure us that mercy will be forthcoming. The woman may weep but God smiles upon her through the music.

48 A chorale of humility, 'Lamb of God, I fall before Thee'.

49–50 Judas admits his guilt, but the priests and elders express their indifference; he casts down the thirty pieces of silver, 'the price of blood', and in bitter remorse hangs himself. Bach shows him no pity; his suicide is simply reported, not dramatised.

51 The ensuing bass aria, again with violin obbligato, seems at first hearing to be almost frivolous with decorative ascending scales and athletic passage-work across the strings. However, knowing Bach's delight in musical symbolism, it is not far-fetched to interpret the rapid ascending scales as the movement of Judas's hand tossing the coins in the air while the ensuing figures show them bouncing and rolling across the floor of the temple. Inevitably, for musical reasons, the passage is extended for far longer than realism would require, but it serves as a springboard for one of the most immediately appealing arias in the whole work.

52 Christ is brought before Pilate; the scene is presented without drama, reflecting His refusal to answer the accusations against Him.

53 A chorale of faith, 'Commit thy way to Jesus'.

54   Pilate offers the people the choice — should he release Jesus or Barrabas? With a dramatic stroke that one might more readily expect to find in a twentieth-century work Bach gives the combined choruses a single dissonant shout of 'Barrabas'. It is an unforgettable moment, the more striking for its shocking abruptness. Asked what shall be done with Jesus they reply 'Let Him be crucified'. The first syllable, CRU- is extended through four bars of 4/4 time with twenty-three notes so shaped that the phrase seems literally to writhe in torment.

55   One of the Passion chorales reappears for the third time (cf. Nos. 3 and 25). It is a compound of amazement that Christ should be willing to suffer so for mankind and incredulity that mankind should so betray Him.

56–8   A contemplation of the essential goodness and compassion of Christ. The format is now well established: a brief recitative from the Evangelist, followed by an accompanied recitative for the soprano with, as in Nos. 9, 18, 65 and 69, a pair of instruments providing the obbligato (oboi da caccia). Then comes the aria, in which the two oboi da caccia are reduced to a more subsidiary role, their plangent sound giving a harder edge to the dulcet tones of the flute — needless to say wooden in Bach's time and therefore less penetrating than the metal instruments of today. Notice the word-painting, the extension of the word 'love' into an encircling embrace and the chromatic fall on 'dying'. (Here Bach and Purcell share a common mastery.) As in all the arias of contemplation time stands still so that the ensuing outcry, 'Let Him be crucified (59) seems like a direct continuation of the closing bars of 54. Bach underlines the point musically by ending 54 with a chord of B major (having started in A minor!) and then beginning 59 in B minor. The CRU- syllable of 'crucified' is extended still further to twenty-six notes, while the higher pitch makes the voices seem more shrill and menacing.

60   The Scourging. Bach distances himself (and us) from the full horror; relentlessly we hear the lashes fall with dreadful regularity but the sound is distant, its harshness softened by being given to strings — those same violins that earlier had consistently provided a halo whenever Jesus spoke. The dotted rhythm is the same as that used in *Messiah* for 'He gave His back to the smiters' though Bach's harmonies are far more intense than Handel's. Both composers use the contralto to describe the scene though again with Bach we have the impression that she is looking back helplessly across the gulf of centuries.

61   The aria that follows continues the rhythmic pattern of the scourg-
      ing even though it is written out in a different notation. Frequently
      there is a short rising phrase culminating in a sharp accent on the
      second beat of the bar. It is surely a cry of pain as the lash cuts ever
      more cruelly. (The aria tells of 'the sacred wounds bleeding'.)

62   Virtually unaccompanied even by the conventional keyboard con-
      tinuo, the Evangelist tells of the mock coronation of Jesus with
      scarlet robe and crown of thorns. In jeering tones the chorus hails
      Him as King of the Jews.

63   The chorale 'O Sacred Head sore wounded'. The chorales not only
      provide an emotional commentary with which the congregation
      could readily identify; they also serve to give musical unity to a
      work on this vast scale. This tune has already appeared as 21, 23 and
      53; it will appear again as 72. In every case Bach provides a different
      harmonisation.

64   The Evangelist tells of the Via Dolorosa and of how Simon of
      Cyrene was chosen to carry the cross.

65–6 In the brief preliminary recitative for bass solo we should notice the
      pathetic three-note phrases on paired flutes that graphically depict
      Christ's steps as He stumbles exhausted beneath the weight of the
      cross. In the aria that follows the obbligato is provided by a viola da
      gamba and though it is obvious from the dotted rhythm that even
      the strong and youthful Simon walks a trifle unsteadily he strides
      out proudly, rejoicing that he can ease the Saviour's burden.

67   The arrival at Golgotha is again described in an exceptionally
      austere recitative, almost without emotion; the ensuing jibes from
      the chorus seem the more hooliganish by comparison as they yell
      'Save Thyself, come down!'

68   Even the thieves crucified beside Him abuse Him, or so the
      Evangelist tells us.

69–70 Again we find the formula, recitative with a pair of instruments
      providing the obbligato (oboi da caccia), followed by an aria
      accompanied by the same instrumental colouring. As in the scene of
      the scourging it is the contralto who is chosen to express the
      universal grief.

          Ah, Golgotha! Unhappy Golgotha!
          The Lord of Glory here 'mid shame and scorn must perish . . .

The reiterated figure in the accompaniment may be intended to represent the mournful tolling of church bells though it could as well be the wringing of hands in sorrow.

The aria returns to the dance format with an almost lilting bass and a gently rocking shape to the melody that suggests a beckoning motion as Christ's hands seem to draw us towards Him. (The notion is not fanciful; the original text reads, in translation, 'See, Jesus holds out His hand to give us strength . . .') 'Come, come' He seems to say, and the second chorus, as though in recollection of their bewildered enquiries in the very opening chorus, again interject 'Come where?' There is an extraordinary tenderness about this episode, a release from the surrounding pain.

71 The Death of Christ. With brief interruptions from a still hostile chorus the Evangelist tells of Christ's last hour. The string 'halo' surrounding Jesus's words is withheld; at this dying moment He is the nearest to being mortal man.

72 The Passion chorale 'Be near me Lord when dying'. The most extreme example of Bach's use of chromatic harmony as a means of intensifying emotion.

73 And now, in comparison to the austere economy so notable in all the narrative passages leading to the crucifixion, we suddenly find an intensely dramatic recitative, vividly descriptive of the rending of the veil of the temple, the earthquake, and the resurrection of the saints. It is shortly followed by what many regard as the most sublime phrase in all music:

'Truly this was the Son of God.'

Within the space of two bars and one beat we find a matchlessly beautiful *melody* in the soprano part, supported by superlative *counterpoint* in tenor and bass, all clothed in *harmony* of memorable richness. It is not merely an affirmation of faith but a perfect fusion of the elements of music itself. It is perhaps worth remarking that in Bach's time it was probably sung by eight singers rather than the hundred or more we have grown accustomed to.

74–5 To a gently murmuring accompaniment of strings the bass soloist tells of the evening hour and the lowering of Christ's body from the cross. As usual in these accompanied recitatives one pattern prevails throughout in the orchestral part. The aria — yet another dance! — has a pastoral air not unlike 'He shall feed His flock' in Handel's *Messiah*. However it is longer and introduces more elaborate figuration in the central section.

76   A brief recitative describes the entombment of Christ. A chorus of priests and Pharisees demands of Pilate that the tomb shall be properly sealed; the music is pompous and self-righteous, becoming indignant in the closing bars.

77   Prior to the final chorus Bach places this masterly little scene in which each of the four soloists in turn is given a farewell phrase interspersed with gentle murmurs from the second chorus — 'Lord Jesu fare Thee well.'

78   The final chorus, for all its expression of tender grief, is a sarabande, not a funeral march. It has neither the dramatic intensity of the very opening chorus nor the majesty of the end of Part I (35). It creates a very personal relationship with the departed Christ, of whose resurrection no mention is made in this Good Friday work. 'Lie Thou softly here' is the culminating phrase and the whole chorus is designed to give a sense of peace. Whitman's 'Come lovely and soothing death' captures something of Bach's philosophy and the feeling we have at the end of this immense work is not one of bleak despair but rather a sorrow that is warmed by a true love of Christ.

BÉLA BARTÓK
1881–1945

Though he was frequently reviled and subjected to malicious and ill-informed criticism during his lifetime, Bartók is now securely established as one of the greatest and most significant figures in twentieth-century music. It is hard to believe that there was a time when one of the most esteemed music critics of the day could seriously write, 'In shunning sentiment Bartók has lost beauty, in shunning rhetoric he has lost reason.' Since Bartók's music is so well organised that every note is meticulously placed, to say that he had lost reason was about as stupid a criticism as it was possible to make; but then every cheap jibe about excruciatingly wrong notes, torturing dissonances and so on was hurled at Bartók, even though he was a superb pianist and a composer whose music had been enthusiastically endorsed by some of the greatest musicians of the 1930s. On the other hand, it would be foolish to deny that some of his compositions do present a daunting challenge to the listener; he was not one to make compromises and it could well be that the very hostility he was forced to endure made his music more openly aggressive than it might otherwise have been. Certainly the work he produced towards the end of his life shows a mellowing that could reflect the increasing esteem in which he was held.

If his music seems strange to us, a prime reason must be that it is derived from a literally foreign source, the genuine folk-music of countries which, centuries ago, were affected by the invasion of Turks from the East. As a young man Bartók made a number of tours of Hungary, Romania and even North Africa in search of authentic folk-music. He amassed a huge collection which made a deep impression on his creative psyche, leaving a fondness for asymmetrical rhythmic patterns, unconventional scales and curiously angular melodic intervals. These attributes spring not from perversity but from a strongly felt identification with peasant music. (It is worth mentioning that in exactly the same period that Bartók was walking through the countryside rescuing music which he believed to be endangered by the encroachment of urban civilization, Vaughan-Williams and Holst were engaged in a similar quest in England.) During those long walking tours Bartók must often have found himself in remote country places at night and he developed an obsession with the nocturnal sounds of nature, the strange noises of insects and birds, the cry of the nighthawk, the almost inaudible rustle of tiny creatures whose restless activity was concealed from the eye by the calm all-enfolding night. His sense of hearing was abnormally acute and it was said that he could pick up sounds from a mile away that a normal person could only hear from a few hundred yards.

The introduction of folk-music as an exotic element within the context of organised compositions is nothing new. Haydn and Mozart frequently incorporated elements of Austrian folk-music into their works, Beethoven could build a string-quartet movement on a Russian folk-song to gratify one of his patrons, while Brahms and Liszt were fascinated by Hungarian folk-music. But even Liszt, himself a Hungarian, tended to present such borrowings in their Sunday best, washed clean, well-mannered, and clad in very fancy dress. Bartók preferred to treat folk melodies and rhythms as truly raw material, emphasising their primitive elements with strongly accented dissonances that, especially in the piano music, help to take the instrument out of the drawing-rooms of high society into a more rustic environment.

Like so many of his fellow-students in the late 1890s Bartók was initially overwhelmed by the influence of Wagner, although in his case Liszt proved equally fascinating. In 1902 he came across Richard Strauss's music for the first time and at once became so fired with enthusiasm that he made brilliant piano transcriptions of some of Strauss's most formidable scores. His first impact as a professional musician was as a quite outstanding pianist; for two years he hardly composed a note. It was as though in his search for a truly Hungarian identity he was trying to shake off the essentially Germanic tradition his pianistic studies had inevitably enhanced. His declaration of musical independence came with a vast symphonic poem called *Kossuth* (1903) whose ten movements were based on the exploits of a Hungarian revolutionary leader of the mid-nineteenth century. Although by no means characteristic of mature Bartók, it was a significant step away from the mainstream of European music. However, his ability to absorb folk idiom without allowing it to become his master enabled him to compose with complete confidence in even the largest forms and his works include three piano concertos, a violin concerto,[1] an unfinished viola concerto, the concerto for orchestra, the splendid 'Music for string instruments, percussion and celesta', the Divertimento for string orchestra, a one-act opera, a major ballet, a dance suite for orchestra, two sonatas for violin and piano, a piano sonata, innumerable folk-song arrangements and transcriptions and, in some ways his most significant contribution to the repertoire, six string quartets. That

[1]An early violin concerto exists, but Bartók incorporated most of its music into the first of the *Two Portraits for Orchestra* Op. 5.

such a man should die in enforced exile and genuine poverty is a sad commentary on an age in which popular entertainers were already able to become multi-millionaires by the exploitation of rather less enduring talents.

Music for String Instruments, Percussion and Celesta
(1936)

This truly unique work serves as an excellent introduction to Bartók's music since it contains virtually all his most distinguishing characteristics, folk-derived melodies and rhythms, a consistent exploitation of patterns based on somewhat angular intervals and an intensely imaginative use of tone-colour. If one asks 'How then can it be unique?' the answer lies in its combination of instruments, a double string orchestra, a considerable battery of percussion instruments including side drum, bass drum, cymbals, tam-tam (gong), xylophone, timpani, a harp, a celesta and a piano. Because the latter instrument has an important part to play it may seem surprising that it is not mentioned in the title, but Bartók, ever logical, no doubt argued that since it has a large number of strings and hammers it falls comfortably into either of the two categories specified, string or percussion. The work as a whole is a perfect example of his ability to balance intellect with emotion; although it is constructed with a notable economy of material, its impact at all times is primarily emotional. Parts of it sound like music for a ghost-story, other sections could be taken for a description of a mist-enshrouded dawn by some remote forest lake, while the finale is an orgiastic gipsy dance.

The first movement combines the classical discipline of fugue with the impressionist technique of tone-painting, for although Bartók gives us no specific clue as to the subject-matter, it is easy to imagine it to be a description of a dawn in which the shapes of trees, rocks and mountains gradually become visible as the sun disperses the early mist. It begins with a single thread of music, almost inaudible on muted violas, its brief phrases rising and then falling by narrow intervals that have a vaguely Eastern flavour.[2] The ensuing entries give an almost pedantic impression of adhering to the academic concept of a fugue, yet the subject is undefined in its tonality while the differing phrase-lengths defy any attempt to enclose the music in a conventional time-scheme such as 6/8, 3/4 or 4/4. Gradually but logically Bartók weaves more and more threads into the texture until it becomes a spider's web of sound. Just as a spider's web is geometrically satisfying so is this music, for each of its lines is built from the same material and all the instruments[3] discuss and explore the same shapes. The growth is slow and

[2]Its second, third and fourth phrases are shown at the first, third and fifth examples on page 41.

[3]Strings only for the first thirty-three bars.

imperceptible, but gradually the great arch of the movement takes form, like some mountain appearing through the morning haze. At the central climactic point, briefly heralded by crescendo rolls on cymbals and timpani and precisely marked by a single stroke on the bass drum, all the strings converge on a single vibrant note (E flat). Beyond the peak of any mountain lies the descent, and so this music must unwind to its ultimate disintegration. The prevailing theme is now inverted, the logical antithesis to the previous ascent, yet the whole concept of the movement is surely imaginative despite the intellectual control of the material. Towards the end the celesta makes its first appearance with a rippling figure that inevitably suggests water. At exactly the same moment the first and fourth violins, three octaves apart, present the original and the inverted versions of the initial theme, a slightly distorted mirror image that surely represents reflections on the surface of a lake. The ripples die down; the movement ends in utter stillness on a single held note.

The second movement is a dance, much more physical in its appeal. The music is designed to be carried on the strong tide of its rhythm in direct contrast to the nebulous shapes that drift through the first movement. From the layout of the music it seems that Bartok may have visualised two groups of dancers since we find many swift interchanges between the two string orchestras. Occasionally the piano assumes a role comparable to a leading male dancer, though not to the degree that it does in Stravinsky's *Petrushka*. The folk element is evident to even the most imperceptive listener, although anyone who attempts to tap their toes in time to the music will have a mortifying experience since the rhythmic patterns are not merely syncopated but increasingly asymmetrical as the movement progresses. Rapid alternations between 2/4 and 5/8 give a strangely lurching gait to the music which, despite the suggestion of happy inebriation, never falters in its forward drive. Even so, Bartók uses all the most masterly tricks of classical musical construction; instruments echo each other's phrases, often in strict canon, they invert them, overlap them and so on, almost as though the composer was openly challenging the critics, daring them to accuse him of academic incompetence when, despite its thrillingly physical impact, the music was so intellectually controlled. One can even detect the basic structure of sonata form with an Exposition, Development and Recapitulation. The end of the Exposition is clearly signalled by two loudly stamped out beats from the timpani (F♯–C♯) followed by a silence. The ensuing Development begins quietly with a considerable exploration of the potential of the more 'feminine' second subject. After some time the pianist introduces a new and forceful idea, quickening the tempo as he does so. Some loud explosive chords of G major (!) followed by a few bars of solo drumming lead to an easily recognisable development of the first subject, a fragment of which soon settles into a machine-like *ostinato* (a multiple repetition of a five-note pattern) while above, piano and pizzicato violins introduce positively jazzy rhythms whose melodic outline proves to be based on the initial groping phrase of the *first* movement, now transformed almost beyond recognition. The excitement gradually dies down through a long passage for plucked strings until the music is reduced to a quiet reiterated drum-beat with an occasional grumble from cellos and basses. Suddenly a solo cello, playing very quietly, introduces a slithering sinuous theme that would serve nicely to illustrate a nature film showing a small eel wriggling out of the muddy bottom of a pond. A little thought reveals that it is a much compressed version of the virile dance theme originally heard in bars 5–7, orchestra I's opening gambit of the movement. Bartók treats this transformed idea as a strict fugue whose academic rectitude is only slightly disturbed by urgent restless drumming from the timpanist. The music gains in tension and excitement as it grows progressively louder, the two orchestras throwing phrases at each other with heightening antagonism. A victory of sorts for orchestra I ensues, marked by a series of rapid descending scale-passages, contracting by a note at a time and ultimately diminishing in tone as well. For a brief moment it seems as though the energy is spent save for a strange whirring trill on the lower strings. With an abrupt broadening of the tempo and a dramatic crescendo we are suddenly precipitated into the Recapitulation, no longer in dispute between the two orchestras, but shared in a combined unison that gives it a tremendous impact. Freely decorated though it may be, it is an unmistakable landmark.

Sweeping *glissandi* in harp and piano signal the arrival of the Coda which, at ever quickening speeds, makes clearly recognisable references to the main themes of the movement. With a touch of humour the music seems to be on the verge of disintegration, only to finish with an abruptly skidding descent.

The third movement is one of Bartók's most remarkable creations, seeming like an improvisation yet tightly organised. So atmospheric is the music that the listener is unlikely to be aware of the overall structure which can be conveyed by this very simple diagram

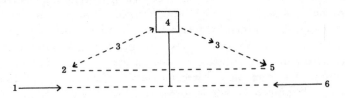

There are six sections in the movement; one and six correspond with each other: section five is a variant of section two, but influenced by (and therefore seeming also to resemble) section three. The fourth section is the centrepiece from which (at bar 49) section three moves away in reverse (retrograde) motion. Six is also a reversal of One even if Bartók is not so fettered by his plan as to make such relationships inflexible. In addition to this ingenious but convincingly symmetrical structure we find several subtly disguised links with the first movement; for instance, bar 2 of the work —

reappears as a simple unison phrase in bars 33–4 of the third movement:

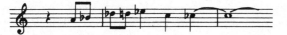

bar 3 of the work —

reappears in equally simple guise in bars 60–3

while the fourth phrase of the work —

appears on celesta and piano at the end of a rippling passage on the celesta which itself recalls its memorable entry in the first movement. Here, more than eighty pages later, is this further reference to the very opening page.[4]

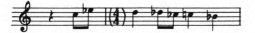

As if these disciplines were not enough, there is also a fugue whose subject is split up and used to introduce the various sections shown in the pattern of numbers on page 40.

Once the music is subjected to structural analysis of this kind there is a danger that our attention may be diverted towards a search for the dry bones; in doing so we may try, quite wrongly, to resist the intensely emotional impact the music is intended to have. The structure is really the composer's concern, a necessary prop for ideas that might otherwise be mistaken for pure impressionism. From the very first notes it is clear that Bartók's prime purpose is to engage our imaginations; the percussion instruments are used with extraordinary inventiveness, suggesting any number of nocturnal

[4] In spite of the curious differences of notations in these pairs of examples, the melodic contours are identical.

visions. Crickets and bullfrogs can easily be perceived, while the passage between bars 20–34 is one of the most spine-chilling examples of ghost music ever written. (According to Bartók's own timing the 'ghost' appears after 1 minute 45 seconds of music.) After the ghost has walked, harp, celesta and piano combine in shimmering *glissandi* that suggests the glitter of moonlight on the troubled surface of a lake. If ever music demanded to be listened to with the imagination at full stretch this is it; read into it what visions you will.

The finale is a complete contrast, a wild gipsy dance whose driving rhythms give the music an intensely physical quality. The form, such as it is, is a rondo, the main theme a bouncy trip down-and-up a scale with a catchy if elusive rhythm. Thrumming pizzicato chords on massed strings suggest guitars, while some of the writing for the piano is surely meant to convey that the player is too drunk to be capable of playing octaves without splitting every note. As is often the case in folk dances there are a considerable number of variations of tempo, episodes where individual dancers show off their particular skills. In such noisy and exuberant company the celesta is out of place and for much of the movement the player joins the pianist to form a piano duet. In addition to the 'gipsy fiddler' tunes there is a hilarious dialogue at one point between the pianist, trying to play a popular song, and the strings who, as one man, decide for no particular reason to practise their scales.

A slower central section, the girl dancers perhaps, leads to a brief but impassioned cello solo; if it is a male courtier, he fails in his intent for the music takes flight in swift upward scales whose irregular rhythms remind us of the opening theme. Suddenly there is a moment of calm as harp and celesta do indeed play that theme, its syncopations ironed out so that all the notes are equal. Did Bartók have in mind the extra careful deliberation with which the really drunk will enunciate every syllable in order to prove their complete sobriety? Perhaps, for the revels resume as wildly as before only to terminate in a general collapse.

Concerto for Orchestra
(1943)

In the autumn of 1940, after an arduous and frustrating journey, Bartók and his wife (a former pupil) arrived in America with the hope of settling there permanently. His health was already a cause for concern and such work as he was able to obtain was not too well paid. The best part of a year was spent researching and noting down a huge collection of Yugoslav folksongs that had been amassed by an American enthusiast and scholar called Milman Parry and which was lodged in the archives of Columbia University. The work was not uncongenial but inevitably it left him little time or energy to compose. A mysterious illness sapped his strength; grants began to run out, and, although he was honoured by various universities, he felt the understandable despair of an unwilling exile.

1 March 1942

. . . And now the bad knews. (sic) Our situation is getting daily worse and worse. All I can say is that never in my life since I earn my livelihood (that is from my 20th year) have I been in such a dreadful situation as I will probably be very soon. To say dreadful is probably exaggerated, but not too much . . . I am rather pessimistic, I lost all confidence in people, in countries, in everything . . . Until now we had two free pianos, a baby grand and an upright. Just today I got the news the upright will be taken from us. Of course we have no money to hire a second piano. So we will have no possibility to study two-piano works. And each month brings a similar blow . . .[5]

(The 'we' refers to his wife Ditta with whom Bartók had given some successful two-piano recitals.)

In 1943 his health deteriorated seriously with nightly fevers and such pain in his joints that he could scarcely walk. Soon he was confined to bed in hospital. In such circumstances he must have found a visit from Koussevitsky the famous conductor a welcome surprise, the more so when Koussevitsky offered him a commission of a thousand dollars to write a work for the Boston Symphony Orchestra. Bartók had some doubts about his ability to cope with such an invitation but the conductor left him a cheque for five hundred dollars and promised that he would receive the rest on completion. Amazingly, Bartók managed to write the 'Concerto for Orchestra' (as he chose to call it) in the space of two months. The decision to call it a concerto rather than a symphony was a compliment to the virtuosity of the Boston players and the work has proved to be a magnificent showpiece for any orchestra that tackles it.

The concerto begins mysteriously with a slow-moving theme on cellos and basses, a quiet shimmering figure from the violins and a faint suggestion of a tune from flutes. It is a formula that one might legitimately compare with the opening of Schubert's 'Unfinished' symphony even though the effect is very different. Schubert's initial theme is designed to be memorable as a tune, 'laid down' to be fully matured in the central development section where it is transformed to dramatic purpose. Bartók's music is a perfect example of the fundamental change of attitude that we find in a twentieth-century composer. His opening phrase is not really a theme in the Schubertian sense; it is

[5]From Halsey Stevens, *The Life and Music of Béla Bartók* (O.U.P., 1953).

deliberately vague, ambiguous in its rhythm, a shape rather than a melody. Certainly it is evocative, suggesting darkness and mystery; but its true purpose is to establish the fundamental importance of an interval, the fourth. (Intervals are measured from the lower note to the higher: thus A—D, B—E, C♯—F♯ are all fourths.) Here, at the very start of the work we find four of them in the first six bars, two rising, two falling.

Ex. 1

The ensuing rustle from the violins is pure tone-painting, a suggestion of a faint breeze stirring the leaves in the dawn mist; two flutes imitate a bird-call — a not too fanciful interpretation since Bartók's love of nature is well documented. Gradually the opening phrase from cellos and basses is extended, still emphasising the fourths as the most important interval. A solo flute offers a vaguely Oriental melody which creates quite a stir in the lower strings. Three muted trumpets accept the flute's suggestion a trifle uncertainly, hesitating at the end of each little group of notes. Suddenly, to thrilling effect, divided violins introduce a passionate melody, derived from, but by no means copying, the flute's first theme. The gipsy influence is very strong here, though not for long; bassoons, followed in turn by all the woodwind, initiate a machine-like repetition of a five-note fragment, consistently rising and whipping up the tempo as it goes. (It is a twentieth-century version of a technique used by Beethoven in his *Egmont* overture, repeating one small pattern a number of times until enough tension has been wound up to cause a break into a new and quicker tempo.) Using the rising five-note pattern as a springboard, Bartók's theme explodes into action.

Ex. 1a

Notice that although this appears to be totally different from the dark opening theme (Ex. 1), there is still a predominance of fourths; bar 1 covers an 'augmented' fourth, bar 2 has C—F followed by the join into bar 3, E♭—A♯; bar 4 is bar 1 inverted, bar 5 has yet another fourth, E♭—B♭. Increasingly in this movement we will find Bartók exploiting this way of establishing 'family relationships' between themes. Ex. 1a proves to be very adaptable and he frequently breaks off one small part (segments 1, 2 or 3) and toys with it, tossing it from one section of the orchestra to another. In amongst the fun and games a single trombone introduces a rather more severe idea, although this too makes extensive use of fourths.

Ex. 1b

This should be tucked away into the listener's memory as it is destined to have a very exciting future.

A contrasting note is proffered by an oboe with a curiously innocent little tune that rocks gently to and fro between one note and its next-door neighbour. It creates an oasis of calm from which we are rudely aroused by a sudden return to the vigorous five-note passage which broke out of the introductory section. (Ex.1a/bar 1) This sweeps through the score with tremendous energy, only to give way to a forceful discussion of Ex.1a/bars 2–3. A clarinet tries to quieten things down with a degree of success, but once again the impatient strings throw in the little five-note phrase, breaking the spell. We have reached the climax of the movement, a marvellous fugue for the whole brass section based on Ex.1b. This is music fit to blow down the walls of Jericho and it culminates with a huge sustained chord that literally seems to burst apart. The little two-note tune returns, this time on a clarinet instead of an oboe; but after a delicately scored interlude followed by a few false starts, Ex.1a makes a very positive reappearance, sweeping all before it. A last outburst from the brass (Ex.1b) brings the movement to an end.

The second movement is called '*Giuoco della Coppie*', or 'Joke with couples'. Is it possible that Bartók may have been inspired by the vision of a sort of musical Noah's Ark? We know he was fascinated by animals, birds and insects so the idea is not wholly frivolous. After a few bars from a side-drum to establish the pace,[6] two bassoons lead off with a pawky little tune in which they consistently stay a sixth apart. Next we have a pair of oboes a third apart, a pair of clarinets a seventh apart, a pair of flutes a fifth apart and then a pair of trumpets a second apart. The intervals are preserved constantly with each pair and I have sometimes wondered whether the different intervals, a third, a fifth, a seventh, and so on, might perhaps represent the different bulk of the animals — wider or narrower as they are. It is a fantasy that has no grounding in scholarship, but Bartók must have had a reason for deciding to arrange the

---

[6]Crotchet = 94, not 74 as shown in the printed score.

music in this unique fashion. One can of course argue that it was a way of showing off the virtuosity of the wind-players in the Boston Symphony, but the music is not really a vehicle for technical display. Britten does that much more consciously in his 'Variations on a Theme of Purcell' ('Young Person's Guide'). The instruments appear in a different order but there too we find a pair of flutes (albeit with a piccolo added), a pair of oboes, a pair of clarinets and a pair of bassoons. However, the differences of character are much more sharply defined, and Britten, especially in the flute and clarinet variations, certainly aims to show off the virtuosity of the players.

In the centre of the movement there is a brief chorale for brass, a few moments of solemnity that only make the side-drum fidgety. But then my Noah's Ark fantasy suffers a blow, for the woodwind procession begins again, this time with *three* bassoons. Next we find paired oboes and clarinets playing together as a garrulous quartet. Bartók rings further changes as the movement draws to its close, the final touch consisting of a delightful fusion of all the various intervals into one harmonious chord. The side-drum beat dies away to nothing: the movement is ended.

The central movement of the five is called *Elegia*. It begins rather as the first movement did with double-basses playing a shadowy theme in which fourths are again conspicuous. Then the ripples start, little fountains of notes on clarinet or flute with a surrounding haze provided by the harp. A piercing high D flat on oboe and clarinet freezes all movement, and then, after a pause, the ripples begin again but this time as though seen in slow motion. Suddenly the mood changes completely as Bartók springs a major surprise on us. Plucked from page two of the Concerto and transplanted onto page fifty-three we find the very phrase that muted trumpets had once offered tentatively before the first passionate outcry from the violins (see page 44). Now violins and clarinets join in this Orientally-slanted melody, dramatically accompanied by sweeping downward scales and massive thumps from the lower regions of the orchestra. The mood grows increasingly agitated and vehement until a huge climax is reached with the return of the gipsy lament that the violins had played so passionately in the introduction to the first movement. Indeed the motto for this central Elegy could well be 'By the waters of Babylon we sat down and wept' for there can be no mistaking the impressions of water nor of a dreadful despair.

That despair melts away in the ensuing movement, the '*Intermezzo Interrotto*', or Interrupted Intermezzo. After a peremptory clearing of musical throats from the entire string section, a solo oboe embarks on a shy little tune with a minimal accompaniment. It has the slightly irregular lilt characteristic of Bulgarian folk-music though there is no reason to believe it is not Bartók's own creation. It is developed in several ways, sometimes by fitting itself against its own image, mirror-fashion. Its character is clearly feminine even though rather demure. Not so the violas who, standing in for an imaginary tenor, sing an ardent love-song. The impression of a serenade is heightened by the harp accompaniment; here, one feels, is a truly operatic conception, but one which is destined to have a rude interruption. A brief reprise of the shy maiden's song slyly disintegrates into a vamping accompaniment of the most banal kind. A solo clarinet introduces a tune composed entirely of descending sequences, each one a little more absurd than its predecessor. As if losing control, the tune begins to tumble over itself only to be greeted by a Rabelaisian 'raspberry' from muted trumpets and shrill woodwind, followed by a cackle of laughter from the clarinets. Two monstrous farts from the trombones form an even more derisive comment.

The significance of this grotesque passage is lost on many a listener today since the object of its mockery is seldom heard any more. It appears that while working on this Concerto Bartók heard Shostakovich's '*Leningrad*' Symphony for the first time. (It was still wartime and the work was being performed quite often to inspire us with admiration for our Russian allies.) Bartók found the prevailing theme of Shostakovich's symphony ludicrously inept in the context of so much human suffering and could not resist the temptation to lampoon it in this admittedly rather childish way. The joke is soon over, and as the musical laughter dies down the 'tenor' theme reappears, gorgeously harmonised. A tender wisp of the 'girl's' tune leads to a brief flute cadenza, surely a nightingale singing to the young lovers; they bid each other good-night and the movement ends as they tiptoe away into the darkness. Purists will no doubt argue that such an interpretation is not supported by any documentation, yet so much of Bartók's music is descriptive, so much is based on folk situations that I feel we are perfectly justified in seeing such images if they seem apposite. Bartók collected innumerable folk-songs describing the joys and pangs of village courtship; the themes in this movement are clearly pastiche folk-songs, the 'voices' of oboe and viola are surely symbols for girl and boy. Indeed, the movement would make a delightful ballet; by calling it an Intermezzo Bartók is certainly inviting us not to take it too seriously.

A short arresting fanfare from four horns in unison shatters the mood; its final note, reinforced by trumpets, gives us a moment to absorb it into our memories since, in due course, we will discover that it has a more important role to play than a butler's announcement that the finale is about to be served. Guitar-like, the violas and cellos start thrumming away energetically, increasing their pace to match the urgent scurry of the violins. The gipsy influence is strong indeed and for quite a time the music relies on the sheer excitement of speed to sweep us along in its wake. Suddenly a single bassoon is exposed in a brief solo, clearly derived from the opening horn fanfare. Other woodwind instruments take up the idea with the intention of launching a decently respectable fugue, but just as it seems to be getting under way there is a complete change of mood. A romantically inclined flute turns the fugue subject upside down, playing capricious tricks with its rhythm; violins, divided into six parts, play a descending sequence of text-book harmonies that suggest we are entering an oasis of calm. It is not to be however, and, goaded on by the woodwind, we are soon swept away into the helter-skelter rush of the opening pages once more. But now a new element appears, so important that its first entry has to be on a trumpet. Beginning with three very positive notes (D♭—A♭—D♭) it grabs our attention even more insistently with an eight-fold repetition of the central A♭. This theme is the real substance of the movement, a fugue of truly classic dimensions even though it may seem far from classical in its presentation. Despite the mad whirl of semiquavers with which he surrounds it, Bartók treats the fugue subject with all the skill of an eighteenth-century contrapuntist; the theme is inverted, it is played in notes of double the value; it is played in notes of half the value; it is treated in *stretto* (with the entries overlapping); it is even developed so as to shed new light on its character. Yet though this is truly a demonstration of academic skills at their best, the enduring impression of the movement is its demonic energy. Even when the fugue subject appears in its final augmentation it is shot through with hurricane scales on strings and wind. To play the work at all taxes the skills of the finest orchestras; for a sick man to have written it in seven weeks is something of a miracle.

Violin Concerto No. 2
(1937–8)

Bartók was first attracted to the idea of writing a violin concerto in 1907; however, he was entering a period of change at the time and was growing increasingly dissatisfied with the frankly romantic idiom — a state of mind shared equally by such contemporaries as Stravinsky and Hindemith. In the end he salvaged what he considered the best portion of the work and incorporated it in the first of the 'Two Portraits for Orchestra', Op. 5. Thirty years passed before he tackled the medium again and then it was only as a commission from the Hungarian violinist Zoltan Székely. Although he was asked to write a violin concerto, Bartók said that he would much prefer to write an extended set of variations, presumably on a Hungarian theme. Székely insisted that as he was paying for the work he had the right to specify its nature; he wanted a concerto, not a set of variations. In the end he got both, for, not liking to admit defeat in an argument over artistic matters, Bartók with some deviousness produced a concerto that is in fact an extended example of variation form. Being a composer of infinite technical resource he disguised his intentions very cleverly. At first hearing, or even on looking at the score, there doesn't seem to be much resemblance between the opening phrases of the first movement and of the finale. The one consists of quiet and somewhat isolated pizzicato notes on the lower strings placed beneath some remarkably simple harp chords — unadulterated B major for the most part. The other has all the strings in unison playing an aggressive phrase that has a kick like a mule. Yet, as we can easily see if we superimpose one on top of the other, the bare bones are identical.

Ex. 1

It is easy enough to dismiss those initial pizzicato notes as a mere preamble, but the violin's entrance clearly brings a theme of considerable importance. Its broad lyrical line is admirably suited to the violin, but then so too is the cheerful dance tune with which, quite unaccompanied, it makes its appearance in the finale. By slightly more Procrustean methods we discover that these two themes, so unlike in character, are brothers under the skin.

The transformation of themes is an old trick and one of which Bartók's great Hungarian predecessor Liszt was particularly fond. It would be laborious to trace the other thematic relationships which exist, but the fact is that there are also similarities of structure between the outer movements of this concerto, similarities of which we may only be aware subconsciously but whose existence gives a satisfying unity of design. One of Bartók's greatest strengths is his feeling for musical structure; whatever the intricacy of detail he never loses sight of the shape of the movement as a whole. In almost every work we find a fascination with shapes, mirror-images, back-to-front versions of themes, arches — they all appear time after time in his music, so much so that one is sometimes amazed that music of such burning intensity can be so meticulously organized.

Considering that it was written in the late 1930s this concerto is a remarkably tonal work. In spite of the harp's initial chords of B major, the

Ex. 2

true key is B minor, a key which both Elgar and Walton also chose for their violin concertos. Like them, Bartók obviously believed that the violin is essentially a melodic instrument for all its brilliance and agility. The opening theme extends for twenty-one bars of which only the first four are shown in example Ex. 2. But then a slightly more restless figure establishes itself, bringing with it an increase in pace; an element of virtuosity becomes apparent leading to the first real climax. Almost as though rebuking the soloist for this bout of exhibitionism, the orchestral violins restate the first theme, or as much of it as suits Bartók's purpose, which is not merely to re-establish the original tempo but to provide a firm reminder of the opening. The soloist seems to accept the hint in the nicest possible way but then, without warning, starts to goad the orchestra with a waspish little phrase which brings increasingly anxious and fluttering reactions from wind and strings alike.[7]

A sequence of crotchets wafting out of the heights brings a period of calm that lulls us into a false sense of security, for suddenly there is a sort of

[7]For those sufficiently interested, this passage too has its counterpart in the finale, as a comparison between bars 56–8 from I and bars 87–93 of III will show. The later version is 'stretched' by a chromatic ascent in the woodwind, but allowing for the differences in rhythm, the two passages are closely related.

screech from the orchestra and, like a falcon swooping down on its prey, the violin has a fierce descending chromatic scale which leads into an agitated episode that only a savage trill on two trumpets can effectively quell.[8] Calm is restored by harp chords reminiscent of the opening; a new theme, a surrogate 'second subject', appears in guileless simplicity. But is it so 'new' after all? Although new in character, the notes themselves were laid down at the very start of the work with the pizzicato bass shown in Ex. 1. Here it assumes an importance that has never been hinted at. It is echoed, after a fashion, by a cor anglais and, a little later, by cellos and basses. For more than forty bars (115–59) peace reigns, the meandering scales on the violin being no more than a twentieth-century equivalent of the type of passage-work found so often in Mozart and Beethoven. Then, just as the orchestra shows signs of total somnolence, 'Enough!' cries the soloist, and awakens everyone with a vigorous finger-exercise straight out of Everyman's Advanced Violin Tutor. This 'practising' passage ('sawing away regardless' to use Sir Henry Wood's unforgettable phrase) continues for some time, even though first a horn and then a cor anglais offers lyrical reminders of the opening theme.

A curious dialogue ensues between the strings — with distant memories of the opening tune in the violins casting a shadow in the basses — and the wind, whose syncopated rhythms have quite a jazzy flavour (182). The soloist seems to want to join the wind and offers some energetic triple-stopping (three-note chords) in exchange. Then, as if realising that such a display of strength is not really needed, the violin embarks on a perfect inversion of the original theme against a quietly shimmering background of harp and celesta. (Notice that the 'finger-exercise' figuration is now given to violas and second violins in turn, an opportunity for a little basic practice that can do no harm.) The soloist breaks off in mid-flight with a terse pattern of three rising notes — actually the lead-in to the first theme — which becomes the basis of an animated discussion in the orchestra. An abrupt halt and a momentary silence lead us to a classic recapitulation with the soloist now presenting the theme two octaves higher than it had been originally and also with some subtle changes in the orchestral accompaniment. As recapitulations go it is fairly strict though there is a characteristic fondness for turning some of the music upside down. A sequence of rapid tightly-knit chromatic groups leads to the substantial cadenza which, in its first stages, is accompanied by lyrical references to the opening theme from bass clarinet to solo horn. It is an easily recognised landmark for, having settled like a particularly vicious wasp on the open string D, the violin experiments briefly with microtones, flattening or sharpening the note by less than a semitone. As might be expected the cadenza is challengingly difficult. It is followed by a

[8]Since the preceding passage (bars 73–91) has flirted with the serial technique of a twelve-note row in both violin and orchestra, this outburst may justifiably be regarded as a scathing rejection of Schoenbergian methods.

condensed summary of the main themes — the jazzy one on bassoons, the lyrical first subject on a solo horn, and other fragments of which one catches only a brief glimpse as they flash by. The movement ends with a solid unison B, reaffirming Bartók's conviction that tonality is not dead. (The thought comes — does so positive an assertion of B serve as a signature for Bartók?)

Székely's wish for a concerto and not a set of variations is openly defied in the second movement which is unashamedly a set of six variations on a theme; there is even a double-bar in the score to show the demarcation between each variation. The theme, a series of short phrases that suggest derivation from a folk-song, is in a slightly distorted version of G major, the fourth note of the scale tending to be sharpened. Variation I is an elegant elaboration of the tune with a minimal accompaniment from pizzicato double-basses and timpani, mere dabs of sound to mark the time. Variation II is virtually a duet for violin and harp, whose rapidly turning figures seem literally to 'run rings' around the soloist. The woodwind provide a relatively static accompaniment. Variation III shows the violin at its most aggressive, goaded by sharp dissonances from a pair of horns. Variation IV adopts a slower tempo with the cellos and basses playing a simplified version of the theme while the violin weaves sinuous coils of notes above. The closing bars create a contrasting mood of absolute calm with the soloist initiating a simple pattern of notes that is imitated in canon by violas, cellos and double-basses in turn. Variation V is a miniature scherzo in which harp and woodwind play a prominent part, while even a triangle and side-drum are enlisted to enhance the distinctly playful character of the music. Variation VI must surely be added to the catalogue of Bartók's 'insect' music with the solo part suggesting the rapid beat of tiny wings. Gradually the movement slows to a halt; with the utmost simplicity the soloist recalls the original theme in a higher octave. The final bar is more like a disappearance than a conclusion.

We have already seen how the third movement begins in Exx. 1 and 2. Although the cheerful little dance tune presented by the soloist leads us to expect a Rondo, the music is actually a large-scale sonata-form movement which is also a variation on the first movement. This it resembles quite closely in structure; for instance the first break into a quicker tempo comes in bar 22 in the first movement, bar 29 in the third. (Since the movements are in 4/4 and 3/4 respectively this means 88 beats as opposed to 87!) References to the first movement become more obvious when the second violins, accompanied by pizzicato strings and harp, launch into a lyrical singing theme which is at once taken up by all the woodwind in unison. It is shortly after this that the variant already mentioned in footnote 7 on page 50 occurs. Not surprisingly there are more opportunities for the display of sheer virtuosity in this movement, but one notably quieter moment is worth mentioning. Easily recognised with its simple accompaniment of triangle, cymbal and harp, it appears to be a totally new theme, lyrical in character even if eccentric in its intervals. On closer examination this too proves to be a remarkably close relation to a theme from the first movement, the flirtation with serialism that was then so rudely received. This time it merely evokes a sort of *frisson* in the strings.

Later in the movement the opening dance tune is converted into a carillon by the brass to tremendous effect, an idea which is picked up quite captivatingly by the soloist towards the very end. Speaking of endings, Bartók's original intention was to finish with a purely orchestral playout but Székely persuaded him that no soloist would really feel happy about this; an alternative was duly forthcoming though both versions are printed in the score. It is curious that similar alternatives are provided at the end of the *Concerto for Orchestra*. Bartók would seem to be the last composer to have had doubts about his music; he had pursued his own path heedless of biting criticism from those who should have known better. Yet in these two cases he clearly had second thoughts; it was characteristic of his integrity that he did not attempt to suppress the original versions but rather to leave posterity to judge.

Piano Concerto No. 3
(1945)

Bartók's first two piano concertos, dating from 1926 and 1931 respectively, were certainly written to suit his own style of playing and to provide him with what Stravinsky would have called 'visiting cards' — works with which he could introduce himself to a wider public as composer and pianist. In this respect he was following in a long line of tradition embracing such varied figures as Mozart, Beethoven, Chopin, Liszt, Rakhmaninov and Prokofiev. Both works treat the piano as essentially a percussion instrument and there is a raw ferocity about much of the writing which antagonised critics and public alike. Nowhere do we find the openly seductive melodies that have brought Rakhmaninov such popularity; the audience is battered into submission rather than cajoled. Although he was a solo pianist of the first rank, this tendency was not particularly apparent in his recital programmes. His repertoire included Scarlatti, Bach, Couperin, Mozart, Beethoven, Chopin, Liszt, Debussy, Ravel as well as his amazing piano transcriptions of Richard Strauss's major orchestral works. Not surprisingly he also included works by such contemporaries as Kodály, Stravinsky, Hindemith and even Schoenberg (despite his pronounced scepticism about serial methods); yet it seems that he did not feel that he had a Messianic role to play with regard to modern music in general. It was his own work, naturally enough, that interested him most, and the fact that his 'official' Opus 1 is a Rhapsody for Piano and Orchestra shows that from the first he visualised himself as the most persuasive advocate for his cause. However, he did not make his task easy whether by the musical idiom he developed or the technical demands he made on himself. The first two concertos in particular are fearsomely difficult to play, calling for exceptional rhythmic precision and steely strength in wrist and finger.

The private life of a composer is not always of any great significance with regard to his art but Bartók's case has a relevant interest. Like many musicians at the start of their careers he was forced to do a certain amount of teaching to earn an adequate living. In 1907 he gained a professorship for piano at the Budapest Academy of Music; although he detested teaching he found himself much attracted by two girl students. The first, Stefi Geyer, was a talented violinist to whom he not only wrote long and revealing letters but also dedicated the abortive violin concerto whose first movement he later adapted as the first of *Two Portraits* for violin and orchestra (Op. 5). It seems that she must have felt that they were too incompatible for a deeper relationship and in February 1908 she wrote him a parting letter. The day he received it he wrote a sad little piano piece called 'Elle est morte'. The heartache was superficial, though, and he found solace in the company of a pupil who had first appeared in his class at the tender age of fourteen. Her name was Márta Ziegler and in the following year (1908) Bartók was already dedicating quite important compositions to her including the aptly named 'Portrait of a Girl'. In the autumn of 1909, when she was in her seventeenth year, they were married; a son, Béla, was born the year after.

In 1923 there was an almost uncanny repetition of the same situation. Once more Bartók became emotionally involved with a piano student in his class. Inevitably the age-gap between them was even wider but he found her charms so irresistible that a divorce was arranged and quickly followed by his second marriage. Ditta Pásztory was a talented pianist and was to remain with him for the rest of his life, giving many concerts with him as a piano-duo.

More than twenty years later, in 1945, Bartók began work on the Third Piano Concerto; this time he was writing not for himself but for Ditta. Although America was not proving to be quite the Promised Land they had both hoped for, there was much to lift Bartók's spirits that year. Not only was Nazi Germany defeated; Bartók was nominated as an honorary member of the new Hungarian parliament and restored to the various official musical posts from which he had resigned when he left his homeland. The Third Concerto is clearly influenced by these crucial events; its opening pages radiate a sense of gentle content, a feeling of 'All's right with the world' that is absent from its two brittle and harsh predecessors. Ironically Bartók did not live to hear it; indeed the final seventeen bars had to be orchestrated from a shorthand score by a devoted disciple of Bartók's named Tibor Serly. (He was also responsible for constructing the Viola Concerto from a number of sketches that the dying composer had been unable to finish.)

The Third Concerto is one of the most classical works that Bartók ever wrote, classical in spirit and in form. In the opening bars the strings set up a gentle undulation of harmonies not unlike the shimmering introduction to Stravinsky's *Petrushka*, though somewhat lower in pitch. Two timpani quietly etch in the dominant and tonic notes of E major (B—E) thereby proclaiming that the music is truly committed to a positive tonality. With both hands in unison, two octaves apart, the pianist begins a long and elegant tune with some elaborate, almost rococo, decorations. Its style resembles a Romanian dance called a *doïna*. Towards the end of the tune the notes seem almost to tumble over themselves, giving an impression of quickening pace even though the tempo remains constant. As is so often the case in Bartók concertos the orchestra takes over just enough of the theme to establish its identity but then proceeds to turn it in new directions.

A striking feature of the piano-writing in this movement is the extensive use of parallel motion between the two hands, whether in single unison notes, octaves or chords. At the twenty-seventh bar the pianist introduces a note of rhetoric that is almost Brahms-like in texture leading to a passage in octaves in which the left hand presents a delayed mirror-image of the right. Bar 54 sees the introduction of a true Second Subject which frequently exploits pairs of falling notes and fluttering trills. A charming dialogue develops between piano and solo clarinet who cuckoo happily at each other as the exposition ends.

The structure could scarcely be clearer for the ensuing Development begins with boldly declaimed arpeggios in A flat major from the pianist and a long extension of the opening theme, now on all the woodwind in unison. This is followed by a more fragmented version for piano solo in B flat major upon which the strings have a few cogent comments to make. Soon the charming second subject reappears (unison in the piano again) its trills setting the woodwind all a-flutter. A sustained and gradually diminishing trill from the violins leads us to a classic Recapitulation, the pianist's hands still moving in parallel but now in paired notes instead of simple unison. Every feature of the original Exposition is recognisable in some form and the movement ends enchantingly in what might almost be described without offence as a sort of cloud-cuckoo-land, so often does that most identifiable of bird-songs seem to appear.

It is unlikely to be pure coincidence that the second movement begins (and ends) with what I have termed the 'cuckoo' phrase. In this new context it serves a very different purpose, no longer a playful frivolity but the beginning of a serenely beautiful phrase of disarming simplicity. Bartók gives the instruction *Adagio religioso*, the only time he uses such a word in all his works; the religious feeling is one of monastic austerity, a warning against an over-sentimental approach for the string-players, who are divided into five-part polyphony without the double-basses. Their opening phrases, fifteen bars in all, die away to silence. The piano enters with a theme that is like a hymn; its reticence can only be compared to the entry in the comparable movement in Beethoven's Fourth Concerto, though Beethoven's music is tinged with a profound sorrow that is quite absent here, as is the sense of conflict between strings and piano that Beethoven exploits to such dramatic effect. So far as I know nobody has ever proffered an explanation for Bartók's decision to write this chorale-like movement. Two possibilities occur to me; first, that it may be a literal hymn of gratitude that the war was ended and his country freed from Nazi domination; second, that he knew he was dying of cancer and that the music, if not exactly a prayer for his own soul, is a reconciliation with the approach of death. Certainly the strings' closing phrase is like a gesture of benediction (54–7).

There follows an extraordinary interpolation, a whirring sound from the strings that suggests the flight of innumerable insects. Oboe, clarinet and piano fill the air with tiny fragments of sound, the nocturnal cries of birds and the little creatures that seldom venture out in daylight. Some of these darting patterns of notes are based on actual bird-calls that Bartók had noted down in Asheville, North Carolina in 1944. Nearly twenty years previously he had written a suite of piano pieces called 'Out of Doors' which he had dedicated to Ditta when they had been married for only two years. Was this movement intended to stir memories for her too? This whole central section is a classic example of Bartók's identification with nature, quite different from the soft 'water-colour' impressions we gain from Delius or Vaughan-Williams, sharply etched but no less deeply felt.

In due course the pianist's opening chorale returns, this time on wood-wind, with an almost Bach-like two-part accompaniment on the piano that now and then dissolves into shimmering runs and trills. There is a moment or two of passion towards the end of the movement but the closing bars again seem like a benediction, the last two chords even saying a peaceful Amen.

The last movement brings an abrupt awakening with a whirlwind rush up the keyboard leading to a strongly syncopated theme. This is the most familiar and popular aspect of Bartók, the stamping rhythms and sheer animal vitality that he exploits better than any other major twentieth-century composer. Yet even in this movement there is an unashamedly classical element, for after the initial energetic dance rhythms have exhausted themselves in a timpani solo, the pianist sets out on a strict fugue, a whim which the orchestra seems happy to follow. This is developed at some length until the pianist introduces another dance tune in octaves, loud and clear. A second solo passage for timpani leads to a new episode, gentler in character and marked *grazioso*. Yet another theme, rather more foursquare in character, appears in the orchestra, provoking the pianist to frenzied scale-passages of great brilliance. After further exploration of the 'gentle' theme, this time on horns to emphasise its pastoral nature, an exciting chromatic scale from wind and piano leads us back to Theme I, more exuberant than ever. A breathless silence precedes the final *Presto*, beginning gruffly on the piano but growing ever more exciting. Bartók was still working on the manuscript score in bed, five days before his death. In his desperation to finish he made a shorthand version of the final seventeen bars, lacking the time or strength to make a full score. The finale gives not the smallest hint that his life was ebbing away fast; it is truly a dance in the face of death, a triumph of the human spirit.

BEETHOVEN

1770–1827

Speculation about who is the greatest composer is a fairly fruitless exercise but it is undeniable that Beethoven was one of the most significant; he it was who extended and developed such major musical forms as the sonata, symphony, string quartet and concerto; he it was who liberated music from classical restraints and opened the way for the Romantic Movement in which composers expressed emotions in personal terms rather than as abstractions. Early Beethoven works take over from Haydn; late Beethoven leads towards Schumann, Brahms and even (in the slow movement of the Ninth Symphony) towards Mahler. To accomplish such a revolution in musical taste required an immensely powerful creative personality; to accomplish it despite the handicap of deafness needed exceptional moral courage.

Although the bulk of the music written by Beethoven in his early years gives little evidence of genius, one work stands far above the others, a work which ironically he was never to hear performed. It is the 'Funeral Cantata on the death of the Emperor Joseph II' composed in 1790. Performances had twice been cancelled owing to the uncooperative attitude of the players who found the music altogether too difficult. A similar fate met the cantata that Beethoven wrote to celebrate the accession to the throne of Joseph II's successor, Leopold II. Surprisingly we have no record of Beethoven's reaction to this considerable setback at a crucial period in his life. He certainly realised that the Funeral Cantata in particular represented an enormous step forward towards artistic maturity; in fact he used a substantial portion of the material in the second finale of his opera Fidelio, a sure acknowledgment that he realised its worth. (The Cantata itself was not performed until 1884.)

It seems quite probable that this double rebuff brought a psychological block in its wake. The effective rejection of two substantial works in the course of a single year must have hurt Beethoven's self-esteem; certainly he continued to compose, but not for orchestra. Apart from the first two piano concertos, a form in which his own mastery of the keyboard assured him of success, all the works written during the last decade of the century were sonatas or chamber-music of some kind. This reluctance to embark on a major orchestral composition is surprising and uncharacteristic. The concept of the symphony as a form had been clarified by such early masters as C.P.E. Bach, Wagenseil, Gassman and Stamitz; it had then been developed with wonderfully inventive powers by Haydn. One would have expected Beethoven to welcome the challenge with enthusiasm, yet even a period of tuition with Haydn in 1792 failed to give him the necessary confidence to do so. He made some sketches for one in 1795 but they proved abortive. If the lessons with Haydn had planted symphonic seeds, they appear to have lain dormant for seven years; with apt historical timing they were to flower with the dawn of a new century in the year 1800, the year of the First Symphony, Op. 21.

Symphony No. 1 in C Major
Op. 21

Following a precept set on many previous occasions by Haydn and his contemporaries, Beethoven begins this symphony with a slow introduction. Although the opening bars may seem undramatic to a modern ear, they are sufficiently unorthodox to have elicited a great deal of comment over the years. It should be understood that the standard way of beginning any major work, whether symphony, concerto, sonata or quartet, was to spell out a sequence of notes or harmonies that would establish a 'home' key, or tonal base. For example, each Mozart symphony begins with a clear declaration of tonality. 'This music,' he seems to say, 'is *in* the key of D major or G minor or C major', as the case may be. Such a declaration is not a mere technicality of interest only to theoreticians; it is vital to the understanding of all the larger musical forms in Western civilisation for a period of at least a century (1740–1840). The 'home' key, or tonic to give it its proper name, served both as point of departure and as ultimate destination. The listener was supposed to be able to appreciate the import of journeys into new tonal centres that contradicted the tonal implications of the original one as well as to savour the satisfaction of returning 'home' after such adventures. At the very start of this symphony Beethoven leads the listener astray by suggesting other 'homes' than the proper one of C major so that when the music does break into a quick tempo we sense a twofold release. Not only is the sustained tension of the Introduction resolved, but also the enigma of uncertain tonality. However, if the Introduction seems to pose the riddle 'What do these pairs of chords signify?' the subsequent *Allegro con brio* supplies an answer. Careful listening reveals a close relationship between the slow opening and the quick music that emerges from it even though the character seems very different.

If the first main theme of the *Allegro* strikes a slightly military attitude with its crisp precision, the second theme is almost operatic in flavour with flute and oboe engaging in a delightful dialogue. The ghost of Mozart hovers in the air, soon to be exorcised with peremptory rhythms that suggest the rapid beat of a side-drum, even though such an instrument was not to find a regular place in the symphony orchestra for the best part of half a century. Out of this brief clash of arms we are suddenly shifted into a world of shadows and mystery. Cellos and basses lead the way, while the strings above offer an accompaniment of gently throbbing harmonies that briefly touch on tonal centres as yet unvisited. The air of mystery imparted by this passage is not simply achieved by playing quietly. The music is mysterious because it ventures into tonalities that contradict the basic components of C major, moving far from 'home'.

During the eighteenth and nineteenth centuries the repetition of the various sections of a composition was standard practice. If the music was for a soloist he would regard the repeat as an opportunity to introduce spontaneous embellishments of his own; if it was for orchestra such an element of caprice could scarcely be allowed, but it is perhaps not too cynical to suggest in those under-rehearsed days that a second try might have been welcomed by all. In such a symphony as this the repeat would be taken from the start of the *Allegro*, dispensing with the slow Introduction. The aesthetic value of the convention was to establish the 'home' key firmly in the listener's mind.

The so-called Development section, the central part of any movement constructed on these lines, begins with three reminders of the first main theme divided one from the other by restless syncopations that give an air of insecurity. Furthermore, the 'home' key of C major is deserted in favour of new tonal centres which shift so rapidly that not one is established with any permanence. Among the most fundamental differences between Western and Eastern music is the exploitation of such changes of tonality and its resultant effect. Eastern music tends to be conceived as a single (even if elaborately decorated) line, whereas Western music is more concerned with harmony and the play of relationships between one tonal centre and another. Hard to understand if one is not a composer is the subtle balance between the conscious and the subconscious processes during the composition of a work. Thus Beethoven's conscious self makes a purely intellectual decision to move further and further away from the 'home' key during the Development by introducing an increasing number of notes foreign to it. However, once these notes begin to appear in actuality they breed a reaction in the subconscious which dictates an emotional response, which in turn will affect the next intellectual decision. To draw a very simple analogy, suppose that one decides for no particular reason to write down the word 'horse'. One then decides (consciously) to add the word 'galloping'. The inner response to the image the two words 'horse galloping' evokes is an emotional one, essentially dramatic, which provokes the next conscious choice of word. If on the other hand one were to decide to add the word 'sleeping' to the 'horse' image, it would evoke a quite different emotional response, and in consequence a different sequel. Comparable to this, although far more complex in detail, is the process by which Beethoven arrives at the considerable 'storm' that takes place in the centre of the movement. By consciously deciding to shift from the 'home' key to remote tonal centres he breeds an emotional (subconscious) response that produces the storm. The point is so significant in comprehending symphonic thought that it needs to be made at this early stage.

The central crisis resolved, the composer re-assembles the original material in the third main section of the movement, the Recapitulation. This should never be regarded as mere repetition for the sake of academic convention; it is a reassessment of the themes in the light of experience gained during the Development. As to the final bars of the movement, they are designed to emphasise the restoration of the 'home' key of C major, as if to assure us that it is no longer at risk.

The second and third movements give a clear indication of Beethoven's transitional state as a composer since the slow movement looks back towards the formal dance-style of the eighteenth century while the ensuing Minuet (so-called) totally discards such conventions. The movements offer a contrast between the academic and the unorthodox, the *Andante* beginning with a demure theme that is treated as a miniature fugue, the following *Allegro molto e vivace* setting off like a whirlwind. Anything less like a Minuet could hardly be imagined and the title must be taken as a joke. The whole conception is totally original; it is in effect the first symphonic scherzo and is the largest comparable movement that he was to write for some time.

As for the finale, it begins with an impressive gesture that turns out to be a hoax, for, like a bevy of hesitant beginners the first violins make no less than five abortive attempts to play a scale, progressing one note further each time. It is a characteristic example of his musical humour that Beethoven would have hated us to take seriously. When at last the movement gets under way it sparkles with wit and vitality. In particular the rising scale that initially seemed to frighten the first violins proves to be a fruitful source of material, whether ascending or descending. Towards the end there are two massive pauses that lead us to expect some great event. Again it is a leg-pull, an amusing exploitation of the effect of anti-climax. The final march, garlanded with scales from the woodwind, is like a children's game. There were no clouds in Beethoven's sky when he wrote this delightful symphony.

Symphony No. 2 in D Major
Op. 36

Sketches for the Second Symphony were begun in 1800 but Beethoven was a slow worker and the germination of any of his major works was a laborious process involving much rejection of preliminary ideas, ideas which often seem incredibly banal but which were ultimately forged into great music. Perhaps the most remarkable thing about the Second Symphony is that it was written during a period of intense personal despair. In October 1802 Beethoven wrote a lengthy letter now known as the 'Heiligenstadt Testament'. Addressed to his brothers, though never sent, it expresses in eloquent

terms the composer's misery at the onset of deafness; the following is a
quotation of less than a quarter of this remarkable document.

> . . . not yet could I bring myself to say to people 'Speak louder, shout,
> for I am deaf.' O how should I then bring myself to admit the weakness of *a
> sense* which ought to be more perfect in me than in others, a sense which I
> once possessed in the greatest perfection, a perfection such as few assuredly
> in my profession have yet possessed it in — O I cannot do it! forgive me
> then, if you see me shrink away when I would fain mingle among you.
> Double pain does my misfortune give me, in making me misunderstood.
> Recreation in human society, the more delicate passages of conversation,
> confidential outpourings, none of these are for me; all alone, almost only so
> much as the sheerest necessity demands can I bring myself to venture into
> society; I must live like an exile; if I venture into company a burning dread
> falls on me, the dreadful risk of letting my condition be perceived. So it was
> these last six months which I passed in the country, being ordered by my
> sensible physician to spare my hearing as much as possible. He fell in with
> what has now become almost my natural disposition, though sometimes,
> carried away by the craving for society, I let myself be misled into it; but
> what humiliation when someone stood by me and heard a flute in the
> distance, and *I* heard *nothing*, or when someone heard *the herd-boy singing*,
> and I again heard nothing. Such occurances brought me nigh to despair, a
> little more and I had put an end to my own life — only it, *my art*, held me
> back. O it seemed to me impossible to quit the world until I had produced
> all I felt it in me to produce; and so I reprieved this wretched life — truly
> wretched, a body so sensitive that a change of any rapidity may alter my
> state from very good to very bad.'

Such inner torment in a Romantic composer would undoubtedly have
produced an equally harrowing piece of music, a literally Tragic symphony.
Beethoven, it seems, was able to exorcise despair by the act of composition
for the Second Symphony is an exuberant and optimistic work that bubbles
over with high spirits. Only in the slow introduction do we find the
occasional sorrowful phrase; even so, it appears to be more a conventional
expressive gesture than a revelation of private grief.

Many Haydn symphonies begin with a slow introduction, a convention that
Beethoven copied in four of his symphonies, including the first two. Here the
introduction to the opening movement is very much more elaborate than that
in the First Symphony. Although it begins in D major Beethoven soon
plunges into alien keys, taking us into a different world where eerie horn-
notes stab through the darkness and rapid ascending scales suggest great
winds blowing through echoing caverns. An eloquent phrase on violas and
cellos seems like a deep sigh, expressing a sorrow that is singularly absent
from the rest of the work, considering that it was written at a time when the
onset of deafness had put the composer into a suicidal mood. After sundry
fluttering trills from flutes and violins, a long sustained A builds the tension
until, with a sudden downward swoop, the first movement proper appears

out of the murk. The main theme is given to the cellos but the swift flurry of notes that flashes through the first violin part from time to time is an important feature that prevents the music from sounding at all pedestrian. A similar interpolation is to be found in the Second Subject, an almost Mozartean march to begin with, though it is subsequently treated in a deliberately rowdy manner. As in the First Symphony there is something of a storm in the middle of the movement but it is clearly not to be taken as serious. More important as an indication of the direction Beethoven was going to take is the Coda, the final section of the movement in which cellos and basses share a majestic ascent that recalls 'The Heavens are Telling' from Haydn's *Creation*. It was a work Beethoven much admired and the passage may even be a conscious tribute.

The idyllic Larghetto which follows seems so relaxed and serene that it is almost impossible to believe that it was written at the same time as the despairing document known as the Heiligenstadt Testament. Here we find the same lyrical character that often appears in Schubert, though he would have been a child of five or six at the time Beethoven composed this. In addition to the wealth of tunes, one of the great delights of the music is its scoring. Trumpets and drums are omitted; clarinets and bassoons in particular lend the movement its special colour. Apart from two ghostly dialogues between the lowest strings and plangent woodwind there is no sign of sorrow.

The ensuing scherzo is crisp and compact, notable for its very individual scoring. The rapid alternation between strings, horns or woodwind is like a practical joke designed to catch the players off their guard, while a comparable trick is played on the audience when, in the central section, the strings come to a complete halt only to be aroused again by a bellowing unison note on wind and brass which should take us all by surprise.

The finale, too, is full of humour, from its initial hiccup to the tiptoe games in the closing pages. With our instinctive feeling that symphonies are meant to be taken seriously it may be hard to accept that even a substantial outburst of orchestral fury proves to be a hoax, but Beethoven's deflation of his own rhetoric is unmistakable. However, the symphony as a whole shows a remarkable unity of themes, not so much four independent movements as a truly organic whole. The scale of the Symphony as a form was ripe for development; the 'Eroica', (No. 3), reveals a remarkable increase in stature.

Symphony No. 3 in E flat Major (The 'Eroica') Op. 55

In the spring of 1804 Beethoven completed his Third Symphony. On the title-page were inscribed two names, his own and (Napoleon) Bonaparte's. The work was meant to be dedicated to the great French revolutionary leader, although it is misleading to take it in any way as a portrait. (One does not write a funeral march for someone who is still alive.) However, when news came that Napoleon had assumed the title of Emperor, the composer flew into a rage and tore the title-page in half, so offended were his republican sentiments. In the end it appeared as 'Heroic Symphony; composed to preserve the memory of a great man, and dedicated to his Serene Highness Prince Lobkowitz' — one of Beethoven's aristocratic patrons. It is ironic that a symphony designed to celebrate a man who stood for revolutionary freedom should ultimately be dedicated to a prince.

After two massive chords of E flat major proclaiming the 'home' key, the most significant theme of the first movement appears in the cellos. Its confirmation of the key is undermined by a disturbing alien note (C sharp) that immediately spreads a feeling of unease to the violins. The almost pastoral mood of the opening is deceptive, as though a sculptor were caressing the stone before striking the first hammer-blow which will hew it into shape. By the twenty-fifth bar we find strongly accented chords that disrupt the even flow of the music; order is re-established with a full-blooded repetition of the first theme. The opening movement is particularly rich in material; the mood changes frequently and yet there is a convincing unity to the conception. Ideas that should be mentioned include an elegant 'conversation' between oboe, clarinet, flute and violins based on a three-note phrase, a leisurely rising tune played by clarinets, a strongly rhythmic and athletic passage for strings and a contrastingly gentle theme in the woodwind that begins with no less than nine repetitions of the same note.

During the Development section the opening theme is transformed in character partly by being shifted into a minor key, partly by being combined with the athletic pattern in the strings. At one point a fugue of sorts begins but it is soon engulfed in a violent storm whose dissonances shake the very foundations of Harmony. The other really outstanding moment in this wonderful movement comes just before the return home to the Recapitulation. The orchestral texture is reduced to a mere whisper from the violins, seeming for the moment to lose all impetus. Faint and evocative, a distant horn-call reminds us of the very opening theme. The suggestion is accepted joyfully by the full orchestra.

A major structural feature of the movement is the extension of the Coda, normally something of a formality. Beethoven launches into it with two strange side-slips in the harmony that must have seemed like a musical earthquake to listeners in 1805. The shock of the unexpected harmonies is emphasised by extreme dynamic contrasts between soft and loud. New light is then shed on the opening theme by a playful counter-melody in the first violins. Only real familiarity can bring a full appreciation of the magnificent architecture of this movement in which order and unity are imposed from within rather than by the application of academic rules.

The second movement is a funeral march suitable for a mythical hero. Note the avoidance of the use of drums, the double-basses supplying a sound that is comparable to the rumble of muffled drums but which is musically more interesting. The immense span of the phrases coupled with the very slow tempo means that the movement is very long, but for those who are prepared to adjust themselves to its measured tread there are ample rewards. Periodically the feeling of grief is softened by episodes in major keys, like warming rays of sun on a grey afternoon.

The Scherzo which follows could hardly be more different, bustling along without a care in the world, its rhythmic vitality unflagging. Excitedly the strings set the rhythm ticking; after six bars of quiet staccato chords, the oboe offers us a cheerful little tune beginning with seven repetitions of the same note. It is taken up in turn by a flute, but for no fewer than ninety-two bars Beethoven avoids a positive affirmation of the 'home' key of E flat major so that when it is finally reached it seems an event of great importance. In due course we arrive at the central Trio, a term that is more apt than usual since it is mostly scored for three horns, one more than he uses in any other symphony except the Ninth where there are four. Although for the most part the mood continues to be exuberant there is, towards the end of this section, a hushed dialogue between horns and strings that establishes a feeling of twilight different from anything else in the symphony. The quiet ending to the central Trio simplifies the transition back to the Reprise, but just when we are liable to feel that Beethoven is merely observing an established convention there is a sudden disruption of the rhythm that takes us by surprise. The whole Scherzo is roughly twice the size of any comparable movement by Haydn, not that direct comparison can be made, so unique is its conception.

The theme of the finale must have been an especial favourite of Beethoven's as he used it in several other compositions including the ballet-music for *Prometheus*. The opening torrent of notes suggests high drama but there are rather different things in store. The strings pluck out a curiously fragmentary little tune punctuated by sudden three-note outbursts from wind, brass and timpani. There are two possible interpretations of this enigmatic passage. It seems that in the Prometheus ballet, the hero breathed life into statues that then took their first faltering steps. One can imagine such a scene to this music but, in the absence of any such programmatic explanation, it is more likely that Beethoven is once again playing a joke on his audience. As the great musicologist Donald Tovey wrote, 'we can almost see Beethoven laughing at our mystified faces'. What we hear is not in fact the real theme of the movement but the *bass* of the theme, a servant wearing the master's clothes. When at last the proper tune appears above this enigma all falls into place.

Soon, as if to apologise for playing such tricks upon us, Beethoven settles down to some severe counterpoint, embarking on a fugue. However, this more serious mood does not last for long. Against a background of swiftly running scales the woodwind present a delightful variation on the main theme. Listeners who look for security will be at a loss in this movement since it shifts from serious to frivolous without warning. For example at one point there is a march, but it cannot be taken to refer to Napoleon since it is soon deflated by a very light-hearted version of the main tune. At another point the fugue-subject is turned upon its head against a comically running counterpoint from the first violins.

Perhaps the biggest surprise in a movement that is full of surprises comes near the end when there is a fundamental change of tempo. A choir of woodwind instruments initiates a slow variation on the main theme. Gradually the orchestra seems to take on the semblance of a great cathedral organ with the main theme transferred to the pedals while the organist improvises an elaborate Postlude above. Then with a sudden memory of the opening flourish we are whipped into a final Presto in which the horns present a hunting version of the main theme. If the final repetitions of the 'home' chord seem too many, Beethoven clearly felt they were needed to establish security after a movement so full of caprice.

Symphony No. 4 in B flat Major
Op. 60

In 1806 Beethoven had already started work on the Symphony we now know as Number Five when he was approached by Count Oppersdorf with a commission to write a symphony, almost certainly with the proviso that it should be in the style of Number Two, which the Count greatly admired. Unwilling to miss the chance of earning a fee of 350 florins, the composer put the C minor symphony aside and wrote the Fourth, seemingly with greater ease than usual. Thematic relationships between the two symphonies offer clear evidence that both works were in his mind at the same time. The first such clue appears in the very opening bars despite the great difference in mood and tempo. The same musical concept, two falling thirds, is to be found in the two symphonies, veiled in mystery in the Fourth, defiant and intractable in the Fifth.

While a number of such similarities may not be immediately apparent, the differences need no emphasis. The two works are a world apart in emotional significance, so much so that the Fourth has always tended to be overshadowed by its mighty neighbours. Nevertheless, the Fourth has magical qualities, and is perhaps the best orchestrated of all the nine. The opening in particular is unforgettable for the beauty of its sound. During the slow introduction the music seems to be feeling its way towards a destination only dimly perceived. At last, after long deferment, a series of brief ascending scale-fragments, crisp and sharp as the crack of a whip, leads us into the main *Allegro*.

The principal theme alternates swift detached notes on the strings with a smooth *legato* phrase on the woodwind. It is like emerging into bright sunlight after the mysterious shadows of the Introduction. As a contrast we find a second group of themes, cheerful little tunes allocated almost entirely to the wind and cleverly (if not obviously) inter-related. Many subtle new developments occur in the central section of the movement of which the most remarkable is the passage leading into the reprise. The violins hover uneasily on two notes for four bars at a time before an ascending flick which evokes a warning grumble from the timpani, a process which is repeated but which ultimately opens the way back to the Recapitulation.

The second movement begins with an important rhythmic figure against which the violins unfold a deeply expressive melody, later to be elaborately decorated. After a second main theme has been introduced by a solo clarinet and then taken up by the full woodwind choir, the double-basses remind us of the initial rhythmic figure; in due course it comes to dominate the scene leading to an astonishingly dramatic descent with each note heavily accented by explosive cannon-shots from the timpani. Out of the tumult emerges the gentlest of phrases, coiling sinuously through the violin-parts. It has been described by a great authority as 'one of the most imaginative passages in Beethoven'. Soon a solo bassoon reminds us of the opening rhythm, though Beethoven might have preferred a horn at this point. (The notes would have been unobtainable on the instrument used in his time.) The closing pages of the movement have a romantic beauty that is virtually unsurpassed in the whole canon of the nine symphonies.

The next movement is vigorous in its rhythmic drive, alternating strongly accented chords with strange ribbons of unison notes in woodwind and strings. As a contrast, the central Trio is mincingly elegant, a parody of the refined conventions Beethoven had clearly lost patience with.

The finale is as exuberant a movement as he ever wrote, almost a study in perpetual motion. Like Mozart and Haydn before him, Beethoven was a more than adequate violinist and there are passages in this symphony that suggest that he was recalling hours of technical practice spent in mastering the instrument. There are also notoriously difficult passages for the double basses as well as a famous bassoon solo. The whole movement bubbles over with good humour and high spirits.

Symphony No. 5 in C Minor
Op. 67

The opening bars of this symphony have become a musical symbol of the image we tend to have of Beethoven, rugged and uncompromising; yet it should be remembered that once the first two phrases have made their dramatic impact, the ensuing passage is more notable for pathos than drama. The music is curiously ambiguous, the falling pattern of each paired interval implying a deep sense of grief, while the driving rhythm seems to forbid such emotional indulgence. There is an almost continual conflict between a cry for pity and the refusal to grant it. Gradually the rhythm generates more and more force until the battering sounds seem literally to disintegrate in a single explosive chord. Horns in unison announce the imminent arrival of the Second Subject, a graceful tune whose poise is destroyed by the all-pervading rhythm with which the cellos and basses doggedly persist. Abrupt chords signal the end of the Exposition, which should be repeated.

The Development section is notable for its fierce concentration on the material so far exposed to us. There is scarcely a note that cannot be traced back to some fragmentary idea in the Exposition. The demonic energy of the rhythm gives a special character to this remarkable movement whose impact is such that it is the most immediately recognisable of all Beethoven's works.

The second movement provides a welcome release from tension. It is a set of variations on a sublimely simple theme which is presented to us by violas and cellos in unison with a few bass-notes sketched in *pizzicato* by the double-basses. The last segment of the tune is lovingly extended by the woodwind, an extension which is at once taken up and amplified by the strings. An unusual feature is the inclusion of a quite independent second theme, a smoothly gliding woodwind tune whose accompaniment in triplet figuration makes us assume that it is the start of a variation on Theme I. The assumption is wrong; the second theme has a clear identity of its own, particularly when trumpets, horns and drums give it a martial air. Doubting phrases on the violins dispel this new confidence, leading us ultimately to the first variation on Theme I. It takes the form of an unbroken stream of notes for the lower strings. Further variations follow, easily discernible even to the untrained ear. Beethoven's original plan for this movement was far more conventional in layout. In rejecting past custom he showed how assured he had become in devising new and yet logical forms.

In all nine symphonies there is not a scherzo more individual than the one we find here. It suggests an improvisation for orchestra, a prophecy of things to come rather than an extension of dance movements from a previous era. Dark and mysterious, the initial theme seems to grope its way forward, uncertain of its destination. Violins bring the music to a complete halt. A second start by the lower strings progresses a little further but is again brought to a standstill. In just such a way will an improviser seem to search for an idea. Suddenly Beethoven strikes out boldly in a new direction, hammering out the theme on unison horns supported by chunky chords from the strings. Even though it is confirmed by the full orchestra this tune also falters, coming to rest on a chord whose waning strength dwindles to nothing. The ghostly opening phrase returns, the music continuing to alternate uncertainty with resolution. In the centre we find a section that combines the scholarly pretensions of fugue with an almost impish sense of humour. Cellos and basses, filled with a confidence so absent at the start of the movement, briskly set the fugue on its way. Later, as though telling us that such academic devices are no longer valid, Beethoven allows the fugue to come apart. Twice the cellos and basses make false starts in an endeavour to get the music back on course. A return to the opening material seems far from secure with various woodwind instruments playing tentative fragments of the previously bold horn theme over an almost inaudible accompaniment. Suddenly all movement is stilled save for the quiet beat of a drum, strangely sinister. In response to its hypnotic throb the violins initiate a weird dance, groping their way upwards step by step. It is an ascent from darkness to light, an ascent that has been hinted at from the very first bars of the movement but which is only accomplished at the last.

The sheer impact of the finale that emerges is enhanced by the addition of three trombones, a piccolo and a contra-bassoon. Perhaps the blaze of sound coming out of a sort of 'aural fog' symbolises a psychological victory over the composer's deafness. Certainly the pure and straightforward harmonies seem to clarify the harmonic vagueness of the preceding passage. For some time the music continues upon its triumphant way, building towards a climax that surely presages some great event. Instead there is a sudden break followed by a hollow ticking sound from the violins; as though a ghost has entered, we hear a spectral version of the horn theme from the previous movement. It is an unforgettably dramatic interruption. Order is restored with the return of the majestic march theme with which the movement began. Towards the end of the symphony the tempo quickens to a headlong rush in which dignity is sacrificed to brilliance, the final affirmation of C major being perhaps over-emphatic in its repetitions.

Symphony No. 6 in F Major (The 'Pastoral') Op. 68

The first movement of this symphony is described in the score as 'The cheerful impressions excited by arriving in the country'; the second is called 'By the stream'; the third is 'A happy get-together of peasants', the fourth is 'Storm', and the fifth 'The Shepherds' Hymn, gratitude and thanksgiving after the storm'. The title 'Pastoral' was sanctioned by Beethoven, though in calling it a 'Pastoral Symphony, or a recollection of country life' he warned against a too literal interpretation with the phrase, 'More an expression of feeling than a painting'. It seems probable that this admonition not to take the pictorial content of the work too literally was prompted by the fear that listeners might misinterpret his intentions. Descriptive pieces were much in vogue at the time but they were mostly trivial and naive, words that can scarcely be used of this delightful but major composition.

It begins with a bare fifth in the bass, the traditional drone-bass of rustic music; above, the violins spell out a simple melody from which much of the material is derived. A notable characteristic of the first movement in particular is the exploitation of the repetition of patterns that we find throughout Nature. The symmetry of leaves on a tree, of flowers, or even of the ripples on the surface of lake or stream, these may well have been in Beethoven's mind as he penned notes that seem to reflect both the infinite similarity and the infinite variety of nature's patterns. After the distraught energy of the Fifth Symphony the mood here is extremely relaxed, a clear symbol of the inner peace the composer found when alone in the country. The harmonies are often sustained over many bars at a time, giving a feeling of a slower pace than the actual pulse of the music would appear to indicate. Long sustained notes in first or second violins shine through the texture like beams of sunlight. The score, like the forest, teems with life, yet the impression we gain is of a great stillness. Towards the end of the movement clarinet and bassoon anticipate the arrival of the little village band which Beethoven parodies so delightfully in the third movement.

Before the peasants' gathering we spend a lazy afternoon by a meandering stream (second movement), unusually scored with two muted cellos lending depth to the sound. The first main theme is notable for its recurring silences, seeming to be literally breathless at the beauty of the scene. The music flows continuously even allowing for these breathing spaces. Despite its length the movement is concentrated in its form, having clearly recognisable First and Second Subjects, a Development section and a Recapitulation. There is an uncharacteristic concession to the purely descriptive on the last page of the movement when flute, oboe and clarinet echo the song of nightingale, quail and cuckoo.

Although it contains an amusing parody of a small village band, much of the third movement is scored with a delicacy that would not seem out of place in more aristocratic surroundings. The opening phrase tiptoes its way in un-supported by harmony; it is answered by a smooth and gentle tune in a contrasting key. Soon a new theme is introduced, rough-hewn, with heavy accents. High horns bellow their approval as scooping figures in the strings suggest the sort of dance where men toss the girls into the air. There is a feeling of robust horseplay far removed from the delicacy of the opening. In due course we hear the little band, depicted with delightful humour, the oboist rhythmically insecure, the clarinettist more accomplished, the horn-player rashly confident in his approach to dizzy heights, the bassoonist cautious and inept. An increase of tempo leads to a second dance-tune, accompanied by droningly primitive harmonies. The movement ends in a panic rush as the peasants realise a storm is about to break.

Without even a final cadence to the preceding music the storm makes its presence felt with a quiet but ominous rumble from cellos and basses. An agitated little figure from the second violins suggests the first drops of rain. Suddenly the storm breaks in its full fury with flickers of lightning in the woodwind and thunderclaps from the timpani. At last it dies away; an oboe sings out a simple melody derived from the first agitated raindrops, now smoothed out into a musical rainbow. An ascending scale on a flute leads without break into the finale. The initial 'hymn' is soon transformed into an ecstatic paean of joy. The movement is part Rondo, part Variations, culmina-ting in a marvellous climax in which shimmering strings convey an impression of blazing sunlight while the wide-reaching phrases in cellos and basses suggest the trunks of great trees, their branches stretching towards the sky. A long descent leads to a quiet statement of belief, more prayer than hymn. A last whisper of breeze stirs through the strings, a distant horn sounds an almost inaudible curfew.

Symphony No. 7 in A Major
Op. 92

After completing the 'Pastoral' Symphony Beethoven was to wait more than three years before embarking on the Seventh (1811). As in the First, Second and Fourth symphonies, he begins with a slow introduction from whose massive first chord a solo oboe tune emerges. Further strong chords mark a gradual accumulation of melodic strands until, in the tenth bar, a rising scale in the strings makes its first appearance. By bar fifteen it has been transformed into an awe-inspiring counterpoint to the initial theme. Soon the woodwind choir presents us with a grave march, almost ritual in character. For some time this and the opening theme seem to compete for our attention until at last the music settles onto the note E natural which is repeated speculatively over seventy times within ten bars. The increasingly wide spacing of these repetitions indicates that Beethoven is teasing us rather as he did at the start of the finale to the First Symphony. At last release comes as flute and oboe delicately mark out the rhythm which is to be the mainspring of the movement. The point made, a solo flute gives us the First Subject, a lilting and joyous tune in very different mood from the Introduction. The movement is notable for its rhythmic drive, there being few moments of repose. Quiet passages there may be but they never lose their forward impulse.

One of the most striking features of this symphony is the unity of rhythm in the various movements, none more insistent than that of the slow movement. Although the rhythm is all-pervading, the harmonic structure is rich. The solemn tread of the opening theme continues for some time until a glowing counter-melody illuminates its dark harmonies from within. The effect is of a grand procession passing by as the full orchestra is increasingly employed. Suddenly the mood changes as clarinet and bassoon introduce a new sustained melody accompanied by gently flowing triplets. It is in the key of A major (after A minor) and seems like a ray of sunshine in a grey sky. Cellos and basses continue to pluck out the initial rhythm but it is relegated to the background as this radiant theme unfolds. The spell is dissolved by a great descending scale through nearly four octaves, plunging us harshly back into A minor. Soon we find a ghostly little fugue in which the players seem to grope their way forward uncertainly. An intense crescendo duly leads back to the first theme, which, after a restatement of the lyrical clarinet tune, brings the movement to a strangely disintegrated close.

The Scherzo sets a new standard for vitality and humour, excelling all its predecessors in rhythmic vigour. The rapid shifts from one tonal centre to another are designed to keep the listener guessing, never able to predict what is going to happen next. The movement falls into five sections, the brisk opening material being interleaved with a rather more static theme derived from a traditional pilgrims' hymn. Woodwind and horns sustain the tune in organ-like tones while the violins hold a bagpipe drone that even has to be stoked up from time to time as the imagined 'pipers' run short of breath. After the hectic scramble of the Scherzo these long-held notes give a sense of great spaciousness.

The last movement displays tremendous energy, with strong accents on the second beat of the bar pounding out the rhythm. There is hardly a moment's respite for the players, Beethoven showing immense intellectual stamina in maintaining such intensity throughout. The final pages must rank as one of his most brilliantly conceived passages for orchestra; the notes seem to fly off the page as we are carried on the flood-tide of his inspiration.

Symphony No. 8 in F Major
Op. 93

As with the Second Symphony, one would never guess from the musical content that this work was written during a period of emotional disturbance — in this case a family row between Beethoven and his brother Johann (1812). It caused much bitterness, yet to judge from the music one would think that the composer was in an exceptionally good humour. The symphony begins without introduction or preamble although at one time a majestic prelude was contemplated. The first theme is almost old-fashioned, a look back perhaps before venturing on into the unknown. However its solid confidence is most wittily undermined as the music grinds to a halt. Preceded by a few apologetic chords and some faintly comical bassoon notes, the Second Subject begins in the distinctly alien tonal centre of D major, a key unrelated to the 'home' key of F. As though admitting to an error, the tune falters, turns awkwardly and arrives deviously at the proper key of C. (Violins play the tune in the 'wrong' key, woodwind put it 'right'.) The movement is full of such musical surprises, Beethoven clearly delighting in catching his audience unawares. One figure based on two notes an octave apart is of particular value in the Development even though it first appears as a most conventional gesture. It is interesting to compare this quietly insistent yet curiously static idea with the dynamic energy displayed in the first movement of the Fifth Symphony. In both works three swift repeated notes lead towards the ensuing strong beat yet the effect is totally different.

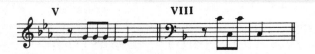

During the development the character of the opening theme undergoes a considerable change, becoming quite tempestuous. Surrounded by hostile chords in the wind and angry figuration in the violins, a fugue of sorts gets under way, though it is far from academic. The tension increases until at last the reprise of the opening theme blazes out in triumph. There are a number of surprises before the movement ends, not least the ending itself which recedes to a mere whisper.

The second movement has a clockwork quality that alludes directly to the inventor of the metronome, an ingenious friend of Beethoven's called Mälzel. The repeated chords give an impression of mechanical regularity, though the melodic fragments that dance to the rhythm are placed in a wittily capricious fashion. There is even a little phrase to illustrate the winding-up of the clockwork spring. Two passages in parallel thirds also deserve mention; they sound suspiciously like a mechanical organ — another manifestation of Mälzel's ingenuity. At the end of the movement the metronome appears to disintegrate in a passage that shows Beethoven's delight in musical humour.

The third movement pays homage to the spirit of Haydn, a deliberate regression on Beethoven's part that makes a striking change from his whirlwind scherzos. A bland central section is notable for an unusually demanding horn-part.

The finale begins with a swift rustling figure from which emerges a nimble dancing tune, beautifully understated. After two brief silences there is a sudden ferocious unison on a wildly unexpected note, not just a joke as it happens but also a seed destined to bear fruit more than 350 bars later when it is used as a pivot to take the music into a distant tonal centre. The whole movement is a brilliant demonstration of how to use a conventional form to prepare traps for the listener. For instance, the so-called Second Subject appears without warning in the 'wrong' key (A flat instead of C). Then during the Development there are several halts followed by false starts as though the players lose all sense of direction. An elaborate Coda, or tail-piece to the movement, makes much use of a slower-moving theme based on five consecutive notes of the scale. It fits against itself in contrary motion, yet any intellectual analysis seems out of place in a movement so full of high spirits. There is not a trace of despair or self-pity in the whole movement; the composer seems completely reconciled to the cruel blow Fate had dealt him.

Symphony No. 9 in D minor (The 'Choral') Op. 125

The idea of setting Schiller's 'Ode to Joy' had come to Beethoven as early as 1793 although the Choral Symphony which incorporates it was not to be completed until the winter of 1823/4. Preliminary work on the symphony was spread over a period of years during which a number of major works were written. In 1808 he had composed the Choral Fantasia, a significant pointer towards the symphony. Not only does its main theme bear a close resemblance to the setting of the 'Ode to Joy'; the ground plan of the work anticipates that of the Ninth Symphony's finale to a remarkable degree. The long piano introduction (which Beethoven improvised at the first perform-ance) might aptly be described as the 'Symphony', using the original meaning of that versatile term. Cellos and basses then offer a theme (as the orchestra does in the Ninth) which is rejected several times (as it is in the Ninth). In the Fantasia the solo piano seems to aspire to the condition of the human voice, precisely what the lower strings attempt to do in the dramatic unison passages that introduce the finale of the symphony. After a period of puzzle-ment and contradiction, the theme at last emerges pure and simple, again a moment that has its exact parallel in the Ninth. Whether Beethoven con-sciously realised it or not, the Choral Fantasia is an experimental version of the later work, though only of its finale. The first three movements are purely symphonic in conception.

In all the preceding symphonies the proclamation of a tonal centre has been of prime importance in the opening bars. Here the music begins as though in a void, the positive affirmation of D minor not arriving until the seventeenth bar. When it does appear the main theme is awesome in its rugged grandeur. It is presented in two versions, minor and major, the North and South faces of the same mountain-peak. Although the movement is conceived on a very large scale, the essential features are very clear. As in the 'Pastoral' Symphony, though to very different effect, the pace of harmonic change is often very slow, giving immense breadth to the music. Much of the material is tragic in mood, while in the Development lies the intellectual core of the movement in the shape of a triple fugue. More than is usually the case the themes of this movement are subjected to emotional changes.

One of Beethoven's most significant contributions to symphonic form was his expansion of the Coda. As we might expect, this movement shows him to have a huge amount in reserve, so much so that (as in the 'Eroica') the Coda is comparable to an entire new development section. Perhaps most remarkable of all is the closing passage, in effect a funeral march. Its foundation is a chromatic wailing bass above which brass and wind proclaim funereal fanfares.

The Scherzo begins abruptly; note the ingenious use of timpani in the fifth bar, the two drums tuned an octave apart — an experiment he had tried in the Eighth Symphony. After two bars of stunned silence a whispering fugue begins, utilising the dramatic octave leap with which the movement began. For no less than thirty-six bars the volume is kept under tight restraint; then a long sustained note on horns and clarinets signals a crescendo. Within seconds the full orchestra is playing at full stretch. Suddenly a radiant new theme flowers, bringing a moment of relaxation. The movement is substantially longer than any of the other scherzos but the material is easy to absorb. Most beguiling is the central section, the so-called Trio, which bears an intriguing resemblance to the comparable passage in the Second Symphony.

The elaborate Adagio which follows is one of Beethoven's most romantic utterances, anticipating Mahler in its profoundly expressive manner. Tender sighs begin the movement, leading to Theme I in which clarinets and bassoons seem to express their approval of each string phrase as though saying 'wasn't that lovely'. These echoes give great spaciousness to the theme which, once it has run its full span, melts into a new tonal centre in which we find Theme II, surely one of the most immediately appealing tunes Beethoven ever wrote. There follow several variations on Theme I, one of which has a particularly elaborate part for the violins. Brief and distant fanfares fail to disturb the immense calm of this sublime movement.

The transition from orchestral to choral music in the finale caused the composer much trouble. The discovery of the solution is revealed in a miniature scenario he jotted down in a notebook.

> This is a day of jubilation, worth singing about . . . (Theme of the first movement) O no, that won't do, I want something pleasanter . . . (Theme of the second movement.) That is no better, merely rather more cheerful . . . (Theme of the third movement.) That's also too tender. Must find something more rousing like the . . . I'll sing you something myself . . . (Theme of the fourth movement.) That will do! Now I have found a way to express joy.

Here, in essence, is the 'plot' of the finale, the actual transition from instruments to voices being facilitated by giving the lower strings a number of quasi-operatic phrases that suggest the inflections of the human voice. The movement begins with a passage of extraordinary violence, a tonal crisis demanding a resolution. Like an operatic hero suddenly appearing on stage, the lower strings declaim their first dramatic phrase. For a second time the orchestral clamour breaks out, for a second time cellos and basses reply. The music then follows exactly the plan Beethoven sketched above, offering us brief snatches of the three preceding movements, each of which is rejected. At last a semblance of the true theme appears to be greeted with an orchestral 'shout' of acclamation. Unruffled, smoothly flowing, the tune finally unfolds, duly to be repeated in triumph.

The process is now repeated with a solo baritone taking over phrases comparable to those previously given to the lower strings. As a suitable verbal introduction to Schiller's Ode, Beethoven chose a simple injunction:

O friends, not these sounds; let us tune our voices more acceptably and more joyfully.

Gradually the chorus is incorporated into the texture, along with a quartet of soloists. From here on the structure of the movement becomes somewhat complex although it is basically a set of variations on the main theme. One of these is a march, with triangle and cymbals adding the clank of swords and the jingle of spurs. Against its steady tread the tenor soloist sings of 'Brothers like heroes to conquest flying'. It is an essentially operatic passage which however is followed by an orchestral fugue of some complexity, itself a variation on the song to joy. After a further affirmation of the main theme there is a silence out of which emerges a great Hymn of Brotherhood:

O ye millions, I embrace ye —
Here's a joyful kiss for all!

There follows a vast section of great solemnity, in effect a slow movement within the finale. It ends abruptly with the simultaneous return of the two principal themes, the 'Song of Joy' and the 'Hymn to Brotherhood'. The two are combined in a brilliant fashion. From a huge climax the music suddenly disintegrates. Strangely fragmented phrases express the feeling of awe in the presence of the very Creator of the world.

The start of the final Coda suggests the running feet of happy children and it may well be that Beethoven had a stage presentation in mind. One of his preliminary notes for the baritone's text reads, 'Today is a day of celebration; let it be celebrated in song *and dance*'. It is a clue not to be lightly disregarded. Certainly the solo quartet has an operatic theme near the end whose innocent gaiety recalls Mozart at his most enchanting. Proclaiming the ideal that all men should be brothers, the symphony draws to its close, an epic ending to a gigantic conception.

(For a more detailed analysis of all the Beethoven symphonies, see A. Hopkins, *The Nine Symphonies of Beethoven*. Heinemann, London, and University of Washington Press, 1981, and Pan, 1982.)

Piano Concerto No. 1 in C Major
Op. 15

Beethoven's earliest public success was as a pianist rather than as a composer; we should remember, though, that the concerts he gave as a young man would have been given on a fortepiano (as it was originally called) hardly different from the instruments of Mozart's day. During his lifetime pianos underwent considerable development, enabling him to enlarge the scope of his keyboard writing so that the musical 'language' of his late works has a far wider range of expression, not to mention more sheer power than anything from his early period. The point is well demonstrated by the five piano concertos, in the first two of which he was compelled to use Mozartean stratagems to solve the problem of balance between soloist and orchestra. Not until he came to write the Fifth concerto did Beethoven have an instrument which, even though he was deaf, he sensed was strong enough to dominate the orchestra. To have written an opening cadenza as forceful as the 'Emperor's' in 1795 (the date of Op. 15) would have been quite impractical since no piano of the period could have achieved the desired effect. That Beethoven was well aware of this is shown by the fact that he wrote three cadenzas for this particular concerto, the third of which is in a 'heroic' style that is far more demanding than anything in the original score. Since concerto and cadenza are separated by a gulf of some fourteen years the difference is understandable, even though in performance the cadenza inevitably seems out of proportion.

In 1784 Beethoven made his first attempt at writing a piano concerto, a work in E flat which can most charitably be regarded as a stage in his apprenticeship. Eleven years later, in March 1795, he was asked to play at a charity concert in aid of the widows and orphans of the Society of Musicians in Vienna. It was to be an important occasion, incentive enough to goad him into completing a piano concerto he had been mulling over in his usual painstaking way for a year or more. With only two days to go before the concert the finale had still not been written and it seems possible that it was the urgency of the situation that brought on a painful attack of colic. Beethoven took to his bed and with a doctor at his side and four copyists in the next room began the frantic rush to get the last movement down on paper. As each sheet was completed it was passed through to the copyists so that a set of orchestral parts could be made simultaneously. When the exhausted composer arrived at the hall to rehearse he found that the piano was half a tone flat. With the resourcefulness of a truly great musician he transposed the entire concerto up a semitone, playing it in B major instead of B♭, a feat that was all the more remarkable when we consider that he could not have actually practised the solo part at all. It is hardly surprising that the experience caused him to take a slightly jaundiced view of the work;[1] he put it aside, revised it a couple of years later, and published it as his Piano Concerto No. 2 in B flat major, Op. 19. The change of numbering was forced on him since meanwhile he had written another concerto, the one which to this day is still referred to as No. 1 in C major, Op. 15.

That Beethoven himself considered the C major concerto to be of greater substance than the one in B flat is indicated by his employment of a slightly larger orchestra, an increase of five players — two clarinets, two trumpets and timpani. The first movement is a march in character even though it begins quietly with strings only. The initial motif of a rising octave provides an instantly recognisable feature, while the swift ascending scale joining the first two phrases also proves itself to be more than a cliché when he makes extensive use of it later. After fifteen bars the full orchestra takes up the march theme with dramatic impact. The influence of Haydn is easily sensed particularly when the horns ascend to a perilous high C, but once he has established a solid cadence on the dominant (G major) Beethoven has a surprise for us. After a moment's silence the second violins murmur a gently rocking figure that suggests G minor; however, the subsequent entry of the first violins (supported by the lower strings) switches deftly into E flat major, a very unorthodox key for a second subject's first appearance. (It would normally be in the dominant.) As if aware that he has committed an indiscretion, Beethoven drifts through various keys, offering us a taste of F minor and G minor in turn before deciding to leave the second subject for the time being. He reverts to the first subject, taking it out of the parade ground and into the classroom by subjecting it to a course of counterpoint. Horns and oboes find this not to their liking and introduce a crisp little march that might have stepped straight out of the pages of a Mozart opera. A stern reference to the initial rising octave from bar 1, now four times repeated, brings this splendidly martial tutti to an end.

[1] When he sent it to be published, the accompanying note said 'I do not consider it to be one of my best'.

A full orchestra with trumpets, horns and timpani would put the small tones of the fortepiano at a considerable disadvantage; Beethoven therefore adopted the solution Mozart had devised, disregarding the orchestral material entirely and giving the soloist a gentle theme that the orchestra is never allowed to touch. Their insistence that the proper matter for discussion is the initial rising octave is met with a brilliant clatter of arpeggios from the soloist; indeed the first acknowledgment of the rising octave theme that we find in the piano part sounds almost derisive, the upper notes deliberately smudged.

The introduction of the second subject enables the soloist to participate on more equal terms, and he accepts it joyfully, adding playful elaborations that interestingly go up to a top F sharp, a note that was unavailable to Mozart. Soon the wind remind us of the Mozartean march tune, an idea which the soloist treats with some energy before embarking on a descending sequence of rotating figures. These, alternating with a more aggressive pattern in chromatic triplets, keep the music humming along in a somewhat facile way until an ascent to a high E, four times repeated, leads us into a different world, expressive and poignant. The spell is broken by a syncopated pattern in strings (and then woodwind) to which a sharply accented rising scale brings a touch of asperity. It is a formula he was to develop to more dramatic effect in the Fifth Concerto:

A sustained double trill from the pianist ushers in a substantial orchestral section in which the First Subject is again treated in a way that shows signs of Haydn's tuition; according to orthodox precepts it comes to a halt with a solid cadence in G, the dominant. There follows the heart of the movement. Encouraged by an orchestral modulation into the unexpected key of E flat, the pianist embarks on what seems like a free extemporisation incorporating flowing arpeggios that range widely over the keyboard as well as lyrical passages in parallel chords. Occasional orchestral reminders of the first few notes of Theme I do nothing to check the element of fantasy that gives the piano part a quite new character. The most magical moment comes just before the Recapitulation when there is a hushed dialogue between horns and piano, an uncanny anticipation of a corresponding duet between timpani and piano in the very closing pages of the 'Emperor'. However, after the truly inventive developments just described, the Recapitulation pursues an orthodox course and the movement ends in the Mozartean convention, that is to say with the orchestra alone playing the final thirteen bars after the cadenza. (I suspect that the convention arose because contemporary audiences almost certainly applauded at the end of the cadenza, just as they still tend to do when a singer triumphantly concludes his or her contribution to an operatic aria.)

The slow movement follows the Mozartean pattern closely, treating the piano as a surrogate soprano with an exceptional technique and range. The conception is essentially vocal even though it frequently goes beyond the compass of any mere mortal. One phrase especially, played as single unaccompanied notes, is lifted almost identically from the sublime *Et incarnatus est* in Mozart's Mass in C minor. However, the main reprise of the opening theme is quite unlike Mozart in its layout. Introduced by a trill that descends chromatically through three notes, it has an almost waltz-like accompaniment that must have seemed quite a new sound at the time. Notable too is the expressive duet between clarinet and piano near the end of the movement.

The finale, a Rondo, is set on its way with a delightfully witty theme stated with delicate precision by the soloist. The orchestra duly repeats it in a boisterously rowdy fashion. After some rapid passages from the piano it is the orchestra's turn to introduce the next episode, a tune whose efforts to sound suave are defeated by hobbledehoy accents on the last quaver of each bar, a gaucherie which the soloist does little to discourage by transferring the theme to the gruffest bass register. An improbable modulation to F minor allows the pianist to introduce yet another theme whose many 'crushed' notes may well be designed to suggest drunkenness, to judge by the violent attack of musical hiccups which immediately follows. (Beethoven's sense of humour was not noted for its subtlety.) Order is restored with the return of the initial theme; as before, it is repeated noisily by the orchestra. The central episode of this outstandingly witty movement is a tune in A minor that sounds strangely Latin-American to modern ears though Beethoven probably thought of it as 'Turkish', the standard term for anything exotic in Mozart's day. (One of the variations in the finale of Beethoven's 'Choral' symphony would have been considered 'Turkish' simply because of its use of percussion.)
  The rest of the movement shows Beethoven amusing himself with further discussion of these varied materials, but the listener should look out for a delightfully novel twist just after the cadenza; a long trill manages to wind itself up a semitone so as to land in the totally alien key of B major, a situation from which Beethoven skilfully extricates himself before the last orchestral version of the Rondo theme. The coda starts with a witty exchange

of scales and fragments of the Rondo divided between piano and wind. The last joke is a mock solemn Amen from oboes and horns, a gesture which is greeted with noisy derision in the final six bars.

Piano Concerto No. 2 in B flat Major
Op. 19

A great number of eighteenth-century piano sonatas begin with a formula consisting of a brief 'masculine' phrase, establishing the tonality, followed by a slightly longer 'feminine' response leading to a suggestion of the dominant. The 'masculine' phrase will then be repeated in the dominant and the response, probably somewhat modified, will lead back to the 'home' or Tonic key. The Second Concerto follows this pattern exactly with a 'heroic' first phrase, a 'tender' reply, a fresh statement of the 'heroic' phrase and an equally ingratiating response. A little surprisingly the tender mood seems to prevail, albeit with a new theme. The heroic theme is then transformed into a quasi-operatic duet between violins and cellos; the feeling here is suppressed but nervous and is soon countered by strong off-beat accents. An excursion into F minor brings the music to a dramatic halt on the dominant (C), thrice repeated *ff*. There is a moment's silence. So quietly that it suggests incredulity, strings and flute offer three D flats, *pp*, as an alternative. A graceful new theme appears in the unexpected key of D flat major, a tonality so outside the conventional scheme of things that it should arouse our surprise. Though it may appear to be the second subject it could prove to be an imposter. Some uneasy murmurings in B flat minor tend to confirm that all may not be well, and there is a certain sense of relief when, after a long and sinuous ascent we reach the 'heroic' opening phrase once more, this time without his female escort. Beethoven develops this brief idea at some length before bringing the tutti to a positive close.

As in the First Concerto, the soloist's entry follows the Mozartean tradition by refusing to enter into competition with the orchestra. The material is in the most fragile area of the early pianos and is quite unrelated to what has gone before. A brief interlude from the orchestra (whose pattern of repeated notes provides an intriguing premonition of the Fourth Concerto) leads to a more positive display by the soloist. This time he does accept the initial 'heroic' phrase, extending it at some length; the passage finishes with a long ascending scale which ushers in the true Second Subject, an ace that was well worth holding back till this moment. Orchestra and soloist discuss it in a very civilized manner until a trill on the piano takes us into an inspired diversion, a free episode in D flat major — the same key that had been planted unexpectedly in the Exposition. More fiery developments ensue in what is pianistically the most challenging passage in the concerto, but the storm abates as a long protracted modulation into the 'proper' dominant key (F) brings us to a powerful orchestral tutti. Here we find the 'heroic' theme in the bass with a new countermelody in the violins.

The pianist re-enters with the same material with which he had begun, though now in the dominant key (F) and sounding the better for it. A quite long development ensues, making clear references to the opening tutti, but to quite different effect now that the soloist is involved. The woodwind make much play with a repeated note theme which increasingly seems as though Beethoven is laying the foundations for the first movement of the Fourth Concerto. At last, as though impatient with the soloist's meanderings, we hear distant reminders of the 'heroic' theme in the strings heralding the actual Recapitulation. From here on matters proceed more or less according to expectation though Beethoven's cadenza, written at a much later date, makes substantially greater demands on the pianist than we find elsewhere.

The slow movement is a true *Adagio*, an extension of Mozart's language rather than a rejection of it. The orchestra has the first statement of the main theme which would not seem out of place in a setting of the Mass. The introductory phrases end with a string unison B to a peremptory rhythm out of which the soloist makes a cunningly contrived entry. The solo passages seldom have a greater density than we would find in Mozart though a reprise of the opening theme in the wind is accompanied by a very individual rippling figuration divided between the hands. The most noteworthy feature of the movement comes near the end. Marked *'con grand' espressione'*, it might be described as an *anti*-cadenza, a passage in single notes of the utmost simplicity yet possessing a spiritual profundity which is the mark of true genius.

Such spiritual matters are banished entirely in the final Rondo, which, if it resembles at all the finale Beethoven dashed off in his sick bed, represents a triumph of the human spirit over bodily ills. The pianist sets off with a gaily syncopated theme, a practical way of setting the tempo if, as I suspect, Beethoven intended to direct the work from the keyboard. As in the First Concerto, the orchestra voice their approval rather noisily; this done, they introduce a more solemn tone to which the pianist pays scant respect. In due course he introduces a rum-ti-tum-ti tune that sounds like a children's game, the more so when the orchestra put in some cheeky 'wrong' notes. The sheer happiness of the movement should dispel for ever the image of Beethoven as a frowning giant. There is even a section whose jazzy syncopations seem like a distant anticipation of boogie, while the ending is one of the best musical jokes Beethoven ever made, so much so that in the final bars we can hear him laughing uproariously at the way he has caught us out.

Piano Concerto No. 3 in C Minor
Op. 37

The Third Piano Concerto is as decisive a landmark in its way as the Third Symphony; both works show the composer widening his musical horizon and stretching established forms in a way that his predecessors had never envisaged. The first two concertos are clearly influenced by Mozart, and do not really extend the demands made on the soloist by all that much. But in this work, written in 1800, one feels that Beethoven is turning his back on the past and looking positively and with new authority into the century that lay ahead. While one might argue with some conviction that both the opening theme and the closing pages of the first movement show some indebtedness to Mozart's great C minor concerto, the scale of the work is substantially larger. Here, for the first time, we find the soloist beginning to assume the 'heroic' role that was to become the hallmark of the virtuoso concertos of Chopin, Liszt, Brahms or Rakhmaninov. The instrument for which Beethoven was writing was not yet capable of the physical domination that we find in the 'Emperor' concerto some ten years later but the aspiration to such dominance is certainly there.

Although we rightly think of Beethoven as a composer whose works were subjected to a long and arduous period of gestation, in the case of the Third Concerto he appears to have carried most of the solo part in his head right up to the time of the first performance as the testimony of a young musician called Seyfried reveals.

> At the performance of his Third Concerto, he asked me to turn the pages for him; but — heaven help me! — that was easier said than done. I saw almost nothing but empty sheets. At the most on one page or the other a few wholly unintelligible signs that could as well have been Egyptian hieroglyphics, scribbled down to serve as clues for him. He played nearly all of the solo part from memory, not having had time to put it all on paper. He gave me a secret glance whenever he was at the end of one of the invisible passages, and my scarcely concealed anxiety not to miss the decisive moment amused him greatly, and he laughed heartily at the jovial supper which we ate afterwards.

(Another unfortunate had a similar experience with Mozart who blithely played the piano part of a violin sonata from a score that showed what the violinist had to do but gave hardly any indication of the pianist's contribution.)

At least Seyfried was kept busy during the orchestral introduction which is the most extensive of all those in the Beethoven piano concertos. Without so much as a preliminary chord it goes straight to the heart of the matter with a theme of almost forbidding austerity.

Notice especially bars 3–4 whose staccato rhythm can easily be taken over by the timpani, instruments which Beethoven liberated from more military chores in a number of works including this concerto, the 'Emperor', the Violin Concerto and the scherzo of the Ninth Symphony.

The opening phrase on strings alone brings an immediate response from the woodwind, equal in length but poised on the Dominant (G) and harmonised with some pathos. Violins now introduce an expressive phrase which appears to be new but which Beethoven almost certainly conceived as a more lyrical version of bar 2; meanwhile cellos and basses give support by stretching the opening three notes so that they read C–E♭–A♭ instead of C–E♭–G. This skilful fusion of two elements of Theme I occurs three times in a rising sequence before falling neatly back onto the tonic chord of C minor. There is a silence. In fact during the next eight bars no fewer than sixteen beats are marked as 'rests'. It is a trick Beethoven had learned from Mozart's example; the gaps are left so that they may be filled in by the soloist in due course. The orchestral Exposition (or *tutti*) in a concerto must differ from the Exposition of a symphony since the composer must avoid showing his hand too openly. While it is important that he reveals the main themes, he must hold back on their development or there will be little left for the soloist to do. In extending the span of the opening tutti to the extent that he does here, Beethoven runs the risk of getting too involved with the material so that he is in danger of writing a symphony with a piano part stuck on to it as pure decoration. (The Second Concerto of Brahms has sometimes been described as 'a symphony with a piano part' by critics who feel that Brahms fell into this trap.) As an instance of what I mean I quote a dramatic episode beginning at bar 36. It is a truly symphonic development of the second bar of the whole work; to make the relationship clearer I have transposed the phrase from E minor to the 'home' key of C minor.

So forcibly is this stated by the orchestra that the soloist cannot really compete; when his turn comes he can only resort to elegant decoration.

Similarly the Second Subject is developed at some length by the orchestra, appearing first in E flat major in the woodwind; the violins seem willing to take it over but then have second thoughts, modulating unexpectedly into C *major* and allowing the flutes to continue with it in that key. A stern reminder of Theme I comes from the bass, is transferred to the upper strings and then confirmed by the wind. An abrupt and positive cadence into C minor leads us to expect the entry of the soloist, eighty-five bars surely being ample by way of introduction. Instead, the woodwind introduce a new and expressive theme beginning with four repetitions of the same chord.[2] Slightly hesitant pairs of notes in the bass bring a suggestion of the 'drum-beat' rhythm from bar 3; once again there is a cadence in C minor. Will the soloist enter this time? 'Not yet' says Beethoven. After a few more moments of apparent indecision he suddenly hurls Theme I at us *fortissimo* in canon; three forceful unison Cs bring the Exposition to an abrupt close.

In a comparable situation, with the orchestra ending so loudly, Mozart would not have dreamed of expecting the soloist to compete. His solution was to establish the piano's identity with a new theme, the soft answer that turneth away wrath (see his concertos in C minor K 491 and D minor K 466). This would not suit Beethoven's new 'heroic' concept; three terse rising scales suggest that the sleeping giant is suddenly aroused; they lead to a powerful statement of Theme I, clearly designed to establish who is master now.

If I seem to have devoted excessive space to the opening tutti, it is not only because of its exceptional importance in this work; all too often the uninformed listener tends to regard the orchestral exposition as a somewhat boring classical formality that defers too long the eagerly awaited entrance of the International Star he has come to hear. (How often do we find ourselves saying 'We're going to hear Pollini tonight' instead of specifying the work he is billed to play.) It is very noticeable that in the post-Beethoven period composers almost invariably brought in the soloist early in the movement as though tacitly acknowledging the audience's frustration at being kept waiting. Even Beethoven did so in his Fourth and Fifth concertos, and he was not a man to compromise. The fact is that the ideal listener should virtually know the opening tutti by heart before hearing a note of the solo part since only then will he appreciate the close relationship that exists between the orchestral exposition and what might be termed the secondary exposition that involves the soloist. In this concerto the Second Subject appears in bar 50; omitting the rhetorical gesture of the three rising scales, there are also exactly fifty bars between the soloist's presentation of Theme I and his version of the Second Subject — this despite a free unaccompanied passage which seems to break the mould completely. Not until more than 190 bars have passed does the music depart radically from the groundplan originally laid down by the orchestra; the moment is clearly sign-posted by the first sustained trill to

[2]It is an interesting precursor of a subsidiary theme in the 'Eroica' Symphony, I, bars 83–91.

occur in the solo part and a modulation into the remote key of G flat major, territory which has been significantly avoided up to this point.

From here onwards the piano part becomes increasingly garrulous, the orchestra being confined for the most part to fragmentary reminders of bar 3. A rushing downward scale extended over four-and-a-half octaves leads to a substantial episode for orchestra closely related to the original tutti. It is cut short by a gesture similar to that with which the pianist had made his initial entry, three rising scales. They appear to be in D major, a key which causes a faint query in the orchestra and a skilful diversion to the more acceptable key of G minor. We have reached the expressive heart of the movement in which the pianist, having reminded us of the opening theme in the simplest way, proceeds to improvise some touching variants on Bar 2.

This whole development is noteworthy for its reticence. In the orchestra we hear constant though subdued references to the rhythm of bar 3 around which the pianist, both hands in unison, weaves elaborate but unostentatious decorations. At last a sudden crescendo and another downward-swooping scale leads to a powerful reprise of Theme I from the full orchestra.

Although this is technically the Recapitulation, within eight bars Beethoven introduces delightful variants such as the mysterious little dialogue between orchestra and strings that is one of the most magical moments of the entire concerto. Even so, a Recapitulation it is and all the important landmarks reappear. As one might guess from Seyfried's nightmare experience turning the pages, Beethoven did not bother to write a cadenza at the time though he did produce one approximately nine years later. It offers a less than perfect solution to the problem but does not lessen the sheer magic of the subsequent orchestral passage. Quiet sustained harmonies from the strings give a nocturnal air while soft reminders of bar 3 are muttered by the timpani. Veiled arpeggios from the piano add a moonlight glitter to the scene. Almost imperceptibly a sense of urgency creeps in until a sudden outburst from the full orchestra elicits a torrent of notes from the keyboard culminating in rising scales through four octaves, an extension of the initial rhetorical gesture that is perfectly placed.

The Largo which follows is remarkable in many ways. First, the key (E major) is almost as remote from C minor as it is possible to be, instantly taking us into a different world; secondly, it begins with an extensive meditation for solo piano, a device that Beethoven uses in no other concerto; thirdly the movement is complete in itself, whereas the slow movements of the Fourth and Fifth concertos are linked by subtle means to the finales; lastly, not only is it the most highly developed of all the concerto slow movements but it is also the most elaborate in ornamentation.

The opening theme, densely harmonised in a way that we would never find in Mozart, is especially notable for a strange *tremolando* effect in the left hand, something we might expect to find in Liszt rather than comparatively early Beethoven. Having been offered a theme of such serene beauty the orchestra take it to themselves, turning it in new directions before giving way again to the pianist. There follows a passage which might almost be mistaken for early Chopin so florid is the writing; an elaborate passage in thirds is succeeded by a highly ornamental run (both hands in unison) which, despite the number of notes packed into each bar must never sound hurried.

A central section gives the thematic interest to the wind in the form of a quasi-operatic duet between bassoon and flute. The piano accompanies with cloudy arpeggios that create an almost impressionistic background. In due course the opening theme returns, this time split between piano and orchestra and with new and even more elaborate embellishments. These ultimately flower into a brief and expressive cadenza. Quietly orchestra and soloist fold the movement away, only to surprise us all with the final chord, a sudden explosion that shatters the dream.

Its function is to plant the third of the scale, G sharp, firmly in our minds, for by a process that can only be described as a musical pun, Beethoven wittily turns it into an A flat and uses it to set the last movement on its way. It is a rondo whose theme is obligingly presented by the soloist and then repeated by the orchestra. After thirty-two bars the orchestra is allowed a substantial tutti during which, at one point, a playful attempt is made to put the theme into C major instead of the minor. The proposal is vehemently rejected, and brass and timpani hammer out a parade-ground rhythm that calls everyone to order. The pianist obliges by practising arpeggios the easy way and then, as if indeed to ask whether this Czerny is really necessary, launches into a deliciously frivolous tune that shows that even a descending scale of an octave and a half can be made into sheer delight.

A little later some Scarlatti-like leaps in the piano part lead the orchestra to attempt to inject a more serious note. While it could not be called a fugue, it is a brief essay in academic counterpoint. The pianist's response is a swift passage in triplets that sound suspiciously like a musical fit of the giggles, out of which a dizzying chromatic run leads us back to the Rondo theme.

It is some time before anything fundamentally new appears but when it does it is worth the wait. Clarinets introduce a lyrical tune in A major which the pianist seizes at the first opportunity. A swift ascending scale leading to a long sustained trill signals the end of this episode. It is time to earn critical respect with a display of honest craft; in suitably hushed tones the cellos begin a fugue giving an air of propriety to the cheeky little rondo tune. Although the other strings take up the subject with proper seriousness, progress is halted as the music marks time on a repeated G — a fugal catastrophe. The G changes to an A flat which the pianist then repeats no less than sixteen times. Suddenly realising that the note can also be regarded as a G sharp, the pianist switches into E major, thereby reversing the 'pun' by which Beethoven had extricated himself from the slow movement. The rondo theme takes on a beguiling new aspect in this alien yet somehow recollected tonality. There follows a typical example of Beethoven's humour which has its equivalent in three other concertos. Using only the first three notes of the rondo theme he makes a number of abortive attempts to get it started again, all to no avail. A derisive cascade of notes from the pianist silences the orchestra, whereupon he shows them how it should be done.

A more or less conventional recapitulation follows leading to a brief cadenza which ends with the same joke that we find at the start of the finale of the First Symphony — a series of ascending scales, climbing a step further each time until, after a fraught pause, the music spills into a happily vivacious tune. Here it is obviously derived from the initial rondo yet the change of character is remarkable and the movement ends in a mood of wild exuberance, the notes spilling over each other like champagne overflowing.

Piano Concerto No. 4 in G Major
Op. 58

It was in March 1807 that Beethoven took his place at the piano to give the first performance of his Fourth Concerto.[3] The audience undoubtedly expected the normal convention of an orchestral exposition or '*tutti*' to be observed, and it is hard for us today to realise what a genuine shock it must have been when he put his hands to the keys and began the work on his own with a phrase of such simple and unaffected beauty that it has remained a landmark in music ever since. A second shock was to follow, for the orchestral entry is not only surprisingly hushed but is also in the 'foreign' key of B major. Echoing but not duplicating the repeated-note theme which is such a feature of the movement, the strings find their way back to the 'proper' key of G major with the minimum of drama; once settled there, they can begin the real exposition. The opening theme is made into a duet between violins and cellos, the lower instruments following the upper line like a shadow — and with the distortions that shadows inevitably bring. The gradual involvement of the full orchestra leads to a tautening of the rhythm and the first climax. The

---

[3]Tovey gives 22 December 1808, but modern scholarship disagrees.

tones seem to melt away and a new theme appears with an accompaniment of repeated notes in triplets; it is in A minor and might easily be taken for the Second Subject were it not that Beethoven has other ideas. At this stage, apart from its rather poignant melodic interest, he uses it mainly as a modulating device enabling him to move smoothly from A minor to E minor, from C major to B minor and from G major to F sharp minor. Returning to the repeated-note pattern of the opening, he begins a slow and beautifully graduated ascent whose purpose is to re-establish the home key of G, a moment that is signalled by a new and much more positive theme proclaimed in some triumph by the full orchestra. Two sustained chords check the forward impulse of the music just when it is in danger of becoming more stormy than the situation really demands; flute and oboe introduce an elegant new turn of phrase based on segments of descending scales which the strings duly copy. Quietly the wind reintroduce the initial theme, to which the violins add an expressive little commentary. A sudden crescendo leads to a strong and dissonant chord in which dominant and tonic are locked in conflict, a conflict which is interrupted by one of the most magical solo entries in all music. Since it is a trick Beethoven plays several times in this movement it is worth explaining in more detail. It is a particularly subtle exploitation of a favourite device among so-called 'classical' composers, by which I mean those to whom tonality, the identity of keys and their relationships one to another, was still an important concept. (It was a concept that was to be gradually eroded in the Romantic era as an increasing use of chromatic — and therefore enigmatic — harmony led to more fluid and rapid shifts from one tonal centre to another.) In this concerto, in which the soloist plays the role of Gentle Persuader rather than Dominant Master, there are several entries which reject the implications of the preceding orchestral phrase, sometimes even directly contradicting it. At this point, the end of the tutti, the orchestral dissonance demands to be resolved; instead, the pianist perpetuates the tension, though in the gentlest manner, by coming in on the note *below* that offered by the orchestra. The phrase climbs teasingly to a playful alternation between C sharp and D, leaving the orchestra to provide its own resolution of the dissonance some four-and-a-half bars later. It provokes a fleeting display of agility from the pianist which is almost instantly turned into a more caressing motif.

A brief reminder of the opening theme from the orchestra is taken up in decorated form by the soloist who then embarks on a quicksilver passage of rapid triplets. The supporting chords in the orchestra might be taken for a mere formality were it not for the fact that they continue to suggest the repeated-note idea that dominates the movement. It is remarkable how, even when the soloist seems to enter into passages that appear to have the spontaneous freedom of improvisation, the orchestral part tethers the music to the opening theme. For instance, an almost Chopinesque flight of fancy in B flat major in the highest register of the keyboard is accompanied by quiet sustained chords in the strings which spell out the repeated-note theme at half speed. In due course, after some glittering passages from the soloist, the strings introduce the true Second Subject which Beethoven has kept in reserve for this special moment of repose. The theme is repeated with slightly prickly decorations from the pianist. Sustained trills with thunderous arpeggios in the left hand lead us back to the material of the orchestral exposition and it is here that Beethoven shows his mastery of concerto form. Bars 29–58 (orchestra only) correspond almost exactly in content and structure with bars 134–64, the essential difference being that from bar 141 onwards the pianist participates with steadily increasing brilliance. Rapid chromatic scales and a double trill sever the link with past procedures, allowing the soloist a brief and expressive meditation on a theme that the orchestra had originally presented as a triumphant paean; soon, however, the orchestra takes charge with a virtually exact transposition of the closing nineteen bars of the initial tutti. This time their dissonance *is* resolved on to a chord of D major (the dominant).

It is at this point that the soloist opens the door to the Development with a magical touch, a soft but absolute contradiction of the previous orchestral chord. Out of the strong orchestral assertion of D major emerges a gently reiterated F *natural*, a denial of D major's most essential attribute (F *sharp*). It leads to a wonderfully mysterious passage whose drifting downward scales reach into a series of unexpected keys. These scales are then transferred to the violins, though nowadays their contribution is often drowned by the pianist's rapid arpeggio figures. On Beethoven's piano they would have seemed a silver lining decorating the much more important orchestral texture, but the modern concert grand has given pianists a weapon with which they can fire more lethal salvoes.

It would be wearisome to catalogue all the events in this remarkable movement but one moment of sheer delight must be mentioned. Having for once asserted authority in a display of uncharacteristic virtuosity, the soloist seems to say 'I didn't really mean to bully you' and offers a new theme of child-like innocence based on five descending notes of the scale of C sharp minor. The effect is so beguiling that we sometimes fail to notice how the cellos and basses subtly relate this to the initial repeated-note theme.

Since the concerto began with the piano alone it is quite proper that the Recapitulation should do so as well; yet even here Beethoven has a surprise for us, for whereas the beginning was disarmingly gentle, the reprise shows a heroic aspect quite unlike anything that has come before. Thereafter events proceed more or less according to expectation, the last surprise being the resolution of the cadenza. Since by tradition this was improvised by the performer, some signal had to be pre-arranged to warn the orchestra to stand by. Custom dictated that this should be a trill on the second note of the scale which, having satisfied himself that the players were ready, the soloist would terminate with a positive thump on the key-note, thus bringing in the orchestra for a final playout in which the piano would take no part. In this work Beethoven again confounds expectation by continuing the trill on the second note of the scale *over* the orchestral entry and then dissolving it into an expressive melodic line. A nostalgic reminder of the opening theme disappears in a cloud of scales which, with gradual reinforcement from the orchestra, build to a final climax.

The slow movement presents us with a unique musical drama, the perfect symbol of the soft answer turning away wrath.[4] The orchestra is reduced to strings only, but they begin with a savage intensity; their stark unisons have something of the character of the introduction to a Handel aria. The ensuing passage for piano is not so much a response as a total disregard for the orchestra's aggression. It is like a chorale, enabling the soloist to withdraw into a world of inner contemplation. Again the strings launch their attack; again it fails to disturb the profoundly spiritual calm of the pianist. The string phrases grow more compact but they only cause the piano part to become a shade more expressive. Gradually the strings, though still in unison, find their resolution weakening; at last, all anger spent, they are reduced to a single pizzicato note. Then, and then alone, do we find an openly emotional phrase for the piano, an expression of grief that culminates in a series of trills beneath which the left hand has some extraordinary chromatic passages which are like the anguished wailing of a lost soul. Faintly, as though repenting their earlier harshness, we hear cellos and basses murmur a fragment of the initial theme. Violins have a brief phrase that is like a heavy sigh; it is echoed by the piano, the first and only time that musical material is shared by orchestra and soloist alike. Three chords of E minor, scored so as to emphasise the darkest tones, bring the movement to an end.

With little respect for our emotions Beethoven breaks the spell with a crisp march that seems to come from a great distance. The soloist takes up the tune, all sadness fled. It is as though Puck has flitted into the Capulet's Tomb, and it takes a moment or two to adjust to this lightning change of mood. In this final Rondo the dialogue between piano and orchestra is totally good-humoured, sometimes boisterous, sometimes witty, occasionally smilingly content. At one point the violas have a beautifully lyrical transformation of the opening theme which is taken up with equal affection by the clarinets somewhat later on. The piano writing calls for considerable agility, but appearances of ferocity should not be taken seriously. Towards the end there is a moment of extraordinary calm and beauty — a passage for solo piano in parallel chords; then, as if to say 'Fooled you again!', a series of trills whips up the tempo and there is a headlong rush to finish the work.

---

[4]Unique that is save for César Franck's almost reprehensible copy in his *Symphonic Variations*.

Piano Concerto No. 5 in E Flat Major (The 'Emperor') Op. 73

The nickname the 'Emperor' by which this work is commonly known would certainly not have gained Beethoven's approval, though it shows the special respect with which it is regarded in musical circles. Here at last it seems as though the piano has come of age and is able to stand up to the orchestra not merely as an equal but as master. Indeed in the opening bars the orchestra is reduced to the level of a lackey opening doors, harmonic doors through which the pianist lets loose a flood of sound. The orchestral chords, three in number, represent the foundation stones on which the tonality of E flat major is built; first the Tonic (E flat), second the Sub-dominant (A flat), and third the Dominant (B flat) with the highest note being the Seventh, thereby ensuring a return to the Tonic. Between each of these majestic chords the piano is given a cadenza of considerable virtuosity, establishing a new relationship quite different from anything Beethoven had employed so far. This dominance established beyond doubt, the soloist is able to relax for a while and allow the orchestra a full-scale Exposition, unusually rich in thematic materials, so much so that I will allocate them letters by way of identification. First comes a march (A) containing two significant features, a swift triplet 'turn' around the key-note, and a martial rhythm ($\sqrt{}$ |) which is reinforced by horns. A clarinet makes an unsuccessful attempt to treat the march-tune more lyrically but the brass and timpani refuse to accept this emasculation. There follows a striking dialogue between horns and trumpets (in unison) and the first violins (B). The theme is simplicity itself, four descending notes of the common chord; the brass spell out E flat major, the Tonic, the violins A flat major, the Sub-dominant. This very four-square motif is followed by a rhythmically more exciting phrase with strongly accented syncopations and aggressive quaver figuration (C). A sudden *diminuendo* leads to the Second Subject (D), a strange almost ghostly march in the totally unexpected key of E flat *minor*. The rhythm is crisp, even mechanical in effect, and it isn't long before the horns correct this breach of musical protocol by smoothing the phrases out and putting them into the more acceptable key of E flat *major*. The triplet 'turn' from the very first bar of the orchestral tutti makes a fidgety appearance in the violins, evoking a grumbling response from cellos and basses; it is enough to set off not a reprise but an *extension* of the initial theme that builds to a considerable climax. Oboes, clarinets and flutes in turn soothe away the tensions with a sequence made up of descending fragments of scales, (E), each four-note group beginning from a higher point than its predecessor. This placatory gesture is soon rejected by the entire orchestra, timpani thundering and trumpets blaring, while violins and woodwind introduce yet another theme (F) whose majestic descending phrases are rudely disturbed by sharp interpolations of the terse martial rhythm from (A). The mood softens as the violins offer us an expressive though compact melody (G), although this too is interrupted by the martial dotted rhythm. It is repeated several times in the woodwind to a strangely dissonant harmony when, summoned by this macabre little fanfare, the pianist makes a surprisingly undemonstrative reappearance with a quiet ascending chromatic scale culminating in a trill. The orchestra is reduced to silence, allowing the piano to change the character of the initial theme from military to contemplative. We barely have time to absorb this for after four bars the rhythm tautens again and an element of virtuosity makes itself felt. It is enough to rouse the orchestra once again; the dialogue between brass and strings (B) is resumed quite forcefully, only to be checked with a gentle reproof by the soloist who then modulates smoothly to what in effect is B major, though for convenience it is written as C flat major. To a slightly athletic accompaniment from the piano, a solo bassoon reminds us of (C), a suggestion endorsed by other members of the wind family. Suddenly the soloist cuts them off with a fiercely accented octave followed by an angry outburst — both hands in unison — that leads to the truly remote key of B minor. It is in this previously unvisited tonality that the second subject (D) now appears; there is a faintly Oriental flavour, the piano figuration suggesting the tinkling of little bells. As though unable to tolerate this unorthodox behaviour any longer, the orchestra comes crashing in with a severely disciplined version of the Second Subject, now in the 'proper' key of B flat major (the Dominant) for the first time. (We can almost hear the sergeant-major's bark, 'Left-Right! Left-Right!') A few magic passes from the piano bring about a bloodless victory; soon the soloist embarks on a thrilling development of the initial theme (A), now compressed into a single bar, with a positive hail-storm of staccato triplets in the left hand to whip up the excitement. This section is a dramatic interpolation into the original structure of the opening tutti, yet after twenty-one bars Beethoven brings us back on course with a decorated version of (E), now on the piano instead of the wind.

In the centre of the movement there is a substantial section for orchestra alone, bars 227–68 being roughly equivalent to bars 62–112 in the Exposition. Both passages are terminated by a chromatic scale from the keyboard finishing on a sustained trill. It is an easily spotted landmark, leading, on this second occasion, to the Development. This is notable for the complete change of character we find in the initial theme (A). By putting it into various *minor* keys, Beethoven deprives it of its proud military air, making it seem forlorn and curiously disoriented. Some abrasive arpeggios in F minor from the pianist (hands in unison again for maximum volume) drag the orchestra out of the doldrums until at last the full wind, brass and timpani hammer out a martial dotted rhythm derived from a fragment of (A). With a gesture of defiance that was unprecedented at the time, the pianist hurls the chord back at them; they repeat their challenge but again back comes the thunderous reply. After the fourth exchange, the piano part struts arrogantly into a victorious sequence of octaves. (Compare the slow movement of the Fourth Concerto where the orchestra is tamed by infinitely subtler means.) For some twenty bars an intense dialogue is engaged between piano and strings as massive scales rise and fall in contrary motion. It is the one place where Beethoven's nerve seems to have failed him; deaf as he was, he could not be absolutely sure that the piano could hold its own against the strings. He therefore directed that they should play only one beat loud, the rest soft. Modern pianists need no such protection and it is far more effective to let the strings play out until, admitting defeat at last, they genuinely give way. The end of the conflict is signalled by a meltingly beautiful version of (G) in the upper register of the keyboard. This is repeated several times in different keys, its serenity unruffled by occasional mutterings from the lower strings. Nevertheless these signs of discontent do ultimately have an effect, and it is the violas who finally provoke the rest of the orchestra to join them in reiterating the swift triplet from (A). A massive chord of E flat tells us we have reached the Recapitulation. The orchestra lays the same three foundation-stones as before, but the piano cadenzas are much more compact than they were at the beginning of the movement.

After the third of these virtuoso passages the orchestra sets out confidently on what we imagine will be a substantial reprise of the opening tutti, but it is not to be. Clarinets, bassoons and horns interpose a lyrical treatment of the second phrase which the pianist then embellishes with trills. At this point we should remember how a clarinet tried to offer an expressive version of the initial march tune, only to be rudely rebuffed by brass and timpani. It was a seed destined to flower 366 bars later, for now the pianist gratefully accepts the idea, extending it considerably and adding a touch of pathos to the end of each phrase. It is the first significant difference between exposition and recapitulation, though from here onwards every landmark should be clearly recognisable.

Two grand flourishes from the piano and heavily scored martial chords from the orchestra lead us to expect a substantial cadenza. Beethoven expressly forbids the performer to improvise one of his own; instead, he provides one of exemplary but unusual brevity which even dispenses with the formality of a concluding trill. The Coda begins with a beautiful shimmering effect high on the keyboard[5] that gradually descends to less ethereal regions. Some final flourishes in E flat bring this immense movement (582 bars) to an end.

After so elaborate a structure as the first movement it is hardly surprising that Beethoven turns to an altogether simpler conception. This is not to say that

---

[5]It is interesting to compare it with an equivalent near the end of the first movement of Rakhmaninov's Third Concerto.

the slow movement lacks profundity but rather that its material is limited to two main ideas, one notably free from ornamentation of any kind, the other elaborately decorated. The first hymn-like theme is announced by muted strings.[6] It is in B major, a key already visited several times in the first movement wearing the disguise of C flat. The last few bars of the opening tune seem almost to disintegrate, creating a sense of expectancy as we wait for the 'arrival' of the soloist. He brings not only a new theme but a new texture, wide-spaced after the warm dark harmonies of the strings. Two descending passages drift downwards in an almost Chopinesque fashion, leading to an openly expressive melody whose sequences might sound trite were it not for the sheer beauty of each curved phrase. Gentle chords from the strings modulate to D major, whereupon the soloist re-enters with similar material, though tinged with sorrow in the second descent. A brief declamatory passage in parallel thirds and sixths leads to a long sequence of trills, steadily rising as they bring us step by step back to B major. For the first time the pianist is given the initial hymnlike theme, accompanied by quiet pizzicato chords from the strings. The tune ended, the piano part is reduced to a gently rocking figure which serves as accompaniment to the third appearance of the 'hymn', this time in the woodwind. Gradually the music descends into the shadows until nothing is left but an octave B quietly sustained on two bassoons. Mysteriously, the music drops a semitone to B flat — now on horns — the change discreetly underlined by pizzicato strings. As though in a dream the piano presents a barely perceived version of the theme of the Rondo-finale. Then, with the bounding energy of a giant refreshed by sleep, it stamps out the vigorous tune that is destined to dominate the last movement.

The form here is a conventional Rondo. The opening statement is followed by a substantial *tutti* expressing enthusiastic endorsement of the piano theme. An important repeated-note rhythm on trumpets and horns should be marked down for future reference. At the end of the orchestral statement the pianist dashes off a few whirligig scales before introducing a more lyrical episode which a bassoon queries wittily. Several exchanges ensue, some doubting, some exuberantly confident until, dismissing the whole affair with a flourish, the pianist introduces Episode Number Two, a happy little tune in B flat major which soon dissolves into rhythmically ambiguous figuration in the highest register of the keyboard. A torrent of broken octaves leads us back to the Rondo theme in triumphant mood.

An intriguing section follows, with the piano chattering away in a rather frivolous manner while the strings have a quiet but earnest discussion of one fragment of the main theme. In unison they affirm its importance but the pianist soon puts a stop to that with a passage that must surely be a musical

[6]Beethoven, no doubt expecting a shortage of violas and lower strings, only asks for the violins to be muted.

representation of laughter. Without warning the theme re-appears, this time in C major. Scarlatti-like leaps emphasise the mischievous mood of the soloist, who ultimately has to be called to order by a peremptory use of the repeated-note rhythm originally established by the brass. This time it is on violas, then clarinets and bassoons, violas again (more angrily) and, lastly, surprisingly quiet horns. In just as capricious a mood the soloist reintroduces the theme *pianissimo* in A flat major before indulging in a dizzy flight of chromatic scales. A further attempt to establish a firmer discipline proves just as ineffective since it merely tempts the pianist to wander into the extremely remote key of E major, a total contradiction of everything E *flat* stands for.

The martial repeated-note rhythm begins to assume an ever greater importance in the orchestra as the piano-writing grows more aggressive. At last, a lengthy trill calms things down; beneath it the strings gently remind us of the magical way in which the soloist had had the first glimpse of the Rondo theme during the closing bars of the slow movement. It is enough to initiate what is in effect a substantial Recapitulation. The remainder needs no comment save for a remarkable passage near the end during which a solo drum taps out the repeated-note rhythm a number of times beneath a descending sequence of expressive harmonies from the keyboard. Having virtually lost all momentum, the music seems about to come to a complete halt. Then 'Enough of that' says Beethoven and whisks us off to the final chords.

Violin Concerto in D Major
Op. 61

The first performance of this great work was given on 23 December 1806. It was not the most auspicious of occasions since both soloist and orchestra were sight-reading, unrehearsed. Since the work was considered to be unreasonably long it was split in two, the first movement being played in Part I of the concert, the remaining two movements after the interval. By way of diversion the soloist, Franz Clement, played a sonata of his own composition to be performed on one string only with the violin held upside down. This circus trick undoubtedly gave great delight to the audience but little joy to Beethoven. The Vienna press gave a somewhat guarded reaction to the work and despite the efforts of several renowned violinists over the years, the concerto never received its proper due until Joachim played it as a child prodigy with Mendelssohn conducting. Meanwhile several publishers had rejected it and no full score was actually engraved until 1894, eighty-eight years after it had been composed.

It shares with the Fourth Piano Concerto an absence of mere technical display, and just as that work began with an unprecedented gesture, the piano playing alone, so does this, the four quiet drum-taps instantly arresting our attention without recourse to drama. The subsequent chorale-like phrase on the woodwind is the most important theme of the movement, not merely establishing the tonality of D major, but also creating a mood of tranquillity that is a cardinal feature of the work. A balancing phrase, also on the wind, leads to the first string entry, a mysterious D sharp four times repeated that momentarily threatens the tonality by directly contradicting the key-note. Order is quickly and firmly restored, but notice how persistent is the four-beat pattern originally established in bar 1. Some straightforward scales in the wind, climbing up and then dipping only to climb again, give us no warning of the storm ahead — a sudden outburst for full orchestra in B flat major, surprising enough to cause a stunned silence after its first and second phrases. In a moment or two the violins reduce the tension with a brief curling pattern, six times repeated; four tick-tock As, echoing the drum-taps, usher in the Second Subject, a serene pastoral tune no different emotionally from the First. (One might expect to find such a similarity of mood in Schubert but it is extremely rare in Beethoven.) This new theme is also wedded to the repeated-note motif whose importance cannot be over-stressed. Horns, trumpets and timpani continue to repeat the pattern in sombre tones while the violins extend the second subject in the *minor*, modulating into the alien key of F major before returning to D. For a moment they stay poised on a unison A; then, as though saying 'I knew it would fit in somewhere,' Beethoven gives us a beguiling justification for that oddly intrusive D sharp, integrating it into the melody so that it no longer seems out of place. The discovery creates quite an upsurge of excitement which in turn leads to an important new theme sung out by the first violins and answered in near-operatic style by cellos and basses. The tutti ends not with a strong final cadence, as we might expect, but with a gentle descent to the dominant (A) which the soloist proceeds to turn in the opposite direction, climbing to a high G before (reversing the grand old Duke of York's historic tactics) 'marching down to the bottom of the hill then marching up again'.

The soloist's identity having been clearly established, Beethoven now begins his secondary exposition. The first twenty-one bars are repeated virtually note-for-note save for the decorations added by the solo violin. Then the rising scales, originally in the woodwind, take on a more agitated aspect in the strings, causing the soloist to make an excursion into various minor keys and to indulge in a considerably more athletic display. A prolonged trill gives the cue to clarinets and bassoons to re-introduce the second subject, now in its orthodox key of A major (the Dominant.) As before, the strings give the theme a touch of melancholy by putting it into the minor, accompanied by somewhat angular figuration in the solo part. The relation-ship to previous events is so clearly established that no commentary is needed for a while. The next event of real significance is again signalled by a sustained trill from the solo violin. Very quietly, the first violins tap out the initial drum-beat rhythm on the note E. (The supposition is that this will prove to be the dominant of A major and lead inevitably to that key.) From the very depths of the orchestra they are answered by a ghostly F natural. This sepulchral voice causes the violins to move upward a semitone to F them-selves. Basses and cellos step after them, rising to G, thereby opening the way for a brief visit to C major. Ascending trills on the violin seem to draw the orchestra upwards until the 'proper' destination of A major is reached, an event which the soloist celebrates with an elaborately serpentine scale passage spread over seven bars.

At this point Beethoven launches us with some violence into a substan-tial tutti that seems to be a more or less exact repetition of the original orchestral exposition, as though from the first *fortissimo* (bar 28). In fact bars 28–101 would appear to correspond exactly with bars 224–98 apart from some variations in orchestration and dynamics. However, there is one pro-found difference; instead of leading us back to the home key of D major, the music heads for the contradictory tonality of C major; far from being a true recapitulation, this entire section is destined to lead us further afield. At the end of a cadenza easily recognisable as a near duplicate of the one that heralded its first entry, the violin moves subtly into B minor and initiates an important new development. The bassoons lead the way with a variant of the very opening theme; in the background the strings constantly remind us of the four drum-taps while the soloist serves a purely decorative function. By halving the value of the notes (thereby doubling their speed) Beethoven gives the impression that the tempo is quickening; the violinist reacts with slightly more agitated patterns, even building up to quite a dramatic climax. There follows the most sublime episode in the whole movement; beneath a caden-tial trill from the violin, horns play four repeated Ds as softly as they can. The music settles into G minor. Against a background of quiet string chords and soft reiterations of the four-beat motif the soloist is given a passage that is as expansive as a Chopin nocturne yet as simple as something by Mozart. This is clearly the emotional heart of the movement, yet despite its rhapsodizing, horns, bassoons and trumpets in turn keep an ever-restraining hand on the music, continually relating it to the very first bar of the work. A long chromatic ascent from the soloist brings us back to broad daylight and a massive re-statement of the opening material, now scored for full orchestra. A more or less conventional recapitulation follows with, in due course, a suitable pause for a cadenza. Beethoven left this to the violinist, though one shudders to think what irrelevant fireworks Clement inserted at the first performance. The cadenza that Joachim wrote in his maturity is still a favourite choice, though over thirty have been published. What we do know

is that Beethoven wanted it to end undemonstratively since the entry immediately afterwards consists of a serene contemplation of the second subject,
virtually unaccompanied. It is a moment of unforgettable beauty whose
effect cannot be diminished even by the convention of a final rush to the
conclusion of the movement.

Although much of the slow movement sounds like a spontaneous improvisation on the violinist's part, the actual structure is organised according to a
very strict plan. The opening theme, on strings only, provides the basic
material for a set of variations. Notice the silences in bars 1, 2 and 5, a clear
invitation to the soloist to provide some decoration. The overall plan can be
shown quite simply:

I   Theme on strings only.
II   Theme repeated on horns, clarinets and strings with expres-
     sive interpolations from the soloist (Variation I).
III Theme on bassoon, violas and cellos with still more elaborate
     decorations from the soloist (Variation II).
IV   Theme on orchestra, *forte*, and reinforced by rhythmic com-
     ments from horns and wind (Variation III).

Having led us to assume that we are listening to a strict set of variations,
Beethoven now breaks free from their restrictive implications. An unostentatious cadenza from the soloist leads us to a completely new theme, sublimely
simple yet deeply expressive. It is an interlude that for the first time in the
movement allows the soloist to lead rather than merely to decorate. Its actual
duration is short in terms of bars though it seems almost as if time stands still.
If we add this section to the plan above and then continue we find:

V   Brief accompanied cadenza leading to
VI   New tune on solo violin (Interlude I).
VII Variation IV, pizzicato strings with soloist shadowing the
     theme in high register.
VIII Interlude II. (Note quiet repeated notes on horns ♪♪♪.).
IX   Elaboration of VI.
X   Return to VIII.

This last section seems about to dissolve into nothingness as muted
horns and then violins give us the faintest possible reminder of the opening
bars of the original theme. Suddenly, and even Beethoven hardly ever gave us
a ruder shock than this, *fortissimo* chords shatter the mood irrevocably,
modulating somewhat obliquely to the dominant of D. A brief cadenza is
demanded of the violinist, though it seems extraordinary that after a move-

ment of such supreme beauty Beethoven should leave this critical moment to the dubious inspiration of the performer. Without more ado, the soloist leads us into the final Rondo.

With only the most rudimentary accompaniment the violin presents us with a theme whose hunting-horn characteristics place the music firmly out-of-doors. After a momentary pause in which the horns do indeed join, the tune is repeated in a higher register, this time accompanied by violins, still so delicately as to seem almost timid. Then, as though they had been in hiding waiting to surprise us, the whole orchestra comes bouncing in with the theme, cheerfully extending it in a boisterously rustic mood. After some twenty bars the music quietens down with no less than eight repetitions of a hop from tonic to dominant, a hop which the soloist copies before initiating Episode I in which the horns establish beyond doubt that 'A-hunting we will go'. Soon the soloist becomes involved in a passage of considerable technical difficulty, the first display of unabashed virtuosity in the entire work apart from what may have occurred during the cadenza. In case this should cause the soloist to lose all touch with the essential matter in hand, violas, violins and cellos in turn offer increasingly firm reminders of the Rondo theme until at last he is compelled to take the hint. A brief pause for breath on a trill, and then the theme is presented again exactly as it was in the opening bars. As before, it is taken up with acclamation by the full orchestra, but this time Beethoven begins to journey away from D major. Brief visits to B flat, E flat, C and F appear to bring him back to D again. 'Do you really mean D?' says the soloist, repeating the notes half-a-dozen times with some disbelief. Comprehension dawns; it isn't D major but the dominant of G minor — same chord, different function. And so we arrive at Episode II, a slightly forlorn tune in G minor whose pathos need not be taken seriously as we discover when it is taken up by a solo bassoon with a vamped accompaniment in the strings. This is Beethoven in what he called his 'unbuttoned' mood, and although the Concerto is habitually regarded with reverence, this movement's spiritual home is the village inn rather than the concert-hall.

The next return to the Rondo-theme is accompanied by a witty dialogue between the orchestral strings and the soloist, each 'raising' the other like gamblers until the violinist sweeps the board with a display of flashing octaves the rank and file can scarcely match. The game begins anew, the theme being presented exactly as it was at the start. (This is unusual for Beethoven; normally he introduces variants.) In fact we soon discover that we are in for a substantial recapitulation of earlier events. Apart from the necessary adjustments to tonality bars 1–88 find their exact match in bars 174–262. In the latter version an expanded treatment of the horn-call from Episode I leads to the cadenza, whose final trill is prolonged for eleven bars beneath which cellos and basses make a number of attempts to bring back the opening theme, gradually losing confidence as the soloist takes no notice of them. Tentative suggestions from the violins lead to a subtle modulation to the surprising key of A flat major and a mischievous reappearance of the theme. By devious means the soloist finds the way back to the home key, handing over to the woodwind with a gesture of aristocratic condescension. The ensuing coda is full of delights; first a dialogue between oboe and violin in which the soloist insists on turning the tune upside down, then some mercurial displays of agility from the soloist followed by some out-of-temper literally 'cross' accents from the orchestra. In the very final pages it seems as though the music is destined to disappear into the distance, so much so that the solo violin is left completely alone. With the delicacy of a butterfly on the wing, the last phrases climb to a high A only to be cut off in mid-flight by two thumping chords from the full orchestra. It is a truly magical ending to a work that knows no peer in its classical perfection.

ALBAN BERG
1885–1935

Serialism

Even today, three-quarters of a century after serialism was devised as one way out of the post-Wagnerian impasse, works written according to the concepts of serial technique need to be explained to a great proportion of concert-goers. Music at the turn of the century was in a Romantic turmoil; Wagner had unleashed extremes of passion hitherto unknown in musical terms. 'Tristan and Isolde' was to other musicians what the discoveries of Freud were to writers; a whole new world was opened and one can trace a direct line of descent from Wagner to early Schoenberg whose gigantic *Gurrelieder* is the ultimate example of post-Wagnerian extension. But not only was the emotional range of music stretching to new extremes; the confines of tonality were crumbling so that it was often difficult to define precisely in which key any specific bar was meant to be — or was it meant to be in *no* key?

Although Schoenberg was essentially a romantic composer, *Gurrelieder* and *Verklärte Nacht* showed him that it was impossible to go further down that particular road; yet he had no wish to make his music less emotional. What he sought was a more satisfactory framework, an inner discipline that would channel these rivers of emotion into some more contained form. After literally years of intellectual struggle he devised a new order for music, serial composition as it came to be known, in which the composer employed what might be described as a totally new grammar and syntax of music. To explain in a few paragraphs a subject which has occupied many a text-book necessarily involves considerable simplification, but briefly Tonal music (pre-Schoenberg) is based for the most part on two concepts of key, major and minor. Key is the generic term for a particular family of notes of which a scale is a step-by-step exploration.

Now in any key certain notes predominate; in the key of C (white notes on the piano) C and G are like the Father and Mother. E is the eldest son and the remaining white notes are the less important members of the family. The black notes in this case would be distant acquaintances, seldom called on in the purest forms of Tonal music. These 'outsiders', chromatic or literally 'coloured' notes, have habitually been used to intensify emotion from pre-Elizabethan days onwards, the historical tendency being for music to become more chromatic as time went by. It may be helpful at this stage to think of key not as a family of notes or even a sort of musical ladder but rather as a mountain with terraces cut around its perimeter. In the latter part of the nineteenth century the clear distinctions between one key and another were beginning to break down, as though the edges of the terraces had become overgrown and nearly invisible. Schoenberg accepted this as an inescapable fact and simply said, in effect, 'there are no more terraces: let us think of the mountain as a whole.' He therefore abolished the Father–Mother relationship and in an attitude of mind that was akin to a sort of musical communism (which was also being born as a political movement at about the same time) decreed that all twelve notes contained within the chromatic scale of one octave were to be regarded as equal. Mention of one octave may be misleading since Schoenberg's vision extends beyond its confines. To him the note C sharp is *any* C sharp; he thinks not of the terraces but the whole mountain. Now if a piece were to be written entirely in D major we might not classify it as 'Seven-note' music but in fact that would be the case; even so, we would not expect those seven notes to be confined within the compass of a single octave. Naturally enough then, though the theoretical basis on which a piece of 'Twelve-note' music is based may be confined to the range of an octave, in practice it is in no way limited to so inhibiting a constraint.

Serialism, or the art of composition through the use of twelve notes related only to each other, is simply a way of thinking, a way of going about the process of organising music, which composition essentially is. Palestrina or Bach (in his fugues, canons or even most of the preludes) organise music according to a fairly strict set of self-imposed rules, rules which are still taught to students as an intellectual discipline rather similar to learning Latin. Schoenberg's rules are actually much freer than Palestrina's or Bach's since they are designed to cater for an intensely emotional style of composition. For each composition a sequence of notes is devised called a Tone-row. It must contain all twelve notes of the chromatic scale though obviously not in the conventional ladder-like order in which we practise them when we are learning an instrument. This row may be conceived in four basic ways, forwards, backwards, upside-down and backwards-upside-down. (The proper terms are Retrograde, Inversion and Retrograde-Inversion but no matter.) A simple analogy is your hand. Hold out your right hand palm downwards; let that be the Tone-row. Now hold your left hand beside the right; you will see at once that the left is the Retrograde of the right: the thumbs are the common starting-point, the journey to the little finger goes in opposite directions. If you want an exact Inversion of your right hand you must turn the *left* hand palm upwards — both thumbs are on the left; turn the *right* hand palm upwards and you get the Retrograde Inversion.

Now no matter how we contort our hands, contracting some fingers, stretching others, bunching them up, putting them sideways or even interlocking them, the *relative* positions of the fingers remain the same. The same principle applies to strict serial music. Suppose we number the twelve chromatic notes 1–12 and decide for the purposes of this particular composition to create this 'row':

$$9 \ 5 \ 4 \ 8 \ 3 \ 2 \ 1 \ 6 \ 7 \ 11 \ 10 \ 12^{1}$$

For the Retrograde version read from right to left; for the Inversion imagine the figures to be upside-down; for the Retrograde-Inversion simply turn the page upside-down and read from left to right in the usual way.

Does this mean that serial music is entirely linear? No, since, as we found with the analogy of the hand, we can put it 'sideways'. In other words 9 5 4 8 could become a chord, 3 2 1 6 a strand of melody, 7–11 and 10–12 could be two consecutive pairs:

```
                        6
         3                    7
    9         2         11  10
    5              1        12
    4
    8
```

This sort of fragmentation can be applied to all four versions of the 'row' and furthermore the whole row may be transposed so that every note loses it original identity while still maintaining its relative position to its neighbours. This means that any given row has forty-eight (12 × 4) possible permutations. Add to this all the complexities of rhythm, orchestration, and the fact that different versions of the 'row' may appear simultaneously and it will be seen that the system is far from rigid. One last supremely important point must be made before we turn to the Berg Violin Concerto: serialism is a procedure, a method of composition; *we are not supposed to be able to trace the workings of the 'row' as we listen*. When a car is running we do not need to see the internal workings of the engine, the gear-box, the drive-shaft or the back-axle; but if the designer had not put them there . . . let us turn to the music.

[1]Treating C natural as 1, this is actually the opening theme of Frank Martin's *Petite Symphonie Concertante*, a twelve-note theme for a *non-serial* work.

Violin Concerto
(1935)

This work, written in the last year of Berg's life, has become a twentieth century classic. Berg was a devoted disciple of Schoenberg's and it is not surprising that the concerto employs serial techniques in its composition; however it is by no means strictly serial, as we shall discover, since the 'row' on which it is primarily based contains strong implications of traditional tonality. Although commissioned by a violinist named Louis Krasner, the work has an almost macabre association with death for Berg was only too aware that he had not long to live and felt that the concerto was in a way his own Requiem. Moreover it is dedicated 'To the memory of an angel'; the 'angel' was an eighteen-year old girl named Manon Gropius, daughter of the famous architect, for whom Berg had a deep-seated affection. When she died of infantile paralysis he felt the loss as keenly as if she had been his own child. We should therefore realise that the concerto was inspired by love and grief rather than a desire to demonstrate a newly developed technique of composition forbiddingly known as 'dodecaphonic'. All the same, some analysis is helpful if only to comprehend the way the craft element in music is used to harness its emotional force.

The basic tone-row or 'series' which Berg uses consists of four traditional three-note chords (triads) to which four notes of a whole-tone scale are added as an appendage:

Ex. 1

(Note-values here have no significance.)

A little thought shows Berg's keen awareness of established musical relationships, for the first two groups are Tonic and Dominant harmonies in the key of G minor while the third and fourth groups are Tonic and Dominant in A minor. The significance of the final four notes will become apparent later.

The concerto begins with a ten-bar introduction in which the violin seems to awaken by symbolically stretching itself. The four open strings, G-D-A-E, are played in bar 2, prompted by the harp. In bar 4 the intervals of a fifth are stretched by a semitone, and in bar 8 they are widened still further.

An extended *rallentando* leads to the true beginning of the movement. This has often been quoted as a transparently clear demonstration of serialism, easy to comprehend precisely because of the essentially tonal nature of Berg's 'row':

Ex. 2

The next entry of the violin spells out all twelve notes of the 'row' as a straightforward rising arpeggio, lingering momentarily on the ninth note. Example 2 is then transposed up a fourth and given to muted brass after which the violin inverts the theme, playing it as a descending arpeggio which is a mirror image of its predecessor. The development of this idea and its many derivatives is very much on classical lines and the musical anatomist can rummage through the score for hours tracing inversions here, augmentations there. For instance bars 47–57 of the solo part — the first point at which the violinist moves into a semiquaver figure urging the tempo forward as he does so — are duplicated exactly as a horn solo in bars 63–70, though at half speed. This augmentation coincides with the first time that a still quicker figure of triplet semiquavers appears in the solo part. A back reference to Ex. 2 is easily spotted when it appears with the original violin parts transferred to flutes and clarinet two octaves higher while the soloist plays the minim figure initially given to the solo double bass. The first section of the work is folded quietly away with numerous references to the arch of rising and falling fifths that occurs in the very opening bars.

Clarinets change the mood to a delicately poised scherzo, their lilting phrase instantly copied by the soloist. Such dialogues between wind and solo violin are the mainstay of this second part in which Berg, ever mindful of tradition, even marks a section as Trio I to be followed later by Trio II. Trio I can be spotted by a spurt of energetic writing for two bassoons and a terse fanfare for two trumpets and trombone. Trio II comes after a spell of triple-stopping (three-note chords) from the soloist and a relaxation of the tempo. A duet for two flutes is a clear landmark here. The orchestra is for the most part used rather sparingly although one aggressive version of the little trumpet fanfare does stand out when it is extended through the full brass section, trumpets overlapping horns, trombones overlapping trumpets.

A curious interloper in this movement is a Carinthian folk-song played in turn by solo horn and trumpet. It is a tune of child-like simplicity and when it reappears near the end of the work at half speed it is perhaps a last sad image of the young Manon Gropius still able to dance before polio locked her limbs in its limp and nauseating grasp.

The second main movement is marked Allegro but with a further instruction that it should be flexible and free like a cadenza. The solo part is ferociously difficult, sometimes playfully capricious against strongly rhythmic patterns in the orchestra. The actual cadenza is occasionally accompanied by cello or viola and its conclusion is greeted by an exuberant outburst from brass and wind. Typically Austrian dance-rhythms keep surfacing, but perhaps the most important thing to listen for is the frequent reference to the pattern of four rising notes that first appeared as 9–12 in the initial series. (It is of course destined to appear in many different registers, low and high.) Gradually the tempo slows, leading through this very sequence into the final Adagio. Here Berg quotes directly an old German chorale, *'Es ist genug'*, originally composed by Ahle (1625–73) but subsequently used by Bach in his Cantata No. 60:

Ex. 3

With great skill Berg integrates this seemingly alien theme into the score; it emerges quite logically since it begins with a four-note whole-tone ascent that corresponds with notes 9–12 of the original 'row'. As the violin plays the first phrase of the chorale a rising coil of notes climbs out of the darkest area of the orchestra, starting on the contra-bassoon. It is a slightly modified version of the original arpeggio with which the violin spelt out the twelve-note 'row'. At this stage it is like a sigh of remembrance as though Berg was metaphorically joining hands with Bach in shared grief and resignation.

> It is enough; my Jesus comes. Now good night O world,
> I go to the halls of Heaven.

Berg himself had only a few months to live after completing the concerto; he never heard it performed. But in the closing pages the music grows in passion and intensity when all the violins join in unison with the soloist as they too share his emotional outburst. Phrases from the chorale keep reappearing, often in strict counterpoint that may be seen as a homage to Bach. But after the passionate outcry of the violins the music gradually disintegrates until there is hardly a whisper left. The last forlorn notes on the violins repeat for a final time the arch-like shape of the open strings we originally heard in bar 2. The open strings are like the bones of the instrument, needing the touch of the human hand to give them life. You cannot use vibrato on open strings; vibrato is vibrance, the vital spark, and with a last sigh from the double basses the spark expires.

BERLIOZ

1803–69

The climate of opinion about the music of Berlioz has changed considerably during the last three decades; once regarded as the eccentric composer of over-ambitious failures, he is now looked on as a man of extraordinary daring who, despite occasional miscalculations, scored some glorious triumphs. The change has partly been brought about by the availability of the music on records; it is hard for us to believe that between the wars a well-known and respected critic could write a book on Berlioz and admit that he had never had the opportunity of hearing the *Grande Messe des Morts*. It used to be said by people who should have known better that Berlioz couldn't orchestrate, that he couldn't write melodies. Even in his own country recognition was slow in forthcoming; listeners found it hard to reconcile the opposing facets of his genius — on the one hand a serene classicism, on the other an intense and explosive romanticism. Stravinsky said that composers are 'inventors'. None was ever more inventive than Berlioz, whose imaginative ear had an uncanny ability to pluck sounds from the air and put them on paper. Not for him the text-book rules of orchestration, the conventional concept of what might be termed orchestral propriety. His anticipation of the twentieth century approach to sound was truly prophetic. Webern once tried an experiment with a Bach fugue, giving each note of its subject to a different instrument so as to disturb all preconceived notions of 'line' and thereby teach us to think of each note as an individual entity. It was a revolutionary approach which caused a furore yet Berlioz had already done it in the 'March to the Scaffold' from the *Symphonie Fantastique*:

W.W.
pizz.Str. Str.arco   W.W.   pizz.Str.   Str.arco   W.W.
                                                           + 8ve.

(Br.)   (Perc.)

The off-beat interpolations from brass and percussion make the effect even more extraordinary. As to his use of timpani, it was so original that it has no parallel in nineteenth century music, whether in building a melodic line in the March quoted above or in the amazing evocation of thunder at the end of the slow movement where he uses four tuned timpani to produce chords unaided by any other instruments.

In the final movement of this unique work he uses tubular bells in an asymmetrical rhythm seemingly completely independent of the starkly harmonised version of the *Dies Irae* that lies beneath. It is a sound we would not be surprised to find in a Stravinsky score but which is almost incredible in a work written a mere eighteen months after Schubert's death and before Tchaikovsky had even been born.

Symphonie Fantastique
Op. 14 (1830)

The Fantastic Symphony not only uses the orchestra in an unprecedented way but also treats the whole concept of symphonic form from a new and very personal angle. Far from regarding the symphony as an abstract musical form, Berlioz used it as a medium for self-projection, seeing himself as the hero-figure much as Richard Strauss was to do generations later in *Ein Heldenleben*.

There are two main sources of inspiration for the work, De Quincey's *Confessions of an Opium-Eater*, which Berlioz read avidly in a somewhat unreliable translation by Alfred de Musset, and (which is far more important) the composer's own love-life. While still a student he became wildly infatuated with an Irish actress called Harriet Smithson whom he had seen playing in what was probably a rather tatty repertory company doing a Shakespeare season in Paris. Against all the odds he did ultimately marry her, though the outcome was less than happy. However, no emotion in Berlioz's life could ever be simple or straightforward, and even his initial feelings for his Irish lady-love waxed and waned in a characteristically inconsistent manner. In February 1830, while he was actually working on the symphony, he wrote to a friend about his beloved. 'She is still in London, and yet I seem to feel her near me. All my former feelings for her are aroused and combine to tear me to pieces; I hear my heart beat, and its pulsations shake me as though they were the strokes of the pistons of a steam-engine.' Not the most romantic of similies, but at least it was up to date since Stevenson's Rocket had first startled the world the previous year. One finds it hard to take such expressions of passion seriously since at the time he had never even spoken to her. A few months later, and still before he'd had any contact with her, disillusionment with his goddess set in. Rumour had it that her morals were less than perfect, and in the final movement of a symphony which was written to glorify his love for her, he turned her into a witch.

The Symphony has an elaborate programme written by Berlioz himself. This is how he describes its five movements:

A young musician of extraordinary sensibility and abundant imagination, in the depths of despair because of hopeless love, has poisoned himself with opium. The drug is too feeble to kill him but plunges him into a heavy sleep accompanied by weird visions. His sensations, emotions, and memories, as they pass through his affected mind, are transformed into musical images and ideas. The beloved one herself becomes to him a melody, a recurrent theme (*idée fixe*) which haunts him continually.

I   *Reveries. Passions*

First he remembers that weariness of the soul, that indefinable longing, that sombre melancholia and those objectless joys which he experienced before meeting his beloved. Then, the volcanic love with which she at once inspired him, his delirious suffering, his return to tenderness, his religious consolations.

II   *A Ball*

At a ball, in the midst of a noisy, brilliant fête, he finds his beloved again.

III   *In the Country*

On a summer evening in the country, he hears two herders calling each other with their shepherd melodies. The pastoral duet in such surroundings, the gentle rustle of the trees softly swayed by the wind, some reasons for hope which had come to his knowledge recently — all unite to fill his heart with a rare tranquillity and lend brighter colours to his fancies. But his beloved appears anew, spasms contract his heart, and he is filled with dark premonition. What if she proved faithless? Only one of the shepherds resumes his rustic tune. The sun sets. Far away there is rumbling thunder — solitude — silence.

IV   *March to the Scaffold*

He dreams he has killed his loved one, that he is condemned to death and led to his execution. A march, now gloomy and ferocious, now solemn and brilliant, accompanies the procession. Noisy outbursts are followed without pause by the heavy sound of measured footsteps. Finally, like a last thought of love, the *idée fixe* appears for a moment, to be cut off by the fall of the axe.

V   *Dream of a Witches' Sabbath*

He sees himself at a Witches' Sabbath surrounded by a fearful crowd of spectres, sorcerers, and monsters of every kind, united for his burial. Unearthly sounds, groans, shrieks of laughter, distant cries, to which others seem to respond. The melody of his beloved is heard, but it has lost its character of nobility and reserve. Instead, it is now an ignoble dance tune, trivial and grotesque. It is She who comes to the Sabbath! A shout of joy greets her arrival. She joins the diabolical orgy. The funeral knell, burlesque of the Dies Irae. Dance of the Witches. The dance and the Dies Irae combined.

Berlioz sticks to this programme with remarkable fidelity although obviously the time-scale of an entire symphonic movement is very different from a few lines of bald description.

The first two bars, for wind only, create a mood of quiet melancholy. The violins then give us the first suggestion of the *idée fixe* which permeates the entire work; as yet we are only allowed a glimpse of a small portion of the theme but the seed is planted in our minds. After a series of profoundly expressive phrases with some extremely effective comments from pizzicato double-basses, the mood changes abruptly as the violins launch a rapid ascending scale which elicits an excited reaction in the other strings. In a single bar Berlioz checks this exuberance and returns to the opening mood. An expansive melody (flute, clarinet and horn in unison) leads us back to another premonition of the *idée fixe*, this time accompanied by decorative figures on flute and clarinet. After a virtual disintegration of the music an important theme on the horn seems to summon us to some significant occasion. An extraordinary pair of chords, literally shivering with excitement[1] and followed by rapid palpitations tells us that the beloved approaches. Her arrival brings us the *idée fixe* in its first complete version:

Ex. 2.

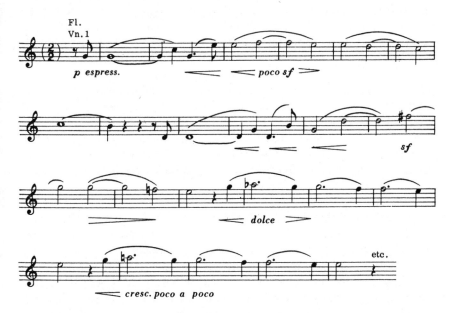

If the tune itself is not amazing, Berlioz's treatment of it is, for instead of under-pinning it with some nice respectable, or even warmly romantic harmony, he gives it a throbbing accompaniment that has the 'pulsations of the steam-engine' of which he wrote. The effect is extraordinary; no living soul could have taught Berlioz to orchestrate or even to harmonise a theme in this way.

Once the theme has been fully stated, the music alternates swiftly between passages of frenzy in the strings and tenderness in the wind; here indeed are the 'delirious sufferings' of which the composer's own introductory note speaks. Even so, he has enough respect for traditional symphonic form to place a double-bar with a 'repeat' sign at the end of the exposition.

[1]The dynamics here are unprecedented in their extreme contrasts: *mf* > *pp* < *ff* — *ppp* in the space of two bars!

The start of the development can be readily identified by a sequential treatment of the first three bars of the *idée fixe* in the lower strings, increasingly distorted as the sequence rises. Soon an extraordinary passage of rising and falling chromatic scales appears, punctuated by loud cries in the woodwind that suggest we are in one of the circles of Dante's Inferno. Three bars of silence (or is it exhaustion?) are broken by a soft note on a solo horn which is greeted with great agitation in the strings. The *idée fixe* returns, this time in the dominant key of G, and given to unison wind covering three octaves. Again the theme provokes an emotional storm which gradually sinks into the darkest regions of the orchestra. At this point an important new theme appears for the first time; it is an expressive oboe solo, the 'return to tenderness' Berlioz mentioned in his introduction. Although the theme itself is new it cannot be separated from the *idée fixe* which persists as a restless counterpoint in violas and cellos. A marvellously sustained crescendo leads to a positively martial version of the beloved's theme, now a veritable Amazon marching in triumph. An *accelerando* with an excitingly striding bass (bassoons and pizzicato double basses) brings us to the ultimate climax of the movement from which there is a gradual disintegration, ending with a sequence of slow sustained chords which are clearly supposed to represent an organ playing. Marked *Religiosamente* they are intended to symbolise 'religious consolation', but after the intense excitements that have gone before, they seem a somewhat perfunctory gesture.

The movement that follows, 'A Ball', is quite properly pure ballet music, beginning with some anticipatory rustlings in the strings and using two harps with notable effect. So far as I know this is the first occasion on which harps were employed in a symphonic score. In due course a deliciously elegant waltz tune appears in the first violins. The orchestration is beautifully economical, the occasional wind chord adding a touch of colour to what is basically a string texture. When the tune is repeated Berlioz shows great ingenuity in handing the 'pom-ching-ching' accompaniment that waltzes demand. With three quavers to dispose of in each bar he gives the first to the strings, the second to the harps, the third to the wind. Only the violins have the tune, but the continually changing colours of the accompaniment give the music a special charm. Three chords from the full wind, horns and strings lead to a sudden change of key (A major – F major) followed by a descending chromatic scale in the cellos. Violins and violas are reduced to a whisper, a tremor of excitement as the *idée fixe* appears on flute and oboe. It is the beloved, waltzing serenely through the assembled company. Clearly she is in the arms of Another since, if we listen to the cellos and basses, we can hear the agitation this vision causes. (The rhythm here is a brilliantly contrived reminder of the throbbing chords which accompanied the *idée fixe* at its first presentation in the opening movement.) As she continues on her way, aloof and unheeding, the waltz theme is divided up between violins and violas, a perfect symbol of the Lover trying to find a path through the weaving pattern of dancers so as to catch a better glimpse of his goddess. A fluttering descent through strings and wind shows his disappointment at not being able to reach her before he is caught up once more in the swirling throng. The waltz continues with continually enriched textures until there is a sudden break, out of which a solo clarinet emerges with a distant version of the *idée fixe*. Does our hero perhaps see his loved one departing in the courtyard below? There is no time for tears as he is swept away in an increasingly animated crowd of dancers.

The third movement is entitled 'Scenes in the Country' and begins with a very evocative duet between oboe and cor anglais, supposedly two shepherds answering each other across the valley. The oboe is required to be played off-stage to give added realism to the scene. To begin with the two instruments are unaccompanied but after several exchanges a barely audible tremor in the violas suggests the threat of rain. There follows a remarkable example of Berlioz' individual approach to orchestration, an extended melody played by flute and first violins in unison without support of harmony. It is a symbol of loneliness, the Lover walking solitary in a deserted landscape. Naturally this extreme economy could not be sustained indefinitely and the texture gradually becomes warmer as the heat of the day makes itself felt. A brief dialogue between the first violins and various individual wind instruments shows our hero listening to the birds. His theme is then taken up by the lower strings while time and again we hear a compact little rhythm (♩♪♪) on the upper woodwind. (Is it a conscious reminder of the quail in the little bird 'cadenza' at the end of the slow movement of Beethoven's Sixth Symphony?)

For some time the music continues in this relaxed outdoor mood when suddenly it is interrupted by a violent shuddering figure on violins and a dramatic outburst from cellos and basses. The woodwind reveal the cause of this emotional disturbance. It is SHE, walking serenely through the fields, as always disregarding the passionate gaze of the onlooker, just as Harriet Smithson on stage playing Ophelia must have disregarded the ardent gaze of Berlioz in the stalls. Indeed the motto of the symphony might well be 'Love unrequited maketh the heart sick'. The Lover's 'reaction' builds to a paroxysm of romantic fervour only to die down in utter dejection as she passes from sight. (Note the extraordinary effectiveness of a single low D flat on cellos expressing a sense of isolation after the impassioned music that preceded it.) Above a gentle pizzicato figure on second violins and violas, a clarinet introduces a new theme which, in time, will prove to be a lyrical counterpoint to the tune originally presented in such simple terms by flute and violins in unison. On this, its second appearance, it has a throbbing accompaniment (the 'pulsating' heart again?) and a sort of *moto perpetuo* in the first violins that is perhaps a symbol of the hero's distraction. The influence of Beethoven is very clear here, though not in the final pages where we hear again the herdsman's pipe (cor anglais only) interspersed with the extraordinary rumbles of thunder already mentioned.

The fourth movement, the 'March to the Scaffold', is an outstanding example of Berlioz' skill as an orchestrator. His demands in this symphony are certainly extravagant — two harps in the second movement only and now extra bassoons, trombones and tubas, cymbals and bass drum. The music of this movement was taken from an early opera of Berlioz, *Les Francs-Juges*. It is possible that the scoring was revised in his maturity, but if not, we should be the more amazed that these extraordinary novel sounds were conceived of in his early twenties when Beethoven was still alive. The opening bars instantly arrest our attention with their menace; two timpani a minor third apart (G–B♭), double basses divided so as to make a four-note chord of G minor, and strange grunts from muted horns low down. A tremendous crescendo from the timpani leads to Theme I, actually a scale of G minor covering two octaves as it descends but so cunningly broken up that we feel it is a genuine melodic line. First stated by cellos and basses in unison, it soon has a descant added by violas (a third higher) and some shrill comments from four bassoons in their upper register. This scale-theme is repeated five times in all with varying counterpoints including, in the fifth version, its own mirror-image.

A rushing scale leads to Theme II, a tremendous march, scored as though for military band. After its first sixteen bars there is a double-bar and an indication that the music should be repeated from the beginning, a gesture towards classical convention that is often disregarded. Shortly after the repeat we find the extraordinary fragmented version of Theme I shown in Ex (1); it is hammered into extinction by the timpani, rising through the four notes G, B flat, D, F and ushering in the return of Theme II. This time the strings are also involved, the violins exchanging a swift and compact little figure which surely represents banners fluttering in the procession. Again Theme I appears in its fragmented version before being transferred to the heavy brass with a flailing motive in the strings that suggests the driver of the tumbril laying about him with a whip to beat off the crowd. Theme I appears in its most massive version yet, punctuated with explosive accents from cymbals and bass drum. An all-pervading dotted rhythm brings increased urgency as the scaffold is sighted. Suddenly, after a series of startling shifts of key (D flat major alternating with G minor), a solo clarinet sings out the first seven notes of the *idée fixe*. The effect is startling, like a sudden close-up in a film, showing the hero's anguished face, his last thought of his beloved before, with a huge crash, the blade of the guillotine falls. Berlioz even depicts the head bouncing across the floor of the scaffold with three pizzicato thuds from the strings. A roar from the crowd (three timpani and side-drum) greets the grisly spectacle, and relentlessly repeated chords bring the movement to an end.

In his original plan for the symphony the finale was intended to be 'a vision of a night of revelry'. In the event it is perhaps fortunate for us that Berlioz turned (temporarily!) against his beloved Harriet on hearing rumours that her behaviour back in London was less than exemplary. (They still had not met.) Deciding to turn her into a witch he composed one of the most astonishing movements in the whole nineteenth-century repertoire, the 'Dream of a Witches' Sabbath'.

It begins with a high shimmering chord in which the upper strings are divided into eight parts while ominous stirrings in the basses suggest the dead moving uneasily in their graves. Unmistakably we hear the flapping of great wings as the witches fly in to the cemetary of a ruined church. There was no precedent for the sounds Berlioz creates in this macabre fantasy; it is, to the nineteenth century, what 'The Rite of Spring' was to the twentieth. Distant fanfares tell us that the leader of the witches is approaching; timpani suggest the sound of a horse's hooves cantering up the path. Grotesquely distorted, we hear the *idée fixe* on a shrill clarinet; it is indeed a nightmare for now the beloved has become a hag, capable of infinite evil. Her arrival is greeted by a great bellowing from the assembled coven. Triumphantly she rides round the graveyard, bassoons cackling their approval and enjoyment. Orchestral bedlam breaks out until there is a sudden hush of expectancy. Cellos and basses take us down into the darkness. Bells ring out from the church tower, eliciting an instant response from one group (violas) which is repressed by a sharp command. Again the bells ring, again the response is checked. It is not yet time to begin the ritual dance; first must come the blasphemy, the perversion of the great Gregorian chant, the *Dies Irae*. First heard on tubas against the irregular clangour of the bells, it is passed on to horns and trombones and then to wind and pizzicato strings, each version seeming more profane than the last. Although the musical content may not be exceptional, the sheer inventiveness of the orchestration is constantly amazing. (It was written thirty-seven years before Moussorgsky's 'Night on a Bare Mountain'.)

At last the Witches' Dance begins, using the theme which had previously been suppressed several times. It is almost disappointing to find it being organised on fugal lines, though violent syncopated interruptions from the brass seem to mock its formality. Academic pretensions are soon forgotten as the music grows increasingly wild. Swift pairs of notes, falling by semitones, suggest cackles of malevolent laughter while, at one point, there is a mysterious descent into the lowest regions of the orchestra and a reappearance of the *Dies Irae*, distant and sinister. A skilfully planned ascent over a long-sustained roll on the bass drum leads to the thematic climax of the movement in which the 'Round Dance' in the strings is combined with the *Dies Irae* in brass and wind.

An extraordinary effect of violins and violas playing *col legno* (bouncing the wood of the bow on the string) leads to the weirdest of all the versions of the 'Round Dance' — woodwind in unison with trills on every principal note.

Once again we hear tubas playing the *Dies Irae* against a series of feverish convulsions in the strings — *pp* to *ff* and back in each bar. The tempo quickens and the movement ends with a touch of banality that is forgivable after the stunning originality that has been evident on nearly every page. Regardless of its subject matter this truly is a Fantastic Symphony, a work of daring that scarcely has a parallel. Had it been written at the end of the century it might seem less astonishing to us now; placed in its historical context it must be regarded as altogether outstanding.

BRAHMS
1833–97

By any standard Brahms had a strange childhood. His father was a double-bass and horn player employed in the Municipal Theatre in Hamburg; his mother, seventeen years older than her husband, was slightly crippled and shrewish of tongue. Money was short with three children to bring up so the young Brahms was expected to earn something towards the family expenses from an early age. One way was to turn out arrangements of popular songs of the day; amazingly, over 150 such potboilers were published while he was still in his 'teens, though he had the good sense to use two pseudonyms, 'G.W. Marks' and 'Karl Würth'. The other way in which he contributed to the family budget was by playing the piano of an evening in a harbour-front brothel. He was an extremely good-looking boy, and the tavern tarts delighted in teasing him. The experience was to have a deep effect upon him psychologically, particularly with regard to his relations to women; indeed, he seems to have been unable to become involved in any deeply emotional (or physical) way with what would have been regarded as a respectable woman, and consorted with prostitutes for all his adult life. It is possible that the disturbing environment of those formative years caused puberty to have been astonishingly delayed in his case. Although we always think of him as heavily bearded, he had no need to shave until he was twenty-four, nor did his voice break until then. In fact it remained unnaturally high-pitched all his life and he schooled himself to adopt an artificially gruff and husky tone so as not to be laughed at.

It does not need a trained psychologist to realise that here we have the perfect recipe for a massive sense of insecurity. However this isn't all, for we have to add the relationship he had with Clara Schumann. As a young man, Brahms idolised Schumann, receiving much needed encouragement and help from the already failing composer. To witness Schumann's gradual deterior-ation into insanity was intensely painful to him, the more so as he had to share his distress with Clara. There is no real evidence that he and Clara ever had an affair, but he felt a deep affection for her that was to endure for the rest of his life. No doubt he would have regarded the thought of any sexual involvement with her with horror; even the idea would have filled him with guilt.

These aspects of Brahms's life as an adolescent and as a young man are enough to suggest that in his inner self he must have had alarming doubts about his virility — the unbroken voice, the lack of facial hair, the instinctive withdrawal from respectable women, plus the moral barrier that separated him from Clara, the only woman to whom he was drawn. Since she was older than him, he was able to turn her into a surrogate mother, thereby giving added strength to the image of her as untouchable. Their artistic friendship endured for nearly forty years, and it was to her that he would always turn for advice on any newly-completed composition.

His first major works, clearly made to measure for his own style of performance, were three massive piano sonatas — Opp. 1, 2 and 5. Each begins in a grandiose and physically assertive manner, calculated to impress the listener by sheer force. It would appear that precisely because he was afflicted with doubts about his masculinity Brahms felt he must prove, if only through his music, that he was a real man, indeed a superman. It is in the Third Sonata that we first sense his symphonic aspirations. Much of the music sounds more like an orchestral transcription than a piano work, most obviously so in the fourth movement (of five), the so-called Intermezzo. There is hardly a bar that does not suggest orchestral colouring; clearly his thoughts were turning towards the symphony as a medium, and it is no surprise that he soon began to sketch one out. Because he lacked confidence in his ability to handle the full orchestra, he initially arranged it for two pianos so that he could hear its effect. The result was unsatisfactory and he couldn't see how to transfer some of the essentially pianistic sounds into orchestral textures. A compromise was reached; he would turn it into a piano concerto. And so, after much travail, the great D minor Concerto emerged. It could hardly have been more disastrous for a composer whose self-confidence needed every buttress it could acquire for support. When Brahms showed the score to his great friend Joachim, the renowned violinist laughed out loud. 'My dear friend' he said, 'you simply can't orchestrate like that. It won't come off.'

If Joachim's reaction was painful to Brahms, the first performance was even more so. Both in Hanover and Leipzig, the concerto was received with no more than a spatter of applause, accompanied by actual hissing from the audience. Brahms was not even given the credit for being a fine pianist, which one needs to be to play this awkwardly written work. The experience scarred him deeply, and during the ensuing years he turned to chamber-music and songs, as well as taking on such undemanding hack-work as the conductorship of a ladies' choir. If he had felt insecure before, his loss of confidence must now have become a serious handicap. His response was characteristic of the man. The list of piano works subsequent to the First Piano Concerto (which was Op. 15) includes Op. 21 No. 1, Eleven variations on an original theme,

Op. 21 No. 2, Thirteen variations on a Hungarian song, Op. 24, Twenty-five variations and fugue on a theme by Handel, Op. 35, Twenty-eight variations on a theme by Paganini (Books 1 and 2).[1]

It is here that psychological considerations provide a useful clue. I have suggested that the first three sonatas were assertions of virility that Brahms felt he had to make. Then came the concerto whose catastrophic failure must have destroyed what confidence he had managed to build up.

The variations were designed to develop his technique as a composer, the beauty of the form being that it provides a constant prop in the structure of the theme itself, its shape of phrase, its sequence of harmonies, and so on. Even in the variations though, there are still times when one feels he is hankering after an orchestra. The Paganini Variations show a particularly determined effort to cure himself of this tendency, their purpose being to explore every facet of piano technique.

It was with such writing that Brahms banished the orchestra from his keyboard, yet still there were problems of insecurity. Even the Piano Quintet caused him considerable heart-searching. It started life as a string quintet, then became a sonata for two pianos before finally emerging in the form we know it today. No other major composer went through comparable periods of indecision. Beethoven might mull over a work for a long period but at least he knew what it was destined to be. Brahms took more than half a lifetime to gain absolute confidence in his abilities, and even then we find traces of insecurity in the self-deprecating little jokes he would make to Clara Schumann when he sent her a new composition. They give evidence of a longing for reassurance. He didn't even rate himself all that highly as a composer; he once equated himself with Cherubini, and on another occasion was heard to remark that he'd give all his compositions just to have been able to write Mendelssohn's Hebrides Overture.

His First Symphony was kept as a secret preoccupation for many years. When he was twenty-nine he sent a first movement (without the slow introduction) to Clara Schumann. Despite her encouragement progress with the remainder was disturbingly slow; even when three movements had been completed he waited for more than ten years before tackling the finale. 'I shall never write a symphony', he confided to a friend in 1870; 'you don't know what it feels like to be dogged by that giant Beethoven.' Not until he was forty-three was the symphony completed, although even then the composer had reservations, making alterations to the two central movements up to the last minute. However, the psychological block which had caused the birth-pangs of the symphony to be spread over nearly twenty years had been broken down and the Second Symphony followed remarkably soon after the First. Once the barrier had been removed a spate of works followed, four

[1] The Sixteen Variations on a theme by Schumann (Op. 9) were written during the period when he was first working on the concerto.

symphonies in all, a second piano concerto, the violin concerto and the Double Concerto for violin, cello and orchestra. Even his relationships with the opposite sex became easier and he derived much pleasure from a warm friendship with a young singer called Hermine Spies who became his favourite interpreter of the Alto Rhapsody. The Third Symphony was written in the year that he met her, 1883, and it seems likely that the happiness she brought him made composition a less daunting task than it had ever been before.

Symphony No. 1 in C Minor
Op. 68

On 1 July 1862, Clara Schumann wrote to Joachim, 'What do you think Johannes sent me recently? The first movement of a Symphony which begins boldly like this . . .' She then jotted down the opening phrase of the Allegro which in the ultimate version emerges from a solemn introduction lasting thirty-seven bars. It is clear then that the introduction was an afterthought, though one in which Brahms skilfully planted materials from which the subsequent allegro seems to grow. The first great arch of sound in this work is tied down to a constantly reiterated C from double-basses and timpani. Violins and cellos climb laboriously upward by narrow intervals while the woodwind and violas move chromatically in the opposite direction; there is a feeling that both lines are striving to escape from the fetters created by the unyielding bass. Release comes through a trill that resolves on to the dominant (bar 9). At once the mood changes with wide-spaced intervals in the wind that are given a little rhythmic pulse by pizzicato quavers in the strings. At the time the phrase seems insecure, as though groping its way, but it is destined to become a gesture of immense power when it reappears in the allegro. A third element in the introduction is easily recognised since it is played by strings in unison, a somewhat bleak version of the notes that comprise the chord of C minor (C–E♭–G) but with the key-note C conspicuously absent. Although it may appear to be of minor importance, it proves to be the seed from which the main theme of the movement grows. The opening arch returns, this time anchored to the dominant (G); cut short after a mere four bars, it is replaced by a brief oboe solo whose wandering path is almost immediately followed by the cellos.

A sudden accent, explosive as a starter's pistol, launches us into the allegro. Although the music is severe in character it has considerable energy, the motive power often being provided by repeated-note triplets that may be a subconscious reference to Beethoven's Fifth Symphony, also in C minor. Strongly accented chords on the secondary beats lead to a fragmentation of the music, its initial ferocity gradually tamed as the strings change from *arco* (bowed) to pizzicato. Two falling fifths — horn solo followed by woodwind — bring us to the second subject group. As if especially aware of the problem of controlling a large-scale symphonic movement, Brahms takes great pains to establish a 'family' relationship between first and second subjects. Thus we find an ascending phrase in the woodwind that is nearly a mirror-image of the *descending* phrase from the very opening bars; beneath it, the cellos offer not the bleak version of a C minor chord we found in the introduction, but a comparable pattern made up from the notes comprising E flat major — though again the critical key-note (E flat) is omitted. The true second subject is an oboe solo which develops into an expressive little dialogue with a clarinet. Against hushed string chords a solo horn suggests an alternative to these caressing phrases which, in due course, is accepted by flute and clarinet; the music comes virtually to a halt.

Violas arrest our attention with a terse phrase of three descending quavers (G♭–F–E♭), quickly taken up by the other strings and developing into a major storm:

Ex. 1

The relevance of this seemingly new idea is shown in the bass, which is an inversion of the main theme. The conflict continues with a reversal of roles as violins and cellos exchange themes. Fierce reiterations of the falling third G♭–E♭ suggest that the exposition is going to end in the unorthodox key of E flat minor but a last minute switch brings us back to C, enabling Brahms to observe the classical convention of a repeat of the allegro section. The second time round the 'switch' takes us to an unexpected B natural and the development begins surprisingly in B major. As before, the common chord theme is notable for its omission of the actual key-note B, the repeated emphasis on D♯–F♯ giving a curious austerity to the music despite its forceful character. This rising third (D♯–F♯) proves to be a significant factor in the development once a solo bassoon (supported by the violas) has slowed it down. A relatively static section follows, only to be interrupted by the ominous three-note pattern in the violas which generates a similar struggle to the one shown in Ex. 1 with the inverted main theme broadened and extended. The forward impetus of the music is checked by a majestic new theme whose expansive phrases are laid out as a dialogue between wind and strings. By giving the illusion of a slower tempo it prepares the way for a number of references to the very opening material of the symphony, a signal that the orthodox recapitulation is within reach. It is a haven that is only attained after a passage of considerable turbulence in the strings.

Conservative as he was by nature, Brahms observes the classic convention of the recapitulation with almost academic punctiliousness and the attentive listener should have no difficulty in following the course of events.

Only in the closing pages are there some surprises when an especially violent outburst leads to a gradual lessening of tension. The final bars are clearly related to the introduction, but the main theme makes its last appearance with the missing key-note (C) now put into place, bringing with it a release into C major and a peaceful cadence.

The second movement, *Andante sostenuto*, shows Brahms at his most lyrical even though the scale is essentially symphonic. The key, E major, follows a famous precedent established in Beethoven's Piano Concerto No. 3 in C minor. Despite the major tonality there is a tinge of melancholy to the music revealed by a tendency to dwell on a flattened third (G natural) at certain points. Such shadows are dispersed by a glorious theme for solo oboe that first appears in bar 17. Once it has run its course the first violins embark on a more floridly decorated melody beneath which second violins and violas weave a contrapuntal imitation. A long sustained note on the oboe introduces yet another idea which is developed further by a clarinet and even commented on by cellos and basses. The relevance of this episode is to be found in the accompaniment, a sequence of gently syncopated chords in the strings whose pattern is derived from the very opening notes of the movement.

Something of a climax is reached when all the strings in unison take up the oboe's second theme beneath a sustained G sharp in the woodwind. A sort of disintegration ensues with four-note fragments passed from wind to strings and back again followed by a sequence of overlapping phrases which succeed in knitting the texture together again. For the first time in the movement we hear the timpani, its quiet rumble heralding the reprise of the opening subject, now in the wind and decorated expressively by unison violins and violas. At last the long-awaited moment arrives, the re-appearance of the sublime oboe melody, supported by the unlikely but effective combination of a solo violin and the first horn. The closing pages of the movement provide an unusual ending that momentarily suggests a sketch for a violin concerto. Did Brahms hope thereby to tempt Joachim to lead the orchestra? The thought is pure speculation but the great violinist did conduct the work in Cambridge a mere four months after the first performance.

A strange feature of the Brahms symphonies is that only in the Fourth is there a true scherzo. In avoiding the conventional display of high-spirited bustle he laid himself open to some criticism and his friend Hermann Levi, a conductor of repute, told Clara that he felt the two central movements of this symphony were more suited to a Serenade. Marked '*Un poco Allegretto e grazioso*', the third movement begins with a gentle tune on the clarinet with little but pizzicato cellos by way of support. The tune is intriguingly constructed from two five-bar phrases, the second of which is an exact inversion of the first. It is followed by a secondary theme scored for a fuller woodwind section featuring descending chains of thirds in a lilting rhythm. The first violins then take over the clarinet's original theme, eliciting a delightful comment from that instrument as they do so.

A modulation to F minor leads to a slight disturbance of the tranquil mood; the strings set up a restless accompanying figure while clarinet and flute in turn introduce a rather more angular melody which is nevertheless shown to be a relative of the initial theme, even if the point is made rather hastily. The disturbance is brief, although it leaves a few ripples beneath the solo clarinet's reprise of the original tune. Suddenly the mood changes completely. A D sharp thrice repeated on unison wind sounds the signal that leads into a Beethoven-like section that is truly symphonic in character. Using only the most concise ideas — repeated notes, fragmented chords — it builds to a considerable climax in which horns and trumpets play a conspicuous part. The whole section is designed to be repeated before the original clarinet tune reappears in the most ingratiating manner. The opening material is reappraised (with some deliciously subtle alterations) before Brahms quietly folds the movement away with a tender reference to the middle section.

The finale is far and away the most substantial movement of the four with an introduction of striking originality. It is an Adagio in Brahms's most sombre mood in which, as in the first movement's opening pages, we catch frustrating glimpses of events to come while as yet remaining unaware of their full significance. For instance, the very first phrase we hear on the violins is a tragically distorted version of the noble tune which ultimately emerges out of the gloom. The broad sweep of the opening bars is interrupted by a strangely breathless figure on pizzicato strings which grows increasingly urgent only to be checked by a return to the darkly brooding opening. Again the pizzicato strings begin their disjointed patterns; this time their flight is more precipitate, leading to a series of swirling figures that flare up to a peak before falling in scattered fragments. With ever-growing intensity the woodwind repeat a three-note phrase E♭–D–C), evoking a thunderous response from the timpani. There is a sudden calm as with great solemnity a solo horn declaims a bell-like theme whose opening three notes are directly derived from the almost hysterical three-note phrases that immediately preceded it. The theme is repeated by a solo flute supported (as was the horn) by tremolando strings. Trombones and bassoons then intone a chorale-like theme which is destined to make an impressive re-appearance towards the very end of the symphony. Again the bell-like tones of the horn theme ring out, their sounds overlapping as bells do. The echoes die away; there is a pause. Then, richly glowing, the great C major tune makes its long-deferred entry, launching the finale on its proper course. Majestic and noble though the tune may be, Brahms does not allow himself to be so carried away by it that he forgets he is writing a symphonic movement, not a rhapsody. The music is tautly constructed according to the precepts of sonata form. Interestingly enough the most fruitful source of development proves to be the second, third and fourth notes of the tune, C–B–C, a concentrated three-note motive whose shape exactly corresponds with the predominant idea of the first movement of the Second Symphony (D–C♯–D).

Once Brahms breaks away from the big C major tune he pitches us into a stormy episode whose semiquaver figuration is derived from the swirling passages that flared up so dramatically in the introduction. As if to confirm this, the flute reintroduces the bell theme, a quotation which is verified by the third horn. The strings now introduce the joyously animated second subject, although its playful mood is soon replaced by a slightly tortuous theme on the oboe that causes considerable perturbation in the strings. A secondary theme on the oboe (dotted crotchets and quavers) can be traced back to the introduction (bar 22), while there may possibly be an allusion to the graceful third movement though it cannot be proved (bars 160–3). Even the ghostly pizzicato passages find a place in the main movement and one can only marvel at Brahms's skill in incorporating all the elements of the introduction into a movement so different in character.

The final Coda is taken at a brisker pace, turning the initially dignified C–B–C of the opening tune into a headlong gallop. Suddenly, and it is surely one of the greatest moments in the symphony, the chorale-like theme from the introduction blazes forth on full brass and strings. Is it perhaps a symbol of victory, a symbol that Brahms had at last conquered the destructive demon of insecurity that for so long had delayed the completion of the work? Perhaps so, for all doubts are certainly banished in the exultant final pages.

Symphony No. 2 in D Major
Op. 73

Brahms began work on this symphony in the summer of 1877; he was staying at one of his favourite resorts, Pörtschach on the Wörthersee, and the idyllic situation seems to be reflected in the relaxed and pastoral mood of this lyrical work. The first movement in particular displays a rare combination of melodic beauty and technical craftsmanship; what seems like spontaneous inspiration straight from the heart is seen on closer examination to be rigorously controlled. The very first page proves to be a rich mine of material; it is shown, reduced to the bare bones, in Ex. 1 on page 132. To the listener this may sound like a continuous melody, discreetly nudged forward by an unassuming bass; to Brahms is is an assembly of fragments each with a potential of its own. The least interesting, 'a' is the most fruitful and in the

Ex. 1

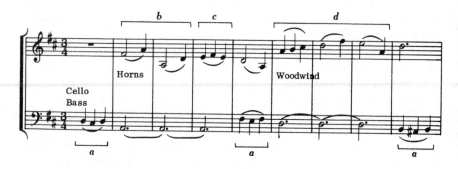

first seventy bars alone this three-note pattern appears more than thirty times in a variety of guises.[2]

The opening phrases suggest an outdoor scene, scored as they are for horns and woodwind alternately. The violins enter almost unnoticed, but once they have risen above the wind they begin a long meandering descent which trails away into silence. A quiet roll on the timpani suggesting distant thunder is followed by three sombre chords on trombones whose potential threat is lifted by gentle reminders of 'a' from the woodwind. The third of these fragments elongates the three-note phrase so that each note is given two beats instead of one (A–G#–A). Then, like a warm ray of sunshine, the violins introduce a free flowing melody whose initial notes are a *compressed* version of 'a'. As the accompanying textures grow richer a solo flute happily copies the violins, extending the tune to new heights. Soon, like buds bursting into flower in the sunlight, fragments based on 'a' crop up in bar after bar until it triumphantly establishes itself again as three crotchets, either in violins or cellos. The climax is short-lived, though it is worth pointing out how changed in character 'a' becomes when it is treated like this:

Ex. 2

This concentrated version of 'a', initially so forbidding, dissolves into a sequence of enchanting musical chuckles on oboes and horns. A richly harmonised string passage modulates smoothly into F sharp minor, the key

[2]It is directly comparable to the three-note pattern C—B—C which plays so important a part in the finale of the First Symphony.

of the second subject. This is beautifully scored for violas and cellos, singing in thirds like a male-voice choir but with the cellos taking the upper part. Meanwhile the violins offer a gracefully drooping accompaniment whose pattern has already appeared a number of times. It is directly derived from the horn theme 'b', again using a compressed version. After some affecting sighs, not to be taken as expressions of true grief, the second subject is taken over by the woodwind and extended in a new direction. With very little warning there is a violent change of mood, a leaping athletic theme in the strings whose jagged dotted rhythm Brahms was to use again to dramatic effect in his violin concerto. The music grows even more turbulent as this taut new rhythm takes hold:

Ex. 3

Each compact three-note unit is based directly on 'a', a truly ingenious example of symphonic development. Soon, as though tumbling over itself, the rhythm becomes syncopated (♪♪♪♪♪), creating a curious tension; cellos and violins in canon begin an emphatic dialogue whose seemingly new theme is derived from the first three notes of 'd'. After the biggest climax so far there is a sudden recession of tone as the second subject reappears, this time with violas taking the upper line. A solo flute provides a decorative *obbligato* in a triplet rhythm which is later appropriated by the first violins. It is yet another derivation from 'a'. Leisurely descending scales bring the exposition to a close.

For approximately 180 bars Brahms has confined his interest almost entirely to the potential of 'a' and 'b', apart from the second subject which has the right to be independent. In the development section he devotes greater attention to 'c' and 'd' although, wisely, he reminds us of the opening theme by giving it to a solo horn in the strikingly novel key of F major. At once an oboe seizes on the single bar 'c' and extends it threefold in a descending sequence. It is an idea that spreads with increasing force through the orchestra. Boldly the first violins propose that the neglected phrase 'd' would make an admirable fugue subject, the more so if it is transposed into the minor. The fugue is taken up with some severity until its progress is interrupted by strident trombones bringing an unusually violent reminder of 'a'. Three-note fragment though it may be, it generates a powerful conflict in which brass and wind insist that our proper concern should be 'b' while the strings emphasise with some passion that it should be 'a' — at twice its normal speed. A detailed analysis of the ensuing section would take several pages and a number of musical quotations but it provides an outstanding example of the way in which 'great oaks from little acorns grow'. There is hardly a single bar in which there is not an allusion to 'a', 'b', 'c' or 'd' in some form though the greatest climax of all comes with a massive unison reference to 'b' (strings and trombones) over a thunderous drum roll accompanied by majestic chords on woodwind and horns. A slow descent on flute and clarinet leads us to the recapitulation, newly orchestrated and delicately embroidered by smoothly flowing string passages. Although the music follows a very similar course to that of the exposition it is full of new details that show that Brahms regarded this part of the movement as much more than a mere convention. The first major surprise is the far earlier appearance of the second subject; the second is the wonderful extension of 'c' on a solo horn that leads by an ingeniously devious route to the Coda. This recaptures the relaxed mood of the opening but in even more lyrical terms; the horn-theme ('b' + 'c') is now given to the first violins who expand it considerably until their 'dying fall' suggests that the final cadence is near. It is at this point that Brahms produces the most beguiling surprise as, with a delicately playful touch, the woodwind recall the chuckling phrase that originally preceded the second subject. Even at this late stage we find new treatments of 'a', notably an almost breathless version of off-beat quavers. The movement ends as quietly as it began, 523 bars which, apart from the second subject, have grown almost entirely from four fragmentary ideas on page one.

At first hearing the slow movement — *Adagio non troppo* — is the hardest to grasp, its form being too episodic to fall into a neat category. The most significant of its four main themes is stated by the cellos at the very beginning and deserves to be quoted at some length:

Ex. 4

Against this expressive theme the bassoons have a somewhat lugubrious counter-theme based on an ascending scale. In the twelfth bar the violins take over the cello theme while the cellos give their greater warmth to the bassoons' rising phrase. Soon a solitary horn begins what seems to be a completely new idea though it is actually derived from the notes marked with a cross in the example above. It appears as if it is going to develop into a short fugue as first the oboes then the cellos take up the idea, but the strings re-establish the latter part of the original cello theme, lifting it to a lyrical climax. Suddenly mood and tone-colour change as the upper woodwind introduce a gently syncopated melody in the dominant key of F sharp major. It is a brief episode, delicately handled. Surprisingly it breaks off in mid-phrase, allowing the strings to intervene with the third main idea, easily recognised by its stepwise movement up the first four notes of the scale. While accepting it in principle, the woodwind change its character com-pletely by putting it into the minor, bringing a restless and disturbed reaction from the violas and cellos. A minor storm develops, ultimately quelled by a return to Theme I. With many variants Brahms continues to explore its possibilities (as well as those of the fugal idea) until trumpets and horns in unison sound an alarm. Reinforced by trombones and timpani, the first violins embark on an energetic figure which proves to be a variation on bar 3 of the original theme. An uneasy peace is restored by recourse to the third theme. Then, after a strange sigh from the strings, the first theme reappears in the woodwind choir, giving it a completely new tone-colour. Sadly the strings fold the tune away and the movement ends with three simple chords of B major.

The third movement is one of the most popular orchestral pieces Brahms ever wrote; indeed an instant repeat was demanded by the audiences at a number of the earliest performances. Although slightly more than half of its 240 bars are marked '*presto ma non assai*' the abiding impression that remains is of the gentle *allegretto* with which it begins and ends. The form is a Brahms invention, an intriguing combination of a rondo, a set of variations and an inversion of the classical Scherzo and Trio. The first impression is that it follows the design the textbooks would call A B A C A; this would make it a rondo with two contrasting episodes. However we do not have to listen too carefully to realise that B and C are both variations on A which puts the movement into the second category. As for the traditional concept of Scherzo and Trio it became (in Beethoven's hands) a pattern of quick-slower-quick-slower-quick. Brahms ingeniously reversed this so that it became slow-quicker-slow-quicker-slow.

The movement begins with an enchanting theme on the oboe accom-panied, serenade-style, by cellos posing as guitars. Violins and violas abstain from joining in; but when they do come in they change the mood entirely. Swiftly and delicately they initiate a fairy dance that Mendelssohn himself could not have bettered. It is based on the framework of the oboe theme even though the pulse is a quick two in a bar instead of a leisurely three. A sudden raucous outburst with strongly marked dotted rhythms may seem to be a new idea but Brahms surely regarded it as a free inversion of the original tune. A delightful chromatic descent through second violins and violas guides us down to the realm of the cellos where, once again, the 'fairy' music reappears. Themes are tossed swiftly to and fro between strings and wind until four calming chords from oboes, bassoons and horns check their flight. As though the whole brief episode had been a fitful dream, the oboe brings back Theme I, beautifully reharmonised. Unison strings seem to offer a mild rebuke, establishing a more serious mood. Their frowns have little effect and within moments there is a quick scatter of notes leading to a delightfully syncopated theme in the woodwind. It is a subtle refinement of the raucous episode that occurred earlier. The strings rough it up a little, causing a chattering response from the clarinets and bassoons; then, to our delight, second violins and violas once again send the music skipping down to the cellos. Unmistakably they produce a tiptoe variation on the original theme which clearly has never been far from Brahms's thoughts. Its reappearance, scored sweetly for strings, is in the surprisingly 'wrong' key of F sharp major, an error which is amusingly queried by the woodwind before it is blandly rectified. Once the tune is reinstated on the oboe doubts creep in and the music shows a fleeting desire to go into G minor. This allows the violins to produce a meltingly beautiful phrase which Brahms may unwittingly have lifted from the slow movement of Mozart's Piano Concerto in A, K 488. The closing bars are the perfect musical equivalent to Shakespeare's

'. . . Parting is such sweet sorrow
That I shall say good-night till it be morrow.'

As if reluctant to break the spell, Brahms begins the finale in a whisper, the string parts all being marked *sotto voce* (in an undertone). The movement is a remarkably elaborate version of sonata form in which the themes are treated with great ingenuity. The first subject is in two sections, the second being an extension of the first. Note how the falling fourths in bars 5–6 provide a pattern for the start of the second part of the theme:

Ex. 5

p sotto voce

(second part)

The opening phrases die down mysteriously; there is a moment's silence. Then, with a calculated shock that would have delighted Beethoven, the full orchestra jubilantly takes up the refrain, extending it with immense energy. Notice how the first bar of the theme is contracted into a concise little group of four quavers (D C# D F#), a usefully flexible pattern which can be made to serve many purposes. After sixty bars a solo clarinet emerges with a calming theme which is taken over by flute and oboe in turn while the strings continue to chatter excitedly about the four-quaver group based on bar 1. A pizzicato arpeggio rising and falling through more than two octaves heralds the arrival of the Second Subject, a broad flowing tune in which violins and violas can revel. Not to be denied, the woodwind choir abscond with it, an action which leads to a rather stormy transformation. Soon a new development makes a strong impression, though it is still a legitimate offspring of bar 1 of the opening tune:

Ex. 5a

The running scales at the end of this example spread like a galloping infection through the woodwind until their exuberance is cut short by some powerful off-beat chords. A brief but exciting episode using a 'Scots snap' rhythm follows. Quite unexpectedly Theme I reappears in its original form, marking the start of the development. (It has been pointed out that the plan of this movement has many points of similarity with the finale of Haydn's 'London' Symphony.)

The first stages of the development are typical of Brahms as he cuts the theme into smaller units which are juggled between the various sections of the orchestra. Turning the theme on its head raises some interesting possibilities, as does a very choppy treatment of the second strand of the theme. Trombones reinforce a substantial climax after which there is a sudden change of mood. A solo flute, accompanied by soft clarinets and a bassoon, introduces what seems to be a new idea. However, a little thought shows us that it is closely related to the opening theme of the movement:

Ex. 6

After this has been exchanged several times between wind and strings, the oboe reminds us of the second part of the opening theme (see p. 136) in the remote key of B flat minor. The forward impulse of the music seems to slacken as we come to a mysterious section in which flute, clarinet and trombone in unison proffer a slow-motion version of the same quotation, causing it to sound not unlike a melancholy rendering of Big Ben's famous chimes. A circling phrase for strings and flute over a quiet drum-roll brings us to the recapitulation. Although all of the material is clearly recognisable, there are a number of subtle changes as well as some shortening of links.

So far, the trombones and tuba have had little of importance to do, but at the start of the Coda they make their presence felt with a richly harmonised variation on the second subject, changing key rapidly from D minor to C major and then to B flat. Three giant chords lead to a sudden recession of tone. A version of the second subject growls away in the bass with Ex. 6 providing an artful counterpoint. The music builds in volume and excitement until a sequence of descending scales in the heavy brass makes us think of a peal of bells. Horns and trumpets make a jubilant fanfare out of the second subject and the movement ends in a blaze of glory. Since the three previous movements each ended quietly this final climax seems all the greater in its effect.

Whenever Brahms felt genuinely pleased with a work he had a habit of making deprecatory remarks about it. On sending the manuscript of this symphony to his publisher he wrote that it was so mournful that it would have to be printed on black-edged paper. To those who knew him such a remark would reveal the special pleasure that comes with the knowledge of a job well done.

Symphony No. 3 in F Major
Op. 90

A gap of five-and-a-half years separates the Third Symphony from the Second, a period of great productivity which saw the birth of a number of important works including the Violin Concerto, the Second Piano Concerto, two orchestral overtures, some chamber works, a dozen songs and two compositions for choir and orchestra. Thirty years before the symphony was completed Brahms had written a scherzo for violin and piano as part of a musical curiosity, a sonata whose other two movements were composed by Schumann and a pupil of his named Dietrich. The sonata was written as a surprise gift for the great violinist Joachim and was inscribed 'F.A.E.', an abbreviation of '*Frei aber einsam*' (free but solitary), a motto which Joachim had adopted as his private philosophy. Brahms at twenty found this unduly misanthropic and adapted it to F.A.F. — '*Frei aber froh*' (free but happy). The relevance of this youthful word-play becomes apparent when we realise that the dominant motif of the Third Symphony is F–A (flat)–F. While the point has often been made, I have yet to read a commentary that admitted that the note A flat in German notation is not A but 'As'. While I accept that the musical motto is significant as a kind of signature, it is my belief that experience had taught Brahms that freedom and happiness did not necessarily go together; the optimistic outlook of the young lion setting out to conquer the world had been replaced by disillusionment and an inner sorrow caused no doubt by his inability to establish an emotionally satisfying relationship with the opposite sex. The F *major* conjunction of the notes F A F was therefore replaced by the F *minor* conjunction F A♭ F. Furthermore, the phrase 'Free *but* happy' carries the implication that happiness is to be achieved *in spite of* rather than *because of* freedom. It is worth pointing out that throughout the first movement the essential major element in the splendidly heroic opening theme (the third of the scale) is 'flatly' contradicted by a determined *minor* third in the bass. Only in the final phrase of the movement is this conflict resolved, a symbol indeed that Brahms had come to terms with life.

> I would know my shadow and my light,
> So shall I at last be whole.
>
> (Tippett: *A Child of our Time.*)

Although the original manuscript was finished in 1883, Brahms was not too proud to make a number of small revisions to the orchestration once he had heard the work played. The symphony is the shortest of the four and it is very possible that the two middle movements were originally planned as incidental music to a dramatised version of Goethe's *Faust*. Woodwind and brass begin the first movement with three massive chords spelling out the F–A♭–F motto theme. The third chord is cut off short and synchronised with what appears to be the start of the first subject, a heroic and passionate tune on violins. Listen, though, to the double-basses, bass trombone and contra-bassoon for it is in their dark regions that you will find the motto; indeed it appears five times in the first twelve bars, ranging through the whole com-pass of the orchestra. A quiet reiteration of four F naturals in the rhythm ♩ ♩ ♩ ♩ ushers in a more relaxed interlude, but in a moment the motto returns, passing from the lower strings to wind and violins and newly harmonised. More repeated notes bring an extension of the interlude followed by a gradual easing of tension. A solo clarinet presents the second subject in the unorthodox key of A major. It is a wayward little tune whose individuality is emphasised by a change of pulse from two-in-a-bar to three. It has a companion, easily recognised by the two detached notes which precede its supple curves, like a delicately pointed toe beating time to the music. As the music dies down to a hushed pianissimo a solo oboe reintroduces the motto, now transposed to A C A. Violins, pizzicato, dissect this into its component parts while descending arpeggio figures in the wind begin to create quite a commotion. The ear is easily drawn to swift flowing quavers in flute, violins and bassoon but meanwhile clarinet and horns keep their minds firmly on the more serious matter of the motto theme, albeit with a changed rhythm. But even this is blown away in the veritable storm that ends the exposition. (Incidentally Brahms expects the traditional repeat which should certainly be observed in this relatively compact symphony.)

The development, once it is reached, continues the turbulent mood; even the wayward second subject becomes agitated with uneasy syncopations hustling it on its way. As for its dance-like companion, it is not only truncated but also inverted. Suddenly order is restored by a solo horn which emerges out of the ruck, turning the initial motto theme (now C E♭ C) into a theme of some nobility. The tempo slows and for the first time since its original appearance the broad 'heroic' tune with which the violins began the movement reappears. The mood is considerably chastened as Brahms seems to tease us with a number of suggestions that recall the theme without getting it quite right. A timpani roll with a big crescendo pulls things together and F A♭ F duly brings us to the recapitulation. Once again Brahms has accomplished the difficult feat of putting essentially romantic ideas into a classical mould unlike those of his contemporaries who found the constraints of symphonic form too hampering. The only substantial surprise remaining in the movement is the quiet ending in which, as has been said, the 'heroic' theme is untainted by disruptive implications of the minor.

The second movement is deceptively simple, more profound in content than its bland opening would have us believe for at its heart lie some of the most awe-inspiring passages Brahms ever wrote. The beginning is plain sailing with the clarinet leading the woodwind through a long and lyrical melody whose cadences win approving sighs from the strings. A decorated variation follows, only to be cut off abruptly and replaced by a strange oscillation between adjacent notes accompanied by gentle dabs of sound on the weaker beats of the bar. Quietly, clarinet and bassoon in unison intone a chant-like melody whose measured accompaniment gives it the feel of a grave procession. This new theme is briefly taken over by oboe and horn before a return to the original tone-colouring. A charming phrase on the strings gives a gesture of benediction that is echoed by the wind. It is here that we reach the mysterious heart of the movement. The essential material could hardly be simpler — a pair of identical notes repeated, the second longer than the first; it is the placing of the notes that produces so magical an effect, now high and clear on violins, now dark and shadowy in the lower strings, now sombre on clarinet and bassoon. Brahms literally conjures with this tiny musical entity so that we never know where it will next appear.

A reversion to the opening theme, elaborately decorated, brings us back into daylight; indeed the music grows quite restless despite the efforts of several woodwind instruments to re-establish the calm and unhurried demeanour of the opening theme. At last the strings slow down their fussy little comments and, as though apologising for causing a disturbance, introduce a glorious sustained melody that has not been heard before. Again we hear those mysterious harmonies before a quiet reference to the opening theme brings the movement to an end.

There is no scherzo. Instead Brahms gives us an elegiac theme in C minor marked *Poco Allegretto*. The cellos are given the tune, accompanied by whisps of arpeggios from violins and violas. Brahms reduces his orchestra to chamber size and there is a disarming quality of gipsy melancholy in the music, a literal song without words whether sung by cellos, violins or solo horn. A central section is mostly scored for wind though the occasional string phrases lend exceptional tenderness. In due course the initial theme returns, different in detail but similar in conception. The closing bars introduce a novel effect with a rising scale in a dotted rhythm that tries to climb to a high C but just falls short of the mark. It is an evasion of the obvious that is typical of the whole movement.

The start of the final *Allegro* bears a resemblance, on paper, to the finale of the Second Symphony since both movements begin with a quiet but urgent theme scored for unison strings. But where the Second Symphony tells of sunlight, here we find music of the night, with clouds scudding across a fitful moon. The opening theme, wind-blown though it is, finishes with a single pizzicato note on the lower strings. Two notes on trombones announce a solemn chorale which may well be related to the mysterious central section of the slow movement. Having made its effect it is abruptly discarded and a typically choppy rhythm sweeps away the last vestiges of the opening theme. For a time the music hammers away relentlessly in C minor until suddenly a heroic theme in C major emerges on cellos and horn. (It was this theme that made Joachim think of Leander swimming the Hellespont to meet his beloved.) The release of a major key does not last for long and soon we are pitched into a stormy episode in C minor. Attempts by the woodwind to reintroduce the opening theme are swept aside with swift ascending scales and the fabric of the music seems to break apart as brass and strings hack out aggressive pairs of quavers over a magnificent striding bass that rises through two octaves.

At last the first four notes of the movement (C B C D♭) are played sufficiently forcefully (bassoons and horns) to make an arresting impression. The opening subject is then transferred to the wind, punctuated by thoughtful chords from the strings which again emphasise the nocturnal character of the movement. Gradually the chords assume greater importance, reducing the theme to four–note fragments. The solemn chorale that had appeared as early as bar 19 tries to establish itself against a considerable battering from the strings. It takes some time to realise that we are in the midst of a recapitulation of sorts although it is far from being a mere repetition of past events. The emergence of the 'heroic' theme on horns (now in F major) confirms that this is indeed a sonata-form movement, though one of great complexity. A sudden cessation of activity warns us that a new event is imminent. Muted violas introduce an ingeniously smoothed-out version of the initial theme, all urgency removed. Soon a solo oboe slows the theme down still further, reducing it to half speed and giving it the romantic warmth of a major key. Rich harmonies on the brass help to give an impression of added breadth even though the strings continue to fuss. But the stormy winds of night gradually give way to dawn breezes as the solemn chorale reappears for the last time. So subtly that at first we hardly realise it, the motto theme (F A ♭ F) from the first movement returns. It evokes a shimmering reflection of its erstwhile heroic companion which now drifts down like a warm ray of sunshine piercing the morning haze. Thus all four movements have ended quietly, a truly unique feature of a remarkable and perhaps underestimated work.

Symphony No. 4 in E Minor, Op. 98

In 1884, at the age of 51, Brahms turned his thoughts towards a possible third piano concerto, having enjoyed a great success with the epic No. 2 in B flat; but, as he put it, 'I don't know whether the two others are too good or too bad but they're certainly getting in the way.' In the event he started on a fourth symphony, completing it in the following year. In his usual self-deprecatory manner he described it as 'a few Entr'actes' and doubted if it would have much appeal. The initial reaction of Hans von Bülow who was to conduct the first movement was a terse message to his agent: 'Brahms Fourth seems to be difficult, very.' Later, after the first rehearsal he wrote, 'No. 4 stupendous, quite original, quite new, individual and rock-like. Incomparable strength from start to finish.'

Basically the first theme of the symphony is a long expansive melody, but Brahms presents it in a very unusual way, each phrase at first being only two notes (see Ex. 1 opposite). These pairs of notes are shadowed by attendant chords in the woodwind, so that if we were to listen to the wind alone we would get a strangely pointillist impression of the melody, little dabs of sound gently nudging the off-beats. As the tune itself begins to coalesce these accompanying chords become more sustained. Soon, however, Brahms

Ex. 1

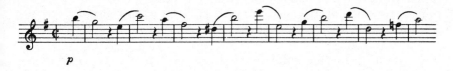

p

breaks the theme into fragments again, this time making it into a dialogue
between first and second violins. Meanwhile the woodwind provide a
counterpoint of flowing scale-passages while cellos and basses play a
shadowy version of the theme.

At the point where the opening theme first began to be a sustained line
Brahms introduced this small unit:

Ex. 1a

compare

It now begins to assume an identity of its own, whether sustained or in the
truncated version also shown in the example above.

A broad sweeping phrase in the strings based on a descending scale leads
us to a brief martial fanfare on woodwind and horns. It announces the entry of
the second subject, a noble theme for cellos and horns with a somewhat
angular accompaniment derived from the preceding fanfare. Violins take
over the theme enthusiastically only to find themselves interrupted by the
fanfare, emphatically stated in unison wind and horns. A strangely fragmented episode follows, pairs of notes alternating between wind and pizzicato strings that remind us of the opening theme without actually quoting it.
In a gloriously lyrical phrase that only Brahms could have written the music
rises to an emotional climax; it is short-lived, but a moment to which even the
most stony-hearted must respond. It provides part of the material for a new
theme in B major, one too many for conventional musical analysis, since its
importance merits the label Third Subject. Easily recognised, it first appears
in unison on flute, clarinet and horn, accompanied by dancing quavers in the
strings. An oboe takes over its second strand which, after a dying sequence,
dissolves into a mysterious sustained chord through which the strings rise
and fall like a swirl of mist. A rumble of timpani and a distant trumpet-call
add a ghostly touch. Tentatively at first but with increasing confidence the
fanfare motive begins to dominate the scene until it reigns triumphant. At the
very point at which we expect a climax of some finality the music breaks off
into two staccato chords. With a complete change of mood flutes and bassoons
offer us falling pairs of notes that might irreverently be described as the call of a

love-sick cuckoo. It signals the end of the exposition; dispensing with the traditional repeat, Brahms moves on into the development. Before we join him it might be worthwhile to have a brief roll-call of the material so far since the movement is particularly rich in themes of potential importance.

Theme I: Falling thirds and rising sixths, the notes grouped in pairs.

Theme Ia: Its 'attendant' — see page 143.

Theme II: The fanfare, usually on woodwind.

Theme III: Obvious choice for true Second Subject; the big cello tune.

Theme IV: Lyrical tune in B major with dancing accompaniment. Extinguished by 'rising swirl of mist' — also important.

The development begins in bar 145 by pretending to be a normal repeat of the exposition; in other words it is identical to the opening of the symphony. The woodwind soon provide their own variation of Theme I, now in G minor, and accompanied by decorative passages in the strings that all spring from Ia. This variation is shortly taken over very forcibly by the strings (B flat minor) and subjected to some very rough treatment. An explosive accent on timpani and horns acts as a strong enough rebuke to silence these clashes. The 'rising swirl' engulfs us mysteriously again, its coils cleverly adjusted to give a suggestion of the fanfare (Theme II) which then appears in spectral form in the woodwind. Several times the swirling arpeggios rise and fall in their nebulous fashion, interspersed with pleading chords on the woodwind. Just as the music seems in danger of disappearing into a fog there is a sudden outburst of the fanfare motive, now peremptory in its command and leading to a passage of unaccustomed severity. With great skill Brahms transforms the tail-end of the fanfare into a more lyrical phrase (clarinets and bassoons in thirds), and places the shadowy version of Theme I above it, gentle off-beat notes in flutes and pizzicato strings.

We are now almost exactly in the centre of the movement (bar 228 out of 440). In a passage whose solemn and mysterious tones can be compared to the heart of the slow movement of the preceding symphony (see page 140), Brahms creates a wonderful sequence of slow-moving harmonies that suggest a sleeping giant. The only melodic interest lies in sixteen derivations of Ex.1a in as many bars. The effect of stillness is extraordinary, as if becalmed in a miniature Sargasso sea. As though in a lethargic trance, the woodwind play the opening notes of the symphony in expressionless and extended form. Again the misty coil of notes rises and falls through the strings. Another sleep-walking phrase from the wind brings a like response. It is an inspired and totally original way of leading into the recapitulation. This is remarkably true to form until the coda is reached, a landmark one can recognise when some violent clashes on the strings emerge from a particularly aggressive treatment of the fanfare theme. Listen in particular for strident horns in thirds, doubled by shrill woodwind. The 'rising mist' arpeggio assumes the ferocity of a dust-storm. Utterly changed in character, Theme I appears as though beaten out on an anvil. The music drives on with irresistible energy and for once Brahms ends a symphonic first movement with a tremendously powerful cadence.

The slow movement (*Andante moderato*) begins with a severe theme on horns and woodwind. The repetitive rhythm gives it the feeling of a solemn ritual while the actual shape of the melody is a marvellous demonstration of what can be done with three consecutive notes, either rising or falling. Clarinets take up the refrain with a discreet pizzicato accompaniment; after a lyrical and expressive extension of the theme the horns re-enter quietly, though surprisingly just as we expect their phrase to be gently folded away there is a crescendo. Clarinets and bassoons in unison remind us of the severity of the opening theme, adding an important and arresting little three-note fanfare at the end. Brahms makes ingenious use of this before bringing us back to the pizzicato strings who take a rather more pessimistic view of the theme. A brief interlude for woodwind leads to an expressive new development as the strings take up their bows for the first time. The opening phrase is smoothed out and imbued with a warmth that has been missing so far; but the romantic mood is destined to be abruptly terminated by harsh triplets in the woodwind. Though it sounds very different, this new figure proves to be an ingenious variation on the opening theme and the pattern of three notes rising, three notes falling is readily apparent. What one does not expect is the transformation that is to come, for the relentlessly hammered-out triplets give birth to one of Brahms's most memorable tunes. Placed side by side like this the relationship is easy to spot:

Ex. 2

This tune, a cellist's dream to play, is elegantly decorated with arabesques from the first violins. It is followed by a period of seeming indecision as paired semiquavers drift through various sections of the orchestra, finally proving to be an apt counterpoint to the original theme, this time given to violas.

Large-scale movements need contrast, and in the centre of this Andante we find a much more aggressive treatment of the initial horncall. Flurries of rapid figuration give the impression of a quicker tempo even though the beat remains the same. The battering triplets return (see Ex. 2) heavily reinforced by timpani, a display of wrath that serves to make the reappearance of the cello tune all the more beautiful. Now it is the violins' turn to have the melody; yet even this gracious theme is given a more heroic aspect by a variant in which the notes fall just after the beat. Clarinets and bassoons restore a feeling of repose before a soft murmuring in the lower strings, darkened by a timpani roll, casts a shadow over the movement. A poignant phrase on clarinets, derived from the opening theme, brings a tinge of sadness, as though Brahms sees the end of the movement ahead and is reluctant to part from it. Horns repeat the very opening phrase, this time richly scored. Quietly and without fuss the movement ends.

It is followed by an exuberant scherzo, all bluster, like Falstaff describing his heroic part in that famous midnight skirmish. The first two phrases, rough-hewn and abrupt, are greeted with an extraordinary leonine roar, after which the rhythm becomes positively bouncy:

Ex. 3

More blustering follows, and then, as though saying 'I hope I didn't frighten you' Brahms transforms Ex.3 into a bland little tune without an ounce of malice:

Ex. 3a

Within seconds the boisterous mood of the opening returns and Brahms amuses himself — and us! — by turning the theme upside-down. The rat-a-tat rhythm shown in Ex. 3 then becomes mysterious while a curiously shaped theme on unison woodwind seems to be leading towards something sinister. Not a bit of it. Instead of mystery we find comedy, a delightful second subject on violins, with laughing scales on the woodwind as commentary (see Ex. 4). This theme is then reduced to a skeleton which in turn becomes a ghost. A sudden crescendo brings back the opening theme which develops into a piece of slapstick humour, leonine roars alternating with timid squeaks from the woodwind. (The dialogue between fortissimo timpani and tremulous triangle shows that we are not meant to take this conflict seriously.)

For a time Brahms continues to use this now familiar material whose salient features are easily recognised. But when for the first time we hear the woodwind choir playing the opening theme as quietly as they can in the remote key of D flat, it is a warning that a change lies ahead. Sure enough, the tempo eases back and a soft little interlude, a mini-trio, ensues. Where the material for it comes from is soon made clear as the full orchestra reverts noisily to the original tempo. We are now just past the half-way mark, and although much that is to come will prove to be familiar, Brahms still has some surprises in store. For instance the smiling second subject is considerably changed in character by tautening the rhythm:

Ex. 4

nor can we fail to notice a magnificent crescendo that builds up over a reiterated drum-beat that continues the same crisp rhythm (♫♪ ♫♪) for twenty-six bars. The humour of the movement is certainly not subtle, but it is of a kind that Beethoven would have enjoyed when he was in what he called his 'unbuttoned' mood.

The final movement is a magnificent demonstration of the craft of composition. Beginning with an impressive eight-bar theme borrowed from Bach's Cantata no. 150, it then offers thirty strict variations followed by an extensive coda. We have seen how in his formative years Brahms wrote a number of sets of variations as a sort of self-imposed apprenticeship. This movement shows the culmination of those hard-earned skills. While it was probably the most taxing to write, it is the easiest to comprehend since the essential framework remains unaltered time after time.

Now this movement has been described both as a chaconne and as a passacaglia. These are old dance forms involving variations on a strictly observed framework. The difference can best be described by thinking of a chaconne as a set of variations on a sequence of *chords* while a passacaglia is an elaborate superstructure built over a repeated sequence of *notes*. A ground-bass is a passacaglia in which the note sequence remains in the bass line all the time. This movement has elements of both forms.

Once the theme has been announced Brahms sets out to prove the basic simplicity of his framework by relating it all to two notes. Six times the horns reiterate the keynote of E before grudgingly admitting the fifth or dominant note of B into the scheme. Meanwhile the opening sequence of harmonies has been repeated by plucked strings, a curiously threatening sound after the blare of brass and wind.

Next the woodwind provide the first of the many lyrical decorations which are destined to flower above this stark frame. From here onwards a catalogue of events is all that is needed.

Variation 3	consists of heavily accented chords employing the full orchestra.
Variation 4	brings an impassioned tune on the violins, the prevailing theme clearly marked in the bass.
Variation 5	A variation on the above with additional wood-wind decorations.
Variation 6	Further elaboration in violins over sustained bass line.
Variation 7	A new rhythmic pattern, dotted quavers and semi-quavers, disrupts the bass line.
Variation 8	Bach-like semiquaver figuration in violins.
Variation 9	Intensified version of above with increasingly important woodwind.
Variation 10	'Breathing' effect of harmonies exchanged between wind and strings.
Variation 11	Variation of above with delicately poised triplets.
Variation 12	Change of time to 3/2, thus extending the length of each bar. A flute solo of ethereal beauty.
Variation 13	Shift to E major; brief expressive phrases exchanged between solo woodwind.
Variation 14	Solemn trombones establish a feeling of almost religious stillness.
Variation 15	An elaboration of above.
Variation 16	Repetition of original theme on woodwind topped by a soaring entry from strings.
Variation 17	Gusting tremolandi with theme on cellos.
Variation 18	'Bending' version of theme, especially in wind and brass.
Variation 19	Bright staccato quavers in dialogue between strings and wind.
Variation 20	Variation on above with triplet quavers.
Variation 21	Full orchestra with rushing scales in strings.
Variation 22	'*Reculer pour mieux sauter*'; a sudden recession of tone with floating off-beat chords in wind.
Variation 23	Theme in brass surrounded by energetic triplet figures.
Variation 24	Ferocious climax with timpani marking each bar.
Variation 25	Variation of above with violins playing counterpoint from Variation 2.
Variation 26	Soft contrast: theme on horns, slightly modified.

Variation 27	'Breathing' chords on woodwind: flowing quavers in strings.
Variation 28	Variant of above with new descant in wind.
Variation 29	Cross-rhythms in wind: off-beat pizzicato in strings.
Variation 30	Final build up to the *Più Allegro*.
Coda	Theme very strong against tumultuous arpeggio figuration in strings. Dramatic rising scale-motif in trombones taken up and developed by strings. The framework of the theme is continued by implication but no longer strictly observed.

Brahms lived for another twelve years after completing this symphony but wisely he never attempted to write another one. It would hardly have been possible to produce a work that could cap this magnificent finale.

Piano Concerto No. 1 in D Minor Op. 15

In June 1854 Brahms wrote to Joachim, 'I wish I could leave my D minor sonata alone for a long time. I have often played the first three movements over with Frau Schumann, but I find that I need even more than two pianos.' In his search for the 'even more' he then set about orchestrating this Sonata for Two Pianos, only to find that the essentially pianistic nature of the material created an insuperable problem. There was nothing for it but to recast the work yet again, this time as a Piano Concerto. Nothing except the First Symphony gave Brahms as much trouble, and three years after we first learn of its existence through his correspondence we hear of it again in tones of disgust. 'You can't imagine what trouble it has given me; it is one botch-up from start to finish and bears all the hall-marks of amateurishness. I am trying to get rid of this and finish it for good.' The trauma of the first performance has already been described (see page 124) and to add to his humiliation Brahms's usual publisher refused to accept the work. It is hard to believe that the score, together with the necessary rehearsal arrangement for two pianos was not published until 1873, fourteen years after the first performance. Yet when we hear the work now we wonder how anyone can have failed to appreciate its intensely dramatic opening, truly music for heroes. Its greatest novelty lay in its starkness, its lack of harmonic padding. At the time the general tendency was for scores to contain ever more notes, more lush harmony, more richness of colour. Had Brahms used the opening material in a Tragic Overture it might have been better appreciated; but it is a concerto, and the essence of the nineteenth-century concerto was athletic display, popularly of a somewhat facile kind.

The opening pages have been described by Tovey as 'one of the mightiest utterances since Beethoven's Ninth Symphony'. Over a volcanic rumble from timpani and double basses the explosive first theme erupts in unison violins and cellos; with its jagged leaps and fiery trills it suggests Mount Etna at its most awe-inspiring, spewing trails of molten lava down its scarred flanks. If the image seems far-fetched it is undeniable that the shattering opening is followed by a phrase so bleak and grief-stricken that it seems to symbolise the aftermath of some great catastrophe (II). It is not hard to imagine it being used to accompany cinematic images of bewildered humans searching the wreckage of homes devastated by the overwhelming forces of Nature. But Brahms was not a Berlioz or a Wagner and, extreme though the emotional contrast may seem at this point, the violins' lament is underpinned by constant (though subtly modified) references to the blazing opening phrase — now reduced to ashes in the cellos. The gulf between violins and cellos grows ever wider until the upper strings seem to disappear in the prevailing cloud. Ushered in by a brief ascent by cellos and basses, a new theme appears (III), the sombre hue of clarinets and bassoons silvered by *tremolando* violins. The key is B flat minor, the darkest corner of the tonal world. The music seems to freeze into immobility before, with a brutal shock, Brahms produces six giant hammer-blows that burst open the door to D minor once again. The first theme reappears; this time violins and cellos are in conflict, goaded on by horns. Out of an angry torrent of descending quavers a rugged four-note phrase emerges (IV). It may seem to be only of passing interest but the Beethoven-like persistence with which Brahms hammers away at it should tell us that it is of some importance, as indeed it proves to be. A fanfare of sorts in strings and wind brings a hint of glory in a brief excursion into D major but it is an unconvincing triumph as the bassoons tell us when they persist in dwelling on such essentially *minor* elements as C natural and B flat. For the second time in this remarkable opening tutti the music seems to be coming to a halt. One feels something must happen to break the deadlock. It does.

Without a trace of virtuosity the piano begins a meditation on the previously aggressive four-note phrase (IV). The left hand plays a passive role, simply taking over a three-note pattern the cellos have just played no less than twelve times. The right hand has a series of gently flowing phrases which have the serenity one might find in the accompaniment to a Bach aria. For fifteen spacious bars there is no sign of storms ahead, but once the left hand begins to duplicate the right the music gathers strength like a tidal wave. Within seconds the tremendous trills of the opening theme become the subject of a titanic conflict between soloist and orchestra, only resolved as the orchestra takes the opening theme and forcibly wrenches it into a new shape.

Over a left hand accompaniment whose angularity precludes any suggestion of tenderness, the piano now has its own version of II. Theoretically in the dominant key of A major, the music is strangely ambivalent, drawn constantly towards the desolation of A *minor*, a desolation which becomes only too clear in the ensuing version in virtually unrelieved E minor. Again the music seems to disappear into the clouds, again the lower strings usher in Theme III. This time the pianist clothes its sad strains in shadowy triplet figurations which are devoid of any hint of brilliance. It is a world of such greyness that we can hardly believe it when a trill starts hesitantly and then begins to blossom as caressing phrases in the orchestra tell us that F major (the true 'relative' major of D minor) has at last been reached. Exerting the true prerogative of a soloist, the pianist now introduces a new theme of great nobility. In time its majestic chords give way to a rippling figure above which we find an increasingly passionate extension of the fanfare that had appeared as a short-lived moment of triumph in the opening tutti. As the piano part dies down a solo flute followed by an oboe echoes the fanfare motif. (At this stage it is pared down to a mere two notes but one should store them in one's mind since they are destined to assume a far greater importance.)

When in due course the strings take over the theme so eloquently presented by the pianist, they quickly build it to a climax. It is here that two horns in unison declaim the fanfare motif in truly heraldic colours — incidentally revealing to the observant listener that its first two notes were actually the seed from which the noble second subject flowered. Against swift running passages in thirds from the piano, quite an exchange of fanfares develops, although in the strings rather than the brass. However, the horns' proprietary rights to such material are not to be denied and after some rhapsodising from the pianist we hear the fanfare in full from a solo horn. It seems to be sounding a curfew of sorts since a beautiful nocturnal episode follows based on an expressive *major* version of III.

If night it is, we are in for a rude awakening for, with a sudden and unwonted display of virtuosity, the pianist launches into a powerful cascade of octaves, derived from the initial two notes of the fanfare. It makes a dramatic start to the development which not surprisingly re-introduces the opening theme, this time surrounded by swirling octave figures from the soloist and subjected to many transformations. Theme II reappears in even darker hue, the tune now in the lower strings, but it is Theme III that undergoes the most striking change. The transformation from introspective melancholy to ferocious energy is accomplished by a dramatic compression. To make the comparison simpler to appreciate I will put the two examples in the same key (see p. 152). Each time that this theme has appeared it has been preceded by an ascending phrase of five chrotchets, a simple example of musical 'joinery' that we assume to be of little importance; but it too now

undergoes a transformation:

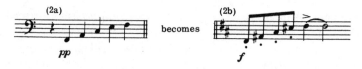

(2b becomes the bass of 1b)

These two insignificant little phrases, 1b and 2b, dominate the remainder of the development. 1b is even made into an enchanting dance, the only light-hearted moment in the whole movement. It is marked by quicksilver arpeggios in the piano part alternating with nimble octaves which no longer have an air of menace. But menace lies ahead as piano and orchestra exchange massive blows centred on the dominant (A). With a thunderous roar the timpani celebrate the return to the tonic key of D minor. Here Brahms has a magnificent surprise; above a continuously sustained D the pianist begins the main theme in a completely contradictory key, a tone above.[3]

The ensuing recapitulation is full of invention such as the orchestra's ferocious treatment of the gently meditative theme with which the soloist made his first entry. Nevertheless, even in new guises, the themes used are all clearly recognisable. A thrilling ascent in violins and woodwind coupled with a striding *descent* in the lower strings leads to more hammer-blows which the pianist parries with dramatic octave passages. These lead logically to an extensive use of the four-note pattern (IV) in the final pages; the movement ends with unrelenting energy and a Beethoven-like insistence that the 'home' key must be established without compromise.

If the tragic character of this first movement was a direct reflection of Brahms's horror at Schumann's abortive attempt at suicide, the slow movement may be regarded as a requiem for Schumann, for over its quiet yet undemonstrative opening theme Brahms wrote the words '*Benedictus qui venit in nomine Domini*'. The scoring, for muted strings with serenely gliding thirds in the bassoons, suggests the tones of an organ, and the music is notable for its restraint and repose. When, after thirteen bars, the piano enters it does so with the two hands doubling up, again suggesting an organ in its density of texture. Quiet exchanges between soloist and orchestra remind one of the

[3]It sounds like E major though in actuality it is the dominant of A minor.

sung responses in a church service. After an especially hushed phrase for strings the piano introduces new material, a spread octave in the right hand initiating a somewhat tortuous and chromatic descent over an increasingly widely spaced left hand part. This, together with certain elements of the preceding passage, convinces me that Brahms is alluding to Schumann's great masterpiece, the Phantasie in C major, Op. 17. A second and extended descent leads to a strange improvisatory passage in which the piano writing is extraordinarily austere, denying any inclination towards sentimentality. Sentiment is briefly suggested by a tender phrase given to a pair of clarinets but is instantly denied by the full orchestra. Again the pianist resumes the bleak and angular style of the previous episode, utterly unlike anything else in the romantic piano repertoire. This time oboes and clarinets in turn are allowed a touch more sentiment before the woodwind choir brings back the 'Benedictus'. This is turned in new directions by the orchestra before the soloist enters as before; but now restraint is cast aside, and the music builds to an impassioned climax.[4] Harp-like arpeggios and timpani-like trills from the piano disturb the tranquillity of the woodwind chorale before the strings exert a calming influence. A brief and wholly unostentatious cadenza (whose quietly ascending trills may conceivably symbolise Schumann's soul ascending to heaven) leads to a last benediction from the orchestra.

The final Rondo puts such private thoughts aside. Out of the same stable as the finale of Beethoven's Third Concerto, it begins with a robust statement of the rondo theme from the soloist. This is taken up with some enthusiasm by the orchestra before a solo bassoon leads the soloist astray into the 'wrong' key of C sharp minor. This deviation causes a moment's hesitation before a possible route 'home' is spotted. A downward plunging scale through four octaves brings the music back on course, allowing the orchestra to reaffirm their belief in the rondo theme. A quiet interlude ensues in which the violins seem to be searching for a tune while the pianist follows after them in a curiously hesitant way. All is well as the elusive second subject at last materialises. It is worth waiting for, a glorious tune in F major whose smooth *cantabile* line offers a marked contrast to the choppy rondo theme.

The strings then have an episode more or less to themselves. Its gentle syncopations die away to nothing. Suddenly an arresting horn-call (shades of *The Flying Dutchman*!) issues a summons not to be denied, and the soloist makes a dramatic return to the scene. The rondo theme duly reappears in full orchestral dress, to be supplanted by a graceful new theme in the violins whose initial rising arpeggio establishes the key of B flat. The pianist shows a certain reluctance to become involved in this, preferring to embark on a long sequence of trills that might well be called 'The Lark Ascending'. However, after a few bars of indecision, an elegantly decorated variation of the violins'

[4]Cf. Schumann Phantasie Op. 17, first movement.

theme does appear. And now comes a truly unexpected episode, a miniature fugue based in the violins' theme though transposed into the minor. Its tip-toe stealth may have been inspired by the ghostly *fugato* in the slow movement of Beethoven's Seventh Symphony. As though aware that this academic excursion might be taken too seriously by his listeners, Brahms doubles the speed of the fugue subject, causing it to sound like a snatch from a Mendelssohn scherzo.

In carefree mood the pianist enters, cleverly combining the horn's summons, the violins' grace, and the rondo's basic shape. A sudden outburst of virtuosity leads back to the rondo theme on the orchestra, the pianist reinforcing the bass with some ferocity. After a fair amount of *sturm*, not to mention *drang*, a soloist offers a modified version of the second subject, now in D minor instead of F major. A dramatic timpani roll and the horn 'summons' tells us that the cadenza, notably absent from the first movement, is now imminent. Marked '*quasi Fantasia*' it has some of the characteristics of a Bach toccata and is far removed from the flashy fireworks offered by contemporary pianist-composers. Even avoiding the convention of a closing trill, it ends with a dying fall that leads into a beautiful extension of the theme originally initiated by the violins. Now in D major, a key unvisited so far in this movement, it allows Brahms to embark on one of those nostalgic twilight codas that were to become one of his specialities. The music becomes even slower as oboes and then horns reveal the pastoral possibilities inherent in a small segment of the rondo theme. Descending trills float dreamily through the piano part before some sweeping scales tell us that Brahms is not going to end quietly after all. As though the players have suddenly glimpsed the time and have no wish to miss their final drink, the music sets off at a much brisker pace heading for the final cadence with an irresistible momentum. It is a fitting ending to a work of quite outstanding originality, so far ahead of its time that it is small wonder that audiences were baffled. There are quite persuasive arguments for claiming it to be the greatest piano concerto ever written, even though the Second is larger in scale and more lavishly endowed with melody, as we shall soon discover.

Piano Concerto No. 2 in B Flat
Op. 83

The considerable gulf between the two piano concertos is evident from their opus numbers, 15 and 83. The second concerto was initially sketched in 1878 but three years passed before the composer put the final touches to the score.

Unusually, there are four movements. Brahms was once asked why he had included the stormy and passionate movement that convention calls a scherzo though it is far from being a jest. His reply was characteristic: 'Well, you see, the first movement is so harmless . . .' Ask any pianist who has wrestled with the extreme technical demands of this most challenging concerto whether he regards it as harmless and see what reply you get. Brahms was much given to such misleading remarks and in one letter described the work as 'quite a little Piano Concerto containing quite a nice little Scherzo'.

The opening bars give little idea of the immense scale of the music that lies ahead. A solo horn plays a theme that has all the romance of a distant view of Camelot:

Ex. 1

(Notice that the first bar consists of three rising notes and, on the fourth beat, three falling notes. Both elements are important and may be treated separately.)

The pianist gathers up an accumulation of chords of B flat major before quietly echoing the last five notes of the horn solo. A second phrase comes from the horn, eliciting a similar response. Woodwind and then strings propose a lyrical extension which turns surprisingly towards the minor. Without a hint of preparation the pianist launches into a cadenza of almost brutal ferocity, the paired right hand octaves seeming like the snapping jaws of a cornered dragon. The cadenza, though brief, covers a huge span, the final bars hammering insistently at the dominant (F) at the opposite extremes of the keyboard. With this giant gesture Brahms establishes the absolute authority of the soloist, just as Beethoven did with the opening flourishes of the 'Emperor' concerto. Yet those who describe this work as a symphony for orchestra with piano have some justification since the orchestra rarely plays a supporting role. Certainly the tutti that now follows is conceived on the grandest symphonic scale. The romantic opening horn-call is transformed into a grandiose march in which the descending triplet soon begins to establish its independence. A 'stretching' phrase on the violins (up a semitone, down an octave) leads to a soaring climax after which there is a gradual lessening of tension. Violins present the graceful second subject over a pizzicato accompaniment from cellos and violas, but after a mere eight bars there is a momentary silence. A swift rising scale pitches us into a violent theme whose jerky rhythms are soon combined with flashing scales. They lead to a stark and forbidding derivative of the initial horn theme, now in D minor and seeming set to stay there. Two convulsive trills force the music back to F, at which point the soloist makes an awe-inspiring entry, enough to command immediate silence. After a brief flourish he begins a free extension of the opening horn-call which increasingly converts the first three rising crotchets into a triplet of rising quavers. An argument ensues, the full orchestra insisting on the 'correct' crotchet figure, the pianist preferring the more athletic triplets. Their differences are settled with a less contentious dialogue which is momentarily obscured by a swirling cloud of notes that range right across the keyboard. Reminders of the second limb of the opening theme are offered by the first flute, but the soloist treats them rather waywardly.

Soon a new theme appears, easily recognised by the initial rhythm, like someone knocking at the door:

Ex. 2

The tiny fragment created by abstracting the second and third notes proves to be enormously important. It is amazing what a great composer can do with so small a unit as a rising semitone, as we are soon to discover. The flute makes the point most graphically while the pianist is given a hair-raising sequence of skips in contrary motion. The rising semitone is then turned into a falling one and treated in a more leisurely fashion (paired crotchets). A more capricious treatment, dancing triplets, is then ironed out by the strings, establishing a relationship to past events that we are unlikely to have realised.

But what of the second subject? Has it been forgotten? 'Certainly not!' says the pianist throwing any pretence at caution aside and introducing a rough-hewn version very different from the elegant phrases the violins had offered in the tutti. An explosive arpeggio brings back the violent jagged theme from the exposition which, having generated a brief conflict with the lower strings, gives way to an obstreperous newcomer. Its stamping rhythms and dynamic energy are immensely exciting and they build to a huge climax in which elements of the opening horn-call can be clearly recognised, whether as chunky chords in the bass, or repeated patterns of descending triplets that leap across the keys.

At last the pianist is given a brief respite as a major storm develops in the orchestra. Referring to both first and second subjects, its relevance is easy to comprehend. A long chromatic descent brings release from the orchestral fury; as though from a distance we hear a solo horn reminding us of the opening theme, now darkened by transposition into the key of F minor. As before, its final notes are echoed by the piano.

At this point Brahms introduces a daring innovation. Cadenzas are normally the exclusive preserve of the soloist and the arresting cadenza that occurs so near the beginning of this concerto would seem to be purely pianistic. We are the more surprised then when its first six bars reappear in a version for piano *and* orchestra. It is a striking effect which leads to an extension incorporating the 'stretching' phrase from the initial tutti. Brief allusions to the compact rhythm that begins Ex. 2 are disregarded by the soloist who introduces a completely new episode in B minor, easily recognised by the fact that the two hands duplicate each other and by the persistence of its dotted rhythm. Soon the woodwind try to establish some tonal stability with strong sustained chords around which piano and strings indulge in a strenuous argument. The crisis is resolved by a *fortissimo* statement of the first three notes of Ex. 1 powerful enough to create a sort of dust-cloud of notes from the piano. Twice more in succession the three ascending notes are stated with the utmost emphasis, settling on the dominant of B flat (F major) and evoking an even more nebulous response. A magically shimmering figure high on the piano finds a subtle route back to B flat; as from a distance we hear the initial horn-call and, almost before we are aware of it, the classic recapitulation arrives.

Although considerably condensed, the material is all familiar until the advent of the coda which is heralded by some extraordinary trills combined with off-beat chords. Suddenly they are reduced to a low grumble in the bass, an effect almost as sinister as the drums at the start of Berlioz' 'March to the Scaffold'. I cannot do better than quote Tovey's description of this wonderful moment: 'Out of subdued mutterings the first theme again arises and hovers, while the air seems full of whisperings and the beating of mighty wings.'[5] After an amazingly prolonged chromatic descent through four octaves of the keyboard the clouds are dispersed by three mighty chords based on the familiar opening theme. The cue is seized on by the pianist who, for the first and only time in the movement, actually plays the initial horn-call, albeit on a heroic scale. A considerable extension of the triplet at the end of bar 1 follows, with piano and orchestra vying with each other in a contest of strength. A long diminuendo suggests the possibility of a quiet ending but it is not to be; a brilliant ascending scale and a clattering trill signal that the end of this truly heroic movement is in sight. The three majestic chords which conclude it were clearly designed to elicit storms of applause and it is a pity that the concert manners of today demand that the movement should be greeted by a silence broken only by a few restrained coughs and a brief murmur of approval.

The material of the ensuing scherzo was originally conceived as a sketch for a violin concerto but Brahms quickly realised that it demanded the greater

[5]D.F. Tovey, *Essays in Musical Analysis*, Vol. III, (O.U.P., 1935).

dominance the piano could give. The movement begins in grim earnest with angrily repeated chords in the orchestra above which the piano part seems to writhe, fighting to get free. After a struggle lasting for 42 bars there is a sudden change of mood as unison strings offer a truce in the shape of a phrase that harps insistently on the note E. As though given its freedom, the piano accepts the offer; an inspired improvisation follows, lyrical and expansive. Even the tiger-like spring with which the movement began is tamed until it is reduced to a gentle rocking figure in the strings. The music dies away to nothing so that the obligatory repeat catches us unawares with the renewal of the conflict.

After the repeat there is an extensive development of the initial phrases, the excitement being heightened by some splendid striding octaves whose majestic chromatic ascent seems to lift the music bodily. The innocent string phrase that once eased the tension is now transformed into something savage with horns baying like some barbaric war-cry. Four full-blooded repetitions of the initial five notes of the movement lead to a sudden transformation as the music shifts into D major. At a slightly steadier tempo the strings proclaim a fanfare-like theme that is type-cast for horns and trumpets. (Their turn will come!) A majestic sequel follows, coming to a cadence of Handelian splendour. The soloist's response is totally unexpected, a variation on the fanfare theme that is fiendishly difficult. The tumultuous octaves we find in Liszt or Tchaikovsky are child's play compared to these, partly because they must be played *pianissimo*, partly because of the angularity of the phrases. (The variation is in D minor, the second limb being in three-part counter-point.) The orchestra say 'Amen to that' with their solemn sequel, now hushed. It prompts a free, almost Chopinesque rhapsody which is called to order by a grave reminder of the fanfare theme from unison strings. A thrilling crescendo brings back the fanfare in its full glory with horns and trumpets joyfully claiming their just rights.

After some quietly pensive chords from the woodwind the pianist reintroduces the initial theme of the movement. It is a curious false start which the orchestra refuses at first to accept. The reason for this becomes apparent after a strangely static passage; it is because the roles are to be reversed. Thus in the true reprise the strings play what was once the pianist's, the piano plays what was once the orchestral part. It is a brilliant way of observing a classic convention while giving it an entirely new tone-colour. Thereafter the movement proceeds on more or less predictable lines, ending with a powerful coda that leaves soloist and audience gasping.

On hearing this concerto for the first time, nobody is likely to forget the impression made by the hauntingly beautiful cello solo which begins the slow movement. It is a literal song without words which the violins, after supply-ing an ethereal descant, cannot refrain from taking over for themselves. Oboe and solo cello then join in an exquisitely tender duet that would not be out of place in *Bohème*. It is an idyllic scene into which the piano enters with an air of reverence, as though anxious not to break the spell. The pianist is then given an improvisatory solo which seems to be divorced from all that has gone before. In fact it is closely related, as the example below reveals. The first two bars show the start of the cello tune (transposed up an octave), while the final bar shows the beginning of the piano 'improvisation'. Transfer the rhythm of the first to the melodic contour of the second as suggested and the relationship becomes clear.

Ex. 3

The next orchestral entry casts a shadow by changing to the minor; this produces a disturbed reaction in the piano part. The trills and swooping arpeggios disguise the closeness to the theme which Brahms still maintains by simply converting dotted crotchets and quavers into notes of half the value. All the skills he had acquired in the numerous sets of variations written in his twenties are brought to bear here, for though the movement is in no way a set of 'variations on a theme' the techniques employed are similar. All the listener need keep in mind is the extraordinary adaptability of this pattern:

It appears most frequently as chords in the right hand, fractionally after the beat.

The central section of the movement is like a nocturne in which a pair of clarinets have a tune of such infinite calm that it seems as though suspended in the air. The pianist's left hand supplies the accompaniment while the right hand follows the outline of the clarinet theme with isolated notes that are like individual stars picked out against the velvety night sky. In twelve bars Brahms says as much as many composers do in an entire slow movement.

Were it not for the sheer beauty of the solo cello tune, its reappearance would seem almost irreverent after this truly profound interlude. The key, F sharp major, might present a problem to a less skilled composer, but a beautifully subtle modulation brings us back to the tonic (B flat major) and a more or less exact reprise of the opening stanzas, elegantly decorated by the soloist. A long ascending trill, richly harmonised, brings this sublime movement to an end.

The final Rondo is one of the most tuneful movements in the entire repertoire with such a prodigal outpouring of melody that it is like an album of musical snapshots, each one more delightful than its predecessor. The first tune dances on air, the sole accompaniment in the orchestra consisting of little sighs of pleasure from the violas. The violins soon take it over to a skipping figure from the piano. The pianist then produces tune number two by toying playfully with the final notes of tune number one. A swift ascending scale in thirds in the unlikely key of D major brings back tune number one which proceeds to show unexpected muscle. An abrupt jerky rhythm from the piano heralds the entrance of the next 'character', clearly a Hungarian gipsy, and a voluptuous one at that. Yet another tune appears, its opening notes a caress followed by a gurgle of delight in rippling thirds. The clarinets show their approval of this one with pizzicato cellos supplying a light-footed accompaniment. We have now had four distinct themes, each one enchanting in its own right. As though this were still not enough Brahms now produces a deliciously silly melody whose rhythm (♩ ♫) is the same in every bar. Once it is taken over by flutes and oboes the pianist is given nimble little comments that suggest peals of laughter.

For more than 180 bars Brahms plays with these tunes, juggling with them so that we are never sure which one will appear next. He then decides that it is time to introduce a rather tougher element, but even that is merely an extension of one fragment of the opening theme. The moment of severity is short-lived and soon the pianist is back with an even more playful version of tune number two. From here on the listener needs little guidance since despite the inventiveness with which they are treated the tunes are always clearly recognisable.

Towards the end of the movement the pianist whips up the tempo with harp-like chords in the left hand and agile octaves (in triplets) in the right. Even this proves to be an ingenious variation on the opening theme, but it serves admirably to lead the final gallop home. If I had to choose one movement from the entire classical repertoire to convince a philistine that a concerto movement could be utterly delightful from start to finish I think I would select this. Small wonder that he felt that to write a Third would prove impossibly difficult.

Violin Concerto in D Major
Op. 77

Like other great composer-pianists before and after him, from Mozart to
Bartók, Brahms wrote his two piano concertos with his own style of playing
very much in mind. A violin concerto was a different proposition and it is
interesting that the greatest composers have rarely ventured on more than
one unless, like Mozart, they were skilled enough to be concert-performers
on the instrument. Fortunately for Brahms he enjoyed a close friendship
with Joachim, one of the greatest violinists of the day, and it was to Joachim
that he turned for advice when it came to writing the solo part of this
concerto. Advice given was not necessarily advice taken and although he left
the composition of the cadenza entirely to Joachim he often preferred his own
original ideas to Joachim's more violinistic 'improvements'. This was not the
case with the two central movements of what was originally intended to be a
four-movement work. 'The middle movements are failures,' wrote Brahms
in the winter of 1878; 'I have written a feeble Adagio instead.' Surprisingly
the concerto was not particularly well received even with Joachim's advocacy
and it took some time for it to be absorbed into the repertoire. In 1894, three
years before his death, Brahms had the pleasure of hearing the concerto
played by a twelve-year old prodigy, Bronislav Hubermann; it was a sign
that the work was no longer regarded as beyond the powers of all but the very
greatest of masters.

Like the Second Symphony, with which it has more in common than a
shared tonality, it was mostly written in Pörtschach where, to this day, one
can see a lakeside café with the proud inscription that 'within these walls the
great composer Johannes Brahms composed his immortal violin concerto'.
The tranquil atmosphere of the beautiful Carinthian lake resort seems to have
brought out the most lyrical aspect of Brahms's genius, and the opening bars
of the concerto breathe contentment. Three significant themes appear
immediately in sequence; the first (I), on unison violas, cellos, bassoons and
horns, spells out the essential notes of D major; the second (II), on oboes with
a gently rocking string accompaniment that suggests the waters of the
Wörthersee, shifts through C major and G major to the dominant of D *minor*;
it is in this darker key that idea number three (III) makes a dramatic appearance with striding octaves in unison strings and wind. With the advent of the
full orchestra, I reappears in the grandest manner, first overlapping itself and
then 'diminished' to notes of half the original value. An impressive descending scale, like a peal of bells, brings us to the second subject group, which like
the first, consists of three distinct themes. The first (A), initiated by oboe and
horn in unison is then extended by the strings, which, having led us to expect
a crescendo, suddenly recede into a remote *pianissimo*. Four unison notes on

woodwind bring a touch of solemnity which a gracious curve fails to dispel. A strangely bleak theme (B) creates a stark change of mood with its plaintive suggestion of G minor. With sudden ferocity the strings produce an explosive theme with an aggressive dotted rhythm (C) which has as its sequel a repeated pattern of four descending semiquavers against which the lower strings and then the wind have a strong marching ascent. This rich choice of material, seven themes of potential importance, is spread over a magnificent opening tutti of ninety bars. Which theme will the soloist choose to make the most effective entry?

At first hearing it sounds almost as if it is a new idea entirely, but the rocket-like arpeggio which shoots upwards through two octaves to the forceful octaves in the second bar is simply a disguise; in fact Brahms has taken the serene opening theme (I), put it into the minor, and changed its character from gentleness to a highly-charged intensity. Fragments of the dotted rhythm (C) seem to goad the soloist to even more strenuous effort until a climactic chord from the orchestra breaks the tension, allowing the violin a long descent through a sequence of arpeggios as oboe and clarinet in turn play a minor and extended version of I. As the violin continues its athletic progress the woodwind make several references to this new development until at last the music is allowed to return to the major key, bringing back the opening theme in something like its original mood. This whole opening paragraph for the soloist could properly be described as an accompanied cadenza and it lasts almost exactly half the length of the initial tutti, forty-six bars as opposed to ninety. A sustained trill tells us that the rhetoric is over and, with masterly placing, the violin is given the original version of Theme I for the first time. Beneath it the violas have an unostentatious accompanying figure which is destined to become gloriously triumphant at a much later stage.

As might be expected from so classically-minded a composer as Brahms, the secondary exposition follows very similar lines to the original tutti although the violin's decorative additions allow the occasional extension of an idea. Theme II duly appears (now in cellos and violas), while the dramatic octave leaps of III provoke a strong reaction from the soloist, whether three-note chords of surprising power or brilliant arpeggios circling round the open E string. A change from busy semiquaver figuration to more leisurely triplets brings us to the second subject group (A) which follows its original course as far as the four solemn unison notes in the woodwind. It is here that Brahms produces a lovely surprise. The brief curving phrase in the woodwind that originally led into the gloom of G minor (B) is now taken over by the soloist and turned into a beguiling new theme (E) of which not even a hint was given in the exposition. One is tempted to call it the true second subject since it is developed at some length by both soloist and orchestra. After thirty bars of enchantment the bleak theme (B) does appear, cold and comfortless. Just as the music seems in danger of coming to a complete halt the soloist launches a vigorous attack with theme (C). For some time battle is joined until a torrent of notes from the violin over a held chord in the wind brings the secondary exposition to a dramatic close.

With an inspired break from tradition Brahms begins the development by giving the full orchestra the version of I which had initially been the soloist's prerogative. Naturally it is shorn of some of the trimmings but is none the less effective for that since now the brass can make striking interpolations which would have seemed overweighty when pitted against a solo violin. Our surmise that E may well be the true second subject is confirmed when violins and cellos enjoy it to the full, even bringing a touch of sunlight into the gloom of B. This theme, up to now an occasional brief patch of shadow, is now taken up by the soloist and developed in a richly expressive manner. Transferred to the orchestra it then gives an opportunity for a delightful new decoration to be exploited, one tiny rhythmic unit (♫) sufficing for no less than twenty bars without creating the slightest feeling of monotony. It is so delicate and graceful that it comes as a real shock when the orchestra, prompted by sudden angry trills from the violin, turn grace into aggression. A short but violent storm breaks out, only to be quelled by a strident chord on full brass and wind. It is the signal for III to reappear, its giant steps marching purposefully through the orchestral bass while the soloist has an extraordinary powerful figure shaped from falling or rising minor ninths. (A—G♯ descending of A—B♭ ascending.) A timpani roll underlines a series of tense allusions to C and I, now thrown into unaccustomed proximity, until the long-postponed but inevitable climax arrives with a triumphant reprise of the opening theme, now clad in martial glory. A calming entry from the violin re-establishes the original pastoral mood and leads us to a classic recapitulation in which every landmark should be easily identified. A short passage for full orchestra based on I allows the soloist a few seconds' respite before the cadenza.

The coda which follows allows the soloist a sublime meditation on the opening theme before whipping up the tempo with a series of fanfare-like flourishes which are based on the unassuming figure originally allotted to the violas as mere accompaniment some 420 bars previously.

The *Adagio*, in the event the last movement to be written, begins with a miniature wind serenade, a clever device calculated to give the listener's ear a rest from string tone. The melody is given to a solo oboe; it is as well that it is so memorable since the ensuing violin solo is entrusted with an elaborate and ingeniously expanded variation, easy to follow if one bears the original tune in mind. At the halfway point there is a seemingly final cadence emphasised by a trill, but just as we expect the music to come to rest there is a sudden rise of a semi-tone and a shift to the alien key of G flat major. For a moment the music seems uncertain of its direction until the soloist takes the initiative and leads the way into a central rhapsody. Despite the increasingly florid decoration in the solo part the music is built on a very simple frame, mostly derived from a single bar of the initial theme. The pattern is easily recognised, a four-note chromatic descent which, by the process known as diminution, doubles its speed.

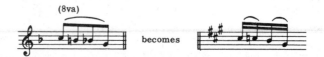

This is further simplified to three descending notes (C♯ B A), a version which encourages a brief but passionate exchange between solo violin and orchestral cellos. After a considerable emotional climax has been generated the oboe gives a gentle reminder of the opening theme. The soloist's contribution at the time is simply a descending scale in 'broken' octaves; on paper it looks boringly pedantic but in performance it is one of the most beautiful moments in a notably expressive movement. Having gracefully acknowledged the oboe tune, the violin part continues its descent with similar figuration. A brief interchange between strings and wind brings us to the coda in which the soloist takes the first three notes of the main theme and extends them in a new direction. The oboe bids a touching farewell to its melody and the movement ends in the twilight mood that is one of Brahms's most personal characteristics.

The finale is a joyous Rondo that pays tribute to the Hungarian folk-music that both Brahms and Joachim loved. The rondo theme is announced by the soloist and then taken up enthusiastically by the full orchestra. A sweeping downward scale introduces a rather less ebullient secondary phrase which turns into a ferociously difficult display of double-stopping (two notes at once) beneath which the lower strings can be heard grumbling that they have been deprived of their fun too soon. Their complaint has some effect for back comes the theme in full orchestral dress, seeming to tumble over itself as the rhythms are cleverly contracted.

It is time for a display of virtuosity and the soloist obliges with flashing bow and flying fingers. A flurry of increasingly rapid scales leads into a bold subject that is basically an ascending scale in octaves, the taut rhythm giving it a military swagger. It is answered by a similar pattern travelling in the opposite direction. These two opposing elements create quite a stir in the orchestra until an apparent deadlock is reached with a number of repetitions of the rising third F♯—A. The soloist resolves the problem by bringing back the rondo theme whose first few notes then become a subject for continued discussion in the orchestra while the soloist shows that practising arpeggios when a student did have some musical value after all. Suddenly bored with memories of past drudgery he introduces a delightful new tune in graceful 3/4 time. At first the orchestra show no interest in this, continuing with their previous preoccupation; but soon an oboe and then a flute accept the lure. The lyrical interlude that follows is suddenly broken up by harshly accented chords which, after a few frenzied scales, lead to the ascending octave theme once more. As before, this provokes quite a storm in the orchestra which is diplomatically resolved by a return to the rondo theme, or rather its less bouncy subsidiary. Again grumbles of discontent in the bass lead to a full-blooded statement of the rondo which is interrupted by a brief cadenza for the soloist.

The music becomes more capricious as delicate trills and flighty arpeggios keep us in a state of suspense. Egged on by the horns, the soloist tries a number of experiments with the opening phrase, finally, in exasperation, cutting loose with a rapid sequence of descending arpeggios. The tempo quickens to a brisk march, causing a change of rhythm in the rondo theme; there is a distinct feeling of heading for home as even the rising octave theme turns into a helter-skelter. But then, just as it seems that we are on the brink of a final cadence Brahms introduces a last poetic touch — a quiet chromatic descent in the woodwind, some brief fluttering phrases from the violin and every indication that there is going to be a surprise ending. In fact the ending is the conventionally loud affirmation of the 'proper' key of D, but the orthodox gesture is made to seem a surprise by the imaginative *diminuendo* which precedes it.

BENJAMIN
BRITTEN
1913–76

Variations on a Theme of Frank Bridge
Op. 10

Britten's talents as a composer surfaced remarkably early, a fact that has been increasingly realised with the publication and performance of boyhood works that had not been publicly available during his lifetime. In the fostering and development of this talent he was extremely fortunate to have studied with a first-class teacher, Frank Bridge, who was himself a composer of substance. Bridge obviously realised that his young pupil had exceptional qualities because he would sometimes give the best part of an entire day to a single lesson. He demanded the highest standards of work; in Britten's own words:

> This strictness was the product of nothing but professionalism. Bridge insisted on the absolutely clear relationship of what was in my mind to what was on the paper. I used to get sent to the other side of the room; Bridge would play what I'd written and demand if it was what I'd really meant. He taught me to think and feel through the instruments I was writing for; he was most naturally an instrumental composer, and as a superb viola player he thought instrumentally.[1]

Britten wanted to show his appreciation of the help Frank Bridge had been to him in a way that would really mean something to the older man. When, therefore, in 1937 Boyd Neel commissioned the twenty-three year old composer to write a work for the Salzburg Festival, Britten decided to write a set of variations for string orchestra on a theme by Bridge. The score is inscribed 'To F.B. A tribute with affection and admiration'. The actual composition took no more than ten days, showing not only that Bridge had taught his brilliant young pupil well, but that now he was fully fledged, and able to tackle the problems of composing at the most advanced level without any help from teacher. The theme Britten chose is a nostalgic little tune in waltz time, with a tender falling phrase like a sigh (see Ex.1 opposite). It can be seen at once that bars 4–6 are themselves a variation on bars 1–3. The next part of the theme is simply a transposition of Ex.1, beginning on C sharp instead of E. There follows a slight elaboration, with poignant F naturals put in as a prefix; but the only significantly new element consists of paired quavers rising to the merest suggestion of a climax (Ex.2).

[1]From 'Music All Around Me' by Antony Hopkins, pp. 42–3. It is an extract from an article that first appeared in the *Sunday Telegraph* in 1964 and was then translated into a broadcast talk and recorded in this form by Benjamin Britten for BBC 'Music Magazine' of 9 January, 1966.

Ex. 1

p con tenerezza

Ex. 2

The work begins with a stirring introduction which focusses almost entirely on the conflict between C naturals in the bass and a perfectly conventional E major chord above. (The reason for choosing this particular mixture is clear enough since it anticipates exactly the way that Bridge harmonises the very first note of the theme.) Over a sustained C in the bass, violins, violas and cellos in turn exchange brilliant fanfares based on E major arpeggios with occasional alien notes thrown in to give added spice. Out of this exciting tumult emerges a ghostly chord on four solo strings. (The Bridge theme is taken from a string quartet.) With tender simplicity the theme begins, its harmonies lightly etched by the guitar-like chords plucked softly by the other players.

The first variation is almost entirely concerned with the passionate phrase shown as Ex. 2 above. Over the rich dark chords of the lower strings the violins muse uneasily on that segment of the theme alone. The supporting harmonies are for the most part fairly orthodox, but presented in that fresh and intriguing way which Britten particularly exploited in his earlier years. In a mere twenty bars this expressive Adagio contains a wide range of emotion.

Variation 2 is entitled 'March', though for the most part it is curiously spectral in feeling, a 'Marche Macabre'. Its material is drawn from the first two phrases of the theme which are compressed so that the falling fifth becomes a fourth (D–A) while the B is flattened. Violas, cellos and basses set off with crisp precision but far from military tread. In the seventh bar, just before a quiet sustained trill in the violins, this derivation of the theme is inverted. Pizzicato interpolations from the second violins make a striking effect as do the piccolo-like trills above. An exciting crescendo brings the march theme to the violins but before long the ghostly patrol disappears into the distance.

Variation 3, 'Romance', is an extended aria for all the violins in unison over a softly vamped accompaniment with a subtle rhythm. The melody is derived from bars 7–8 of the theme. Once again Britten modifies the first interval, this time stretching it to a fourth. A change of rhythm is all that is necessary to complete the disguise.

Ex. 3

(The second part is transposed to simplify comparison.)

The tune is so easy to listen to that we may fail to realise that during the first four bars the pizzicato bass follows the exact pattern of Bridge's theme (bars 1–6).

Variation 4 is called 'Aria Italiana', a title that suggests an operatic love-song of the more sentimental kind. But Britten's parody is more blistering than that: he visualises one of those frantically busy operatic arias where the heroine, surrounded by countermarching troops, exhorts her loved one to deeds of derring-do, phrased with all the virtuosity at her command. The theme is forgotten except for the initial impulse provided by the falling fifth. Such genuine musical wit is a rarity and this variation caused huge delight at the first performance in Salzburg.

Variation 5, 'Bourrée Classique', is also based largely on the falling fifth that begins Bridge's theme. Here it is flogged mercilessly on the two open strings A–D. There is more than a touch of Prokofiev in this and it may be that the parody is intentional if a mite malicious.[2]

Variation 6 provides a Viennese Waltz as a compliment to the Austrian audience to whom the work was first to be performed. Neither '*Rosenkavalier*' nor '*The Merry Widow*', the music moves swiftly with a violin part that suggests the empty gossip of society ladies in a smart café. In the first bar we hear the ubiquitous falling fifth. Thereafter the material is mostly derived from bars 7–8 of Bridge's theme. First it is fashioned into a chromatic loop of notes which is extended in various ways. It then appears as a langourous melody in the middle strings, the initial rising third being repeated several times before being allowed to flick down to the end of the phrase. It is one of the longest of the variations and is technically one of the most challenging.

Variation 7 is an extraordinary 'Moto Perpetuo' which bears little relationship to the theme. It is basically a single strand of notes, unharmonised, as though we were suddenly able to hear one giant string instrument of infinite

[2]Donald Mitchell proposes Stravinsky as the target though I feel the young Britten would have respected him too much to satirise him.

range — music for a superhuman Paganini striding across a dozen strings.

The eighth variation, 'Funeral March', is the most profound in content. A drum-like rhythm in the bass harps persistently on Bridge's falling fifth; but the melody above is also based on a falling fifth, though now the intermediate steps are filled in to make a partial scale. Scooping *glissandi* suggest cries of lamentation and the influence of Mahler (whom Britten greatly admired) can be felt in almost every phrase.

Variation 9, 'Chant', is a strange interlude with eerie harmonics casting a chill that seems to inhibit movement save for some restless fidgeting in the violas. It is like a winter landscape in which we see a starving animal scratching in the snow in its search for food.

Variation 10 is called 'Fugue and Finale'. The fugue subject is an urgent and breathless transformation of bars 1–6 of Bridge's theme, but it is the treatment of the material that makes this fugue truly unique. It is the very essence of fugal composition that the music should accumulate part by part so that in a fugue for quartet we hear first one, then two, then three, then four lines with a texture that consequently grows in density as each part is added. Britten's fugue *looks* like a fugue on paper; one can see how violins, violas and cellos enter in turn. But the *sound*, as in the 'Moto Perpetuo' is like a single strand, even though the fabric is made up from many overlapping fragments divided between the various instruments. With the entry of the double basses the fugue subject is put aside and replaced by suggestions of a grotesque march. The falling fifth becomes more and more insistent until rushing scale passages seem to sweep the sound away. Double basses descend to their lowest E, setting up a throbbing pulse. As though in a whisper the fragments of the fugue begin to assemble, this time in several different keys. With a stroke of sheer magic the original theme appears as if in a dream, surrounded by the continuous rustle and murmur of the elfin fugue. At last the players all converge on one note which grows in intensity until it is like a searchlight beam, only to fade away again into near darkness. With great tenderness Britten begins a long farewell to the theme, an extended coda whose final bars lead us to expect a quiet ending; but a sudden gust of wind seems to scatter the pages away leaving the orchestra no option but to converge on a final impressive unison.

The Variations were an instant success and proved to be the foundation of Britten's international reputation. Within two years they received fifty performances in Europe and America. They remain one of the truly outstanding works in the string orchestral repertoire.

CHOPIN
1810–49

Piano Concerto No. 2 in F minor
Op. 21

Although this work is still habitually referred to as the Second Concerto it was actually the first that Chopin wrote. He was only nineteen at the time and undoubtedly regarded such an ambitious project as a necessary passport to the fame he hoped to attain in more cosmopolitan capitals than Warsaw. He had already shown outstanding qualities as a teenager and his teacher, Elsner, wrote in his diary that his young pupil had opened 'a new era in piano music through his astonishing playing as well as with his compositions'. A trip to Vienna in July 1829 made him realise the relative poverty of musical life in Poland but all the same he greatly impressed a number of distinguished musicians who heard him. 'All these Germans (sic) are amazed by me', he wrote to his family, 'and I am amazed at them being so amazed by me.'

The concerto cost him immense labour, partly because, despite his youth, he was forging a completely individual style of writing for the keyboard. The first book of studies (Op. 10) was occupying him at the same time and while each study is concerned with one particular aspect of technique the whole set show an astonishing originality in their pianistic layout. The concerto was first performed on 17 March 1830 and although he had an inadequate instrument which was sometimes swamped by the orchestra he scored a huge success with the audience. A second performance on a better piano was at once arranged for 22 March. One of the critics wrote, 'Chopin does not play like others; he gives the impression that every note passes through the eyes[1] to the soul, and that the soul pours it into the fingers.'

The concertos have both been criticised for the lack of interest in the orchestral parts, but it should be realised that Chopin was not trying to emulate Beethoven. He was writing at a time when the piano was becoming the dominant instrument. Great pianists enjoyed the adulation given to pop-stars today and the public was eager to be dazzled by feats of virtuosity. Chopin was known to play his concertos as solo works, dispensing with the orchestra. He was passing through a period of indecision; was he to be a pianist who composed or a composer who performed? It is an intriguing comment on musical fashion that when in the following year he arrived in Paris, he received a letter from his revered teacher advising him that playing the piano was only the beginning of a career; he would be wise to turn his talents to opera since the piano concertos of Mozart and Beethoven were already forgotten! We may consider ourselves fortunate that the advice was disregarded.

[1]The custom of playing from memory in public had not been established.

The F minor concerto actually begins with a substantial orchestral exposition, considerably longer incidentally than anything to be found in the concertos of Schumann, Liszt, Tchaikovsky, Grieg or other less admired composers of the mid-nineteenth century. The opening bars may be quiet, but their softness is misleading; it is not weak but rather an expression of aristocratic melancholy, soon dispelled by defiant chords for full orchestra. The first eight bars will in due course be accepted and elaborately decorated by the pianist, but quite a substantial portion of the opening tutti belongs to the orchestra alone. Admittedly we are given a taste of the second subject, but it assumes a somewhat martial manner which gives a very false impression of its romantic potential. After a rousing sequence built from a more athletic phrase the music dies down, creating a sense of expectancy. With a wonderfully commanding phrase covering almost the entire span of the keyboard the soloist makes a dramatic entrance. A brief fill-in from the left hand allows us to recover from the shock and then, in the most lyrical style, we hear the piano version of the opening orchestral phrase. A cynic might dismiss it as little more than an act of courtesy since once the gesture has been made the soloist introduces a completely new theme, soon to be decorated in characteristic fashion with exquisite roulades.

A passage of pure development follows, based essentially on alternations of dominant and tonic harmony. But where a classical composer would have been content to use conventional scales or arpeggios as decoration over an orchestral foundation, Chopin shows his extraordinary flair for inventing new ways of presenting such basic materials. Each group of notes has some subtle twist, a change of shape here, an unexpected chromaticism there; and although to the heedless ear the piano part may seem like aimless chatter, there is hardly a phrase that does not contain implications of melody. The beautiful arabesque of single notes that leads into the second subject is a perfect example, an extended arpeggio-like figure that skilfully avoids any obvious pattern. (Pedants may identify it as a 'dominant ninth' but that gives little hint of its magic.)

The second subject is greatly extended in the piano part, ending with a feather-like run and a sad cadence in C minor that Chopin marks '*con duolo*'. Within two bars 'grief' is replaced by 'resolution' — *risoluto*. It marks the beginning of perhaps the most memorable episode in the movement which, after modulating through several keys, leads to a captivating tune that has a suggestion of fairy bells chiming in a summer breeze. A surging left hand marks a change of mood and the music builds to a heroic climax.

A substantial orchestral interlude follows, enabling the soloist to mop his brow; its relationship to the original exposition is curious, as though Chopin vaguely remembered how it went but couldn't be bothered to check it. The next solo entry produces a beautifully simple variation on the opening theme, the two hands in unison. However, the air of simplicity is misleading, and within moments the pianist becomes involved in a passage of extreme agitation. The technical demands are formidable without the more blatant exhibitionism we find in the Liszt concertos. A brilliant descent in chromatic thirds reinforced by the left hand leads to a short orchestral interlude which is the cue for a recapitulation of sorts, much shorter proportionately than what we would find in a Beethoven concerto. Surprisingly the movement ends with orchestra alone as though the youthful composer was determined to show that this was music to be taken seriously.

There is little that needs to be said about the slow movement except that it is one of the most beautiful Nocturnes that Chopin ever wrote, a literal Nocturne for piano and orchestra which, like several of the similar works for solo piano, has a dramatic central section by way of contrast. Five bars of orchestral introduction suffice to set the scene before the pianist embarks on the most ravishing melody. One feels that here is a permanent record of what Chopin's improvisations must have been like; however elaborate the decorations may be there is a sense of spontaneous invention so that at moments one can almost see a smile on Chopin's face as he causes his listeners to gasp at the fluency with which he embroiders an otherwise conventional cadence. In the centre of the movement the strings begin an agitated *tremolando* on the chord of A flat minor; above, there is an impassioned recitative for piano, the two hands in unison. It is a remarkable piece of writing in the grand manner of heroic Romanticism. With modern pianos there is no need for the strings to stay as quiet as is indicated in the score; the drama should be shared. At last, all passion spent, an enchanting bell-like chime from the piano leads us back to the opening theme, even more elaborated. The movement ends as quietly as it began, a totally remarkable achievement for a nineteen-year old composer.

The finale is a rondo in the style of a mazurka. The piano leads off with the main theme which the orchestra comments on without saying much of consequence. A second version of the theme follows with some skips that Scarlatti would have appreciated; the formal close on the orchestra merely confirms the key of F minor.

The first episode follows, beginning with a downward rush that has a slight similarity to the pianist's initial entry in the first movement. A delightful variation on the rondo ensues, now in A flat major, with a continuous flow of triplets that cover a wide range of the keyboard. Once again the orchestra rounds off, this time with a rustic rhythm that effectively takes the music out-of-doors. The pianist now presents the second episode which is a theme with a suggestion of a horn-call about it. Chopin had already become very interested in Polish folk-music, and the second limb of this tune must be modelled on a folk-dance. It too becomes the subject for brilliant variations before reappearing in the rather unexpected key of C major. The music loses impetus for a moment before a long chromatic descent from the upper reaches of the keyboard leads neatly back to a reprise of the rondo theme.

A solo horn-call seems briefly to anticipate Richard Strauss, a sort of 'Till Ready-spiegl'. It is the signal for the coda in which the horn-call is taken over by the pianist's left hand while the right dazzles us with glittering figurations that seem to be the musical equivalent of laughter. The entire concerto bears out Elsner's opinion that Chopin had opened a new era in piano music; to have done so when he was still virtually a student underlines the remarkable individuality of his genius.

DEBUSSY

1862–1918

Although Debussy was in no way exploited as a child prodigy he certainly had enough innate talent to be one. In July 1874, shortly before his twelfth birthday he played the formidably difficult F minor concerto of Chopin in the advanced piano class of the Paris Conservatoire. It was the compulsory set-piece for the top prize that year and despite his extreme youth Debussy gained an honourable mention. Two years later he won the Second Prize for piano and it was confidently predicted that he would win the First Prize the following year. It was not to be, for despite his natural gift the idea of being a concert-pianist had no great appeal for him; besides, as he grew older his style became increasingly eccentric. A fellow-student, Gabriel Pierné, described Debussy's playing while he was still in his teens:

> He used to astonish us with his weird playing. I don't know whether it was due to native awkwardness or timidity, but he used literally to throw himself at the keyboard and exaggerate every effect. He seemed to be in a violent rage with the instrument — to treat it with impulsive gestures, breathing noisily as he performed difficult passages. He had a habit of emphasising the strong beats with a sort of panting or raucous breathing. These faults became gradually less noticable and at times he produced marvellously soft and delicate effects. These qualities, good and bad, gave his playing a very individual character.

Debussy won many distinctions at the Conservatoire but he was a far from model student, failing his harmony exams year after year owing to his refusal to obey the academic rules. He exasperated his teachers yet they could not deny his talent; some regarded him as a dangerous influence who might corrupt his fellow-students by the unorthodoxy of his ideas.

A curious musical link was established when, at the age of seventeen, he became resident pianist to a wealthy Russian widow, Nadezhda von Meck, who for years had been Tchaikovsky's patroness. She kept a trio of musicians on her staff to entertain her, and night after night the young Frenchman would play chamber-music or piano solos to while away her lonely evenings.

She took him with her to Florence, Venice, Vienna and then north to Moscow. It must have been a dream-like experience for the still adolescent youth, coming as he did from a semi-working-class background where the prospects of foreign travel must have seemed remote. No doubt it helped to cultivate his love of the exotic, not to mention his contempt for conventional behaviour.

By modifying his highly individual style to suit the conservative taste of the jury he managed to win the coveted Prix de Rome in 1884, entitling him to a two-year sojourn in Rome to further his studies. He found the enforced stay abroad irksome and failed to meet all the conditions that the prize imposed. Soon after his return to Paris he became involved with a pretty young blonde called Gabrielle Dupont; they shared a penurious existence together for nine years though Debussy, ever susceptible, was a less than faithful lover. In 1897 his philanderings caused Gabrielle to attempt suicide. Debussy was contrite but the damage was done and two years later he married one of Gabrielle's friends, Rosalie Texier, having given a piano lesson in the morning to be able to pay for the wedding breakfast. Over the previous few years he had been persevering with his major project, the opera '*Pelléas et Mélisande*', but other works, notably '*Prélude à l'après-midi d'un faune*' and the '*Nocturnes*' for orchestra, had been completed and established his growing reputation.

The preliminaries to the first performance of '*Pelléas*' were marred by a violent quarrel between the composer and the author, Maeterlinck, whose wife had been considered for the title-role. Characteristically Debussy had started to rehearse with another singer without saying anything, so enraging Maeterlinck that the two men were nearly involved in a duel. Meanwhile Debussy's marriage showed signs of losing its initial bloom since Rosalie had little comprehension of his music. In 1903 he began a liaison with a banker's wife named Emma Bardac which was soon to cause a scandal that shocked even his Bohemian friends. In the summer of 1904 Debussy left his wife and joined Mme Bardac in an apartment she had bought for them. A few months later Rosalie tried to shoot herself and was taken to hospital with severe chest injuries. That Debussy could continue to compose in the midst of such melodrama demonstrates the supreme egotism of genius; but even he was not insensitive to the antagonism his actions had aroused. Faced with a damaging divorce suit he and Mme Bardac fled to Eastbourne to escape from what he described as 'this tedious fuss'. It was there, within the sound of the sea, that he completed his orchestral masterpiece *La Mer*.

The first performance took place on 15 October 1905, exciting more controversy than enthusiasm. Many of the audience were openly hostile to Debussy since the scandal was still in the forefront of people's minds. Even so, some of the Parisians' disappointment may well have stemmed from the fact that the title led them to suppose that the music would be more openly descriptive than it is. The critic of '*Le Temps*' said, 'I neither hear, see nor feel the sea;' but for all its evocative qualities '*La Mer*' is not a descriptive tone-poem such as Richard Strauss might have written. It is no accident that Debussy called the work 'Three symphonic sketches', sharing the attitude Beethoven had shown in the 'Pastoral' symphony when he said it was 'more an impression of the countryside than an actual painting'. The titles of the three movements, 'From dawn to mid-day on the sea', 'Play of the Waves' and 'Dialogue of the wind and the sea' are sufficiently vague to allow one to fill in images for oneself. (Erik Satie made a classic joke at the first rehearsal when, referring to the period 'from dawn to mid-day' in the first movement, he said he particularly liked the bit around half-past ten.) It was not until the London première in 1908 that *La Mer* was fully appreciated; Debussy himself conducted and, despite considerable nervousness caused by his lack of experience with the baton, he steered the orchestra through the intricate score with notable success. Nevertheless *The Times* critic seemed to have reservations:

> For perfect enjoyment of this music there is no attitude of mind more to be recommended than the passive, unintelligent rumination of the typical amateur of the mid-Victorian era. As long as actual sleep can be avoided, the hearer can derive great pleasure from the strange sounds that enter his ears if he will only put away all idea of definite construction or logical development.[1]

Just how misleading this suggestion is we shall now discover.

---

[1] E. Lockspeiser, *Debussy* (Dent, 1936).

'La Mer'

1. 'De l'aube à midi sur la mer'

The movement begins as quietly as possible; harps set up a gentle alternation of adjacent notes (F♯—G♯) which are then given a little rhythmic flick by muted cellos. It scarcely seems important enough to be called a theme but its rhythm is like a signature which appears a number of times whether the paired notes are rising or falling. Violas have a slow ascent based on rising fourths which prompts a high shimmer on violins like the first tentative streak of sunlight in the grey dawn-mist. The 'rhythmic flick' appears several times in various woodwind instruments; muted trumpet and cor anglais in unison offer a longer phrase, easily recognised by the five repeated notes with which it begins. It is worth remembering since it spans the whole work. A long descent through the strings leads to a slightly more animated section in which the 'rising fourths' phrase gathers momentum. Daylight breaks through as second violins and violas begin a rippling figure which certainly depicts the surface of the water stirred into motion by a gentle breeze. Cellos have a continuously retiterated pattern not unlike the one that Mendelssohn uses so effectively in the 'Hebrides' overture. Above these repeated wavelets four muted horns have a long melancholy theme whose modal scale gives it a hint of plainsong. Debussy has the habit of throwing fragmentary themes into the score so that as we listen we may find it difficult to gauge their ultimate importance — a plaintive tune for oboe and solo cello in unison, a swift rise and fall on a flute that suggests the flight of a bird skimming over the waves. But as the strength of the breeze clearly increases, the 'plainsong' theme in the horns becomes more prominent while glittering figures in the woodwind suggest the white crests of the waves sparkling in the sun.

There is a momentary lull before a remarkable passage for cellos, divided into four parts — Debussy specifies sixteen players. Their energetic new theme, starting with the 'rhythmic flick' from the introduction, soon spreads to other sections of the orchestra, first the woodwind and then, more powerfully, woodwind and horns. Meanwhile the waves gather force unmistakably as the strings pound out an exciting repetitive rhythm. A gradual *diminuendo* tells us that the wind is losing its edge though the water remains choppy. Cor anglais and trumpet recall the theme from the introduction, the one with five repeated notes to begin with; skilfully Debussy reintroduces other fragments from the opening pages, clearly recognisable to us now, even if not to *The Times* critic of 1908. A patch of haze (cor anglais and cello in unison against sustained string harmonies) leads us to suppose that the movement will end quietly, but suddenly the mist is dispersed by a glorious blaze of sunlight as the full brass lend their weight to the orchestral mass.

2. 'Jeux de vagues'

This movement serves the same function as a scherzo in a symphony. It is less substantial than the outer movements and a little more openly pictorial. The orchestration is both scintillating and translucent, a textbook of delicate effects that have often been copied but never surpassed. Nobody can have taught Debussy how to put these sounds on paper, how to imagine them with such assurance. By putting it into its historical context we can better judge the individuality of Debussy's style. Stravinsky's *Firebird* has something of the same inventiveness, but in 1905 Stravinsky was still a student. If Debussy had a rival it would have been Richard Strauss who had produced most of his large-scale tone-poems by 1900. *Don Juan*, *Tod und Verklärung*, *Zarathustra*, *Till Eulenspiegl* and even *Don Quixote* are all late nineteenth-century works. Without disrespect to Strauss, for all his brilliance he was extending a Wagnerian style, adapting it to his own purposes. Debussy had struck out in a much more individual way, consciously shaking off all traces of Wagnerian influence. His harmony is much more elusive than that of Strauss, who tends to glory in the common chord, even though his rapid and frequent shifts of key disguise the fact. When Debussy uses common chords he tends to move them in parallel motion as blocks of sound; elsewhere his use of the whole-tone scale (six consecutive intervals of a tone) gives an enigmatic 'off-centre' quality to every harmony.

Thematic analysis is hardly worth while in this movement. After a brief shimmering introduction a cor anglais produces the most important fragment, an upward flick of four notes which then flowers into a nimble, vaguely oriental theme. First cousin to this is an idea that is easily spotted since it begins with two trills on unison violins. A tortuous phrase for horns leads to a swiftly pattering rhythm on flutes and clarinets. Almost everything thereafter is derived from one or other of these initial materials. The beauty of the music lies not in the themes but in the kaleidoscopic colour, constantly shifting as indeed the reflections of light on water do. Surprisingly the movement ends with a whisper.

3. 'Dialogue du vent et de la mer'

It is in this movement that Debussy fully justifies his use of the word 'symphonic' in the subtitle, 'Three Symphonic Sketches'. Much of the material is culled from the slow introduction to the opening movement, yet it also has some strongly defined themes of its own. After some menacing rumbles that tell us a storm is building up over the horizon, the woodwind introduce the first of these; it is instantly repeated at a higher pitch with the added strength of horns. Growling bassoons and chattering cellos should not distract us from listening to cor anglais and clarinets who recall the 'rhythmic flick' from the very opening of the work. The memory once awakened, a solo trumpet confirms our recollection with a very positive version of the theme from the second page that originally began with five repeated notes. These are now dispensed with as unsuitably hesitant. A swift succession of urgently rising scale fragments in the strings gives a vivid suggestion of waves rushing towards the shore.

Suddenly, above the angry tug of the swell, the woodwind begin a hauntingly beautiful phrase whose first two notes, a falling semitone, are derived from the 'rhythmic flick' in the introduction. The tune is long drawn-out by Debussy's standards, but in the background one senses the racing tide. Soon the strings begin a wildly tossing figure against which we hear Neptune's horn-call summoning the winds to whip up the seas. Bassoons and pizzicato cellos build up the excitement by reiterating the theme from the introduction which has now shed its initial repeated notes for good. Repeated several times, this theme builds to a huge climax. Debussy seldom uses the full orchestra so that when he does the impact is that much greater.

A chromatic descent through trumpets, horns and trombones in turn leads to a lull in the storm. (Notice the high solo cornet's reference to the 'rhythmic flick' theme from the opening). There is a soft mysterious trill on low clarinet and bassoon before softly but majestically the horns introduce a solemn new theme, richly harmonised. It is destined to play a crucial part in the final climax although at this stage we only hear it twice. Soon it is time for the other great theme of this third movement to return, the long haunting tune beginning with the falling semitone. Now it is on flute and oboe with an altogether less agitated accompaniment — a murmur on harps and a high sustained note on violins. A glockenspiel produces a playful variant which is copied by horns and woodwind in turn. At last the strings are allowed to bring their full expressive power to the 'falling' theme. It is an emotional high-spot not to be missed.

For a while Debussy throws his various themes into disorder, as though different currents were converging in a rocky cove; but by this stage they should all be easily recognised. The strings whip up the excitement with increasingly urgent figures until a majestic climax is reached as the solemn brass theme reappears like the God of the Seas arising with his trident from the waters. A short swift coda, again derived from the introduction, brings this truly symphonic movement to an end. It marked a new stage in Debussy's development, showing that not only could he handle the largest orchestral forms with complete authority, but that he had new light to shed on traditional concepts of musical structures.

'Nocturnes'

In 1892, at the age of thirty, Debussy began to compose '*Trois scènes au crepescule*' (Three twilight scenes). The first movement was intended to be called 'A study in grey' but the inclusion of a solo violin part, surely unsuitable for such a role, showed that Debussy lacked a clear vision of the work. With the fastidious self-criticism that he applied to his music, if not to his morality, he scrapped the project, retaining only the best of the ideas for possible future use. They emerged some five years later in *Nocturnes*, a set of three wonderfully descriptive pieces which, though they lack the symphonic strengths of *La Mer*, yield nothing to it in terms of the imaginative use of tone-colour. The composer himself provided an introductory note which freely acknowledges the frankly descriptive nature of the music.

> The title *Nocturnes* is to be interpreted here in a general and, more particularly, in a decorative sense. Therefore it is not meant to designate the usual form of the nocturne, but rather all the various impressions and the special effects of light that the word suggests. *Nuages* renders the immutable aspect of the sky and the slow, solemn motion of the clouds, fading away in grey tones lightly tinged with white. *Fêtes* gives us the vibrating atmosphere with sudden flashes of light. There is also the episode of the procession (a dazzling fantastic vision) which passes through the festive scene and becomes merged in it. But the background remains persistently the same: the festival, with its blending of music and luminous dust, participating in the cosmic rhythm. *Sirènes* depicts the sea and its countless rhythms and presently, amongst the waves silvered by the moonlight, is heard the mysterious song of the Sirens as they laugh and pass on.[2]

Although the full score was published in 1900 a subsequent edition printed twelve years after the composer's death shows a number of important modifications he made in the light of experience. A detailed study of the two scores might prove a fruitful subject for a thesis but need not concern us here since the original version is no longer played.

1. 'Nuages' (Clouds)

If there is any truth in the maxim 'Great minds think alike' supporting evidence is to be found here since the opening harmonic sequences, bleakly scored for clarinets and bassoons, are remarkably akin to Stravinsky both in timbre and idiom. (In fact, whether Debussy consciously realised it or not, the melodic curve of the initial phrase was lifted note for note from a

[2]Ibid., p. 189.

Mussorgsky song called 'Sunless', an act of petty larceny that was also committed by Stravinsky in '*Le Rossignol*'.) After two static chords on divided violins beneath which there is a far distant rumble of thunder from the timpani, the opening phrases are resumed by muted strings, richly divided into eight or more parts. There is a passage in Joyce's *A portrait of the artist as a young man* which provides a wonderfully exact parallel to this music: '. . . the slow-drifting clouds, dappled and sea-borne, . . . voyaging across the deserts of the sky, a host of nomads on the march . . .'

Gradually the texture increases in density as though the clouds are forming into sky-mountains, their peaks tipped with an illusion of snow. A plangent little theme on the cor anglais appears from time to time, an expression of loneliness; a recurring pair of notes on unison horns depicts the siren of a small tug as it chugs its way down river.[3] On the whole the woodwind have a relatively small contribution to make until a solo flute introduces a more openly lyrical melody in F sharp major; doubled by harp it brings a ray of sunshine into the grey sky. It is echoed by a solo string trio but is soon lost in the prevailing mist. There are few pieces in the entire orchestral repertoire in which less appears to happen and yet there is a magic about the sheer sound which casts its own especial spell.

2. 'Fêtes' (Festival days)

The second movement is far from Nocturnal in the usual romantic sense; it may be a night scene, but it is a scene of noisy revelry at one of those fairgrounds which to this day the French so enjoy. An exhilarating tarantella-like rhythm sets the mood while whirling runs in the woodwind suggest helter-skelters and merry-go-rounds. The pace is hectic as crowds swirl round the numerous side-shows, only arrested for a moment by a strident brass fanfare and a roll of drums — perhaps the stentorian voice of the ringmaster in the circus-tent. Woodwind suggest the excited chatter of the spectators in brilliant repeated triplets (note the 15/8 time signature, five beats to the bar) as the music continues its headlong rush. At one point a long swaying theme in unison wind may represent a group of drunken revellers walking with arms linked through the heedless crowd. Suddenly, as a considerable climax is reached, there is an abrupt change of mood and tempo. As from a great distance we hear the thump of drums and the tread of marching feet. It is the band of the Garde Républicaine approaching in ceremonial dress.

[3]Other commentators maintain that the chromatic melody on the cor anglais represents the ship's hooter, an insult to Debussy's ear when the horns provide so much more accurate a description. The mistake presumably arises through a reported conversation between Debussy and a friend, Paul Poujaud; Poujaud doubtless confused cor anglais with '*cors*' – horns.

The gradual crescendo as they come nearer is marvellously graded by systematic augmentation of the orchestral resources. With the addition of trombones, tuba and a martial side-drum, Debussy skilfully reintroduces the whirling scales from the start of the movement, as though hordes of children are rushing alongside the band to get a better view. Arrived at their destination, the bandsmen halt and put down their instruments. The opening music resumes, not quite so noisily as before since presumably the band has attracted too much attention and the stalls are relatively deserted. Soon the carnival is in full swing again with one important newcomer in the shape of a striking theme given to the violins. It is related to the triplet quavers that dance attendance on it, though not an exact augmentation. Gradually the crowds depart; tender farewells are exchanged between oboe, flute and bassoon; a drummer from the band beats a brief tattoo as he disappears into the distance; lights flicker and die as the streets finally empty.

3. 'Sirènes' (Mermaids)

As though in preparation for *La Mer*, 'Sirènes' describes a moonlit seascape in which the voices of mermaids cast a supernatural spell. To achieve this effect Debussy employs a small choir of sixteen female voices, an additional expense which concert promoters tend to resent. The voices sing a wordless chant for which the composer does not even suggest specific vowel-sounds. The most important theme appears first on a solo cor anglais, a favourite instrument in Debussy scores; it is easily recognised by the triplet embellishment on the second note and by its sad chromatic fall. It appears a number of times in diminished form before becoming a hypnotically repeated pattern in the violins.

A gently undulating melody appears in the voice-parts; notice especially a version for mezzo-sopranos alone with an extraordinary depiction in the strings of the glitter of moonlight on water. A sweeping scale rising through two octaves leads to a brief climax in which the horns have an important two-note figure suggesting the sound of conch-shells blowing. Debussy's use of pairs of adjacent notes is extraordinarily inventive, and here we do find an apt comparison with *La Mer*. As befits a moonlit scene the colouring is mostly subdued, *piano* or *pianissimo* being the most frequently used dynamic. The absence of significant themes would seem to be a severe handicap but it is in the nature of Debussy's genius that he can engage our interest by the constant play of colours rather than by memorable tunes. We may not find ourselves singing as we leave the concert-hall, but we will find that we have been put into a trance of sorts and that our minds are filled with such sounds as were heard on Prospero's island.

Images
(1910–13)

There is something inherently respectable about writing a symphony or a concerto, and if a composer writes exactly the same amount of music in the guise of a symphonic poem, we tend to assume that in some way it is a work of lesser stature. To deny a composer the highest rank because he never wrote a symphony is about as silly as to say that a man could never be a first-class citizen unless he owned a frock-coat. The symphony was the great monumental form of the late eighteenth and early nineteenth centuries. By 1880 it had largely been replaced by other forms, and what symphonies there were were frequently graced with explanatory titles so that the composers could get the best of both worlds by gaining the prestige attached to the word symphony while not actually adhering too closely to the form. Debussy is a perfect example of a composer who was clear-sighted enough to realise that the classical forms, based as they were on conflicts of tonality, were of little use to him. But the sheer work involved both spiritually and physically in the creation of works like *La Mer* or the orchestral *Images* was just as great — greater in fact, for there was no ready-made mould into which he could pour his ideas.

The full score of *Images* runs to 205 pages of exquisitely conceived orchestral colour. Debussy had in mind a somewhat vague scheme of associating these pieces with three countries, England, Spain and France. The Spanish part, which is longer than the other two combined, is itself divided into three sections. The first movement seems to have been the one that gave him the greatest difficulty in that he ultimately left it uncompleted. (The orchestration was finished by André Caplet.) It is called '*Gigues*', a title to which he originally added the word 'Tristes'. 'Sad Jigs' seem to be a contradiction, but then contradictions would appeal to a mind as subtle and elusive as Debussy's. It starts in utter stillness, and anything less jig-like it would be hard to imagine — nor less English for that matter.

An oboe d'amore, its tones rather more individual than the ordinary orchestral oboe, plays a sad little tune which hardly disturbs the vague misty background. There's still little sign of a jig, even a sad one.

Even when Debussy shows his hand more openly the only thematic shape to appear is a falling third. But just as skilfully as any symphonist, Debussy takes this shape and converts it into a more sharply defined rhythm. If the ensuing melody vaguely reminds you of a folk-tune called the Keelrow you're entirely justified — it's meant to. It is indeed the only element of 'English-ness' in this very French score, but it's there for a purpose, just as there are Spanish rhythms and melodic shapes in the movements that are associated with Spain.

The jig begins to fall into shape, the rhythm becoming firmer and more clearly marked. But the music seems to be of two minds and part of the fascination of this very under-estimated piece lies in the way Debussy preserves two conflicting and apparently irreconcilable moods simultaneously. The sad piper's tune reappears, but the dance-rhythm fidgets along underneath it.

To examine the scoring in detail would be the work of hours; we take Debussy's orchestral virtuosity for granted nowadays but one only has to look at any one of its pages to be struck by the extraordinary delicacy of calculation which went into them. Here a chord is scored for four desks of violins only, another for three; there a single note on the harp is marked *piano* but stressed; a solo viola is matched with a high bassoon; every sound is imagined with such exactitude and such finesse, and this applies all through *Images*.

Part Two, the so-called 'Iberia', is the most popular. It is divided into three distinct sections, but despite the very large orchestra Debussy uses, the sound is never coarse or ostentatious. The rhythms too, though they obviously have a markedly Spanish flavour, are wayward and unpredictable, the melodic lines being deliberately stretched across the accompanying figures in such a way as to prevent the shapes from ever being trite.

The first section of 'Iberia', *Par les rues et par les chemins*, conjures up a picture of Spanish villages. Now, descriptive works are liable to be episodic, whereas symphonic works demand repetition and development. Debussy's 'Iberia' is infinitely more symphonic in its approach than, say, Rimsky-Korsakov's *Capriccio Espagnole*. The actual material in this movement is treated with a remarkable economy and discipline. Of course the outlines are not defined in the old manner of first and second subjects, bridge passages and the like, but there is the sort of continuous drive that one expects from a symphonic movement, and the themes are inter-related; these are not impressionistic sketches dashed off in an impromptu fashion, but beautifully controlled compositions, full of conscious craftsmanship, and an avoidance of cliché that is quite remarkable. Debussy even denies himself the easy satisfaction of a grand slam finish to the movement, the final chord being allotted to just two clarinets.

The second section, *Les parfums de la nuit*, is an evocation of the sounds and perfumes of a Spanish evening. It is the quintessence of Debussy, with little in the way of a climax in the whole of its span; *piano* or *pianissimo* appear in nearly every bar, a constant demand for restraint from conductor and players alike. It is music of suggestion rather than statement, of distance rather than proximity. There is not a single *forte* until the fourteenth page and even that is short-lived.

Melodies, such as they are, tend to be fragmentary, and are usually made from three or four adjacent notes. A brief climax near the end leads us to suppose that there might be a positive ending but the music dies away, leaving the final phrase to a solo violin and flute in unison, merging without a break into the third section. This, 'the morning of a public holiday' according to the title, skilfully blends the sound of church bells into the score, a touch of realism that could scarcely be avoided. The movement serves the function of a scherzo but, colourful and gorgeous though it is, it is still music of suggestion and under-statement. To start with, the spell of the langourous evening lingers on and one can imagine the composer being disturbed from sleep by the distant throb of drums, the sound of voices and footsteps in the street below. Soon the violinists and viola-players in the orchestra are instructed to hold their instruments sideways like guitars, and the combined strings produce a wonderful thrumming rhythm in this '*marche joyeuse et alerte*'. Shrill clarinets suggest the amateur efforts of a village band, though a solo fiddler shows surprising accomplishment. Once again, though, the avoidance of any real vulgarity is extraordinary and within moments the sound is sharply suppressed as if the disturbed sleeper had slammed his window shut to keep out the unwelcome sounds. The gesture is in vain for soon we join the throng in the village square; for once Debussy allows himself the indulgence of a grandstand finish.

The final *Image*, 'Rondes de printemps', appeared long after the others. It is headed by the inscription 'Vive le mai! Bienvenu soit le mai avec son gonfalon sauvage'. (Hail May! Welcome May with its wild banner.) Perhaps because Debussy was ravaged by cancer it presents a less than idyllic view of Spring and a critic of the time castigated him for writing such 'wintry dances'. As if to emphasise his disassociation from the conventional view of springtime, Debussy makes extensive use of a popular song 'Nous n'irons plus au bois', subjecting it to distortions that sometimes disguise it effectively from an inattentive ear. There is also an early allusion to a nursery song 'Do, do l'enfant do'. They are tunes that must have had a special appeal for Debussy since both appear in one of his most famous piano pieces, *Jardins sous la pluie*. Although the orchestration is as brilliantly individual as ever, there is a feeling that inspiration was flagging and the composer admitted that he had had to struggle to finish the work. The constant pain he suffered from the malignant disease that was to destroy him must have made composition an ever more arduous labour; if 'Rondes' is less than a total success, it is still a notable monument to human courage.

DVOŘÀK

1841–1904

Few composers better illustrate the American belief in the 'rags-to-riches' fairy story than Dvořák; how suitable, then, that towards the end of his life he should have been invited to America to become director of the recently founded National Conservatory of Music in New York. Did the governors of that august-sounding institution realise that they were appointing the son of a village butcher who had been brought up in the depths of the Bohemian countryside more than forty miles from the nearest city? Butcher and inn-keeper though he was, Dvořák's father was clearly a remarkable man who had taught himself to play both violin and zither. He gave young Antonin every encouragement to learn music from the village schoolmaster who, by good fortune, was enough of a musical Jack-of-all-trades to be able to give the boy a solid foundation on violin, viola and organ. When the child was still only twelve years old he was sent to live with an uncle some distance away, partly to learn German (an essential asset if ambitions were to be realised) but also to study music more intensively. Although he had already set his heart on becoming a musician there was a time when any such prospect hung in the balance. His father had become virtually bankrupt and insisted that his son should return and learn the proper trade of butchering; there was surely more money and security in meat than in music. Fortunately the uncle had seen the boy's dedication at first hand and offered some financial help towards his training; thus it was that one autumn day in 1857, the sixteen-year old boy and his father set off in a farm-cart to travel the forty-five miles to Prague where he was to enrol in the organ school. He made no great mark as a student — his report said he was 'weak in theory' — but became a good enough viola player to join an orchestra which played popular music in the city's smartest restaurants. In time it formed the nucleus of the Czech National Opera orchestra and it was in the somewhat claustrophobic en-vironment of the opera-pit that Dvořák really learnt the art of orchestration in the most practical manner. The salary may have been pitiful but the experience was beyond price. Every spare penny from his meagre wage was spent on manuscript paper and for eleven years he ploughed a hard furrow for himself, composing quantities of music, most of which he would burn to save money on fuel.

The conductor of the opera-orchestra was Smetana and it was from him that Dvořák acquired a belief that the folk-music of his native country could be a proper source for a composer to draw on, even in concert works. The influence of Wagner had threatened to engulf Dvořák's natural musical inheritance and no doubt he felt for a time that childhood memories of music he had enjoyed with his father had little relevance for a serious composer. After fruitless years the first work to establish him as a composer of potential interest was a fervently patriotic *Hymnus* (Op. 30) for chorus and orchestra. Its enthusiastic reception gave him much-needed encouragement and his first published composition, Six Songs, was issued in the same year (1873). Despite these propitious omens he continued to consign even quite substantial works to the flames, exercising ruthless self-criticism towards everything he wrote. One early opera, *King and Collier* was not merely destroyed, but entirely re-written with not so much as a single aria carried over into the new version. The première was highly successful but the opera subsequently foundered owing to its feeble libretto. However, Dvořák's name was becoming known and in 1875 he was given a small government grant in recognition of his talent.

It was at this crucial time that his work first came to the notice of Brahms who was to prove to be an important influence in more ways than one. Mutual admiration of each other's music was gratifying, but more to the point was the older composer's standing in Vienna, the musical capital of Europe. It was Brahms who persuaded Simrock, his publishers, to take an active interest in Dvořák's music, thereby putting him on the road to international fame. By 1877 he was able to devote his energies entirely to composition though it was perhaps unfortunate for posterity that the opera theatre held such a fascination for him that much fine music was squandered on ill-chosen libretti. With growing recognition came greater confidence though four symphonies were held back for later revision; this led to considerable confusion since the sixth symphony to come from his pen was published as No. 1, the seventh as No. 2 and the fifth as No. 3. Only symphonies 5–9 were published during his lifetime.

In 1892 Dvořák was invited to become director of the newly founded National Conservatory of New York for the enormous salary of $15,000 a year. He spent three years[1] in America during which he wrote some of his finest music including the ninth symphony 'From the New World' and the cello concerto which many regard as his greatest masterpiece. In spite of the acclamation he received he became desperately homesick and was only too glad to return to the less demanding pace of life in Prague. Although world-

[1]He took five months' 'home leave' in 1894.

famous he preserved a peasant simplicity, one of his pleasures being to wander round the railway marshalling-yards looking at steam engines. (Amateur psychologists may like to ponder the difference between Brahms, who had a large collection of toy soldiers, and Dvořák with his passion for trains.) Honours were showered on him in the closing years of his life[2] but he was not one to sit back and rest. The search for a satisfactory libretto continued and the last three major works he wrote were all operas, of which only *Rusalka* has acquired a place in the operatic repertoire outside Czecho-slovakia. Orchestral music and chamber music were his true domain, his feeling for orchestration being so felicitous that orchestral players have a special affection for his music, so gratefully is it written.

---

[2]He was the first musician to be made a member of the Austrian House of Lords!

Symphony No. 8 in G Major
Op. 88

In August 1889 Dvořák was hard at work on a piano quartet, destined to be his Op. 87. 'Three movements are finished already', he wrote to a friend, 'and the finale will be in a few days. It's going unexpectedly easily and the melodies simply pour out of me.' The quartet was actually completed on 19th August. Barely a week later he began to jot down ideas for a new symphony; clearly the days of burning manuscripts were over. On 6 September he began the first draft of the opening movement, finishing it by the 13th. Three days later he had composed the second movement; the third was completed on the following day and the fourth by the 23rd. The entire symphony was fully scored by 8 November, a striking feat of creativity from a composer who had failed to achieve any recognition until he was thirty-two.

Although Dvořák clearly specifies G *major* as the key, the symphony actually begins in G minor, a surprise that must have set the critics' pencils scribbling at the first performance. When we consider the speed at which the symphony was composed it may even be that when the splendid opening theme came into his mind Dvořák was not entirely sure whether the music might stay in the minor or not. Certainly part of the charm of this work lies in the way that ideas seem to pop out one after the other, a broad singing tune for cellos, a little bird-call on the solo flute, an introductory fanfare for the strings and so on, all done with the facility one might bring to writing a letter rather than a major work of art. In fact the first six pages of the score can justifiably be classified as an introduction in which the most important element turns out to be not the long cello tune but the frail little flute solo which immediately follows it. This is duly confirmed by the horns who take over the flute's theme with considerable vigour while the strings are still busy playing 'curtain up' music. The introduction is terminated with a sharp rap on the timpani and an explosive unison D from the full orchestra. Cellos and violas set out boldly on a theme that could serve as a model for a national anthem, (see Ex. 1) though its seriousness of purpose is somewhat deflated by the frivolous little bird-call on the flute. A few bars of good-natured knockabout lead to a powerfully reinforced statement of the flute tune, now far from frail. Dvořák spins out its last three notes by several repetitions passing from clarinets to bassoons, from violas to horn solo; then, after a momentary pause, the strings introduce a beguiling new theme that rocks to and fro from F♯ to G♯, nudged forward by a capricious little curve from the cellos. It has such instant appeal that one is tempted to identify it as the true Second Subject at once, but the slick labels of conventional analysis are hard to apply in this most *un*-conventional movement and we soon find an even more likely candidate in the woodwind. It is easily recognised, drawing attention to itself with a dotted rhythm on the up-beat followed by an upward leap of an octave. The strings proceed to explore its possibilities in quite a serious way with striding octaves in the basses and trombone enforcing some interesting modulations by their relentless rise. An impasse is reached on the dominant of B major, at which point the woodwind produce a ravishing new melody. (Had he not recently written 'the melodies simply pour out of me'?) Since this is the sixth clearly identifiable theme to appear in sixteen pages of score it seems absurd even to contemplate calling it a Second Subject, but it is greeted with such obvious enthusiasm by the full orchestra that we cannot discount its importance. Only time will tell us if it has a major role to play. However, there can be no doubt that the little flute tune is a principal character since the brass now give us a forcible reminder of it, even though it is shorn of its rather flippant tail. Muted trumpets, timpani and horns take turns at reducing it to a mere rhythmic pattern as the music grows ever quieter.

Anyone fortunate enough to be following a score will notice that Dvořák has ruled a double bar-line down the page at this point. It is a small gesture of acknowledgment that if he were writing a classical symphony this is where the repeat of the exposition would come. 'But don't let's bother with that' he seems to say and pushes on into the development with what sounds remarkably *like* a repeat. Back comes the broad cello tune in G minor; back comes the frail flute bird-call. Just as we are gulled into thinking that he has observed the classic convention of a repeat the music begins to venture into new territories. The flute theme is smoothed out and turns into a dialogue with an oboe during which there are some disagreements about the proper tonality. Meanwhile the cellos assume the role of an ageing cuckoo. This avian episode is rudely interrupted by a tremendous blast from the full orchestra followed by a phrase that sounds uncommonly like a call to arms. The once frail flute theme is conscripted into the military by bassoons and lower strings and there is a general feeling of urgency if not emergency. Clarinets and violas hum their way through the tune I described as a potential national anthem (to which the flute adds a brisk fife-like counterpoint) before Dvořák seems to decide that it's all getting a bit too frivolous. The bassoons begin a study in strict counterpoint, taking the preceding theme at double speed and initiating a remarkable passage of a fugal nature in which the subject-matter goes through a series of ingenious transformations as shown in Ex.1 on p. 196. Swift descending scales in triplets add to the excitement and the fugal exercise culminates in a huge climax in which horns and trombones make dramatic use of the first three notes of the minor/crotchet version (the third line of Ex.1).

There follows the most truly symphonic section of the movement in which bassoons, horns, cellos and basses hammer out the third transformation of the theme shown above while the violins have an intense version of the original flute bird-call, now in E minor and with its flippant ending converted

Ex. 1

into energetic rising arpeggios. A sudden restoration of G minor, reinforced by trombones and timpani, brings back the opening theme of the symphony, now resplendent on trumpets despite being battered by a Force Nine gale in the strings. Although it is the sort of climax that seems to have been lifted straight from Tchaikovsky, Dvořák emerges unscathed as it dies down, allowing a solo cor anglais to restore the original flute tune to its former shape. Clarinet and flute in turn voice their approval though the flute still tends to treat the theme with some caprice. The recapitulation which has arrived in this unorthodox manner dispenses entirely with the 'national anthem' tune and pushes on impatiently into the second subject group. Familiar friends reappear and the movement is rounded off with an exciting coda which makes enterprising use of the dotted rhythm that stems from the innocent-sounding bird-call that seemed so insubstantial when it made its first shy appearance.

It is worth saying that the truly symphonic part of this movement does not really materialise until the second half. There was a real danger that with such an abundance of themes the work would just ramble on with no cohesion, but Dvořák's laboriously acquired skills came to the rescue, enabling him to exert the more intellectual disciplines which symphonic movements need.

The slow movement appears to be based on a piano solo written earlier in the same year called 'At the old castle'. It is like a miniature tone-poem and clearly reflects Dvořák's love of the country with its frequent suggestions of bird-song. The opening phrases have a touch of pathos, a nostalgia perhaps for childhood days in the little village where he had been brought up. A falling two-note pattern persists in the flutes until it is unexpectedly transformed into a strong gesture in the strings as though the persistence of the figure had become irritating. In a moment the frown disappears, dispelled by one of the most enchanting episodes even Dvořák ever wrote. The strings have a series of little descending scales in C major like a minute chime of bells while the wind instruments extend a long line of melody that soars lazily as a kite in a summer sky. A violin solo confirms the outdoor feeling of the music as fluttering *tremolandi* in the second violins suggest the rustle of leaves. Then, as though Dvořák had said 'This is a symphony, not a divertimento,' the idea is extended by the full orchestra with a thrilling ascent in horns and trumpets leading to a majestic climax.[3]

The opening music returns with the order of events somewhat changed, but the falling two-note pattern in the flutes and the rather doleful clarinet phrases are familiar enough by now. What is new is a more impassioned development of the initial theme, now treated in quasi-operatic fashion with a duet between cellos and violins of the kind that usually sees the hero tearing himself from his lover's embrace to go to a certain but honourable death. Reiterated trumpet calls heighten the drama and for a moment it seems as though we may be heading towards a dramatic finale. In a trice the crisis is resolved and to everyone's relief the lovely C major tune returns, now on strings instead of woodwind. As the movement unwinds towards a peaceful cadence there is one more brief eruption of violence, but it is soon soothed away by the ubiquitous two-note motif.

The ensuing movement can hardly be called a scherzo as the tempo, *Allegretto grazioso*, makes clear. It is rather a charming Intermezzo, a dreamy waltz to be danced on a terrace in the moonlight. The rippling accompaniment in the woodwind suggests the splash of water in a nearby fountain while occasional dancing staccato notes in the strings rival Mendelssohn in their fairy-like delicacy. As if these delights were not enough, Dvořák introduces a central section in G major in which flute and oboe offer a tune which is unashamed of its simple peasant stock. While the tune itself is disarmingly unsophisticated the accompaniment is extremely subtle rhythmically with approving little taps on the drum falling in unexpected places. The tune is enjoyed to the full by the rest of the orchestra before a reprise of the first section. As for the final coda, it presents a nimble variation on the central section, a technique Dvořák

[3] I have not seen the piano pieces Op. 85 but presumably this passage relates to 'the Old Castle'.

may have copied from the comparable movement in Brahms's Second Symphony. All set for a boisterous finish, Dvořák surprises us with a sudden hush and a final chord that is like a sigh of sheer contentment.

The trumpet fanfare that opens the finale was added as an afterthought but it certainly arrests our attention. The form of the last movement is essentially a theme with variations, with a slight inclination towards a rondo. The cellos spell out the theme in two clear-cut eight-bar phrases, each of which is repeated. The first variation follows immediately, still led by the cellos while variation two proves to be a somewhat rowdy version for full orchestra. Variation three allows the flute an opportunity for a more graceful approach but such subtleties are soon displaced by another outburst from the full band. A rough-edged unison passage for strings leads to the episode that would more properly belong in a rondo since it is in C minor and has only the most tenuous connection to the theme. It degenerates into the one passage where Dvořák's inspiration seems to have flagged, a sequence built on notes a third apart that sounds like a children's counting game. It is more reassuring when trumpets and horns reintroduce the opening fanfare in a harmonised version; it is then put through some strange distortions over a striking sequence of harmonies before the strings treat it with furtive disrespect.

The return of the theme in more lyrical guise gives us a recognisable landmark and some tranquil variations provide a welcome contrast of considerable beauty. A gradual *ritardando* leads us to expect that the movement may end in a Brahmsian twilight, but having given the impression that sleep is imminent Dvořák rudely arouses us with a lively blast from the full orchestra and sweeps us off to a boisterous if abrupt finish. The very last bar is silent, a musical joke which it takes a subtle ear to appreciate; in fact one more note is required to complete the rhythmic pattern. By depriving us of it Dvořák makes the ending seem a trifle more precipitate.

Symphony No. 9 in E Minor
From the New World
Op. 95

Once Dvořák had arrived in New York in September 1892 he quickly settled down to his duties as director of the new National Conservatory. Although his surroundings must indeed have seemed like a New World to him he was determined not to neglect composition; first he had to put the finishing touches to a cantata 'The American Flag', a work composed more out of a sense of duty towards his hosts than from genuine inspiration.[4] He had brought with him his most recent composition, a most original setting of the Te Deum, conceived as a miniature symphony with sections corresponding to slow movement and scherzo in addition to the two outer movements. His patroness, Mrs Thurber, tried hard to persuade him to write an operatic version of *Hiawatha*, a poem which he already knew and admired in a Czech translation, although his many visits to England had compelled him to become quite fluent in the language. He was quite taken with the idea and filled several notebooks with sketches, one of which was to bear fruit in the middle section of the slow movement of the symphony.

Four months after his arrival he began serious work on the symphony, finishing the first three movements in short score in less than three weeks. Orchestrating them occupied him off and on through the spring of 1893; the finale was written and scored in May. The following month his family joined him and together they set out for Spillville in Iowa where there was a Bohemian settlement. It was quiet and peaceful and the presence of so many of his countrymen made him feel at home. Yet even though it was supposed to be a holiday the urge to compose was irresistible and he was soon at work on the F major string quartet. The entire quartet was written between 8–10 June. The autumn brought a reluctant return to the city where, in December, the new symphony had its world première in Carnegie Hall.

'The papers say that no composer ever had such a triumph', wrote Dvořák to his publisher. 'Carnegie Hall was crowded with the cream of New York society and the audience applauded so much that, like visiting royalty, I had to take my bows repeatedly from the box where I was sitting.'

The symphony begins with a slow *pianissimo* introduction, the tune being given to the cellos. In the fourth bar there is a sudden explosively accented note on two horns in unison, a seemingly inexplicable interruption of which more anon. The cello phrase is repeated at a higher octave by a solo flute. The stillness is again shattered, this time by a violent abrupt phrase on all the strings, five times repeated, and punctuated by *fortissimo* timpani and shrill woodwind chords. Peace is restored. Flutes and oboes have a cheerful snatch of syncopated melody which is followed by a significant phrase for horns and lower strings which heaves its way out of the deep and sinks back again. (It is the seed from which the main subject of the symphony is to grow, but we are not to know that at the time.) The pattern is repeated, building to a climax swiftly reached and swiftly repressed. The first movement proper is about to begin.

In all honesty I must admit that the explanation of this introduction I am about to offer has no documentation of any kind to support it, nor have I ever

[4]It was not performed until after he had left America.

heard it suggested by anyone else; yet I am convinced that these opening pages are a description of Dvořák's first arrival in New York harbour. The first quiet cello phrase shows him awaking, aware that the ship is still at last after the long Atlantic crossing. The ship's siren sounds a peremptory blast — the horns in bar 4. Dvořák draws the curtain from his porthole, letting in the daylight — the flute tune — and hears the tremendous clatter of the anchor-chain being lowered — the violent string and timpani passage. The ship settles in the calm water as a passing cabin-boy whistles a cheerful little tune — the woodwind phrase; a lazy swell lifts the ship momentarily, perhaps in the wash of a passing steamer — the rise and fall in horns and strings — ropes are thrown to the quayside (a comparable phrase to the 'anchor-chain' but at a higher pitch) and with the final crescendo the ship is slotted into her berth. Seasoned traveller though he had become, the arrival in New York must have made a deep impression on Dvořák, and I see no reason why he should not have recalled the experience in musical terms. The hypothesis fits so neatly and I can see no real *musical* justification for the sundry violent interruptions that occur to disturb the peaceful atmosphere of the opening phrases.

A famous horn-call provides the first subject of the ensuing *Allegro molto*. Dancing attendance on it is a little subsidiary theme in thirds on clarinets and bassoon. The two ideas are repeated with a changed ending. Four brass chords lend their massive support to the strings as they extend the horn theme further, turning its last four notes into a sequential pattern that builds to a notable climax. The initial theme is confirmed in its importance by trombones and horns, *fortissimo*, after which the strings make a long and joyful sequence out of the subsidiary fragment. After some swift byplay between the violins and their deeper-voiced brethren the music gradually calms down to prepare the way for a new idea. Given to flute and oboe in unison, it is in the unexpected key of G minor. It certainly has a folkish flavour but Dvořák vehemently denied that any of the themes were actually based on Negro or Red Indian folk-music. The second bar, oscillating between A and C, should be particularly noted as it is to be used extensively in the near future. The tune itself is duly taken over by second violins over a rustic drone bass before being transferred to the cellos and basses. It is at this point that the little oscillating phrase from the second bar assumes such importance, providing the basis for a continuing pattern which extends over some eighteen bars before taking on an altogether happier mien in G major. Meanwhile flutes and clarinets are clearly supposed to be imitating the chirruping of birds while an expressive phrase in the bass seems to give a sigh of present content tinged with past sorrow. Sweet as a cradle-song, the strings have a gentle rockabye to introduce the true second subject. It is an enchantingly unpretentious little tune for solo flute which wishful thinkers have somehow persuaded themselves to have been influenced by 'Swing low sweet chariot'. It seems unlikely that if Dvořák meant it to be a quotation he would begin it with the fourth word. (One might as well claim that Brahms's Fourth Symphony was inspired by

'Pop goes the weasel' since its first two notes are identical to those allotted to 'weasel' in that equally famous tune.) Violins are quick to seize the chance of playing the flute melody against gentle syncopations from clarinets and bassoons. A short climax is generated in which even the trombones lend their added weight to the second subject, perhaps making us realise for the first time that both the first and second subjects begin with the same rhythm ♩. ♪|♪ ♩.|.

After the obligatory repeat the development begins with a slight distortion of the second phrase of the flute's tune — the dominant (D) is sharpened, a point which Dvořák makes four times to get us accustomed to it. Since D sharp is the so-called 'leading-note' of E major, it enables him to make an easy transition to that key. The second subject now becomes the topic of discussion between various contrasted instruments, horn, piccolo, trumpet and, in a quickened agitated version of its first four notes, in the cellos. Meantime the oboes remind us of the almost forgotten subsidiary to the first subject. The cellos' abbreviation of the second subject assumes greater importance with a four-fold repetition in the violins leading to a dramatic reappearance of what I described as the 'lazy swell' in the introduction, now as vigorous as the initial horn theme (trombones and lower strings). Horns have a notable distortion of the second subject as the mood of agitation mounts. Soon we are caught up in an orchestral storm, possibly a memory of the Atlantic crossing, in which trombones convert the opening theme into a giant wave while shrill strings describe the gale-force winds. One can scarcely miss the trumpets' insistent repetition of the abbreviated fragment from the second subject which, as the storm subsides, turns out to be a convenient little pattern to fit against some more expressive treatments of the first subject. These make a useful bridge to lead into a formal recapitulation. It follows predictable lines until a sudden blast for full orchestra in which trumpets and trombones present a battle of wills between second and first subjects; the violins have an exciting new version of the first subject, compressed to half its normal length and piled up in an ascending sequence which then descends in a fierce chromatic scale. Four trumpet-calls seem to sound an alarm as the movement hastens forward to a dramatic finish.

The second movement is one of the best-known in the entire repertoire with its touchingly simple cor anglais solo and its dramatic references to the opening allegro in its central section. (The fine progression of harmonies at the start may well have served as a model for Rakhmaninov in the slow movement of his Second Piano Concerto, so similar in conception are the two introductory phrases.) Muted strings take over from the final impressive brass chord preparing a soft bed of harmony on which the cor anglais tune can lie in comfort. In its original version this tune was significantly different in detail, and much the poorer for it.

Ex. 1

The change from pairs of equal quavers to the dotted rhythm we now know made a world of difference. In the second limb of the tune the addition of a clarinet moving in parallel a tenth below is a masterly idea, giving a dark shadow to the cor anglais' expressive tones. Note too the way in which a quartet of clarinets and bassoons fold the tune away, tenderly repeating the last five notes, first as an exact copy and then twice as slowly as if reluctant to leave it alone. The opening sequence of harmonies is repeated in the wood-wind and then the strings embark on a variant of the melody which seems to lose its way before the cor anglais puts it back on course. Muted horns hold us in suspense for a moment, leading to a change of mood and content. In his sketches for this constrasting section Dvořák originally suggested the title 'Legend', perhaps thinking to put it to some different purpose. Flute and oboe present the tune together, circling round the first three notes of the scale of C sharp minor. (The cor anglais theme is in D flat major; this central section could be said to be in D flat *minor* but such a theoretical key would present awkward problems of notation.) The accompanying strings suggest the rustle of leaves in the forest and, as is so often the case in Dvořák's music, we have the feeling that the music belongs out of doors rather than in the formal surroundings of the concert-hall.

A third theme makes its appearance, a veritable funeral procession in character with its sombre theme on clarinets and the measured tread of double-basses. It may have been suggested by a forest burial in *Hiawatha* but there is no need to try to relate it to a specific incident. Themes two and three are both presented again in different orchestral colours before the woodwind, led by a solo flute, break in with a series of cheerful bird-songs. They may at first seem both irreverent and irrelevant but a moment's thought shows that they are directly related to the cor anglais tune, quickened in tempo and somewhat compressed.

Ex. 2

Innocent bird-song is swiftly transformed into a minor volcanic eruption as trombones break in with a powerful version of the main theme from
the first movement while the violins forcibly remind us of the opening notes
of the second subject from that movement and the woodwind offer a shrill
condensed version of the second phrase which rightfully should follow. Thus
we find four thematic fragments combined, three from the first movement
and one from the second — since the trumpets insist that the cor anglais tune
should be our proper concern. The combination is ingenious enough to
justify showing it in simplified score:

Ex. 3

This fusion of the two movements soon resolves into a reprise of the cor
anglais theme; peace is restored. Once again the violins seem to lose their way
during the second part of the tune. Their momentary lapse is more than
compensated for by a gloriously expressive phrase that they have on their
own before the return of the solemn opening chords brings the movement to
a deeply satisfying close.

The scherzo is popularly supposed to have been inspired by an American-
Indian warrior's dance although it is doubtful whether Dvořák actually saw
one. Certainly we can imagine the timpani to be tom-toms, and the dissonant
chord which the strings repeat over thirty times between bars 8–19 is clearly

designed to represent the thudding of feet on the bare earth. (It is an intriguing precursor of the famous repeated chords near the start of Stravinsky's *Rite of Spring* though the primitive Russian tribe is considerably more savage and ill-tempered.) The actual theme is made up from fragments, at first in the woodwind with the clarinets following a bar behind their shriller brethren, secondly in the first violins with the seconds providing a swirling counterpoint. The full orchestral version that soon follows is immensely exhilarating with the theme in the bass and an interesting new countermelody in the form of a syncopated chromatic descent.

With the central 'Trio' we return to Dvořák's native land as flute and oboe introduce a tune that has all the hallmarks of a Czech folk-song. (Note the interesting rhythm in the string accompaniment.) After the cellos have been given a tantalising taste of this eminently singable tune Dvořák works his way back to the opening material which duly comes to what sounds like a very rousing finish. Whispered references to the opening pattern tell us that there is more to come — or is this a surprise coda? The surprise comes from the cellos who unexpectedly remind us of the horn-call from the first movement. The quotation ends with a slight distortion which is queried by several instruments in turn. The violas then offer the same reminder and again the distorted ending is questioned by flute and oboe. However, the violins realise the potential of this novel ending and, smoothing it out a little, turn it into a delightful accompaniment to 'Trio II'. This proves to be another folk-dance with a skipping rhythm. 'Leave out that nonsense about my having made use of original American melodies' wrote Dvořák to a former pupil who was going to conduct the work; and here is a tune that confirms the point for it is pure Czech. It has a second part whose nimble grace tells us that it is for the girls to dance rather than the men. There follows a delicious alternation of trills between strings and woodwind which may be interpreted as cooing turtle-doves or giggling dancers according to personal preference. The 'Trio II' tune then returns rather more elaborately orchestrated.

According to classical precedent the main part of the scherzo is then repeated. The Coda gives the horns the opportunity to introduce another variant on their original theme from the first movement, causing the woodwind to remind them that they're still in the scherzo; but the quotations from the first movement gather strength with a solo trumpet even producing an elongated version of the original second subject. Then, like a toy engine running down, the movement appears to lose its momentum. There is a moment's silence after which Dvořák slams the lid with an abrupt *fortissimo* chord.

The finale is marked '*Allegro con fuoco*' ('with fire'). The introduction prepares for the entry of the main theme in a manner reminiscent of a circus with its rather too obvious widening of intervals; but once the theme arrives on horns and trumpets it proves to have genuine grandeur. The strings, left on their own, are hard put to it to match the splendour of the brass and welcome the added reinforcement from the wind. But soon the full orchestra becomes involved in some frankly rustic music which shows Dvořák's peasant upbringing rather too obviously. Redemption comes in the form of a lovely clarinet solo which creates an atmosphere of absolute peace only occasionally disturbed by impatient cellos.

The next episode for full orchestra in this loosely constructed movement does have a hint of 'Black and White Minstrel' about it with its thumping 'clap hands' rhythm in the timpani part and its 'ragtime' quavers in the violins and flutes. It is the only real concession to Americana and lacks the quality the fine opening theme has led us to expect. A brisk episode follows, mainly led by the strings, during which we become increasingly aware of a phrase which may irreverently be referred to as 'Three blind mice'. (They don't run very far but they crop up all over the place.) After tiptoeing their way through the strings, *pizzicato*, they appear in delightfully elegant dress in the woodwind, the third note handsomely decorated with a trill. As though this is all becoming too frivolous, horns remind us of the splendid initial theme but fail to impose a more serious approach on the rest of the orchestra. In fact the cellos and basses take all the dignity out of the theme by playing it double speed, though not loudly enough to draw attention to their lack of respect.

This leads to another ingenious combination of ideas: the violas play around with the disrespectful version of the theme from the last movement: flutes and clarinets summon a memory of the slow movement's theme, grafting on to it part of the *last* movement's theme at its proper speed: violins and then cellos remind us of a fragment from the Scherzo. Three movements are thus related to each other, a fusion which Dvořák enjoys sufficiently to extend for several pages. The only significant theme to be missing is the initial horn-call from the first movement; sure enough, after a suitably impressive build-up it makes a stirring reappearance, only to be displaced by a long delayed return of the true theme of this rather too episodic finale. In a climax that Tchaikovsky could not have bettered, trumpets and then trombones proclaim its dominance. Once the point has been hammered home Dvořák can afford to relax; quieter versions ensue until the violins can bring their warmest tone to the second subject, the one that had originally appeared as a clarinet solo. Gradually the music eases back in tempo as a far more expressive form of the 'Black and White Minstrel' tune appears in the woodwind. (Don't miss a delicately humorous transformation of the initial horn-call which bubbles up in the bassoon parts.) A solo horn ascends to a perilous top E in another reminder of the 'motto' theme — as the initial horn-call from the first movement has now proved itself to be. (It appears in all four movements.) An exciting fanfare on horns heralds a more massive extension of the 'motto' after which the main theme of the last movement reappears in its full glory on trombones and horns, surrounded by the peasant dance which, when it first appeared, had seemed a little too rustic for its context. As the excitement mounts Dvořák produces a master-stroke of invention, the opening harmonies of the slow movement utterly transformed. This huge climax gradually subsides as little fragments of the preceding movements drift past like leaves blown in the autumn wind. Against soft pulsating beats from the timpani a solo horn has a lengthened version of the main theme which is then copied by the full orchestra. At a slightly slower tempo the trumpets have a strangely distorted ending to the comparable phrase while trombones remind us of the initial horn-call from the first movement for the last time. In a final sprint for home the tempo quickens; a triumphant conclusion is certain — or so it seems. Yet the very last chord contains a surprise since, though it is cut short in the strings, wind and brass hold it for a long chord that fades away to the quietest possible sound. If, as I believe, the opening of the symphony symbolises his arrival, was this gradually diminishing chord a sub-conscious expression of Dvořák's wish to see New York recede on the horizon as he made his homeward journey?

Violoncello Concerto in B Minor Op. 104

Although Dvořák wrote the cello concerto during the latter part of his stay in New York he altered the finale substantially after he had returned home. Rather as Brahms had turned to Joachim for advice when writing his violin concerto, Dvořák sought help from a renowned fellow-countryman called Hanuš Wihan to whom the work is dedicated. Wihan certainly helped over some of the finer points of cello technique but composer and performer fell out when it came to the matter of cadenzas. Wihan wanted to insert a cadenza in the last movement to show off his undoubted virtuosity; Dvořák couldn't stand the idea and even wrote to his publisher forbidding any alterations without his express permission in case Wihan went behind his back. In the end the first performance was given in London on 19 March 1896 by Leo Stern.

Since the cello is much larger than the violin, and since there are fewer cellists than violinists in an orchestra, one might be forgiven for assuming that a cello would be louder and more penetrating than a violin. Therefore it should in theory be easier to write a cello concerto than a violin concerto, if only because it should surely be able to dominate the orchestra more easily. In fact, noble though its lower register undoubtedly is, when matching a solo cello *against* an orchestra a composer will tend to use its middle and upper range practically all the time. Problems of balance are far more acute in a cello concerto than in a violin concerto, which may be one reason why there are fewer of them. Considering what a wonderful instrument it is, the cello is surprisingly short of repertoire; there was never a golden age for cellists, as there was for violinists in the seventeenth and eighteenth centuries, or pianists in the nineteenth. There is a notable lack of concertos by the really great masters, Beethoven, Mozart and Brahms or in our own day Bartók or Stravinsky. Casals and, more recently, Rostropovich have inspired a number of works, but one wonders how many will take a permanent place in the repertoire. There is little doubt, though, which is the greatest nineteenth-century cello concerto; it must surely be Dvořák's. He had actually written one thirty years previously, but he never orchestrated it, and clearly regarded it as an apprentice work. Maybe it bore no immediate fruit, but down in the subconscious, it must have planted not so much a seed as a veritable acorn, for there is no questioning the splendour of the work that ultimately appeared in his maturity.

The start is unassuming enough, rather similar to the beginning of Tchaikovsky's Fifth Symphony in its colouring, with sombre clarinets spelling out a theme, accompanied by the lower strings. It's as though Dvořák was preparing our ears to start listening in a lower register than usual.

(Notice that the third bar, which is to prove especially significant, is itself a variation on bar 1.)

Violins and violas now take over, largely concentrating on the shape and rhythm of bar 3; within moments a substantial crescendo has built up and we are confronted with the opening theme in majestic splendour. It is also turned into a dialogue of sorts so that strings and wind alternate, one echoing the other. Gradually things quieten down, although the cellos try to start an insurrection with a rising scale which is duly copied by the woodwind. This theme sounds more important than it is since Dvořák makes no further use of it. It is merely a way of delaying a little further the entrance of the second subject, surely one of the most beautiful horn solos in the concerto repertory. The second part of this 'song without words' is taken over by a clarinet and then extended further by other woodwind instruments. After so lyrical a passage the outcome is a little surprising, a burst of rustic revelry which one feels belongs more to a set of Slavonic Dances than a cello concerto. It's almost too naive, as though Dvořák was saying 'Well, I'm only a simple country chap at heart you know'. And so he was of course, which is one reason why his music is so delightfully accessible. However, it's worth pointing out that this particular rustic dance doesn't appear anywhere else in the movement, as though even he may have thought 'Perhaps I shouldn't have . . .' The bucolic outburst soon dies down, resolving onto a quiet chord of B *major*, darkened by low trombones and a soft timpani roll. In a passionate and resolute style the soloist enters with the opening theme, subtly suggesting B major but actually on the dominant of E minor. The strong three-note chords give an epic quality to the music while the dotted rhythm of the third bar is soon made more impetuous by an ingenious transformation, here transposed for ease of comparison:

The increase in excitement finds release in a brief cadenza for the soloist into which Dvořák inserts fanfare-like figures which, for the sake of balance, are given to the woodwind in preference to the brass. A rising sequence of trills, against which flute and clarinet continue to remind us of the opening theme, leads us to a delightful variation. To the careless ear it may sound like a new theme but, as is shown in (b) in the above example, it is clearly derived from Theme I. Carried away by the sheer pleasure of this discovery, Dvořák develops it into a little episode on its own until, after a high trill on the dominant (F♯) the soloist returns to the proper matter on the agenda by recalling the opening phrase *fortissimo*. A graceful and ornamental descent leads to the second subject which the soloist understandably appropriates to himself. After this noble theme has run its full course a newcomer appears in the shape of a new theme for woodwind; it rocks gently between two adjacent notes while the soloist has a delicately fluttering accompaniment that demands great agility of bow and finger.

Yet another tune emerges from Dvořák's fertile mind as the fluttering triplets cease; it is a derivative of the 'rocking' theme but is very different in effect. It seems so spontaneous a development that it is hard to believe that Dvořák rejected three alternatives before arriving at this, the most satisfactory solution. Clarinet and flute give the tune their blessing with a beautiful counter-melody. As if aware that he has been dabbling with irrelevancies for long enough, the soloist begins a dramatic climb whose ultimate aim is a return to the opening material. This is achieved by a number of references to a compressed version of the opening four notes (♪♪ ♩), ending with a plunge to a low D.

The full orchestra responds with a grandiose treatment of the opening theme over a reiterated 'pedal'[5] D in the bass. There is a gradual *diminuendo* enhanced by a remarkable solo for the third horn-player whose descending

[5]A 'pedal-point' in the bass is a note that is sustained regardless of the harmonies above.

arpeggio covers a span of two-and-a-half octaves. Though it is nerve-racking for the player, it is intended to tranquillise the audience, preparing us for a considerable change of mood. Cellos and basses seem to pull the opening phrase down into the shadows. Another ingenious variant of the opening phrase has a momentarily disturbing effect, first in the cellos and then the violins, but the ultimate purpose of this section is to bring us to the true heart of the movement, a deeply felt contemplation of Theme I in the remote key of A flat minor. Above a barely audible accompaniment from the strings the soloist extends the tune by doubling the length of the notes and, in conjunction with a solo flute, turns it into a miniature elegy.

As though awakening from a dream, the cello plays a gently oscillating figure which provides a persistent accompaniment to a new theme in the woodwind. Its first three notes establish a relationship to Theme I but it is a cousin several times removed. A sudden timpani roll provokes a more energetic reaction from the soloist until, with a great wash of sound, the orchestra overwhelms the soloist just as he makes a sensational glissando climb (in octaves) to a high B. It is here that Dvořák shows his willingness to defy convention if he so chooses; a normal recapitulation would have to begin with at the very least an acknowledgment of the first subject's importance. Dvořák bypasses this completely and begins his recapitulation with a full orchestral version of the lyrical second subject. It is of course accepted gratefully by the soloist who thereafter follows a fairly predictable course. The final coda re-establishes the importance of the first subject which, in the closing bars is turned into a triumphant fanfare by the brass.

The slow movement is unusually rich in material, so much so that it seems unnecessarily pedantic to label themes that flow so naturally one from the other. First to appear is a folk-like melody on the clarinet, soon to be echoed by the soloist. Notice how a dangerously static moment in the clarinet tune is filled with a graceful arpeggio from the cello — a perfect example of the way the composer of a concerto will leave a 'pocket' in the orchestral part for the soloist to fill. After the third of these arpeggios the mood changes from simple song to heartbreak as the cellist has a descending sequence that anticipates the moving lament in the finale of the Elgar cello concerto. It leads to a tearful sequence of paired notes in which the music seems to sob in unrestrained grief. As if in consolation the clarinet brings back the opening theme, only to be forcibly interrupted by a ferocious outburst on the full orchestra in G minor. The interruption may last for only four bars but it effects a total change. The cello begins a passionate song whose opening phrase descends through five notes of the scale (D—G). It is a quotation from one of Dvořák's 'Four Songs' Op. 82. The composer had just heard that his sister-in-law, a charming young actress called Josefina Kounicová, was seriously ill; the quotation seems to express his longing to be back in his homeland so that he could be with her. (There is a further quotation from the

Op. 82 songs in the finale, inserted into the coda as a memorial to her after Dvořák had learned of her death.) The 'sobbing' motif returns, as does the violent G minor phrase on the orchestra; indeed, the movement alternates between the lyrical and the passionate.

The stroke of true genius is the cadenza which appears just after the horns have given us a solemn reminder of the opening theme. (Note the 'muffled drum' effect in cellos and basses.) The cadenza begins with the solo cello meditating freely on the opening theme; but after a few bars it is joined by several wind instruments which unmistakably imitate the sounds of the countryside. A flute warbles like the nightingale; bassoons croak like bullfrogs; a pair of flutes coo like doves. This sudden evocation of the country shows Dvořák's dissatisfaction with the urban environment and his intense longing for the rural peace of his homeland. As such it is strangely comparable to the second movement of Bartók's Third Piano Concerto (see page 56) which, like this work, was written far from home.

In the final pages of the movement there is a return to the opening material and even a feeling of some consolation. Six bars from the end there is a sudden pang of sorrow, followed by an ethereal descent in harmonics and a lingering farewell on the clarinet.

The finale begins as a march very much in the manner of Tchaikovsky. Over the distant left–right tread of cellos and basses the horns offer a sketch of the main theme, leaving the finer details to be filled in by the soloist. An exciting if somewhat conventional build-up leads to the solo entry, a sturdy tune in B minor which Dvořák clearly intended to be the basis for a rondo. The orchestra endorse it with enthusiasm and the first episode duly follows — somewhat skittishly, it must be said, after the resolute character of the theme. Within less than thirty bars the rondo theme is back, first on flute and oboe over skirling trills from the cello and then on strings and brass. It is at this point that the rondo framework begins to weaken since Dvořák embarks on a series of episodes which delay the return of the theme for nearly 190 bars. The first intervention is a 'marche militaire', unrelated to anything that has preceded it. The soloist's attempt to match the power of the orchestra is not all that convincing so, with positively feminine guile, the 'march' is converted into a tender caress calculated to melt the heart of any soldier. One of Dvořák's typical 'rocking' tunes appears on a solo clarinet, enchantingly teased by the cello. This delightful flirtation is prolonged for some time until the cellist tires of the game and launches into some agile triplet arpeggios which, after considerable cavorting, lead back to a reprise of the 'marche militaire' — now in D major instead of B minor. By a slightly devious route the cellist finds the way back to the rondo theme, sneaking it in so that we hardly notice; the orchestra does, though, and gives it a rowdy reception.

The exuberant tag the violins attach to its tail is repeated several times and then cleverly ironed out to introduce yet another episode at a more moderate tempo. Here again we find the composer drawing on the resources of the folk idiom. As the tempo quickens once again the flute has a particularly naive tune which the cellist disregards entirely, preferring for once to show off the fluency of his technique. The orchestra continues to concentrate on the folk material but the cellist becomes increasingly capricious. At last the rondo theme reappears, but this time the soloist toys with it, arousing the ire of the violas as he does so.

A solemn fanfare on the brass puts a stop to the frivolity and leads to the truly inspired coda which has the lilting tenderness of a lullaby. Its gentle rocking themes effect a skilful marriage between the rondo of the finale and the opening bar of the first movement. (A clarinet and then a horn make the point clear to those who haven't spotted the relationship.) As the music slows to a majestic tempo a magnificent chorale rises through the orchestra only to be swept away in the whirlwind final page.

There had been many cello concertos before this but none had explored so wide a range of emotion nor been so richly endowed with melodies. As long as there are cellists to play it, it will remain a firm favourite and justifiably so.

ELGAR
1857–1934

One evening, back in the closing year of the nineteenth century, a still relatively unknown English composer was recovering from a long and trying day's teaching by improvising gently on the piano. It wasn't his instrument really; he was a violinist. But one can't believe that his playing would have been unmusical, even if he hadn't got a facile technique. Anyway, the theme that came into his mind and out through his fingers was a slow one, tinged with melancholy. Her attention caught by a tune she'd never heard before, his wife asked him what it was. 'Oh, nothing', replied Elgar 'but I might be able to do something with it.' And then, for no particular reason except a flight of fancy, he started to amuse himself by imagining how some of his musical friends might have treated the theme. For instance, there was a man called Nevinson, a cellist, with whom Elgar used to play trios for pleasure. That very evening Elgar imagined how an amateur cellist would approach the theme, and there and then he improvised on the piano to show his wife.

Her reaction was to suggest to Elgar that he'd hit upon a brand new idea for a work, and straight away they made a game of it, he playing the theme in various ways and she guessing who he was imitating. And so this English classic was born, the whole work being written within a fortnight. The Enigma Variations were to prove a most significant breakthrough for Elgar. The first performance, in June 1899 under Richter, was hailed as a triumph, and the work was soon in the repertory of European orchestras. Here's Elgar in a letter to his close friend A.J. Jaeger who worked at Novello's the publisher:

> Since I've been back I have sketched a set of Variations on an original theme: the Variations have amused me because I've labelled 'em with the nickname of my particular friends — you are Nimrod. That is to say I've written the Variations each one to represent the mood of the 'party'. I've liked to imagine the 'party' writing the var. him (or her) self and have written what I think *they* would have written — if they were asses enough to compose. It's

a quaint idea and the result is amusing to those behind the scenes and won't effect the hearers who 'nose nuffin'. What think you?[1]

But though the Variations had scored a great success at their first performance, Richter and others, including Jaeger, had expressed misgivings about the ending. Elgar's reaction to the criticism is fascinating in its mixture of schoolboy slang and serious musical talk. Again he's writing to Jaeger:

> As to that finale, it's most good of you to be interested and I like to have your opinion. I have my doubts as to some of the rest 'cos it's generally *suggested* to them. Now look here, the movement was designed to be concise. Here's the difficulty of lengthening it. I could go on with those themes for half a day but the key G is exhausted. The principal motive (Enigma) comes in grandioso on page 35 in the tonic and it *wouldn't do* to bring it in again. Had I intended to make an extended movement this would have been in some related key, reserving the tonic for the final smash. In deference to you I made a sketch yesterday but the thing sounds Schubertian in its sticking to one key. I should really like to know how you heard that Richter was disappointed. He criticised some of it but not the end. The actual final flourish was spoilt in performance . . . You see there's far too much of this sort of thing said. Somebody wants to find fault and in course of conversation says 'the end did not please so and so, I find it very poor, *don't you?*' The other chap hadn't thought of it at all but says 'Yes, it's very abrupt' and so it goes on. This sort of thing is of no value to me. What *you* say is your own opinion and would be given on anybody's work. All the other fellows would never have made a remark if the work had been written by any great man. If I find, after New Brighton that the end does not satisfy me, I may recast the whole of the last movement but it's not possible to lengthen it with any satisfaction, I fear. If I can find time to make a readable copy of my 'end' I'll send it to you and then you'll see how good E. Elgar is at heart.[2]

In fact the revised ending proved to be a significant improvement and Elgar admitted that Jaeger's judgement had been right. (The mention of 'page 35' in the letter above suggests that Jaeger had been given a piano reduction since in the full orchestral score the 'grandioso' passage would have been at least a hundred pages later.)

Although Elgar had written a considerable quantity of music in the years prior to 1899 he had remained a 'local' composer whose works were not widely known. He earned a none too handsome living doing a variety of musical jobs, mostly with amateur musicians; he was for a time organist at St George's Church, Worcester; he conducted various local choral societies and orchestras; he played the violin in the augmented orchestra that was assembled for the Three Choirs Festival and once, in 1884, played under Dvořák's baton. His marriage in 1889 was an important step for him for his

[1] Basil Maine, *Elgar: His Life and Works*, p. 86 (Bell, 1933).
[2] Op. cit.

wife had some means of her own and gave him some freedom to escape the worst of the musical drudgery which had been his lot. With her encouragement they moved to London, hoping for greater things; but the unknown from a rural cathedral city found little response in the capital and in just over a year they returned to the country they knew so well and settled in Malvern. It was a difficult time for them both. Elgar, the son of a piano-tuner and shopkeeper, had married the daughter of a Major-General, Sir Henry Roberts, KCB. They made an oddly assorted couple within the rigid structure of Victorian society; furthermore Elgar was a Catholic in a staunchly Protestant community. However, success began to come his way in the mid–1890s, mostly with choral works such as 'King Olaf' or 'Caractacus', compositions which reached London or Leeds but which still had no international standing. The 'Enigma' Variations were to change all that. It seemed as though he had suddenly found new confidence in his ability, and the enthusiastic endorsement of Hans Richter, the great conductor, gave him the feeling that he was now fully equipped to tackle the major musical forms. Self-taught as he was, he had forged a style that was uniquely his own, indebted to no 'school'; to achieve this from so unpropitious a background confirmed that here at last, for the first time since Purcell's day, was an English composer to whom the word genius could honestly be applied.

Variations on an Original Theme for Orchestra
Op. 36

Enigma

Dedicated to my friends pictured within.

Malvern 1899

The word 'Enigma' was added to the manuscript score in pencil, apparently as an afterthought. In the programme note which he wrote for the first performance Elgar set a riddle which has caused much food for thought for those with a taste for codes and ciphers.

> The Enigma I will not explain — its 'dark saying' must be left unguessed, and I warn you that the apparent connection between the Variations and the Theme is often of the slightest texture; further, through and over the whole set another and larger theme 'goes', but is not played. . . . So the principal Theme never appears, even as in some late dramas — e.g. Maeterlinck's *L'Intruse* and *Les Sept Princesses* — the chief character is never on the stage.

It is the mention of 'another and larger theme' that has tantalised musical scholars ever since, for it is a musical impossibility that any specific tune could fit against the Theme *and* against all the variations. A number of solutions have been proposed[3] ranging from 'Auld Lang Syne' to abstract conceptions such as 'Friendship'. Elgar was fond of anagrams, acrostics and word puzzles. The name of his house, 'Craeg Lea', is an anagram of his own name and his wife's initials, C.A.E.[4] An early composition dedicated to some friends called Gedge used their name as a basis for the musical material — 'Allegretto on G.E.D.G.E.'. I am therefore inclined to favour an ingenious solution proposed by Vernon Jones in an article for the Royal Academy of Music magazine, the summer issue of 1970. He shows how the theme, if transposed into A minor, becomes a musical translation of the name of Elgar's daughter Carice, which itself is a contraction of his wife's names Caroline Alice. Since the final variation is headed EDU, a pet name for Elgar that his wife had invented, it seems quite likely that the 'larger theme' that 'goes' with all the variations is family love. The snag to almost every solution is the authentic story of Elgar improvising the theme at the piano; it is inconceivable that he would by chance have hit upon a melody that would fit in perfect counterpoint against another tune as different in character as 'Auld Lang Syne', even though, by somewhat Procrustean methods 'Auld Lang Syne' can be

[3]See *An Elgar Companion* ed. Christopher Redwood (Sequoia, 1982).

[4]Or possibly *Carice, Alice, Edward*, incorporating his daughter, wife and himself.

adjusted to fit against the 'Enigma'. But many musicians have played the musical spelling game that makes tunes from letters — for instance Schumann's ABEGG Variations, Ravel's '*Menuet sur le nom d'Haydn*' and '*Berceuse sur le nom de Gabriel Fauré*', not to mention a number of compositions based on B.A.C.H. Knowing this, and taking into consideration Elgar's love of word-puzzles, is it not quite possible that Elgar jotted down the musical equivalent of his daughter's name, perhaps to delight her on some future occasion, and then began to improvise around those notes? '*I might be able to do something with it*': 'might be able' to write a piece depicting his daughter, or perhaps amuse her by describing friends she would also know? When Elgar first played the completed work to his wife he exclaimed 'Japes!' as he began, which, together with 'High Jinks', was a favourite expression. Yet on another occasion he wrote that the opening bars of the theme depicted 'the loneliness of the artist'. As Elgar's stature as a composer grew he became increasingly irritated by any discussion of the 'Enigma' and it may well be that what started as an intimate family game proved to be unsuited to more public exposure. Since the riddle has no definitive solution it is as well that we should not dwell on it too long; the music stands on its own merits as the sole English orchestral masterpiece to emerge from the nineteenth century.

A glance at the theme (see below) shows that it falls into three sections, six bars in G minor, four bars in G major, then a reprise of the first six bars plus a final bar which momentarily touches G major again. Thus the tonality of theme is itself 'enigmatic'.

(Notice the numerous directions to the players that are characteristic of Elgar: '*ten.*' is an abbreviation of '*tenuto*', 'held' or 'lingered on': '*Mesto*' means 'sadly'.)

An unusual feature of the theme is the absence of first beats in the two G minor sections, an absence which makes their provision in the central part all the more effective. What is not shown in the example is the glorious counter-tune which surges up in the middle register in bars 13–16. The last note is sustained by the violins who then provide an expressive two-bar link that feels its way back to G minor and Variation I. Very properly, since it was at her behest that the work came to be written, it represents Elgar's wife, Caroline Alice. The silent first beats of the theme are now filled in, giving it an air of greater confidence while the delicately syncopated arpeggios in unison violins and cellos suggest her moving quietly about the house anxious not to disturb the composer. Oboe and bassoon have a quite prominent little figure with a triplet rhythm; destined to reappear in the finale, it was apparently a fragment that Elgar used to whistle to show his whereabouts. The variation grows to a sudden impassioned climax in the middle, revealing the depth of feeling this very devoted woman aroused in him.

Variation II is notoriously tricky to play and supposedly represents a pianist friend called H.D. Steuart-Powell who was in the habit of 'limbering up' at the keyboard by dashing off a few technical exercises. The music is a mischievous caricature since Steuart-Powell would select rather facile passages, whereas these patterns are extremely awkward. The theme doesn't appear until the eighteenth bar when it makes a somewhat grumpy entrance in the bass, as though Elgar was saying 'Why can't we get on with it?'

Variation III portrays Richard Baxter Townshend, an author of boys' books who delighted in amateur theatricals. The oboe has a cheeky if slightly breathless version of the theme, now all in G major; it describes Townshend playing the role of an old man and adopting a senile falsetto voice to do so. This would cause much mirth since his normal voice was very deep, as a bassoon shows towards the end of the variation.

Variation IV uses the full orchestra for the first time. The theme is hammered out — no time for rests! — while the G major section becomes a whirlwind. It seems that W. Meath Baker was a rather choleric country squire who tended to treat his house-guests as though he was a commanding officer. Here he gives the orders for the day and sweeps out of the room, leaving his friends at the breakfast-table laughing affectionately at the display. (A jocular little section for woodwind.) His reappearance at the end is good-natured bluster.

Variation V begins with a grave new melody on the violins beneath which the lower strings and bassoons play the first part of the theme, now in C minor. Richard Arnold, son of the poet Matthew Arnold, was serious in bearing but witty in speech; both aspects are vividly conveyed, the gravity by the strings, the wit by the woodwind. The music moves smoothly without a break into the next variation, Ysobel. The archaic spelling is a scant disguise for Isabel Fitton, an amateur viola player who had been a pupil of Elgar's. As an affectionate tribute to her there is a prominent part for solo viola. The theme, reduced to fragments, is given to the bassoons but our attention is inevitably drawn towards the gracious viola tune and the smiles of approval that the clarinets seem to give as the 'pupil' explores unaccustomed heights.

Variation VII is technically one of the most demanding for the orchestra. The first four bars allude to the rhythm of the theme but in a very abrupt and alarming manner; the rising phrases that follow are derived from the central portion of the theme and, when given to the trombones, sound positively menacing. The explosive timpani rhythms give the impression that Troyte Griffith was extremely ill-tempered. In fact he was one of Elgar's closest friends, although he had a habit of blurting out unexpected remarks. The portrait is therefore unexpected, but its air of ferocity should not be taken seriously. Elgar himself offered this explanation:

> The uncouth rhythm of the drums and the lower strings was really suggested by (his) maladroit essays to play the pianoforte; later the strong rhythm suggests the attempts of the instructor (Elgar) to make something like order out of chaos, and the final despairing 'slam' records that the effort proved to be vain.

It would seem that Elgar was not the most patient of teachers . . .

Variation VIII is one of the most enchanting episodes, putting the framework of the theme into the major and changing the rhythm into a flowing 6/8. The piquant little trills on the oboe followed by delicate staccato figures on the flutes describe Winifred Norbury's characteristic laughter, light-hearted but refined. The variation ends with a phrase that is warmly affectionate. Its final note is held for a long pause, the tonic of G major poised to be transformed into the third note of the key of E flat.

So begins Variation IX, 'Nimrod', its name being a typical Elgarian pun. Nimrod was 'the great hunter' of mythology, and 'hunter' in German is 'Jaeger'. A.J. Jaeger worked at Novello's, the music publishers, and was more than a dear friend to Elgar; he was also someone on whom he could rely for totally honest criticism as well as unflinching support. He idolised Beethoven and would often discuss Beethoven's music with Elgar as they walked together on the Malvern hills. It was for this reason that 'his' variation begins with a subtle allusion to the slow movement of the 'Pathetique' sonata:

Beethoven (transposed)

Elgar

This noble theme is orchestrated in such a way that the sound accumulates; the first eight bars are for strings only. Woodwind and horns are then added to enrich the texture, while a soaring counterpoint in cellos and violas recalls the passionate phrase that appeared towards the end of the original theme. A soft timpani stroke signals an ingenious new treatment of bars 7–10 of the theme in which it is inverted by violas and cellos. Then, after a sustained crescendo the 'Nimrod' theme is heard for the third time, now with full orchestra. The penultimate phrase is repeated three times with ever-increasing intensity. The last three bars demand a quite extraordinary diminution of tone from the fullest *fortissimo* to an almost inaudible *pianissimo*.

Elgar described this famous variation as 'a jolly fine tune. It's just like you,' he wrote to Jaeger, 'you solemn wholesome hearty old dear.' The heartiness is not evident but the solemnity is such that the piece has acquired an almost religious significance.

There follows an Intermezzo which cannot really be regarded as a variation although the first entry of a solo viola may be an allusion to the rising phrase in bar 7 of the theme. The name at the top of the page is Dorabella, a reference to one of the characters in Mozart's '*Cosi fan tutte*', which perhaps Miss Dora Penny may have appreciated. If she was anything like as charming as the music she must have enchanted everyone who met her. Elgar said that the music suggested 'a dance of fairy-like lightness' and the delicate trills on the violins and the fluttering phrases in the wind do give an impression of gossamer wings hovering in the twilight. The soft sustained lines on solo viola or flutes are a master-stroke of scoring. A contrasting episode beginning with a swift upward scale from the violas takes us by surprise and for a moment or two the music shows greater animation. Notice particularly the contributions from the woodwind; every note counts and the whole Intermezzo is a supreme example of the fastidiousness of Elgar's scoring.

Variation XI is a curiosity. Supposedly a portrait of Dr. George Sinclair, the organist of Hereford Cathedral, it is more concerned with his bulldog Dan of whom Elgar was immensely fond. He even used to write fragments of music in the Sinclairs' Visitors' Book to illustrate Dan's mood of the day. On one occasion Elgar and Sinclair were walking by the river Wye when Dan slithered down the bank and fell in; he paddled frantically back towards dry land, scrambled out, shook himself and gave a triumphant bark. 'Set *that* to music' said Sinclair. 'I did' said Elgar after the variation had been written. Bar 1 shows Dan falling in, bars 2–3 show him paddling back to safety, the swift chromatic run in bar 4 is the dog shaking himself; clarinets, bassoons, horns and lower strings provide the bark in bar 5 and we even hear the chink of a triangle to capture the sound of Dan's name-plate medallion on his collar. The whole incident takes less than ten seconds but it provides Elgar with material for a brilliant variation. The dog's paddling becomes synonymous with Dr. Sinclair's nimble pedalling, the full brass grab hold of the theme and make it sound like a cathedral organ playing a fanfare; a musical joke becomes a virtuoso showpiece that is entirely relevant to the theme. Particularly ingenious is the compression of the theme in bars 2–3.

Variation XII depicts a cellist friend, Basil Nevinson, who used to play trios with Elgar and Steuart-Powell (see Variation II). Not surprisingly it opens with a cello solo. The other cellos soon join in to share the broad singing melody whose relationship to the theme is easy to comprehend.

Variation XIII is headed with three asterisks and the word 'Romanza'. The only reference to the theme is a gently rocking phrase on a pair of violas. Elgar's own note reads: 'The asterisks take the place of the name of a lady who was at the time . . . on a sea voyage. The drums suggest the distant throb of the engines of a liner, over which the clarinet quotes a phrase from Mendelssohn's "Calm sea and prosperous voyage".' There is a small mystery here. In later years Elgar himself pencilled in the name of Lady Mary Lygon, later to become Lady Trefusis. It seems though that Lady Lygon was not at sea in the first months of 1899 when Elgar was orchestrating the work since she and Winifred Norbury both went to his home to have tea on 21 February. If anything it was Elgar's memory that was at sea since it has recently been suggested that the asterisked lady was Helen Jessie Weaver to whom Elgar had been engaged some sixteen years earlier. Owing to religious differences the engagement came to nothing but Elgar was deeply affected by their enforced separation. Helen Weaver subsequently went to New Zealand, and it was no doubt because he was thinking of her at the opposite end of the world that he quoted the Mendelssohn phrase in this way.

The second appearance of the Mendelssohn quotation, on trombones and low trumpets, is truly impressive, perfect music for a film shot of a great ocean liner ploughing tirelessly across an infinite sea.

The finale, Variation XIV, is headed E.D.U. which, as we have seen, was his wife's pet-name for Elgar. (The full stops are certainly there to mislead the over-curious.) It starts as if it might well be a 'Pomp and Circumstance' march, though none of them had yet been written. The music symbolises the enormous gain in self-confidence which came with the writing of this work. The first references to the theme come in the brass after two powerful chords for full orchestra. Some way in, the brisk tempo eases back as cellos refer to the rising central phrase of the original theme; set against it is a new melody which Vernon Jones shrewdly points out spells E D U according to the musical 'alphabet' playfully used by many composers.

This theme spreads through the orchestra as the central section of the original theme becomes more openly displayed. Suddenly the full brass produce the theme transposed into the major, a moment of triumph celebrated with a magnificent descending scale in counterpoint. The music increases in tempo then breaks off for a momentary pause. Softly the march begins again, building more rapidly than before. Abruptly it halts in mid-flight and the music seems to freeze on a low E flat. Loud and clear we hear the triplet figure from Variation I, the private signal that Elgar used to whistle to his wife. We hear a distant echo and then, ever faithful, she appears — an exact quotation from her 'portrait' in the first variation. It is an oasis of calm in the excitement of the finale. Soon the music gathers impetus as though Elgar himself were striding with quickening steps towards the goal of recognition too long withheld. The theme reappears majestically, the orchestra now reinforced with the organ. The final climax is immense with the trombones proclaiming the first five notes of the theme in a hugely drawn out version. Small wonder that the work has retained its popularity ever since its first triumphant performance.

Introduction and Allegro for Strings (Quartet and Orchestra) Op. 47

The majestic opening bars of this splendid work do little to suggest that it was inspired in the first place by the sound of a few Welsh voices singing in the distance. Elgar was taking a holiday at the time and, so far as is known, had no particular project in mind; but the distant music touched a response which lay dormant in his mind. Some time later he was sitting one evening on his beloved Malvern hills and again he heard Welsh voices from far off. The sound was too remote to be able to identify the tune with any accuracy but one interval, a falling minor third, seemed to predominate. Fascinated by the elusiveness of the sounds and perhaps feeling that the dual experience was a prompting that he should not disregard, he took out the notebook he habitually carried round with him and jotted down a tune with a distinctly Welsh inflection (see top of page 223).

At that moment he probably had no particular idea as to its possible use but as he mulled it over it must have seemed especially suited to string tone. That decision made, he set to work on a most original plan, paying homage to the baroque concerto grosso by contrasting a solo string quartet with a larger

body of strings while at the same time writing what could be described as a gloriously free extension of the traditional concept of Prelude and Fugue. A postcard to his friend Jaeger, dated January 1905, reads: 'I'm doing that string thing in time for the Sym. Orch. concert. Intro. and Allegro — *no working-out* part but a devil of a fugue instead, G major and the 2nd. divvel in G minor.'

'That string thing' was finished on 13 February and performed at the Queen's Hall the following month, proof if needed of Elgar's ever-growing confidence. It is an extraordinary work, reconciling a variety of ideas that hardly seem to belong to the same world. The tempo fluctuates wildly, as it often does in Elgar's music, while ranging in emotion from majesty to tenderness, from frankly sentimental to fiercely intellectual and all within a span less than that of a symphonic first movement.

The first four bars, (I) are as grand a proclamation of the key of G minor as has ever been devised. Having made the point in so powerfully rhetorical a way, the main body of strings yields gracefully to the solo quartet who offer a brief contrasting phrase, (II) in which the rhythm 𝄽 should be especially noted for future reference. The 'orchestral' violins take the hint but the listener should pay greater heed to the lower strings whose rather sombre curve (III) is due to appear in a very unexpected role later in the work.

$p \prec sf \succ p$ *dim.*

For four bars quartet and orchestra contemplate Theme I in a somewhat sweetened version and then, impatiently, the quartet moves on into II which, this time, is picked up with rather more emphasis by the orchestral violins, the sombre counterpoint of III now more intense in feeling. With a sudden and magical change of mood the solo viola from the quartet allows us to hear the 'Welsh' theme which was the genesis of the whole work. It is duly taken over by the main body of strings building to a climax of great warmth before dying away mysteriously as though receding into the night. A powerful crescendo on a single chord brings back Theme I, slightly modified, and terminated by three massive chords; as the last of these dies down we hear the quartet quietly meditating on the 'Welsh' tune. So far then these have been four distinct ideas, only one of which has been allowed to develop at any length; it is truly an Introduction in which the characters make their identities clear, each so different from the other.

But now there is a distinct change as the orchestral strings begin to develop II at greater length. Occasional interjections by the quartet attempt to sentimentalise it, but the 'orchestra' always moves the tempo forward again. Notice too how Theme III emerges from the depths, appearing in the violin parts for the first time. A sudden crescendo out of nothing halts the music in mid-flight. A new subject appears, (IV), instantly recognisable by its non-stop chatter of semiquavers. Treated at first as a dialogue between the quartet and the main body of strings, it builds to an exciting climax that spills over into a torrent of descending scales. Without any prior warning Theme I appears triumphantly in unashamed D major. An impassioned new theme grows out of it with an exhilarating striding bass. Brilliant scale-passages show off the violinists' technical skills; they lead to an agitated figure that opens out in contrary motion. It is a moment worth remembering for it is due to be repeated at a later point with a different sequel. Here it leads to a rather more lyrical version of Theme I which gradually subsides as the quartet again offers a tender reminder of the 'Welsh' tune. The music appears to come to a complete halt.

If we are to take the words on Elgar's postcard to Jaeger at their face-value it would seem that he had second thoughts here for the 'devil of a fugue' makes its unexpected entry in G minor, not G major as he suggests. Nor does there appear to be a second fugue; presumably he decided that one was sufficient. Whatever the truth of the matter the fugue is remarkable enough in itself. Beginning on the second violins it has a curiously hopping gait with sudden little upward spurts of notes that suggest a cloak swirling around a slightly grotesque figure. The entries would have been approved by Bach himself although the gradual infiltration of smooth legato lines deprives the theme of some of its spikiness. It is the entry of the quartet that brings the greatest surprise for instead of joining in the fugal dance they bring back Theme III which, amazingly, provides a perfect counterpoint to the continuing fugue despite its very different mood. The compositional problems that Elgar sets himself in the development of the fugue are very challenging, the more so for one who had never been through any conventional course at a conservatoire or university. After some striking examples of contrapuntal ingenuity the music gradually loses its forward thrust and the fugue subject makes an exit via the basement. Like a whisper, fragments of the 'chattering' theme return. With a sense of release a recapitulation of sorts begins, picking up the music at a point which was originally ten pages in. Familiar landmarks pass by, easily recognised since each element has so clearly defined a character. At the 'contrary motion' climax already mentioned Elgar plays his ace. Instead of the reversion to Theme I which we had previously, he offers a grandiose version of the 'Welsh' theme, no longer tender and distant but blazing with fervour. It is one of the richest examples of string orchestral writing in the entire repertoire and must lift our hearts however often we hear it. Some soaring fanfare-like figures bring the work to a conclusion that combines brilliance with nobility. 'I have finished the string thing and it's all right; of course, it will take you some time to get used to it, but it will sound really wholesome and bring out much tone from the strings.' So wrote Elgar after he had completed the score; those of us who have 'got used to it' find it a good deal more than 'wholesome'. 'Totally inspired' would be a better description of a work that can be classified as one of the greatest ever written for string orchestra.

Symphony No. 1 in A flat
Op. 55

To Hans Richter, Mus. Doc.
True Artist and true Friend.

These words appear on the title page of Elgar's First Symphony and Richter repaid the compliment handsomely when, at the rehearsal for the first London performance in December 1908, he began by saying to the orchestra, 'Gentlemen, let us now rehearse the greatest symphony of modern times, written by the greatest modern composer — and not only in this century.' Elgar had cherished the idea of writing a symphony for ten years; he had even contemplated following the precedent of Beethoven's 'Eroica' by relating the work to a contemporary hero, General Gordon. 'The Gordon thing possesses me but I can't write it down yet,' he wrote to Jaeger at one time. Perhaps it is as well that the plan was dropped; somehow the title 'Gordon Symphony' sounds amateurish. In the event the First Symphony turned out to be purely musical in concept with no suggestion of a programme. It is a long work taking some fifty minutes to play, but Elgar handles this largest of pure musical forms with great assurance. Prior to its composition he had suffered a long period of depression; he felt, with some justification, that the musical establishment in England had not yet given him due recognition. For example in 1908 Stanford had written a book of essays largely concerned with English music without so much as a mention of Elgar's name. Admittedly he had been given the professorship of music at Birmingham University but his duties there were not sufficiently practical to hold his interest; lectures on music were no substitute for conducting performances of his own works. Perhaps in an effort to rejuvenate his tiring muse he turned to some music he had written as a child of fourteen. Reworking the material with the skill of a mature master the fifty-year old composer produced two charming suites called *The Wand of Youth*. The relatively simple task gave him some relaxation so that at last he felt ready for the daunting task of writing a symphony. Considering its length it is remarkable that the work was written in two months, June/July 1908. The orchestral score was completed in the Autumn, the first performance given in Manchester in December. Within a year the symphony had been played over a hundred times, a response which must have delighted the composer even though he was so exhausted mentally that for several months he could not bear to hear a note of music. For relief he turned to chemistry, which fascinated him, or the occasional game of golf which he thought 'a grand game because you can think of nothing else when playing'.

The orchestra can certainly think of nothing else when playing this symphony since it is a work demanding virtuosity from every player. The opening pages give little hint of the perils ahead; two preliminary bars for timpani and low strings are like an initial clearing of the throat before making a speech. Elgar then gives us a magnificent tune with a hymn-like character.[5] At the first statement its tone is subdued, the texture virtually confined to two parts — the tune and a solemn marching accompaniment. The second 'verse' is scored for full orchestra and is richly harmonised until the closing bars which die away to a quiet sustained A flat in the bass. A tune as complete as this is not really good symphonic material since it is already fully grown; it leaves no room for development. (Schubert had a similar problem at the start of his great C major symphony.) It is not really surprising then that mood and tempo change abruptly as the 'true' first movement begins. The surprise lies in the key, D minor, a violent contradiction of the unadulterated A flat major that has preceded it.

The new theme (I) surges restlessly against a curiously angular bass, quickly reaching a climax before breaking into an urgent sequence in the strings goaded by off-beat chords for wind and brass. (I) returns in cellos and clarinets, now in G minor; it again climbs to a peak from which the descent is made to seem more precipitous by a change of the rhythmic pulse from 2/2 to 6/4. (This means that each 'beat' is subdivided into three instead of two, thus giving the impression of an increase in speed.) Gradually the agitation lessens, making way for a more relaxed theme (II) in the first violins. It is a precursor of the second subject, anticipating its shape but not its full span. That materialises a moment or two later, easily identified by the octave rise to a high A and the more leisurely descent. The music becomes increasingly lyrical, drifting through several keys while isolated dabs of sound from the flutes give a suggestion of scattered raindrops. Just as we think that peace is restored, an element of unease creeps in; the brass re-enter the fray (note the

[5]See Ex. 2 for a later version in C major.

high trumpet part) provoking an extremely vigorous response from the violins, leaping upwards in a sequence of mounting fifths. Rapid-fire chromatic scales in trumpets and trombone are the signal for a descending cascade in the strings out of which emerges a fragment of I. It is no more than a reminder and much more dramatic use is made of a phrase which originally appeared as a subsidiary to theme II. Here are its two versions, the first so discreet, the second so forceful:

Ex. 1

The tempo eases back and as if from a great distance we hear the very opening theme on muted horns; it seems to grow quite logically from the second part of the example above as a comparison of the first four notes will show.

Ex. 2

This reminder of things past signals the beginning of the Development which takes up more than a third of the movement. It starts with a 'wailing' motif on strings that has not appeared before, but a reversion to the 6/4 pulse causes some anxiety. The woodwind parts become notably more active, soon infecting the strings with their swiftly running figuration. Fragments of II appear in wind, horns and strings in turn, but they are shortly displaced by a strange new pattern whose awkward gangling shape proves to be surprisingly fruitful.

Ex. 3

It is the intrusion of such seemingly irrelevant passages that have laid this symphony open to criticism. It has been described as 'shapeless', 'sprawling', 'an improvisation rather than a symphony'. On being asked to account for its diffuseness Elgar exclaimed, 'All this is beside the point because I *feel* and don't invent. I can't even invent an explanation.'

To catalogue every happening in this extensive Development would be wearisome; the sounds alone should be thrilling enough. All the same we should not fail to recognise the dramatic re-entry of the second subject, its initial rising octave stretched to a tenth, its character transformed as the timpani thunder beneath it. There is also a remarkable expansion of Ex. 3 that goes from *pp* to *fff* in three bars. At a later point the music loses all momentum, coming to a virtual halt; quietly the 'wailing' motif reappears, ethereally scored. It is a useful landmark warning us that the recapitulation is about to begin. Although Elgar accepts the convention willingly enough, he finds plenty new to say; after the unmistakable re-entry of the rhythm shown on page 223 on horns and trumpets we should stand by for the extensive coda. We can hardly miss the imposing gateway that leads to it — three downward steps on bass trombone and tuba followed by a dramatic rising arpeggio in the violins.

The opening theme of the movement makes a ghostly appearance played by the back desks only of the strings while the 'wailing' motif provides a tender counterpoint. As the texture thickens again the opening phrase becomes more prominent until it appears radiant in the strings and wind. The gangling figure Ex. 3 crops up briefly but fails to establish any authority. Inevitably we sense that the movement is nearing its close as the tempo grows more and more relaxed. The end, when it comes, is almost inaudible, just two clarinets and a hushed pizzicato note from cellos and basses.

The second movement is a brilliant scherzo in which Elgar's earlier skills as a violinist stood him in good stead since the violin parts are superbly written to show the instruments' agility to the greatest advantage. After four introductory bars the first violins begin a sort of *moto perpetuo* figure which, though extremely quiet, fairly crackles with energy. The woodwind interpolate a less excitable phrase as the violins seem to pause momentarily as if to take breath. Soon the strings set up a more aggressive pattern which is skilfully divided between them. The wind, abetted by muted trumpets, respond to the challenge. Then violas and clarinets introduce a firmer footed idea beginning with the same note repeated three times. There is a vaguely martial feel to this, a brisk march for light cavalry rather than plodding infantry. The sound increases layer by layer until the high trumpets provide a fitting climax. The aggressive string pattern begins again, this time with horns giving a hard edge to the overall shape. The advent of the full orchestra plus a clash of cymbals heralds a new theme descending by thirds from a top A; it is a striking anticipation of an important theme in the violin concerto which

Elgar was to write two years later.[6] Strongly rhythmical chords from the full orchestra bring us back to the opening *moto perpetuo*, now played by unison strings, a passage that must have brought a smile to Elgar's face as he put it on paper. 'High Jinks' indeed for the cellos particularly!

After this exhibition of virtuosity the music appears to slow down by the simple process of doubling the value of notes. Flutes change the mood completely with a cheeky but casual little tune which is the equivalent of the Trio in a classical Scherzo. Clarinets (in thirds) offer a companion theme which has a touch of Dvořák about it. The violins find it irresistible; so do we all when it turns out to make a perfect counterpoint to the bustling *moto perpetuo*, now in violas and cellos only while the flutes whistle away cheerfully far above. For some time Elgar rings the changes on by now familiar themes, alternating the march with bustling semiquavers or even combining the two. The cheeky theme appears in full military uniform only to be displaced by a fairy troop. At last fatigue seems to set in as the semiquavers of the *moto perpetuo* are turned into triplets and then into crotchets. (Flutes and oboes in unison far below a sustained violin chord.) Gradually the music disintegrates until nothing is left but a quietly sustained F sharp in violins and violas.

Without a break Elgar leads us into the ensuing Adagio, a slow movement of which Richter said, 'ah, this is a *real* Adagio — such an Adagio as Beethoven would 'ave writ'.[7] And here we must pause for a moment to appreciate the amazing ingenuity Elgar shows. First let us take a look at the *moto perpetuo* from the scherzo, remembering that it should be played as fast as possible.

Ex. 4

Ex. 4a on page 230 shows the beginning of the Adagio; close comparison reveals that the actual notes are identical even though the outline is heavily disguised by the change in note-values. Elgar himself makes the point clear a few bars later when half of the second violins and violas are given Ex. 4 to play in equal semiquavers, although of course at the much slower tempo. Meanwhile the first violin part has developed into an impassioned melody of Mahlerian intensity. One of the most interesting things about this sublime

[6]See Ex. Ia on page (232).
[7]See W.H. Reed, *Elgar* (J.M. Dent, 1939).

Ex. 4a

movement is the contrast between long sustained melodic lines and tiny wisps of phrases. The influence of bird-song is apparent and despite the difference of idiom it seems to have much in common with Dvořák in its evocation of nature's beauty. Two solemn chords on trombones with a mutter from the timpani announce a soaring melody which has descending scales as a counterpoint. Notice also the extravagantly ornamented dialogue between clarinet and solo violin. Further reference is made to the opening theme before a coda of exquisite tenderness introduces yet another theme in this richly endowed movement. In the very closing bars there is a stroke of genius in the orchestration when muted trombones, timpani and harp are mingled together in the softest possible blend. The little triplet figure with which they interrupt the strings' elegy looks like a fatal miscalculation, but Elgar's touch is absolutely sure and the effect works to perfection.

A sudden blast of sound would have been too cruel a way of breaking the spell of this remarkable movement. Elgar tactfully begins his finale with a slow introduction whose opening bar should be barely audible. Bass clarinet and cellos seem to lift a curtain revealing a darkened stage. (Their notes incorporate the first bar of Ex. 3). Bassoons and pizzicato cellos present a ghost of a theme, all bones and no flesh. Faintly we hear a memory of the opening theme of the symphony, so faint indeed that it seems in danger of being blown away by a sudden flurry of notes from flute, harp and bassoon. Trombones take up the spectral march; the strings give a more forceful reminder of Ex. 3; there is another abortive attempt to introduce the opening theme. The music seems to be in a limbo, uncertain of its direction. After a moment's silence the solution is found; a rushing scale pitches us into the finale proper with a theme whose obsessional insistence on one rhythm (♩ ♪) is a stern corrective to the deliberately amorphous introduction. (The constant repetition of one rhythm is so characteristic of Elgar that it seems presumptuous to call it a weakness; we shall find it again in the finale of the Second Symphony and in the first movement of the Cello Concerto. Whereas repeated rhythms are acceptable as an accompaniment — as in Holst's 'Mars' — they become dangerous when they occur in the actual theme.) The dotted-crotchet-quaver pattern continues unbroken for twenty bars, forty times in all, so that when the music does break out one has a sense of escape to freedom. After some further developments the 'spectral march' from the introduction appears, crisply confident and building swiftly to a climax. The obsessional rhythm returns for another eighteen bars before the horns start a game of 'Hunt-the-march' that spreads through the brass in thrilling style. After some time the excitement dies down and once more the back desks of the strings give us a distant reminder of the opening theme, slightly altered. It has a wonderfully soothing effect on the 'march' which is promptly converted into a lyrical melody by the violins. Violas and cellos follow in imitation while the harps provide a rippling accompaniment. This new treatment is developed at some length leading to a fine climax.

The obsessional rhythm returns but with added interest in the shape of a sustained line in the horns. More excitement is whipped up with the march theme, urged on by fanfares from horns and trombones. As a final apotheosis the opening theme returns in glory, the surrounding arpeggios seeming like banners dipping in salute. It is a fitting climax to a work of the grandest stature, the first great symphony ever to have been written by an Englishman.

Concerto for Violin and Orchestra
Op. 61
(1910)
'AQUÍ ESTÁ ENCERRADA EL ALMA DE . . . . .'

This brief Spanish quotation, 'Here is enshrined the soul of . . . .', is inscribed on the dedicatory page of the concerto. It is a second Enigma that has caused much speculation. The five dots would seem to have some significance and it is unfortunate that the two most likely candidates to occupy the space both have names with five letters in: Alice and Helen. At one time Elgar wrote to a friend of whom he was particularly fond, Alice Stuart-Wortley, and told her that she was the one whose soul was enshrined in this intensely romantic work. But towards the end of his life, after his wife had died, Elgar confided to his close friend Ivor Atkins that the concerto had been inspired by Helen

Weaver, the girl to whom he had been briefly engaged in his mid-twenties.[8] White lies are a convenient way of concealing painful truths; men in their fifties are only too likely to have nostalgic memories of early romances. It seems quite probable to me that with his wife still alive — and his devotion to her is not in doubt — Elgar might well have used a harmless affection for Alice as a cover to hide a more profound feeling he had experienced nearly thirty years earlier. The cadenza in the third movement, a unique feature of the concerto, is a profoundly expressive contemplation of past events in a musical sense, a survey of the principal themes steeped in nostalgia. Helen Weaver was an accomplished violinist and I do not find it the least improbable that Elgar's cadenza was a musical symbol of 'If only . . .' There are many crossroads in all our lives and when it comes to affairs of the heart which of us does not at some time contemplate what might have happened if we had chosen an alternative?

Following the great precedents established by Beethoven and Brahms, Elgar begins his concerto with a substantial orchestral exposition, a classical convention which had fallen out of fashion by 1910. Even by Elgar's generous standards the first movement is unusually rich in material and there are no less than six clearly identifiable themes in the exposition. The 'first subject' group contains four, the 'second subject' a mere two; however, the continuity of the music is such that there is no impression of bittiness while subtle relationships between some of the themes help to preserve unity.

The opening phrase has an easily recognisable contour but it is worth noting that nowhere in the entire work does the solo violinist play these actual notes.

The two-bar phrase is immediately repeated in a slightly modified version, more powerfully orchestrated. Its first subsidiary (Ia) follows at once, its descending pattern mirrored by a comparable ascending shape in the bass.

[8]See Enigma Variations, Variation XIII.

Again there is a slightly modified repetition before the announcement of (Ib) whose initial rising semitone (F♯–G) shows at least that it is a member of the same family.

Since this phrase is only a single bar it merits a four-fold repetition to balance the preceding patterns, but whether by modulation or by ornamentation each repetition introduces some variation. The entrance of the fourth theme (Ic) brings a change of mood. Although the melodic line continues to be lyrical there is a slightly sinister counterpoint on horns while a timpani roll adds a further touch of menace.

This is the first of these four themes to be developed at some length, sixteen bars in all. A slight *allargando* (broadening) makes room for the true Second Subject (II).

This too is considerably extended, the initial rising phrase being common to every variant; then, as though saying 'I've indulged myself long enough', Elgar quickens the pace and introduces the sixth theme (IIa), its rhythm strongly marked.

Another roll on the timpani accompanies the return of Ic, its two elements changing places so that the 'sinister' horn counterpoint now appears on top on violins and oboes. Waspish trills and swift ascending scales heighten the tension, summoning the trombones to make an impressive appearance. Theme I reappears in a more agitated mood and builds to a climax notable for some sensational writing for the horns. Ia makes its strongest effect yet, the rising bass reinforced by a tuba. Suddenly calm, the violins repeat Theme I, awaiting a reply. It comes from the soloist who, in a notably original entry, finishes off the orchestral phrase, bringing it to rest on a darkly coloured chord of B minor.

Although Elgar had been a professional violinist at the start of his career, it is likely that in his fifties his playing skills had considerably deteriorated. He therefore turned for practical help to W.H. Reed, a fine player who was for many years leader of the London Symphony Orchestra. In a very fascinating essay about the early birth-pangs of this work Reed describes the genuine delight that the novel entry of the soloist gave to the composer.[9]

Elgar was always very lavish with his printed instructions to performers and there is hardly a bar in this work that does not have a *crescendo* or *diminuendo*, a *tenuto* on one vital note, a change of tempo or any one of the wide range of dynamics between *ppp* and *fff*. There are six indications of tempo changes in the first nine bars of the solo part, showing that while Elgar wanted the soloist to adopt an improvisatory style of playing, the improvisation should be strictly according to Elgar rather than a matter of personal caprice.

Having rounded off the orchestral tutti in so satisfying a manner the soloist begins a quiet rumination beneath which the violas offer a tender reminder of the opening theme — a touchingly beautiful 'Lest we forget'. Soon the soloist arouses himself from this trance-like state and launches into a powerful statement of Ia, joining it seamlessly to Ic. This is developed quite extensively by soloist and orchestra with increasingly elaborate ornamentation in the solo part. Displaced from its original position, Ib now comes to the fore, exciting a somewhat breathless and agitated response from the soloist, not to mention a figure that is borrowed from the 'Introduction and Allegro'. The solo part grows increasingly athletic with wide sweeping scales covering two octaves or more. At last a fleeting reference to IIa brings a release and with touching simplicity the solo violin presents us with the second subject, shorn even of the dotted rhythm. The melody, seeming like a folk-song in its total lack of pretentiousness, is extended in a passage of notable beauty which, rather surprisingly, brings the Exposition to an end.

A sighing recollection of Theme I from the violins signals the start of the Development which soon involves a new theme. Accompanied by restless syncopations on horns and a quiet rumble from the timpani, it strides purposefully through wide-spaced intervals. The orchestral violins will have none of it and offer instead a neatly contracted version of Theme I.

[9]Reprinted in *An Elgar Companion*, pp. 251–7 (Sequoia, 1982).

This proves to be very productive and leads to the first open display of virtuosity from the soloist, rapid and aggressive chords that were revised several times before appearing in their final spectacular form. Having arrived at last on an altitudinous top C sharp, the soloist has a dazzling chromatic descent beneath which oboes and clarinets make four frustrated attempts to reintroduce Ic. It is the cue for an extensive orchestral tutti which effectively reduces the soloist to silence for a while. This centrepiece treats the material more dramatically than has been the case so far. First there is a full orchestral version of Ic; next a complete transformation of the tender second subject. Having put it into the minor with majestic new harmonies, Elgar extends it upwards on unison horns and clarinets while the violins have a turbulent passage in triplets which even continues as fragments of Theme I pass by in the woodwind. The music broadens as the first phrase of II is built into a four-fold sequence which spills over into more brilliant triplets in unison strings, harried by off-beat chords in brass and wind. The effect is almost overwhelming and one wonders how the voice of a single violin will make itself heard against such a volume of sound. Needless to say Elgar has things under control and the reappearance of Theme I in the violins has the necessary calming influence. The soloist takes over the pattern of the first three notes of I turning it into a descending sequence. A beautifully free improvisatory passage now begins while the orchestra offer expressive reminders of II. The soloist finishes his extempore style by returning to Ic in a substantially slower tempo. As the speed quickens again clarinet and violin engage in a dialogue while a restless figure like a sudden gust of wind surges through the strings. We are now in a recapitulation of sorts in which we find many recognisable features — a reworking of Ib and, in due course, a more passionate version of II. Passionate though it may be, it ends with a phrase of touching simplicity.

A soft timpani roll and the sudden menace of trombones brings an agitated reaction from the soloist with Ic and soon we sense that the pace is increasing as Elgar sees the final cadence ahead. The writing for the soloist grows ever more brilliant until we reach a suggestion of a cadenza. It is an indulgence Elgar denies himself, saving it for the last movement. A quick sprint for home brings the movement to an end.

The slow movement begins with an unaffected tune of great simplicity, its smooth flow interrupted in the second and fourth bars by curiously static chords from the woodwind. After a mere eight bars the solo violin enters not with the melody but with an independent inner part; it is a surprise as ingenious as the initial entry in the first movement. As the phrase shifts into the minor the soloist joins the orchestral violins briefly, only to leave them in a wonderfully ethereal ascent to the topmost register of the instrument. A new theme appears in the strings, mystical and reverent. This too comes to a halt on a sustained chord of E major. (Note how subtly Elgar darkens the harmony by dividing his cellos and adding a discreet roll on the timpani.) Over this chord the soloist offers a phrase of profound beauty that rises and falls again like a sigh. The strings disregard it, repeating their previous phrase a little tentatively. The soloist is not to be denied, however, and extends the sighing phrase into a melody of great warmth accompanied at one point by trombones, a blend of sheer genius on Elgar's part. This arouses a passionate outburst from the orchestra, positively Wagnerian in intensity, to which the soloist adds a searing comment.

A brief reminder of the opening theme serves to cool the passions. A capricious element now enters into the solo violin part as the music eddies to and fro. The orchestra is anxious to stress the importance of their secondary theme (to which the soloist adds a deeply expressive extension), but soon the capricious figures begin their tantalising dance again. A restoration of order comes from the horns and once more the secondary theme reasserts itself, freely decorated by the soloist. There is a particularly poignant episode in B flat minor in which a solo horn reiterates a mournful falling sixth, but in time the opening theme returns.

Although the movement appears to be loosely constructed, one may regard this as a recapitulation. From here to the end the music is unashamedly lyrical. The capricious element is banished; every phrase is profoundly expressive. Indeed it is hard to think of a single slow movement which can rival it in its exploitation of the violin as a 'singing' instrument.

From a purely formal point of view the finale is the most original of the three movements. Basically it is in a loosely constructed sonata-form but room is made for a substantial quotation from the slow movement before the remarkable cadenza which surveys material from the whole concerto.

We hardly have time to hear a soft rustle on the strings before the soloist starts a swiftly spiralling climb up the arpeggio of B minor. (After the unorthodox B flat major of the slow movement it is important to restore the 'proper' tonality.) From the outset it is clear that this movement is aiming to exploit technical virtuosity to a greater degree than its predecessors. The first significant theme does not appear until the twenty-eighth bar when the orchestra, determined 'to get a phrase in edgeways' against the soloist's perpetual chatter, interrupt the flow with this very positive statement (I).

Instantly it is taken over by the soloist who then reverts to the bustling semiquavers to provide a nimble variation. The orchestra restates the theme even more firmly but the soloist playfully rejects it, preferring to play 'catch-me-if-you-can' with clarinet or flute. Tiring of the game, he allows the orchestra to introduce a fine new theme which was briefly suggested earlier but disregarded.

This is treated majestically with some counterpoint from the brass but the soloist remains unimpressed by its seriousness, responding with sparkling scales and a positively flirtatious little phrase in elegant double-stopping. Having toyed with us in this enchanting and very feminine manner Elgar now introduces the second subject, a tune easily identified by the three repetitions of its first note. The orchestra gives a rather melancholy tinge to this tune but the soloist refuses to be downcast and embarks on some delightful variations. For a moment the 'flirtatious' phrase aspires to the grandeur of Brahms, only to become even more enchantingly capricious.

The initial spiralling arpeggios return, indicating the start of the development. The material follows very similar lines to the exposition, one significant difference being a powerful version of I played by the violin alone in three-note chords (triple-stopping). As before the orchestra has a brief but impressive tutti based on II; as before the second subject is introduced by the soloist, though this time the orchestra is allowed to relish it to the full.

The next significant landmark is signalled by a sequence of trills in the violin part culminating on a high sustained F sharp. Richly harmonised, the orchestra brings back the second main subject of the slow movement, inspiring the soloist to rhapsody. Just as the emotion seems about to become overwhelming there is a sudden scurry in the strings as though Elgar was sweeping away all thoughts of romance. The soloist produces a bold version of I above the rushing strings followed by a sequence of trills which brings back a brief reference to II. This is soon extended by the orchestra and unexpectedly scaled down until it is reduced to little more than a sigh. We are at the threshold of the cadenza which, far from being a firework display, is profoundly expressive. It begins with a touch of sheer magic, a ghostly reminder of Theme I from the first movement, just six notes. The soloist has a different recollection and with infinite tenderness suggests Ic (see page 233), extending it lovingly. Suddenly we hear a completely new sound, never used by any composer before; it is a harmony sustained by a soft thrumming as violins and violas play their instruments guitar-style. Against this mysterious background the violin wafts arpeggios upwards, lingering time and again on the falling third E–C♮. Once this wonderful meditation on Ic is ended it is the turn of the second subject from the opening movement. The mere reminiscence is enough to start an ornate extemporisation which alternates swift flights of notes with impassioned double-stopping. Virtually the whole time there is some orchestral support, usually a murmur but occasionally moved to share moments of exceptional intensity. Only towards the end of this unique section is the violinist left to muse alone. A soft trill beckons the strings back with a whispered reminder of the slow movement's secondary theme which seems to merge naturally into the comparable theme from the first movement. Then, with greatly intensified emotion, the orchestra again recalls Theme I from the first movement to which the soloist this time gives the logical response.

The rustle from the strings and the spiralling arpeggios bring us out of the dream and the final coda begins. Here too Elgar has a surprise for us for the tender second theme from the slow movement, so emotionally treated in the cadenza, is transformed into a broad singing melody that strides out energetically. The orchestra also gives us a stirring version of the rather neglected second subject of the finale — the theme beginning with the same note thrice repeated. A sequence of rough-hewn chords on the orchestra marked *strepitoso* (noisily) is cut short by a dramatic roll of drums such as might herald the last and most daring act of a circus acrobat. The soloist obliges with the triple-stopping version of I (see page 236), drawing each chord out to the full. Horns and cellos proclaim a simplified but triumphant version of the very first theme, now translated into the major, as the soloist provides some glorious fanfares to bring the work to a heroic conclusion.

Symphony No. 2 in E Flat
Op. 63

In addition to the conventional title the full score carries the following inscription:

Dedicated to the memory of His late Majesty King Edward VII

At the foot of the page there is a further sentence:

This Symphony, designed early in 1910 to be a loyal tribute, bears its present dedication with the gracious approval of His Majesty the King.
March 16th 1911

On the inside of the fly-leaf there is a brief quotation from Shelley:

Rarely, rarely comest thou, Spirit of Delight!

The death of King Edward VII while Elgar was actually working on the symphony caused the dedication to be modified in this way. The first performance was given on 24 May 1911 and earned the seal of Royal Approval by the award of the coveted Order of Merit the following month. Curiously enough the première was received with less enthusiasm than Elgar had expected and afterwards he remarked to the leader of the orchestra 'What's the matter with them, Billy? They sit there like a lot of stuffed pigs.' It seems that the 'Spirit of Delight' was absent on that occasion, though the relevance of the quotation is characteristically enigmatic; does it greet the arrival of the Spirit or bemoan its absence?

At the end of the score we find the words 'Venice — Tintagel, 1910–11', but it is now known that sketches for the symphony date back to 1903. In December of that year one of Elgar's dearest friends, A.E. Rodewald, died in Liverpool. Hearing of his sudden illness Elgar at once journeyed north but arrived too late. He was distraught by the tragic news and wandered aimlessly through the streets unable to believe that the man who only two months previously had been his genial host in Bettws-y-Coed would never again help him with proofs, never offer valued criticism nor encourage him in his recurrent periods of depression. Unable to face the jouney home, he ended up in a room at the North-Western Hotel where he unashamedly wept. It was almost certainly this personal loss, so deeply felt, that resulted in the 'funeral march' in the Second Symphony, since the score was completed *before* the death of Edward VII.[10] If we relate the Shelley quotation to Elgar's nostalgic recollection of his friendship with Rodewald it makes a great deal more sense than if we try to associate it with the inevitably remote figure of a monarch.

The first movement, *Allegro vivace e nobilmente*, begins with an immensely energetic theme whose frequent syncopations give it an impression of tumbling forward impetuously. Like the overture 'In the South', which he had written some six years previously, it shows the influence of Richard Strauss in the sheer exuberance of the writing — the pagan whoops on the horns for instance which are a striking feature within seconds of the start. It is hard to pick out the most significant themes from the welter of sound with which the symphony begins but it is worth noting Elgar's love of contrary motion; if the violin phrases rise, the bass will tend to fall and vice versa. After more than forty bars of intensely animated music the pace slackens a little as a curiously angular pattern of triplets passes down from violins to violas. A new theme appears which one is tempted to hail as the second subject;

[10]W.H. Reed maintained that the slow movement was written subsequently but early sketches disprove this; it could well be that Elgar rescored the movement in a grander way after the King's death.

however it is extremely unstable harmonically with two shifts of tonality in each bar. (G major to E flat, A flat to the dominant of D minor, G minor to the dominant of E flat — and all in the space of four bars!) It is this wayward refusal to settle down that makes me prefer to call it a bridge passage (a swaying rope bridge . . .) since it seems to be the origin of a much calmer theme for the cellos, the first extended lyrical tune of the symphony. Beginning with a sustained B flat in the high tenor register, it climbes by stages to a top F, although Elgar curbs delusions of operatic grandeur by the restraints of *dolce, delicato* and frequent warnings to make instinctive *crescendi* small. The restless uneasy figures of the 'bridge' disturb this brief period of calm and soon the full orchestra is involved in strongly accented chords marked *Impetuoso* followed by a giddily see-sawing pattern that is whipped on by brilliant triplets in the trumpet parts. The tempo quickens again only to ease back slightly as we reach a huge climax with more conventional battle-calls from the trumpets cutting through the general hubbub.

Some respite is offered with the emergence of some soft harp chords though there is still some uneasiness in the strings. Then, as the agitation dies, quiet string chords drift downwards in a strange ghostly interlude. There are still murmurs of unrest but the effect is nocturnal, veiled in mist through which the occasional swift chromatic run suggests a bird winging its way back to its nest high above. A barely audible rumble from timpani and bass drum adds a touch of menace. Only the cellos seem confident as they spin a golden thread of tone, yet even their theme seems to lack a conventional sense of key. It is not surprising that the first audience was puzzled for this was a very different Elgar from the one who had bewitched them with the violin concerto. That had tunes in abundance, but could this cello theme, surrounded by strangely groping harmonies, be called a *tune*? (Tune or not, it is as well that we should stow it in our memories since it is destined to appear nearly a hundred pages later in the middle of the scherzo.) The drum-beat slows as the ghostly interlude continues until it dies away to nothing but sombre clarinets and bassoons. The strings remove their mutes and a revival begins with a repeated phrase in the lower reaches; it spreads to the wind then to the horns. Within eight bars animated figures from the earlier section of the symphony sweep through the orchestra. The tempo quickens as the music grows more violent; imposing unisons from horns and trombone summon an awe-inspiring climax of extraordinary intensity that leaves us literally gasping. Although we are unlikely to realise it at the time, it is the start of the recapitulation, and after a moment's silence we are pitched into the second full bar of the initial theme, the preceding cataclysm having been a hugely magnified version of the first bar. (Even the prolonged B flats on horns and trombone are a giant extension of the very first notes of the symphony.)

It would be unlike Elgar to give us a literal recapitulation and there are many additional touches even though the basic framework is clearly recognisable. The most noticeable difference is the omission of the 'nocturnal' section. As it is, bell-like harmonics on the harp give us due warning that the coda is imminent. It introduces a sustained tune on the violins that we have not heard before. Its emphasis on flattened sevenths (D flats in an E flat major context) gives it a sense of yearning and for a moment or two we wonder if Elgar will follow in Brahms's footsteps by giving us a twilight ending. But no; the restless rhythms begin to surge again and the final bars flare up like a consuming fire.

The Larghetto which follows is for the most part a very controlled expression of grief. A few introductory bars from the strings set the mood and then flutes, bass clarinet, trumpet and trombone present the main theme with the greatest simplicity. Against this sustained threnody quiet but weighty chords on the second and fourth beats suggest the solemn tread of a funeral procession. (It is by such means that Elgar may have given a public face to private grief diminished by the passing of the years.) Soon the violins take over the melodic interest, bringing their more openly expressive tones to a more elaborate theme. After ten bars the initial theme returns now on horns and trombones alone; but it seems that we catch only a glimpse of the *cortège* at this moment for after one phrase the interest shifts to the woodwind with a gently rocking motif that is like a sad lullaby. ('Come lovely and soothing death . . .')

For the first time the strings are left completely on their own with a new theme beginning with a rising fifth that soon reaches out to become an octave. At first in three parts only and sounding like choral writing rather than orchestral, it soon grows more impassioned, building to a strong *forte* phrase which is echoed almost inaudibly — such an effect as may come naturally in a great cathedral. Suddenly the music seems to be racked by paroxysms of anguish as scales, trills and arpeggios sweep through the string parts while the darker woodwind have a theme that is heavy with grief. Unison horns extend this further until the music spills over in a passionate outburst out of which emerges one of Elgar's noblest tunes. The key, F major, brings release from the wrought-up tension of the preceding pages; it is a passage that rivals 'Nimrod' in its solemn beauty, but unlike 'Nimrod' it finds no reconciliation in the end. Softly oboes and then clarinets bring back the 'sad lullaby' which, by a brief extension, leads into a reprise of the first main theme. Despite the essential simplicity of the tune the texture here is very complex. In the bass we find a constantly reiterated figure in this rhythm ♪ ♫ ♩. Meanwhile divided violins, violas and cellos have dense clusters of harmony, four notes to a beat, over solemn chords for brass and harps reinforced by drums — all off the beat. But the truly inventive ingredient, the touch of genius, is a forlornly wandering oboe part, almost like a sad version of 'Jesu Joy', flowing with complete freedom through the deliberately measured rhythms that surround it.[11] Out of this grave processional comes a

[11]The thought comes that this might by a symbol of Elgar's aimless wandering on that private via dolorosa in 1903.

passionate theme from the violins; we have heard it once before as early as the nineteenth bar, but not with such emotional intensity. The horns seem to give a solemn rebuke to this almost operatic display of grief and the strings, repentant, return to the quiet three-part 'choral' theme. From this point on there is the sort of reprise that is needed in a symphonic movement on this scale. After the anguish comes the noble tune that I compared to 'Nimrod', now in its 'proper' key of E flat. This is no funeral march but a triumphant cry of 'Death where is thy sting, Grave, thy victory?' Even so the movement ends not in glory but in sorrow as the awareness of bereavement strikes a cold chill into the heart.

The third movement is labelled Rondo on the score instead of the more traditional Scherzo. Its components are extremely simple to grasp; the first could be described as a flick of a theme:[12]

Ex. 1

while the second once again employs Elgar's favourite rhythm:

Ex. 2

The first section, which is repeated, is concerned entirely with Ex. 1 and its derivatives. Despite the initial suggestion of Puckish humour there is a frenetic haste about some passages that gives the music a nail-biting intensity and although the raucous appearance of Ex. 2 may seem to suggest the entry of Bottom and his fellow-rustics into a fairy glade, the music is too harshly driven for comedy. Even when this second theme is treated more delicately the constantly shifting tonalities are unsettling, so much so that when the first theme returns on flutes and oboes it is cruelly distorted. After some scampering chromatic runs in the woodwind the violins produce a new theme against

[12]Elgar said that he had heard the phrase from a group of itinerant musicians in the Piazza San Marco in Venice.

a barrage of three-note patterns derived from the very first bar. These and subsequent derivations are very obvious even to the untrained ear since the initial 'flick' is instantly recognisable.

After one particularly energetic passage of hustle and bustle the woodwind propose a change; it is an innocent enough little theme:

Ex. 3

It is not developed in any significant manner but it keeps nudging its way into the score as though determined to stake a place. The strings disregard it entirely as they start on a new episode that has the naiveté of a nursery song. Still the wind persist in their interpolations of Ex. 3 until at last the violins are forced to acknowledge it — once!

In due course, after some stalling in the strings, the rondo theme returns. As it does so, the second violins add a new counterpoint that seems of little importance:

Ex. 4

Gradually it displaces the darting flicks of the rondo, lengthening the span of the phrases. The timpani begin a softly insistent beat, the only warning that we are about to be thrust into a nightmare. Against an extraordinary throbbing pulse Ex. 4 is transformed into the long cello tune from the 'nocturnal' section of the first movement (see page 240). There too it was accompanied by the rumble of drums, but now the beat is relentless. Elgar is said to have had in mind the lines from Tennyson's 'Maud':

> The hoofs of the horses beat,
> Beat into my scalp and my brain.

This theme from the first movement is transferred from the violins to trombones in a passage of astonishing drama. The 'hoof-beats' pound out on the heavy percussion while fragments of the rondo theme seem to hurl themselves against this unwelcome invader. One can see why Elgar avoided the word Scherzo, for this is clearly no jest. As the shattering tumult dies down we even hear faint allusions to the drifting string harmonies from the 'nocturne'. At last the music comes to a complete halt on a sustained dissonance from horns and bassoons. Almost tentatively Ex. 2 reappears, as though emerging from hiding. Soon it gains confidence and initiates the semblance of a reprise. What differences there are are self-evident but inevitably the rondo theme regains its eminence towards the end. When Elgar described this work as being 'on a totally different psychological plane from that of the first symphony' he must surely have been thinking of this movement in particular; the central section is the most disturbing passage that he ever wrote. In a letter he wrote to Alice Stuart-Wortley he said, 'I've just put the last notes to the third movement and very wild and headstrong it is . . .'

These are not words one would be likely to apply to the finale which begins with a theme that glides along '*con dignita*', scored darkly for bass clarinet, bassoons, horns and cellos. (The horn-section had some justification for their complaint that it was extremely difficult to play, though the modern instruments of today's orchestras ease the problem somewhat.) Once more Elgar lays himself open to the criticism of sticking closely to one rhythm; it may be that since the symphony was completed in Tintagel the music was inspired by the tireless sweep of the waves. The secondary theme that follows has a more energetic spring to it, leaping through a fifth, a sixth and then an octave before falling back again. It has the most unusual instruction '*ff ma dolce*' (very loud but sweetly). By this time Elgar had written his three oratorios as well as such early choral works as 'King Olaf' and 'Caractacus'. I only mention this because his treatment of this new theme tends to follow the precepts of traditional choral practice with a first entry on tenors, then altos, sopranos and so on. In other words although it is certainly not a fugue, it follows a fugal concept. It builds to a fine climax emphasised by a splendid ascent in the trombones and a brilliant martial figure in trumpets and horns. A gradual broadening leads to the true second subject, a fine expansive tune which fully deserves Elgar's often used instruction '*Nobilmente*'. It runs its full course without interruption until, having come to a peaceful cadence, the cellos give us a brief reminder of the opening theme.

It is a cue for the development to begin. With a complete change of texture Elgar begins an agile treatment of the leaping secondary theme with athletic counter-subjects that remove all suggestions of choral music. The music makes increasing demands on the virtuosity of the players, the string parts being especially brilliant. At the climax the trombones (abetted by timpani) present an abrupt staccato version of the opening theme that quite changes its character, an act of aggression which the strings soon do their best to mollify. Just to show it can be done Elgar then combines the smoothly rolling first theme with its leaping subsidiary, although as a symbol of reconciliation both are now hushed.

A new theme now appears (III) starting high on the violins and falling by intervals of a fifth and a fourth through just over two octaves. It proves to be an effective new counterpoint to the first theme and the two are worked together for some time. (Do not miss a demanding pizzicato passage for the cellos which must lead to sore fingers at any lengthy rehearsal.)

The recapitulation in this relatively conventional movement is easily recognised although the participation of III gives it the appearance of novelty. Anyone who has absorbed the material of the exposition should have no difficulty in appreciating the reappearance of now familiar themes. As one would expect, the '*Nobilmente*' subject is re-stated majestically, after which an even bigger climax suggests that the symphony is heading for a triumphant conclusion. Surprisingly the flames flicker and die. A quiet drum-roll and the re-emergence of the first theme signal the beginning of an unexpectedly tranquil coda to which the harps lend a golden sheen. The tempo slows as though indeed all passion is spent. Elgar was steeped in Shakespeare, and the Duke's lines — 'That strain again! It had a dying fall' — would suit these closing pages admirably. Only one concession is made to convention, a fortissimo chord for full orchestra that seems to court applause. But then 'too vulgar' thinks Elgar and marks a long diminuendo until only strings and a few woodwind are left fading to silence.

Concerto for Violoncello and Orchestra Op. 85

Despite its impressive opening phrase I doubt if in the whole repertoire of concertos there is one so reticent, so essentially introverted as this. It was written in the aftermath of four devastating years of war during which Elgar had of necessity composed various patriotic works such as *The Spirit of England* and a set of songs to Kipling's words called *The Fringes of the Fleet*. These were performed with scenery and action at the London Coliseum until Kipling for some obscure reason withdrew permission for his poems to be used. The composer, now in his sixties, was growing weary and retreated to a cottage called Brinkwells in a beautiful part of Sussex. As though reflecting his wish to escape from public life, from rousing patriotic concerts and from the constant reminders of the huge death toll across the water, he began to write chamber music — a violin sonata, a string quartet and a piano quintet. These works represent a huge reaction from the orchestral splendours of the symphonies; they are intimate and restrained, the private thoughts of a man in his sixties who sensed perhaps that his creative fire was on the wane.

These same qualities prevail in the cello concerto which he actually began in the last month of the war. The first performance was given a year later on 27 October, 1919. The audience was in the mood for something more spectacular and only those who knew Elgar well fully appreciated the work's unique character. Even Donald Tovey, normally the most perceptive of writers, stresses its humour rather than its pathos, drawing the dangerous analogy of 'slipping on a banana-skin' as he describes a passage in the last movement.

The work begins with an arresting declamatory passage for solo cello which the woodwind make an abortive attempt to copy, quickly suppressed by a 'Hush' from the strings. The initial recitative continues with an expressive ascent whose final note dissolves almost imperceptibly into a gently meandering theme for the violas, completely unaccompanied. Here surely is a symbol of Elgar wandering alone through the Sussex woodland thinking of the numerous friends who had met a painful and frightening death in the endless massacres that had turned France into a human slaughterhouse. Most unusually for Elgar the music is almost devoid of expression marks as though true feeling must be kept behind a mask. (The time for weeping comes at the end of the work.) The soloist takes over the orchestral phrase as discreetly and unostentatiously as a couple, long-married, might link hands wordlessly as they stroll along a favourite path. Richer harmonic support from the orchestra brings greater intensity of tone from the soloist who, with a magnificent ascending scale summons a brief majestic tutti. It lasts for a mere six bars, too massive for a theme of such intimacy. The soloist resumes as before and then, with the utmost simplicity, brings the phrase to rest with two pizzicato notes and a final sustained low E.

Clarinets and bassoons now introduce a pastoral phrase that is not so much a dance as a recollection of one. It is a memory the soloist seems to share, a memory tinged with sorrow for days that can never be recaptured. The orchestral participation is tactful and sympathetic but if we listen to the cellos and basses we can hear the suggestion of a salon orchestra in this strangely haunted ballroom, full of memories though the furnishings are bare. The cello part grows more passionate but elicits no response. The vision fades and the wandering theme resumes its leisurely pace. The ascending scale — the one concession to virtuosity in the whole movement — again rouses the orchestra to a show of strength but it is even shorter-lived and almost before we are aware of it the movement has died away to a single held note in the bass.

Three plucked chords from the cello remind us of the opening recitative; they are cut off by a dramatic orchestral gesture. A strange miniature cadenza follows, as though the soloist is searching for a suitable theme for a scherzo. A restless little fragment is tried and then rejected with two pizzicato chords —

tried again, and again rejected. Yet again we find this curious indecision; then, as though in exasperation at this mental block the pizzicato chords are wrenched aggressively into a brisk ascent culminating in an extraordinary cry of anguish (now 'bowed') as though the very idea of writing a happy-happy scherzo is more than can be endured. Two more tentative attempts are made before the movement at last gets under way.

It proves to be a strange sort of scherzo, a will-o'-the-wisp movement that flits and darts like a dragon-fly. The orchestral part is minimal, only occasionally chasing after the soloist in imitation of some especially notable flight. Only one phrase seems to have real flesh on it, a characteristically Elgarian theme that is at once endorsed with healthy enthusiasm by the orchestra. (It is their first *forte* in the movement!) Within seconds the cello returns to its *moto perpetuo* style of playing. Indeed there are only two elements in this movement, the dragon-fly motif and the brief Elgarian phrase; even that is never allowed to develop at any length and the movement ends its hovering flight by coming to land most elegantly.

The slow movement is only four pages long compared to the fourteen of the violin concertos. It is scored for two clarinets, two bassoons, two horns and strings. It has scarcely a *forte* in the orchestral part and little visible contrast. Yet so deeply felt is the emotion that time seems of little consequence; perhaps only the Cavatina from Beethoven's Op. 130 Quartet says so much in so concentrated a form. Eight introductory bars set the mood; then, with the last beat of the eighth bar the main theme begins. Apart from a single bar's rest the cello line remains unbroken for the rest of the movement. One falling phrase needs to be stored in the memory so that we may better appreciate its return towards the end of the concerto. Otherwise all we have to do is to surrender to this sublime meditation.

The orchestra begin the finale purposefully with a brisk march rhythm but the soloist declines to share their mood and turns their crisp little theme into a declamation. A brief cadenza ensues, culminating in a brilliant rush into the extreme upper register. Having thus established total dominance, the soloist sets the march going at a slightly steadier pace. The strong accents on the second beat of every alternate bar give the music a splendid forward thrust and the wind and brass welcome the chance to show a bit of muscle after their long silence. For a moment or two we are in a mood of Pomp and Circumstance but the cellist, as if saying 'we've done with marching now' takes a capricious turn and introduces a more lyrical theme with a delightfully skittish tail. Elgar develops this in a series of sequential repetitions which, in due course, are treated as material for variations in a continuous pattern of semiquavers. The orchestral accompaniment is kept very light so that every note of the solo part can be heard. At last the soloist tires and has a charming 'sit-down-and-rest' phrase on descending minims. 'You take over' he seems to say, and the wind do so with the little march theme. Gaining confidence, it begins to spread through the orchestra until a rocking arpeggio figure from the soloist magically transforms the march into a light-footed dance. It is the happiest moment of the whole concerto, a symbolic emergence from the rigours of war.

There is a tiny gap after three stamping chords and then the cello resumes the first theme in a recapitulation of sorts. Again the orchestra is given the chance to show its full strength — rare in this work, and again the cellist resorts to caprice to change the mood. But a sustained timpani roll, the first in the movement, casts a sudden shadow and all the spring suddenly goes out of the music. Five repeated C sharps plucked on the double basses sound like a funeral drum. Strings and soloists together share a phrase of heart-breaking poignancy as though Elgar was questioning the propriety of writing cheerful music when so many millions had died in the mud and filth of Flanders. The ensuing lament is one of the most profoundly expressive passages in the cello repertoire, the more so when a quotation from the slow movement makes its unforgettable appearance. The cynical might argue that Elgar overplays his hand here by too many repetitions of the wailing chromatic phrases, but the cynical have not experienced the grief that Elgar was expressing for all those whose loved ones had been killed. The last note of this heart-felt lamentation dies away to silence; then, solemn and majestic, the very opening phrase of the concerto reappears. Two explosive chords like gunshots over a grave interrupt its progress, but it continues on its way, even though it is not too fanciful to suggest that the phrase seems to shed tears as it descends to a dramatic low E. As though from a great distance the crisp little march tune begins again, though the soloist is too wrapped in grief to be able to respond to the change of mood. But the rhythm grows more insistent until, almost unwillingly, the cello is forced to join in. It is a coda that seems almost indecently short after so profoundly moving an episode but 'life must go on' it seems to say, even if only to deny Death the added satisfaction of dragging the living into the pit of despair.

CÉSAR FRANCK

1822–90

Franck's talent for music manifested itself at an early age although the family had been noted for producing painters of quality for a number of generations. His father earned his living as a banker but was a keen amateur musician. Every encouragement was given to the young César to develop his innate abilities and he made his first concert tour in his native Belgium when he was still only eleven years old. At fifteen he was admitted to the Paris Conservatoire where after less than a year's study he played the Hummel Piano Concerto in A minor so expertly that he seemed certain to gain the first prize. However there was also a compulsory sight-reading test. Hoping to impress the examiners Franck read the piece flawlessly while simultaneously transposing it down a third. The jury were astonished except for Cherubini who, jaundiced pedant that he was, claimed that the rules had been broken and that Franck should therefore be failed. Only the vehement protests of the other professors persuaded Cherubini (who had the final say as Director) to agree to make a special award, a *Grand Prix d'Honneur*.

Franck was to become the greatest organist in France but despite his prodigious gifts he was not appreciated by the powerful musical Establishment and for a long time his sole income came from the church and from teaching private pupils. Times were difficult in Paris with the political disturbances of the second revolution and, later, the Franco–Prussian war. Franck would habitually rise at five-thirty in the morning to give himself time to compose before setting out to give the daily round of lessons. Not until he was well into his forties did acknowledgement of his qualities as a composer begin to come. At the age of fifty he was offered the post of organ professor at the Conservatoire where he soon became adored by his pupils and disliked by the staff; his method of teaching was too liberal and too unorthodox to be acceptable to narrow academic minds. His modesty was such that he was incapable of promoting his works yet he continued to compose on an ambitious scale. Only the enthusiasm of his devoted pupils enabled many of his compositions to be performed at all, and when a grudging government finally awarded him the order of Chevalier of the Legion of Honour it was for his abilities as an organist, not as a composer.

In 1887 his pupils organised an entire concert of his works but insufficient rehearsal and Franck's inexperience as a conductor prevented it from being a success. He was not to receive a real public ovation until 1889 when his String Quartet was performed at a concert of the *Société Nationale de Musique* which, incidentally, Franck himself had founded some years previously. The persistent calls for the composer at last persuaded him to take a bow. The next day the sixty-eight year old Franck said to his pupils, 'You see, they are beginning to understand me.' Recognition had indeed come, though cruelly late for the following year he died after months of illness. Although posterity has denied him the status of true greatness, a certain number of his works have retained their place in the repertoire. Of these the violin sonata, the piano quintet and the Symphonic Variations show him at his best, while his bequest to organists is considerable. Liszt declared that Franck could have had no equal as an improviser since Bach himself and it is our loss that recording had not been perfected in his time so that his inspired improvisations could have been preserved for later generations to marvel at.

Symphonic Variations for Piano and Orchestra

The Variations, which are played without a break, are based on three themes, two of which are heard in the initial dialogue between the orchestra and soloist. The conception of the opening is remarkably similar to the slow movement of Beethoven's Fourth Piano Concerto, a resemblance of which Franck must surely have been aware; since Beethoven's mould is soon broken, the point is not worth labouring. It is enough to say that the opposition between aggressive strings and conciliatory piano simplifies the listener's task since the two themes are so different in character that they cannot be confused. Here then are themes I and II.

Notice that the strings have a *diminuendo* in their first phrase, a concession that Beethoven certainly does not allow in his G major concerto.

The dialogue is repeated at a higher pitch after which the orchestra, subdued but obdurate, continue to develop their theme, the offbeat chords above emphasising the gradual increase in tension. Meanwhile the piano intervenes with romantically expressive phrases designed to avert any more open conflict. The orchestra remains unmoved by the piano's protestations and in time the dotted rhythm of Theme I becomes powerful enough to persuade the pianist to accept it as well; however the alternate phrases still express argument rather than agreement. The sudden flare-up soon subsides and after a rippling arpeggio from the piano we meet Theme III. Its first presentation is not all that encouraging; woodwind and pizzicato strings present it rather drily over a quiet drum-roll.

A brief linking passage from the piano brings us to Variation I. It is for piano alone and is an extension of Theme II, more lyrical, more impassioned and accompanied by a figure in the left hand that is a Franck hallmark.

At their next entry the cellos and basses continue to grumble away about Theme I. The piano's renewed attempts to calm their irritation come to nothing and the orchestral part builds to a considerable climax. The dispute between soloist and orchestra is renewed but it is a contest which the piano easily wins. A brief orchestral link offers several hints that it's time to give more serious consideration to Theme III. So begins Variation II, in a far more expressive version than the one shown in the above example. It is a theme with many silences in it, silences which are soon to be filled in the delightful second part of the variation. For the first time pianist and orchestra are reconciled and in an enchanting dialogue they share the theme turn and turn about.

Another variation follows at once with violas and cellos turning Theme III into a fully sustained melody while the pianist is given a delicate accompaniment of 'raindrop' chords. No sooner is this section ended than another variation begins. It involves quite wide skips in the piano part which centre round reiterated C sharps — the dominant of F sharp minor. With the increased participation of the orchestra this becomes much more resolute, leading into a powerful new variation in which the melodic shape of III is combined with the rhythmic drive of I. Were it not in 3/4 time one would think of it as a march; certainly it is 'heroic' in concept, developing into quite a menacing storm. However this is not a work in which the pianist readily accepts the role of hero-figure and an extension of this variation soon follows with the strings quietly continuing the 'march' version of I-plus-III while the pianist has a sort of 'skater's waltz', with dancing triplets and bell-like upper notes. Gradually the music slows down for the two central variations which structurally serve the purpose of a slow movement.

At a much slower tempo the pianist begins a softly rippling figure in F sharp major. Tempting though it is to give all our attention to this dreamy nocturnal music, the heart of the matter lies in the cellos who are given a beautiful variant of III, dark in tone and deeply expressive. The second half of the variation is shared by the woodwind and occasional pizzicato chords from the strings though the piano figuration remains constant throughout.

A return to F sharp minor reduces the pianist to a purely accompanying role whose harp–like figures give the cellists sympathetic support in the next variation. Here the material is taken from II, now extended and converted into a profound sigh. Muted strings provide a hazy background which modulates through several keys before finally coming to rest on a wide-spaced chord of C sharp major. A subtly disguised chromatic scale enables the pianist to escape from the hypnotic arpeggio figures which have persisted throughout the variation. A trill rouses the woodwind from their slumber with dancing crotchets that are derived from III, while the lower strings offer a far more cheerful version of II, its angular intervals smoothed out, all sadness banished.

Infected by the new mood, the pianist joins the woodwind with a happy clatter of chords before embarking on a free episode in which the left hand figuration from Variation I plays a vigorous part. Three bars of piano solo prepare the way for the next variation, a carefree treatment of I whose nimble athleticism is a sheer delight. The orchestra takes over for a few bars in much rougher fashion, but the pianist woos them with a new tune in which the two hands move in parallel chords. Down in the orchestral bass there is a cleverly sketched version of III. A brief orchestral tutti produces yet another treatment of II, sinister and exciting. It breaks off abruptly having built to a dramatic peak.

As if in gentle rebuke, the pianist now has an extended episode of a lyrical character loosely derived from I. Although it isn't at all dramatic it has an intriguing rhythm in which the right hand is playing in 6/4 while the left hand is in 4/4. It gives a slight unease to an otherwise conciliatory passage.

The entry of a flute with the cheerful dancing version of II is enough to produce a change to a more frivolous mood. The rhythmic ambiguity of the piano part is resolved into a nimble waltz which fairly flies over the keys. In due course there is an easily recognised reprise of two of the more joyous variations and the work ends with Theme II transformed into a peal of bells. Apart from its purely musical qualities this work shows Franck at his best since although the craftsmanship is brilliant, three concise themes being all that he requires, there is throughout a feeling of spontaneity so that one imagines that each variation was improvised on the spot rather than being the product of purely intellectual decision.

GRIEG
1843–1907

Grieg inherited his musical talent from his mother who, although not a fully professional musician, was sufficiently gifted to play in concerts in Bergen. She began to give piano lessons to young Edvard when he was still only six; his natural tendency was to improvise in a rather formless way, searching for beautiful and exotic chords. He once wrote that his happiness at discovering a dominant ninth (CEGB♭D) knew no bounds. Hearing him dreaming away at the piano his mother would come in and reprimand him, redirecting his thoughts towards more systematic study of the pieces he was supposed to be learning. Since Grieg at the time nursed a childish ambition to be a pastor who could harangue congregations from the pulpit he saw no reason why he should play the piano other than for pleasure. A significant turning-point came when Norway's most famous violinist, the delightfully named Ole Bull, became acquainted with the Grieg family. He it was who took an interest in the fifteen-year old's attempts at composition and urged his parents to send him to Leipzig for proper musical tuition.

It was not an experience which Grieg particularly enjoyed although he did strike up a friendship with a fellow-student from England called Arthur Sullivan. He soon realised that his mother's dilatory approach had caused him to fall far behind the standard required; much though he hated the drudgery of technical exercises and theoretical study he began to work feverishly to make up lost ground. The result was a complete breakdown and a severe attack of pleurisy which left him with one lung permanently impaired.

During the summer of 1864 Grieg spent some time at Ole Bull's country home on the island of Ostery. Although he had an international reputation as a concert violinist, Ole Bull was a true Norwegian at heart and had a profound conviction that the folk-music of Norway should be the proper source of inspiration for any Norwegian composer. This was a welcome philosophy to young Grieg who had been stifled by the conservatism of Leipzig where Chopin and even Schumann were regarded as dangerously 'modern'. To hear the violinist whom he idolised playing folk-songs and dances with such fervent enthusiasm fired Grieg with a determination to find a new path, untainted by the German school. From then on, he decided to concentrate on establishing a specifically Norwegian style of composition. Another young musician called Rikard Nordraak encouraged him still further, and Grieg began to mount his own concerts in various cities, and even founded a Norwegian Academy of Music when he was still only twenty-four. He was married the same year. The following summer, soon after the birth of a baby daughter, Grieg composed the piano concerto. (1868).

A grant from the Norwegian Government enabled Grieg to visit Rome where he met Liszt, at that time the most renowned musician in Europe. It was on a second visit to the Liszt household that the famous episode concerning the piano concerto occurred. Grieg described it vividly in a letter home.

> I had fortunately just received the manuscript of my pianoforte concerto from Leipzig, and took it with me. Beside myself there were present Winding, Sgambati, and a German Lisztite, whose name I do not know, but who goes so far in the aping of his idol that he even wears the gown of an abbé; add to these some young ladies of the kind that would like to eat Liszt, skin, hair, and all, their adulation is simply comical. . . . Winding and I were very anxious to see if he would really play my concerto at sight. I, for my part, considered it impossible; not so Liszt. 'Will you play?' he asked, and I made haste to reply: 'No, I cannot' (you know I have never practised it.) Then Liszt took the manuscript, went to the piano, and said to the assembled guests, with his characteristic smile, 'Very well, then, I will show you that I also cannot.' With that he began. I admit that he took the first part of the concerto too fast, and the beginning consequently sounded helter-skelter; but later on, when I had a chance to indicate the tempo, he played as only he can play. It is significant that he played the cadenza, the most difficult part, best of all. His demeanour is worth any price to see. Not content with playing, he at the same time converses and makes comments, addressing a bright remark now to one, now to another of the assembled guests, nodding significantly to the right or left, particularly when something pleases him. In the adagio, and still more in the finale, he reached a climax both as to his playing and the praise he had to bestow.
>
> A really divine episode I must not forget. Toward the end of the finale the second theme is, as you may remember, repeated in a mighty fortissimo. In the very last measures, when in the first triplets the first tone is changed in the orchestra from G sharp to G, while the piano part, in a mighty scale passage, rushes wildly through the whole reach of the keyboard, he suddenly stopped, rose up to his full height, left the piano, and with big theatric strides and arms uplifted walked across the large cloister hall, at the same time literally roaring the theme. When he got to the G in question he stretched out his arms imperiously and exclaimed: 'G, G, not G sharp! Splendid! Splendid!'

In the event it was a pianist called Edmund Neupert who gave the first performance of the concerto, although it was perhaps ironic in view of Grieg's nationalist feelings that it was given in Danish Copenhagen. Grieg himself soon acquired a very considerable reputation as a pianist and as a conductor and was much admired in England, France and Germany as well as in his homeland. On one of his trips to London a newspaper diarist noted that audiences for his concerts had started to queue at eleven in the morning. If his standing is not so high today as it was in his lifetime it is because his genius failed to develop in the larger musical forms of concerto, symphony or opera; nevertheless the piano concerto has greater claims to originality than it is usually allowed, as a closer look should reveal.

Piano Concerto in A Minor
Op. 16

Since this concerto has suffered from becoming too well-known, it is worth while to place it in its proper context. It was written just over twenty years after the Schumann concerto and fourteen years before the Tchaikovsky. Looked at in this light one can begin to appreciate its genuine originality. Grieg was only twenty-five when he wrote it, and although he had written a symphony while still a student — recently unearthed and recorded — it is extremely unlikely that he had ever heard any of his music played by an orchestra. The fact that he revised the orchestration a number of times in later years gives proof of his insecurity.

After a preliminary drum-roll the piano has a brief cadenza, a fine rhetorical flourish that establishes the tonality of A minor very positively. The woodwind then announce the first subject material which comes as two contrasting ideas, the first crisp and detached, the second smooth and sustained; the strings shadow both of these tunes, only coming to the fore during the repetition of the second stanza. This whole exposition (only twelve bars in all) is then repeated by the piano with relatively little assistance from the orchestra. Suddenly there is a complete change of mood as the pianist launches into a capricious passage that suggests an elfin dance and it is here that Grieg shows an individual idiom that he certainly did not learn in Leipzig. (Without documentary evidence one cannot be certain but it seems very probable that it was passages such as this and the dance-finale that prompted Ibsen to invite Grieg's collaboration in the dramatised version of 'Peer Gynt'.)

A descending scale in chromatic thirds leads to a duet between oboe and piano which, having reached a momentary climax, dissolves into the lyrical second subject. This is given to the cellos[1] with a soft accompaniment from trombones and horns; each short phrase is approved by the woodwind in a charming way. The pianist takes over the melody with slightly Chopinesque decorations, extending it substantially in a rising sequence which increases in passion and intensity until it explodes into an exciting display of octaves in the right hand which, after a rather trite cadenza, leads into an orchestral tutti in C major. This is derived from the very first notes of the piano part though their effect is naturally very different. The cellos and basses have an important response which is an ingenious development of the first subject that takes just its first five notes as a starting point. A big *crescendo* leads to a trumpet fanfare which is very similar to a famous passage in Tchaikovsky's Fourth Symphony, an allegation easily made but which one hastily withdraws on learn-

[1]Liszt advised Grieg to put it on the trumpet!

ing that the Grieg was written nine years earlier. Even so, such passages offended Debussy in his capacity as music critic. He said that he could not understand 'why it should be broken up by martial trumpet-blasts, usually announcing the beginning of nothing more than a languishing little tune'. Grieg would no doubt have replied that the 'trumpet-blasts' give the movement a heroic stature that it would otherwise lack for it is undoubtedly true that in general the movement is more of a lightweight than its dramatic initial gesture would suggest.

Three quiet pizzicato chords lead us into the development which begins with a lyrical treatment of the first part of Theme I from flute and horn in turn. A melancholy version of the second limb of the theme follows, an exchange which is repeated in a different key. Suddenly the brass arouse us with a powerfully different approach to the same theme which elicits a tremendous arpeggio from the pianist covering almost the whole range of the keyboard. It is now the turn of the second part of the theme to be developed in a series of rising sequences. Trombones and wind interrupt with an angry statement of the first bar of the main theme against hammering triplets from trumpets, horns and timpani. Twice the pianist responds to the challenge with double octaves that are derived from the opening cadenza, but the crisis is soon resolved and in a moment we are at the start of the recapitulation, easily recognisable when the soloist takes up the opening theme exactly as before. The development section is therefore quite unusually short, a mere twenty-eight bars, or, if we include the orchestral tutti as well, at most forty-four.

A strict recapitulation follows, only differing by the necessary modulations that bring the second subject into the 'proper' key of A major. A five-bar outburst from the full orchestra heralds the arrival of the cadenza, musically the finest part of the movement. It begins in a freely improvisatory style much indebted to Liszt both in style and harmony; there is then a splendid development of the first theme with wide-spaced arpeggios in the left hand. It reaches a climax with a descending cascade of double octaves followed by a massive treatment of the same theme, its progress interrupted by thunderous rumbles in the bass. A greatly augmented version of the second part of the theme then appears, surrounded by a positive torrent of notes. Gradually the storm subsides and a series of trills finally fades into near silence as the orchestra enter with a most expressive version of the second part of the theme. A short coda rounds off the movement beginning with a seemingly new tune on oboe and bassoon in unison. It is enough to suggest an inversion of the initial cadenza to the pianist who, having made the point quite wittily, brings the movement to a resounding conclusion with a majestic restatement of the opening bars, giving them a finality that would have been quite out of place at the start of the work.

The slow movement is notable for the beauty of the orchestral theme with which it begins. The first phrase, four bars in length, is in D flat major. By a simple process Grieg then repeats it, starting on the second degree of the scale; this effectively transposes it into E flat minor, giving it a markedly more poignant quality. A series of shorter phrases follows, their chromatic harmonies very similar to César Franck in style. Yet all the large-scale works of Franck, the symphony, the quartet, the violin sonata and so on come from a later period and apart from Wagner Grieg should be given credit for being one of the very first composers to use harmony of quite such chromatic richness. Certainly he must have had a considerable influence on Delius.

The entry of the solo piano brings an elaborately decorated alternation of tonic and dominant, naive in harmony but sophisticated in ornamentation. Strong bell-like accents are the most original feature. The whole nine-bar sequence is duly repeated at a higher pitch before flute and clarinet start to remind us of the opening theme. This time the piano adds swathes of colour to the orchestral texture and a substantial *crescendo* leads to a majestic statement of the original theme by the pianist with a skilfully contrived cello part following in its wake a bar later. The second portion of the theme is continued in the orchestra with nicely harmonised comments from the soloist. A brief coda with bird-song trills from the piano brings this essentially lyrical movement to an end.

Without any interruption Grieg begins his finale with a staccato rhythm on clarinets and bassoons that recalls a similar moment in Beethoven's Fourth Concerto, albeit with a very different outcome. An arpeggio shoots rocket-like across the keyboard and sizzles down to earth in a brilliant descent. A strongly rhythmic accompaniment begins in the left hand telling a Norwegian audience that Grieg is going to incorporate a favourite national dance, the *halling*, into the concerto. The pianist develops the theme at some length before the orchestra is permitted to express its rather noisy appreciation.

A new episode in the solo part seems to suggest the entry of a particularly nimble dancer. It is a passage that demands considerable dexterity from the pianist who must feel a certain relief when it gives way to a more sustained tune in crotchets. One of the characteristics of the more energetic type of folk-dance is for individual dancers to take turns in showing off fancy steps of their own devising, the men in particular trying to excel each other in athleticism. This movement suggests such a dance quite vividly since the episodes, short in themselves, follow one another in rapid succession. Next to appear is a very virile theme with a military rhythm; it is announced by three C major chords but quickly subsides as the orchestra takes over the thematic interest. The rhythmic pattern here (three repeated crotchets followed by four semiquavers) is taken directly from the first piano solo though the effect is rather different. Accompanied by fluent arpeggios from the pianist the orchestra builds up a stirring sequence which culminates in a powerful tutti. It is interrupted abruptly by the pianist who is allowed a brief cadenza before restarting the *halling* even more energetically than before. At last the dance ends in a general collapse.

An almost imperceptible shift to F major enables Grieg to change the mood entirely as a solo flute introduces a pastoral melody whose tranquil beauty suggests a lakeside scene at dawn. The shimmering string accompaniment is played *sul ponticello* (the bow very close to the 'bridge') an effect which conveys not just brightness but the icy clarity of sunlight reflected off a glacier. The soloist duly takes up the same theme in an expressive improvisation. A solo cello sustains the bass notes, an ingenious device to aid the relatively weak effect of the sustaining pedal on the pianos of the 1860s.[2] This central section occupies quite a substantial portion of the movement and the theme is destined to reappear in much more heroic guise at the end of the movement.

First, though, we must have a return to the dance. More tactfully than we might expect the woodwind quietly awaken us from our reverie with the tap-tap rhythm. The piano responds and a classic recapitulation follows for some eighty-two bars. At this point the *halling* is transformed into something far more serious with sweeping scales in the orchestra and Lisztian rhetoric from the pianist. An exciting orchestral crescendo leads to a bravura display of double octaves which one can imagine Liszt sight-reading with particular relish. There is a brief silence and then, with a change from 2/4 to 3/4, the final section begins. The tempo is quicker — *quasi presto* — and the dance is changed to another national favourite, the *springdans*. There are definite reminiscences of Schumann here in the sudden shifts of accentuation and in the rapid modulations. As the pianist executes a swift downward scale covering the whole span of the keyboard, trumpets give a ceremonial welcome to the splendid coda, a triumphal version of the central tune, now transformed from the dawn-song of a lark to a patriotic hymn. It was in this section that Liszt hailed the G natural with such enthusiasm; those of us who regard the concerto as altogether too predictable would do well to remember how original it seemed to Grieg's contemporaries, even to one so daringly innovative as Liszt himself.

---

[2]It was reliably reported that Schumann would improvise for an hour at a time without ever changing the pedal.

HAYDN
1732–1809

Although the names of Haydn and Mozart are often loosely coupled together
they could scarcely have led more different lives. Mozart through force of
circumstance was a prodigious traveller from early childhood onwards;
Haydn was most fortunate in his patrons and hardly travelled at all until the
latter part of his life when he enjoyed two hugely successful trips to London.
Mozart died in his mid-thirties, poverty-stricken; Haydn lived to be seventy-
seven and was well provided for for almost the whole of his adult life. Mozart
was a public performer accustomed to the acclaim of audiences in the concert-
hall or the opera-house even though applause did not necessarily bring
adequate financial reward; Haydn mostly performed to small select groups
invited to a princely palace and was quite overwhelmed by the experience of
public concerts in London. But perhaps the most significant difference came
about through Haydn's long attachment as resident musician at the court of
the Esterházy family, for there he had a permanent orchestra at his disposal
with which he could experiment as he liked in matters of orchestration.

Although Haydn had a sound musical education at a choir school he had
none of Mozart's prodigious gifts as a child. Indeed his first adult years were
something of a struggle during which he scraped a precarious living teaching
and playing in small orchestras at aristocratic parties. Not until he was
twenty-six did he find regular employment with a Viennese nobleman,
Count Morzin. He had already developed great fluency as a composer and
had a number of works to his credit including sonatas, concertos, quartets,
church music and even his first essay at opera. The appointment to Count
Morzin's household would not have come unless Haydn had already given
proof of his abilities; but within two years the Count had to cut down his
establishment for financial reasons and Haydn found himself jobless. It was to
prove a most fortunate dismissal for the following year he was engaged by
one of the wealthiest Princes in Europe, Paul Anton Esterházy. He remained
in the service of the family for nearly thirty years during which time he was
required not only to compose but to act as musical director in the Prince's

private chapels and opera theatre. Winters were spent at Eisenstadt, some thirty miles from Vienna, summers at Esterháza in Hungary where Paul Anton's successor, Prince Nicolaus, built a magnificent palace that was rivalled only by Versailles. It was in such protected surroundings that Haydn was able to work without either financial worries or the distractions of a public life. Even so, his works gained recognition in other countries and in 1784 a set of six symphonies was commissioned by a young French aristocrat for performance by the finest Parisian orchestra, *Le Concert de la Loge olympique*. By then Haydn had become one of the most celebrated composers in Europe and his music was frequently performed in Germany and France, though it should be remembered that such performances gathered no royalties. The Paris commission brought an offer of twenty-five *Louis-d'or* for each symphony, a sum which seemed 'un prix colossal' to Haydn who up to then had received no specific payment for the numerous symphonies he had written as a matter of course for his royal patron. However, the most significant commission was to come after the death of Prince Nicolaus in 1790. The new Prince, another Anton, cared little for music and disbanded his orchestra; to Haydn he gave not only his freedom but a generous pension. The gratified composer left Esterháza for Vienna with the prospect of a new, more independent life-style opening before him. News of his availability brought a number of invitations of which the most important was the most informal. One morning, without even a preliminary request for an audience, a German violinist who had established himself as a successful impresario in London arrived at Haydn's apartments. 'I am Salomon of London,' he said; 'I have come to fetch you to England'. With this historic summons came a contract for £1,200 for six symphonies, an opera and twenty lesser compositions. By the standards of the day it was an enormous sum and Haydn willingly accepted.

He bade a tearful farewell to Mozart, with whom he had struck up a warm and admiring friendship. Mozart had of course spent nearly a year in London as a child and asked Haydn how he would manage when he spoke not a word of English. 'My language is understood all over the world' replied the older man. It was a remark justified by events for he was to score a huge success with London audiences. He and Salomon arrived there on 2 January, 1791. Six days later Haydn was writing to a woman friend in Vienna:

> My recent arrival in London caused a great sensation and I was giving newspaper interviews for three days running. Everyone wants to know me. I've dined out six times already, and if I wanted, I could be entertained every day. But I must consider my health first, and also my work. Everything is terribly expensive here. I wish I could fly for a time to Vienna to have more quiet in which to work, for the noise from the streets outside is intolerable.

The first concert of the series Salomon had planned was given early in March; it caused a sensation, earning ecstatic reviews in the newspapers.

Haydn thrived on the unaccustomed adulation he received on every side and was easily persuaded to stay for a second season. In July, 1791, he was given an honorary Doctorate at Oxford; meanwhile he had cultivated wealthy friends with country estates where he could escape from the 'intolerable noise' of the streets and compose in peace. The demand for his music was such that his pen was kept busy providing new works. An added zest to his visit came when he fell in love with a widow, Rebecca Schroeter, whom he would happily have married had he not left a Frau Haydn in Vienna. (His marriage was one of the less successful aspects of his life.) At the end of his two-year stay he had earned as much as would have taken him twelve years in the service of the Esterházys. After returning to Vienna in 1792 he paid a second and equally successful visit to England in 1794. The following year found him back in Austria once again attached to the Esterházy household. (He was persuaded to do so by a second Prince Nicolaus.) His duties were not arduous and he turned his attention increasingly to religious music, producing some magnificent settings of the Mass as well as *The Creation* and *The Seasons*. His last works were for string quartet, although in the final six years of his life his faculties diminished and further composition was beyond him. All the same, to have continued composing with ever increasing brilliance until he was nearly seventy was remarkable enough and it is clear that the English visits gave him a stimulus that inspired him to heights that he might not otherwise have attained.

Sinfonia Concertante in B flat
for oboe, bassoon, violin and cello
(1792)

As a musical form the *Sinfonia Concertante* was a direct descendant of the *Concerto Grosso* of the Baroque period, a work in which a small group of players was given a more virtuoso role than that of the supporting orchestra. Audiences enjoyed the display of any especial talents in the orchestra and such works were very popular. Noting the enormous success of Salomon's Haydn concerts, a rival organisation, 'The Professional Concerts', offered a contract to one of Haydn's pupils, Ignaz Pleyel,[1] then resident in Strasbourg. London audiences were perpetually hungry for novelty and it was hoped that the arrival of a newcomer on the scene would do something to displace Haydn in their affection. Haydn swiftly defused any potential sparks by publicly embracing Pleyel and applauding his compositions warmly; but, since Pleyel had scored his greatest successes with his *Sinfonie Concertanti*, Salomon no doubt suggested to Haydn that he would best dispose of the opposition by writing a comparable work. The autograph manuscript shows that it was composed in considerable haste although in no way to its detriment.

The blend of instruments is unusual. The most obvious choice would be to place a string quartet or wind quartet in opposition to the orchestra but Haydn of all people had a dislike of the obvious. (The symphonies are full of experimental ideas as, for instance, the point in the finale of No. 60 where the violins have to re-tune their lowest string before proceeding.) The instruments he chose as soloists offer several options, whether as a pair of woodwind and a pair of strings, as an oboe and a cello matched against a violin and a bassoon, or simply as a quartet with two unmatched treble and bass pairs.

The opening exposition is forty-eight bars long but the solo quartet are by no means idle. Salomon, as leader, would have played the main orchestral part as well as his solo contributions, but there are moments when all four soloists are given passages that stand out from the main tutti. The work is not a concerto but a symphony with concerto elements and Haydn is careful to establish this convention quite early.

The first bars are unusually lyrical; he usually has a preference for something more positive but here we find a phrase which might suitably introduce an operatic aria. However it is instantly followed by a passage for full orchestra (including all four soloists) to which horns, trumpets and

---

[1] In all probability Pleyel was responsible for the theme on which Brahms based the so-called Brahms-'Haydn' Variations.

timpani give a splendid bounce. A busy tutti comes to a close on the dominant (F major) in bar 18. The implied modulation is contradicted at once by a gentle phrase which coincidentally would make a perfect response to the very opening theme. It is treated as an elegant conversation-piece by the solo quartet with the added participation of the first violins. Sixteen bars later the full orchestra rejoins the fray with a back reference to the 'bouncy' theme into which the quartet interjects a cheeky comment. A very positive cadence in B flat signals the end of the orchestral exposition.

The soloists now begin an elaborate discussion of the opening material with the violin and cello parts in particular showing a greater element of virtuosity. An expressive little phrase in F minor provides a momentarily touching contrast, but it should be taken no more seriously than a heroine's 'attack of the vapours' and Haydn wittily switches back to bustling frivolity. (The violinist's ascent to a high B flat tells us what an exceptional violinist Salomon must have been.) A cadenza-like passage in which all four soloists show their dexterity in playing scales ends with the conventional trill that warns the orchestra to stand by for action. A substantial 'symphonic' tutti follows, ending, or so it seems, with the same cadence in the dominant. Typically, Haydn foils expectation with a sudden shift into the totally unheralded key of D flat major. A wonderful development of the opening theme now materialises in which Haydn draws upon his substantial operatic experience. Apart from the advantage of sheer range that instruments have over voices, it is laid out exactly as an operatic quartet might be. It is the first moment to touch our hearts rather than merely to entertain us. And then, just as we are thinking 'how beautiful', the bassoon reverts to comedy with a grotesque skipping phrase which dispels all pathos. A progression of trills from the two wind players leads us towards an emphatic cadence in quite the 'wrong' key — the dominant of G minor, whose F sharps totally contradict the proper tonality of B flat to which we should have been heading by rights. The Gordian knot is severed by the violinist who with a brief (unwritten) cadenza steers us back into home waters.

It is a strange way to approach a recapitulation but that is what we now find, bars 163–80 being exactly comparable to the first eighteen bars. At such moments we should be on our guard since Haydn regards predictability as synonymous with laziness. He by-passes fifty-one bars and picks up the thread at the point where previously he had given us a moment or two of pathos in F minor. It is now in B flat minor but the substance is the same; indeed it continues on orthodox lines towards the traditional pause that precedes the cadenza in a solo concerto. Such cadenzas were normally improvised by the performer in Haydn's day but that would clearly be impractical with four soloists. The easy solution would have been to omit the cadenza entirely, nor would he have been censured for so doing. Instead he gives us a brilliantly contrived cadenza for all four players, thirty-four bars of music that marries expressive beauty to virtuosity while humour dances attendance on them both.[2] Even the final trill has an element of surprise, for the bassoon cannot resist the temptation to throw in an extra arpeggio just as we think that the resolution is upon us. The closing tutti is brief and to the point, reasserting the tonality of B flat from which the solo quartet has strayed delightfully during the cadenza.

The slow movement is in Haydn's most elegant style, the essentially simple theme being lavishly decorated. Perhaps even more than the first movement it shows us what outstanding players Haydn had at his disposal. One should remember that oboes and bassoons in his day were far less perfect mechanically than modern instruments yet in the first eight bars we find that a top B flat is expected from the bassoon and a top D (twice) from the oboe-player. Such notes are extreme for the instruments and even today's players would regard them as a challenge. The cello part ascends to the high E an octave and a bit above 'middle' C while also containing some very rapid accompanying figures which demand great fluency.

The movement begins with a four-bar phrase which is treated as a duet, first for violin and bassoon and then for oboe and cello. Violin and cello are then paired together and after a short transitional passage mainly for violin they present us with a second subject in the dominant, the violin now accompanying the cello. This tune has a subsidiary extension whose brief phrases evoke elaborate comments from violin or bassoon. The appearance of the opening theme on the full orchestra for the first time serves as a central landmark after which the preceding material is presented anew with the individual roles exhanged. Towards the end of the movement we are kept in suspense for a long silence before a tiny coda in which the horns have a dangerously high entry. (Haydn's horn writing is often extremely demanding; even in a symphony as early as No. 5, written in the late 1750s, he produced a horn-part which is one of the most challenging in the whole symphonic repertoire — and this for valve-less 'natural' horns which were notoriously tricky to play.)

The finale begins with a spirited tune that shows the composer in his most rustic mood; starting with everyone in unison, it ends in rumty-tumty fashion with a deliberately silly cadence. With mock solemnity the violin declaims a vocal-type recitative that sounds like a stern admonishment to abandon such frivolity. After a slightly stunned silence, the orchestra begins again as before only to be checked in mid-flight by further admonitions from the solo violin. In case anyone should be so obtuse as to take this seriously, Haydn then gives the violin a delightfully mischievous phrase that almost seems to be giggling as it goes on its way. This new tune, a derivative of the opening theme, is

[2]Had Mozart perhaps shown him the miraculous cadenza for soprano and wind instruments in the '*Et incarnatus est*' from his C minor Mass? It might have served as a model.

taken up with enthusiasm by the full orchestra. From this point on Haydn exploits the contrast between the solo quartet and the full orchestra to great comic effect. Soon the violinist embarks on a tricky solo that is the musical equivalent of a tongue-twister, a solo which the bassoonist courageously tries to match. Each member of the quartet is given a chance to display his technical dexterity, the most fearsome challenge being given to the cellist. The tutti which follows this is built around a descending chain of notes around whose measured steps fragments of the opening theme dart and play. A brief excursion into minor keys leads into a huffing and puffing tutti which clearly fails to blow the soloist's house down since the cello sets them dancing again at once. The music continues happily until suddenly halted at a portentous pause. Again the violinist assumes the mantle of an oratorio singer and again the attempt to be serious dissolves in laughter. Soon the quartet begins an absurd slow-motion trill, all four of them in unison; the rest of the players cannot refrain from joining in. It is a signal for a last display of high-spirited virtuosity from the quartet, violin and cello in turn climbing to such dizzy heights that Haydn gives them silent beats to enable them to find the right place on the finger-board. The final tutti is notable for some two-octave skips in the violin parts that even *look* comically awkward to play as well as sounding hilarious. The whole movement is a remarkable display of musical wit; it is immense fun to play as well as to listen to.

A new concertante from HAYDN combined with all the excellencies of music; it was profound, airy, affecting, and original, and the performance was in unison with the merit of the composition. SALOMON particularly exerted himself on this occasion, in doing justice to the music of his friend HAYDN. (*Morning Herald*, 12 March 1792)

A new Concertante, for a Violin, Violoncello, Oboe, and Bassoon was performed for the first time with admirable effect. The solo parts were finally contrasted with the 'full tide of harmony' of the other instruments, and they were very ably sustained by the respective performers. (*Morning Chronicle*, 12 March 1792)

Symphony No. 94 in G (The 'Surprise')

Simple as a nursery-rhyme, the slow movement of this symphony has rebounded against its creator by becoming too well-known. Thousands of children must have had it thrust upon them as a first introduction to so-called 'classical' music, probably coupled with the apocryphal legend that the loud bang that interrupts its tiptoe progress was put in by Haydn to wake up any old ladies in the audience who might have dropped off to sleep. He himself denied this, saying that he merely wanted to surprise his audience with something new. The surprise bang is a very small part of a large symphony, though a part that has caught the popular fancy ever since. Needless to say it isn't a surprise any more and I can't help wishing that Haydn had left a note in the score giving the conductor leave to insert something different at each performance. A ting on a triangle would make a nice change and would cause people to sit up more effectively now that they know what to expect. The trouble about such a noticeable feature is that it attracts a disproportionate amount of comment. Like a pretty daughter in a family of plain boys the slow movement has hogged all the attention; for all too many of us the rest of the symphony is relatively unknown.

Haydn wrote this work in rural Hertfordshire where, on his first triumphant visit to England, he stayed for a couple of months with the family of a banker. 'I work hard', he wrote to a friend in Austria, 'and when in the early mornings I walk in the woods alone, with my English grammar in my hand, I think of my Creator, my family, and all the friends I have left behind.' This letter itself contains a surprise, for just as you think he's going to say how homesick and miserable he is, he says: 'How sweet this bit of liberty really is! I had a kind Prince, but sometimes I was forced to be dependant on base souls. I often sighed for release, and now I have it in some measure.'

Although he was caught up in a whirl of social life, Haydn could not forget his obligations as a composer, and every now and then he would withdraw from the scene for a few weeks to dash off another symphony. Numbers 93 and 94 were written in the early spring of 1792 and were received with the habitual ovation which Haydn was to know everywhere he went in England. The London Symphonies give us an interesting insight into the standards of orchestral playing at the time; Haydn makes considerable demands on the players. He was an eminently practical musician, and would never have doubled up flutes, oboes and bassoons on the very first page if he hadn't been confident they would play well in tune.

The slow introduction we find here was his normal way of beginning a symphony, a hangover from the earlier suite from which the form had developed. The first phrase from the woodwind is like a caress to which the strings give a nodding approval. A second and sweeter caress follows which also brings a smile from the strings. The interest now passes to the cellos who begin a somewhat tortuous ascent, opening doors to several different tonalities on the way but never staying for long enough to settle until they regain the dominant of G. An isolated phrase from the first violins leaves us in mid-air waiting for the expected resolution into G major. It is at such moments that Haydn proves himself a true master of surprises far more subtle than the crash in the slow movement. The first subject of the ensuing

Vivace assai ('rather lively') appears with great delicacy in the 'wrong' key of A minor before having second thoughts and reverting to the proper tonality of G. The safe arrival at this desirable goal is greeted with enthusiasm by the full orchestra whose bouncing 6/8 rhythm and lusty brass give a hunting flavour to the music. After seventeen exuberant bars the violins are suddenly left on their own save for some fragile support from the other strings. They seem unnerved by the situation and play the same bar three times before breaking off, as if hoping someone will come to their aid. The lack of offers causes them to go back to square one and start again with exactly the same routine as before. Once more the return to G major is hailed as a cause for rejoicing, but this time the tutti effects a proper modulation to the dominant, D major.

According to convention the repeated As we find at this point should lead into the second subject which without a shadow of doubt should be in D major. Haydn scorns convention and produces three 'surprises' in the space of two bars. First of these is the non-appearance of the second subject, second the substitution of D *minor* for D major, third a rapid shift to the alien key of F major — and all with the first subject cheekily usurping the rightful position of the second. Not surprisingly this causes some consternation and for a while there is an impression of chaos in the orchestra as the violins rush around in D minor or the lower strings and woodwind try to force their way back to a respectable dominant (A) from which there is a chance that sanity — in the shape of D major — will return. It does, although the displaced accents seem to indicate a rather bumpy landing. The violins take up their position on the dominant (A), seemingly ready to make amends for their earlier indiscretion; surely this time the second subject will appear . . . But no. Like a kitten trying to catch its own tail, they twirl round and round with a phrase whose deliberate banality is underlined by the 'vamped' accompaniment which continues patiently underneath. (It is an early example of the old music-hall accompanist's 'till ready' fill-in). At last, twenty-six bars late, the second subject does appear, all neat and tidy and anchored firmly to a sustained D in the bass. It skips happily along with the insouciance of a child until a bit of an argument breaks out in the woodwind. All is well, though, as the full orchestra heads for a glorious cadence in D major that will bring the exposition to a proper and satisfying conclusion. But does it? Only by showing what convention would dictate can I reveal how unconventional Haydn is. This is what we might rightfully expect, the first three bars being Haydn's.

All very fine but all very obvious. This is what he actually does — and how well deserved the nickname 'Surprise' seems when we encounter such diversions:

Admittedly landing up on these repeated B naturals does facilitate the conventional repeat of the exposition since that is the note the *Vivace* started on; but the total avoidance of a proper cadence at this point leaves the violins in mid-air. Where should they go from here?

Haydn's solution brings another extraordinary surprise, a smooth modulation into C major, a key which nobody would ever predict in such a context. As though to confirm that he really means it, he spells out the scale of C in a unison phrase for wind and strings; but then doubts creep in and in a marvellously imaginative passage the strings drift in and out of F minor before settling back into C. A sudden blast from brass and wind produces a dramatic shift to D minor and for some thirty bars there is a veritable storm in which modulations from key to key are too frequent to be listed. Heavy accents mark the majority of the main beats and the mischievous geniality of the previous music seems to be forgotten.

The sudden emergence of quiet repeated Bs on the violins gives us some reassurance that a way back may be found. They sound like raindrops and when the first subject makes its welcome return the addition of a flute an octave above is like a pale ray of sunlight. It is the beginning of a recapitulation in which, though the material is familiar, there are still surprises for the attentive listener. For instance Haydn's little joke of leaving the violins on their own and then breaking off in bewilderment is omitted completely. There is also a delightful new event when four detached chords seem to be bringing the movement to a conclusion. Low horns give vent to a tuba-like note that sends the violins loping upwards to start yet another game with the first subject, a game that the woodwind then enjoy on their own. The second subject duly makes a graceful last appearance before a rousing tutti puts an end to a remarkable movement.

The famous slow movement is a set of variations on a C major theme. It is ironic that the sudden *ff* chord from which the symphony gets its name was an afterthought of which there is no sign in the original autograph. Haydn was particularly concerned that the second-beat crotchets in bars 2, 4 and 6 should be fully sustained in a basically staccato context; he therefore marked *ten.* for *tenuto* (held) on each one. The theme itself is simple enough to need no description except to underline that it only contains one modulation — and that to the adjacent dominant (G).

Variation I gives the theme unaltered to the second violins, adding a neat and elegant decoration in the first violins which are joined by a flute in the second phrase.

Variation II brings a fundamental change of character, a shift to C minor and a much stronger version of the theme. The initial severity is quickly mollified by an apparent switch to A flat major in the strings, a deception which is soon explained as it turns out to be an intermediate step on the way to E flat major. This fails to bring the peace one might expect and the second half of the variation is extremely dramatic. References to the theme are confined to its first five notes while agitated figures in the violins soon spread to all the strings as brass and timpani add their considerable force to the score. A sweeping upward scale in full strings and woodwind suddenly leaves the first violins out on their own. As if not quite certain how to extricate themselves from the situation, they have a rather tentative little phrase which at least enables them to reach Variation III.

This features a delightfully stuttering oboe who gains confidence when he is joined by a flute. Together they provide an enchanting descant to the theme.

Variation IV covers the theme with glory, trumpets, horns and timpani bestowing full military honours on it while the violins stand in for the cavalry. With the audience reeling from the sudden assault, Haydn plays one of his most characteristic jokes — a change of mood so sudden that one suspects the players may have turned two pages by mistake. Out of the hurly-burly emerge the strings *pianissimo e dolce* with a smoothly gliding version of the theme that changes its character completely. As though resentful of this seductively feminine intrusion, the gentlemen of the military summon their forces to bring the variation to a rousing conclusion — or such is their intention. Heading for a final cadence they are brought to a sharp halt by a diversionary chord that holds us all in suspense. Tentatively the strings suggest a way out and then relax onto a series of cushion-like harmonies of a positively voluptuous kind while oboe and bassoon say a fond farewell to the theme. The movement ends like the Cheshire cat, so that all that is left is the smile on Haydn's face.

The term *Menuet* which Haydn applies to the third movement is a meaningless gesture towards convention since the indication of the tempo, *Allegro molto*, clearly precludes any possibility of courtly dancing. In fact he is preparing the way for the Beethoven-type Scherzo not only in the speed of the music but also in its humour. The first eight bars are rustic in the extreme with their rum-ti-ti accompaniment and very basic harmonies. Beware, though, for another surprise is imminent; instead of matching eight bars with another phrase of comparable length Haydn extends the second stanza to ten bars. The repetition of these first eighteen bars gives us an opportunity to enjoy its lack of symmetry. As if to compensate for those extra two bars he then gives us a three-bar phrase followed by a six-bar one, a defiance of the laws of proportion which causes quite an upset. Accompanied by strident chords on the woodwind, the violins hop through a swift sequence of keys, G minor, E flat major, C minor, and back to the dominant of G, all in the space of eight bars. The music breaks off, uncertain of where to go. Flutes and oboes have a flick of a phrase that seems to ask 'Up here?' Bassoons and a solo cello reply 'Or down here?' Neither is right, as the orchestra confirms by returning full of confidence to the opening theme, confidence that is misplaced since in the eighth bar the music grinds to a halt. Somewhat chastened, violins and wind make a couple of abortive attempts to get started again. Help is forthcoming from flute, cellos and basses and the main part of the 'menuet' is concluded with the aid of the brass and timpani.

The central Trio features bassoon and violins in unison, an unusual match to say the least, so much so that in the second part the bassoon seems to miss his cue and the violins have to circle round D several times waiting for him to catch up. The normal repetitions of the 'menuet' are duly observed in a movement that is too easily taken for granted.

'The Finale is one of the most sophisticated examples of a sonata rondo that Haydn (or anyone else) ever composed.' I quote the opinion of H.C. Robbins Landon, the great expert on Haydn's music, who goes on to describe it as 'a phenomenal movement'. The term 'sonata rondo' should perhaps be explained. Rondo form involves a recurring theme with intervening episodes, usually described in the textbooks as ABACADA. (B, C and D will most probably be in related but contrasting keys while A always represents a return 'home' to the original or 'tonic' key.) A 'sonata rondo' combines elements of sonata and rondo forms; it should have three sections, (corresponding to the exposition, development and recapitulation of a sonata-form movement) as well as two episodes of which the first will probably reappear in the dominant key while the second consists of a further development. We should realise that such forms are not rigid and may be manipulated in a number of ways by composers of genius.

The tempo of the finale is very brisk, *Allegro molto*, and the first theme slips by so quickly that it is just as well that Haydn instantly repeats it with the addition of a flute to give extra brightness to the subdued violins. The tune has an extensive second limb with a nice 'double take' in the middle. In the thirty-eighth bar we find the first tutti, notable for the fiery runs in the violin parts (here in unison for maximum brilliance). At one point there is an oblique reference to the first subject, now in the dominant (D), but for the most part the intention is to leave us breathless. A sudden break and a silent bar seem to confirm that the violins have indeed run out of steam. A quiet pizzicato bass and a dancing rhythm in the second violins announce the arrival of the second subject, graciousness personified. As with the first subject we are given two opportunities to hear it before another exhibition of virtuosity by the violins brings the exposition to a brilliant close.

The emphatic D major chords which end the exposition are quietly contradicted by the three C naturals which follow. In a trice we are whipped back to the first subject, a move calculated to fool the more knowledgeable listener into thinking that Haydn has observed the convention of repeating the exposition. We are soon shown that the assumption is wrong when he takes a drastic short cut. The original first subject material occupied thirty-seven bars before the first tumultuous tutti. At this later point we are given a mere eight bars to assimilate what has happened before the tumult begins again. After twenty-nine extremely energetic bars the music breaks off, makes several comic false starts, and then gets back on the rails again with a return to the main theme. After another eight-bar spell the entry of brass, timpani and full woodwind signals a shift to G minor, an event which leads to an almost frenzied series of modulations into a number of totally alien keys. After a searing climax everybody drops out except for the first violins who, finding themselves thus exposed, scuttle around for a little before finding safety in a reprise of the initial rondo theme, here given new colour by the participation of flute and bassoon two octaves apart. Once again Haydn takes an ingenious short cut by omitting twenty bars from his original plan, but the second subject duly makes its gracious entrance, complete with the preliminary silent bar. However, its proper termination is rudely interrupted by trumpets, horns and timpani.

A new treatment of the rondo theme now appears, woodwind thirds over a soft timpani roll with strumming pizzicato violins adding a comic effect. Suddenly the timpani roll grows louder, bringing a startled reaction from the full orchestra who plunge into E flat major without a hint of warning. After a noisy few bars the first violins extricate themselves neatly from an awkward situation and lead a joyous return to G major. This solution is received with jubilation by all and sundry, especially the timpanist who looses off a cannonade in celebration. And so this remarkably inventive movement finishes; 'Laus Deo' says Haydn at the end of the score, 'Praise to God' being a more pious expression of gratitude for reaching the end than 'Thank God'.

The effect on the audience of the day was stupendous and Haydn related how the cry of 'Encore' came from every throat. How disappointed he would have been to feel that the symphony would become so famous for the wrong reason — a practical joke in one bar of the slow movement, and an afterthought at that.

Symphony No. 98 in B Flat Major

There are many unusual features about this symphony, the first of which is the key of the Introduction — B flat minor. For technical reasons to do with intonation it is probably the least used key in music and without extensive research I can think of only one symphony in the entire repertoire that is actually *in* B flat minor and that is Walton's First. Since tonality was so important an aspect of all musical forms in the eighteenth century, Haydn must have realised that to begin a work in this manner would be appreciated as unusual to say the least. Furthermore the Introduction is exceptionally powerful and severe in character with all the strings declaiming the main theme in unison, each minim being marked with a heavy accent.

Notice the abrupt cut-off in the fourth bar and the dramatic pause that follows. The phrase is then repeated in a modified form, *piano*. After a second pause we find another modification of the opening phrase, this time with the original fierce dynamics intensified by an angry trill. Two brief chordal passages in dotted rhythm bring this impressive introduction to a close. It seems to be designed to prepare us for matters of grave import; how typical of Haydn it is when we discover that it is an elaborate hoax, for the *Allegro* that follows is delightfully entertaining. Despite its totally different mood Haydn evolves it from the introduction with great skill, as a comparison with the previous example will show at a glance.

The change to B flat major contributes greatly to the transformation, but so do the slurs in the third bar, so different from the stern crotchets in the Introduction.

   Towards the end of his life Haydn had become increasingly concerned with unifying his larger orchestral works. Slow introductions were a relic from the days of the French *'Ouverture'*, the opening movement of the orchestral suites from which the symphony as a major form was partly derived. (The Italian overture or '*sinfonia*' was normally in three sections, fast-slow-fast.) Although Haydn had a great fondness for slow introductions, he felt instinctively that there was a danger that they might seem irrelevant to what followed; thus it was that in Symphonies 90, 97, 98 and 103 we see a positive effort to establish a recognisable thematic link between the introduction and the main part of the movement.

The first movement of this symphony is conceived in the broadest terms that Haydn could envisage. Once the link shown above has been securely established (with a captivating variant the second time round), the full tutti is used for the first time in a robust confirmation of B flat major. After some considerable activity the music settles onto a sustained C enabling him to modulate convincingly to the anticipated dominant key of F. We are justified in expecting the second subject to appear at this point, but Haydn surprises us by returning once again to his opening theme, extending it in a number of ingenious ways. Not for the first time in his music we hear echoes of Mozartean opera, as for example in the pleading voices of the strings and the peremptory interruptions from wind and brass. A tinge of F minor casts a momentary shadow which is brusquely dispersed by some energetic passages for strings and wind.

The second subject is one of the strangest aspects of the symphony since it sounds more like a transition than a theme. Accompanied by throbbing strings, it consists essentially of four semibreves on a solo oboe (C, C♯, D, B♮). The rest of the orchestra show little sympathy for it and the exposition ends with brilliant triplets cascading through the violin parts. The dominant key, F major, is firmly underlined by the closing chords. It is a point worth making since the first bar of the ensuing development brings a shock.

Contradicting the preceding tonality completely, Haydn re-introduces the first subject in what seems like D major; that it turns out to be the dominant of G minor in no way lessens the surprise. Then, as if feeling that this is no way to carry on, he cranks the music up a semitone and tries the theme out in E flat major in much more positive tones. This is the signal for a quite remarkable demonstration of contrapuntal skill in which the first three notes of the theme are made into the basis of a free fugue whose running counter-subject gradually dominates the scene in a bustling quaver run that keeps the violins fully occupied for thirty-two bars, 256 quavers non-stop! A more sustained section follows as a much-needed contrast, descending expressively at last to the recapitulation. Although this follows a fairly predictable course, the second subject is allowed a little more scope than before while the coda introduces a new treatment of the opening theme with the off-beats pounded out with some gusto.

The second movement, a deeply felt *Adagio*, has in its opening bars a suggestion of 'God Save the King' which may indeed be a subtle compliment to Haydn's hosts. Yet the emotional content corresponds poorly with any such gesture and it seems more likely that the movement is a private lament for Mozart's death, an event which had seemed a grievous loss to Haydn. (The idea was put forward by Donald Tovey.) Certainly there are a number of passages which have a truly Mozartean flavour once the violins introduce the second main subject. The softly repeated woodwind chords which seem to give a blessing to each violin phrase are a device Mozart frequently used in operatic arias, as are the little hesitations which give such poignancy to the melody.

The central part of the movement brings a storm of anguish with the serene opening phrase cruelly distorted in the bass — surely an unlikely treatment to be meted out to the National Anthem? The storm ceases as abruptly as it had begun and the opening phrases return with the addition of an expressive new counterpoint from a solo cello. The initial serenity is hard to regain after the emotional upheaval in the centre of the movement and even when the two oboes sing the opening theme in a mellifluous duet the string parts show a continuing unease. The final harmonisation of the opening phrase is tinged with extraordinary pathos and the movement ends with two *pianissimo* chords. This in itself was extremely unusual for Haydn who, having grown accustomed to the English habit of applauding every movement, would normally end even the most touching *Adagio* with a loud chord regardless of context.

The *Menuet* has a certain roughness about it that is different from mere rustic cheerfulness. First beats are accented with an upward scoop that has a whiplash effect while the extensive use of brass and timpani removes the music from the ballroom. In other words it is a truly symphonic movement whose impact the occasional gentler phrases do little to soften. The central Trio is more forgiving, with its naive melody scored as a duet for violins and bassoon, yet even this innocent little tune is roughly handled in a weighty unison for full wind and strings. One cannot help feeling that Haydn was beginning to resent the convention that demanded a 'menuet' now that he had attained his freedom from aristocratic patronage.

Although the last movement is marked as a *Presto* 6/8, its unusual stresses can most easily be described as one-two-THREE-four, one-two-THREE-four, the 'THREES' standing out not as accents but as the only sustained notes in this nimble-footed theme. Nimble it may be in the hands of the violins or a solo oboe, but the full orchestra attack it with the exuberance of a party of drunken males at a hunting lodge. Three separate chords on the dominant (F) arrest the dance in mid-flight. There is a momentary silence and then the violins make three tentative attempts to get things started again. It is such a witty idea that it is almost as though Haydn is winking at the audience. 'This is fun' he seems to say, and then lets the flute and violin proceed, light as a ballerina. Her toes are swiftly trodden on by the raucous throng who, judging by the oboes and bassoons, appear to have a collective bout of hiccups.

A second subject appears, trying to inject a vestige of calm; but it is soon whisked away in a rising swirl of triplets. The passage that follows has the sort of enchanting silliness we more readily associate with Rossini. It simply consists of fragments of scales over a galloping accompaniment, now here, now there, like the insistent calls for Figaro in 'The Barber of Seville'. A sudden outburst of 'Tally-ho's' from the full orchestra must have delighted the hunting fraternity in the London audience while the coy response from the violins no doubt gave equal pleasure to their wives. The exposition ends riotously with dominant harmonies slapped on top of a tonic bass — and 'the Devil take your rule-book'.

A silent bar with a pause over it allows any shocked academicians time to recover their equilibrium, only to be bowled over again by Haydn's next move. Having ended the exposition in F major he now begins a delicate oom-pah accompaniment in the strings in the foreign key of A flat major, while Mr Salomon toys playfully with the Rossini-esque theme on his own. He too gives the audience a wink with three confidential asides. They are greeted with a roar of appreciation from unison strings and wind, whereupon the flute joins Salomon in the game. 'Enough fooling' says Haydn, and launches a massive tutti that could be mistaken for Beethoven at his angriest. The music literally grinds to a halt, uneasily swaying between D and C sharp before settling on D for a long pause. 'What shall we do next?' is the question that hangs in the air. Well, in moments of such grave crisis what can a fellow do but go oom-pah oom-pah in another key (E flat) and whistle a careless tune — which is just what the solo violin seems to do. It doesn't seem quite right, though, so it is followed by a slightly embarrassed silence. He tries again but still seems to be getting nowhere. There follows a delightfully witty link which haltingly finds the way back to the original tune, still treated as a violin solo.

This restoration to normality is greeted with loud acclaim by the full orchestra, hiccups and all. Something like an orderly recapitulation follows, but just as we think the movement is about to end, Haydn breaks off in mid-phrase. Picking their way with the care one expects from the barely sober, the violins embark cautiously on the theme, '*Più moderato*'. It is one of Haydn's best jokes for he uses a slower tempo to make the music seem faster.[3] The steadier beat enables the players to pack more notes into the bar, and after a mere seven bars of groping from the violins, the whole orchestra sweeps into a torrent of semiquavers that must have overwhelmed the audience. Yet even now this astonishing composer has not finished with us. Twice more the music breaks off abruptly. Then, as the violins again play the tune at the slower tempo, a glittering figure appears on the piano, played by Dr Haydn

---

[3]Beethoven uses a similar technique to much more serious purpose in the finale of his Op. 110 piano sonata.

himself to the huge delight of those present. Its merry tinkling has a musical-box effect and must have seemed as novel as the famous celesta solo in Tchaikovsky's 'Dance of the Sugar-plum Fairy'. Although Haydn directed his symphonies from the keyboard, it was unheard of for the instrument to be featured in this decorative capacity. The symphony ends with eleven more exuberant bars from the full orchestra, a fitting close to a masterpiece in which humour, intellect and sensibility have combined to give us a musical feast.

Symphony No. 101 in D Major (The 'Clock')

As with the 'Surprise' symphony, the public reputation of this work tends to rest unfairly on the slow movement. (So far as I know nobody has yet tried to call Beethoven's Eighth Symphony the 'Metronome' even though to do so would at least have more substantiation than to call the Fifth Piano Concerto the 'Emperor'.) In Haydn's case the many nicknames attached to his symphonies came about purely because of the sheer number that he wrote. When a composer produces 104 works of the same genre it does create problems of identity and it is only fair to say that such soubriquets as 'Clock', 'Surprise', 'Drum-roll' or 'London' do have some value in helping instant recall. The objection that Haydn himself would surely have raised is that the nickname often draws attention to a relatively unimportant feature.

The introductory *Adagio* is in D minor and would seem to be in a totally different mood from the extremely lively movement that follows. In fact the seeds of both first and second subjects of the main movement are planted here, though the relationships are perhaps easier to comprehend through the eye than the ear. Here is the opening of the *Adagio* and its derivative.

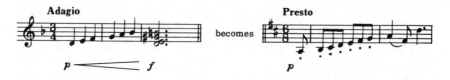

And now bars 5–8 of the second violin part followed by its transformation some 73 bars later:

Thus although it may be said that 'coming events cast their shadow before' the solemnity of the Introduction in no way prepares us for the frivolity that lies ahead. What we should be aware of is the subtle way in which the 'shadows' lengthen, for Haydn begins with a four-bar phrase, follows up with one of eight bars and ends with eleven bars. This lack of symmetry is a notable characteristic of Haydn's style and when the *Presto* begins we should realise that it is far more sophisticated than its dancing rhythm suggests. Two phrases of five bars are followed by one of three, one of eight and one of four — scarcely a predictable pattern. What *is* predictable is that the delicacy of the initial presentation will be offset by a display of full orchestral strength. This comes to a halt on the dominant chord of A, leading the gullible listener to suppose that the second subject is about to appear. Foiling expectation in his usual mischievous way, Haydn proceeds to give us quite an extensive development of the first subject, twisting it this way and that until it comes to an abrupt stop.

Scored with extreme delicacy, the second subject makes its appearance. Frail though it may seem, it is destined to dominate the central section of the movement, something it can do without offence since it represents no real change of character. (This shows no lack of invention on Haydn's part but rather an increasing preoccupation with unity within a movement.) The tail-end of the second subject shows a curious cessation of activity as though the music suddenly loses its way before joyfully resuming its skittish dance. The exposition ends on a much more positive note with a bold descending figure quite different from anything else in the movement. Having reached base by climbing heavy-footed down to a low A, it discharges a couple of rockets into the air which explode into five cadential chords. The sparks sizzle down in two swift but quiet descending scales; to go back to the obligatory repeat all Haydn has to do is to reverse the direction of the scale. (Omission of the repeat means the loss of this delightful pun.)

The development begins with an urgent though whispered discussion of the second subject initiated by the second violins but soon spreading like gossip through all the strings. It is with some shock that we suddenly find ourselves plunged into the very 'wrong' key of C major. As if the world has indeed gone crazy, the first subject promptly appears upside-down. Somehow a way out of this impasse must be found and Haydn begins a tiered sequence of modulations using a pattern derived from the second subject. Higher and higher he climbs until an exciting climax is reached, swaying perilously between F sharp major and B minor. The strings extricate themselves with a bustling unison passage which seems to have found G major after a fashion, but a sudden blast from brass and timpani blows them off course again. Eight terse chords from the full orchestra tell us that B minor it has to be. As though they can scarcely believe it, the strings spell out the notes of a B minor chord in slow motion. It is a moment of extraordinary magic. Violins and flute again begin to discuss the second subject in hushed tones but soon there is a rapid crescendo towards an immense dominant seventh chord through which hurtles a descending scale. There is a silence, enabling us to absorb the fact that this chord is indeed the gateway back to the tonic key of D major. We stand by for the recapitulation.

It is all very well to identify where we are in the overall plan of the movement but Haydn is in far too inventive a mood to be content with a slavish repetition of past events. After seventeen bars — or roughly seventeen seconds! — he changes course with a sudden lurch into D minor which causes considerable agitation. The passage to the second subject is now very much stormier than it was in the first place but it is also very much shorter — fifteen bars from the diversion just described instead of the original forty. Needless to say the orchestration is changed, cellos now taking the place of violins. Haydn seems intoxicated with his material, constantly finding new tricks to play with it. There is one particularly subtle passage near the end where the violins mutter away on their lowest string in a state of indecision before being prodded on their way by four chords on horns and bassoons. As for the ending, it could scarcely be more brilliant, deserving the storms of applause which so delighted the composer but which we are now too good-mannered to bestow.

The second movement has the slow tick-tock accompaniment from which the symphony derives its name. Above it the first violins begin an elegant and courtly dance-tune, extremely aristocratic in its manner after the sparkling ebullience of the first movement. Yet even here Haydn plays a little joke on us for the beautifully poised four-bar phrase is matched by an equally beautifully poised four- . . . sorry, *five*-bar phrase. As the music continues into the next stanza the dynamics are surely humorous in intent, the dainty dotted rhythm of the first two beats followed by a clumsy *forte* on the next two, as though an accomplished girl dancer finds herself lumbered with a fat and arthritic partner. A long sustained note on a solo oboe introduces a new touch of colour as the violins provide an extension of the rhythm of the first bar of the tune, building it up in sequences until, after taking a slight stumble, it returns to the first phrase once more. (Note the addition of a flute and the extra pizzicato chords in the viola part, previously silent.)

After the affected manner of this somewhat foppish theme the last thing we would expect is a stern-faced excursion into G minor, but that is what happens. Complete with horns, trumpets and drums, the orchestra embarks on a dramatic and fully symphonic episode whose only connection with the previous music is the rhythmic pattern ♫♫ which now, instead of mincing along, acquires a severity more suited to a passage from an oratorio. Indeed, as the music progresses to the intensely dramatic centre it seems like a setting of the *Dies Irae*. There is no logical or programmatic explanation for this truly extraordinary passage, but it gives a potent demonstration of what I call the two-way process of composition. Haydn makes an intellectual decision to go into G minor; once there, the very sound of the music generates an emotional reaction deep in his inner self that demands release in this extravagant display of power.

The return to the 'Clock' theme seems positively irreverent after this storm, the more so with the enchantingly eccentric orchestration Haydn now provides. The tick-tock figure is given to flute and bassoon more than two octaves apart while the effect of a musical toy is enhanced by the combination of flute, oboe, bassoon and first violins. One of the delights of the palace at Eszterháza was a puppet-theatre and this section of the movement might aptly be described as a Puppet Serenade. It comes to a stop exactly as marionettes do; there is a silence. The second violins begin the tick-tock figure on G and B flat. Not another excursion into G minor surely? No; it is even more of a surprise, a shift to E flat major. The violins make a brave attempt to reintroduce the opening theme in this new key but it only leads to trouble. There is a minor crisis which is resolved to everyone's evident relief by a return to G major, the 'proper' key for the theme, now in a much more robust mood. Just as the music seems to be fining down to its original daintiness there is a violent intrusion of heavy brass and pounding timpani that must have had the ladies clutching their escorts in terror. 'Didn't really mean it' says Haydn, and allows the movement to trickle away into silence.

Before we move on to the Menuetto is is worth pointing out that the form of the slow movement is wholly original; it is part Rondo, part Theme and Variations. But the stormy central section gives it a symphonic weight that neither term adequately conveys. Donald Tovey, that eminent musical scholar, describes it as having 'an audacity and genius without parallel in earlier or later music'. Some clock!

The Menuetto scarcely deserves its Italian diminutive since it is the longest of all in the Salomon symphonies. The theme, rather square and solid at first hearing, is artfully constructed. The first beat of bar 1 is a D, bar 2 an E, bar 3 an F sharp, bar 4 a G, bar 5 an A, bar 6 a B — at which point he seems to say 'that's high enough for the moment' and gently slides back to E. The phrase begins anew as if it is going to be a straight repetition; instead it climbs by a quicker and more direct route to a high E, taking an extended and tortuous path down again to the dominant (A). Some rough syncopations confirm this to be a genuine modulation rather than a brief call on a neighbour. This first section of 28 bars is duly repeated according to the convention of the time.

The following passage shows some intriguing contrasts between quiet chromatic phrases in the strings accompanied by soft drum taps and a pastoral response from oboes and horns. This is extended in a richer texture before arriving back to Theme I in a lengthened version.[4]

There follows a Trio of rustic charm in which the strings set up an

[4]The two sections of the Menuetto are respectively 28 and 51 bars in length.

unchanging 'drone' accompaniment above which a solo flute acts the part of a
shepherd-boy's pipe. (The resemblance between this and the corresponding
part of Beethoven's First Symphony is so striking that it lays the latter open to
a charge of petty theft.) The first time the flute tune occurs the accompanying
harmonies refuse to budge even when propriety demands that they should;
furthermore the 'rustic charm' is rudely dispelled by a rowdy interruption
from the full orchestra. The second time round the strings pay more attention
to the flute and make the required adjustment to the harmony, except for the
cellos and basses, who are too idle to change. In the second portion of the Trio
there is a would-be elegant duet for flute and bassoon in which one feels that
the peasants are mimicking the affectations of the gentry. Soon the violins
have a deliciously comic 'cadenza' in which they get hypnotised by one
circling phrase, ultimately repeated seven times. The rest of the orchestra
come to the rescue with the greatest confidence only to fizzle out in a
bewildered way leaving an embarrassed silence. The rustic 'drone' begins
again in a rather tentative manner, the sense of insecurity justified when the
horns plonk down a bottom D a bar too early. The whole Trio is a 'village
band' joke comparable to the one in Beethoven's 'Pastoral' Symphony
written fourteen years later.

The finale, *Vivace* starts with deceptive innocence. For once the tune is a
symmetrical one of two four-bar phrases of which we need to remember two
fragments marked below.

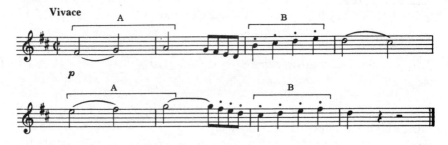

This artless tune is duly repeated, after which there is a twelve-bar sequel
which plays at modulating into new tonalities without really getting anywhere; Theme I then returns to reassure us that nothing alarming has
occurred. At such moments we should be on our guard, for with a thump on
the timpani and a blare from the brass Haydn straightens our backs up with
whipcrack phrases on the violins. Unison strings then begin a crisp development of B, doubling its speed as the trumpets sound a call to arms. A brisk
skirmish follows out of which a single oboe emerges unscathed, cheerfully
piping its repeated Es. The strings offer a second subject of sorts, so akin to
the opening theme that it could be taken for a variation. Some confusion is
generated when the first violins lose their place and play across the beat for six

bars. It is just after this that we are given the first inkling of the tremendous events that lie ahead. Against a brilliant running counterpoint in violins and flutes the lower strings (reinforced by the brass) turn A from Theme I into massive footsteps which then become a jogtrot of tremendous energy.

After a pause for breath a new episode begins, altogether calmer in mood and based on the twelve-bar sequel already mentioned; here again it seems anxious to modulate but horns and violas supply a firm anchor. Slyly, so that we hardly realise it's happening, the violins introduce a devious version of Theme I, a piece of frivolity which is forcibly corrected by the full orchestra — the first time the theme itself has been played at all loudly. A swifter variation soon follows but this is no time to sit back with a confident feeling that we've heard all this before. For the next fifty bars we are battered by a fierce storm in D minor, as great a shock as the one in the centre of the slow movement. It ends as abruptly as it began.

Haydn now begins a double fugue[5] where the dextrous mastery of contrapuntal skills rivals even that of Mozart. (The young Mendelssohn may well have studied this closely before writing the brilliant fugue in the last movement of his Octet.) The whole fugal episode is played as quietly as possible until a brief crescendo summons the full orchestra, *fortissimo*. The ensuing tutti seems to be heading towards the final cadence but Haydn cannot resist a last leg-pull. Tenderly he says farewell to his theme with a new harmonisation that gives it a suggestion of a tear. Twice he detaches the fragment B from the theme. Will the music end on tiptoe? 'No!' says Haydn, and doubling the speed of B turns it into a dazzling sequence of ascending quavers that lead us towards the triumphant close.

Symphony No. 103 in E Flat (The 'Drum Roll') 1795

The more we know the Haydn symphonies, the more amazed we should be by his unflagging inventiveness. The very first bar of this work — a simple drum roll — was totally original and, so far as I know, has not been duplicated in later times. It is followed by a quiet sustained phrase for bassoons, cellos and basses that within the idiom of the eighteenth century has a mystery comparable to the start of Schubert's 'Unfinished'.

[5]Two subjects sounding at once but both being treated fugally.

Soft wind harmonies provide a modulation to the dominant with the last two notes of the above; a phrase of similar length takes us back to the tonic. Violins take over from the lower strings, the theme in the 'firsts' being followed by tentative steps from the 'seconds'. Gradually the texture thickens slightly, ending with a unison descent through the arpeggio of C minor to a low G, nudged disturbingly by the adjacent A flat. There is a pause.

Seemingly indifferent to this mysteriously veiled opening, the strings begin a perky little dance, *Allegro con spirito*. Its two brief phrases are repeated an octave lower before the full orchestra offers a joyous comment which continues in a carefree mood for some time. The oboes' contribution is worth noting as they pick out a phrase on their own, provoking a wriggle of delight from the strings. A loud drum-roll and a sustained brass chord serve as a useful landmark to help us identify a significant moment we could easily miss. Without drawing attention to it in any way, Haydn gives this phrase to his violins:

A comparison with the opening theme (see above) shows how close the relationship is, yet Haydn, having made the point to his own satisfaction, passes on happily to the second subject. The tune is folk-like in character and has the most unsophisticated of accompaniments. The end of the exposition has an unmistakable air of finality.

The development begins with a tightly woven web of counterpoint based on fragments of the '*con spirito*' theme. This continues with growing energy until it is brought to a sudden halt on the dominant of C minor (G). Cellos and violas begin an obvious reference to the opening *Adagio*, turning it into an ambling accompaniment against which the violins offer the sort of fragmentary phrases that Beethoven was to use so effectively. Again there is a halt and a brief pause. An enterprising new development of the first few notes of the '*Allegro*' leads us to a reprise of the second subject, now in D flat major and instantly recognisable with its pizzicato bass. Its peasant origins are soon obscured in some symphonic hullabaloo that need not be taken seriously since Haydn arrests it in mid-flight. There is another pause, a feature of this movement, followed by a perfectly proper recapitulation. As we have grown to expect, the road to the second subject is considerably shortened. However, just as things seem to be going along according to plan there is an extraordinary upheaval, a musical earthquake of shattering force that ceases as unexpectedly as it had appeared. With a master-stroke of ingenuity Haydn brings back the opening *Adagio*, the initial drum-roll now seeming much more sinister in such a context. In the ensuing coda he returns to the *Allegro con spirito*, openly revealing its relationship to the introduction. There have been shocks enough and sixteen brisk bars end the movement.

While we often describe Haydn's themes as being *like* folksongs it is not often that we can know precisely whether he was drawing on childhood memories, quoting songs that were still current in Austria or Hungary during his adult years, or simply inventing them *à la mode*. In the case of this slow movement (and in the finale) it is possible to be more specific and researchers have established that the two themes on which Haydn wrote an elaborate double-variation movement both came from the district of Oedenburg, the nearest town to Eszterháza. Rather than quoting the folk-tunes exactly, Haydn used them as a starting-point, continuing on more interesting lines after the first few bars. Since one theme is in C minor and the other in C major they are easily distinguishable even though the actual melodies are rather alike in shape; indeed at a first hearing one might mistakenly presume that the second tune is a legitimate, if rather free, variation on the first.

The form of the movement is simple enough:

Theme I	(C minor) in two sections, both repeated.
Theme II	(C major) in two sections, both repeated.
Theme I	Variation 1, no repeats.
Theme II	Variation 1, violin solo with repeats.
Theme I	Variation 2, first section only repeated.
Theme II	Variation 2, no repeats.
Coda.	

There are several points worthy of comment. Notice the gruff sound of the double basses, tuned down to an exceptional low C to give a suitably rustic trudge to the accompaniment. Theme I is initially for strings only; Theme II highlights oboes, bassoons and horns to give it a quite different tonal colour as well as a different tonality. Theme I, Variation 1 sees little change in the string parts but new interest is added by solo wind instruments. Theme II, Variation 1 has a highly decorative violin solo, a further opportunity for Salomon to show his skill though Robbins Landon suggests that in this case Haydn was writing for his friend Viotti.

Theme I, Variation 2 is altogether different, with brass and timpani conscripting the humble peasant tune into the army. The second portion involves some very brilliant passages for the violins. In contrast Theme II, Variation 2 is rather frivolous, with perky oboes and an ornithological flute. Towards the end of the variation note the strangely growling bass. The music then breaks off on an ascending phrase and there is a little pause before the delightful coda in which we find ingenious imitative counterpoint in the strings, a humorous dissection of the subject and a salvo of artillery near the end.

The Menuetto is notable for the sharp rhythmic kick that occurs in alternate bars. This is a real country dance and one can easily imagine the stamp of heavy boots and the slap of horny hands on *lederhosen*; in fact the tune itself is almost certainly meant to be a yodelling song. The second section begins rather timidly as though the aristocracy are slightly alarmed by this rowdy display; but with the return of the initial rhythm Haydn plays a nice joke on us since the dancers are no longer together, the lower strings lagging a bar behind. This produces a flustered reaction from the violins who take some time to get back in line and re-start.

The central Trio begins with a gracefully curving figure which is passed from hand to hand, possibly representing the flags or coloured ribbons that are often used in folk-dances. A curious little passage based on repeated quavers conjures up a picture of girls running tiptoe to their appointed places for the next part of the dance, but the main feature here is the transparent delicacy of the texture in comparison to the boisterous rusticity of the Menuetto.

The final movement is remarkable for its concentration on one theme virtually throughout. Only in the first movement of Beethoven's Fifth Symphony do we find a comparable limitation of themes, although to very different purpose. Curiously enough both composers use themes that exploit repeated notes:

Haydn begins the movement with a quiet passage for two horns suggesting the lure of the chase to his English audience. It could have been a mere prefix but turns out to have an additional function as accompaniment to the theme above. This too is based on a Croatian folksong, suggesting that despite his huge popularity in England Haydn's thoughts were beginning to turn homewards.

The omnipresence of the theme makes it extremely difficult to pick out any notable landmarks, but one point that even the tone-deaf would notice is the first tremendous climax in which full brass and timpani join forces with the rest of the orchestra. Out of this considerable eruption emerges a quiet tapping figure on violins and violas, preparation we feel sure for a second subject. But no; refusing to make way for any such intruder, the cellos come in with Theme I yet again, eliciting a confirmatory response from the flute. The tapping accompaniment continues as the cellos and basses set out on a mysterious journey that ultimately produces a mirthful reaction from the full orchestra. Theme I now seems momentarily to lose its way as the strings grope around by semitones; however, they are soon put right by their colleagues and after a typical Haydn pause the development section begins. (One might mistake it for the recapitulation but the movement is conceived on a very large scale and though the material may seem not overimpressive, Haydn is astonishingly inventive in his treatment of it.) The actual arrival of the recapitulation is very clearly signposted with the entire orchestra (save for the timpani) stamping out four repeated Gs.

The final coda makes the most of the opening horn call, now doubled by trumpets and wind as the timpani whip up the excitement by playing at ever increasing speed. To have based 386 bars of music on one short theme may seem to be carrying economy to a ludicrous level, but the movement is a splendid justification of Haydn's self-imposed restriction, and we are swept along on the flood-tide of his inspiration.

HOLST

1874–1934

To have been a composer in Britain at the start of the twentieth century must almost have seemed an act of vainglorious folly. English music was scarcely substantial enough to have any real quality of its own; it was all imitation Brahms or Mendelssohn dusted over with a touch of old Celtic at times to give it a native flavour. This may seem a mite harsh to such pioneers as Stanford, Parry, Cowan or McCunn, but the verdict of posterity has been to relegate them to a position of very minor importance in the European scene. In the circumstances it is hardly surprising that those composers who had sufficient individuality to fill the gap that had been empty so long were at first beset with dreadful uncertainties. There was no real tradition to draw upon, no receptive climate of opinion, no belief that 'our' music could ever be as good as 'theirs'. And yet, with a quiet faith that somehow the dawn had come at last, men like Elgar, Vaughan-Williams, Delius and Holst got on with the business of composing, sometimes with little assurance that the notes would ever be played, unless by amateurs whom they themselves could direct.

It was Holst who had one of the hardest struggles to find his true identity, to shake off the imprinted suggestion of what music ought to be like, and to isolate and reveal his own remarkably individual personality. His first venture into opera was a harmless lightweight called *Lansdown Castle*, written in his 'teens and showing the influence of Sullivan; this was at a time when Grieg was a 'modern' composer, so much so that Holst's father couldn't stand the sound of the *Lyric Pieces*. But father and son shared an enthusiasm for the Gilbert and Sullivan operettas, and Holst was to follow up his boyish essay in the form with a one-act opera called *The Revoke*. In May 1893, he went up to London to study; after the quiet of Gloucestershire it must have seemed a dizzily new world. He was overwhelmed, most especially by Wagner. He was assailed with all the usual delusions of grandeur that are liable to unbalance young men of talent. He embarked on a three-act epic opera called *Sita*. It was to take him seven years of labour, and so far as I know it has never been performed. Holst later described it with characteristic frankness as 'good old Wagnerian bawling'. The libretto was his own adaptation of a Sanskrit legend; Imogen Holst, his daughter, gives this brief description of the story:

> '. . . Scenic effects and stage directions have a grandiose disregard for the practical difficulties of the producer. The action takes place in the ravine of a jungle or on the banks of a raging torrent into which the villain is hurled in the last scene. There are several furious battles: victims are killed and wounded: gods appear on a distant mountainside, lit by the shining moon or by the pearly light of dawn: hordes of devils enter, bearing flaming torches: a chariot with winged horses appears and mounts into the air during a flash of lightning. Everything is planned on a suitably colossal scale. The long-enduring soloists have to compete with an enormous orchestra in their efforts to provide the volume of tone demanded by the composer. When the heroine appears and catches a first glimpse of the man who is destined to be her husband, she flings back her shoulders and greets him by name on a high-held fortissimo A over a tremolo crescendo from the full orchestra . . .'[1]

It doesn't need a lot of imagination to realise the fantastic labour involved in getting an opera on this scale down on paper; what one tends to forget is the consuming demon that makes a man do it with so little hope of reward. The demon was there all right, but it had to be tamed, and this huge score was perhaps like the first mad uncontrolled gallop of an unbroken horse, a gallop that by exhausting the creature, makes it more tractable.

Only by being aware of this background can we appreciate the extraordinary originality of Holst's next venture into opera, *Savitri*. The three acts were whittled down to one; that one was to last a mere thirty minutes; there were only three characters, and the orchestra was reduced to a mere twelve players. The spectre of Wagner had at last been laid, but what temptations must have been resisted in the process.

Savitri is an Indian fable concerning a battle of wits between Death and a woman; Death comes to take the woman's husband, Satyavan, and strikes him down; but she welcomes Death, and so moves him by her gentle courtesy that he offers her a gift. The gift she asks for is life; Death grants her the gift, but she then shows him that life is untenable without her husband. Death recognises defeat, and her husband is brought back to life.

Holst begins this with the voice of Death calling to Savitri, and it must have been very tempting for him to colour the words with sombre chords and the ominous beat of drums. But in the end, in that lonely time when the composer has finally to decide, he took his courage in his hands and dared to start the opera with no orchestra, no overture, no drums, not even the figure of Death standing tremendous against a backcloth. Just a voice, offstage, unseen.

The economy of this writing in 1907 was quite staggering. It was an age

---

[1] Imogen Holst, *The Music of Gustav Holst*, O.U.P., 1951.

of supreme orchestral voluptuousness, and here was Holst, without any real incentive except a self-imposed process of purification, denying himself all the rich trappings of sound which make it so much easier for a composer to seduce the ear.

Now, *Savitri* is to English music what *Pelléas et Mélisande* is to French, for Debussy was going through exactly the same struggle to escape from Wagner's influence. It was a struggle that Strauss didn't attempt to make, for he accepted the Wagnerian mantle, merely stretching its fabric in certain directions. But this is where it is essential to be aware of the isolation of the English composers that I mentioned earlier. In comparison to *Pelléas Savitri* may seem a small achievement; it would be foolish even to try to put it in the same rank. But then Holst was not a genius of Debussy's stature either; he had to find himself, and it took a far longer, more intensive search to forge for himself the proper language for his thoughts. He hadn't finished with big forces entirely for *The Planets* had still to be written, with the remarkable assurance in handling a large orchestra that it shows. Yet the most individual passages in *The Planets* are not the loud or brilliant parts but the bleak austerities of 'Saturn', and it was this secret that perhaps he discovered when he was writing *Savitri*.

There are certain weaknesses in Holst's music, an overdependence on rather trite repetitive figures for one, occasional banalities of harmony for another; but all through his life he was wrestling with them, trying to shake off unwanted influences, but equally searching for positive sources of inspiration and stimulation. He was perhaps at times led off course by his sudden passions for non-musical subjects like Sanskrit or astrology; but it seems that he needed some touchstone of this kind to spark off his creative energy. Seen against the great panorama of European music of the last seventy years, he is inevitably dwarfed; but once one appreciates how heavy were the odds against him one can only admire the resolve with which he pursued his aim. Initially he was dependent almost entirely upon amateur performers if he wanted actually to hear any of his music, and there are moments, even in his mature works, where the critical listener becomes aware of the mark this left on him. Increasingly it came to seem as though he was a man standing between two rooms, one full of amateurs, the other filled with professionals. His heart belonged to the first, his destiny lay with the second. With his innate modesty and shyness he was never happier than working at Morley College, St. Paul's Girls' School or at the festival at Thaxted that meant so much to those who participated in it; yet he knew that his genius must lead him to heights that could only be shared with professional musicians; he had to leave his beloved amateurs behind him, but he found it very hard to do. The easy road would have been to have settled down at St. Paul's where he could enjoy the adulation of a devoted staff and the unalloyed happiness of working with the young. Instead, with admirable pertinacity and despite the real agony of acute neuritis in his hands, he continued to look towards remote horizons. The journey from the boyish opera *Lansdown Castle* to the bleak tone-poem *Egdon Heath* was arduous, but it was a road on which he found more than music; he found himself.

The Planets
(1914–17)

Holst was in his fortieth year when he began work on what was destined to become the most popular of all his compositions. He was apprehensive about tackling the symphony as a musical form, nor did the concerto, with its emphasis on virtuosity, have much appeal for him. He needed some extra-musical stimulus to spark off his creative energy; rather surprisingly, since astrology did not then have the popular appeal the tabloids have given it today, he found it in the subject of the planets whose seven differing characteristics provided him with a justification for writing seven symphonic movements. Ironically he began work on Mars in May 1914, finishing the first sketch with prophetic timing just before the outbreak of World War I. Owing to his poor health he could not be considered for military service; thus he was able to continue working on this immense project in the sound-proof room that had been specially provided for him at St. Paul's Girls' School in Brook Green, Hammersmith. (All three locations were to provide titles for lesser compositions.) However, progress was frequently interrupted by the demands of regular teaching and the work with amateur choirs and orches-tras that brought him such satisfaction. In the event it was virtually three years before he was able to complete the massive score. Parts of it he tried out with piano duet and organ aided by members of staff or the more talented girls in the school. By 1918 Holst was convinced that he might never even hear the work in its proper colours. A summons to Salonika[2] to organise music for the troops made the prospect of performance seem even more remote. Then came a Hollywood-like gesture that composers might dream of but which seldom materialises. Balfour Gardiner, a minor composer with considerable private means, decided to give Holst a parting present. He hired the Queen's Hall, the London Symphony Orchestra and a young man called Adrian Boult to put on a private performance of *The Planets*. Holst was naturally overwhelmed by the experience, and legend tells how during 'Jupiter' the cleaning ladies cast aside their brooms and scrubbing-brushes

[2] Salonica in Holst's letters.

and danced in the aisles, a spontaneous reaction which showed how effectively he had reached the hearts of the common people.

Ever his own most severe critic, Holst did not regard *The Planets* as his best work, preferring the restraint of *The Hymn of Jesus* or his ultimate masterpiece, the remote and austere *Egdon Heath*. One evening he returned to his lodgings in Kensington with a look of dejection on his face. His landlady, Mrs Pattison George, inquired solicitously what was troubling him. 'I have become popular,' he said in tones of self-denigration; '*The Planets* is to be performed in the Queen's Hall.' He was genuinely alarmed at the prospect of public appearances, much preferring the friendly but restricted circles of St. Paul's or Thaxted. In fact critical opinion has remained divided. The brilliance of the orchestration is indisputable, as is the composer's ability to sustain a mood through long slow movements without monotony or boredom. But there are weaknesses in the construction—too much reliance on repeated rhythms and sequences, a tendency to pad at times, and a naive belief that asymmetrical rhythms are inherently more compelling than symmetrical ones, as though there is some special magic about five or seven beats in a bar. Such technicalities are of little concern to audiences and, with the increasing familiarity brought about by recordings, the work has grown in popularity to such an extent that it is now regarded as one of the great landmarks in the twentieth-century renaissance of English music.

I   Mars, the Bringer of War

There is an implicit conflict here between the relentless forward impulse of the reiterated rhythm and the slow heave of the menacing motif in the brass. The repeated Gs continue their ominous beat for thirty-nine bars of 5/4, above which Holst builds a steadily increasing mass of harmony punctuated by strident alarums from tenor tuba, trumpets and horns. Their tauter rhythm enhances the tension until a great climax is reached, a sustained D flat major chord against pounding C naturals. It is the signal for a new development. Horns, trumpets and trombones introduce a phrase in parallel cords that uncoils as sinisterly as a giant python. Joined in turn by woodwind and strings, it builds to an even bigger climax out of which emerges a stamping crotchet rhythm that seems to acknowledge a debt to Stravinsky's *Rite of Spring* in its primitive quality. A solo tenor tuba proposes a new melody which elicits a welcoming fanfare from the trumpets. The tuba theme spreads through the orchestra until it develops into a conflict of will between tuba and trumpet, the tuba daring the trumpet to climb a step higher in each peremptory phrase. A swift flurry of notes from wind and strings leads us to a huge sustained chord which gradually dies away. Quietly the serpentine coils worm their way upwards from the very depths as a side-drum taps out brief reminders of the initial rhythm, reminders that grow more emphatic until at last the whole orchestra hammers out the opening rhythmic pattern. In terms of musical form this could be regarded as a recapitulation of sorts, much reinforced. Indeed from here to the end of the movement there is no new material save for a brief patch of static (if extremely tense) harmony, and the final explosive dissonances.

When Holst was composing this movement, banging out its violent discords on his landlady's piano, she remonstrated with him. 'It's so ugly, Gustav!' she said. 'But war is ugly' was his response, 'ugly, but grand too. That is how I feel it and that is how I *must* write it.' To our ears today the dissonances may not seem all that alarming but even so the music has an awesome power that can leave us genuinely shaken.

II   *Venus, the Bringer of Peace*

After the powerful rhythmic drive of Mars the Venus music brings a feeling of stillness that is instantly conveyed by the opening horn-call. (Is there an echo here of the first notes of Weber's *Oberon* overture?) The response comes from four flutes and three oboes whose close-packed harmonies soon resolve into a hypnotically repetitive alternation of chords above which glockenspiel or celesta offer brief reminders of the opening flute phrase. The entry of the strings with a rather too conventional arpeggio in the cello part is less magical, and the central section of the movement is relatively weak in content. Imogen Holst shrewdly pointed out that when her father was unsure of himself 'he would put in a *poco accelerando*, as if he were nervously trying to get over the ground as soon as possible.'[3] A return to the initial tempo brings a restoration of quality while some lovely rippling figuration on harp and woodwind adds new interest. The final unwinding of a circular pattern in the celesta part is particularly effective, with divided violins placed an octave above the flutes.

III   *Mercury, the Winged Messenger*

This movement, a true scherzo, shows Holst at his most inventive; despite the very large orchestra he had at his disposal (or hoped to have!) the music is nimble and delicate. There is an intriguing ambiguity in the harmony which alternates swiftly between two contrasting keys, B flat major and E major.[4] From these conflicting entities Holst fashions an interesting scale, Bb–C–D–Eb–E♮–F♯–G♯–A–Bb etc. Its two components are divided equally between two instruments giving a truly 'mercurial' effect as they flash past. One such

[3] *The Music of Gustav Holst*, p. 43.
[4] Britten exploits the identical tonal conflict in the opening bars of *Les Illuminations*.

composite scale terminates with a solo violin playing a high E natural upon which it fidgets for a while as harp, celesta or woodwind toss in perfectly conventional three-note chords in unconventional juxtaposition. The solo violin is replaced by an equally restless glockenspiel while, from time to time, the delicate texture is rudely shattered by cursory phrases on raucous woodwind or horns.

At the suggestion of the solo violin a new theme makes its appearance; as a melody it makes little progress but it takes the fancy of a number of instruments in turn—oboe, flute, celesta, clarinet, second violins—until it becomes positively radiant in full orchestral colour. It is a central climax that goes straight to the heart, only to tantalise us by dissolving into mysterious pauses before the flickering phrases resume their nimble dance. Here we sense the basically classical structure of the movement, for is this not the return to the opening that follows the central Trio of traditional scherzo movements? However, Holst is not content merely to repeat what has gone before and the remaining part of Mercury, while similar in purpose, has some new and more complex elements, notably some unison flurries in the strings that provoke an excited response from the woodwind. The fidgety rhythm originally on a solo violin or glockenspiel now becomes a timpani solo; the central tune makes an abortive attempt to reappear but is soon swept away by a remarkable ascending scale in the woodwind that rushes from bassoon depths to piccolo heights in four-and-a-half bars. It is like a playful gust of wind that sweeps all before it, leaving only a few scattered fragments to drift back to earth in its wake.

IV   *Jupiter, the Bringer of Jollity*

A brilliant staccato figure on the strings serves as both introduction and accompaniment to the first main theme whose somewhat heavyfooted syncopations suggest that Jupiter has already spent some time in the company of Bacchus. Despite its immense vigour there are moments here where Holst's inspiration flags. For example there is a fanfare-like motif initiated by four horns in unison which suffers from rather trite repetition, at one point coming to a complete halt as though uncertain where to go. All is forgiven as horns and strings in unison produce a splendidly rousing tune which surely provoked the spontaneous 'knees-up' among the cleaning ladies.

Suddenly the pulse changes to a sturdy 3/4 as the horns—all six of them now—belt out a new theme that has a suggestion of a bell-chime about it. It is repeated a further five times with striking changes of orchestral texture until things are brought to an abrupt halt on a massive chord of F sharp major. A dramatic exchange between brass and timpani leads to a few quiet references to the opening material over a curious thrumming effect from violas and cellos, a rapid pizzicato repetition of the same note that is much harder to do than one might imagine from just looking at the notes.

Enter the Big Tune. Although it irritated him profoundly, Elgar must have realised that it was almost inevitable that the central theme of his *Pomp and Circumstance March No. 1* would have words fitted to it and end up as 'Land of Hope and Glory'. The theme that Holst introduces into the middle of Jupiter offers an equally open invitation, with the important difference that he himself used it as a setting to the hymn 'I vow to thee, my country' some years later. It was a tacit if perhaps reluctant admission that here, in the middle of a virtuoso work designed for 'professional' orchestral players, Holst's association with 'amateur' performers exerted an inescapable influence. There is no denying that it is a fine tune, devoid of sentimentality. But it fits uneasily into this context, the ensuing mock fanfares seeming trite and frivolous by contrast. (It is interesting to compare this with another Elgarian tune, 'Nimrod' in the *Enigma Variations*, a truly instrumental conception that is wonderfully integrated into its surroundings.)

The third section of 'Jupiter' is a reprise of the first, albeit with some changes of key. A final coda reintroduces the central tune in the deepest register surrounded by fountain-like cascades of notes, but the reference, though solemn, is brief, and the movement finishes with a flash of brilliance.

v   *Saturn, the Bringer of Old Age*

'Saturn' is not merely a slow movement; it takes us into a different world which no English composer had entered before. Two chords toll gently to and fro; upper and lower notes are a ninth apart while the scoring (two flutes, bass flute and harp harmonics) gives an unearthly tone-colour that Stravinsky himself might have envied. Beneath, double-basses heave a huge sigh which in due course elicits a doleful response from the violins. The repetition of the flute chords gives a feeling of timelessness while the string phrases convey a sense of utter desolation.

Pizzicato cellos and basses introduce an ostinato figure of four notes oft-repeated which literally bring us back to earth. After the sheer magic of the opening the ensuing slow march seems something of a cliché even though the trombones give it a spacious majesty. The return to the tolling flute chords takes us back to the magical world of a distant planet; but soon its austere landscape begins to seem menacing as the heavy brass take over from the flutes, building an immense crescendo which spills over into a sudden clangour of bells. The pace quickens and for a moment or two there is a genuine feeling of terror which even the stark opening theme (double-basses) does little to dispel. The moment is short-lived however and we are soon back with the sad tolling of the flute chords.

A change of key and pulse brings some relief as though some distant sun had brought a touch of warmth to the frozen planet. From this point to the end of the movement the music is altogether less forbidding. The long drawn-out string phrases still speak of desolation, but glistening harp figures suggest the gentle tinkle of icicles jangling in the wind. Gradually the violin parts ascend to higher registers until at the last we are left with a bare E minor chord, faint but clear yet once more devoid of warmth. Had Holst lived to see the actual photos of a lunar landscape, I doubt if he would have changed a note of this remarkable piece.

VI *Uranus, the Magician*

In symphonic terms this movement might be described as a second scherzo. The first four notes, impressively declaimed by trumpets and trombones, are of great importance thematically, an importance that is underlined by an immediate repetition at a quicker pace from tenor and bass tubas and a rapid-fire comment from the timpani. Three bassons begin a grotesquely lolloping dance which spreads through the orchestra regardless of the awesome gestures of the initial 'magic' theme. (One is inevitably reminded of the *Sorcerer's Apprentice* with its contrast between the hoppity broomsticks and the commanding figure of the magician.) Despite the brilliance of the orchestration the thematic material in this movement is distinctly homespun and Holst's daughter, Imogen, is positively scathing in her comments on it in the admirably detached book she wrote on his works. Nevertheless, the uncritical listener is sure to be swept along with the big march tune which ultimately emerges as a great climax. The sheer volume is tremendous, with the full brass urged on by pounding rhythms from two timpanists. Suddenly an organ glissando (!) sweeps the noise away as if by magic leaving nothing but a mysteriously quiet string chord hanging in the air. Harp harmonics spell out the opening 'magic' theme as though from an immense distance. A second summons elicits a bustling response from grunting woodwind, angry tubas and frenzied timpani. A violent dissonance reveals the full power of Uranus, a formidable magic spell whose repercussions die away chord by chord until there is nothing left but the silence of space.

VII *Neptune, the Mystic*

By any standards this is a quite extraordinary piece of music. A footnote in the score instructs that 'the orchestra is to play *pp* throughout', an exhortation that would seem to invite disaster from the point of view of audience appeal. Furthermore, Holst's own score has a reminder in pencil—'*dead* tone, except the clarinet after Fig. 5'. Orchestral players do not like to play *pianissimo* throughout, nor do they appreciate being asked to play with 'dead' tone. As though the sheer size of the orchestra was not obstacle enough to the prospects of a performance of a work by a still relatively obscure composer, Holst required (in this movement only) a six-part chorus of female voices who, he said, 'should be placed in an adjoining room, the door of which is to be left open until the last bar of the piece, when it is to be slowly and silently closed. The chorus, the door, and any Sub-Conductors that may be found necessary are to be well screened from the audience.' That such a requirement substantially reduced the number of halls in which *The Planets* could actually be performed mattered little to Holst; his sole concern was to achieve (albeit by a somewhat crude method) an effect of sound gradually receding towards the threshold of inaudibility. Nowadays we are so accustomed to electronic fades that we may not fully appreciate the originality of Holst's conception.

The movement begins with a flute and bass flute drifting in parallel motion through a theme whose 5/4 metre gives a feeling of rhythmic ambiguity. A high shimmering chord on harps gives an icy glitter to the scene. The entry of violins and violas signals an increase of activity in the woodwind, whose gently undulating figures shift constantly from E minor to G sharp minor and back again. These two conflicting tonalities are crucial to the movement which, despite the firm restraint of *sempre pianissimo* (always very quiet), develops a series of rippling arpeggios in celesta and harps that suggest light reflected off the surface of a frost-bound world. The ripples slowly subside and die. Through a long sustained chord of E minor a simple chant-like phrase gropes its way upward from cellos to woodwind and on to the horns. For the first time we hear soprano voices, a sustained high G, almost imperceptible, and so unexpected that it seems an illusion. The important clarinet solo appears, the first theme to show any warmth or expressive appeal. It plants a seed from which the unseen voices flower into melody, almost unaccompanied except for the soft sighing of low flutes. The voices are momentarily interrupted by a further shimmer, a soft flurry of wind that sends snow crystals skimming over the ice. The distant voices begin their eerie alternation of high chords, gradually receding until we feel that we are no longer hearing but imagining the sound. It is an ending of spell-binding magic, unforgettable in its effect.

As a somewhat prosaic postscript it is worth offering a counter to those critics who have tended to dismiss *The Planets* as thin gruel in comparison to *Petrushka* or *The Rite of Spring*. In this movement alone there are a number of truly prophetic passages, not merely anticipating possibilities now fulfilled by electronic means, but looking forward to such works as the Bartók *Concerto for Orchestra* (third movement) or the extraordinary closing moments of the Second Act of Benjamin Britten's *Peter Grimes*.

IVES
1874–1954

An introductory survey

Genius is not a word to be used lightly; indeed it is a quality difficult to define. Given talent and application in any art a child can duly progress to the stature of a mature professional artist, able to command respect. But genius is something beyond talent, occasionally so far beyond that lesser mortals are unable to recognise it. When Weber said that Beethoven was ripe for the madhouse when he wrote his Seventh Symphony it was a refusal to acknowledge genius. The well-known definition 'the infinite capacity for taking pains' fails to convey the sheer courage that accompanies genius. Most of us are hemmed in by an invisible barrier, the barrier of what we believe to be possible. It is a barrier that is partly erected by the conventions of the society we inhabit, partly by technical knowledge. Whether we are concerned with carving wood, playing an instrument, applying brush to canvas, stringing words together or using actors on a stage there comes a point where this barrier inhibits further invention. Though he may refuse to accept it consciously, the normal person knows in his innermost self that the barrier exists and even, if he has great talent, may spend much of his time within touching distance of it. The true genius disregards the barrier and heedless of public opinion passes through it, breaking new ground that, once charted, we in turn may enter with our earlier fears dispelled.

Not surprisingly, a genius is seldom a comfortable person to be with; exploration is a lonely venture and the product of his art may continue to seem strange or obscure for a considerable time. We are all aware of the tribulations suffered by the greatest artists before their genius came to be acknowledged; Picasso, Epstein, Stravinsky, Bartók, Wagner, Joyce—the roll of honour is long and an indictment of the common man's ability to appreciate the uncommon. Yet of all the composers to whom the word genius can unhesitatingly be applied, none can be stranger than the American, Charles Ives. Born in Connecticut in 1874 he lived to be eighty; not until he was seventy-one did he hear even a single one of his compositions for full orchestra. Two years later he received the Pulitzer Prize for his contribution to music, a belated tribute to a spare-time composer who had made a substantial fortune in the insurance business while at the same time developing an entirely original musical language. Admittedly the quality of his music is uneven, but the same could be said of Beethoven, Verdi, Schumann or Wagner.

Now, much has been made of Ives' amateurism, but he actually studied for a music degree at Yale University, though at a time when its entire music department consisted of one room containing a piano and a blackboard. His teacher was Horatio Parker, an able and conscientious musician, albeit lacking in creative imagination. Ives was shrewd enough to play the academic game, realising that it was useless to show Parker the sort of music that his restlessly experimental mind was already beginning to explore. In 1898 he submitted his First Symphony in order to acquire the respectability of a musical degree. It is a work that gives virtually no indication of the fantastically original language he was ultimately to forge for himself. The symphony is more than competent, the scherzo in particular having a Mendelssohnian charm as well as some exemplary fugal writing calculated to delight an examiner's eye. But had Ives progressed no further than this his name now would be as little known to the world at large as that of his teacher. The most detectable influences are Wagner and Dvořák, and it is worth remembering that Dvořák had been director of music at the New York Conservatoire from 1892–5. Since Ives began to compose his symphony in 1897 it seems probable that he had heard a good deal of the Czech composer's music.

Despite a diet of Wagner at the 'Met.' and Tchaikovsky at Carnegie Hall, Ives was soon to shake off all such European mainstream influences and turn nearer to home for inspiration. Encouraged by an eccentric father to think for himself, he decided that any music he wrote should reflect life as it was rather than a world of myth and legend. He listened to the military bands, the revivalist meetings, the kids yelling, the carousel at the circus, the honky-tonk piano, the traffic, the lady next door playing her 'cello, the milkman, the chaotic disorganised sounds of the everyday life surrounding him. But he also heard the music of the spheres, the slow breathing of the sea, and the earth moving a little beneath the weight of mountains; all these sounds he wove into thick tapestries of music.

An early song, 'Circus Band', written in 1894, has such a bouncing vitality that it could easily be transferred into an American musical of the 1940s; few of the audience would sense anything out of place. However, Ives had no wish to follow directly in the steps of Sousa; as he matured he became increasingly sceptical of music that had too immediate an appeal since one of his prime beliefs was that anything achieved too easily was somehow second-best. Even the act of listening to music he wanted to be a challenging experience; the wallpaper music that nowadays floods restaurants and public buildings would have sickened him. Yet, and this is where the paradox of his music lies, he also welcomed material of the humblest kind. For instance he loved to hear a big congregation singing hymns with fervour; but his ultra-perceptive ear was also fascinated by the groaners, the ones who couldn't make the top notes, who persistently sang flat, or just sang the tune wrong. It gave a blurred edge to the line which was an exact musical equivalent to one of the tricks of the Impressionist painters, colour spilling beyond the confines of the outline into the adjacent area. Because it was true to life, Ives wanted to reproduce it, though not simply by having a big choir and instructing some of the members to sing off-key. He aimed to capture and put down on paper all the vagaries of rhythm and pitch that happen accidentally and then transform them into something permanent.

The Orchestral Set No. 1, which bears the title *Three Places in New England* is one of his best and most characteristic works, as imbued with pride in America as any poem by Walt Whitman. The first movement is a sort of musical soliloquy inspired by a statue on Boston Common of Colonel Shaw, a hero of the Civil War who led a regiment of coloured soldiers to help free their brethren in the South. For a long time the music sustains a mood of hazy stillness. There is little at this stage to suggest soldiers or war; Ives' imagination, and consequently the music, is still under the spell of the statue by St Gaudens, seen presumably in a autumnal haze with no one around to disturb his thoughts. But then as though from an immense distance of time and space a memory awakes in Ives' mind. It is a tune known at the time to every American child, although its first stirrings in the orchestral texture are elongated, distorted, as though it were a shadow stretched to unnatural length by the early rays of sunshine. If we listen attentively to the violin parts we hear a ghost-like version of 'Marching through Georgia'. Progressively, just as if the enshrouding mist disperses, the tune becomes clearer until the opening phrase appears quite openly on a solo clarinet. It is this gradual emergence of the familiar out of a quiet but complex web of sound that provides the *raison d'être* of the piece.

The second movement of the Orchestral Set, 'Putnam's Camp', takes us to a different war when the American settlers were fighting off the British. Not far from Ives' home lies a small park (now a memorial) where General Israel Putnam and his Continental soldiers made their camp. 'Long rows of stone camp fire-places still remain to stir a child's imagination,' wrote Ives, and it was through a child's eyes that he 'saw' the event described in the music. A preliminary note in the score gives us a detailed account of the composer's vision:

> Once upon a '4th July', some time ago, so the story goes, a child went there on a picnic, held under the auspices of the First Church and the Village Cornet Band. Wandering away from the rest of the children past the camp ground into the woods, he hopes to catch a glimpse of some of the old soldiers. As he rests on the hillside of laurel and hickories, the tunes of the band and the songs of the children grow fainter and fainter;—when— 'mirabile dictu'—over the trees on the crest of the hill he sees a tall woman

standing. She reminds him of a picture he has of the Goddess of Liberty,—but the face is sorrowful—she is pleading with the soldiers not to forget their 'cause' and the great sacrifices they have made for it. But they march out of camp with fife and drum to a popular tune of the day. Suddenly a new national note is heard. Putnam is coming over the hills from the center,—the soldiers turn back and cheer. The little boy awakes, he hears the children's songs and runs down past the monument to 'listen to the band' and join in the games of dances.[1]

All this is in the music, including the rowdy bands playing on the Fourth of July. The apparition of the woman is done magically with a single blurred chord, held in a moment of stillness by the strings until, in the far distance, a march begins, dispelling the mood.

It is in this movement that Ives brought back to vivid life a childhood memory. His father, George, delighted in musical experiments of the most unorthodox kind. He was a band-leader, and on a famous occasion arranged for two bands to march towards each other from opposite ends of a baseball ground playing different music in conflicting keys. Their gradual but relentless convergence towards a chaotic clash of harmony and rhythm and its equally gradual dissipation fascinated the young Ives and he later determined to try to reproduce the effect on paper, thereby creating daunting problems for conductor and orchestra. Here we find one of the two 'bands' playing in a different key, a different rhythm and a different tempo (one-and-a-third times as fast) from the other. We think of experiments in stereophony as a comparatively recent development, enhanced by the introduction of electronics into the concert-hall, but Ives anticipated this and many other aspects of music that we assume belong to a post-war age.

The composition of the *Three Places* was spread over a period of more than a decade, from 1903 to 1914, but the listener is not aware of any fundamental change of style despite Ives' delight in experiment and innovation. The third movement is the least dramatic, inspired by a walk along the Housatonic river at Stockbridge where Ives, not long married, took his young wife for a romantic stroll. At the music's core lies a sustained tune of great simplicity which Ives was later to arrange as a song for voice and piano. Around this central thread the orchestra weaves a complex web of delicate, almost inaudible sounds, painting the perpetual movement of the water gliding by, the murmur of leaves, the quiet restlessness of nature when moving water brushes past reeds and bullrushes gently clash in the summer breeze. At times we hear a suggestion of distant hymn-singing coming from a church across the river. Musical radical though he was, Ives' compositions frequently turn towards traditional forms of worship.

One would imagine that as a part-time composer spending his routine days in a busy insurance office Ives would have concentrated his remaining

---

[1] From the score of *Three Places in New England*, p. 20, paragraph II.

energies on one work at a time, but even the most casual glance at the chronology of his compositions shows us that often he must simultaneously have had several different manuscripts in varying stages of completion. In 1908 he put the finishing touches to one of his most profound works, *The Unanswered Question*. It is a perfect example of his fascinating individuality. In the background is an immensely slow string-sound, so timeless as to be like the surface of the moon. It has no change of tone throughout the movement, and Ives called it 'The Silence of the Druids, who Know, See and Hear Nothing'. Seven times in all, a trumpet plays a strange atonal pattern of notes which Ives calls the Perennial Question of Existence. Six times 'the Fighting Answerers (flutes and other people)'—to use Ives' own phrase—seem to hunt for the invisible solution, increasing in agitation until at last, with a mocking rejection of the trumpet's recurring theme, they surrender and depart. At the end we are left with the continuing string harmonies, serene and unruffled by the dispute, a triumph of consonance over dissonance. It is not too far-fetched to say that this remarkable composition anticipates conceptions that were not more fully explored until the advent of Stockhausen. Since it pre-dates even *Petrushka*, let alone *The Rite of Spring*, it is a truly astonishing achievement.

Of the symphonies the one known as *Holidays* is perhaps the most representa-tive. Ives chose not to give it a number since, as he put it, 'These movements may be played as separate pieces . . . or lumped together as a symphony.' The four movements date respectively from 1909, 1912, 1913 and 1904. The finale was therefore written first, before any idea of using it as part of a symphony had entered the composer's head. Labelled 'Thanksgiving and/or Forefathers' Day' it clearly reflects Ives' early days as an organist in certain passages of string-writing that bear a likeness to Vaughan-Williams—of whose music Ives had certainly never heard although they were almost exact contemporaries. Even so, the first part of the movement contains some highly individual writing for glockenspiels and celesta whose delicate bell-like sonorities had never been so exploited by any previous composer. Scored for a large orchestra and chorus[2] the movement ends with what Ives described as 'a praise.'

The symphony is sub-titled 'Recollections of a boy's holidays in a Connecticut country town' and the first movement is inscribed 'Washing-ton's Birthday'. Like the other three movements, it begins with very quiet slow music, an apparent weakness of structure that even the most impercep-tive listener might be tempted to criticise. Ives would argue that all days begin the same, with the emergence out of darkness into light, a fact so obvious that he would feel no need to be defensive about it—not that he was really defensive about any of his music. He was a supreme example of the

[2] Not used in the preceding movements.

creative artist pursuing his own way, regardless of every kind of mockery and ignorant criticism.

Washington's birthday falls in February and the opening movement stresses not only the dark of a winter morning but the cold as well. Yet though Ives' harmony is often complex and extremely dense in texture, it is quite wrong to suppose that he has no feeling for melody other than quotations of American popular song. Certainly he makes liberal use of such quotations; they are as much a part of his heritage as English folk song was to Vaughan-Williams, something to acknowledge with affection and pride rather than an apology. But if we examine those melodic lines that are clearly his own, they are usually lyrical in character, even though their outline may be deliberately blurred.

As though from a church spire seen faintly through the low-lying mist of early morning, bells softly chime in characteristically irregular rhythms. The sound patterns grow more dense and then the mood changes abruptly, just as if one had come in from the cold street to a house brilliantly lit, with a log-fire blazing and a party in full swing. Such sudden changes of mood and style are disconcerting until one sees their complete pictorial validity. You *can* have a warm, brightly lit house surrounded by a cold outer darkness and we accept such juxtapositions all our lives. Put us into a concert hall, though, and our minds tend to become inflexible. Familiarity enables us to accept the striking contrasts between aristocratic and peasant music that we find in Haydn symphonies. Ives would maintain that his contrasts were much the same in spirit, though he cannot resist teasing us by incorporating a 'Jew's Harp' into the orchestra. (Shades of Leopold Mozart's sleighbells in his Divertimento in F or Papageno's little Pan-pipes in *The Magic Flute* . . .)

Typically, Ives, having almost affronted us by the naive simplicity of the initial dance-music, builds it up into a texture of increasing complexity until it becomes virtually chaotic. But is there any sound much more chaotic than sixty or seventy people in a room, all talking and laughing, drinking and dancing, until the nearest neighbour becomes inaudible in the welter of noise? And when the party's broken up and one sits with the last few chosen guests around the dying fire, isn't there, even in these cynical days, a sense of old-world peace, so that even the sentimental strains of 'Home Sweet Home' strike an evocative note? To round off the movement and send the closest friends happily into the darkness outside what could be more suitable than a snatch of 'Good-night ladies'?

Now in a sense, if one wants to be critical, it could be argued that Ives set himself an impossible task by incorporating such home-spun material into scores that elsewhere are extraordinarily unorthodox and challenging. It is certain that he did not do it to court popular appeal. Wealthy and successful business-man that he was, he could afford to disregard critical opinion. Throughout his music there is an extraordinary nostalgia for a lost boyhood in small-town Danbury, even an imaginary boyhood dating back to years he had only heard about from his father's tales. The ballads, hymn-tunes and folk-songs that crop up so surprisingly yet frequently in his major compositions are vital threads that linked him to the dream-world of a vanished childhood. In an entry in a personal notebook dated June 5, 1914, he wrote 'each day I fear I may get further and further away from my boytime dreams'.

The *Holidays* symphony is the most open confession of this aspect of Ives' personality, and the third movement, 'Decoration Day' continues the trend with fragments of 'Swanee River' and 'Taps' incorporated into its considerable complexities. But the greatest difficulties remain to be surmounted in the final movement, 'The Fourth of July', a work which passes so far beyond the bounds of what had been thought possible that it makes *The Rite of Spring* seem almost easy. Admittedly there are many quotations from the huge store of patriotic or popular songs of the day, but they are jumbled together with a wild abandonment that defies every rule of musical propriety. As Ives wrote, 'I remember distinctly when I was scoring this that there was a feeling of freedom as a boy has, on the Fourth of July, who wants to do anything he wants to do, and that's his one day to do it.' His own programme-note must be unique for its racy breathless style.

> It's a boy's '4th'—no historical orations—no patriotic grandiloquences by 'grown-ups'—no program in his yard! . . . His festivities start in the quiet of the midnight before and grow raucous with the sun. Everybody knows what it's like,—if everybody doesn't,—Cannon on the Green, Village Band on Main St., fire crackers, shanks mixed on cornets, strings around big toes, torpedoes, Church-bells, lost fingers, fifes, clam-chowder, a prize-fight, drum-corps, burnt shins, parades (in and out of step), saloons all closed (more drunks than usual), baseball game (Danbury All-Stars vs. Beaver Brook Boys), pistols, mobbed umpire, Red, White and Blue, runaway horse—and the day ends with the sky-rocket over the Church-steeple, just after the annual explosion sets the Town-Hall on fire.[3]

Although Ives admitted that not every detail here described could actually be found in the score, the words do give an impression of the amazing vitality of the music. Yet at the very end of the work, after the welter of sound has battered us dizzy there is a touch of sublime impracticality as Ives calls for a choir to sing one verse of a hymn.

> God, beneath Thy guiding hand
> Our exiled fathers crossed the sea
> And, as they trod the wintry strand,
> With prayer and praise they worshipped Thee.

It's a climax that is truly exalting, but he resists all temptations to prolong the moment, allowing the music to die away to nothing in a series of orchestral amens that seem to linger in the air for eternity.

[3] Quoted in Frank R. Rossiter, *Charles Ives and his America*, Gollancz, 1976.

Ives wrote a considerable quantity of religious music, all of it deeply felt; but many of his compositions remained unfinished since he never took the least notice of what one might call his obligations to posterity. The claims of his business career often made it impossible for him to complete his vaster projects. But the work he rated highest was his setting of the ninetieth Psalm: 'Lord thou hast been our refuge.' The entire piece, and it's a long setting, is built on top of a slowly reiterated low C, like the omnipresence of God. It's scored for organ and bells only and is rightly regarded as a masterpiece of choral writing. It is considerably more straightforward in many ways than much of his music but its truly visionary quality is there for all to hear. Let Ives himself have the last words:

> If a Yankee can reflect the fervency with which his gospels were sung—the fervency of Aunt Sarah, who scrubbed her life away for her brother's ten orphans, who, after a 14-hour work-day on the farm would hitch up and drive five miles through the mud and rain to a prayer-meeting—her one articulate outlet for the fullness of her unselfish soul—if he can reflect the fervency of such a spirit, he may find there a local colour that will do all the world good. If his music can but catch that spirit by being a part with itself, it will come somewhere near this idea—and it will be American too.[4]

---

[4]Quoted in Henry and Sidney Cowell, *Charles Ives and his Music*, O.U.P., 1955.

JANÁČEK
1854–1928

Although dates are often of little real importance, the period from 1854–1928 witnessed amazing changes in music. It is worth considering what it must have been like to have been born in the 1850s in a rural backwater of central Europe and then to live long enough to experience a world transformed in the 1920s. If one had been a student when Wagner, Brahms, Liszt, Tchaikovsky and Dvořák were living giants, dominating the musical landscape, how did one adjust to the revolutionary era of 1910–20 when virtually every conception about the language of music went through fundamental changes that must have seemed strange and disturbing to a man in his sixties? To survive such a period without getting left behind and being regarded as old-fashioned presupposes a mind of powerful originality. Such a man was Janáček. As if to underline the significance of his life-span his first opera, `Sárka`, dating from 1887, was not actually performed until 1925, by which time, despite extensive revisions, the composer must have felt it had originally been written by someone else.

Virtually everything about Janáček is extraordinary. Apart from Charles Ives, no composer waited longer for recognition; he was over forty before his first significant work appeared, over sixty before his music was heard by an appreciable public. Yet the last twelve years of his life were strikingly productive, his music showing no signs of having been written by someone whose whole upbringing had been in the nineteenth century and who was forty-six in the year 1900. For much of his life, he remained an obscure unknown; but the lack of recognition did nothing to dissuade him from writing, and he continued to compose large-scale works, even operas, when there seemed little chance that they would be performed. Success, when it did come, was the result of a curiously haphazard incident when a perceptive and artistic man happened to be walking in the country, and passed a house where a woman was singing some completely unfamiliar music. The stranger was so impressed by that he was compelled to find out what it was. Discovering that it was by Janáček, a name he'd never even heard, he had the persistence to go to the managers of the opera-house in Prague and tell them they must give this unknown composer a hearing. Janáček at this time wasn't a student at the threshold of a career, but a mature man of some sixty-one years. Now in fact, although the literary gentleman hadn't heard of Janáček, the opera-management had, since he had written a number of works which had already been performed in Prague or Brno. But the music had never really been acknowledged as anything very special, and it was only in the last twelve years of Janáček's life that the Czechs realised that they had a national genius in their midst. One of the main obstacles that deferred his recognition was the personal enmity of Kovařovic, the conductor of the National Theatre in Prague, whose music Janáček had scathingly (if rather unwisely) criticised back in 1887. Kovařovic had actually seen an amateurish and inadequate performance of *Jenůfa* when it was first tried out in the provincial city of Brno (1904), and it seems that he had not been impressed. The ardent pleas of Janáček's newly-found advocate caused him to reconsider, and so it was that twelve years after it had been written *Jenufa* came to be performed properly. It scored an instant success, providing the composer with a recognition too long denied and, incidentally, ending a damaging feud that had lasted for thirty years.

The triumph of *Jenůfa* brought a substantial alteration to Janáček's way of life. For many years he had depended on teaching and choral conducting for a living. In 1881 he had married a piano pupil shortly before her sixteenth birthday. Not surprisingly the relationship, presumably based on a passing infatuation, failed to bring lasting happiness; indeed an early separation so affected Janáček that he was unable to compose for some four years. Once he began to write again he was increasingly drawn towards opera, foolhardily ambitious though it may have seemed as a medium;[1] but together with these aspirations came an intense new interest in folk-song and it was this that enabled him to shake off the Germanic influence imparted to him during his studies in Leipzig and Vienna. Arduously, constantly revising, he began to develop a style that he could feel was truly his own. It tended to exploit rather succinct melodies, repetitive patterns, ambiguous tonality, and the modal scales characteristic of Moravian folk-song. His obsession with opera caused even his instrumental music to be influenced by the speech-rhythms of his native tongue. By the time he was sixty he had written a great deal of music, but though he was respected as a fine local musician in Brno he had made scarcely any impact on the outside world.

Jenůfa changed all that. 1916 might not have seemed an auspicious year to mark the start of an international reputation, but productions were soon arranged in Vienna and Berlin and a contract signed with the highly reputable Universal Edition. With success came a fluency and confidence that had

---

[1] It is worth noting that Dvořák succumbed to the same temptation, though never with such spectacular success.

hitherto eluded him, and though he was now at an age when most men think of retirement, Janáček began to compose as though his life depended on it.[2] His creative energy was partly fired by a passionately felt though platonic relationship with Kamila Stösslová, a married woman thirty-eight years younger than he, but someone who filled the emotional gap that his sterile marriage had created. He wrote to her almost daily for eleven years sharing his most intimate thoughts. She remained comparatively aloof but there can be no doubt that she provided the inspiration for the remarkable sequence of works that he produced in his closing years. They were *The Diary of One Who Disappeared*, a cycle of twenty-three poems for five singers and piano, *Ballad of Blaník*, a symphonic poem, the operas *Káta Kabanová*, *The Cunning Little Vixen*, *The Makropoulos Case*, and *From the House of the Dead*, *The Wandering Madman* for soprano solo and male chorus, two string quartets, a wind sextet called *Youth*, written to celebrate his seventieth birthday (!), a Concertino for piano and six instruments, a Capriccio for the one-armed pianist Otakar Hollman, a set of eighteen 'Nursery Rhymes' for nine singers and small orchestra, the *Sinfonietta* and the *Glagolitic Mass*. Such productivity would be remarkable for a man in his thirties; to have composed on such a scale between the ages of sixty-two and seventy-two is nothing short of astonishing.

Only in recent years has Janáček's true stature as an operatic composer been fully appreciated, but he is now accepted as a master whose nationalist idiom serves as no barrier to the expression of emotions that touch all our hearts, regardless of heritage.

Sinfonietta

When Janáček was already seventy-two years old he received a commission to compose some fanfares for a gymnastic festival. Ideas for this relatively trivial task may well have begun to germinate in his mind when they received an additional stimulus through a happy afternoon spent in the company of his beloved Kamila. Strolling together through a public park in her home-town of Písek they heard the sound of a military band. Following its martial strains they found a bench and sat together in the sunshine to listen to the open-air concert. Janáček was utterly content, sitting with the woman he loved with such strange and undemanding devotion, and the combination of her presence and military music released a flood of themes which took shape within the space of three weeks. The fanfares that had been asked for expanded into a

---

[2] 'I finish one work after another, as if I were soon to settle my account with Life.' Janáček in a letter dated 30.xi.1927.

major composition lasting some twenty-five minutes. Its title, *Sinfonietta*, is one of the most misleading in all music, suggesting as it does a light-weight work for chamber orchestra. With the sort of self-deprecation that we associate more with Brahms, he wrote to Kamila that he was just finishing 'a pretty little Sinfonietta with fanfares'. What he didn't say was that it was scored for a very large orchestra augmented by nine trumpets, two bass trumpets and two tenor tubas; furthermore it was to be in five movements— 'Fanfare', 'The Castle', 'The Queen's Monastery', 'The Street', and 'The Hall'.

' At first Janáček toyed with the idea of calling it 'Military Sinfonietta', intending to dedicate it to the Czech Army, a proud and independent force at last now that his country had been freed from German domination. On second thoughts he made it a tribute to the town of Brno where for so long he had received the acknowledgement denied him elsewhere. Composed as it was for a popular occasion, the *Sinfonietta* is musically less demanding than the operas, and the sheer glory of its sound has an overwhelming impact.

In the first movement, 'Fanfares', the musical material is extremely simple—bare consecutive fifths on the two tenor tubas and a repetitive rocking pattern on the nine trumpets. A break into 3/4 time introduces some more active patterns which are interwoven in such a way as to 'set the wild echoes flying'. Janáček avoids all the conventional rhythms that are associated with military calls or ceremonial fanfares, and instead uses his brass almost like bells. He relies on the splendour of the sound to hold our interest, rather than giving us complicated themes interlocked in contrived counterpoint. There is a rough-hewn simplicity about it that gives the music a very special quality of its own.

The second movement is scored for a completely different combination of instruments, woodwind, trombones and strings. Initially two clarinets play a particularly important part with a rapid accompanying figure that is very characteristic of Janáček. It's a familiar enough pattern dating back to Mozart's time or even earlier, but the actual combination of notes he uses, plus the unusual sound of the clarinets in so curiously exposed a position again provides a novel and instantly intriguing sound. The clarinets are never ensnared in a web of string tone, their bright and clearly defined pattern spinning merrily over trombones and bassoons two and a half octaves beneath. This introductory passage proves to be quite brief, soon giving way to a cheerful little peasant song scored for oboes or flutes with trombones and tuba supplying a somewhat hobnailed accompaniment. The form of this movement complies with no established tradition. It's more like a string of tunes linked together by certain factors that they have in common, a melodic shape, a rhythm, an accompanying figure, whatever it may be. All the tunes have the simple direct appeal of folk-music, and there's virtually nothing in the way of working-out or development in the normal symphonic sense. Brahms would have been very puzzled by it; he might have enjoyed the tunes, but he would have found the orchestration altogether too bare, and the form haphazard to a degree. But while it's difficult to find any satisfactory way of labelling the music except by rather weakly saying theme one, theme two, theme three, theme four and so on, there is a feeling of shape and of climax. Janáček accomplishes this by a technique of merging like with like, so that there is a feeling of continuity even when new tunes are introduced. This he achieves partly by giving his themes rather similar rhythms, partly by the accompanying figures. Certainly there is a central climax when for the first time we hear the full orchestra; but it dissolves in a flurry of references to the opening clarinet pattern and a reminder of the oboes' peasant tune.

The third movement, named after the Queen's Monastery where Janáček had served as a boy chorister, is the first to exploit strings in a conventional way by using their lyrical sustaining quality. But here, as in the first movement, Janáček deliberately repeats his phrases, thereby giving them the character of folk-songs. There's little of the travelogue about it, and his approach is not consciously descriptive in the way that a composer like Respighi's would have been, given a similar title. The individuality again lies in the scoring as bass clarinet and tuba sustain a low E flat a couple of octaves away from the nearest string sound. Janáček's orchestration is full of comparable touches designed to prevent the slightest trace of sentimentality from creeping in. Once more we find variations of pace between relatively short sections, while a boisterous and irreverent tune on the trombone may be a reminder of boyhood pranks when the composer was a chorister.

The fourth of the five movements is called 'The Street', a non-committal title that tells us little about what sort of street Janácek had in mind—a grand boulevard, a slum, a quiet residential mews or what. In fact no further clue is needed as the trumpets kick off with a jaunty tune that conjures images of cheeky errand-boys rather than languid aristocrats.

Janáček repeats this tune time after time, varying its instrumentation and its pitch, and occasionally whipping the music up to a faster tempo. But he's made his own set of rules and it would be misleading to suggest that this is comparable to the scherzo of a normal symphony. The fact is that this work is much nearer to being a suite than a sinfonietta, as Janáček must certainly have realised while he was writing it. His most positive concession to a larger concept of form is the way in which he re-introduces the most important themes from the first movement in the finale. There are even suggestions of themes from other movements, although the generally folk-like quality of the tunes makes it easy to imagine relationships that may not necessarily be intended.

Certainly the busy accompanying figure that we heard so much of in the second movement reappears, but Janáček uses this so much in his other compositions that I don't think we should attach too much importance to it. There are some splendid skirling noises suggesting a sort of bagpipes, and then the opening fanfares return to bring the movement to a triumphant conclusion. It is impossible to force this work into any orthodox mould, but the music is so direct in its appeal that the prop of conventional form is scarcely needed. Its main feature is its extraordinarily individual tone-colour. It is quite free of all the usual clichés found in most arrangements of folk-music or pseudo-folk-music for orchestra. It is clear, bright and unsentimental, perhaps even a little crude at times; but its vitality is remarkable, the more so considering Janáček's age when he wrote it.

Glagolitic Mass

Written in the same year as the *Sinfonietta* (1926), the *Glagolitic Mass* shows a similar disregard for convention. Substantial though it is, it was composed in the space of a single month although Janáček had first thought of writing a major liturgical piece some five years previously. In the event he produced a setting that sounds more pagan than Christian in its rejection of all the traditional conventions of church music. He even rejected the orthodox Latin text, preferring to use the ancient Slavonic alphabet known as Glagolitic which was used in very early religious writings. Here lies one significant clue to Janáček's approach, for his use of an archaic language seems to have prompted him to stress the primitive basis of religious faith. (Stravinsky's *Symphony of Psalms* written two years later shows a similar aim.) Although not conventionally devout—'No believer till I see for myself' he would say—Janáček had been trained as a chorister and many a time as his attention wandered during the long services his eyes must have been drawn to the mosaics and icons that are such a feature of Byzantine art, icons that portray haunted faces staring with black hungry eyes from their gilded prisons. There is nothing smug or cosy about the Byzantine concept of religion, and a sensitive child must have been deeply impressed by the pain and torment in the Saints' expressions and by the emaciation of Christ's body as its weight drags cruelly from the bleeding hands. Here lies the other clue to the music's almost pagan character, pagan because of the barbaric splendour of some of the writing.

The work begins with an introductory fanfare whose sonorous writing for brass tells us that the sounds of the *Sinfonietta* still lingered in the composer's mind. The material is again very simple, centring on the tonic and dominant notes of E flat, over whose 'major' implications a flattened seventh (D flat) raises a doubting question-mark. This opening motif is converted into a constantly revolving pattern in the strings beneath which the brass fanfares continue. Woodwind introduce a gentler theme which grows in magnificence until it is declaimed in majestic harmony by trombones. Typically Janáček creates a sense of unity between opposing themes by using the 'revolving' patterns as an accompaniment to both. Having begun in E flat, the introduction ends a semitone sharper, in E major; in the very last bar the hitherto flattened seventh is raised, possibly a symbol of affirmation of faith.

There follows a Kyrie Eleison. It begins with a gruff angular theme in the cellos, punctuated by trombone chords. Its halting progress is interrupted by a wild scurry of notes on violins and clarinets, a cry of terror that seems to give a vivid justification for the prayer 'Lord have mercy upon us.' The moment of fear is short-lived and an oboe restores the opening theme which is soon taken up by the choir. It is a theme consisting of a mere six notes that provides an especially clear demonstration of Janáček's method, for in one form or another it appears forty-two times in the first twenty-nine bars. It is replaced by a four-note pattern which recurs just as obsessionally, mostly as an accompaniment to the first soprano solo. These repetitions give the music a starkly primitive character—a secret Stravinsky also discovered—but such is the individuality of the orchestral colour that we are never bored.

The ensuing Gloria begins as a soprano solo whose accompaniment alternates between a suggestion of the distant clang of bells and a child-like melody on the clarinet. The music is deliberately naive in the way that Chagall is naive, unashamed of its peasant heritage. The entry of the choir brings an increase in fervour. Suddenly the tempo quickens as whirling patterns of notes interlock throughout the orchestra; it is the music of flames, not the slowly burning flame of a hallowed devotion but the hot blaze of fanaticism. A return to the original tempo eases the tension but with the next entry of the soprano soloist the accompaniment again becomes agitated. Gradually the music is dominated by a powerful gesture, a simple rising fifth which nevertheless makes a tremendous effect. It suggests a forest of hands raised in supplication, but the increasing desperation of the music seems to tell us that these prayers are to a heedless God. The final Amens are punctuated by silences as though the congregation of the world awaits a sign. ('No believer till I see for myself . . .?')

All the same, a Mass without a Credo is unthinkable. Needless to say, Janáček defies convention by starting his setting with a brisk little theme on cellos and bass clarinet whose terse rhythms seem far from devotional. Again we find brief patterns predominating although the tenor soloist does introduce a more lyrical element in the central section. With the return of the opening instrumental theme a strange thing happens; four times, at widely spaced intervals, the choir sings 'I believe' (*Veruju*); each repetition is quieter than its predecessor the last being marked *ppp*. Is this again an expression of doubt, or would it be more charitable to interpret it as an indication of increasing reverence?

A substantial orchestral interlude follows, exploding dramatically into an extraordinary organ solo of savage intensity. The orchestral section surely symbolises the crowd baying for Jesus to be crucified, just as the organ solo must be designed to convey the agony of the crucifixion. A tremendous climax for organ brass and timpani reminds us of the Kyrie, as though entreating mercy for what mankind did to God's own Son. There is a brief pause. The subsequent change of mood allows the women's voices to tell simply of the resurrection on the third day. Soon we hear again a quiet and expressive statement, '*Věruju*', and a long sustained trill in strings and wind suggests a vision of the Holy Ghost. It is the nearest approach to convention in the whole work, dispelled after just eight bars by a reappearance of the somewhat rustic theme with which the Creed began. Lyrical solos from tenor and bass affirm their faith in the Catholic church, after which choir and orchestra end gloriously with a belief in the life everlasting.

The start of the Sanctus is almost Bach-like with paired quavers above a reiterated bass-note. Soprano, tenor and bass in turn have an extraordinary swooping phrase which possibly symbolises the waving of palms. The orchestral part grows increasingly important in this section as brass fanfares resound through the vaults of Heaven. Also worth noting is a descending phrase of four consecutive notes ('Blessed is He') which is taken in turn by each of the four soloists—even the alto, silent until now.

The sixth section, Agnus Dei, allows us for the first time to hear the choir unaccompanied for brief spells. The intervening orchestral texture is wide-spaced with muted trombones in the bass and high violins far above. With the renewed entry of the soloists the music becomes far more chromatic in character than at any previous point and it remains for the chorus to restore the mood of simple piety with a gentle repetition of their initial phrase.

There follows an extraordinary intrusion, an extended organ solo built almost entirely on one phrase, a discipline which in no way disguises its ferocity. It seems that there was a tradition that the celebration of Mass should be followed by an organ postlude; but though Janácek had himself excelled as an organist in his youth, one cannot imagine that even his wildest improvisations were so strange as this almost sacrilegious outburst. It is capped by a processional *Intrada* for full orchestra to which brass and timpani give a martial air while blazing trumpet fanfares contradict the wailing violins. The final cadences are abrupt and unforeseen, a fitting ending to a work that occupies a unique position amongst the innumerable settings of the Mass. It is totally original in its conception, in Janáček's words: 'Free from the gloom of the motifs of monastery cells, free from the echoes of imitative parallelism, Bach's fugal 'tangles', Beethoven's pathos, Haydn's playful-ness . . .'[3]

---

[3] See Ian Horsbrugh, *Leoš Janáček*, David & Charles, 1981.

KODÁLY
1882–1967

The encouragement given by parents to a child can make a substantial difference to the upbringing of a musician even though a true gift for music will somehow come to fruition despite adverse circumstances. To have been born the son of a station-master in rural Hungary might seem less than an ideal preparation for a career as a composer, but Kodály was fortunate to have a father who was a keen amateur violinist and a mother who was a competent pianist. From early boyhood, young Zoltán became involved in music-making at home and there was always chamber music to be heard in the Kodály household whenever the father had some spare time. But after one of the moves necessitated by a change of job, the Kodály family found there was no longer a neighbour who could play the cello. It was a sad loss; cellists don't grow on trees. So Zoltán (who had already dabbled with the piano and the violin) bought himself a 'How to play the cello' book, borrowed an instrument and set out to teach himself. This he did to such good purpose that he was soon able to join in the musical evenings. He even came to the rescue in another way. His father had a set of parts for the Haydn quartets, which he much enjoyed playing. The cello part was mislaid, during yet another of the moves, and there was no score available in the remote Hungarian country-side. So young Kodály would sit down of an evening, spread out the three other parts on the dining-room table, and puzzle out what he thought the cello part ought to be. Apparently his musical insight was such that when at last a replacement cello part was acquired, it was found to be not all that different from the one he had deduced. Chamber music at home naturally led to a preference for composing works for small groups of players. While still a student, Kodály wrote a quartet, apparently of a rather Brahmsian kind, a string trio and sonatas for both violin and cello. But even in those early years, he was intensely interested in Hungarian folk-music, and his friendship with Bartók, almost his exact contemporary, was to confirm this interest. Together they started a vast collection of Hungarian folksongs, music which was to influence both of them to a marked degree. (It was at just about this time that Holst and Vaughan Williams were doing the same thing in England.)

A few months' study abroad helped to widen Kodály's musical horizon, but his spiritual home was Hungary and he was happy to return there and embark on a mainly academic career which at least provided him with a modest salary. Meantime he continued to compose and in collaboration with Bartók, by now his closest friend, founded a society to promote the performance of new Hungarian music. Political upheavals caused him to lose his post as deputy director of the Academy of Music and for two years life became a real struggle. But then, in 1923, when he was already in his early forties, he had his first great triumph, a triumph that was to put his name so securely in the front-rank of central European composers that from then on he never really looked back. The occasion was a festival of contemporary music held in Budapest in November 1923 to celebrate the fiftieth anniversary of the joining of the two cities of Buda and Pesth. Kodály's contribution was the *Psalmus Hungaricus*, a substantial choral work for tenor, chorus and orchestra which he had written with remarkable fluency within a period of eight weeks.

The Hungarian Psalm is based on a text by a sixteenth century Hungarian poet, Mihály Vég; the writer had translated the fifty-fifth Psalm, which is concerned with the persecution of the Jewish people, and subtly modified it so as to make it more applicable to his own race and time. In this way he made its emotions more intense, more valid to the audience he was addressing. Kodály, who was a nationalist through and through, found in Mihály Vég's text a truly national inspiration, even though the work begins with references to King David and Jehovah. It makes a fascinating sequence of artistic regeneration, the fifty-fifth Psalm being renewed and brought up to date in the sixteenth century, and then once again refurbished in the twentieth by the addition of music. Kodály uses his large orchestra with the greatest skill considering that the work is only his Opus 13; although his previous compositions for orchestra were very few, his assurance is absolute.

The success of *Psalmus Hungaricus* brought Kodály international recognition and he soon after produced the opera *Háry János* from which he derived an orchestral suite which was taken up with enthusiasm in Europe and America. Thereafter he continued to compose until the last year of his life although his music nearly always shows a strong Hungarian bias. Despite the great divide of post-war politics he managed to maintain the respect of both sides and there can be few other artists in any field who can claim to have received Honorary Doctorates in Moscow and America, East Berlin and Oxford. Although he cannot be classified as Bartók's equal, Bartók had the highest regard for him, saying that his works were the most perfect embodiment of the Hungarian spirit. A gifted linguist and a dedicated researcher into ethnic music, Kodály also made a most notable contribution to musical education in Hungary. The 'Kodály Method' was adopted in virtually every school in the land, and the enormous number of choral works he wrote with amateurs in mind have delighted choirs the world over and will doubtless continue to do so since while they are extremely effective, they do not present insuperable difficulties. His devotion to folk-music ensured that he never climbed onto the fashionable band-wagons of the avant-garde; indeed his style remained remarkably consistent throughout his long life.

Háry János
(1927)

This orchestral suite, derived from Kodály's opera of the same name, is famous for its very opening bars, a graphic musical depiction of a gigantic sneeze. However skilfully it may be devised it is only fair to say that such attempts at literal description could equally well serve a different purpose—a giant wave perhaps, or even, in a film score, a suitable accompaniment to the discharge of one of those great catapults with which the Roman armies would bombard ancient citadels while Charlton Heston gallops across the desert seeking reinforcements. Once we know it is meant to be a sneeze we can admire the skill with which the composer achieves so unlikely an effect; the question remains—why do it? According to Hungarian folk-lore, any tale preceded by a sneeze is likely to be either untrue or grotesquely exaggerated; here then is a musical joke whose significance a Hungarian audience would appreciate at once.

Háry János was a legendary Hungarian soldier from the Napoleonic wars who was renowned not for his valour but for his Falstaff-like propensity for wearing a hero's cloak to which he had only the most delusory right. A man who claims to have conquered Napoleon's army more or less single-handed invites scepticism, but Kodály does not wish to make his 'hero' nothing but a figure of fun. Just as we know that Falstaff must once have been a good soldier so Háry János stands as a symbol of the Hungarian military tradition of gallantry; despite his exaggerated tales there was a foundation of courage and truth in him once. His better qualities are made very clear by the music that immediately follows the sneeze. Rather in the manner of Bartók, the music accumulates gradually in a nearly fugal manner, giving the discipline of counterpoint to phrases that essentially spring from the material of folk-song. But even if the implications of a fugue are easily recognised, the academic form is not strictly observed. The texture gradually thickens until the full orchestra is playing, the treatment of the initial theme growing increasingly impressive until it is declaimed powerfully by horns, trumpets, cellos, and violas while, above, brilliant woodwind figuration suggests a dazzling sunrise. It is not the introduction one would expect to a piece describing a comic hero; but just as Elgar couldn't depict Falstaff without writing genuinely heroic music, so Kodály must regard his hero as someone of worth.

By contrast, the second movement is purely descriptive. Called 'Viennese Musical Clock' it is an intriguing concatenation of bell-sounds through which occasional themes emerge, a symbol perhaps of the mechanical figures that process around such masterpieces of medieval craftsmanship as the clock-face of Wells Cathedral.

In the third movement we come to an aspect of the work that (to non-Hungarian ears at least) deserves consideration on aesthetic grounds— the use of that traditional Hungarian instrument the cimbalom. Apart from the purely practical problem it presents, since cimbalom players are not to be found in every orchestra, is the intrusion of such an instrument welcome in the concert-hall or does it become too self-conscious an assumption of nationalism, as though one could not write a Scottish Symphony without employing real bagpipes? Nowadays electronic sound has accustomed us to the weirdest of noises, but actual folk-instruments do not always blend successfully with the conventional orchestra and the cimbalom might easily have seemed an inept intruder with its tendency to sound like a slightly out-of-tune harp played with a fork and spoon. Kodály shows true genius here, for he introduces this exotic stranger into the orchestra so subtly that we are hardly aware of its presence, even though musically this is the most profound and moving episode in the whole suite. It is based on a true folk-song which Háry János sings as a duet with his sweetheart in the opera. His voice is represented by a solo viola, hers by an oboe, but between the verses of their song comes the soft breath of night breezes and the rustle of leaves; it is these sounds that the cimbalom conveys so graphically and its very individual sound has the effect of transporting us from the concert-hall into the open air.

As the 'duet' develops, the music grows more virile, and here the cimbalom sounds almost like the clash of sword and shield—not in combat but in one of those colourful folk-dances in which the men dress as warriors to impress the village maidens. Once, many years ago, I had a meal at a country inn not far from Zagreb; outside, in the moonlight, a troupe of male dancers in gorgeous apparel circled ghost-like on the grass, their swords catching moonbeams out of the air. It was like a ritual rather than a dance, a scene that Kodály's music would have fitted perfectly.

The next movement brings us down to earth with a deliberate sense of anti-climax. It is the absurd episode in which Háry János supposedly defeats Napoleon. It is a field-day for the brass, but for all their huffing and puffing, the material they are given to play is far from heroic. Horses may trot, harness may jingle, but this regiment is not meant to be taken seriously. The battle rages; oceans of blood (or is it Hungarian ketchup?) stain the field, but Kodály makes it quite clear that he believes not a word of this tale, and we share his delight in such preposterous lying.

The ensuing 'Intermezzo' is more straightforward, just a rousing folk-dance based on typical Hungarian rhythms. The most interesting feature is the mingling of the powerful melody on the strings with a regular pattern of equal notes on the cimbalom as it provides a chattering commentary. It is comparable to the blurring of an outline that a painter might give to convey an impression of motion. Several other tunes appear in this movement and it is perhaps worth underlining that while it is enjoyable enough as pure dance music it has something more behind it—pride, tradition, call it what you will; perhaps 'a sense of ancient glory' is not too dramatic a phrase.

In the last movement we see not the glories of the past but the jokes of the present. The Emperor who now makes his entrance surrounded by witless sycophants cannot be taken seriously as a regal figure and one senses that Háry János, the old veteran, sees disconcertingly clearly that while this Emperor may at least have clothes there's little else to be said for him.

All nations must have their comic soldiers; Schweik is probably the most famous, while Bruce Bairnsfather's versions of Tommy Atkins, the un-forgettable gallery of Giles cartoons, or more recently the lunacies of M.A.S.H. show that even modern wars can be made more bearable by laughter. Yet the music of Háry János is more than satire and cynicism, more than a comic story or a cartoonist's quip. Somewhere within can be found the very essence of a nation: 'His work proves his faith in the Hungarian spirit. The obvious explanation is that all Kodály's composing activity is rooted only in Hungarian soil, but the deep inner reason is his unshakable faith and trust in the constructive power and future of his people.' (Béla Bartók)

Dances of Galánta
(1933)

On the route from Vienna to Budapest lies the small Hungarian market-town of Galánta. Kodály knew it well from his childhood days and it was there that he heard his first gipsy-band. The sound fascinated him, so different from the domestic chamber-music he was used to at home. Some forty or more years later he was to immortalise this memory in an orchestral work that must be placed among the very best of its genre, the *Dances of Galánta*. Based on authentic gipsy themes culled from a book of Hungarian dances published as early as 1800, Kodály exploited his great skill as an orchestrator in dressing the somewhat primitive material in gorgeous colours.

Cellos declaim the first theme unaccompanied. Their opening phrase in the tenor register is followed by a swift flurry from the upper strings as though a herdsman's song had startled a flight of birds. A solo horn repeats the cello phrase which again evokes a flurried reaction from strings and piccolo. The theme is then extended on woodwind or violins, punctuated curiously by brief agitated murmurs whose shape is directly derived from the preceding 'bird-flight'. Gradually a solo clarinet takes over a more commanding role until, regardless of the increased activity in the rest of the orchestra, it emerges from the ruck with a considerable cadenza. Two quiet pizzicato chords provide a cadence to this elaborate introduction; a brief upward scale from the clarinet leads us into the first main dance, unmistakably Hungarian in accent with a beautifully poised accompaniment that lays stress on each second beat and clips short each fourth. In a sudden upsurge of passion unison strings take up the melody, horns, cellos and basses providing rich harmonic support. The scoring here is a constant delight, richly sonorous but with many changes of colour. A long descending sequence of chords on divided violins brings the dance to a close.

A new, gently pulsating rhythm on pizzicato strings indicates the start of the next dance whose melody appears sinuously seductive on a solo flute. After a brief exchange between strings and flute, timpani and triangle point the rhythm, encouraging the woodwind to add fancy decorations to the tune. Soon a magnificent climax is reached as full wind and strings bring back an extended version of the first dance, now supported by an impressively striding bass. Notice how in due course the cellos cannot resist joining the upper strings in the melody, adding a darker strand to the texture. Surprisingly this section ends quietly, making way for the next dance which is set on its way by an oboe with a cheeky little tune, accompanied with extreme delicacy. Occasionally the tempo fluctuates capriciously as though one group of dancers grows impatient. A brief helter-skelter leads back to a majestic variant of the first dance which, however, soon dies away.

Urgent but quiet syncopations set our feet tapping as a new dance begins, far more active than its predecessors. It is a typical example of 'gipsy-fiddling', its exuberance spreading through the orchestra like wildfire until the dancers seem to collapse in an exhausted heap. The tempo slows as horns and bassoons seem to pant for breath after such a display of energy. The clarinet introduces a more graceful dance to which the violins soon add a more skittish variation. Once again the 'panting' motif appears on the horns until, over a quiet but insistent Left-right-left-right from the timpani the final dance is launched. It is extremely nimble with swiftly whirling semiquavers serving as counterpoint to a more bucolic tune. The rhythmic drive is irresistible and it must be hard for a concert audience to refrain from dancing in the aisles. At the very peak of excitement there is a sudden silence; with a touch of true genius, Kodály summons back the first dance over a delicately rustling shimmer from violins and violas. It is a moment of sheer magic, ending with a rising sequence of trills from the clarinet which seem to be climbing to unattainable heights. With a whoop of excitement the full orchestra crashes in and rushes impetuously through the final three pages.

Some six years later Kodály wrote a Concerto for Orchestra, but although it is a more than competently written work it fails to attain the sheer brilliance we find here; the *Dances of Galánta* are not merely tuneful; they are a challenge to the virtuosity of any orchestra. The clarinet part in particular is especially demanding and any conductor who omits a special gesture of thanks towards the clarinettist is positively churlish.

LISZT

1811–86

Had Liszt been born two years earlier, his life-span would have extended from the death of Haydn (1809) to the birth of Stravinsky (1882). The hypothesis may seem a little fanciful but it does make one realise the huge changes that came about in music during the nineteenth century. Such changes were due not merely to revolutionary ideas about the function of music but also to the extensive improvements made in instruments. Most of the wind and brass instruments underwent substantial developments that opened up new possibilities for composers to exploit in their orchestral scores; but in some ways the most significant alterations were made to the piano, which was given a greater compass and a far bigger tone. A comparison between Beethoven's Fourth and Fifth Concertos makes the point vividly, but more was to come. Indeed, the period from approximately 1830 to 1900 was to prove the Golden Age of pianism, just as the seventeenth century had been the Golden Age of the violin. The point is worth making since Liszt built his phenomenal reputation on his abilities as a solo performer, so much so that to this day he is revered as probably the greatest pianist of all time. Such a reputation would have been impossible to achieve had he been born in the era of the silver-toned *fortepiano* for which Mozart and Haydn wrote. An attempt to play Liszt's concertos on a Mozart-period instrument would be farcical, leading to frustration for the performer and destruction for the piano.

Liszt's father, Adam, was a versatile musician who was employed by the same Esterházy family who for so long had been the beneficent patrons of Haydn. Delighted by his son's natural aptitude, he gave him every encouragement; soon the child was astonishing audiences with his prodigious gifts, not merely as a pianist but as a sight-reader and improviser. Although far from healthy, the boy was taken to Vienna where Czerny gave him intensive tuition, building up his stamina with a ruthless concentration on the physical aspects of piano technique. After two years of dedicated study the twelve-year old Liszt was already being compared to the greatest pianists of the day.

Father and son set out on a concert tour that was reminiscent of the travels of the child Mozart, to whom Liszt was often compared. While the Paris Conservatoire refused to accept foreign students, however gifted, the Parisians took the young Liszt to their hearts. More important than their adulation was the gift of a new grand piano from its maker, Érard; its action was a great improvement on any of its predecessors and it enabled him to produce effects previously unheard.

For four years Liszt experienced the spurious glamour and wearying strain of the travelling prodigy, an unnatural adolescence that led to a virtual breakdown of his health. His father's death while they were on tour in France left the boy stranded in a foreign land. He returned to Paris, sold his piano and resolved to give no more concerts. His reputation was already so great that even though he was barely sixteen he could earn an adequate living by teaching, a task made more congenial by the fact that most of his pupils were daughters of the aristocracy of much the same age as their youthful master. With one of these, Caroline Saint-Cricq, he fell in love, but any possibility of marriage was firmly crushed by her father. Liszt was heart-broken and sought refuge in religion with the spiritual guidance of the Abbé Lammenais. But though he may have seriously contemplated entering the priesthood, the glittering world of the Parisian literati was too attractive for a young man to desert, and in 1831 he encountered three influences more crucial than the Church could offer, Paganini, Berlioz and Chopin. The dazzling virtuosity of Paganini fired Liszt's enthusiasm for playing in public; he began to practise feverishly, rebuilding his neglected technique on the foundation that had been so securely established in his childhood. His return to the concert platform caused a sensation and he and Chopin, both from Eastern Europe, became twin monarchs of Paris society, welcome in every aristocratic salon. It was at such a gathering that he met the Countess Marie d'Agoult. Her husband had little interest in the arts and despite three children the couple were virtually estranged. The Countess was overwhelmed by Liszt's striking good looks and his genius at the keyboard; after a few months a mutual fascination flowered into a passionate relationship which resulted in the birth of a child. In 1835 the two of them eloped to Geneva, causing a notable scandal which the Comte d'Agoult affected to disregard.

Marie was a powerful influence for good in Liszt's career since she encouraged him to turn his talents more seriously towards composition. The birth of a second child added to the couple's notoriety but Liszt cared little for bourgeois opinion. A trip to Italy prolonged the idyll for a little while but Liszt grew restless under the yoke of domesticity and began travelling again, giving charity concerts in Vienna to raise money for flood-relief in his native Hungary and also to pay for a suitable monument to Beethoven. Inevitably the adulation of women led to other affairs; while Marie remained the recurring theme in the Rondo of his life, the intervening episodes offered more spice. For seven years he went from one city to another, winning such acclaim that he was treated as royalty. Everywhere he went women fell for him—princesses, singers, dancers or even a pianist called Camille Pleyel for whom in former years Berlioz had conceived a typically violent passion. In the circumstances Liszt can hardly be blamed for catering to the demands of an adoring public whether in the concert-hall or the bedroom. To cauterize the wound inflicted on her pride Marie d'Agoult wrote a novel called *Nelida*, a thinly disguised account of her notorious affair in which the 'hero' Guermann stands in for Liszt with little credit. (Liszt petulantly described it as 'a stupid invention'.)

It was during his third concert tour in Russia that Liszt met the other truly significant woman in his life, Princess Carolyne von Sayn-Wittgenstein. Wealthy and married, she was twenty-eight, eight years his junior. A series of exceedingly passionate letters from her pursued Liszt from place to place on his tour and he found it no hardship to accept her invitation to stay at Woronice, one of her several estates. Surprisingly, considering the way she had thrown herself at him, she was profoundly religious and, in conversation, rekindled in Liszt an inclination towards the Church which had long lain dormant. He decided to renounce his career as a pianistic lion and concentrate on creative work as a composer. The following year, 1848, he was appointed Honorary Kapellmeister to the Grand Duke of Weimar, a post which enabled him to have an admirable orchestra at his disposal. Needless to say he still relished female company and set up his residence in a hotel with a French lady companion. The arrival of the love-lorn Princess from Russia created a situation which had its farcical side; Liszt had hurriedly to despatch his French paramour and, after a decent interval for tears to dry, join the Princess in the Ducal Palace. She was a plain lady, described candidly as 'small, dark and ugly', but posterity should be grateful to her for she took firm command of Liszt and made him settle down to the serious business of composition. During the twelve years that they lived together she bore him three children while he gave the world two concertos, two symphonies, the great Piano Sonata in B minor and a number of lesser works.

With immense pertinacity, which even involved a personal trip to the Vatican, the Princess managed to arrange a divorce, though Liszt was totally unsuited to marriage as a way of life. At the very last moment her plans were thwarted by relatives who resented the prospect of Liszt laying legitimate hands on her considerable personal fortune. Broken-hearted, she became a recluse, spending the last twenty-five years of her life writing a monumental attack on the Vatican that ran to twenty-four volumes of turgid prose and muddled thinking.

Although Liszt expressed a romantic passion for Carolyne in his Will, it seems unlikely that their relationship was mutually loving. All the same he soon began to be assailed with some remorse for his Don Juan-like existence. Once more he turned to religion and attached himself to a Dominican monastery near Rome, seriously intending to take Holy Orders. In 1865 he received his first consecration and assumed the habit of an Abbé. It was not a wholly convincing role and he soon tired of its restrictions. The temptations of the flesh were renewed by a liaison with a nineteen-year old Russian Countess, Olga Janina. At first Liszt resisted her blandishments but in time he succumbed to her beauty, only to suffer a fit of contrition afterwards. The repentance was not long-lasting, and together Olga and Liszt went to Hungary. Their romance ended in a scene that even a Hollywood script-writer could scarcely have imagined, with Olga attempting to play Chopin's G minor *Ballade* at a society concert. Three times she broke down, earning her master's public scorn; having failed to commit suicide she then attempted to kill Liszt and herself, but fortunately made as much of a hash of the attempt as she had of the *Ballade*.

A perceptive contemporary said of Liszt that he was 'Mephistopheles disguised as a priest'; the dichotomy of his nature was a cross he had to bear and that he found increasingly painful with the onset of age. Yet if his morality was deplorable, his generosity towards others was unstinting; he gave lessons free to talented pupils and, despite the material success of his period as a virtuoso, lived frugally in his closing years. His most valued friend was Wagner, his son-in-law, whose music he admired immensely. When he heard of Wagner's death he was heard to murmur 'He today, I tomorrow . . .' Three years later he died in Bayreuth during the annual Wagner festival; the legend of his pianistic prowess lives on to this day even although he voluntarily terminated his career as a virtuoso when he was only thirty-six.

In assessing the ultimate value of Liszt's music one needs to take into account the strange duality of his nature. The public demanded sensations and in catering to their wish he wrote much that was flashy and meretricious. But within the showman lurked a mind that possessed an awe-inspiring sense of exploration, of pushing forward the boundaries of music in directions that nobody else had dreamed of. This prophetic mood seemed to accompany thoughts of death or the devil, as we can see in a series of remarkable compositions such as *Pensée des Morts*, *Funerailles*, *Totentanz*, *Malédiction* and the *Faust* symphony. Most outstanding in sheer originality are some comparatively slight pieces he wrote towards the end of his life. Lonely and perhaps repentant, he was much occupied with thoughts of death. He was living for a time in Venice, and the sight of the funeral gondolas swathed in black moved him profoundly, so much so that he wrote two pieces called *La Lugubre Gondola*; unlike most old men though, he didn't look back. With what was surely one of the most remarkable examples of prophetic vision in the whole history of music, Liszt's ageing eyes pierced the veil of the future. While his contemporaries were adding more and more notes to their scores in riots of Wagnerian extravagance, Liszt composed these strange austere little pieces, which look forward to the world of Debussy and even Bartók. For example, in the first Funeral Gondola piece, we hear the gently rocking waves in the left hand, and the sad timeless chant of the gondolier above. Harmonies clash ruthlessly; the music wanders in a vague timeless manner, for death is no longer romantic, no longer filled with splendid ceremony. It is a forlorn emptiness, and here carried on the waters is but the shell of a man on a last voyage to nowhere.

Such strange rarities lead one to speculate what a giant of a composer he might have been if he had given himself time to develop his harmonic and rhythmic originality. His output was prodigious but too much of it consists of elaborate transcriptions of other composers' work designed to astonish a public hungry for sensational display. In a way there could have been no one better suited to write a Faust symphony, for the richness of his talent led to an artistic downfall which a return to religion reversed, if only in part.

Faust Symphony
(1854)

I 'Faust'

It is hardly surprising that certain legends have had a recurring fascination for composers. In the early days of opera a much-used plot was the story of Orpheus and Eurydice. Obviously it is particularly suited to music since the hero is both singer and lute-player. But in the nineteenth century there was another legend that was constantly being used by musicians and that was the story of Faust. Since Goethe's drama on the subject, better known on the continent than Christopher Marlowe's much earlier version, over fifty composers have written music that is associated with the Faust legend in some way, whether in the form of operas, overtures, incidental music to a stage production, or simply using poems such as Gretchen's spinning-song which Schubert set for voice and piano. But with all due respect to admirers of Gounod's opera, the greatest musical work to be inspired by Goethe's play is Liszt's tremendous Faust Symphony. Two of the greatest landmarks of Romantic music in the symphonic field are the Berlioz *Symphonie Fantastique* and this *Faust Symphony* of Liszt's, and it's only poetic justice that Berlioz should have dedicated his symphony to Liszt, and that Liszt should have dedicated his *Faust Symphony* to Berlioz. Thus did two giants of the age salute each other across the years, for roughly twenty-five years separate the two works.

Now it is a sign of genius never to stop learning, and one of the most remarkable things about Liszt was that in spite of his phenomenal success as a pianist he never gave up teaching himself to compose. Even as late as 1850, when he was thirty-nine years old and acknowledged as an international figure, he was constantly seeking practical advice on orchestration from fellow-musicians such as Raff and Conradi, both of them much lesser figures, but sound technicians. Many of his works were orchestrated by others, but then he would go over the score scrupulously, correcting, adding and re-composing so that often his compositions were totally revised three or four times before he was satisfied. The final version can always be said to be truly his, since by then the work of his amanuensis had been completely overlaid with his own alterations. How he had time to do all this remains an unsolved mystery, especially with the constant travelling that he did; but one thing we do know, and that is that wherever he went, three books went with him,—his prayerbook, Dante's poems and Goethe's Faust. He even kept copies of all three in every room of his house at Lake Como, so that he could put his hand on them at all times without delay. They were for him what Shakespeare and Virgil had been to Berlioz. This immense influence of literature was a characteristic of the age. In its breakaway from classical forms music needed some substitute for the previously established props of sonata, rondo or fugue. Composers hoped to find this by using literary programmes, by relating themes to characters, even by literally telling stories in music. Liszt was a supreme master of this new approach and the *Faust Symphony*, which lasts over an hour, sustains our interest throughout by a process he made very much his own. Instead of developing themes in the classical sense, he transformed them, changing their character completely while preserving their original outline. Schubert had done this in his *Wanderer* Fantasy, Berlioz had done it in the *Symphonie Fantastique*. But in both those cases the themes are rather dragged in by the scruff of the neck in the later movements. Liszt solved the problem of integrating the numerous versions of his basic themes so that they seem utterly convincing in their new guises.

There are three movements, the first one called Faust, the second Gretchen and the third Mephistopheles. Essentially they are character studies, but the Faust themes appear throughout, as though we are meant to see how the other two touch upon his life. Two of the most important themes appear on the very first page. The opening sequence might be described as Faust, the magician and sorcerer (Ex. 1) Since it uses all the notes of the chromatic scale, enthusiasts for serial music have been quick to seize on this as the first true twelve-note theme, but I doubt if Liszt consciously thought of it in such a way. What is clearly intentional is its avoidance of any defined tonality; it is in a musical limbo, a symbol of a lost soul.

In response we have a forlorn phrase on the woodwind (Ex. 2). This could be interpreted in a number of ways—perhaps it is Faust's dissatisfaction with his lot, perhaps the futility of his desires, or even a comment from outside, from Liszt himself as one might say, on the folly of Faust's aspirations. Whatever its literary significance, it is one of the most important

Ex. 1

themes, and is destined to go through a number of transformations. It is quite misleading to interpret these changes as a narrative. This is a true symphony and the events are all musical. Try as we like, we can't force this music into the shape of the Faust legend. This is a portrait of Faust, and in it we see his weakness and his moment of decision, we see him at the height of his intellectual power, we see him arrogant and triumphant, we see him fearful and doomed. Above all we see him redeemed by the love of Gretchen and rescued from his terrible bargain with the devil. Think if you like, then, of Faust in his cell brewing magic potions, share a sense of decision as the music whips into a brisk allegro, feel the spell come to fruition as it storms back on trombones through a welter of orchestral sound. Do not be surprised, though, if, like Faust's dreams, such specific images crumble, for the strength of this music lies in itself, not in its imagery, and its power is such that it would fire our imaginations just as much even if it were called by a completely different name. Once the movement gets under way the sheer drive is breathtaking and even Tchaikovsky, a master of the orchestral whirlwind, never bettered these pages.

A gradual relaxation of intensity leads to a slower section with mysterious string figuration wafting upwards like coils of smoke while the woodwind announce a less tormented version of Ex. 1. A sequence of plaintive sighs from cellos and violins leads to the first transformation of Ex. 2. Sweetened by an altogether prettier harmonisation, it now becomes a thing of grace and beauty.

Ex. 2

Again, it's dangerous to assume that this represents Faust doffing his hat to a lady or anything as absurd. Liszt's interest here is to find out how the *theme* responds to this different treatment. He wants to see what its possibilities are, used as a melody. They prove to be considerable, the elegant phrases punctuated by expressive rising comments from the violas. As the music grows more impassioned its course is interrupted by a strident fanfare on horns and trumpets reinforced by woodwind.

One of the first rewards of Faust's pact with Mephistopheles was to mingle with the mighty, the confidant of kings. This material triumph is expressed by a splendid brass theme which is presented with Wagnerian grandeur. (It is one of a number of passages which suggest a Wagnerian influence though in fact it was Wagner who was indebted to Liszt. The Faust theme that begins the symphony (Ex. 1) appears almost identically in the second act of *Walküre* while the so-called 'Kiss' motif that comes at the end of the same opera closely resembles a climax in the finale of Liszt's great work. Even the opening three notes of *Tristan* may well be derived from Liszt since they occur extensively throughout the symphony.[1] The progress of the 'triumph' theme is interrupted by an agitated version of Ex. 2, no longer forlorn, and Liszt combines these two very different ideas with considerable skill.

For some time the music continues in a state of high excitement until a peremptory command on the heavy brass calls a halt. Exx. 1 and 2 reappear in their original form; slightly extended, they dissolve in sighs; a solo bassoon plays a lugubrious phrase that ends in darkness. There is a moment's silence. Against a gently throbbing accompaniment Liszt combines Exx. 1 and 2 in a passage that is the sorrowful heart of the movement. The ensuing developments are magical in their imaginative exploitation of Ex. 1, but they contain a further interest—a confident use of 'whole-tone' harmonies whose invention is normally attributed to Debussy.

Something like a symphonic recapitulation now appears although there are a number of new episodes that the attentive listener will appreciate. This first movement runs to 120 pages of score, but despite the essentially Romantic character of the material and the considerable contrasts of tempo it is a true symphonic movement. The unexpectedly quiet ending, heavy with sorrow, conveys Faust's tragic predicament with deep understanding, so much so that we feel that Liszt, perhaps without realising it, is painting a self-portrait. 'Isolation is bad for me. I feel I have no strength left in me. I live in a state of utter discontent. My past years seem so shameful, so pitiable—yet in my solitude I cannot work. My time is almost wasted. I agitate and torment myself in vain.'[2] Such was the intimate revelation of a man who had the world at his feet.

---

[1] One of Liszt's songs, 'Ich möchte hingen', anticipates almost exactly the opening phrase of *Tristan*—by ten years!

[2] From Anthony Wilkinson, *Liszt*, Macmillan, 1975.

II   'Gretchen'

In general, virtue is more boring to portray than vice, a fact which artists recognise as clearly as do newspaper editors. Consequently Liszt obviously lavished all his skill on the 'Gretchen' movement so that it wouldn't seem to sag after the thrills of the first part of this great triptych. Its orchestral colours are delicately conceived in terms of solo groups of instruments, there is a rich web of melody and counter-melody; what is perhaps even more dramatic evidence of Liszt's care in this movement is that it's one of the few works that he wrote out in full score straight away, and then revised hardly at all. (Although the entire symphony was written in an amazing two months in 1854, Liszt characteristically continued to revise and improve it during the ensuing seven years.) The first few pages present the most important themes scored almost entirely for woodwind. After an introductory section notable for its exploitation of what came to be known as 'the Wagnerian turn' (a four-note group circling around a central note), a solo oboe presents a lyrical melody accompanied in a very individual way by a solo viola. Flute and clarinet extend the theme accompanied by a solo violin so that the impression of chamber-music is continued, a striking contrast to the dramatic orchestration of the first movement.

In due course the interest is transferred to the strings; but it seems as though Liszt is particularly conscious of the dangers of sentimentality in this movement and he seldom allows the string section to indulge in open displays of emotion. Their loveliest moment comes with the introduction of a new theme, easily recognisable from the three repeated chords with which it begins. Even this is soon transferred to the woodwind choir, the instruction *dolce amoroso* being clear evidence of the composer's intentions.

The tender and idyllic quality of the movement is suddenly disturbed by the dramatic intrusion of Ex. 2 from the first movement. The theme is played by horns, marked *patetico*, while an agitated rhythm in cellos and basses tells us of Faust's beating heart as he sees Gretchen, beautiful but unattainable. After a sequential and increasingly anguished treatment of the phrase another theme from the first movement makes a second appearance. Originally it wore a very impassioned garb as a quasi-operatic dialogue between the woodwind instruments and the lower strings. Nobody could deny the intensity of feeling behind this music (Ex. 3).

Liszt's treatment of this same theme when he comes to the second movement is completely different. Three solo cellos pour their respective hearts out while flutes and harp etch in a delicate and flowing background of harmony. This isn't just a theme transformed but Faust himself transformed by Gretchen's beauty, his craving for power subdued by her unaffected loveliness.

If one is to criticise this music at all, one could say that Liszt (like

Ex. 3

ff   *espress. ed appassionato molto*

Tchaikovsky) is a little too ready to accept sequences—repetitions of the same phrase at different pitches—as a means of building a musical structure. But the people who criticise Liszt on these grounds would never think of making the same allegation about Bach yet he constantly uses sequences. The only difference lies in the musical content of the phrase that is repeated. Liszt's music is more blatantly heroic in its conception. Yet the beauty of the orchestral texture should be compensation enough; one must remember, too, that this is a very large canvas, and the symmetry of these repetitions helps us to find our bearings in it. It's far more important to be aware of the transferences of material from movement to movement than to worry about sequences. For instance, we have already heard a disturbed version of Ex. 2 during the course of this second movement. It soon appears again in a section of positively Wagnerian sensuality; Faust's love for Gretchen sweeps away all doubts and fears, and that theme, once so empty and forlorn, is now imbued with warmth. However, the evil power that lies in wait for Faust at every turn casts a chill over the music, which disintegrates in a series of sighs from the first violins, faintly echoed by the harp.

Exquisitely scored for a quartet of solo violinists, the initial Gretchen theme reappears against an elaborately flowing counterpoint. Indeed, a notable feature of the movement is the impression of light given by the scoring, the lower strings being seldom used except in the most discreet manner. After a reprise of the '*dolce amoroso*' theme the movement ends ethereally with high sustained chords on divided violins and a gently curving descent in the violas which seems like a caress.

III   '*Mephistopheles*'

The introductory phrases in the final movement of this epic symphony could well be derived from the finale of the *Symphonie Fantastique*—remember that the work is dedicated to Berlioz. But the tempo is far brisker and lacks the brooding menace that Berlioz conveys so wonderfully. Although the title 'Mephistopheles' is authentic, Liszt shows considerable subtlety, not to mention psychological insight, in refraining from giving us an actual theme for the third character in this symphonic drama. Instead, he uses further transformations and distortions of the various Faust themes, so that we get

the impression that Mephistopheles is present in Faust himself. This anticipates the discoveries of Freudian psychology by a number of years, but also it
seems a much more convincing way of dealing with the problem than merely
resorting to rather obvious horror music of the sort that we hear in Dracula
films. Anyway Mephistopheles isn't like that. He's a very sophisticated
demon, suave and persuasive as indeed one would expect him to be.
Throughout the movement the Faust themes recur, and the keyword to
describe them here is really mockery. Mephistopheles seems to be laughing at
Faust, seeing him as but a pawn in the eternal game with men's souls as the
prize. In fact we can hear his laughter depicted quite near the beginning of the
movement.

But throughout the movement we can only be astonished by the
ingenuity—one might almost say diabolical ingenuity—that Liszt displays in
presenting these already well-tried themes in still further guises. For instance,
Ex. 2 is broken up into small fragments which are then scattered through
various instruments anticipating a later musical development that was to find
its ultimate and logical conclusion in Webern.

A little more obvious, but still enormously exciting, is another treatment of the same theme a bit later on. Here it lies in the murky depths of cellos
and basses, building up to a climax which bursts into incadescent showers of
notes, before the theme ultimately reappears once more in its fragmented
version. But without question the most remarkable development of Ex. 2 is
its conversion into a fiendish fugue whose angular and distorted treatment is
totally remarkable for the 1850s. (There is a somewhat comparable episode in
the earlier B minor piano sonata but here the working-out of the subject
matter is more extensive and elaborate.) To analyse the movement in detail
would take an entire chapter with a dozen or more music examples to show
the ingenuity with which Liszt handles a commendably small number of
themes. While it is an additional pleasure to appreciate the intellectual skill he
displays, there is enough excitement to sweep the listener along on a
flood-tide of orchestral sound.

Originally the symphony ended as a purely orchestral work, and it can
still be performed that way. But three years after he'd finished the score, Liszt
apparently grew dissatisfied and felt the need for something extra at the end.
Indeed, the original ending does sound rather abrupt, even after an hour's
music. Inevitably he turned to Goethe where he found at the end of Act II of
the Faust drama a so-called 'mystic chorus'. It is a mere four lines long and
was deftly translated by Louis McNeice in these words:

> All that is past of us was but reflected:
> All that was lost in us here is corrected:
> All indescribables here we descry:
> Woman's divinity leads us on high.

Thus, by implication, Faust is redeemed by a woman's love, an ending that doubtless appealed to Liszt's romantic temperament. By characteristic repetitions, he spins this out for a number of pages, scoring it for tenor solo and male voice chorus. It is indeed an apotheosis—a solemn and yet triumphant ending to a symphony that is one of the greatest musical monuments of the nineteenth century.

Totentanz *(Dance of Death)*

One of the essentials of being a good listener is to be aware of what is remarkable. This implies that one also has to be sufficiently knowledgeable to know what is *not* remarkable, for one can only appreciate unorthodoxy against a background of the orthodox. By remarkable I mean an unexpected twist of harmony, a moment of especially imaginative orchestration, a particularly memorable melodic phrase or a visionary step into the future. An accurate feeling for period adds enormously to the pleasure of listening; for example, the Berlioz *Symphonie Fantastique* would seem much less extraordinary had it been written fifty years later. One could scarcely find a better instance of this aspect of music than *Totentanz*, a set of variations for piano and orchestra on the great medieval chant 'Dies Irae'. By any standards it's a remarkable composition; the name *Totentanz* or Dance of Death prepares us for something out of the way and Liszt doesn't disappoint us.

The inspiration for the work came as far back as 1838, when Liszt, passing through the Italian town of Pisa, went to see some magnificent frescoes by Orcagna called 'The Triumph of Death'. His imagination, like that of so many of the Romantics, was fired by anything with a touch of the macabre or morbid and he tucked them away in the back of his mind as a possible idea to be worked on. Eleven years later, in 1849, he had completed the first version of the score. Although one tends to think of Liszt as a slick composer, winning the applause of the mob with flashy pieces designed to show brilliance and little else, he actually worked very slowly at his major works; for instance the composition of the first piano concerto was spread over twenty-six years, the second concerto took twenty-two and *Totentanz* took ten. Obviously these scores were not always in his mind; a first draft would be completed and then lie dormant on a shelf for perhaps ten or more years. Liszt would then play it over, possibly at the request of a friend, and start revising. This process would continue off and on for anything up to another decade. It makes it virtually impossible to date his works with any accuracy, which is why I stress that *Totentanz* is remarkable by any standard; of course, the earlier we fix the date the more extraordinary it becomes. If the opening with its stamping chords and harsh dissonances really came into his mind as early as 1838 it's almost unbelievable. It might genuinely be mistaken for Bartók, and its exploitation of the bass resonances of the piano is unprecedented.

Once the 'Dies Irae' theme has been thoroughly established, Liszt sets out on the first variation, putting a ghost-like version of the chant in the bass and accompanying it with two lugubrious bassoons, like a couple of friars discussing a funeral in reasonably detached and cheerful tones.

Now while it is true that some of the variations rely too much on rather cheap pianistic tricks (glissandi for instance), one has to weigh such things against the strikingly prophetic and original writing that we find in such places as the third variation which seems to anticipate Rakhmaninov's *Paganini Rhapsody* by nearly 100 years.

A little later on Liszt begins a sizzling fugue, using the piano like a Hungarian cimbalom. I said 'begins' a fugue because all thoughts of academicism are soon put aside in the general excitement. In fact, he even stops numbering the variations from this point on, so great is the momentum of the music.

Liszt's use of the bass sonorities of the piano is always remarkable, but never more so than near the end of *Totentanz* where he hammers out the theme low down. Collossal scales streak from end to end of the keyboard against these extraordinary sounds, and if one makes the imaginative effort to put oneself back in time to the period when this was first performed, one can realise what a savage impact it must have made. It was, outwardly at any rate, an era of great refinement, and one can imagine many listeners feeling that music as sheerly physical as this was an assault upon the senses too violent for propriety. While it may not be great music, it is the product of a startlingly original mind which establishes a quite new relationship between piano and orchestra.

The Piano Concertos

There is a difference between heroism and bravery, a difference that is not unlike a sort of class distinction. We live in an age when bravery has been made to seem a commonplace by the directness with which it is reported. The man who defuses a bomb in Belfast is watched, almost clinically, by the television cameraman; the fireman who drags an old man from a burning building knows glory for as long as the next day's papers carry his picture and is then forgotten; every now and then, when a lifeboat capsizes or men die in a coalmine, our imaginations are sufficiently touched for the impression to strike home for a day or two.

What is the difference then between a hero and a courageous man? Perhaps it is more to do with the cause for which the act of bravery was committed than the act itself. If you believe in a cause sufficiently fanatically, an act which the rest of the world condemns will seem heroic to your supporters. Heroes must defy death itself in the risks they take, but they must defy it for a minority. The bomb disposal man, the fireman, the lifeboat crew act for us; they are doing our dirty work because, we secretly think, it happens to be their job, not ours. In the epic sense, they are not heroes and perhaps this is one reason why, in an increasingly prosaic yet monotonously ghastly world, we have come to mistrust heroes and even relish destroying myths. The men who dared to seem larger than life, Lawrence of Arabia, Churchill or whoever, must, if possible, be cut down to size.

The Piano Concerto No. 1 in E flat major offers a supreme example of the pianist as hero-figure. The dramatic orchestral opening, presenting the main theme in unison, is allowed a mere four bars before the soloist interrupts with a leaping octave passage which quickly evolves into a massive cadenza in the contradictory key of C major. At the end of this pyrotechnical display the orchestra, their initial aggression tamed, again offer the main theme; once more they are interrupted, this time with a more expressive phrase though still one that leaves us in no doubt who is the master.

The beginning of the Second Concerto in A major could scarcely be more different, a quiet sustained Adagio in which the orchestra seems to be preparing the way for an operatic aria to be sung by a lovesick heroine in tearful mood. The pianist's initial role is, then, to accompany the orchestra, not to dominate it, while the first cadenza is only a few bars long and serves as a transition into new and admittedly more dramatic material.

The genesis of the two works is worth studying. In the case of the First Concerto the preliminary sketches date from 1830, but Liszt went on revising it for a quarter of a century; in fact, the first performance wasn't given until 1855, with Liszt as soloist and Berlioz conducting—one of those occasions one feels that would have been worth the price of a black-market ticket. But whereas the two piano concertos of Brahms come from widely separated periods of his life, those of Liszt are almost contemporaneous; the second concerto which was begun in 1839, was also revised over a number of years and had its premiere in 1857, just two years after the first. Although in many ways a better and more interesting work, it has never taken the public fancy in the same way as the E flat concerto, largely because the pianist as hero-figure has been so seriously demoted by the composer. (Incidentally, as if to confirm the reduced importance of the soloist, Liszt did *not* play the piano at the premiere of the second concerto; he conducted). But could two works of the same genre, and actually constructed on a similar plan, possibly begin more differently?

Form is a necessity in music and without some sort of inner discipline in his works the composer gets as lost as his listener does. Whatever faults Liszt may have had, he was a great formal innovator. He seems to have been worried most by the four-movement plan of the classical sonata or symphony. Might it not be possible to make these movements more closely related to each other? Beethoven had pointed the way in his Fifth Symphony, and even more dramatically so in the Ninth. But in Beethoven's case the references from one movement to another were more in the nature of quotations; the themes were transplanted from movement to movement, but they didn't really change their content. Liszt saw a more theatrical vision than that. Imagine a serial story with a hero who gets into all sorts of situations; obviously he'll behave differently whether he's fighting a giant or courting a princess. But he's the same man. Liszt saw the possibility of submitting a theme to all kinds of different emotional stresses, rather as one does in a theme and variations; but by enclosing these different episodes in a grander musical scheme, he'd avoid the patchiness of variations. The solution he devised therefore was a large-scale continuous movement within which substantial contrasting sections would be placed as an approximation to the traditional concepts of slow movement, scherzo or finale. Thus in the First Concerto we find a slow nocturnal section in B major whose lyrical theme is transformed into both a gloriously heroic declamation and a nimble scherzo. (The use of a triangle in this passage has occasioned much comment, most of it derogatory.) The same 'nocturne' serves as the basis for the brisk march in the finale which also manages to include material from each of the preceding sections.

The same approach is to be found in the Second Concerto although the joins are rather less obvious and the element of display substantially less. But the first 'virile' theme is presented in a most original manner with a series of abrupt chromatic spurts in the left hand which are like pianistic snarls. As for the opening section, any suggestion of sentimentality is dispelled completely when it is converted into a splendidly heroic march. These changes of character make for adventurous listening if one is prepared to follow Liszt's thoughts rather than to be merely dazzled by the profusion of notes.

If we accept, as I think we must, that Liszt came in on the floodtide of Romanticism, we also have to accept that he went out on the ebb—that, perhaps more than any other nineteenth-century composer, he saw the directions music was going to take. Pieces like the *Totentanz*, the *Malédiction*, *Pensée des Morts* or the much later *Nuages Gris* and the 'Funeral Gondola' all show an almost uncanny prophetic vision, in which, gradually, the excesses of Romanticism were stripped away, leaving a style that was totally uncompromising. Using this analogy of the tides, the two concertos represent the turning-point, the change of direction; and perhaps the first necessity was to reduce the stature of the hero-figure, hence the vastly different style of piano-writing. Now I'm not saying Liszt was even conscious of this at that moment of his life, although he certainly became increasingly aware of it. Only in the perspective of history can we begin to appreciate Listz's genius;

the relationship of soloist to orchestra was to change radically in the twentieth century, as the concertos of Prokofiev and Bartók show—though not Rakhmaninov; he perpetuated the nineteenth-century hero-myth, which is one reason for his popularity. But the trend has been to make the pianist not so much a soloist as a more important member of the orchestra; as I suggested in my definition of the difference between the hero and the brave man, by putting the pianist more into the orchestral scene, you deprive him of his heroic status because he is no longer a heroic minority of one against ninety. It's a brave man who plays a Bartók concerto but, when we leave the hall, we remember him for how well he fought rather than for how great a victory he won. In the first concerto of Liszt, the pianist is a hero-figure throughout; even in the most lyrical passages, he is the ardent lover, whose seductive powers always prevail. And when battles have to be fought, he rides his charger into the enemy ranks, confident of victory.

It's interesting to note that in the last pages of the second concerto the thematic interest is given almost entirely to the orchestra, while the piano acts as an extra percussion instrument, a sort of glorified cymbal, bashing out the rhythm.

It may be only a personal view, but for me the significance of the second concerto lies in its transitional nature, in its indication that, even as early as the mid-nineteenth century, Liszt realised that something would have to be done to reduce the overwhelming dominance of the soloist that more powerful pianos had made possible. Proof of this can also be found in his orchestration, which often gives a single woodwind or string instrument the melody and reduces the soloist to an accompanying role. It was like the gradual erosion of a monarch's powers, an historical inevitability. All the more remarkable, then, that it was the greatest monarch of the keyboard who realised that necessity and voluntarily relinquished his throne.

LUTOSLAWSKI

1913–

In any survey of the history of music one is bound to notice that different countries have had periods of special glory at different times. The seventeenth century was a Golden Age for England and Italy, the eighteenth for Austria, the nineteenth for Germany and the first two decades of the twentieth for France, particularly if one includes Stravinsky as an émigré to France to share the honours with Debussy and Ravel. Of course this is only a generalisation and is not meant in any way to suggest that individual composers in countries I have not mentioned did not make a significant and substantial contribution. The only reason for making the point is that I suspect that when historians in the twenty-first century look back on the twentieth they will be compelled to devote a special chapter to Polish music, for in spite of the virtual destruction of Poland by the Nazis and its subsequent oppression by the Russians or their lackeys, Polish composers have flourished to an extent never known previously. Three names in particular stand out, Lutoslawski, Penderecki and Panufnik. (The last has settled permanently in England and become a British citizen but that has not altered the Polish inheritance which shows in his music.) Although all three use contemporary idioms to express themselves through music, they have managed to communicate to a wide and international spectrum of audiences. They are not dependent on minority cliques to propagate their works nor on sycophantic claques to applaud them. Such works as Penderecki's *St Luke Passion* and Lutoslawski's Cello Concerto have had an overwhelming effect on audiences the world over, while Panufnik has become the favourite contemporary composer of the London Symphony Orchestra whose own committee has taken the rare step of commissioning major works from him, so satisfying do they find his music to perform.

No Polish composer can have been unaffected by the traumatic experiences of World War II, when Warsaw was sacked with a ruthlessness that Genghis Khan himself could not have surpassed. Hopes of freedom after the holocaust were cruelly destroyed by the heavy hand of Soviet Russia, and

Panufnik, at one time officially regarded as one of Poland's greatest composers since Chopin, found the political situation intolerable and fled the country. Lutoslawski remained and by skilful diplomacy managed to stay in the system while at the same time maintaining a degree of personal freedom. His international reputation is now such that he is regarded as a national asset and can organise his life as he pleases. A fluent linguist, suave in manner and elegant in appearance he is a desirable if unrepresentative ambassador for a communist regime.

Brought up in a cultured and musical family, Witold Lutoslawski showed a great gift for music while still a young child. Although he was later to study mathematics at Warsaw University, the lure of music was too strong and he quickly turned to composing and teaching as a profession. During the years before the outbreak of war he produced a number of compositions, some of which gained prizes of considerable prestige value. When the Nazis invaded Poland, Lutoslawski quickly volunteered to serve in the Polish army. He was slightly wounded and taken prisoner; on the way to a prisoner-of-war camp he managed to escape and, mostly under cover of darkness, walked some 200 miles back to Warsaw where he remained until its destruction. During this period he and Panufnik formed a two-piano team, earning a living of sorts playing in a coffee-house-cum-nightclub called 'Kawiarnia Sim'. One of their show-pieces was a brilliant set of *Variations on a theme of Paganini* (1941) in which Lutoslawski showed great resource and ingenuity in finding yet more to say about the famous A minor Caprice.

In the post-war era he was more or less compelled to write for popular consumption; adopting the pseudonym of 'Derwid', he produced a number of pieces of light music for Polish Radio. Educational music, film scores, incidental music for drama poured from his fluent pen, but his more personal and serious compositions were banned as 'decadent'. Meanwhile he began to devise an idiom that would ultimately bring him artistic satisfaction; after the death of Stalin, a degree of artistic freedom was again allowed and during the next ten years he produced a number of major works of increasing importance. Their principal novelty was the 'aleatoric' element which introduces a system of organised improvisation into music. At certain points members of the orchestra will be given repetitive patterns to play in an improvisatory and unsynchronised manner, producing a random effect which would be impossible to write down in specific notation since it will inevitably differ at every performance. In Lutoslawski's hands this apparent abrogation of responsibility works very well since the 'formless' passages are simply moments of confusion within a well-ordered structure, rather comparable to the seemingly unrelated shapes which spin out of a black background to form the title of a television programme.

Although the *Concerto for Orchestra* dates back to 1954, it is a work that serves as a wonderful initiation into certain aspects of 'modern' music. To have included it in this Companion may cause surprise in some circles where it will now be regarded as positively old-fashioned; however, there are few works which I would recommend more wholeheartedly to those who feel they want to widen their musical horizons since its appeal is dramatic and immediate. It may not have acquired the status of Bartók's similarly titled work and its composer has now developed a more challenging style; but it is often a composer's early works that are ultimately the most enduring and I suspect that in years to come this Concerto will acquire the wide popularity it deserves.

Concerto for Orchestra
(1954)

I *Intrada*
II *Capriccio, Notturno e Arioso*
III *Passacaglia, Toccata e Corale*

When he first began work on this Concerto Lutoslawski's position was still rather precarious. Political pressures were being brought to bear all the time, and he'd already had his First Symphony banned from performance because it didn't meet the aesthetic dictates of the party. This was ironic because at the time Lutoslawski was basically a traditionalist, and this Concerto marks the end of a period in his life. After he'd finished it (and it took him four years) he was to push forward into far more avant-garde techniques. In a sense, then, the work is a compromise; it's based on very simple folksong-like material which Lutoslawski handles with extraordinary virtuosity.

Now, one of the complaints most heard about modern music is that people say they don't know where they are. As if to mock this attitude, Lutoslawski begins the first movement of his concerto with 111 repetitions of the note F sharp, and ends with 138 repetitions of the same note, albeit high up on a celesta instead of low down in the timpani. It gives a strong feeling of traditional tonality even though Lutoslawski isn't really a tonal composer in the strict sense of the word. Over this anvil-like reiteration of one F sharp, the cellos begin a tune, starting with a very short phrase, then getting a little longer each time, like a plant visibly growing in one of those speeded-up films that are so fascinating to watch (Ex. 1).

This very compact idea is not only destined to grow; it is also the seed from which material will develop in other movements, whether as flying fragments in the scherzo or as a ground bass in the slow movement. The one

Ex. 1

small unit in bar 3 of the example can thus help to give unity to a work lasting half-an-hour, though admittedly the relationships are tenuous and not to be compared with the thematic transformations of Liszt, Berlioz or Tchaikovsky. They are there for the composer's benefit rather than ours.

The pattern extends and multiplies over the constantly reiterated F sharp until at last a huge climax seems to cause the music to break apart. More nimble figures now appear, their dancing rhythms periodically interrupted by explosive *pizzicato* chords from the strings. Against this urgent bustle massive chords are built up step by step in the brass, great block structures that are instantly memorable so that they can easily be recognised when they appear at later stages. The whole central climax is immensely exciting, demanding great virtuosity from the players. At last the tumult dies; there is a moment's silence. A soft mysterious chord ushers in a reprise of the opening material, the reiterated F sharp now high and clear on the bell-like celesta. Although continuing to be pianissimo, the sustained string chord gradually grows more dense until it contains thirteen notes. The repeated F sharps peter out; the movement ends, the harmony as soft yet dense as a snowdrift.

The second movement, *Capriccio, Notturno e Arioso* is in three main sections, a scintillating caprice filled with the scarcely audible rustlings of the night, an Arioso whose strong broad melody deserves no diminutive, and a return to the opening material. It is a twentieth-century equivalent to the 'Queen Mab' scherzo of Berlioz or the *Midsummer Night's Dream* overture of Mendelssohn. Immensely difficult to play, it demands extreme agility from strings and wind alike. It is akin to Bartók in its suggestion of an insect world. Amongst the whispering and scurrying a high solo violin floats a lyrical fragment derived from Ex. 1. Suddenly the heavy brass makes its first appearance as three trumpets in unison proclaim the first phrase of the Arioso. The effect is dramatic in the extreme and it isn't long before a powerful dispute takes place between brass and strings, while woodwind chatter in increasing excitement. This central section finally disintegrates with two low chords on strings and brass against which a rapid-fire rumble from the timpani sets the pulses racing for a return to the opening material. Transferred from the heights to the depths, it creates a markedly different effect even though the patterns are very similar. The movement ends with some wonderful drumming exchanges between five percussion players with muttered comments from the double basses.

Out of total silence the first tentative notes of the ensuing Passacaglia appear, deep and mysterious. The basic theme, oft repeated, is in a virtually unsullied D major with only an occasional sharpened fourth (G sharp) to add a little spice. Feather-light arpeggios from a piano usher in the notes of a simple A minor triad, one at a time. Above this very traditional framework a solo horn has a tortuous but impassioned melody. Gradually, as one would expect in a Passacaglia, the textures grow more complex over the reiterated bass. Rapid figuration in flutes and oboes takes our minds back to the second movement without actually quoting it. As strings and brass begin to place ever greater emphasis on the Passacaglia theme, flying scales in the wood-wind convey a near-hysterical agitation.

The basic theme rises into the brass as unison strings introduce a new and passionate counterpoint whose inflections reveal a gipsy inheritance. Then, as the tempo quickens, a more urgent figure of rapidly repeated notes pervades the orchestra, battering at the Passacaglia theme which rides out the storm on a clarion trumpet. At last the tension eases and the Passacaglia ends on high violins at the opposite end of the tonal spectrum from where it had begun.

The so-called Toccata that follows begins with two abortive attempts to set it into motion. Then, with a blast from the trombones and a choppy rising scale, we are away. Not as rapid as the central Capriccio, the music nevertheless has tremendous driving energy although the violins at times are called upon to sustain a long melodic line against considerable opposition. In time the music is calmed and oboes and clarinets present the first phrase of the Corale, eliciting a gentle and lyrical comment from a solo flute. Gathering density rather than volume, the chorale works its way through different sections of the orchestra, each phrase crowned with glittering figuration from celesta, harps and piano. A fugue of sorts develops, its dancing crotchets unleashed by a single flute; but its progress is far from academic, and Lutoslawski increases the excitement by whipping up the pace until it develops into a gallop. The final pages see a return to the chorale in the brass against skirling tremolos in wind and strings. It is a finish calculated to leave the players exhausted and the audience exhilarated, showing the composer to be an absolute master of orchestration. The overall structure of the work is clearly defined so that even the uninitiated listener can recognise a number of significant landmarks. It may not be quite in the same class as Bartók's magnificent *Concerto for Orchestra*, but it runs it a very close second.

MAHLER
1860–1911

In comparison to those of Berlioz, Liszt or Wagner, a biography of Mahler does not make enthralling reading. As a boy he was a sufficiently gifted pianist to be regarded as something of a prodigy though his talents were not exploited in concert tours. His career as a student at the Conservatoire in Vienna was not outstanding, although he did win the composition prize in 1878 with a piano quintet in which he himself played the piano part. He received no lessons in conducting since it was not part of the curriculum, but he did study harmony and counterpoint with Bruckner whom he greatly admired, so much so that years later he subsidised the publication of Bruckner's works by voluntarily forfeiting all his own royalties. His fellow-students almost to a man idolised Wagner whose star was shining ever more brightly in the musical firmament; Mahler stayed a little apart, enthusiastic over the music but not over-impressed by the theatrical aspect. Nevertheless he felt that opera might well be his proper métier and with the encourage-ment of a talented sixteen-year-old—Hugo Wolf no less—he began to sketch an operatic treatment of the legend of *Rübezahl*, a mythical character in the mould of Puck or Robin Goodfellow. (The subject had already been treated operatically by several German composers.) Mahler never completed *Rübe-zahl* though it seems that he felt a lasting affection for some of the music. Instead he turned his attention to an elaborate concert-work for soprano, alto and tenor soloists, chorus and two orchestras, one on stage and the other so placed that though the players' parts were marked *fortissimo*, the audience should hear them only as a distant *piano*. It was a wildly impractical project for a young and unknown composer, and in fact Mahler had to wait twenty years before *Das Klagende Lied* was performed. All the same, it was a work that had great significance for him and he confided to a friend that he really looked on it as his Opus 1. At the time of writing it he had high hopes that it might win him the Beethoven prize for composition but it failed to do so. Although it is uneven in accomplishment, this early cantata is a significant harbinger of things to come and it can be said to be the first example of

Mahler's true musical identity.

Since composition was no way to earn a living, Mahler was compelled to turn to conducting; in 1881 he was appointed to the theatre in Ljubljana in Yugoslavia, a position that involved a wide range of music from Beethoven to ballet, Mozart to Johann Strauss. Despite his youth and small stature, the company found that he was a hard taskmaster who would accept nothing but the best. He soon gained their respect and in the course of a single season raised the standards of performance by a considerable degree. His second appointment, to the opera-house at Olmütz, was a less rewarding experience. Mahler made no attempt to ingratiate himself with either the management or the singers, nor did he care that they laughed at his vegetarian diet and his refusal to drink alcohol. He would not allow performances of Wagner or Mozart (though he adored both) since he felt the company could not do justice to their music. He described the experience as 'suffering for my great masters'.

The following season he moved on to the opera-house at Kassel where he found himself in a humiliating position subordinate to a lesser musician than he was. He became the musical dogsbody of the theatre and, seeking consolation in his wretchedness, fell deeply in love with a young actress. The affair inspired his first important song-cycle, *Lieder eines fahrenden Gesellen* (Songs of a Wayfarer), songs that dwell more on the sadness of unrequited love than on the joy of its fulfilment. From this cycle he was to derive material for his First Symphony.

The early stages of Mahler's career as a conductor were often painful, but with moves to Prague and then to Leipzig things improved and he was at last given the opportunity to show his prowess as an interpreter of Wagner and Mozart. At the age of twenty-five he made a big impression in Prague with a performance of Beethoven's Ninth Symphony, an experience which undoubtedly had as deep an effect on him as on the audience. His inclination towards big forces was certainly encouraged and he began work on his massive First Symphony, an occupation that became so absorbing that he started to neglect his duties at the opera-house, thereby earning the disapproval of the management. For the first time the cruel irony of Mahler's life became apparent for however brightly the creative fire burned within, he was compelled by circumstances to be a part-time composer. The greater part of his life was spent in conducting, a career which brought him international acclaim at the highest level, acclaim which for a long time was denied him as a composer. Yet time-consuming though it was, there is no doubt that the enormous experience he gained while working with orchestras was of great benefit to him as a composer since his mastery of orchestration was one of his greatest talents.

A chronicle of his life as a conductor would take a book of its own; Budapest, Hamburg, Vienna, London and America in turn applauded his mastery in the opera-pit though, not surprisingly, he aroused the antagonism of some of the more conservative critics who found his interpretations too overtly emotional. One marvels at the energy of a man who, so occupied with bringing music to life through others, could also find time to create a new world of sound for himself. The Second Symphony, the so-called 'Resurrection', cost him immense labour. It seems determined to challenge Beethoven with its heroic scale and choral finale, but, vast though it is, it is worth observing that the material of two movements is partly derived from two songs that he had composed, taken from a collection of German folk-lore called *Des Knaben Wunderhorn* ('Youth's Magic Horn'). This book had a profound influence on Mahler from his childhood days and served to nourish his essentially romantic, if morbid, imagination. Although he surely considered himself as primarily a symphonic composer, he found it hard to separate himself entirely from the prop of words; whether this was the result of his intense association with opera, or simply a need for some metric framework, it is hard to say.

Like the Second Symphony, the Third requires soprano and contralto soloists and a chorus. It is conceived on an even more gigantic scale. The first movement alone lasts for nearly forty minutes—as long as Beethoven's Fifth in its entirety! Instead of the conventional four we find six movements (he even contemplated a seventh) while the orchestra is gargantuan. A tentative programme which Mahler subsequently withdrew called the symphony 'A summer morning's dream'. This suggestion of a Delius-like idyll could scarcely be more misleading since in the first movement 'Summer marches in' with a positively martial swagger. The collage of march-tunes, fanfares, student choruses and rustic folksong is like a Viennese version of Charles Ives. 'Summer marches in singing and resonant in a way you can't imagine' wrote Mahler to Anna von Mildenburg, his one-time mistress.

After the immensity of the first movement the second and third are relatively light-weight. Mahler gave them rather coy titles—'What the Flowers on the Meadows tell me' and 'What the Animals of the Forest tell me'. Here we find evidence of another paradox, the combination of a powerful intellect and a childish naiveté in the same mind. It is this juxtaposition of opposites that often causes resistance to Mahler; to the unsympathetic ear the dramatic passages can seem pretentious while the lyrical tunes bring a touch of bathos unsuited to their context.

Having drawn on the material of an early *Wunderhorn* song in the third movement, Mahler turns to Nietzsche's *Zarathustra* for his fourth, another contrast of extremes.

'O man, take heed!
What does the depth of midnight say?

. . .

Desire longs for eternity—
Deep, deep eternity.'

This deeply felt movement, given to a contralto solo, is followed by a transformation of mood—'What the angels tell me'. A choir of boys' voices sings a three-note bell-chime to the words 'Bimm-bamm' above which a group of girls tell of 'three angels singing a sweet song' to a tune whose instant charm is reminiscent of Humperdinck's *Hansel und Gretel*. It is a movement of light that displaces a movement of darkness, the children's voices giving it a freshness that offers a new experience in the symphonic repertoire.

The ensuing Finale, 'What Love tells me', is calm and serene, a vision nearer to *Parsifal* than *Tristan und Isolde*. Richly divided strings begin with an almost religious theme, a quiet hymn of thanksgiving for the healing power of love, though later chromaticisms hint at more passionate ecstacies. At the end of a symphony that lasts a full ninety minutes it must have taken courage to risk a slow movement, yet to have done otherwise would have been to destroy the message of the work. 'All is dissolved in Peace and Being' wrote Mahler of this movement, and one feels that his tormented soul did find some respite here despite the pounding timpani and brazen fanfares of the final page.

Not long after completing this mammoth work Mahler's conducting career took a significant turn when he became director of the Vienna Opera (1897). The anti-Semitic climate would have prevented a Jew from holding a post of such prestige but he had prudently embraced the Catholic faith—although more for political than spiritual reasons. Although Christianity held some emotional appeal for him, he was essentially pantheistic in outlook, as the programme of the Third Symphony reveals. Fully appreciating the scope now given him, Mahler drove himself mercilessly in Vienna, greatly enlarging the repertoire of the opera company and in due course taking over the direction of the Vienna Philharmonic concerts as well. His autocratic manner earned him many critics, especially when he openly tampered with the scores of established masterpieces such as Beethoven's 'Choral' Symphony. He defended such actions by pointing out that orchestras had greatly changed since Beethoven's day and that he was simply adjusting the balance to accommodate the increased number of strings.

Despite a schedule that would have exhausted lesser mortals, Mahler gave himself no rest. After taking the Vienna Philharmonic to the Paris World Fair in 1900, a trip that cut short his already brief holiday period, he returned immediately to his villa at Maiernegg on the Wörthersee to begin work on his Fourth Symphony. Not surprisingly it is on a less monumental scale than its giant predecessors. Essentially pastoral in nature, it explores a less extreme range of emotion. The original plan of the Third Symphony included a seventh movement, 'What Childhood tells me', and it is not too far-fetched to suggest that the Fourth Symphony is a more comprehensive working-out of this previous vision. Once more we find a dependence on words, the last movement requiring a soprano soloist whose voice should have a child-like purity.

Although the beginning of the first movement with its suggestion of jingling sleigh-bells seems to be descriptive in intent, the movement as a whole is in a particularly rich sonata-form with no fewer than five clearly identifiable subjects. One need hardly say that a large orchestra is required, but it is used economically, more for the range of tone-colour it provides than for its mass. Mahler's search for exotic sound shows clearly in the second movement where he writes an important part for a solo violin tuned a tone higher than normal to produce a special and slightly macabre tone-quality. He had in mind a legendary fiddler called 'Freund Hein' who supposedly led the dead upon their journey to the afterworld—Austrian dead, we may assume, since the rhythm of the dance is characteristic of the *Ländler*. The slow movement is a set of variations which also contains allusions to material from earlier movements while the last shows a child's vision of Heaven with St. Peter looking on approvingly as Martha goes about the homely but essential business of baking bread. The gentle final cadences, so different from the cataclysmic endings of the preceding symphonies, give this work a special character rare in Mahler's music, contentment. Perhaps without realising it he was saying a tender farewell to the innocent happiness of childhood, a happiness which he himself might not have known but which the *Wunderhorn* poems had brought so vividly to life in his imagination.

The year after completing the Fourth Symphony and when work on the Fifth had already begun, Mahler met a beautiful and talented girl called Alma Maria Schindler. She was nineteen years his junior but an instant rapport was established; within five months they were married. His love for her was genuine and intense, the first real breach in the egocentric wall with which he had surrounded himself; she on the other hand was something of a *femme fatale*; already infatuated with her composition teacher Zemlinsky when she met Mahler, she readily changed her affections to one she felt was the greater genius. (She outlived Mahler by fifty-three years and was successively the mistress of Kokoschka, the wife of Walter Gropius, by whom she had the daughter to whose memory Berg's Violin Concerto was dedicated,[1] and, after a divorce, the wife of Franz Werfel, the author.) Despite a somewhat stormy relationship which at one time drove Mahler to seek help from Freud, the marriage provided the composer with new inspiration and he embarked on a sequence of four immense symphonies with ferocious energy. Performances of his works were becoming much more frequent and these no doubt fired him with an ever greater belief in his destiny. After one spectacularly successful performance of the Third Symphony he made a very revealing remark: 'I have beaten Strauss, who is all the rage here, by yards.' It clearly mattered to him that he should be thought the greatest living composer; indeed a driving force of such a kind might well explain his predilection for the gargantuan forms his music took.

[1] See Volume 1, page 108.

The Fifth Symphony, much of it composed during the first happy months of his marriage and copied out by his young wife, begins with a funeral march (a burial of his past?) to which the second movement is a thematically related but turbulent sequel. There follows a Scherzo which might be described as an Austrian *Ländler* promoted to symphonic status,[2] after which the famous *Adagietto* provides a perfect miniature slow movement for the much reduced forces of strings and harp. The finale, which is also thematically related to the preceding movement, is Mahler's most 'academic' display of composer-craft, a complex Rondo with a substantial fugue thrown in for good measure. It is as though he had determined to rid himself of the prop of words, to write 'pure' instrumental music; even so, several themes in the symphony echo phrases from songs that he was writing in the same period.

In 1903 Mahler began work on the colossal Sixth Symphony which incorporates a portrait of Alma in the second main theme of the opening movement and a depiction of children playing in the Scherzo. (Their first child, a daughter, was still a baby some nine months old.) But meanwhile, to Alma's distress, he had been working on a cycle of songs concerning the death of children, *Kindertotenlieder*, fragments of which filtered into the scores of both the Fifth and Sixth symphonies. Whether by coincidence or by some strange prophetic vision the immense last movement of the Sixth Symphony contains three literal hammer-blows, the blows of Fate which finally crush the hero-figure. Tragically Mahler was to experience such blows not long after, for in 1907 he was forced to resign from the opera by the machinations of an anti-Semitic caucus; he then found that he had a heart condition that could easily prove to be serious; worst of all and hardest to bear was the death of his first daughter at the age of four and a half. Alma's superstitious forebodings had been realised.

Meanwhile, before these tragic events, Mahler had completed the Seventh and Eighth symphonies, the latter a vast choral work based on the ancient Christian hymn 'Veni Creator Spiritus' and a setting of the final scene of Goethe's Faust. This astonishing composition, the so-called 'Symphony of a Thousand', was written in two months of feverish inspiration. It was, he was convinced, his greatest work, and the tumultuous acclamation which greeted its first performance (in Munich) was the more fitting since, though he could not have known it, it was the last time that he was to conduct in Europe.

With the termination of his long association with the Vienna Opera, Mahler had accepted an invitation to go to New York. During the remaining few years of his life he continued with the demanding career of a star conductor, regularly alternating between America and Europe and somehow finding time to write *Das Lied von der Erde*, the Ninth Symphony and the

---

[2] Cf. Ravel: *La Valse*.

unfinished Tenth. Ever a perfectionist, he also made extensive revisions to nearly all his earlier symphonies, profiting from the experience of a number of performances.

The Ninth Symphony is perhaps the most prophetic of Mahler's works even though at times it looks back to *Das Lied von der Erde*. It begins with a slow movement lasting twenty-five minutes or more that Alban Berg described as 'the most heavenly thing that Mahler ever wrote'. Deeply emotional though it is, perhaps its most remarkable feature lies in the coda where the usual large orchestra is fined down to chamber music size as though the composer was tacitly admitting that he no longer needed enormous resources to express himself adequately.

There follows the almost inevitable *Ländler* with two contrasting Trios; there is a somewhat spectral quality about the movement at times, while the instruction 'rather clumsy and rough' suggests a dance for Caliban rather than Puck. Satire and parody are a recurring feature of Mahler's music as he openly admits by calling the third movement a *Rondo-Burleske*; he even seems to be mocking himself since themes can be traced back to both the Fifth and Third symphonies. While it is tempting to the musical analyst to see such relationships as deliberate, it may be that certain melodic shapes are so characteristic of the composer that they reappeared without him being aware of it. Nevertheless, cross-fertilization from the songs to the orchestral works is undeniable. None is more touching than the one which occurs in the final Adagio of the Ninth Symphony when high violins produce an echo of one of the *Kindertotenlieder*. There is an aching sorrow in this movement which has led Michael Kennedy in his penetrating study of Mahler[3] to suggest that the composer may have regarded it as a requiem for his little daughter and for the brothers and sisters to whom he had been deeply attached.

The Tenth Symphony was left unfinished although Mahler made extensive preliminary sketches. For thirteen years Alma refused to allow them to be seen, possibly influenced by the anguished annotations he had scrawled in the margins of the score, cries from the heart directed to her. Subsequently the manuscripts were released and after immense and dedicated labour the English Mahler scholar Deryck Cooke brilliantly deciphered the sketches and produced an impressively convincing performing edition. It is an affirmative work which scotches the over-sentimental view of Mahler's closing years which prevailed for so long.

Driving himself as hard as he did, Mahler succeeded in cheating death for several years, and one cannot help wondering if he would not have been wiser to give up conducting altogether when the first symptoms of heart trouble disclosed themselves. As it was he never heard *Das Lied von der Erde* or the Ninth Symphony. He died in May 1911 at the age of fifty, leaving behind a major contribution to the symphonic repertoire whose full impact has only

[3] *Mahler*, J.M. Dent, 1974.

really been felt in the last two decades. Once regarded with some suspicion as a self-indulgent neurotic who never knew when to cry 'Enough!', he has now taken his rightful place as a visionary composer whose message speaks more powerfully to each succeeding generation.

Kindertotenlieder
(1901–4)

In 1834 the German poet Friedrich Rückert suffered a heartbreaking loss; his two younger children died during an epidemic of scarlet fever. He sublimated his grief by writing a sequence of poems called *Kindertotenlieder*, or 'Songs on the death of children'. In 1901 Gustav Mahler came across these poems, and, deeply moved by their touching simplicity, set three of them to music. The following year he married and in due course had a child of his own. Three years later, in 1904, his second daughter was born, and it was in that summer that he set two more of the poems, making the cycle we now know of five songs in all. At the time he must have been perfectly happy, and it should be established quite clearly that the emotional intensity of his settings was prompted entirely by the poems, and not by any personal situation in his life. (A comparable tragedy was to come later.) A composer is by nature a sensitive being, and Mahler's response to these poems reveals a quite understandable ability to identify himself with the poet.

The songs were designed to be sung by a baritone for, after all, the poems were written from the father's viewpoint; but contraltos and mezzo-sopranos have taken them into their repertoire as well, for their tender and expressive grief is equally suitable to be expressed by a woman. Mahler meant them to be performed with orchestra, but a piano version is quite practical although inevitably loses some variety of tone-colour.

The first song faces up to the fact that life will go on, the sun will continue to shine whatever grief the father may feel. Mahler begins his setting wonderfully simply with a bare two-part introduction scored for oboe and bassoon. His avoidance of the potentially over-sentimental sound of strings is notable; they are used with extreme economy, and most of the melodic phrases are given to wind instruments or the horn. There is one particularly touching sound in his first song, which comes several times—the little bell-like chime of a glockenspiel, which I suspect Mahler put in as the echo of a child's toy. Only for one brief passage of half a dozen bars does the music really become impassioned; for the most part there is a sort of numbness in sorrow which is more moving than some more overt display of emotion could ever be.

The second song, though still philosophical in content, is directed more personally towards the dead children, especially the memory of the expressive power of their glances, like 'dark flames'. The music begins with a Tristanesque phrase which reminds us how absorbed in Wagner's music Mahler was. But despite the passionate first few bars, the scoring is again for the most part remarkably restrained. The vocal line is in the grand Germanic tradition of song, though with phrases of a sensuous loveliness that can have seldom been surpassed. One, in particular, goes dangerously near the borderline of sentimentality, but Mahler at once counterbalances it with a more austere moment. There is a master-stroke at the end; for some little time the music is in undiluted C major, the final three notes of the voice part actually spelling out the notes of the common chord of C.

These that are eyes today, in nights to come will be stars.

The thought is beautiful but does it really bring comfort? 'No' says the orchestra and folds the music back into C minor with a last sad cadence.

The third song sounds as though it might have been influenced by Hugo Wolf with whom Mahler had been a close friend in their student days. The music is like a sad little march as the father remembers how, when his wife entered the room, the bright happy face of the child would come peeping in behind her. It is as though a game is being remembered, a game that will never be played again.

In the fourth song the father indulges in a fantasy: 'the children have only gone out—they will soon be home again—do not be anxious—it is a beautiful day.' The scoring is richer, with horns reinforcing the strings as though the vision of the children 'on the heights in the sunshine' demands a greater warmth in the orchestral texture. But it is in the final song that the orchestra makes the greatest contribution. The alternative version for piano is ineffectual here with left hand trills making a poor substitute for the vivid colours of the orchestral score. The background to the voice-part is uneasy and turbulent, brilliantly depicting the storm referred to in the poem.

In this weather, in this storm, I would never have let the children go out.[4]

Gradually the tension eases until once again we hear the little chime of the glockenspiel. Does Mahler perhaps imagine the father to be standing in the children's nursery, idly touching one of their toys? The delicate sound leads to a most tender and moving conclusion:

Watched over by God's hand, they are resting, as if they were at home with mother.

[4] Translation by William Mann, 1959. Published by EMI Records.

This cycle of such mourning, shot through as it is by a deep sense of personal grief, ends in the major key with some of Mahler's loveliest music. It is like a cradle song, and one feels that the distraught father has found some sort of peace at last despite the bitterness of his loss.

The musical significance of the *Kindertotenlieder* is considerable since it is a sort of seed-bed from which a number of symphonic themes were to grow. This was not unusual for Mahler, and the first three symphonies in particular all have themes that can be traced back to individual songs. Donald Mitchell has pinpointed these with painstaking accuracy in his definitive study *Gustav Mahler, the Wunderhorn Years*,[5] and it is he who identifies the precise phrase from the first song of the *Kindertotenlieder* that reappears in the first movement of the Fifth Symphony, as well as revealing the close relationship between the second song and the famous *Adagietto* in the same work. More astutely he traces a line from the last song of the cycle to the finale of the Sixth Symphony. Finally, as we have already seen (on page 63), even as late as the Ninth Symphony echoes of this song cycle lingered in Mahler's mind when he quoted the very phrase (from the fourth song) which describes how beautiful the day is in the mountains where the father imagines the children still to be.

Symphony No. 3 in D Minor (1893–6)

The Third Symphony provides an easy target for anyone antipathetic towards Mahler's music. In the first place its demands indicate a sort of megalomania; what orchestral management will willingly provide four flutes, all doubling on piccolo, four oboes, cor anglais, three clarinets, two E flat clarinets, bass clarinet, four bassoons, one doubling on contrabassoon, eight horns, four trumpets, four trombones, tuba, six timpani requiring two players, a massive percussion section, two harps, strings, a contralto soloist, a women's chorus, a children's choir, and off-stage a posthorn and a set of six bells? Secondly, the proportions seem eccentric to say the least; the first movement lasts nearly forty minutes after which the composer requested an interval. The remaining five movements constitute the second half of the concert and together take not a great deal longer than the first. The thematic material covers the entire gamut from nobility to vulgarity, from the profound to the naive.

[5] Faber & Faber, 1975.

At the time of writing the work, which occupied him for three summers, Mahler was emotionally involved with and subsequently engaged to a singer named Anna von Mildenberg. In one of many letters he wrote to her he said: 'My symphony will be something such as the world has never yet heard! The whole of Nature finds a voice in it, and tells of such secret things as one may perhaps divine in a dream. I tell you, I myself get an uncanny sensation at certain points, I feel as though I hadn't written this myself.'[6] An unsympathetic reader might dismiss this as the ravings of a madman and indeed Mahler's aspirations were regarded as virtually lunatic by some contemporary critics. In Munich a respected writer vented his spleen on 'the complete emptiness and vacuity of an art in which the spasm of an impotent mock-Titanism reduces itself to a frank gratification of common seamstress-like sentimentality'.[7] I am not sure what it means but it would seem to be unfavourable!

At one stage Mahler gave descriptive titles to each of the six movements; the first was 'Pan awakes; summer marches in'. If his original intention was to start quietly in the manner of Debussy's Faun, he obviously had second thoughts for the symphony begins with eight horns in unison proclaiming the principal theme *fortissimo*, a rude awakening . . . The theme (Ex. 1) has not unjustly been compared to the big C major tune that begins the finale of Brahms' First Symphony, a resemblance Mahler must have been perfectly aware of but which clearly didn't bother him.

Ex. 1

In conventional terms one would be tempted to label this the First Subject, but the construction of the movement is far from conventional and this theme does not actually reappear until page 78 of the score. However, it does serve as a source for a number of derivatives, the final fragments bracketed as (a) being especially fruitful. After so resolute a beginning it is a surprise to find the music sinking almost immediately into darkly brooding harmonies which die away to near silence, leaving nothing but a vaguely menacing rumble on the bass drum. Trombones and tuba pick up its rhythm

[6] Quoted from Kurt Blaukopf, *Mahler*, Allen Lane, 1973.
[7] Slonimsky, (ed.) *Lexicon of Musical Invective*, Coleman-Ross Inc., 1953.

(♩ , ♫♩ ♪) as gurgling bassoons introduce the first derivation from (a). Oboes and clarinets have a striking leap of an octave which evokes a startled response from muted trumpets in unison. A rushing upward scale in the lower strings (marked '*wild*') leads into a broad impassioned phrase. These basic materials suffice for some time, punctuated by strident interruptions from trumpets or horns whose splendid fanfares conjure up images of Austrian castles perched on rocky crags.

A second solo passage for bass drum leads to a change of mood, a pastoral theme on a solo oboe accompanied by swaying harmonies in the wind and softly shimmering strings. (It is this tune that Mahler parodied grotesquely in the Ninth Symphony, third movement.) A solo violin briefly extends the theme before being interrupted by sharply accented triads from the clarinet. A mysterious passage for percussion only disintegrates into silence and a long pause.

A double-bar and a change of both time-signature and tempo would seem to indicate that everything up to this point has been an introduction, offering us samples of things to come. A repetitive, almost funereal, accompaniment begins, based on the terse rhythm shown above; against its monotonous beat a solo trombone launches into a passionate declamation in which his colleagues are ultimately compelled to join. This strange recitative-like episode is terminated by a shudder from the woodwind and a mighty clang from a gong. As though momentarily exhausted, the music sinks down to an almost inaudible low D on cellos and basses. It is in their deepest register that the pastoral oboe theme now reappears, tempting us to call it a Second Subject in the accepted form of the classical symphony. Such a solution would be altogether too restrictive for Mahler's plan for he soon introduces some completely new material of an unashamedly trivial kind (Ex. 2).

Ex. 2

This cheeky little tune leads into a march, but for children rather than soldiers, skipping lightfooted as they go. Soon more and more people join the happy parade until with a sudden blare the horns cut in with an irreverent version of Ex. 1 against which the violins have a joyous descant. Before long we gain the impression of a great crowd singing in spontaneous unison, but the universal jollity is cut short by sweeping upward scales like a sudden gust of wind. Against a fierce tremolando from the strings the horns remind us of the abrupt phrase (a), extending it into a powerful recitative that matches the earlier passage for trombone without exactly duplicating it. An abrupt but arresting little trumpet call should perhaps be mentioned in any list of important 'subjects' but it can hardly fail to be noticed.

At the centre of the movement there is a period of calm, easily recognised by the appearance of a trombone solo which Mahler actually marks 'Sentimental'. Fragments of themes drift by on cor anglais or solo violin; whirring trills in the strings create a dust haze through which a trumpet sounds a military command; a piccolo whistles a pert reminder of Ex. 2; a bassoon tries to remember Ex. 1 and gets it all wrong. This whole passage is a collage rather than a development section and anyone who has paid due attention to what has gone before should have no difficulty in recognising a number of familiar themes even though they may be slightly altered in shape or character. In particular the 'unison song' that provided the previous climax is given a far more lyrical treatment.

This gentler mood is dispelled by the cellos and basses who introduce a comically 'learned' version of Ex. 2, now in the minor, and donning Bach's wig in an attempt to fool us into believing that a fugue is imminent. This elicits chortles of mirth from the woodwind and some cheerful Hoorays from the horns. The ensuing section is by far the most continuous in the movement, no longer subject to the sudden and erratic changes which have tended to disconcert the conservative listener. In due course Exx. 1 and 2 are combined in dextrous counterpoint until at last swirling scales in the strings sweep the remaining themes away leaving only the rattle of a side-drum to hold our attention. It is as clear a signal as we could wish for to herald the recapitulation; once more the eight horns proclaim Ex. 1 in its full glory and for a time we can sit back, content to identify the observance of a classical tradition in what has seemed a heretical movement.

The first departure from the previous plan comes when the solo trombone reminds us of the 'sentimental' theme. Soon the music comes to a halt. Three times the cellos and basses seem to clear their collective throats in an endeavour to say something. What should it turn out to be but the 'children's march' which proceeds jauntily on its way with increasing rowdiness. Once again we get the impression of a great unison song; once again the song is interrupted by sweeping scales. But this time they lead to brilliant and triumphant fanfares; high summer is come in glorious pageantry 'singing and resonant in a way you can't imagine' as Mahler said.[8]

SECOND MOVEMENT: *'What the Flowers on the Meadows tell me'*

'It's the least troublesome movement I've ever written' wrote Mahler, and

---

[8] On finishing the first draft, Mahler is reported to have said: 'The title "Summer marches in" no longer fits the shape of things in this introduction; "Pan's Procession" would be better . . . Satyrs and other rough children of nature disport themselves in it.' See Donald Mitchell, *Gustav Mahler, The Wunderhorn Years*, Faber & Faber, 1975.

after the immense span of the first movement this ensuing *Tempo di Menuetto* seems lightweight indeed. It may seem strange that a composer in the 1890s should deign to write a genuine Minuet, but Mahler was very concerned that conductors should not mistake his intentions, not only marking it *Grazioso*, but also *Sehr mässig* (very moderate) followed by the exhortation 'Don't hurry' with an exclamation mark. A solo oboe presents the first theme with a minimal accompaniment from pizzicato violas or cellos. This lasts some nineteen bars without departing from A major. The first violins then introduce a slightly more active measure with a hint of F sharp minor only to find it seeming to dissolve in a curious chromatic descent. They soon recover from this setback and embark on a warmly expressive melody that only an Austrian could have written.

A change to 3/8 gives an impression of a quicker tempo as repeated triplet chords bring a new chirpiness to the music; there is a suggestion of birdsong in the air and a gradual accumulation of activity. Oboes and clarinets in unison have smoothly flowing runs like sudden gusts of wind setting the flowers nodding in the sunlight, the colours forming a kaleidoscope across the meadow. It is a brief disturbance and the 'Austrian' theme soon returns to restore calm to the scene. A second disturbance produces rather more agitation though the scoring remains delicate. Mahler actually described this as 'a whirlwind sweeping over the meadow shaking the leaves and blossoms so that they groan and whimper as though crying for salvation',[9] but it is rather too melodramatic a picture to match what we hear. A playfully capricious violin solo leads us back to the opening minuet, somewhat modified, and the movement ends quietly with birdsong in the flutes and amorous sighs in the violins.

THIRD MOVEMENT: *'What the Animals of the Forest tell me'*

Although Mahler gives the indication *Scherzando*, this movement is far from being a Scherzo in the Beethoven tradition. The beginning is artless in the extreme, harking back to an early *Wunderhorn* song about the death of the cuckoo.[10] The transparent scoring favours the woodwind while at times there is a curiously ambiguous alternation between major and minor harmony. Suddenly, as though fed up with the rather trivial decorative passages in the violins, two horns in unison belt out a clod-hopping theme which startles a passing donkey—a close relative of the one in Mendelssohn's *A Midsummer Night's Dream* Overture.

The music becomes distinctly coarser as it breaks into 6/8 time, a round

[9] Neville Cardus, *Gustav Mahler, his mind and his music*, Gollancz, 1965.
[10] *Ablösung im Sommer.*

dance for the farmyard stock rather than the elusive creatures of the forest. Sustained trills signal a general exit leaving a solitary bassoon to hop uneasily across the gap of an octave. Flutes reintroduce the opening theme, now more elaborately decorated. Soon Mahler brings in the heavy brass as reinforcements, their ponderous syncopations giving a very rustic flavour to the dance. (A stunning chromatic descent in unison horns, trumpets and trombones brings an irresistible suggestion of 'A-tishoo, a-tishoo, we all fall down!') Triplet figures in the horns grow increasingly rowdy over a 'jungle drums' effect in the timpani, but then flutes bring back a plaintive version of the opening theme. Suddenly a trumpet-call arrests our attention; violins freeze on a sustained chord as in the distance we hear a post-horn. Despite the Wagnerian echoes this is no demi-god but Man intruding into the animal kingdom. He seems a cheerful fellow but his long solo brings a slightly timid response from flutes and violas, while a second post-horn solo supported now by horns sets the violins trembling.

Tentatively the round dance begins again, gradually gaining confidence. A repetition of the chromatic descent in the brass leads into a running passage for the lower strings which Mahler marks *Grob!* (Coarsely). The music gains in sheer exuberance until once again it is stilled to hear the posthorn solo. Divided strings make a serene comment leading us to expect a twilight ending to the movement, but Mahler has a considerable surprise in store. An excited murmur begins in the strings; a bird-call from the very beginning of the movement grows increasingly insistent in the woodwind leading to a huge chord from which harp arpeggios sweep downwards like the flight of angels' wings. Against a persistent beat of drums a tumult of brass fanfares builds up to a stunning climax, bringing a movement which began as a naive miniature to a dramatic conclusion.

FOURTH MOVEMENT: *'What Man tells me'*[11]

In comparison to all that has gone before the scoring of this movement is amazingly economical. Mahler asks that it should be 'Very slow, mysterious and extremely soft (*ppp*) throughout'. Nearly forty bars are poised on a sustained 'drone' bass—D and A—above which a pair of horns offer a solemn melody in thirds punctuated by eerie harmonics on violins and harps or a sad bird-call on an oboe ('Like a Nature-sound'). Cellos and basses begin with a low murmur, rocking gently to and fro between A and B flat. The first harmonies come as the alto soloist sings her initial invocation, 'O Mensch!' The eight horns add a muted four-part comment which confirms that there is a direct quotation from the second page of the symphony, the 'darkly

[11]Mahler originally called this 'What the twilight tells me'.

brooding harmonies' which follow immediately after the powerful opening theme (see p. 67). There is a silent pause and then the 'drone' bass begins its mysterious hum, modelled on the opening bars of Beethoven's Ninth Symphony but so very different in effect.

For text Mahler turned to Nietzsche's *Also sprach Zarathustra*:

> 'O man! Take heed!
> What says the midnight hour?
> I slept, I slept—
> From deep dreams I awake:
> The world is deep,
> And deeper than the Day knew.
> Deep is its woe—
> Joy—deeper still than grief.
> Woe speaks: Begone!
> Joy yearns for eternity—
> For deep, deep eternity.

The alto phrase for 'Take heed' (*Gib Acht!*), twice repeated, is like a profound sigh. For a moment or two it seems that the singer cannot continue as the horns gently prompt her with the melody; but then she joins them, turning the phrase to the minor on the last syllable of 'Mitternacht'. It is then that we hear the infinitely sorrowful tones of the oboe, 'the bird of night'.[12] The music slows almost to a halt and then resumes the sad refrain. At the mention of Day (*der Tag*) violins interpolate a deeply expressive line whose tender yearning is stifled by the haunting bird-call.

The opening phrases return, giving the impression of a second verse to the song. A solo violin adds poignant comments to the singer's line. The other violins rekindle the previous expressive interlude but this time the soloist joins them, reaching towards the peace of eternity. Again we hear the sad bird-call, once, twice, and then suddenly distorted in an anguished descent. The gentle rocking motion of the opening bars resumes, slows and, almost inaudible, dies away to silence.

The movement takes a mere 11 pages out of a score totalling 231 but it is here that the true heart of the symphony lies.

FIFTH MOVEMENT: *'What the angels tell me'*

The change of mood is so abrupt that it comes as quite a shock, the more so as for the first time we hear a choir of boys' voices. Mahler must have realised he was taking a considerable risk by following a movement of such profound seriousness with anything as potentially banal as 'Bimm-bamm, Bimm-

---

[12] Mahler's own phrase.

bamm' sung to a three-note chime. Since he also uses real bells one would think that the voices might be regarded as a dubious extravagance. Little boys in a concert-hall are not necessarily a convincing substitute for cherubim, though cherubim were clearly what he had in mind. A solid four-square tune from the woodwind introduces the angels' song, sung by a three-part female choir.

> Three angels sang a sweet song;
> The sound rises towards heaven.
> They rejoice for St. Peter is free of sin . . .

As I have already suggested, the style of the music is very near to Humperdinck's delightful opera *Hansel und Gretel* with cheerful counter-points in dotted rhythm giving a crisply starched edge to the flowing vocal lines. A four-bar interlude for the lower strings and harp leads to a change of mood as the alto soloist sorrowfully asks 'And should I not weep O kindly God since I have broken the Ten Commandments?'.[13] The bell-chime passes to the female choir, its notes more solemn. Occasional flurries of semiquavers rise through the woodwind parts, possibly symbolizing the errant sinner straying from the path of righteousness. All restlessness is stilled as muted strings accompany a hymn-like phrase—'O come and have pity on me'. The clamour of the 'bells' increases as the boys' voices return and the orchestral texture fills out. Only twice—and that briefly—are the voices unaccompanied, the second time to the significant phrase 'Liebe nur Gott in alle Zeit' (Love only God for evermore.) It is a phrase echoed by the boys as for the first time they sing words instead of their 'Bimm-bamms'. The music becomes more joyous as a pair of trombones in unison stand in for the Heavenly trump. We expect a loud ending but it is not to be and the 'bell-chimes' fade away leaving a single high F in the top soprano part. The orchestral support to this final note is an intriguing example of Mahler's fastidious aural imagination—a *pianissimo* harmonic in violas, single harmonics in the two harps, a soft F on a glockenspiel and, strangely, four piccolos in unison an octave above the voice marked *f* $\diagdown$ *ppp* one way of ensuring that there really is a *diminuendo* in this closing bar.

Sixth Movement: *'What Love tells me'*

The Love Mahler tells of in the title (all of which he subsequently suppressed) is Divine not sensual. The movement begins very quietly with divided strings playing with the intimate quality of chamber music. The smooth progression of the melody gives it a devout character so that we feel we might

---

[13] The second half of this phrase also appears in the finale of the Fourth Symphony.

well be listening to the introduction to a Benedictus in a setting of the Mass. Mahler's directions read, 'Slowly; calmly; with feeling', and it is a long time before he allows a dynamic louder than *pianissimo*. The first emotional climax is signalled by the entrance of the horns whose sustained crescendo provokes an impassioned reaction from the violins who soar up to a high B flat only to die away to nothing a few bars later. After a long static pause the cellos introduce a new, more chromatic melody, richly harmonised. Mahler extends this into the violins, but after a series of dying falls the opening theme returns, newly coloured by a descant in the woodwind.

A key-change to E major intensifies the emotion as violins begin yet another melody beneath which gently throbbing syncopations in the violas add a touch of unease. A phrase-by-phrase description of events in this movement is relatively valueless as it is a perfect example of Mahler's technique of continuously extended melody. It is easy for the listener to be carried along on the virtually unbroken melodic line and to respond to the increasing richness of sound as the eight horns add their considerable weight to the orchestral texture. A fine central climax creates a core of tension which slowly dissolves on a long sustained unison C sharp. The hushed mood of the opening returns, but this time it is not sustained for so long. A carefully tiered crescendo leads to an even bigger climax, notable for an anguished phrase in the horns and violent stabbing thrusts from unison trumpets. Here, one feels, is the dark night of the soul; comfort and consolation come with a chorale on a solo trumpet. Inevitably and majestically the music builds towards its immense final cadence, a glorious proclamation of D major which makes a fitting ending to this gargantuan symphony, 'Not with crude power,' says Mahler, 'but with muted noble tone'. It is an affirmation of faith which effectively dispels the despair of the Fourth Movement.

Symphony No. 5 in C sharp Minor (1901–2; revised 1907–9)

The association of music with a film can have a somewhat corrupting effect which it takes a long time to overcome. For how many years after seeing *Brief Encounter* did audiences continue to see images of Celia Johnson and Trevor Howard meeting in railway station buffets whenever they heard Rakhmaninov's Second Piano Concerto? When will the slow movement of Mozart's great C major Piano Concerto cease to be known as the *Elvira Madigan* theme or the *Adagietto* from this symphony fail to conjure up memories of Dirk Bogarde mooning round Venice hoping to catch a glimpse of a blonde youth? Yet it is undeniable that Visconti's use of Mahler's music in the film *Death in Venice* made many new converts to the symphony, though since the *Adagietto* takes up only five pages out of a total of 243 there was plenty left to discover for those who made the effort.

A brief consideration of some of the other movements raises some interesting questions; for instance, we find a funeral march to begin with and a scherzo-waltz as a third movement. There are of course honourable precedents in Beethoven's *Eroica* Symphony or in Tchaikovsky's Fifth. Inevitably the funeral march prompts the enquiry 'Whose funeral?' Is it for an unknown warrior, a hero, a nation, an era, for the hopes of man, for a lifestyle? Certainly Mahler's funeral march begins with every sign of being military, the opening trumpet sounding a sort of Last Post; but it isn't long before the violins are playing a tune not far removed from Kurt Weill, and it is easy to imagine Lotte Lenya singing it to a bitter and cynical lyric contrasting the harsh actuality of death with the meaningless pomp and ceremony with which the dead are interred. The title 'Funeral March' is incontrovertible in its suggestion of a public ceremony, but the moment that tune arrives it seems as if Mahler has identified himself with the person rather than the occasion. In televisual or cinematic terms he's moved into a close-up of the dead man's face, and we no longer think of him as a general or a statesman, but a man, once a schoolboy, once a lover, once a typically fallible human being. The procession goes on its way, but every now and then Mahler tugs at our heartstrings by taking another look into the coffin itself.

Here perhaps is the clue to the enigma of Mahler's style as a symphonist. Over and over again we find this dichotomy between the epic nature of the conception and the essentially personal nature of its realisation. If his aspirations as a composer put him onto a pedestal, his humanity keeps pulling him down to rejoin us ordinary mortals. He is so aware of life around him that it keeps breaking into his own inner life. The greatest composers have the capacity to become so totally involved in the process of writing that they can cut themselves off from everything except the music. They withdraw. Paradoxically they then produce something that seems to have universal implications. Mahler couldn't divorce himself from surrounding realities to this degree. Even his obsessional revisions show this, for he was so concerned with the practicalities of performance that he was always trying to find better solutions to their problems.

If we turn now to the scherzo-waltz, there is a notable difference between the approach taken by Tchaikovsky and Mahler. Both realised the need to replace the Minuet of hallowed tradition with something more apposite to the times; but the Minuet was an aristocratic dance whereas the waltz was more bourgeois. Tchaikovsky solved the problem by writing a waltz that belongs more to the ballet than the ball-room; in a word it has 'class'. Mahler doesn't even allow himself that much of an artistic justification; his waltz openly belongs to the Viennese café, and how does one reconcile café-music with a huge symphonic score? Another point worth making is that Tchaikovsky's waltz-movement is a complete entity, while Mahler's is only a fragment of a huge movement lasting just on eighteen minutes. In trying to find some phrase which would explain this movement or indeed the whole symphony satisfactorily, it's impossible to disregard the populist aspects of the music. Much of it is quite openly descriptive and it's useless to pretend otherwise. But descriptive of what? This is where my opening remarks about the association of films and music begin to become relevant to the argument. Mahler's symphonies are so long that it's hard not to hear them as a series of individual events, a loud bit, a sad bit, a fierce bit, a languorous bit and so on. This waltz-scherzo, all 819 bars of it, divides only too readily into episodes. If we start putting imaginary pictures into it, making it as it were into a film-score, it becomes irritating simply because the subject-matter changes too rapidly. Mahler's own view was obviously more comprehensive than that, like seeing a city from a helicopter rather than through the window of a taxi. It may seem trite to say the symphony is about Life with a capital L, but if we accept (as is inevitable) that parts of it really are café-music, then it may be helpful to suggest that Mahler is concerned not with the scene but with the cast. If we look at a Breughel painting of some village feast it's easy enough to take in the whole concept of the picture at a glance. But once we start to look closely, every face shows a different character; the more we look, the more we realise how positively Breughel identified everyone on a crowded canvas from children to grandparents. Pursuing the analogy into music, I believe that the explanation for the seemingly inconsistent style of this huge movement is that Mahler, whether consciously or not, is concerned not with the sounds of café-music or balletic waltzes or even country *Ländler*, but with the infinitely varying emotional states of the people who are dancing, eating, conversing or courting *in* the cafés, ball-rooms or village-inns. The creative artist is a form of sensory receiver; his all-embracing eye takes in the whole scene and then re-creates through his medium, be it painting, music or literature, a reaction that may either be specific or generalised. If it's specific, it's easy for us to identify; if it's generalised it's harder for us to share the vision.

There can be no doubt that Mahler was a visionary. For him, music unquestionably had a message in so far as it was a means of communication, a communication of feelings so intense that to put them into words would be an embarrassment. But a visionary isn't the same thing as a dreamer. Hugely experienced in the practical realities of working with orchestras and in the opera-house, he was immensely critical of his own work, constantly revising and altering, an attitude he shared with two of his great Romantic predecessors, Liszt and Berlioz. Berlioz certainly would have understood Mahler's approach towards the symphony as a musical form, his own *Fantastic Symphony* being the nearest approximation to Mahler's concept that one can find from an earlier period. But Berlioz gave us a detailed programme, planting images in our mind beforehand, whereas Mahler begins his Fifth Symphony with a funeral march but will not tell us whose funeral it is. Mahler's aspirations are so often heroic in the extreme, but he doesn't spend all his time on the mountain-tops; he'll sit beside us in a café, watch a street-band, drink a pint of lager in a village inn; but while he shares these simple pursuits he talks to us of fire and tempest, of dragons and demons, of heroic legends and impossible dreams. The language is so vivid, the voice so compelling that we are compelled to listen. Only afterwards do the doubters ask 'Was it really true?'.

FIRST MOVEMENT: *Funeral March*

Although the orchestra required is slightly smaller than was needed in the Third Symphony—six horns instead of eight and only three oboes, clarinets and bassoons—it is still fairly extravagant in its demands. As in the Third Symphony, Mahler begins with an arresting brass motif, but here we find a single trumpet instead of eight horns in unison. Its summons is resolved with a tremendous chord for full orchestra which dies away, leading us to expect a quiet contrast. But no; the solo trumpet continues with a dramatic theme accompanied by short spurting phrases that have a striking impact. Again the music comes to a halt; again the chord dies; again we are surprised by the sequel—pounding triplets that seem determined to outdo the start of Beethoven's Fifth Symphony in their severity. Convulsive trills in the strings sink shuddering through a chromatic descent as unison horns blare out a curiously angular phrase which takes a sudden plunge into their deepest register. Trombones, quieter now, announce a solemn rhythm which is gravely echoed by the bass drum, with soft tam-tam (gong) and timpani lending additional weight but not volume. (In Mahler's original version he used the percussion too heavily; Alma complained that she could hear nothing else and years later Mahler wrote, 'I fail to understand how I could have blundered like a novice'.)

The immensely impressive introduction over, violins and cellos embark on the main theme, a song-like lament sparsely accompanied by isolated pizzicato notes from the double-basses. The sobbing cadences die away in the cellos; trombones again make their solemn comment. The initial trumpet-call now reappears, no longer unaccompanied. It causes a violently agitated reaction in the strings with scales that swoop and plunge like giant banners whipped by the wind. Despite these additions this section may be regarded as equal to a classical repeat, for we soon recognise all the features that appeared in the opening forty-five bars. New developments occur when the wood-wind take over the melodic line with an expressive new counterpoint added by the cellos. The measured rhythm in the trombones gives a feeling of unity, but though Mahler dispenses with voices in this symphony, the music continues to be so essentially lyrical that one feels that it is song-based. It therefore comes as no surprise to find that one phrase is taken note for note from the first of the *Kindertotenlieder*. Quiet trombones and percussion bring the funeral procession to an end. Distantly we hear a trumpet seeming to echo the opening summons.

It receives a startling response as, without warning, Mahler launches into a wildly impassioned section in which the violins give vent to hysterical grief. Cellos and basses continue the idea of a march with a stolid 'Left-right' tonic-dominant bass but, reverting to my film analogy, the violins show us a close-up of a woman's face contorted in anguish. Meanwhile a solo trumpet has a most unmilitary phrase, a cry of pain and protest. The whole ensuing section is something only Mahler could have written, so intense is the emotion, so uninhibited the expression of grief. No stiff upper lip here, and it is understandable that such passages initially met considerable resistance in Anglo-Saxon quarters.

The opening trumpet-call restores some measure of self-control and we soon find a recapitulation of sorts though with many variations. For instance, the main theme no longer appears on unison violins and cellos but on flutes, oboes and clarinets; instead of a long *cantabile* line, however, we find broken phrases of four notes at a time. At one point the opening trumpet-call is given to solo timpani, a cue for the violins to begin a new theme we have not heard before. Mahler extends this at some length with an eloquent counter-melody from the first horn. A huge chord screws the tension almost to breaking-point but passion is nearly spent and the great wash of orchestral sound slowly subsides as the trumpet sounds its initial motif for the last time. The final disintegration brings no hint of consolation; no stranger movement ever began a symphony, nor left us so ill-prepared for what follows.

SECOND MOVEMENT: *'Stormy, agitated, with the greatest vehemence'*

With the utmost ferocity, cellos and basses, reinforced by bassoons, stab out an abrupt phrase that circles round three notes. It is followed by an explosive chord. After several repetitions of this, the woodwind let out a tortured scream. Angry scale-passages scurry through the strings interspersed with yelps from the horns. A rocking figure, whose dotted rhythm momentarily suggests Elgar, seems to establish a foundation for something less chaotic but it doesn't last and the music continues in an intensely disturbed mood, a notable feature being a two-note motif which lurches unsteadily from side to side. Soon all six horns give us a forcible reminder of the initial three-note pattern. A sudden slither downwards through the entire woodwind section leaves us breathless with only a barely audible drum-roll to keep our pulses racing. Quite unexpectedly the tempo reverts to that of the Funeral March as, after a few preliminary flutterings in the wind, the cellos begin a variation on one of the principal themes from the first movement. The clarinets' counter-melody is ingeniously derived from a violin tune that appears in the turbulent central part of the Funeral March, a typical example of the cross-fertilization from movement to movement that so preoccupied Mahler. The long melo-dies continue in an almost unbroken line but against them, time after time, we hear two fragments, one suspiciously reminiscent of the predominating rhythm in Beethoven's Fifth Symphony (♪ ♫ ♩), the other a slower version of what I called the woodwind 'scream', now a poignant cry extending over a minor ninth.[14]

An intense crescendo sustained through four bars leads us back to the wild mood that began the movement, although this time the hysteria is somewhat abated. The treatment of the material is comparatively short, the downward 'slither' more tortuous. Again we are left with a quiet drum-roll, destined to continue for some time. Against its chilling murmur the cellos have an eloquent cadenza, full of yearning. It brings us back to the tempo of the Funeral March and a reprise of the previous slower section. Horns now take the place of cellos in leading off with the tune but Mahler does not allow himself the indulgence of a straightforward repetition. Instead he embarks on a completely new development, easily identified by the parallel thirds moving in close chromatic intervals in the woodwind. The instruction 'From here on no more dragging' warns conductors not to wallow in emotion. The time for that comes later when, in a phrase of infinite tenderness in B major, the music does return to the tempo of the Funeral March.

A more active figure in the bass involving a little triplet figure introduces a note of asperity, dispelling sentiment. Within moments the music builds to an intense climax, capped by a thunderous beating of timpani and a majestic phrase for horns and trumpets in unison. It is a signal for a return to the agitation with which the movement began though it can scarcely be termed a conventional recapitulation. At least its various components are familiar by now until a huge and dramatic coda begins. (An easily recognisable landmark is a tremendous drum-roll followed by three harp *glissandi* and an upward rush in the violins.) The brass-writing at this point is magnificent, while swirling scales and arpeggios in the strings add to the excitement. We are all set to finish in a blaze of glory but that would be too obvious for Mahler and the movement fades to nothing, those yearning ninths raising a last despair-ing gesture before the single quiet drumstroke that ends the movement.

Mahler asks for a long pause before the next movement; during it we should try to recall the majestic brass passages, almost a chorale, for they are due to reappear in the Fifth Movement, a link that should not pass unnoticed.

---

[14] This three-note motif is taken from the First Movement.

THIRD MOVEMENT: *Scherzo*

Interestingly Mahler labels this Part II as well as Movement 3, indicating that he looks on the first two movements as essentially one, the second being an elaborate fantasia on themes from the first. As I have already suggested, the movement has certain stylistic incongruities which are hard to come to terms with. Mahler himself was acutely aware of the problems he was creating. In a letter he wrote, 'The Scherzo is the very devil. Conductors for the next fifty years will take it too fast and make nonsense of it—and the public? Heavens, what are they to make of this chaos in which new worlds are forever being created, only to crumble into ruins the moment after? What are they to say of these dancing stars, of this primeval music?' Fanciful language, rather different from the self-deprecation Brahms would adopt when writing about his latest creation.

Mahler's directions are very clear: 'Robustly, not too fast'. Even as early as the fifth bar comes a reminder, 'Don't hurry'. The initial flourish on four horns leads us to expect heroic deeds but the first horn[15] soon disabuses us, leading the way into a country dance accompanied by clarinets and bassoons giving a passable imitation of an accordion. First violins join in enthusiastically with a waltz that stands halfway between Johann and Richard Strauss—too wide-ranging for the first and not voluptuous enough for the second.

Violas suddenly strike up confidently with a rather awkward pattern and then, realising that they are on their own, seem to lose heart; squealing clarinets interrupt them before the violins offer what seems to be a rather drunken phrase partnered by clumsy bassoons and lower strings. Flutes in thirds add a much-needed touch of grace to the proceedings before the horn intrudes rowdily as before.

A detailed chronicle of events in so vast a movement (819 bars) would be wearisome since the themes are easy to comprehend. The problems are aesthetic rather than intellectual. For instance an unashamedly 'popular' café waltz, scored with the utmost delicacy, is rudely interrupted by a knockabout brass quartet who bring back the opening theme. The viola passage that had seemed curiously out of place previously is taken up *fortissimo* by the violins—'*wild*' says Mahler!—and turned into a pseudo-fugue that one can only imagine to symbolise a crowd of drunken students aping their professors. Gradually its angularities are smoothed out until the woodwind convert it into a fluid accompaniment to a gliding waltz to which one trumpet-player shows no respect. A quarrel breaks out in the strings which is quelled by four tremendous blasts from the horns; abortive attempts by the solo horn to get the dance going again meet with no response. But then the waltz is taken up at a rather more cautious tempo by pizzicato strings; a bassoon has an attack of

---

[15]Described as 'corno obbligato', emphasising the solo nature of the part.

hiccups, an oboe bashfully ('schüchtern') tries to join in.

The waltzes come and go almost as if at random, one passage (after a long trill in the woodwind) taking on a nightmare quality. There is a tiny pause and then the opening flourish reappears. It is the start of one of Mahler's recapitulations in which the events of the exposition tend to be condensed, newly orchestrated, and then treated in new ways. In general the texture is richer, returned to the concert-hall from the café. The solo horn still shows a wish to be the centre of attention but, just as it seems as though everyone will finally fall asleep, a bass drum sets up a dance rhythm that has the dancers back on their toes. The music quickens; horns whoop, trumpets reel drunkenly, trombones sing in raucous harmony. With two excited leaps the movement ends.

FOURTH MOVEMENT: *Adagietto*

Since the film *Death in Venice* this has undoubtedly become the most widely known and probably best-loved of all Mahler's works. A mere 103 bars, it is far the shortest of his symphonic movements and might fairly be described as an orchestral song. Its opening phrase is derived from the second of the *Kindertotenlieder*, 'Nun seh' ich wohl', while the final climax quotes another setting of a Rückert poem, 'Ich bin der Welt abhanden gekommen'. The orchestration of the movement for strings and harp is also very similar to that of 'Nun seh' ich wohl'. Mahler may have dispensed with the human voice in this symphony but such quotations are a clear indication that it was never far from his mind. Little need be said about the structure of the movement, the more agitated central section simply being comparable to a contrasting verse in a *Lied*. A point worth making is that Mahler covers the score with detailed instructions to the players as though deeply concerned that the music should be played with all the shades of expression he requires; it is an obsession he shares with Elgar, whose scores are also notable for his reluctance to trust the performer's intuition. If I quote the dynamics alone in six consecutive bars—forget about the notes!—they show:

Observe that there are eleven 'hairpins' ($<$ $>$) and two 'cresc.' but that the loudest dynamic is *p*. Here speaks Mahler the conductor as much as the composer and one feels that he dreads anyone else taking charge.

The movement, though it is often performed on its own, should properly be regarded as an introduction to the extensive Finale which follows.

FIFTH MOVEMENT: *Rondo-Finale*

The first horn sounds a long A, almost as if usurping the oboe's privilege of 'tuning' the orchestra; quietly, the first violins echo it an octave lower. These two false starts are enough to break the mood of the Adagietto and the horn makes a more positive move with three commanding notes. Somewhat irreverently the bassoon proposes a theme of a rather trivial kind. It is taken from another of Mahler's songs, 'Lob des hohen Verstandes' (In praise of learning), an ironic joke on the composer's part since the song refers to a contest between the cuckoo and the nightingale with a donkey acting as judge. A clarinet gives a hesitant reply; the bassoon makes another cheerful proposition which, after a rousing interpolation from the horn, the clarinet accepts with a show of reluctance. 'Motion carried!' says the oboe, and with that this brief preliminary conference is ended. The time has not been wasted, for in the space of twenty bars Mahler has shown us the main materials of the movement.

Taking their cue from the oboe's final phrase, the horns now set this complex finale on its way with a theme whose subsequent contrapuntal treatment shows us that the ghost of Haydn was peeping over Mahler's shoulder. As if acknowledging the eighteenth-century influence, the cellos begin a lively fugue whose nimble subject follows a surprisingly academic course. While it continues to bustle along, our attention should be directed to two counterpoints, one a descending scale:

Ex. 1

the other a direct reference to the introductory dialogue between horn and bassoon:

Ex. 2

A change of mood comes as the violins toy with the four descending notes with which the horns had launched the movement proper, while, in turn, the woodwind produce a beautifully smoothed-out version of Ex. 1.

After a few bars in which the music temporarily disintegrates, a solo trumpet restores order with the 'Motion carried' oboe-theme. The violins take the hint and re-start the 'Haydn' theme, complete with rustic drone in the bass. Once again we find Mahler giving us his own individual treatment of the classic repeat of the exposition—the same but different, the fugue now appearing slightly earlier in the scheme and in the new key of B flat. This time it is not worked out nearly so extensively and soon gives way to an expressive theme on the violins. With something of a shock we realise that this is the tune from the *Adagietto*, even if somewhat disguised.

Its initial four rising notes are soon subjected to a rather undignified treatment, being made to tiptoe around in the company of three melancholy blind mice. (I am not suggesting that Mahler was quoting the English nursery rhyme, but it is an easy way of identifying an important new element.) So long as we carry that preliminary little conference between horn, bassoon, clarinet and oboe in our minds, the ensuing pages should present no difficulty since one or other of their themes is always in the foreground, usually accompanied by bustling quaver figuration derived from the fugue. For all its length, this is one of the most tautly constructed movements Mahler ever wrote, truly symphonic in the way the material is developed. It is the ingenuity of the counterpoint that is one of its most notable features and even the more relaxed passages usually involve the combination of several different thematic ideas.

After the first deployment of the full orchestra (uncharacteristically delayed until bar 483) a massive descending scale in the brass leads to a change of tempo and a new departure. The music becomes less contrapuntal, more openly rapturous; the four descending notes which began the movement become passionate and lyrical. The trumpets then reveal that these same notes can be extended into Ex. 1, now made marvellously expansive. The rapture dies as cellos and basses once more attempt to get the fugue under way, but this time it excites little interest in the rest of the orchestra who prefer to treat it as a jolly counterpoint to Ex. 2. This theme marches through the brass with increasing dominance until we reach the second major climax of the movement. It is followed by a quieter section, a more serene discussion of the 'Haydn' theme, in which even the contrabassoon is allowed more say than usual.

For more than forty bars the scoring is almost entirely for wind, horns and the lower strings. The re-entry of the violins is extremely quiet but exhibits signs of impatience. Against a chirpy counterpoint from the woodwind the parody of the *Adagietto* reappears and is taken up in turn by violas and cellos and then by the woodwind. Amid increasing excitement the trumpets sound an alarm and, with a thunderous roar from the timpani, Ex. 1 appears in majestic splendour in the full brass with the fugue subject dancing attendance upon it in unison strings.

Bass drum and cymbal clash alert us to the crowning moment, the reappearance of the brass 'chorale' from the second movement. The subsequent gallop for home must inevitably seem a sop to convention though it serves its purpose well enough, guaranteeing a standing ovation for orchestra and conductor alike. Anti-Mahlerites may try to decry the last section as a gigantic ego-trip, but no musically educated person can dismiss this finale, for Mahler was never to excel it as a display of sheer craftsmanship. The handling of a very limited number of completely 'tonal' themes is wonderfully inventive, while the climaxes, beautifully placed, are never over-extended. Bruno Walter, one of its most noted exponents, described it as 'a masterpiece that shows the composer at the zenith of his life, his powers and his craft'.

Das Lied von der Erde
(The Song of the Earth)
(1907–9)

Although Mahler did not number this work as one of his symphonies, it is symphonic in scale, a song-symphony for tenor, contralto and full orchestra lasting an hour. The text comes from a book of German translations of Chinese poems; but to call them translations is misleading since Hans Bethge knew not a word of Chinese, creating a slim volume of some eighty poems from the study of already existing versions in German, French and English. The book, entitled *The Chinese Flute* came into Mahler's possession in 1907 and it seems that the poems struck a sympathetic chord in his mind almost immediately since he began the work in the summer of that year. His original choice of title was somewhat morbid, 'The Song of Earthly Woes' (*Das Lied vom Jammer der Erde*) since the first song is called 'The Drinking Song of Earthly Woes' (*Das Trinklied vom Jammer der Erde*.) Initially he selected seven poems but in the end he merged the last two into one; nor did he shrink from modifying the text where it suited his purpose, especially at the end of the cycle where he extended the original poem and even changed its metre. The songs are given alternately to the two soloists, 1, 3 and 5 to the tenor, 2, 4 and 6 to the contralto. With the obvious intention of giving some thematic unity to what might easily have become six quite separate movements, Mahler makes ingenious use of a very simple 'motto' theme (Ex. 1).

This should be regarded as a pattern rather than the specific notes A–G–E though it is in that guise that the violins state it with considerable emphasis in bars 5–7. Of all the movements the first is far the most heavily scored, making extreme demands on the singer, who is in grave danger of being

Ex. 1

drowned in the orchestral tumult. The poem, whose Chinese original was by Li-Tai-Po, celebrates drunkeness as the cure for all human woes:

> Already wine sparkles in the glass
> But don't drink until I have sung a song to you
> A song to free the soul from grief.
> When sorrow comes the soul's garden is laid to waste;
> Joy and song fade and die.
> Dark is life and dark is death;
> Master of this house, your cellar holds much golden wine;
> Here is my lute—lutes play, glasses empty;
> At the right time a full beaker of wine is worth more than all the riches of the
> world;
>
> Dark is life and dark is death;
> The sky will stay blue, and the earth will long exist and bloom in Spring,
> But you, O man, how long will you live?
> You have less than a hundred years to enjoy the little pleasures of this world.
> See there! in the moonlight a wild figure crouching over the tomb.
> It is an ape; listen to its shrill cries cutting through the scented air.
> Now take the wine, now is the right moment.
> Empty your golden beaker on the ground.
> Dark is life and dark is death.

Perhaps the most significant line is the one that says 'Dark is life, and dark is death'. It's a melancholy philosophy, and the exuberance of the opening music would seem to be at odds with it. But it's the key to the whole work for all that, so much so that Mahler repeats it three times in this first movement; in fact, they are the last words we hear in the opening section. Each time the phrase recurs the music quietens, the voice part loses its forward impetus. Moreover, the repetitions are ingeniously planned so that each one is a semitone higher than its predecessor, shifting from G minor to A flat minor and then to A minor, an eloquent symbol of a growing despair that the copious draughts of wine fail to dispel. But if the singer is destined to end quietly, not so the orchestra, for, in a last convulsion, the music flares up once more to end as impetuously as it had begun.

From these explosive sounds Mahler takes us into a different world for the second song, 'The lonely one in Autumn' (*Der Einsame im Herbst*). Taking his cue from the first line, 'The autumn mists drift blue over the lake', he introduces a gently undulating phrase in the violins over which a solo oboe projects an expressive melody that begins with the 'motto' pattern twice repeated—now D–C–A. Although it appears a number of times, usually on flute or oboe, our attention is more likely to be caught by the vocal line, consisting largely as it does of descending or ascending scale passages. The keynote here is restraint, save for a brief moment when a single loud chord provokes a cry of despair:

> Sun of love, will you never shine again
> To dry my bitter tears?

The oboe repeats its mournful little theme, the violin phrase coils and uncoils like the drifting mist. There is no consolation.

The third movement is more an intermezzo than a scherzo—an enchanting song, affectionately depicting some of the pleasures of a civilised, still youthful existence.

> In the centre of the little pool stands a pavilion of white and green porcelain;
> A jade bridge arches towards it like a tiger's back
> In the little house friends in fine garments drink, talk, and compose verses.
> Their silken sleeves slip back, their silken hats slide happily askew.
> On the still surface of the little pond charming mirror-pictures show,
> Everything in the pavilion of green and white porcelain stands on its head,
> The bridge seems like a half moon, with the arch reflected,
> While friends in fine garments drink and talk.

Here we find Mahler the miniaturist, scoring the music with great delicacy, the violins graceful, the woodwind sometimes chattering excitedly but always with decorum. The 'motto' theme is subtly concealed in the voice part (e.g. '*Stiller, stiller*') but we need not concern ourselves with worries over the form; the appeal of the music is instant.

The contralto matches this in the fourth song, which describes a group of young girls picking flowers by a river on one of those marvellous sunlit days, when the grass seems the deepest green you ever saw, and the little streams find their busy ways down the hillsides to the lush pastures below. Again the scoring is beautifully delicate with the chatter of girlish voices, the song of birds and the ripple of water inextricably mingled together in the accompaniment.

But suddenly this idyllic picture is shattered by an immense blast of sound from the full orchestra and Mahler commits what seems one of his stranger indiscretions. It's as though he had thought to himself, 'Here I am with this huge orchestra, and I'm scoring everything for little groups of woodwind; I must use everybody or they'll wonder why they're here.' And in the middle of this slight song about young and innocent people we find an orchestral outburst that would not be out of place in his most dramatic symphonies. Is there perhaps something in the poem to justify this violent change? Only a reference to some young men passing by on horseback; one horse is especially frisky and tramples down the flowers with its hooves, tossing its mane. Mahler's imagination seems to have run riot at this point, providing music more suitable for a regiment of cavalry. It is interesting to note that he originally considered a baritone as an alternative to the contralto, an option that might have affected his judgement here. Yet the ending of the song is exquisite with an orchestral coda of the utmost charm.

The fifth song returns to the topic of drink, 'The Drunken Man in Spring'. (*Der Trunkene im Frühling.*) It begins cheerily with skirling wood-wind and bragging horns. Notice the cocky version of the 'motto' pattern that appears shrilly in the woodwind just after the tenor's first phrase. Violins have a swaying phrase which suggests the dubious hero reeling on his way. The tempo slows as he addresses a bird in a tree; 'Has Spring arrived?' A piccolo obligingly replies, and on the words 'Spring is here' (*Der Lenz ist da*) a positive choir of birds bursts into song. Here we find none of the dark undercurrent of sorrow of the first song and the music ends in joyous exuberance.

The final song, 'Farewell', is the longest, and surely the most perfect. It is a meditation on the finality of parting, and man's ultimate loneliness.

> The sun sinks, evening comes, the moon sails like a silver ship through the
> > blue lake of the sky.
> The world sleeps.
> I stand in the shadows waiting for my friend, to bid him a last farewell.
> I long to be beside you, my friend, to share the beauty of this
> > evening with you.
> Where are you? You leave me here alone too long.
> O Beauty! O love-drunk, life-drunk world!

After a long orchestral section, in effect a funeral march, the friend arrives at last and is asked where he is going, and why—why must it be?

> He spoke, his voice choked with tears:
> In this world Fortune has not been kind to me.
> I shall wander in the mountains, seeking peace for my lonely soul.
> In Spring the earth will come to life and everything will be green again;
> And the far distance will shine clear blue—always, always.

There can be few passages more forlorn than the first phrases of the alto here, spaced as the voice is between a long-held low C from the cellos and a single flute high above, echoing the initial lament of the oboe.

Like so many composers, Mahler was particularly in tune with nature, and much of this final scene (you can't really call it a song) consists of musical imagery of natural sounds—the murmur of water, birdsong and the like. Often a solo instrument, oboe, flute or cello, is projected against the most insubstantial background so that the music has the delicate understatement of a Chinese painting. But the real glory of the work lies in its final pages which, perhaps ironically, are the most transparently simple that Mahler ever wrote and yet the most profoundly moving. Every phrase seems to express a heartfelt longing though there is hardly a trace of the richly chromatic harmony we found in the *Adagietto* of the Fifth Symphony. Those who are interested in such matters will notice that flutes and oboes quietly muse over an inverted version of the 'motto' pattern now E–G–A. But as the movement dies away into silence we are haunted by the alto's heartbreaking repetition of the word *Ewig* (Eternally), a sigh dragged from the innermost depths of the soul.

Although Mahler was still to write the Ninth Symphony and the unfinished Tenth, he knew very well he was living on borrowed time. He did not live long enough to hear a performance of *Das Lied von der Erde* but he could not have left a more poignantly beautiful valediction than this closing movement. Shorn of all excess, it speaks with such direct simplicity that its message goes straight to our hearts, leaving an impression that, once heard, can never be forgotten.

MENDELSSOHN

1809–47

We live at a time when the prodigious young make the headlines, mostly in sport. Teenage girls set world records in swimming, play tennis at top level, or seduce millions with their skills on the horizontal beam. A fourteen-year-old boy can take on and defeat Grand Masters at chess, though in fact that isn't a new phenomenon. In a more artistic field the National Youth Orchestra or the European Community Youth Orchestra can attain a standard that challenges some of the greatest orchestras in the world. All the same, I am prepared to maintain that nothing any teenager has ever done in sport, art, literature or music can rival the sixteen-year old Mendelssohn's achievement in composing his Octet for Strings; it must remain an unsurpassable landmark since it represents perfection, and one cannot outshine that.

It's as well to remember that Mendelssohn at sixteen was far from being an owl-like swot. He was an excellent swimmer, a good horseman, a beautiful dancer; he delighted in a work-out on the parallel bars and even persuaded his father to build him a small gymnasium; he would have been a more than proficient skater had he not disliked the cold. With all this he was fluent in several languages and a gifted artist, to say nothing of being stunningly handsome. As for his musical gifts, they were truly prodigious; compositions poured from his pen, symphonies for strings, operas, chamber music, songs, concertos, sacred music, there was hardly a form he hadn't explored by the time he was fifteen. Naturally many of these early compositions were derivative, much influenced by the models he most admired; such apprentice works were an essential part of his development. In writing them he acquired the facility that was to become his trademark, a dangerous facility as it turned out though he wasn't to know that at the time. Yet it is certain that the exquisite craftsmanship shown in the Octet could have been achieved in no other way, for his touch is so sure that it can truly be described as masterly, and nobody can be a master without first serving an apprenticeship of sorts. Surprisingly the Octet doesn't seem to have caused the major sensation one might have expected, perhaps because it was first performed at a family occasion where the listeners had come to expect something prodigious with each new work. Even so they must have appreciated that the combination of craftsmanship and imagination was here fused in such a way as to produce something astonishingly individual.

In the year after this remarkable achievement he composed the Overture to *A Midsummer Night's Dream*, another work to which the word 'perfection' has frequently been applied. Yet it is interesting to note that the incidental music that he wrote for the same play seventeen years later shows no apparent change in style, no development of a stronger and more individual personality. It is a phenomenon worth considering in more detail.

There's a tendency nowadays to think that the international jet-set musicians, commuting from Europe to America and back again, recording, televising, conducting one day in Vienna and the next in London, are something new. They aren't. The only things that are different are the means of travel and the radio, television and recording aspects—which, after all, are only a different way of giving concerts. Musicians in the nineteenth century were often afflicted with the same Flying Dutchman syndrome that we see in the perpetual travellers of today, and the pressures seem to have been every bit as great. Of them all, Mendelssohn appears to have been one of the most hectic. He was in constant demand as conductor, composer, pianist and organist. For instance in August 1837, some five months after he had been married, he found himself in London for his fifth visit to England. He was on his way to Birmingham where he was to conduct *St. Paul*, his latest oratorio. On 10th September he played the organ, appropriately enough, in St. Paul's Cathedral. The great crowd of listeners refused to leave, marvelling at his brilliance, especially in pedal passages. (Mendelssohn used to say he practised these so hard that he found himself 'walking' pedal passages down the street, which conjures up a delightful vision). In the end, the vergers went up to the organ-loft and bribed the organ-blower to leave his post, as being the only way they could get the crowds to disperse. On his arrival in Birmingham, Mendelssohn was busy rehearsing choir and orchestra for the oratorio; but at the opening concert of the Festival he not only gave a brilliant extemporisation on the organ, but also conducted the *Midsummer Night's Dream* Overture. Yet next day, he rehearsed and conducted *St. Paul*, and the following evening gave the world première of his Piano Concerto in D minor, playing the solo part himself. That was on a Thursday. On Friday morning, he played the Bach *St. Anne* Prelude and Fuge at an organ concert, before catching the 11.30 mail-coach to London. He reached London by midnight, and on Saturday morning was guest of honour at a reception where he was given a silver snuff-box, suitably inscribed. Soon after midday, he caught the stage-coach to Dover, thereafter travelling non-stop to Frankfurt where he arrived three days later. There he was joined by his wife, and together they journeyed on to Leipzig. Arriving there at two in the afternoon of 1st

October, he conducted a concert at six in the evening. Yet, at times he must have wondered whether it was all worth while. Later that month, in a letter to his brother he said:

> The more I find in my vocation of what is termed encouragement and recognition, the more restless and unsettled they become in my hands, and I cannot deny that I often long for some rest. Very little remains of performances and festivals and all that personal stuff. People shout and applaud, but it passes so quickly, without leaving a trace; and yet it absorbs as much of one's life and strength as the better aims, or even more. Once one has gone in, it is impossible to get out half way.[1]

The cry of the artist, caught on the treadmill of his own success. The constant strain took its toll, and in January 1838 he complained of complete deafness in one ear, pains in his head and neck, and general ill-health. But the concerts went on, whether as conductor or performer, and it's surprising that he found time to compose a note.

This aspect of Mendelssohn's life is worth stressing not only for its contemporary parallels but also because it may well have had some bearing on why he never quite achieved the greatness as a composer that the astounding works of his boyhood promised. Having a sheer technical facility in composition that had probably only ever been matched by Bach and Mozart, he must have found it only too easy to fall back on technical resources when time pressed so heavily upon him. Despite all the travelling and performing, he continued to compose; one would expect the music itself to show some evidence of the perpetual strain, but curiously enough it doesn't; it presents a beautifully polished surface to the world in which not a note is ever out of place. Everything works with a smooth precision that could not have been excelled by a master of harmony and counterpoint living a life of ease in a quiet university. Compare his music to that of Berlioz or Tchaikovsky and we find an almost total absence of real passion; there's none of the romantic agony, the overt drama. Yet craftsmanship of such exceptional quality is not to be discounted and although much of his prodigious output has now fallen out of favour, there remain a few works of such perfection that they will never lose their place. His tragically early death at the age of thirty-eight was almost certainly precipitated by the continual demands that his enormous popularity inevitably brought. The question remains: might he have been a greater composer if his upbringing had been less privileged, his gifts as a performer less exceptional?

To a considerable extent, Mendelssohn reflects the society in which he lived, particularly its manners and affectations. Although it represented only a small proportion of the total population, it was a society that preserved a facade of remarkable elegance, seemingly unaware of the appalling

---

[1] G. Selden–Goth (ed), *Mendelssohn Letters*, Paul Elek, 1946.

inequalities on which it still rested, despite the French Revolution and its brave talk of Liberty, Equality and Fraternity. The relationship between music and politics is sometimes suspect, but I think it not irrelevant to Mendelssohn. The great composers of an earlier period, Haydn, Mozart and Beethoven in particular had all known what it was like to suffer poverty and hardship. Professionally, they mingled with their aristocratic patrons, but they had come from humble backgrounds and must often have been aware of the social barriers of class. Certainly Mozart's father, Leopold, was a shameless social climber, knowing only too well where to seek the butter to spread on the rather meagre loaf that was all even his talented son could earn. By comparison, Mendelssohn was cushioned from reality, brought up in wealth and comfort, never having to struggle and, most important, immediately acceptable for his social background. His dazzling gifts gave him the entrée to every salon, but the point is that he would have been welcome even if he couldn't have played a note. I doubt if the same could have been said for any of his great predecessors. It seems, then, that with such a sheltered upbringing, it was almost inevitable that the superficial refinement of social life should cause Mendelssohn to reject the provocative and disturbing elements of music which Beethoven had unleashed, and which had been so warmly welcomed by such a born rebel as Berlioz. Berlioz was a provincial too, a bone-poor student fighting for hard-earned recognition. He was six years older than Mendelssohn, but far behind him in finding acceptance by the public. Mendelssohn himself was not able to understand Berlioz at all, saying that he couldn't believe that impartial people would take pleasure in discords or be in any way interested in them. 'If that sort of stuff is noticed and admired,' he said, 'it is really too provoking.' Even to Chopin he adopted a faintly patronising attitude, although he admired him enormously as a pianist. He made a very revealing remark or two in a letter, disclosing the slight snobbery which was an automatic reaction to a Polish émigré.

> Although we live in different worlds, I can get on famously with such a man, while I cannot get on at all with the demi-semi-people. Sunday evening was remarkable. Chopin made me play over my oratorio, and when between the first and second part he butted in with his new Études and a new concerto (to the amazement of the Leipzig people) it was just as though a Cherokee and a Kaffir had met to converse.

It seems then that Mendelssohn realised that he was not cut out to be a trail-blazer, though he claimed confidently to be a radical. Yet it is interesting that while Liszt and Schumann were always acting for the avant-garde, supporting new works that held a challenge for the listener, Mendelssohn's great enthusiasm was for Bach. His heroic efforts in mounting a performance of the *St. Matthew Passion* when he was a young man of twenty are well known. It was his devotion to the classics that made him value craftsmanship so highly, and of the craftsmanship there is never any doubt.

Overture: 'The Hebrides' (Fingal's Cave) Op. 26

It was in 1829, when he was twenty years old, that Mendelssohn first visited England. After some successful concerts and much socialising in London he and his companion, Karl Klingemann, set out to tour Scotland. Conditions there were still extremely primitive except in such great houses as Blair Athol. After a narrow escape from drowning in Loch Lomond, when a sudden storm nearly caused their rowing-boat to capsize, they continued to journey through the Highlands.

> To describe the wretchedness and comfortless, inhospitable solitude of the country, time and space do not allow; we wandered ten days without meeting a single traveller; what are marked on the map as towns, or at least villages, are just a few sheds huddled together, with one and the same hole for door, window and chimney, for the entrance and the exit of men, animals, light and smoke. . . . The rooms are pitch-dark in broad daylight, children and fowls lie in the same straw, many huts are without roofs altogether . . .[2]

Mendelssohn finished this gloomy catalogue with an assurance that despite everything they had thoroughly enjoyed their tour and would not forget it as long as they lived.

A boat-trip to the Hebrides and the island of Staffa left Mendelssohn miserably sea-sick; even so it was to prove a source of amazingly spontaneous inspiration. A letter dated 7th August, 1829 says: '. . . in order to make you understand how extraordinarily the Hebrides affected me, the following came into my mind there:' and sketched out on hand-drawn staves is a remarkably detailed first version of what we now know as the 'Hebrides' overture even with indications of the orchestration. In the following month, writing from London, he tells his sister that he has nearly finished a string quartet (Op. 12), and that he then intends to begin his 'Reformation' Symphony, his 'Scottish' Symphony and 'the Hebrides affair as well'. Progress on these ambitious plans was halted when he was involved in a nasty accident. The cabriolet in which he was travelling overturned, throwing him out onto the road; the main part of the carriage fell on his leg and was then dragged forward by the frightened horse. His injuries caused him to be bedridden for two months and prevented him from being present at his sister's wedding for which he had written a special organ piece. In the following year extensive travels through Germany, Austria and Italy

[2] Ibid.

provided him with considerable diversions and it wasn't until 30th December 1830, that he was able to write, 'The Hebrides is completed at last'.

The overture begins with a quiet sustained F sharp on the violins, beneath which cellos and violas play a vitally important figure (A) suggesting the gentle rocking motion of the boat as we set out on our journey to Staffa. For two bars the key is B minor; clarinets then superimpose an A onto the violins' F sharp and the tonality shifts to D major; two bars later oboes add a C sharp which produces yet another change of key, this time to F sharp minor. The next two bars provide a modulation to E minor; thus in the first eight bars the music touches on four different keys, a procedure that subtly conveys the ever-shifting surface of the water without recourse to drama. As the music progresses, we sense the sudden impact of a larger wave lifting the boat like a giant hand, but such moments are brief and are invariably followed by a shimmering figure on the violins that suggests the glitter of sunlight on the white-capped waves.

Softly repeated notes on a pair of trumpets usher in the second subject, a gracefully rising theme on the cellos whose occasional hesitations may be intended to convey the rise and fall of the prow of the fishing-boat that took Mendelssohn on this so productive journey. Violins duly take over the theme only to find themselves suddenly becalmed on a high D, against which the flutes reintroduce the initial fragment (A). Its reappearance generates considerable excitement and within seconds we find the first orchestral tutti which combines Neptune's fanfares in the brass with turbulent waters in the lower strings and a modified version of (A) in flutes and violins. It makes a splendid climax, tautly enough constructed to be truly symphonic while at the same time being powerfully descriptive.

Trumpets and horns emerge from the ruck to be lost in the shimmer of strings. Extensions of (A) are passed through violas and cellos but our attention is more forcibly arrested by a whole series of peremptory fanfares. After a number of exchanges between wind and brass the cellos exercise a calming influence with a phrase derived from the second subject. For a moment there is complete stillness before the violins have a gentle descending phrase that proves to be a smoothed-out version of (A), now in G major instead of the variety of minor keys to which we have become accustomed. Violas provide a slightly disturbing undercurrent that suggests that rough waters may lie ahead. A solo flute denies the implication but an ominous rumble from the timpani sets the mast swaying against the darkening sky. Soon we find the opening fragment (A) developed in a characteristically brilliant fashion, its smooth contours made choppy and abrupt. The music at this point is perilously near to a jocund scherzo in *Midsummer Night's Dream* vein, but sustained notes in the oboes create an uncanny tension that brings a note of menace. Strident fanfares on horns and woodwind in turn summon the tempest and for a few moments the seas rage furiously around us.

The storm is short-lived and dissolves in a sustained trill on violins and clarinets; violas and cellos bring back (A) in its original form, a solo flute adding a soothing comment. We can be forgiven for assuming that this is equivalent to a symphonic recapitulation, but Mendelssohn has other plans in mind. A long descending sequence of harmonies in the strings leads into a section of great beauty in which a solo clarinet, later joined by his partner, seems to extemporise a lovely variation on the second subject. The key, B major, has been kept in reserve for this special moment and it creates a wonderful feeling of tranquillity.

An impatient trill from the violins disturbs the mood and soon the music is whipped up into the most violent passage of the whole overture in which the rushing semiquavers in unison strings depict the waves surging angrily around Staffa's rocky cliffs. The ending is sudden and unexpected, a sequence of abrupt chords through which we hear the same quiet sustained F sharp with which the work began, played now on trumpets, a master touch that suggests a wan beam of sunlight piercing the clouds. A clarinet briefly reminds us of (A), a solo flute has a rising phrase like a gull soaring towards the cliff-top; three pizzicato chords tell us the journey is done.

After its first London performance in May, 1832, the critic of *The Athenaeum* said that as descriptive music it was a decided failure, a remark which might be taken as a tribute to the perfect construction of an overture whose few compact themes are treated with a mastery that could not be excelled. Wagner might have produced a more dramatic sea-picture or a more imposing vision of Staffa's rock-formations, but it is doubtful whether any of Mendelssohn's contemporaries would have produced a more perfectly proportioned or economically constructed work.

Symphony No. 4 in A Major (The 'Italian') Op. 90

In 1832 the Philharmonic Society of London commissioned Mendelssohn, then twenty-three,[3] to write a symphony, an overture and a choral work, an acknowledgement of how widely his fame had spread even at such a comparatively early age. A long and happy journey through Italy had already inspired him to begin work on an 'Italian' symphony and the additional incentive of a fee of a hundred guineas for the three works(!) was enough to

[3]According to Donald Tovey, Mendelssohn had actually finished the composition of the symphony when he was only twenty-two.

make him hasten its completion. Uncharacteristically he maintained that the writing of it cost him bitter moments but of this there is no sign in the effortless flow of the music.

The symphony begins with swiftly repeated chords in the woodwind which serve as a bustling accompaniment to the exuberant first subject on the violins:

Ex. 1

This theme dances along for twenty-one bars before the woodwind rob the violins of the first five notes, turning them into a miniature fanfare by sustaining the fifth note for three beats. This fragment proves to be very useful, though the theft causes an excited (though not indignant) reaction in the strings. Contrary motion scale passages of gradually widening compass lead to a triumphant reprise of the first subject, now more heavily scored. There is a brief chattering altercation between woodwind and strings before an interesting variant on the first theme appears in cellos and basses only to be outdone by the violins in their most brilliant register.

Having established the 'dominant' key of E major with several forceful chords in wind and brass, Mendelssohn embarks on a nimble 'bridge passage' whose staccato quavers remind us of his special aptitude for 'fairy' music. Clarinets and bassoons in thirds soon introduce the second subject, a tune that sets out to be a smooth contrast but which is given a slight feeling of breathlessness by the frequent quaver rests which interrupt its flow, while the second violins and violas continue to give a sense of urgency to the music with a galloping accompaniment. The second subject is repeated by flutes and oboes and then ingeniously extended by the violins over a long and increasingly exciting timpani roll. Once the inevitable climax is reached the tone of the music becomes calmer, gradually quietening down until, for a moment or two, violins and cellos are left on their own, enjoying a tender, vaguely operatic cadence. Distantly a solo clarinet sounds a reminder of the opening theme slowed down to half-speed; it is a summons that cannot be disregarded and the violins duly respond with considerable eagerness.

Mendelssohn's classical instincts make him feel the need to repeat the Exposition, but he does introduce a novel linking passage to lead him back to the start. Conductors who omit the repeat deprive the audience of this charming episode in which the violins have a gracefully turned melody over a sustained bass, a well-planned and desirable respite before the return to the energetic opening music.

The development section begins with an unexpected shift to A *minor* which in turn moves to D minor, a somewhat unorthodox move whose delightful eccentricity is compounded by the introduction of a totally new theme:

Ex. 2

Mendelssohn proceeds to treat this as a miniature fugue without making any undue concessions to text-book propriety. It is a perfect demonstration of his great technical facility as a craftsman, creating a joyous situation when the woodwind try to call the strings to order with a forceful reminder of the opening theme. 'Don't worry, we'll get to it in time', say the strings while happily continuing with their contrapuntal studies. Four times they are reprimanded by wind and brass in turn before they agree to return to the proper agenda—Ex. 1, now in the alien key of C major. Having conceded the point with several bewildering shifts of tonality, the strings overcome the opposition and persuade the whole orchestra to join in a bouncy version of Ex. 2, thereby promoting it to the position of prime importance in the central section of the movement. An amusing conflict develops as Ex. 1 tries to reassert its authority, finally achieving victory with some thumping C sharp major chords and a triumphant descent in the initial rhythm.

There follows a wonderfully imaginative section in which the natural impetus of the music is held right back. Cellos and basses quietly reiterate low C sharps; above this anchor-note the remaining strings ruminate over the possibilities of C sharp major, F sharp minor or even D major as potential starting-points for a return to the opening material. A long sustained note on a solo oboe is like a searchlight beam pointing the way. As the excitement begins to build up in the strings, clarinet and horns in turn issue the summons that will ultimately lead to the recapitulation.

The achievement of this classic landmark is clearly defined and Mendelssohn, being the well-mannered composer he is, duly provides us with the second subject in the 'proper' key, albeit on violas and cellos instead of clarinets. (Notice the happy interplay between flute and clarinet, a delicious new touch.) In due course Ex. 2 reappears, this time in the wind and without any academic pretensions. Towards the end of the movement the tempo quickens and the first violins in particular are required to display agile fingers. The closing bars show an ingenious new derivation from Ex. 2, now put firmly into place as it establishes the home key of A major beyond all doubt.

The first movement finishes on a chord of A. The slow movement begins on a unison A several times repeated but darkened by brushing gently against the adjacent B flat. Cellos and basses begin a continuous measured tread, *quasi pizzicato*, above which violas, bassoons and oboes extend a sombre melody in D minor. The movement is said to have been inspired by a religious procession Mendelssohn saw when in Naples and the initial unison phrase may well be supposed to represent monks intoning a fragment of plainchant. The second 'verse' is given to the violins, subtly blended with flutes to give an organ-like effect.

A new strand is taken up by the first group of instruments and, as before, is repeated an octave higher by violins. There is an artless simplicity about the conception that makes it instantly memorable. Once the wistful melody has run its full course the strings are left on their own to introduce a delicately poised extension of the opening 'plainchant'.

The mood becomes less austere as the clarinets lend their expressive tones to a new theme in A major. It is like a ray of sunshine and the violins are quick to respond to its warmth. A strongly emphasised reprise of the opening litany seems to act as a rebuke and the melancholy march resumes its measured pace. The movement is remarkably compact and completely free from any romantic excess, revealing once more the essentially classical attitude that Mendelssohn showed towards his art.

This is even more apparent in the ensuing minuet, for that is what it is even though he avoids actually labelling it as such. It is as though the Beethoven scherzo had never existed; all is grace and elegance, the scoring in a direct line of descent from Mozart. The 'trio' evokes woodland glades with its soft horn-calls; here, we feel, Mendelssohn pays another visit to the fairyland of *A Midsummer Night's Dream*, the music striking a more positive note as the mortals come on the scene and then returning again to the court of Oberon. It is an exquisite piece of writing, beguiling in its simplicity. The minuet duly returns according to classical convention although Mendelssohn scorns a literal repeat, adding a number of felicitous new touches. At the end of the movement we hear the 'horns of Elf-land faintly blowing' once more, before the violins gently fold the movement away.

Gentle is certainly not the word for the final movement, a brilliant and lively dance known as a Saltarello. A few loud introductory bars awake us violently from forest fantasies before a pair of flutes set the dance nimbly on its way. Violins keep up an insistent drumming rhythm which finds its way down to the bass as more and more instruments become involved. (Mendelssohn was too fastidious to use a tambourine, a temptation few composers would have resisted in a similar context.)

A strong unison phrase in the strings offers a contrast to the jiggety rhythm while stamping chords conjure up a vivid image of the dancers' movements. Horns mark time on repeated crotchets as the violins unfold a new theme whose sinuous shape suggests girls weaving their way between the momentarily static males. Then, with a touch of magic, the violins have a more sustained line, a single dancer, perhaps, of special beauty whose graceful movement excites a buzz of applause from the woodwind. For a moment or two a sort of chain-dance begins in the strings at Firsts, Seconds and Violas chase each other in quick succession. The flutes will have none of this and reintroduce the opening theme, now at a higher pitch. For some time the music continues to use material that should be familiar by now, but then a sequence of trills in the woodwind leads us into a new development.

It is strictly speaking a Tarantella, the dance that was supposedly a cure for the tarantula's otherwise fatal bite; the victim danced nonstop until the poison was sweated out. The violins begin this rotating theme quietly to a tip-toe accompaniment from the lower strings. It passes in a continuous stream from one section to another, never louder than *piano*, even when after a long absence the wind feel compelled to join in. The gradual accumulation of sound thereafter is brilliantly contrived until at last the pattern breaks, exploding into the original Saltarello rhythm.

Towards the end of the movement the woodwind seem to try to calm the ever-restless strings but their urgent rhythm persists until the very final chords. A notable feature of the movement is that it maintains its minor tonality to the end while sacrificing nothing in the way of brilliance or wit. There can be few symphonies that begin in a major key and end in the minor and perhaps it was this unconventional design that caused Mendelssohn some unease. For all its effectiveness he was known to have been dissatisfied with the finale, and it is interesting to note that he withdrew the symphony after the first performances and prevented its publication during his lifetime. Although numbered as the Fourth of his symphonies it was actually completed before the 'Scottish' (No. 3), but it is only fair to say that he had written no less than twelve symphonies in his youth and that the Symphony No. 1 in C minor with which he made his London début was composed when he was fifteen. A rare talent indeed . . .

Violin Concerto in E Minor
Op. 64 (1844)

Of all the works of Mendelssohn's adulthood the Violin Concerto is generally considered to be the most flawless. It may lack the heroic stance of the Brahms or the technical challenges of the Tchaikovsky; but it is one of those compositions where everything seems perfectly in place. Despite his extraordinary facility the concerto did not come easily to him; he felt its first stirrings within him in 1838 when, in a letter to the notable violinist Ferdinand David, he wrote, 'I would like to write a violin concerto for you for next winter; one in E minor is in my head and its beginning gives me no rest'. Six years elapsed before these first seeds bore fruit, but even then Mendelssohn was curiously indecisive. In a further letter to David, dated 17th December, 1844, he tells of a number of modifications he has made, altering and lengthening the cadenza, changing the end of the first movement, worrying about the pizzicato accents in the theme of the *adagio* (sic). After expressing some of his doubts he wrote, 'Do not laugh at me too much; I feel ashamed in any case, but I can't help it; I'm just groping around'. More detailed queries follow and the letter ends, 'Thank God the fellow is through with his concerto you will say. Excuse my bothering you but what can I do?'

Not a trace of these uncertainties remains in the finished work which seems effortless from first to last. The opening is far more original than is generally realised, dispensing with the convention of an orchestral introduction and thus setting a model for such widely differing works as the concertos of Sibelius and Bartók. A quiet murmur of strings and a sustained wind chord provide a gentle background of E minor above which the soloist projects the main theme, whose unashamed lyricism continues unbroken till the upbeat to the twenty-fifth bar. Three staccato chords in the orchestra galvanise the soloist into greater activity so that swiftly running triplets soon become the order of the day. A passage in rising octaves, repeated in decorated form, leads us to a fairly substantial orchestral *tutti* which takes up the main subject, giving it a rather more aggressive character. A sudden recession of tone allows the violins to introduce a transitional theme of a slightly more angular nature which the soloist is quick to take over. After a number of twists and turns the key of G minor is established and flute and violins offer a wistful little melody which the soloist disregards, preferring to display his dexterity at playing swiftly repeated thirds in a virtually chromatic ascent. As the solo part grows more challenging the orchestra is reduced to a purely accompanying role. Gradually the excitement dies down as the rhythms change from triplets to ordinary quavers and then, after a beautifully poised high B, to a slow descent in crotchets.

The violin part settles onto its lowest note, the open–string G, a touch of sheer genius, for above this unique monotone accompaniment, the flutes and clarinets give us the first hearing of the tender second subject, a tune of beguiling simplicity that is instantly memorable. Not surprisingly the soloist takes it over, extending it considerably, either by providing a descant to the wind or indulging in flights of fancy above the cushioned harmony of the strings.

A charming reminder of the first theme now appears in G major but the soloist quickly abandons it in favour of capricious arpeggios in triplets. A series of ascents by narrower intervals leads to a sudden thunderous chord in the orchestra, a signal that we have been pitched into the true Development section. It provokes an impassioned response from the violin based on a stretched version of the opening theme. The orchestral 'roars' diminish in ferocity as the violinist plays an Orpheus-like role, but an aftermath of agitation persists as the angular transitional theme hastens on its way, urged on by chattering quavers in the woodwind. Soon the soloist adopts a more flowing style as various members of the woodwind try out some adaptations of the opening theme's first few notes. Greater confidence comes as the first violins join in, moving firmly into E major. The soloist in due course agrees that this could be productive and makes a couple of soothing passes in that key. But then a wonderful thing happens. The supporting harmonies drift away, initiating some subtle changes of key. In the most expressive passage of the whole movement the soloist begins a descending sequence that modulates through several keys before coming momentarily to rest on a low D sharp. The orchestra rouses us from this reverie with a call to action based on the now familiar modified version of Theme I; within moments the violinist launches into the cadenza which is brilliantly integrated into the movement both at its beginning and its termination. Its placing, at roughly the half-way point, is highly original and leads us to expect that the movement will be unduly short. Mendelssohn's solution to the structural problem this poses is brilliant, for the flying arpeggios which end the cadenza continue in the background as the orchestra re-enters with a full Recapitulation. From here on everything is clearly related to past events, the only surprise being the absence of the soloist from the emphatically repeated E minor chords with which the movement ends—or rather, seems to end.

In days past there was a time when audiences could not resist the impulse to applaud at this point, thus destroying one of the most magical touches in the whole concerto. Out of the full orchestral chord emerges a single held note on a solo bassoon; after an expressive pause it shifts up a semitone from B to C, a rise which is copied at different pitches by flute, violas, second violins, firsts and then cellos in turn. It is as subtle a way of arriving at C major as could be imagined. This new destination safely reached, the strings set up a gentle accompaniment above which the soloist has a tune of extraordinary purity. It has the simple unaffected beauty we associate with Mozart's slow movements, yet it is no pastiche, not even an affectionate parody. Here we find the essentially classical nature of Mendelssohn's muse; the music comes to us free of any trace of romantic self-indulgence.

The melody continues unbroken for forty-two bars before timpani, trumpets and horns warn us of a change of mood. A new and more disturbed theme appears in the orchestra, quickly building to a climactic chord. The soloist responds by taking over both melody and accompaniment in a first concession to virtuosity; but though technically challenging, it is wholly relevant and cannot be looked on as a mere pyrotechnical display.

Release comes with a return to the initial theme, though some agitation lingers on in the accompaniment. Calm is restored with an exquisite ascent to a high C, a peak which is followed by a beautifully tiered descent through three octaves down to the rich tones of the G string. The closing bars are decorative without any excess of ornamentation and the movement ends with a simple affirmation of C major.

Perhaps realising that too sudden an arousal from such perfect serenity would be unkind, Mendelssohn provides a brief lyrical introduction to the finale, an orchestral equivalent to the charming vignettes of Schumann's *Kinderscenen*. Its closing bars are something of a tease, prolonging the suspense before a brisk fanfare sets the finale on its way. The violin capriciously refuses to have anything to do with these military aspirations and after four flicks of disdain begins a fairy dance, visiting once again the world of Titania and Oberon that had so fascinated the composer since his adolescent years. (See Music Ex. 1, upper line.) The accompaniment is necessarily extremely delicate, mostly in flutes and clarinets to provide a tonal contrast to the violin solo.

The playful mood continues for over forty bars until a sudden brilliant ascending scale from the soloist encourages the full orchestra to bring in the triumphal march which the initial fanfares promised but which has been so long postponed. The attempt at majesty cannot be sustained though and the 'fairy' theme keeps interrupting, like Puck flitting round Theseus' throne. In the end a happy compromise is reached as the 'march' goes on tiptoe while the violin part scampers around in a delightful display of high spirits.

At last, as though tiring of all this activity, the violin introduces a lyrical sustained tune of great elegance which later proves to be a perfect counterpoint to the nimble 'fairy' theme.

Ex. 1

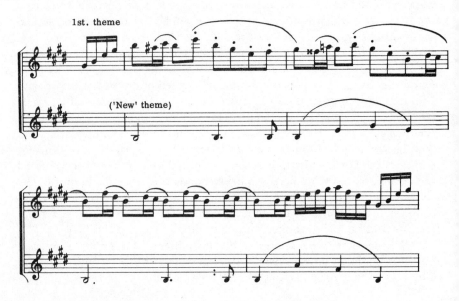

This fusion of contrasting ideas appears at the beginning of the Recapitulation which follows the classic pattern. Imposing brass chords over a *fortissimo* timpani roll seem to herald a cadenza, but it is a mere four bars long, trills rising through two octaves, beneath whose penultimate note a solo clarinet cheekily pinches the 'flicks' with which the soloist began the movement. From this point on one senses that a final gallop for home is imminent, and though Mendelssohn does not ask for an accelerando, few soloists can resist the temptation to push the tempo on during the last few pages. Their reward does not come with applause alone, for the concerto is so superbly written for the violin that it must be one of the most satisfying works in the entire repertoire from the performer's point of view. Above all, this finale is a supreme example of totally happy music. Poor health prevented Mendelssohn from conducting or even attending the first performance which was given by Ferdinand David on 16th September, 1844. Three years and one month later Mendelssohn died at the age of thirty-eight, burnt out by the demands of an exhausting career in which his versatility and brilliance proved ultimately to be destructive.

MOZART

1756–91

Few children can have known so unnatural an upbringing as the young
Mozart. He was the seventh child of Leopold and Anna Maria Mozart, but
only he and one sister, 'Nannerl', survived; the other five children all died in
infancy or soon after. Mozart's precocious gifts revealed themselves at a very
early age and there is a well-authenticated story that when he was still only
four he was discovered industriously writing music. His father assumed that
it was nothing but childish doodling but a friend of the family, Andreas
Schachtner (a professional trumpeter), looked more closely and found that it
was a genuine attempt at composition with proper harmonies and modulations. Leopold, amazed, observed that the music was too hard for anyone to
play whereupon the child replied, 'It has to be difficult because it's a
concerto'. Not surprisingly the father, himself the author of a notable treatise
on violin-playing, did everything he could to nurture this prodigious talent,
the more so as the sister was also an exceptionally gifted keyboard player.
Under his expert tuition the two children were soon ready to play in public
and so began a remarkable series of tours which took the family to almost
every European city of importance. Although the children enjoyed the
acclaim of the aristocracy it was a cruelly taxing existence, with arduous
journeys in lumbering stage-coaches, often so cold that straw was littered on
the floor to keep their feet warm. Meanwhile a small portable clavichord was
taken with them, not merely to pass the time but to keep their fingers well
exercised.

When he was eight, Mozart, by then an experienced traveller, was
brought to London for a stay of some fifteen months. An English connois-
seur called Barrington wrote an extensive description of a test he gave to the
child:

> Happening to know that little Mozart was much taken notice of by
> Manzoli, the famous singer, who came over to England in 1746, I said to
> the boy, that I should be glad to hear an extemporary Love Song, such as his
> friend Manzoli might choose in an opera.

The boy on this (who continued to sit at his harpsichord) looked back with much archness, and immediately began five or six lines of a jargon recitative proper to introduce a love song.

He then played a symphony[1] which might correspond with an air composed to the single word, *Affetto*.

It had a first and second part, which, together with the symphonies, was of the length that opera songs generally last; if this extemporary composition was not amazingly capital, yet it was really above mediocrity, and shewed most extraordinary readiness of invention.

Finding that he was in humour, and as it were inspired, I then desired him to compose a Song of Rage, such as might be proper for the opera stage.

The boy again looked back with much archness, and began five or six lines of jargon recitative proper to precede a Song of Anger.

This lasted also about the same time with the Song of Love; and in the middle of it, he had worked himself up to such a pitch, that he beat his harpsichord like a person possessed, rising sometimes in his chair.[2]

The word he pitched upon for this second extemporary composition was, *Perfido*.

After this he played a difficult lesson, which he had finished a day or two before: his execution was amazing, considering that his little fingers could scarcely reach a fifth on the harpsichord.

His astonishing readiness, however, did not arise merely from great practice; he had a thorough knowledge of the fundamental principles of composition, as, upon producing a treble, he immediately wrote a base under it, which, when tried, had a very good effect.

He was also a great master of modulation, and his transitions from one key to another were excessively natural and judicious; he practised in this manner for a considerable time with an handkerchief over the keys of the harpsichord.

The facts which I have been mentioning I was myself an eye witness of; to which I must add, that I have been informed by two or three able musicians, when [Johann Christian] Bach, the celebrated composer, had begun a fugue and left off abruptly, that little Mozart hath immediately taken it up, and worked it after a most masterly manner.[3]

It's clear from this that Mozart must already have been familiar with the operatic repertory of the day. His first efforts at composing opera came when he was twelve; indeed, during his adolescent years he wrote a number of them, *La Finta Semplice, Mitridate, Lucio Silla* and others equally unknown. The libretti were usually very poor, dramatic interest minimal. Opera was at its most artificial, concerned with mythological heroes with little basis in reality; no real depiction of character was needed since all that was required was a vehicle for singers to display their virtuosity. The phrase 'Stand and deliver' was more applicable to opera-singers than to highwaymen. The

[1] 'Symphony' was the term commonly used for the introduction to an aria.
[2] This corresponds almost exactly with Pierre Monteaux's description of Stravinsky playing *Le Sacre du Printemps* to him for the very first time!
[3] Erich Schenk, *Mozart and his times*, Secker & Warburg.

sentiments expressed in entire arias could indeed be encapsulated in a single word such as 'Perfido' as the infant Mozart clearly realised.

Most of his adolescent years continued with a pattern of concert tours across the face of Europe while at the same time he composed a large number of works which his father hoped would curry favour with the influential patrons of the day on whom musicians were almost wholly dependent. At times his youthful talents earned suspicion or envy though in general singers and instrumentalists who worked under his direction were quick to acknowledge his exceptional gifts. The strain of travelling and performing with scarcely a pause inevitably took its toll and his health suffered. Even so his teenage years were probably the happiest of his life with much achieved and every prospect of a glorious future.

Leopold's employer and patron at the time was the Archbishop Sigismund von Schrattenbach, an undemanding prelate who minded not at all that his principal court musician spent most of the year away from Salzburg travelling with his prodigiously gifted son. But in 1771 Schrattenbach died and his successor, Count von Colloredo, took a far less lenient attitude. Leopold was told quite firmly that he must attend to his proper duties; as for his son, he should be grateful for a post as assistant at a salary of 150 florins a year. It was a wretched sum and though Mozart tacitly accepted the situation by writing a number of *divertimenti*, symphonies and some church music, he began to look elsewhere for a more sympathetic employer.

It is one of the supreme ironies of music that one of the greatest composers the world has ever known was conspicuously unsuccessful in obtaining a position suited to his talents. Neither Munich, Mannheim nor Paris could find room for him; various schemes to gain support from private patrons came to nothing and Mozart was compelled to live a somewhat hand-to-mouth existence, depending on commissions for individual works to meet the requirements of some specific occasion. Acclaim was easily achieved by his dazzling performances as a pianist but the reward often came in the form of *objets d'art* or watches rather than much-needed money. (At one time Mozart used to wear breeches with five pockets in them with a watch in each—a sardonic hint that he had quite enough already.) His lack of financial acumen caused his father much distress though Leopold did his best to provide some support from his own rather meagre salary.

Between September 1777 and January 1779 Mozart stayed away from Salzburg, always hoping that he might find more congenial employment in a bigger city. Nothing of substance materialised and at last he was compelled to admit defeat and return to the service of the disagreeable and unappreciative Colloredo. Reluctantly Mozart settled down to such hum-drum duties as teaching music to the cathedral choir-boys or playing the organ in the Archbishop's private chapel. Meanwhile he continued to compose works suited to the terms of his employment, though the Sinfonia Concertante for violin, viola and orchestra (K. 364, 1779), a true masterpiece, reveals a profundity that Colloredo probably failed to appreciate. A commission for an opera for Munich came as a welcome relief and Mozart responded with his first really mature opera, *Idomeneo*. Although the characters are cardboard and the plot lacking in credibility, the music sustains a consistently high level of inspiration, so much so that it is sometimes regarded as musically the finest of all his operas. Shortly after its successful first performance Mozart was summoned to Vienna where Colloredo was playing a formal visit. A violent clash of personalities ensued with the Archbishop determined to put Mozart in his place as a servant, while the composer was equally resolute in his demand for the respect due to his talents. Three times he petitioned for his discharge, three times he was bluntly refused. The situation became explosive and culminated with Count Arco, Colloredo's personal chamberlain, literally kicking Mozart downstairs. It was a bitter humiliation that he could not accept; he resolved to stay in Vienna and forge an independent career for himself.

The immediate need was for a home and he went to lodge with the Weber family, for whose eldest daughter, Aloysia, he had conceived a passion some years previously. By this time Aloysia had married and had become an opera singer of some distinction. In his embittered state it was only natural that Mozart should seek consolation in female company; he seems to have found it in the person of the third of the four Weber sisters, Constanze. Although she was only eighteen, she was a responsible and kindly girl; within months they were married despite Leopold's objections. Mozart broke the news by letter adding a typically tongue-in-cheek postscript: 'My wife is nearly 91'—meaning she was just 19. The union was plagued by the same devastating infant mortality that Mozart's own parents had endured; out of six children born between 1785 and 1791 only two survived. By the standards of the day the marriage was a reasonably happy one and some of Mozart's letters to his young wife are touching in their tender almost child-like affection. Intellectually she was very much his inferior but she had a fine soprano voice and inspired what is possibly the most beautiful aria he ever wrote, the 'Et Incarnatus Est' from the C minor Mass he composed (but failed to complete) as a thank-offering for their wedding.

Mozart's decision to strike out on his own came in 1781. Justifiably he felt he could make an adequate living from commissions, subscription concerts and, if need be, a little teaching. With his literally international reputation he must have felt that an appointment to a royal household would soon materialise. In fact he had to wait until 1787 before any such invitation arrived; it came from the Emperor Joseph II who, on Gluck's death, had a vacancy for a court composer, primarily to write dance music to be played at the lavish balls which entertained the aristocracy. Mozart accepted for a modest salary of 800 gulden a year—Gluck had been paid 2000! It was the only regular income Mozart had for the remaining four years of his life and, feckless as he was with money, it was quite inadequate to sustain him and a wife whose health had been severely weakened by too many pregnancies.

Financial and domestic problems may have dogged him for a decade but they did not stop him from pouring forth an almost unbroken stream of masterpieces. His prowess as a pianist and the public demand for novelty caused him to develop the piano concerto to an extent undreamed of by his contemporaries, while his genius for the theatre revolutionised the concept of opera. It is possible that his humiliating experiences as a 'servant' in Colloredo's employ made the plot of *The Marriage of Figaro* especially attractive to him since it is certainly the first opera in which the servants consistently outwit their masters. But though the operas were immediately successful, they brought no steady income; publishers were unscrupulous in pirating music and there were no performing rights to supplement a paltry salary. ('Too much for what I have done but too little for what I could do' wrote Mozart on a receipt to Joseph II's treasurer.) In the last years of his life Mozart was driven to write pathetic begging letters to a banker friend asking for loans which he would repay with interest once his 'prospects' were realised. They make tragic reading, for here was a man who gave the world so much to treasure that one can scarcely believe that society could treat him so ungenerously.

To convey Mozart's unique qualities as a composer is almost impossible; there was a period when he was regarded as a light-weight in comparison to Beethoven. Denis Matthews was once handed a cheque for playing a Mozart concerto with the words, 'It seems a lot of money to pay just to hear you play a lot of scales . . .' It is true that Mozart does employ the formulae current during his period, the accompanying figure known as the Alberti bass, decorative passages made up from scales and arpeggios, embellishments and trills. But behind this elegant facade lies a troubled spirit which makes its presence felt in subtle dissonances and poignant harmonies, 'the tears behind the smile'. His melodies seem disarmingly simple because they go directly to the heart of the matter, whether it is sorrow or gaiety. The proportions of his music are always superbly balanced even though the perceptive ear is frequently beguiled by surprises unnoticed by the casual listener. His operatic ensembles are extraordinary demonstrations of contrapuntal mastery coupled with human observation. He has Haydn's wit and Beethoven's profundity; if he is too well-mannered to allow the open display of passions that became acceptable in the latter half of the nineteenth century, it does not mean that he did not feel them just as strongly. It is the economy with which he achieves his effects that is so impressive; the famous criticism made by the Emperor, 'Too many notes, Mozart, too many notes', was singularly inapposite, for if we compare Mozart with those who came after him, we find that he could express everything that they wished to 'say' in music but with less rhetoric and fewer notes.

The Piano Concertos

Mozart did not invent the keyboard concerto, but the twenty-three that he wrote span the most important creative period of his life from 1773 to 1791. The harpsichord had been promoted from its humble supportive role in a number of concertos by Bach, most of them adapted from violin works. Bach's eldest son, Carl Philipp Emanuel, was the first major composer to exploit the newly developed 'fortepiano', and was so enamoured of the instrument that he wrote forty-seven concertos. It is unlikely that Mozart had come across any of these while he was still only eight years old, but during his childhood stay in London he came under the influence of Johann Christian Bach, youngest son of the great Johann Sebastian. The 'London Bach', as he was known, was greatly taken with the precocious child and formed a paternal friendship which left an enduring mark. At the time the fortepiano was just beginning to displace the harpsichord in popular esteem although the two instruments co-existed for a short period. (C.P.E. Bach actually wrote a double concerto for harpsichord, fortepiano and orchestra to exploit the essential differences between the two instruments.) When he was ten years old Mozart took three sonatas by J.C. Bach and arranged them for piano and orchestra. It was an exercise suggested by his father to develop a feel for this rapidly emerging form. The adaptations are surprisingly inept by Mozart's standards though they served a useful purpose while the family was on tour since they required little rehearsal. Further essays of a similar kind followed on the return to Salzburg in 1767, often using a single sonata movement by composers whose names mean little to us now—Honauer, Raupach, Eckard or, more familiarly, C.P.E. Bach. This second series employs a larger orchestra, strings and two pairs of wind instruments, and for some time four of the works were thought to be genuine Mozart compositions. In fact he did not compose a concerto of his own until he was seventeen. A further five followed during the Salzburg period, but once he had settled in Vienna he was quick to write three more since they were the most likely works to bring him popular success. Between 1784 and 1786 he wrote another twelve, each a masterpiece in its own right; but the Viennese public proved to be fickle and his drawing power as a solo pianist diminished. Even so, he produced two more concertos in 1788 and 1791, the second of which, K.595 in B flat, seems to renounce virtuosity almost entirely. Its intimacy belongs more to the world of chamber music, as though Mozart had come to accept that fame and fortune would continue to be denied him and that he might as well write for himself alone.

The form of his concertos is remarkably consistent, but if the structure remains the same, the inventiveness within the framework is unflagging. The first movements are all in sonata form. With the exception of K.271 (in which the piano makes a brief premature entrance) they begin with an orchestral tutti which presents the main subject as well as other material of importance. The second contrasting subject may appear in either the tonic or dominant key or it may be withheld for the soloist's benefit. Sometimes we find a 'false' second subject, in which case it may not reappear until much later in the work. Once the orchestral exposition is completed, the piano will enter, and it is at this point that Mozart shows great ingenuity. Sometimes the piano part will emerge almost by stealth with a decorative passage that runs through the closing bars of the tutti; at other times the orchestra will come to a halt, leaving room for the soloist to take over the main subject; a third option that occurs in the most profoundly serious concertos such as the D minor (K.466) and the C minor (K.491) is for the soloist to take a completely independent line, disregarding everything that the orchestra has had to offer. This is not mere caprice but a brilliant solution to the fundamental problem of balance that Mozart had to face. The piano for which he was writing was a silver-toned instrument that was quite incapable of dominating an orchestra by force. An orchestral exposition with a powerful ending might well make the soloist's entry seem puny by comparison. Adopting the Biblical principle of the soft answer that turneth away wrath, Mozart would make a virtue of the fortepiano's frailty by giving it a theme full of pathos which would remain its exclusive property. For instance in the great C minor concerto (K.491) the soloist *never* plays the opening theme, while the orchestra, as though by mutual agreement, never usurps the pianist's initial phrases.

During the secondary exposition the true second subject will duly appear, usually in the soloist's hands since it will almost certainly be lyrical in character. Whenever the orchestra is given something of importance the soloist will either drop out for a moment or two or supply decorative passages that serve as a silver lining. In the development section the thematic interest often lies in the orchestral part and it is at such points that the soloist is most likely to introduce an element of display. New themes may well appear, often in remote keys, but the piano writing seldom involves chords of any density since Mozart consistently avoids any contest of strength between soloist and orchestra. For the most part he demands agility in the right hand, support in the left, though he was enough of a virtuoso to realise that an audience could easily be impressed by brilliant unison passages or by challenging runs in the left hand.

The recapitulation will be compressed and build to the classic suspense chord that heralds the cadenza. Fortunately for us, Mozart wrote out a number of these for the benefit of other performers and they give us a good indication of the sort of thing he would have improvised on the spot. The accepted cue to alert the orchestra was a sustained trill on the second note of the scale resolving onto the keynote. The closing bars were almost always given to the orchestra alone.

The slow movements of the concertos show an astonishing variety even though most of them are marked 'Andante'. The differences lie in the melodic line, which may be touchingly simple or disturbingly tragic, in the harmonies, which may be dulcet or anguished, and in the texture, which may be transparent or richly opaque. In the great C minor concerto we find an exquisitely simple 'aria' for piano alternating with a serenade for woodwind. In the D minor concerto (K.466) a tender Romance is interrupted by a stormy interlude that could well be called a Toccata. More commonly we find the piano part aspiring towards the quality of the human voice, frequently engaging in quasi-operatic duets with individual wind instruments. The form may consist of variations, a rondo, sonata-form or a free fantasia.

The finale—Mozart only uses three movements in his concertos—is usually a rondo, often with two themes of more or less equal importance. The opening bars are sometimes given to the soloist, if only to set the proper tempo. Unlike the first movements, which do share certain structural characteristics, the finales are liable to spring surprises on us—a sudden change of tempo, a modulation to a remote key, even an alteration of the basic pulse as for instance in K.271 where a hectic Presto in 2/2 time suddenly changes into a seductive Minuet in 3/4. (The headlong flight of the movement has already been interrupted by a capricious cadenza that alternates between Andantino and Presto). If variety is most conspicuously to be found in the finales, it is nevertheless unwise to make any generalisations about the concertos since it was a form that inspired Mozart to constant experiment. This brief survey began with the assertion that Mozart did not invent the piano concerto; more remarkably he perfected it in the relatively short period of eighteen years. There are no works more perfect in every detail than the finest of these concertos; they may have their rivals but they cannot be excelled.

Piano Concerto in E flat Major *K.271*

The numbering of the concertos can cause confusion since for a long time four of the student exercises mentioned previously were classified as Mozart's own work; consequently this concerto, properly No. 5, is often known as the Ninth. This is the most individual of the Salzburg concertos and it has a number of original features. It was written in January 1777, the year of his twenty-first birthday and it could be said to symbolise his true coming-of-age as a composer in this genre. A French woman pianist, Mlle Jeunehomme, was passing through Salzburg at the time, presumably as part of a concert-tour. Mozart, not easily impressed by other artists, must have taken to her, for he coined one of his characteristic nicknames, addressing her as 'Jenomy'. She asked him to write a concerto for her and this superb work was the result.

It begins with a bald unison statement of E flat major from the orchestra.[4] Such declarations of tonality were a standard opening gambit and their energetic masculinity was expected to elicit a soft feminine response. The response certainly comes but not in the orchestra; instead, Mozart allows the pianist to reply, a move that defied convention and that was not to be equalled in originality until Beethoven, in his Fourth Concerto, astounded his audience by beginning the work with the solo piano. This brief exchange between orchestra and soloist is so unexpected that Mozart instantly repeats it before embarking on an orchestral tutti of some substance. Harmonically unadventurous, it spends some time alternating between dominant and tonic, the interest lying mainly in the bass. A descending scale from the violins leads us to a graceful second subject that uses a B flat as a stepping-stone to higher things.

Ex. 1

This theme is developed further by the first violins over a running commentary from the seconds and a delicately sketched bass. Horns and oboes introduce a more martial air, causing considerable agitation in the string parts, so much so that the music grinds to a virtual halt on a strident dissonance before order is restored somewhat hesitantly in the violins. Some chirpy fanfares bring the exposition to a close though here too Mozart has a surprise for us. Instead of delaying the soloist's entry until the opening tutti has been tidied away, he gives the pianist a sustained trill on a high B flat while the orchestra still has four bars left to play. It's like a warning bell telling them that it's time they stopped. Dutifully they do so but only for three bars. Just as the soloist seems safely embarked on a completely new theme, the orchestra interrupts with a reiteration of the very opening unison phrase. The soloist obliges with the proper response but then begins to play a brilliant and witty variation on the ensuing material from the orchestral exposition. Considerable dexterity is called for before the activity dies down and the pianist graciously condescends to acknowledge the second subject (Ex. 1),

---

[4] It is strangely similar to the opening phrase of his very first symphony, written in London at the age of eight!

now in the dominant and treating F as the stepping-stone. The same extension follows, though with a more soothing accompaniment; and then, as though jealous of such delights, violins and oboe take over the tune while the piano supplies a chuckling accompaniment. Such subtle exchanges were a relative novelty not to be found in the concertos of Mozart's predecessors.

A fairly elaborate excursion ensues before the horns summon us back to the parade-ground and a reprise of the little martial episode from the opening tutti. As before, it comes to a halt with a crisis chord to which the pianist now offers a soothing rejoinder. With great skill Mozart has steered his way back into the material of the exposition (now in the dominant) having led us to believe that he had put it behind him.

The true development is heralded by a re-statement of the opening dialogue. It is the signal for the soloist to begin a joyous game of hide-and-seek with one fragment (Ex. 2).

Ex. 2

Time after time it appears, always in an unexpected place, with the trill often growling away in the lower depths while the initial fairy trumpet-calls come from the tree-tops. Intellectually it is a highly concentrated development of one fragmentary theme but in fact it is a musical joke such as Beethoven would have delighted in.

A further example of Mozart humour comes with the recapitulation when roles are exchanged, the pianist taking the E flat proclamation, the orchestra giving the 'feminine' response. It is this feminine phrase that Mozart now develops extensively in the piano part, modulating swiftly through several remote keys before returning to the 'home' key and a reprise of the second subject. The principal materials are then reassessed until an emphatic extension of the very first bar prepares the way for the cadenza. It seems that Mozart didn't trust Mlle Jeunehomme to rise adequately to the challenge so he wrote one himself, no empty display but a further working-out of the main themes.

A last surprise is still in store for, after the orchestra have greeted the cadenza with enthusiasm, the piano makes a further entrance with the same sustained trill that appeared near the end of the exposition. This time it dissolves into an E flat arpeggio, as though to say 'Enough!' The hint is taken and a few staccato chords confirm the ending of this wholly remarkable movement.

The ensuing *Andantino*[5] is in C minor, the first movement in a minor key to appear in Mozart's concertos. First and second violins, both muted, begin with a very closely knit canon, the seconds exactly copying the firsts, but a beat behind. With the entry of horns and oboes on a unison G the strings begin to move in contrary motion before the phrases seem almost to disintegrate. Once more the strings resume their shadow play but the soloist disregards them entirely, offering instead an expressively ornamented line whose improvisatory quality is a wonderful foil to the academic severity of the canon in the orchestral part. An unexpected modulation into E flat major in the orchestra prepares the way for an extensive piano solo in this more congenial key. A brief interpolation from the strings tries to bring back the second part of the opening material which the pianist promptly puts into the minor in a rather tearful way. It is a touch of sadness soon forgotten as the writing becomes increasingly decorative. But then, as though acknowledging that the orchestral material does have some merit, the soloist ends this paragraph with a beautifully simple reference to the closing phrase of the orchestral introduction.

Eight bars of orchestral music follow, providing the soloist with new material to develop in a characteristically elaborate way. Soon an arpeggio figure in the bass gives added depth to the music and for a short while we seem very near to Beethoven in style and content, a likeness enhanced by the quite weighty accents in the orchestral part. A triplet figure in the right hand drifts down from the highest register of the keyboard to come to rest in C minor. For the first time in the movement the soloist touches on the initial violin theme. It serves as a reminder to the orchestra who resume the opening music together with the piano descant. For some time Mozart gives us the equivalent of a recapitulation with the significant difference that the E flat major episode is truncated, unable to resist the dark influence of C minor. At one point there is a particularly expressive exchange between the piano and the first violins which the orchestra interrupts with a more formal display of grief.

Mozart then provides a cadenza of profound beauty, developing themes in a truly inspired way that must have made Mlle Jeunehomme regard him with awe. He even has a false ending, for the traditional trill dissolves not into an orchestral tutti but into three bars of extreme pathos such as might accompany the 'Lachrymae' in a Requiem. One impassioned phrase from the orchestra does little to ease the pain and the movement ends sorrowfully save for the final cadence, a stern confirmation of C minor.

The finale brings so abrupt a change of mood that it can take us by surprise even after several hearings. For nearly forty bars the piano keeps up a non-stop chatter before allowing the orchestra to join in the fun; such a long

---

[5] A little faster than Andante.

solo at the start of a movement is quite exceptional and the long-delayed orchestral entry seems determined to establish a firmer grip on this mercurial material. Having done so, the violins introduce a frivolous little theme which the soloist is delighted to take over. A climax of sorts is reached as the strings move outwards in opposite directions over a forceful unison F in oboes and horns.

The pianist promptly introduces a new figure whose exuberance is hardly affected by an abortive attempt to get a fugue under way in the strings. A fleeting concession to academic propriety, it is quickly jettisoned, allowing the piano to continue its happy burblings unimpeded.

At last, as if impatient at this continuous display of agility, the orchestra seizes a swift unison phrase from the soloist's grasp. We expect a substantial tutti but instead the soloist cuts them off with a totally unforeseen cadenza which includes a number of complete changes of tempo. After teasing us with this whimsical caprice, Mozart brings back the opening material exactly as it was, though the oboes do have a delightful premature entry before the rest of the orchestra re-establish some authority.

The pianist then introduces a new episode which enables the music to modulate into a series of different keys, mostly in the minor by way of a change. A brief cadenza in the shape of a sinuous descent to a low D flat leads to the most dramatic surprise of the movement, nothing less than a minuet with four variations, each more elaborate than the last. Yet another cadenza provides a way back to the opening material in a compressed form and the remainder of the movement is a résumé of what has gone before with the order of events slightly changed. A special touch worth noting is the appearance of the theme on oboes and horns to a pizzicato accompaniment while the pianist trills happily on a high B flat for eight bars. In a movement full of surprises even the ending is unorthodox, for the last refrain grows quieter and quieter until it almost disappears. Almost, but not quite, for two thumping chords are tacked on at the end to bring this remarkable concerto to a triumphant conclusion. Not for several years was Mozart to write anything so audacious as this highly original work and one would love to know what success Mlle Jeunehomme had with it when she returned to France. Mozart was to follow her there not long after, but it was an ill-fated journey tragically marred by his mother's death.

Piano Concerto in G Major
K.453

1784 was an astonishingly productive year for Mozart even by his almost superhuman standards. One concerto, K.449, was finished on 9th February, another on 15th March, a third on 22nd March and this one, K.453, on 12th April. Two more were written between September and December and, as though these labours were not enough, he also wrote two sonatas, a string quartet and a quintet for piano and wind for a pupil named Babette Ployer for whom Mozart must have felt a special affection since he had already written a concerto for her (K.449). The orchestra, a pair each of flutes, oboes, bassoons and horns as well as the usual body of strings, provided him with a rich palette of tone-colour which he exploited to wonderful effect in the slow movement.

The violins begin the first subject without any preliminaries. The occasional dotted rhythms suggest a march, but there is a difference between a march and a walk and this music has no suggestion of ceremonial pomp about it; it is definitely a walk, jaunty and carefree. The first phrase gains a delightful murmur of approval from flutes and oboes; it is followed by a neatly contrived modification, alike in rhythm but different in contour. Two more positive gestures capture our attention before the violins produce a curiously static phrase obviously designed to leave an opening for the soloist to fill. Suddenly there is a change of mood as the music does become more military in character. A few swirling runs lead to a climax with repeated D naturals giving pointed emphasis to the dominant while cellos, violins and violas overlap in a swaggering theme. It breaks off abruptly leaving the woodwind with an angular figure that is going to prove very important. At this point it serves as a bridge passage leading to the second subject, an enchanting tune notable not only for its sensuously beautiful harmonies but also for the breathing-spaces which, when it is repeated, are filled with wistful echoes. Just when we think that Mozart will be unable to resist taking this tune further there is a surprising switch to E flat major, a move which provokes an agitated response. Some forceful chords seem about to terminate the exposition but Mozart has other ideas. Cellos and basses throb gently on the key-note G while above them the violins have an exquisitely poignant phrase beginning on a G *sharp*. The phrase is repeated with a melting descent from the woodwind but even this does not exhaust the riches of this wonderful exposition for the violins produce a lilting theme of great elegance which is deftly syncopated before some staccato chords do bring the tutti to a positive close.

With a ripple of pleasure the soloist takes over the opening theme. For some time the music follows the course of the exposition closely but, as might be expected, the two static bars in the string parts are filled in with decorations by the soloist, at first with lingering syncopations and then with a more agile running passage. An interesting example of Mozart's concern for balance follows: bars 16–22 of the opening tutti are marked *forte* and scored for full orchestra. We now find an exactly comparable passage marked *piano* and much more delicately orchestrated so as not to swamp the piano. Soon the pianist breaks free from the original structure, taking a nimble if slightly devious route to A major—actually the dominant of D. Mozart now surprises us with a completely new theme of irresistible charm. Is it perhaps the true second subject? One might think so, but the supposition proves to be false for the 'original' second subject from the orchestral exposition will make a proper appearance in due course. Meanwhile we should be content to have such a bonus offered to us. Certainly the oboes and bassoons are only too happy to filch a phrase from the piano part, repeating it no less than four times.

A magnificent sequence of modulations follows with descending arpeggios in the piano serving to decorate an elegant dialogue between flute and oboe with pertinent comments from the bassoon. All the thematic interest lies in the orchestra and it is a pity that in many recordings of the work our attention is directed rather too forcibly towards the piano arpeggios which should be pure filigree. Easily recognised, the angular phrase from the exposition reappears, first in the piano and then the woodwind. It serves its original function, preparing the entrance of the second subject. The soloist's presentation of this beguiling tune is free of ornament and has that child-like innocence which so often leads people to think, wrongly, of Mozart as a Dresden china figurine. The tune is repeated in the woodwind with the piano supplying the little echoes that give the theme a touch of wistfulness.

Some pure decoration follows, ending with dramatic rising scales and a cadential trill. The orchestra accepts this as a cue for a show of strength, taking up the 'military' theme from the exposition with some vigour. There follows the most remarkable passage in the whole movement. A sudden shift of harmony takes us mysteriously into the remote key of B flat major. The soloist provides an accompaniment of delicately floating arpeggios in triplets while the woodwind have a long series of gracious exchanges, all in crotchets. Soft sustained chords in the strings outline the harmonies for us as Mozart sets out on this strange journey through a series of keys. The sequence is shown in Ex. 1. Even the most insensitive ear must surely be aware of the mysterious nature of this progression. The final chord of Ex. 1 may look like B major but Mozart soon shows us that it is the dominant of E minor. 'Well, at least that's settled', we think, but then quiet but restless syncopations in the strings lead us astray once more and we are suddenly transported into the even more unexpected key of C minor. A plaintive fragment of a tune appears in the piano part, uncertain of its destination or even of which octave it should

Ex. 1

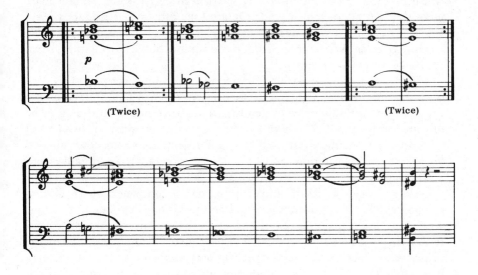

be in. Horns on a sustained D provide it with a useful tonal anchor though the phrases remain forlorn with their somewhat distorted versions of the dominant of G minor. Four soft chords in the woodwind offer reassurance that we are nearer 'home' than we imagine. 'My goodness, so we are!' says the soloist and slides effortlessly into a recapitulation of the first theme.

As might be expected, the ensuing pages cover familiar ground although with several felicitous new touches, particularly a more extensive use of what I have called the angular theme. The preparation for the cadenza is especially unusual, harking back to that sudden plunge into E flat major which had caused some agitation in the original exposition. Mozart's own cadenza is remarkable for its musical content, only occasionally allowing flashes of virtuosity. The subsequent orchestral entry is a stroke of pure genius, not the expected loud affirmation of G major, but a quiet throbbing in the bass above which the violins place the yearning G sharp which tugged at our heartstrings shortly before the pianist's very first entry. Not until Beethoven's Fourth Concerto was the problem of bringing in the orchestra again solved with such magical subtlety.

The slow movement—'Andante not Adagio' warned Mozart—is surely unique in its construction. It begins with a five-bar phrase of the utmost simplicity which nevertheless is profoundly moving;[6] it ends on the dominant and then pauses for a moment leaving us wondering what the sequel will

---

[6] It is worth comparing with the slow movement of Schumann's Piano Sonata in G minor.

be. In the course of the movement this 'motto' phrase appears five times, and on the first four occasions it not only leaves us in suspense but is followed by increasingly unpredictable events. Only on the fifth appearance do we find the logical answer to the enigma it poses. Here, then, is a completely original construction, derived from the Rondo concept but not following the normal course of a rondo movement.

The first episode is for orchestra alone, beginning with an expressive oboe solo. Soon flute, oboe and bassoon are involved in a quasi-operatic trio of ethereal beauty supported by gently rocking harmonies in the strings. The dissonances here are bitter-sweet, D sharp against E, C sharp against D, but each arising from the most elegant counterpoint. Repeated notes on two horns an octave apart bring a more forceful gesture, but it soon dissolves into a plaintive sigh from the strings. There is a momentary silence.

Enter the piano with the initial 'motto' phrase complete with its enigmatic ending. Out of the silence emerges an impassioned episode in G minor with wide leaps spanning an octave and a half.[7] The woodwind briefly resume their 'operatic' trio only to find their material commandeered by the pianist who proceeds to extend it in the most elaborate way. The music may be written down, but it gives an impression of spontaneous improvisation. The 'plaintive sigh' reappears in the woodwind and is even intensified by the soloist. A halting ascent divided between wind and piano leads to the third recurrence of the initial 'motto', now in G major instead of C and, for the first time, scored for woodwind. In this key the final chord is D major, the dominant of G. In direct contradiction the soloist begins the next episode in D *minor*. Starting simply, the writing grows increasingly elaborate, developing an intensity which the woodwind interpolations are powerless to check. The piano part finally breaks off on the dominant of C sharp minor, a point so far from 'home' that the subsequent orchestral modulation back to C major seems almost magical. Calm restored, the soloist plays the 'motto' theme once more. The ensuing pause seems more tantalising than ever.

Without warning we are plunged into E flat major with even wider-flung phrases covering two-and-a-half octaves. After so heroic an entry, the music loses heart and drifts forlornly into C minor. Some solace comes with the little operatic scene in the woodwind, to which the piano now adds a fourth 'voice'. Two rising chromatic phrases lead into another surprise, a genuine cadenza, a further demonstration of Mozart's improvisatory powers. (It even includes a brief prophetic vision of the slow movement of the Schumann piano concerto!) At the conclusion of the cadenza the woodwind proffer the fifth version of the 'motto' theme, subtly tinged with sadness. The soloist's response supplies the long-deferred sequel which seems like a benediction. The movement ends with the orchestral sigh which delicate ascending scales from the keyboard can do nothing to comfort.

---

[7] These would almost certainly have been filled in by any performer in Mozart's time.

On 27th May, 1784 Mozart bought a starling as a pet. Passing through a street market his ear had been caught by its precocious song which he duly noted down with the comment 'Das war schön!'

Ex. 2

Take out the pause and the sharp sign in front of the G and you have the theme of this finale, or at least its first phrase. (The bird so endeared itself to Mozart that when it died he buried it in his garden with an epitaph in verse.) In its final form the theme has a number of *acciaccatura* or 'crushed-notes', no doubt intended to imitate the chirpiness of the bird's song. The form of the movement consists of a theme with five variations, the initial presentation of the theme being allocated to the orchestra alone.

Variation I belongs mostly to the soloist though the first violins do occasionally show their approval by imitating a particularly appealing phrase.

Variation II leaves the theme with the orchestra, allowing the pianist to show off the dexterity of each hand in turn in a torrent of triplets.

The next variation breaks free from the constraints of the theme. The woodwind are the first to offer some ingenious alternatives which the pianist duly takes advantage of, supplying what might be termed a variation on a variation.

Variation IV takes us into a new world, mysteriously shadowed and touched with the poignancy the key of G minor always seems to have in Mozart's work. The string-writing is almost ghostly, while the pianist's response produces an anguished line whose tortured angularity must have seemed as strange to eighteenth-century ears as Bartók did to his contemporaries.

Variation V restores conventional tonality with a thump, the first full orchestral sound in the movement. Eight bars of such noisy presumption is quite enough for the pianist and (s)he assumes command with a sustained trill on a high D—that starling again?—with the theme in the left hand. The orchestra continue to have symphonic aspirations but are duly tamed by some delicious chromatic figurations from the piano. There is a half-close followed by a pause.

Very quietly, in the mood of a brilliant operatic finale, Mozart begins the final section at the much quicker tempo, *Presto*. Horns and bassoons urge the music forward with hunting calls. For the time being the theme is forgotten in the general excitement. A moment to be noted is a sudden hushed unison in the strings above which the pianist plays joyous ascending scales; and then, against a busy chatter from the keyboard the woodwind pile up an amazing sequence of harmonies which, having reached their summit, disintegrate in a shower of arpeggios from the soloist. Amongst all this hilarity the theme must not be totally forgotten and it reappears undisguised in the piano part, only to have its tail twisted by the woodwind. After a further working-out of the 'operatic' material Mozart has a final witticism in store as the pianist stealthily plays the theme to a delicate pizzicato accompaniment. After this tiptoe excursion only the last five bars are marked *forte*, a concession to popular demand that invites the ovation this brilliant work deserves.

Piano Concerto in D Minor
K.466

The amazingly productive year 1784 was barely over when Mozart began work on this concerto, completed early in February 1785. It represents a new stage in his development, exploring emotional depths that are not only more intense but also disturbing in their implications of tragedy. The orchestral exposition is like no other in all his works, the restless syncopations conveying a feeling of deep anxiety which his innate good manners can scarcely conceal. If Mozart had written incidental music to *Macbeth*, the first thirty-two bars of this concerto would have served admirably as a prelude to the first scene with its ominous rumblings in the bass and the uneasy effect of the continuous syncopation in the strings. The other most unusual feature is the abandonment of the convention of two contrasting phrases early in the exposition. Here we find a relentless concentration on one rhythm for fifteen bars while the menacing fragments in the bass gather increasing momentum until, in bar 16, the tension is at last released with explosive force. (Horns, trumpets and timpani give this tutti a truly symphonic scale.)

When, after a dramatic break in bar 32, the second subject is at last revealed, it is scarcely allowed to flower as a melody. Minim chords suggest the beginning of a chorale but their suitability is immediately queried by an interrogatory phrase from the flute; three times this brief and still unsettling dialogue is repeated, each time at a higher pitch. The truth is that the first part of the exposition has cast so ominous a shadow that a relaxed or lyrical second subject cannot hope to flourish; this one, such as it is, disintegrates into a sequence of brief exchanges between first and second violins before a violent storm breaks out, a tumult of sound that rises in an irregular pattern to a tremendous climax in which D minor and E flat clash as though in battle, harried by an agitated phrase in the strings that has an air of desperation.

Beethoven at his most awe-inspiring could hardly exceed the sheer power of this climax, though the pleading gestures that quickly follow reveal the essentially operatic nature of Mozart's approach—the heroine begs for mercy as the sentence of death is pronounced. Once more the storm breaks out, first in the bass and then in pounding quavers in the violins. There is a quality of ferocity in the music that we seldom find in Mozart and, as if realising the danger of dwarfing the soloist's entry, he breaks off abruptly, offers a brief gesture of conciliation, and then rounds off the exposition with a more lyrical though still despairing phrase.

The opening bars of the piano part disregard everything that has gone before. There is a notable simplicity about the shape of the phrases, a restraint that admits sadness but refuses to indulge in an open display of emotion. This theme will remain the exclusive property of the soloist and it is interesting to note that the instant the orchestra join in, even though unobtrusively, there is an agitated reaction in the piano part.

The secondary exposition begins, easily recognised as the strings re-introduce the restless syncopations of the first page. After a mere four bars they are joined by the piano, at first in a purely accompanying capacity but gradually becoming more important as the emotional temperature rises. A climax is reached with a dramatic passage in broken octaves in the left hand punctuated by emphatic chords in the upper register. Even so, Mozart must have felt that the fortepiano lacked the sheer volume required and it is the orchestra that hammers out the last few bars of this section. There is a momentary silence followed by the appearance of the second subject, now divided between orchestra and piano in an elegant dialogue. A few bars of nimble passage-work lead to a new and more significant event, the arrival of the true second subject, a far more convincing theme than its predecessor, and one that is duly taken up by the orchestra in its first display of amiability. In spite of occasional brushes with G minor or D minor, the music remains in the more relaxed key of F major for some time. Admittedly the soloist does have one passage which recalls the storm from the orchestral tutti but the music seems much less menacing without the force of the full orchestra. After a fair amount of activity which reasserts his dominance the soloist has a cadential trill and hands over to the orchestra.

The ensuing eighteen bars refer back to the less disturbing elements of the opening exposition and, since the music remains in F major, the feeling of anxiety is still allayed; indeed the soloist's next entry sheds a new light on his initial theme which, translated into the major, now seems positively radiant. However, clouds soon gather to disperse this sunnier mood as the syncopated rhythms which began the concerto reappear in the strings. A shift to G minor creates a more intense emotional reaction in the solo part and one of the fascinations of this section is to observe the subtle changes that Mozart brings to a theme whose melodic contour remains basically similar at each appearance but whose emotional content continually varies. A sudden descent through three octaves of E flat major leads to the heart of the development in which the piano has wide-ranging ascending arpeggios countered by downward torrents based on dominant sevenths. Each pair of bars establishes a new tonality, the framework being:

E flat major, shifting to	(*Piano ascending*)
the dominant seventh of	(*Piano descending*)
F minor, shifting to	(*ascending*)
the dominant seventh of	(*descending*)
G minor, shifting to	(*etc.*)
the dominant seventh of	
A major, which becomes	
the dominant seventh of	
D minor, the 'home' key	

Beneath each 'dominant seventh' bar the orchestral bass reiterates the abruptly ascending triplet which created so ominous an effect at the very start of the work. After so many modulations Mozart takes his time to assert his final arrival at the proper destination, allowing the music to die away over grumbling octaves in the bass. And then, suddenly resolute, a chromatic ascent in octaves leads into the recapitulation.

Although it starts familiarly with the original opening passage, the soloist now becomes involved by the end of the eighth bar, helping to whip up the excitement with a clatter of broken octaves. In due course the second subject appears in its dialogue version between orchestra and piano. There follows a considerable compression, enabling the soloist to introduce his 'personal' second subject at a much earlier stage. No longer carefree, it is now in D minor; indeed from this point onwards the movement seems to grow increasingly tempestuous. The soloist has no further respite until the nine bars immediately preceding the cadenza, and the formidable challenge the piano part provides gives us a clear indication of Mozart's prowess as a pianist, since he intended the work for himself. Unfortunately this means that he never bothered to write out a cadenza, a chore he was only prepared to do for the benefit of pupils or patrons. It is interesting that Beethoven found it worth his while to write one, and though it contains some stylistic anachronisms it offers an exciting glimpse of the convergence of two great minds.

After the cadenza the storm rages anew with the full orchestra repeating the most turbulent passages from the opening tutti. By Mozart's usual standards this orchestral coda is exceptionally long but the greater surprise lies in the quiet ending. It is as though the last flames flicker and die leaving little but dust and ashes; all passion is spent and the ensuing Romance comes as a much needed solace.

Mozart calls the second movement 'Romanza', a suitably vague term that was frequently used at the time. In fact the movement is a spacious Rondo whose recurring theme appears in two sections, both of which are proposed by the soloist and seconded by the orchestra. The time-signature, *alla breve* or two-in-a-bar, is a warning against an over-sentimental approach, a warning too easily disregarded by pianists for whom the suggestion of Romance has a hypnotic quality. Although the exchange between soloist and orchestra may seem to be a polite formality, Mozart can still surprise us by extending the second orchestral response from the expected eight bars to an unforeseen fifteen.

A little surprisingly he stays in B flat major (the tonic key) for the quite extensive episode which follows. In essence it is an aria in which the piano stands in for an idealised soprano voice with a superhuman range. All the interest lies in the right hand with the left hand supplying only the most rudimentary bass. The orchestra's role is confined to pure accompaniment for no less than twenty-eight bars, at which point the rondo theme reappears exactly as before. The orchestra duly shows its approval by repeating the opening stanza, but just as we expect the second part of the refrain to fill its allotted place in the scheme, Mozart has a truly startling surprise. A brilliant toccata-like passage dispels the serene mood; rapid figures in the right hand give a whirring effect while the left hand creates an impression of a dramatic duet by passing swiftly from treble to bass and back again. To add to the drama the music is now in G minor with an emphasis on woodwind tone that gives a harsher, far from 'romantic' quality. At one point in this remarkable section the general direction of the solo part changes from ascent to descent and we find that while the right hand continues with its spinning pattern, the left hand has a series of striding arpeggios which cover the entire range of Mozart's piano from the highest note to the lowest. Gradually the storm subsides as the number of notes to the bar are reduced from twenty-four to sixteen and then from twelve to eight, a loss of momentum brought about by simple mathematics. At last the rondo refrain returns, but now the piano has both stanzas without the interpolation of the orchestra. The tension unwinds and a touchingly simple coda brings this most unusual Romance to an end.

The finale, also a Rondo but in a very different style, has the rare indication 'Prestissimo', or 'as fast as possible'. The soloist sets the tempo with a flashing upward arpeggio that is like the spring of a jungle predator. There is no joy here; a demonic energy drives the music forward so that we feel that emotions that were bottled up in the first movement are now allowed to run riot. Indeed the syncopations that characterised the first movement exposition appear in even greater agitation as an ascending chromatic scale (in minims) seems to be opening a giant doorway to the abyss into which Don Giovanni ultimately fell.[8] Audiences of the day must have been astounded to

---

[8] The 'judgement' scene in the opera is in the same key—D minor.

find such ferocity in the last movement of a concerto, normally a cue for relaxation and mirth.

Whether by chance or design, the soloist, after this orchestral mael-strom, seems to have a variant of the initial entry in the first movement, the A–C sharp-D progression being common to both; but since it could also be said to be derived from the opening phrase of the finale one should not read too much significance into this. The frequent rests give the theme a breathless quality and it is soon swept away with a return to the opening rondo subject. A shrewd alteration of one note in the bass (C sharp becomes C natural) allows Mozart to modulate into F major, a move which brings some emotional relief even though the activity is unabated.

Suddenly, as if from nowhere, the pianist produces a completely new theme in F minor whose humdrum accompaniment gives it a somewhat rustic air. The woodwind take it over briefly before coming to a harmonic impasse out of which the pianist tries to wriggle his way. The deadlock is broken and for the first time in the movement there is a suggestion of laughter. A virtuoso passage culminating in a trill brings out the sunshine with an enchanting tune in Mozart's wittiest vein. Surprisingly it comes from the orchestra:

Ex. 1

The soloist feels that this is too good to be left to the working classes and happily appropriates it; yet within seconds the smile is wiped off our faces with a striking return to the initial rondo theme, no less savage than it was before. The orchestra respond with a compressed version of the opening tutti, after which the piano initiates a substantial development of the two main themes. (The presence of such a development justifies the term *sonata-rondo* to describe the form of the movement.) The development is shared between piano and orchestra, often in rapid altercation. It is lengthy but easy to follow since the actual thematic material is very concise. At last Ex. 1 reappears, though it is now curiously ambivalent in tonality, aspiring to D major but constantly pulled back into the minor. This indecision is not finally resolved until after the cadenza—which on no account should anticipate the reconciliation to come. Most unusually the cadenza ends not with an orchestral postlude but with a last statement of the initial rondo theme by the soloist, a statement that he himself cuts short with some dramatic chords.

There is a silence. Horns quietly sound a 'dominant' A and then the oboe comes dancing in with Ex. 1, now in D major and completely at ease. The soloist happily takes it over, causing general rejoicing in the orchestra. Slower-moving harmonies allow us to relax even more as the piano part chatters away inconsequentially. The woodwind play games with Ex. 1, eliciting such hoots of pleasure from the horns that they ultimately spread through the whole orchestra as though everyone must share in the relief that the storm is over.

In the period in which he lived Mozart could scarcely have ended this concerto in the grim mood in which it began; his audiences liked to be entertained, not harrowed. (Even Brahms in his massive concerto in the same key felt compelled to end on a more optimistic note.) Where Mozart is so skilful is in his use of tonality; until the joyous coda begins there has not been a single bar in the entire work that could be said to be in D *major*, and it is this final emergence into the sunlight that registers so strongly to even an untrained ear.

Piano Concerto in C Minor
K.491

In the early spring of 1786, Mozart composed two piano concertos whose emotional content could scarcely be more contrasted. The one in A major, K.488, has a first movement that is all sunlight, a central Adagio whose tender melancholy has a suggestion of a serenade sung by a lover who knows that his cause has little hope of fruition, while the finale bubbles over with exuberant high spirits. This concerto, one of the most instantly lovable works he ever wrote, was completed on 2nd March. Within twenty-two days he had finished the C minor concerto, once aptly described as the first symphony with piano. The sunny introductory theme of K.488 is replaced by a stern unison opening filled with menace; the slow movement has some of the most elaborately scored passages for woodwind that he ever wrote in a concerto; the finale is a set of variations on a theme whose severe austerity is only occasionally mellowed by more yielding harmonies. The orchestra throughout has a more important part to play than is usual in the concertos, a factor which he seems to have had in mind from the first since he chose the largest forces available with horns, trumpets and timpani to reinforce the woodwind and strings.[9]

The opening theme is strikingly unusual, notable for the angular distortions which, while accepting the tonality of C minor, seem also to be resisting it by introducing a number of foreign notes.

Ex. 1

The effect of the oboes' entry above these stark unisons is extraordinarily poignant, but then any indulgence in self-pity is swept away by the dramatic repetition of the theme at full orchestral strength. For twenty-two bars Mozart treats us to an awe-inspiring display of sheer power so that we may well wonder how the frail voice of the fortepiano will be able to make any impression. A new theme now appears, easily recognised with its three repeated notes followed by a rising octave. Scored for solo oboe with support from two bassoons, it offers a total contrast to the preceding storm. It soon evolves into a beautiful demonstration of Mozart's skill in counterpoint with descending scale passages flowing smoothly from one instrument to another while the threefold repetition initiated by the oboe continues to make its presence felt, albeit with a new ending tacked on to it. This gentle interlude continues for some twenty-eight bars before it is engulfed in a fierce reprise of the opening theme, now given to the bass. Its fury dissolves in a plaintive sequence of three-note phrases, circling through narrow intervals against which the woodwind offer comments based either on descending scales or ascending chromaticisms. A taut and astringent dotted rhythm provides yet another element in this unusually rich and varied tutti in which five distinct themes can be identified even though the transition from one to another is so smoothly accomplished that all might be said to be related.

[9]It is the first concerto in which he uses pairs of clarinets *and* oboes.

None of them proves to be exactly to the soloist's liking for here, as in the D minor concerto, Mozart gives the pianist material which avoids competition with the orchestra. However, although the first entry seems to be completely new, closer examination reveals that it is subtly derived from the orchestral exposition; the quaver descent in the second bar has been hinted at a number of times in the woodwind, while the three repeated crotchets in the third bar have featured prominently as a 'second subject', even though in a rather different treatment. For eighteen bars the piano part sustains a mood that is both withdrawn and submissive, far indeed from the romantic concept of the soloist as hero-figure. The orchestra responds brutally with an aggressive re-statement of Theme I—but only for six bars, for on the seventh the pianist steals a phrase from them, extending it with wide leaps that span an octave and a half or more. For the first time the orchestra begins to accept an accompanying role as the piano introduces a long decorative passage in semiquavers that ultimately unwinds into the key of E flat major. Here we meet the true second subject which Mozart has held back especially for the soloist. The four falling quavers with which it begins establish a satisfying relationship with several previous events and the theme is duly approved by an oboe and a clarinet who decide that it has the makings of a charming duet.

A substantial development follows, offering the pianist considerably more opportunities for virtuosity, while the wind instruments are given circling phrases that are of more thematic importance. Step by step a rising sequence leads us towards a climax that finally resolves on a cadential trill. With notable generosity Mozart now produces a gracious new theme which passes in a descending chain through oboe, clarinet, bassoons and horns in turn. One might regard it as a charming orchestral interlude, but then the pianist takes it over, adding delightful embellishments so that we are compelled to ask can this be a *second* 'second subject'?[10] (Unfortunately Mozart is less than helpful to the aspiring musical analyst since this theme reappears in the recapitulation *before* the 'other' second subject, while its transposition into the minor gives it a far more serious mien.)

Once this pretty diversion is over a solo flute brings back Theme I in the rarely exploited key of E flat minor,[11] accompanied by a fairly active piano part. The music is soon on the borderline between sharp and flat tonalities, the scales of F sharp major and G flat major being identical on the keyboard although different in theory. (String players can actually make the difference audible, but even pianists find a different emotional response to the extreme sharp and flat keys. For example one could not imagine César Franck choosing to write the last section of the Symphonic Variations[12] in G flat

[10] Two helpings from the sweet trolley are not unknown.
[11] Keys with numerous flats created serious problems of intonation.
[12] See Vol. I, pp. 251–3.

instead of F sharp; even though the notes would be the same the 'feel' of
F sharp is much brighter.) As though aware of the tonal no man's land into
which he has wandered, Mozart gives us a very unusual sight in the score
with pianist and strings playing in F sharp major while oboe and bassoon
stick manfully to G flat. A descending sequence of diminished sevenths,
a chord that 'belongs' to no key, enables him to regain the desirable haven of
E flat major, an arrival that is confirmed a number of times as if to restore
some stability to the proceedings.

A two-bar cadential trill rounds off this section, at which point the
orchestra produces an interesting modification of the second part of Theme I,
less distorted than it was at first, and, a little surprisingly, staying in E flat
major. Nineteen bars later the pianist reintroduces the pattern of the original
solo entry, no longer as forlorn as it was initially, since it, too, is now in the
major. It is a release from sorrow that is short-lived for a brief interjection
from the woodwind shifts the music back into the minor, a move to which
the pianist's left hand in particular gives an eloquent response. Theme I
reappears powerfully in the orchestra, initiating an extensive development
section that sustains an extremely troubled mood for several pages. Such
momentary silences as the soloist is allowed are filled with agitated syncopations from the orchestra. At last a cascade of scales leads to a point that we can
identify with some conviction as the recapitulation. Even here Mozart has a
surprise for us for the emphatic orchestral statement is cut short by the
soloist. However, despite the compressions and changes of key, the material
from this landmark onwards is familiar.

An interesting example of Mozart's use of musical shorthand occurs just
before the orchestral tutti that leads up to the cadenza. For four bars the
pianist is given an arpeggio figure that rises and falls through two octaves;
suddenly the semiquaver figuration ceases and is replaced by a single dotted
minim in each of the ensuing four bars. An examination of the original
manuscript shows that these bars come close to the end of a page; there is
simply no room for the arpeggios to continue. Mozart therefore noted the
outer notes only, trusting the intelligence of the performer to understand
their significance. There is no doubt whatever that the semiquaver figuration
should continue.

Sadly, Mozart left no cadenza; with material of such dramatic potential
one would love to know what he might have done in the way of improvisation. That it was unorthodox we can be fairly sure for the conventional final
trill to cue in the orchestra is omitted; indeed the orchestral entry is unusually
stormy, appearing to snatch an octave passage of great power from the
soloist's hands. For twenty-two bars the orchestra continues, apparently
heading for the final cadence by a route already charted at the end of the
original exposition. Yet again Mozart surprises us for at the very moment
that we expect the movement to finish the pianist re-enters with a sequence of
gently rippling arpeggios, against which the woodwind make a series of

neatly interwoven references to the second part of Theme I. Despite the menace of a sustained rumble from the timpani the movement ends *pianissimo*, an extraordinary refusal to bow to convention by earning easy applause.

The slow movement has an unusual tempo indication for Mozart, *Larghetto*. After the storms of the first movement the simple unaffected beauty of the E flat major theme is like balm to the anguished spirit. The initial four-bar refrain for solo piano is repeated by the orchestra, the woodwind seeming concerned to hush the over-emphatic strings. The pianist then begins an extension of the tune which, as is often the case, has more of the character of an operatic aria than a passage from a concerto. (It invites ornamentation of some sort from the performer.) After a pause, the opening phrase returns and is gently folded away with a cadence of some finality.

The ensuing episode is elaborately scored for the wind section; although it is deeply expressive, the new key of C minor and the occasional swift roulades for flute or bassoon bring a feeling of agitation that is at odds with the serenity of the opening. The soloist accepts the change of character, providing elaborate variants of the woodwind phrases. Then, as if repenting these somewhat extravagant gestures, he returns to the sublime opening theme. This time Mozart only allows us four bars before producing another episode. The woodwind are again predominant but the key, A flat major, is less disturbing than C minor while the soloist's variations are more lyrical. For a third time the initial rondo theme appears, complete with its 'operatic' extension. Over a strangely pulsating bass from a deep-voiced french horn the woodwind produce delicious sighs and fluttering scales to which the soloist adds a graceful comment. This closing section is truly aristocratic music, all elegance and affectation with only a fussy bassoon disturbing the calm like an over-solicitous waiter clearing the table for the next course.

The finale is less precipitate than usual, a set of variations on a rather sedate theme that stands on the borderline between serious and comic, rather like Osmin's arias in *Il Seraglio*. The two sections of the theme are repeated, enabling us to absorb the very clearly defined harmonic scheme which is preserved virtually intact through the first three variations. The third of these generates a more martial character with its strongly dotted rhythms and aggressive triplets in the left hand of the piano part. All is forgiven in the fourth variation which takes us into A flat major and a light-footed dance scored for clarinets and bassoons with occasional support from the horns. The change of character is considerable even although the relationship to the theme remains clear.

Variation five, almost solely for piano, is musically the most remarkable, a return to the opening key of C minor, its previously clear outlines now distorted by poignant chromaticisms that add greatly to the emotional intensity. There is a real feeling of despair here, and the subsequent emergence into C major through the good offices of oboe and bassoon brings a sense of release from pain that is duly welcomed by soloist and audience alike.

The seventh variation brings a return to C minor and a clear reminder of the theme in its original form. (The pianist's interruptions are pure decoration adding nothing of significance.) A short cadenza, left to the soloist to provide, leads into the final variation which breaks capriciously into 6/8, changing the tears of variation five into chuckles of delight. Even so, the entrance of the orchestra brings a more sombre note and it cannot be said that joy is unconfined; indeed the closing bars of the piano part seem to move increasingly into the shadows, shadows from which the final upward rush in the orchestra extricates us with some brusqueness. Neither in the first nor the third movement is Mozart in the mood to make concessions and we cannot help being taken by surprise by the endings of both. Here is a concerto in which entertainment is a very secondary consideration; if his effete audience found it too strong meat, so much the worse for them.

Piano Concerto in B flat Major
K.595

Although we do not know for whom this, the last of Mozart's concertos, was actually intended, it seems probable that he had a pupil or friend in mind since, had he written it for himself, it would almost certainly have provided more opportunities for the display of virtuosity.[13] It is in fact one of the most restrained and intimate of his works in this genre, bringing the spirit of chamber music into the concert-hall. Trumpets and timpani are banished; one flute and a pair each of oboes, bassoons and horns are all that is required to augment the usual complement of strings. The work was finished in January 1791, a mere eleven months before his death, but it is falsely sentimental to see its reticence as in any way a withdrawal from life. He was affected not by premonitions of the future but by recollections of the past, for the previous two years had been the most disastrous he had known, so much so that the fount of inspiration had almost dried up. Dogged by financial and domestic worries, his inability to find any post worthy of his genius was like a running sore, damaging to his pride and to his health. If in such circumstances the absence of extrovert display comes as no surprise, the sheer beauty of the work seems the more remarkable; yet it is the beauty of autumn rather than

[13] The fact that he played it on 4th March, 1791, need not invalidate this supposition; his provision of cadenzas is strong evidence that he had another performer in mind.

summer and though at a casual hearing the music may seem carefree enough, any deeper acquaintance will reveal its underlying sadness.

Symptomatic of this is the very beginning of the concerto. Innumerable works of Mozart and his contemporaries begin with a formula—a strong unison phrase to establish the key, followed by a more openly expressive and quiet rejoinder. Here the positions are reversed. After a quiet introductory bar (itself a very unusual feature) the violins propose the key of B flat in the most lyrical way. Their soft and gracious utterance elicits a terse military response from unison wind and horns—exactly the type of phrase one would normally expect to open a work. The violins plead their cause even more tenderly but meet with the same brusque reply. Refusing to be provoked, the strings continue to proffer their gestures of conciliation until, in bar thirteen, they startle us with a sudden flare of temper which momentarily recalls a phrase from the finale of the 'Jupiter' Symphony, completed two and a half years previously. It is enough to bring about a measure of agreement between the two sections of the orchestra who now begin a neat exchange of civilities which, however, are terminated by another flurry of notes from the strings and strongly marked rhythms from the wind.

The lead into the second subject is a little tremulous but the theme, once it materialises, covers a wide span in a descending scale; its second element is curiously chirpy, almost bird-like; but then the descending scale appears again, tinged with sadness by its minor inflections. There is a sudden change of mood as a quiet but urgent figure begins in the strings, swiftly building to a climax and then receding again. (It is the sort of pattern that Rossini was often to employ in his overtures.) There is a feeling of anticipation and excitement in the air but Mozart is not yet ready to introduce his soloist. Instead he turns again towards the minor with a wistful theme in the violins. It finishes with a serpentine coil of quavers which is taken up with increasing emphasis, ending with a touch of almost military authority. The exposition might well have ended here but Mozart is in no mood for bravado and tacks on a couple of graceful little phrases that greet the soloist with a curtsy instead of a salute.

With such undramatic material there is no need to give the piano an independent entry; we therefore find a decorated version of the lyrical violin theme which began the work. The brief fanfare with which it had been interrupted becomes a quiet nod of approval from the strings. The music is in Mozart's most limpid vein until the arresting 'Jupiter' theme excites a more active response from the soloist. A short bravura passage follows, rounded off by a couple of vehement bars from the full orchestra. Since these originally prepared the way for the second subject, we are justified in supposing that it will reappear at this point. Instead, the soloist makes an unexpected excursion into F minor, introducing a heart-rending phrase of such beauty that neither the flute nor the oboe can resist the impulse to add an expressive descant. The bulk of the orchestra shows little sympathy with a harsh interruption in unison. With delicate wit the soloist transforms their anger into an enchanting dialogue between the two hands, its outline etched in by pizzicato strings.

This episode is soon over and Mozart puts us back on course by returning to the 'exchange of civilities' from the exposition, now divided between piano and flute. With little fuss the second subject re-enters, only to be brushed aside by the 'Rossini' pattern which the pianist clearly enjoys. It is a moment of frivolity which sombre chords on the woodwind do their best to quell, though with little effect on the pianist.

A short orchestral tutti follows, more turbulent in mood than anything we have experienced so far. Its final bars are hesitant, uncertain which path to follow. We are unlikely to guess their destination, B minor, a key which is a direct denial of all that is essential to the 'home' tonality of B flat. It is the start of one of the most remarkable development sections in all Mozart. There is nothing fundamentally new or irrelevant yet everything is changed, whether it is the function of individual phrases, their relationship to each other, their proportions or their tonality. To list each happening would be laborious, but any listener who has properly absorbed the original exposition can scarcely fail to appreciate the ingenuity with which Mozart rearranges it. Not once in forty-nine amazingly inventive bars is there a single phrase in B flat, so that the ultimate arrival at the reprise brings a very special feeling of release from suspense; yet in the whole passage there are only two bars of *forte*. (Four half-bars to be precise!) It is a masterly demonstration of the powers of under-statement such as one might expect in a string quartet but not in a concerto. (The statistically-minded may care to note that Mozart pays fleeting visits to no less than eleven keys during this *tour-de-force*.)[14] After so adventurous a journey it is hardly surprising that the recapitulation follows an orthodox course, the only remaining surprise being the quiet ending.

The slow movement begins with a phrase that speaks of that 'sweet sorrow' which Juliet felt as she bade Romeo good-night. Its melting refrain is taken up by the orchestra before the piano embarks on one of those sublimated 'arias' which are such a feature of these movements; but it is only allowed to take wing for eight bars before returning to the opening theme. Its ruminative melancholy evokes two profound sighs from the orchestra; but then the tone becomes more impassioned, temporarily silencing the soloist.

Another and more extensive 'aria' follows with a discreetly throbbing accompaniment from the strings. In due course a rising sequence of trills leads us back to the opening (rondo) theme which is once again followed by the first 'aria'. Now comes one of the strangest sounding passages Mozart ever wrote: the piano has the theme exactly as it was before, but the tune is doubled at the same octave by a solo flute and an octave *lower* by the violins.

---

[14] B minor, C major, C minor, E flat major, E flat minor, F sharp major, A flat major, F minor, G minor, G major, D minor. Several are visited twice.

Add a slight discrepancy of notation which makes it appear as though 'they're not together' and you have a positively eccentric experiment which puzzles performers to this day. The remainder of the movement presents no such problems, its closing bars so serenely beautiful that any soloist must feel reluctant to break the spell by embarking on the final Allegro.

This has a loping gait that is far from being a jig. True, there is a suggestion of the 'hunting' movements that were popular at the time, but we are riding decorously with the ladies, side-saddle. The occasional noisy incursions from the orchestra should not be allowed to destroy the essential delicacy of the music. It is worth noting that a few days after completing the concerto Mozart used the recurring theme of the finale for a song, 'Sehnsucht nach dem Frühlinge' (Yearning for Spring), and the vital word 'Yearning' gives us an important clue as to the tempo. The superficially happy theme drifts into the minor from time to time, casting a shadow that can only be shaken off with some effort. A detailed analysis would be wearisome since the music lacks complexity, behaving according to the well-established principles of a rondo. An illuminating comparison can be made between this movement and the finale of Beethoven's Piano Concerto No. 2 in the same key. Beethoven's music appears bouncy, vigorous and witty, full of youthful confidence. By comparison Mozart seems rarified and infinitely subtle. One feels that he had come to accept that try as he might he was not going to impress a heedless aristocracy; it was one thing to be their darling as a child prodigy but an altogether different matter to be accepted as an adult genius of disturbing versatility. This concerto is not a farewell to life itself but it is perhaps a farewell to the role of public performer. To quote the great Mozart scholar Alfred Einstein, 'It is so perfect that the question of style has become meaningless'.

The Symphonies

Lacking the inestimable advantage of a resident orchestra such as Haydn had throughout most of his maturity, it is almost surprising that Mozart produced the number of symphonies that he did—more than fifty if we include perhaps a dozen youthful works now presumably lost for ever. His first essays in the form date from a very early period when, as an eight-year-old in London, he came under the influence of Johann Christian Bach. As we might expect such childhood works as the First Symphony (K.16: Dec. 1764 or Jan. '65) are short in duration and show a lack of adventure in the treatment of the material; but they were to set a useful pattern for him to follow, although at this stage three movements was the norm. By a charming coincidence the slow movement of the First Symphony contains a four-note motif (*do-re-fa-mi*) which, allowing for transposition, exactly corresponds with the opening theme of the last movement of his final symphony, the 'Jupiter'. Thus a single strand links the first and last symphonies, spanning virtually the whole of his creative life. (A. Hyatt King in his book *Mozart in Retrospect*[15] has traced twelve other works of Mozart's in which the same motif is to be found. It seems likely that it was originally given to the child as part of an exercise in counterpoint and that it remained lodged in his memory. There are other instances of childhood seeds bearing fruit in later years; a theme from the Symphony in B flat (K.22, 1765) reappears in *Figaro*.)

Although J. C. Bach had the strongest personal influence on Mozart at this critical early time, all his early symphonies follow what we now call the 'Italian' style.[16] It was derived from the opera-house and was essentially a development of the Overture, itself often called a *Sinfonia*. A brisk first movement with two markedly contrasting ideas would be followed by an expressive slow movement with a short and brilliant finale to round things off. (This last was usually a Rondo with two contrasting episodes to serve as foils to the recurring theme.) The extra Minuet inserted before the finale was a German innovation which in due course came to be accepted almost universally, the more so when it was transformed into the more exciting Scherzo.

The prime purpose of the symphonies Mozart wrote during his adolescence was to serve as 'samples' such as a commercial traveller might tout in the hope of gaining commissions. Since his travels took him to Italy it was only politic to write works that would appeal to the Italian taste. Between 1770 and 1773 he produced no fewer than twenty-seven symphonies; most were written to a formula and must have cost him little effort, but individual movements occasionally stand out from the rest, giving indications of the mastery that was to come. The year 1773 seems to have been something of a turning-point; a stay in Vienna during the summer enabled the still impressionable Mozart to hear a great deal of music that stimulated him to new thoughts about the art of symphonic writing. Haydn's compositions in particular were a revelation, causing the younger man to realise the potential of counterpoint, especially in final movements. Here was a challenge that was to bring a new maturity to Mozart's orchestral works and he responded with three symphonies that show a considerable advance on their predecessors; that in G minor (K.183) is profoundly disturbing, exploiting agitated syncopations, extreme contrasts of volume and violent accents; the C major symphony (K.200) is less openly emotional but has many points of originality with a conspicuous horn part in the Minuet and an exceptionally brilliant

[15] O.U.P., 1955.
[16] J.C. Bach had himself studied in Italy under Padre Martini.

finale. As for the symphony in A (K.201), it must surely be counted as the gem of the three, as we shall see in due course.

The advent of the Colloredo regime and the return to Salzburg caused Mozart to turn away from the symphony as a musical form; his philistine employer demanded lighter fare, serenades and divertimenti. But in 1778 a commission for a symphony came from Paris, bringing with it the opportunity to write for a substantially larger orchestra than he had previously employed. Mozart knew that the Paris orchestra was second in reputation only to that of Mannheim, where he had been introduced to clarinets for the first time and where the standard of performance was such that Dr Burney had described the orchestra as 'an army of generals' (1772). The symphony Mozart produced to impress the Parisian audiences was in certain respects 'made to measure'; the bold unison opening catered to their liking for a strong attack—*le premier coup d'archet* (the first stroke of the bow); the brilliance of the orchestration was designed to show off the virtuosity of the players. When told that the slow movement was too long for comfort, he accepted the criticism with a good grace and quickly provided an alternative. He dispensed with the Minute and, taking a leaf from Haydn's book, composed a finale that included a fugal section so as to show off his skill as a contrapuntist. He had high hopes that a wealthy patron might be sufficiently impressed to offer him a worthwhile post, but nothing of interest was forthcoming.

On his return to Salzburg he wrote two more symphonies (K.319 and K.338), the first a relatively light-weight work scored for a necessarily smaller orchestra, the second a more significant reflection of his Parisian experience. Both were originally planned as three-movement works but on his move to Vienna to make a bid for independence, Mozart added minuets and even revised the scoring by writing extra flute-parts. Although the remaining symphonies belong to his Viennese period two are associated with other cities, the 'Linz' (K.425) and the 'Prague' (K.504). The influence of Haydn becomes increasingly apparent when, in the 'Linz' symphony, we find (for the first time in Mozart's symphonies) a slow introduction; however, although Mozart was willing to learn from Haydn in matters of structure, the idiom and the emotional content remained very much his own. The 'Prague' symphony (1786), written for the city where he scored his greatest public successes with *Figaro* and *Don Giovanni*, again reverts to the three-movement format, but this in no way diminishes its stature which is of the finest.

Nearly two years separate the 'Prague' symphony from the final great trilogy, symphonies 39–41. They represent one of the most remarkable feats of composition ever accomplished since they were composed in less than two months—a period in which Mozart also wrote quite a substantial number of lesser works. They form an astonishing crown to his career as a symphonic composer, a career that extended from child prodigy to mature genius and which in sheer variety of achievement has never been rivalled.

Symphony No. 29 in A Major
K.201

The opening of this symphony is a magical example of the way in which genius can transform a commonplace idea. In essence all that Mozart does in the first eight bars (plus one beat) is to progress up the first four notes of the scale and back again: A–B–C♯–D–C♯–B–A. But while these may be the bare bones, they are given the most seductive flesh, a dropping octave followed by a tenderly caressing figure that literally seems to stroke the principal note.

Ex. 1

Meanwhile the lower strings provide a soft bed of harmony that helps to give this phrase an unforgettable allure. Who would suspect that after a few bars of musical chit-chat from the violins this enchanting theme would become a topic for strenuous argument between the upper and lower strings, the violas and cellos insisting on their rights even though they are half a bar behind? The conflict is resolved rather noisily, leaving nerves frayed, as the sudden alternations between *p* and *f* reveal. A striding bass brings us to the threshold of the second subject, an innocent little tune whose initial repeated crotchets suggest that here is a song in the making. The violas seem to play tenor to the violins' soprano, adding approving echoes at the end of phrases. A sudden outburst from the full orchestra causes a brief disturbance but soon the music becomes even more operatic with a loving exchange between first and second violins followed by a delightful 'quartet' suitable for some ditty about birds in the springtime. This quasi-operatic episode is dismissed sternly as altogether too frivolous and the exposition ends with a 'no more nonsense' establishment of the dominant key of E major. A graceful gesture for violins alone leads us back to the beginning for the mandatory repeat.

It is a gesture that is put to more serious purpose at the beginning of the development, switching the tonality to D major. Development is really the wrong word to use for Mozart makes only the most cursory reference to any previous events. There is a certain amount of interplay based on rising or falling scales followed by a stormy descent into F sharp minor. In a moment of spontaneous caprice Mozart introduces a completely new theme in the first violins with the simplest of 'vamped' accompaniments. Once again we feel the lure of the opera-house, the more so when this brief 'aria' develops into an 'ensemble' in which the suggestion of voices is almost irresistible. (Mozart was engaged in writing the opera *La finta giardiniera* at much the same time.)

After this diversion Mozart can afford to have a formal recapitulation, following the plan of the exposition closely except for the alterations needed to bring the second subject into the 'home' key. One surprise awaits us, though, a coda which begins with a note of enquiry from the violins. 'Should we finish here?' they seem to ask. 'Not yet' says Mozart and proceeds to interlock Ex. 1 at three different levels, violins, cellos and violas overlapping at half-bar intervals. A rousing finish solicits applause, something that is still missing in so-called 'authentic' performances today but which Mozart would have been dismayed not to receive.[17]

The Andante that follows is a pastoral sonata-form movement without the conflict of moods that the word sonata usually implies. Mozart asks for the violins to be muted, a request that should probably be passed on to the violas as well with orchestras of the quality we now have. (Violas in eighteenth-century opera-houses were said to be the last refuge of horn-players who had lost their teeth!) The music is beautifully poised, with a rhythm that conveys a lazy reluctance to move from one principal note to the next. (It is something of a paradox to find that double-dotted quavers here suggest languor whereas in Handel or Purcell they would demand a vigorous treatment.) The four-bar melody with which the movement begins is taken over by the second violins, giving the 'firsts' the opportunity to provide an enchanting descant. The intrusion of oboes and horns is handled with great delicacy, confirming the outdoor serenade character of the music. In the fourteenth bar the violins introduce a more sustained melodic line which, having flowered briefly, breaks off with a sigh. First and second violins exchange whispered confidences before a more elaborately decorated third subject appears, too important to be written off as a mere *codetta*. That comes with a sudden change to a triplet rhythm in the violins.

This new rhythmic pattern proves to be very important in the central section of the movement, which again is more like an episode in a rondo than a true development. The softly buzzing trills in the violins suggest the hum of insects in a summer garden, while the long-sustained notes on horns or oboes give a feeling of stillness that prevents the prevailing triplets from sounding fussy. (It is possible that Mozart was influenced by a symphony of J. C. Bach that exploits a similar figure.) The final coda brings a surprise, a sudden *forte* that is like a summons, perhaps calling us in from the garden to take part in the ensuing Minuet.

---

[17] He even expressed his delight when an audience applauded a modulation in the *middle* of a movement!

Despite its air of formality this is a highly original movement. The first phrase, a duet for the two violin sections, is almost tentative; but then its daintiness is mocked by a sudden blast for full orchestra. An elegant curtsy is likewise parodied, whereupon oboes and horns in unison hammer out a somewhat uncouth rhythm. Knowing Mozart's feelings about his ungracious employer, it seems possible that he is having a sly dig at the ill-mannered and clumsy-footed aristocrats, for each graceful feminine phrase is followed by a coarse response. Even the smoothly flowing Trio is disfigured by grotesque accents on the third (theoretically weakest) beat of the bar as though overfed and drunken men are tripping over their own toes. Remember that this symphony was written shortly after Mozart had returned from a summer in Vienna, a return he must have found particularly irksome since for the first time he felt the repressive atmosphere that came with Colloredo's accession to power.

The fourth movement is a fiery *Allegro con spirito* whose opening theme is subjected to intensive development at a later stage. There is a youthful exuberance about the music that makes it positively sizzle with excitement, while the conspicuous horn parts are clearly designed to conjure up reminders of the hunt. The second subject is notable for the curious flicks in the first violin part, as though the players were fanning themselves after their initial exertions, leaving the theme to their colleagues in the second desks. Notice also the dramatic ending to the exposition, a scale that fairly rockets into the air after a pause to light the fuse.

The essentially operatic nature of Mozart's thought is demonstrated clearly in the development when a fine duet is enjoyed between the basses and the violins, the 'male' cellos and basses, domineering and arrogant, the 'female' violins cowering in the face of such a display of wrath. As for the final Coda, it is easily recognised since it begins with a grand gesture, the only time in the whole movement when the opening theme is played by all the strings—and oboes—in unison. The last 'rocket' is a test of nerve for players and conductor alike and must have caused the eighteen-year old Mozart much amusement in rehearsal.

Symphony No. 38 in D Major (The 'Prague') K.504

If the opening bars of the Symphony No. 29 can be described as ingratiating, what we find here is something altogether different—'forbidding' might be a suitable word to convey the austere severity of the initial gestures. The additional forces used—flutes, bassoons, trumpets and timpani—all make their presence felt with the first awe-inspiring note, a massive unison D that starts loud and is instantly suppressed. The four curt phrases that follow are like a giant clearing his throat, and it is worth pointing out that up until the second beat of the third bar we have no way of knowing if the music is going to be in D major or D *minor*. The Adagio tempo and the harsh unisons tilt the balance in favour of the minor, so much so that when the strings timidly spell out the arpeggio of D major in bar 3 the assumption is instantly contradicted in the following bar by a ferocious assertion of B minor; the strings then make a placatory gesture by offering G major, to which the woodwind make a forlorn response in E minor. The point is worth stressing, for Mozart's dramatic sense has caused him to jettison two of his most reliable formulae— a clear statement of tonality and a symmetrical balance between masculine and feminine aspects of the opening material. Here we find not only an introduction whose scale is comparable to that of Beethoven's Second Symphony, but one whose lack of tonal stability is even more striking than the notoriously enigmatic opening to Beethoven's First. If we accept that the first two bars, however arresting, are tonally ambiguous, we must also realise the startling surprises involved in establishing four different keys in the next four bars, while the expected soft-loud-soft-loud symmetry is destroyed by that last forlorn woodwind cadence.

Violins now begin a strangely wandering line that makes an unconvincing attempt to establish D major, only to find itself drifting into E minor. A slow chromatic descent in unison violins seems to be heading for D major once more, but again expectation is foiled and the phrase tails off into B minor, a deviation which is sadly confirmed by the flutes and oboes. As if determined to break this compulsion to move into minor keys, the whole orchestra produces a massive cadence into G *major*. It is an option the woodwind refuse to accept, but hope dawns in the following bar when a cadence into D major really does seem inevitable, even though the quietness of the phrase may suggest a lack of absolute conviction. Any doubts we may have are fully justified for we are suddenly and brutally plunged into D *minor*, a move which provokes an agitated and fearful response from the violins. And now the symmetry does become relentless, with massive chords like hammer-blows alternating with cries for mercy. With each blast from the full orchestra the tonality shifts again, passing from B flat via its dominant to G minor and then through the always enigmatic diminished seventh to A. An impassioned lament from the strings—D minor again—is interrupted by chromatic wails from the woodwind while the timpani add their menace in a continuous rumble. Gradually the music seems to disintegrate although the tonality is no longer in doubt; the symphony may be *in* D major, but up to this point only three bars (3, 11 and 15) have actually been in that key. This introduction is an overture fit for a tragedy; with what delight Mozart must have decided to turn so fierce a frown into a smile, for what follows is high comedy, taking us completely unawares.[18]

The slightly uneasy syncopations with which the violins begin the main part of the movement (*Allegro*) suggest that the emotional disturbance generated by the introduction has not been entirely forgotten, but by the fifth bar the repeated notes quicken into a patter not unlike the happy little theme that emerges from the solemn introduction to *The Magic Flute*. Horns and trumpets greet the transformation with a joyous fanfare, though we should also take note of the flutes and oboes whose octave rise followed by a descending scale will prove to be more important than we imagine. A solo oboe tries to introduce a note of pathos but to little effect and soon the second violins and violas are chattering excitedly about the *Magic Flute* rhythm while the first violins offer a fragment of a theme which would appear to have some potential. (In fact Mozart finds that its first three notes (A–F♯–D) are enough to provide him with a springboard for some dramatic developments at a later point.) With a whirling figure in the strings and strongly accented offbeats the music develops new energy, driving forward forcefully towards a loudly repeated unison A. By all the normal standards of symphonic structures this should herald the arrival of the second subject, but Mozart is no longer hidebound by any established conventions. The surprise he has in store for us will be appreciated only by a listener knowledgeable enough to anticipate what *ought* to happen and to whom, therefore, a return to the opening material will come as a shock. What should be even more of a surprise is the extensive development we now find of the *Magic Flute* rhythm, and it is at this point that we can hear how productive the little three-note motif mentioned above can be. Four brilliant ascending scales are a landmark that we can scarcely miss, warning us that the second subject is due to make its delayed appearance. Its fundamental shape is anticipated by three graceful little gestures in the violins; the theme itself is playful in its teasing rotations of a recurring pattern. An unexpected excursion into A minor encourages the bassoons to join in, and it is they who, after some chromatic vacillation, restore the subject to its proper key of A major. The violins, not to be outdone, produce a delightful descant before the 'whirling' pattern jerks us out of these trivialties and, with the help of its subsidiary ideas, brings the exposition to a vigorous close.

By this time Mozart's conception of what development really implied had matured enormously. Instead of the charming but largely irrelevant episode that he gave us in the Symphony No. 29 we find intricately woven counterpoint shedding new light on material culled from the exposition. The example of Haydn's mastery is here used to good purpose as for nearly thirty bars he occupies himself almost exclusively with three fragments—the

---

[18] This juxtaposition of moods is exactly comparable to Beethoven's Second Symphony, also in D.

rising octave and descending scale first heard on flutes and oboes in bars 7–9 of the Allegro, the repeated note pattern I have described as the *Magic Flute* rhythm and the whirling figure that first initiated a more energetic mood. He juggles with these with consummate skill, whether as closely-knit canons or by combining one with another in unsuspected ways.

The central climax to the development comes with those emphatically repeated unison As which misled us earlier into thinking the second subject was imminent; but Mozart has not exhausted his material yet. Having dropped in a brief reminder of the beginning of the movement in case it has slipped our memory, he continues to toy with the first two of the three fragments that have been in the foreground so long. A neat exchange between bassoons, oboes and flutes leads to the emotional highspot of the movement, a marvellous descending sequence in the violins that drifts down through several minor keys, gently nudged on its way by violas and cellos until it floats down to the softly syncopated D from which the exposition began. We have reached the recapitulation, which follows a reasonably predictable if somewhat truncated course. Excited quavers on horns, trumpets and timpani proclaim the final coda, displaying all the power Mozart can muster and bringing this extraordinary movement to a brilliant conclusion. Since the largest possible sound is demanded, it may be an appropriate moment to drop in a contentious word about 'authenticity'. It is probable that on only one occasion in his life did Mozart have the chance to conduct a really large orchestra. It had forty violins, ten violas, eight cellos, ten double-basses and no less than six bassoons. The wind instruments were all 'doubled', an ambiguous word in that it could mean the normal two of each or, as I suspect, the normal complement 'doubled', that is to say four of each. At the least, then, the orchestra numbered eighty players (including horns, trumpets and timpani), a number which today would be regarded as grotesquely over-inflated. According to Mozart 'It went *magnifique!'*

The second movement is a Pastorale whose gently lilting 6/8 rhythm is almost like a cradle-song. The deceptively simple opening is soon decorated with lingering chromaticisms which add expressive depth. Five repeated unisons on woodwind and horns provoke a tiny crisis but all is smoothed over by the violins. Long meandering passages of semiquavers suggest a flowing stream, and Mozart, usually more of a townsman than a country boy, here comes very close to the mood of the slow movement of Beethoven's *Pastoral* Symphony. This is especially noticeable towards the middle of the movement and at the end, where the violins have paired notes with intervening silences; there is surely a suggestion of birdsong here. There is even a brief shower of rain as, for a moment or two, smooth legato phrases are displaced by a spatter of staccato notes and a sudden *forte*. Analysis of such a movement is an insult to the listener; there are some exquisite examples of counterpoint, but they are inserted as a bonus, not designed to challenge our intellects.

The absence of a Minuet is a quirk for which no satisfactory reason has ever been found; perhaps Mozart was simply pressed for time; perhaps he felt in no mood for dancing after the delicious languor of the preceding movement. The breathless urgency of the finale conveys something more than mere high spirits, for though the beginning is witty and mercurial, the first passage for full orchestra brings occasional rising sevenths (D–C♯) whose angularity is disturbing, almost painful. A delicate interlude for woodwind moving through D minor to F major is swept away in an intense tutti that has the ruthless drive we associate more readily with Beethoven. The fit of temper is short-lived and it is the violins alone who lead us into the second subject— pure comic opera in which it is almost impossible not to hear imaginary singers enjoying some farcical situation to the full. A solo flute calls us back to the first subject which once again explodes into an unexpectedly violent outburst. Is it to be taken seriously? The violins say not, as they unloose a nimble pattern of triplets which dissolve into giggling trills. The first part of the movement (in fact a sonata-form exposition) is rounded off with a cheerful if noisy affirmation of A major, the 'dominant' key.

A remarkable development ensues with roaring chords putting frightened flutes and oboes to flight. Soon the strings begin a serious discussion of the opening rhythm, modulating through various keys until first the oboes and then the bassoons seem to ask whether it isn't all getting a bit too serious. A recapitulation of sorts begins, though Mozart is unable to resist the temptation to scare us again with his leonine roars. Familiar phrases flash by until, at the last, the violins are called on to make ever more spectacular leaps before bringing the work to a triumphant conclusion. There is a fascinating ambiguity in this finale, for one can imagine two very different interpretations, one displaying the wit, the other showing a sort of desperation, the frenzied dance of a clown who must make us laugh despite a breaking heart.

Symphony No. 39 in E flat Major
K.543

Estimates vary as to the precise time it took Mozart to write the final great trilogy which crowns his contribution to the purely orchestral repertory. What we do have as firm evidence is the completion dates of the scores; Symphony No. 39 was completed on 26th June 1788, No. 40 on 25th July, No. 41 on 10 August. Since he was occupied with other compositions at the same time we can but marvel at the speed with which the work was done;

there is surely no need to quibble about weeks or days. What is as remarkable is the quite different character of three works written in such close proximity.

Like the 'Prague' Symphony the Symphony in E flat begins with a slow introduction, a device that is common in Haydn but rare in Mozart; here, though, we find a solemn majesty which makes the Adagio all of a piece, whereas the introduction to K.504 is, as we have seen, profoundly disturbing. The symphony begins with three impressive gestures, massive chords in ceremonial rhythm linked by echoes from the woodwind and descending scales in the violins. In bars 7–8 the violins have a hesitant phrase that gropes its way upwards as though in search of the 'proper' tonality before returning to the safe haven of the dominant. The next eight bars are securely anchored to what is known as a dominant pedal-point as horns, trumpets and timpani hold firmly to B flats regardless of what may be going on around them. Cellos and basses give additional emphasis with a measured rhythm whose insistent pattern (♩ 𝄾 ♩ 𝄾 ♩ 𝄾 ♩ 𝄾) will ultimately spread to almost the whole orchestra. Meanwhile clarinets and bassoons sustain organ-like harmonies in support of a solo flute whose three-note phrases are more expressive in effect than they would appear to be on paper. Murmuring scales glide softly downwards in the violin parts, emotionally neutral. But when brass and timpani erupt with a strident version of the pervasive dotted rhythm this same scale pattern is transformed by the lower strings so that it seems like a monster heaving itself out of the deep. The music grows more powerful and more dissonant, one violent clash between C and D flat being hammered home with a persistence that must have had the audience wincing at the ugliness of this 'modern' music. (*A History of Modern Music* published in 1862 has as one chapter-heading, 'Extinction of all traces of the old tonality in the works of Mozart' (!)) Surprisingly, after such a display of power, the introduction ends with a quiet, slow-moving gesture which disintegrates into two isolated chords. Such musical silences are almost always like a question-mark; what will follow? Few would guess rightly, for an introduction suitable for a reigning monarch leads to the entry of a young princess.

With striking economy the graceful theme is presented with minimal accompaniment, an unsupported line for violins whose first three notes are echoed by horns. The mood is more akin to a minuet of the most elegant kind than to a normal symphonic first movement, indeed elegance is the key-word to describe these curving phrases which seem to bow and curtsey to each other. Particularly unusual for Mozart is the lack of any contrast in material or volume for twenty-eight leisurely bars. The change, when it comes, is violent and startling, a sudden blast from the full orchestra that gives us a very different view of E flat major. Wide leaps spanning two octaves or more impart a special vigour to the violin parts, while their murmuring scales from the introduction are transformed into angry torrents. Emphatically repeated chords in woodwind and brass mark the beats with a Beethoven-like insistence, a comparison which becomes even more valid when we find a number of repetitions of a driving rhythm much used in the *Eroica* symphony (♫♫♫).

The second subject appears abruptly, as though a door had been slammed on the preceding clamour. It contains three elements, a sinuously descending phrase for the violins, a delicately poised reply from the woodwind and a sustained melody for strings with a pizzicato accompaniment. The tranquillity these charming ideas brings does not last for long and soon we are plunged into an orchestral storm which ends as abruptly as it began. Its final rhythmic pattern, the one comparable to the *Eroica*, appears less confidently in G minor at the start of the development. It is an abberation that earns an instant reprimand from the whole orchestra who, with some coarseness, switch to an oblique view of A flat major. 'That'll do nicely' say the strings, gently reintroducing the third element of the second subject. The respite lasts for a mere thirteen bars before battle is joined between basses and violins, each hurling the *Eroica* rhythm at each other with the utmost ferocity, shifting their ground as they do so until the struggle breaks off at the very threshold of C minor. There is a bar's silence so that players and audience alike can regain their breath. Three pleading phrases from the flute cry 'Enough!'—and indeed it is, for seemingly from nowhere the graceful first subject reappears. Amazingly there has not been a single reference to it since it was so rudely interrupted 159 bars previously; there can be few other symphonies that show so total a disregard for what appears to be the main theme.

The recapitulation follows a more orthodox pattern, making the small alterations necessary to bring the second subject into the home key but providing only a brief final flourish to serve as a coda.

The second movement (*Andante con moto*) starts with deceptive simplicity, four short phrases sharing a common mood but separated from one another by brief silences. This opening sentence is repeated. Mozart then shifts Phrase I to the lower strings, closes the gap so that Phrase II presses close on its heels and initiates a rising sequence which spills over into a long extension of the prevailing rhythm. He then finishes this second section with a return to the opening sentence, now subtly altered but preserving the original proportions.

Four repeated chords from the woodwind lead us into a totally unexpected drama, an impassioned phrase in F minor with an agitated accompaniment. This may be described academically as a 'transition' but if so it is a stormy voyage. Repeated B flats in the violins restore some stability as the woodwind and lower strings attempt to revert to the opening theme, but another storm blows up, with choppy chords in the wind and a heroic dialogue in almost Handelian style between upper and lower strings. An unsupported phrase for the first violins extricates us from this conflict, leading to a moment of pure magic. Above a gently rocking accompaniment the woodwind build up layers of counterpoint of melting beauty, each entry beginning with four repeated notes. (The material is derived from the two-bar link that led into the first 'storm'.)

Theme I now returns, though with a number of new additions such as a descant in the violins and descending chords in the woodwind that are like a chime of bells. A striking new modulation leads to the alien key of B minor; the stormy 'transition' begins once more, taking an adventurous route back to the safe harbour of A flat. (High repeated E flats on violins will give you your bearings.) The 'Handelian' dialogue is resumed, as is the lovely interlude for woodwind, but the movement contains no more alarums though the final loud cadence is a trick learnt from Haydn, designed to ensure that the audience would applaud.

The ensuing *Menuetto* is certainly Haydnesque, a dance for countryfolk rather than pampered dandies. It is unusually robust for Mozart, horns and trumpets thumping out the rhythm with rustic vigour. The central Trio confirms the impression, with Mozart's beloved clarinets playing an artless tune over a simple strummed accompaniment. Here, one feels, is a little village band very similar to the one which Beethoven so wittily parodied in the scherzo of his Sixth Symphony; since they can only muster two good players the rest are given as little as possible to do.

That type of joke does not apply to the Finale, which demands virtuosity from every section of the orchestra. Its catchy little theme is first presented by violins alone but is quickly taken up by the full orchestra. Soon the violins are caught up in a fearsome passage that must have given Mozart malicious delight as he wrote it down. The clap-hands simplicity of the accompaniment draws all the more attention to the strenuous exertions of the fiddle-players. Once the texture thins out some extraordinary things happen as fragments of the opening theme flit through the woodwind in the wholly foreign key of F sharp major. (The syncopations in the first violins, always behind the beat, can be put down to sheer breathlessness.) A full tutti follows these flutterings, complete with donkey hee-haws in the violin part that anticipate Saint-Saëns' 'Personages with long ears'.

The development gets off to a false start, followed by a puzzled silence. 'Shall we try A flat?' say the violins; but then with an extraordinary shift the music slides into E major, the ultimate contradiction of the 'home' key of E flat. This deviation from all normal procedures brings chaos in its wake and for the next few bars the music skids crazily from one key to another.

Clarinets and bassoons begin a hymn-like passage that seems to pray for salvation as the violins nervously scoot from G minor to D major and then to D minor. 'There must be a way back' is the thought in their minds; once it is found, relief is expressed by a joyous reprise of the theme, in the right key at last. A recapitulation follows in which we are the victims of much the same practical jokes, extra stress on the 'donkey' motif showing Mozart's delight at making asses of us all.[19] Towards the end of the movement the strings have a unison version of the theme that exudes propriety; gloriously rich harmonies then give promise of a triumphant ending but there is one last joke in store. Instead of a conventional cadence Mozart cuts off a phrase in midflight, as abruptly as if one had lifted the needle off a record. If there was ambiguity in the finale of the 'Prague' symphony there is none here; it is surely one of the wittiest movements in all music. That it is followed by the pathos of the G minor symphony is an extraordinary demonstration of the range of Mozart's genius.

Symphony No. 40 in G minor K.550

The absence of trumpets and timpani from the score of this symphony suggests at once that Mozart had a more intimate conception in mind than he had felt when embarking on its great predecessors. Originally the work was scored for one flute, two oboes, two bassoons, two horns and strings. In one of his rare revisions Mozart re-scored the wind parts at a later date, virtually replacing the oboes by clarinets and giving them a more supporting role. He also hit upon an ingenious idea that anticipated nineteenth-century practice; instead of having the two horns tuned to the same key and therefore limited to an identical series of 'natural' notes, he chose to put one horn part in B flat and the other in G, thereby giving himself more scope for their involvement. A further novelty, most unusual for the period, is the division of the violas into two parts in the initial accompanying figure.

It is probably true to say that only in one other symphony, Beethoven's Fifth, do we find a first movement that surpasses this in its concentration on one fragmentary idea whose interest is primarily rhythmical. The first four notes of Beethoven's C minor Symphony are perhaps the best-known in all classical music; Mozart needed only three—Eb–D–D to the rhythm of two quavers and a crotchet.[20] The rhythm occurs twelve times in the first nine bars, occasionally with an extra crotchet added to carry the phrase forward. Now, falling semitones in Mozart, and indeed in most composers' music, are a symbol of pathos when slow and agitation when fast. Here we have a supreme example of a theme that is on the borderline of tears but is given no

---

[19] The idea may seem far-fetched but the MSS of the horn concertos are covered with derisive, humorously intended remarks aimed at the performer, 'Signor Ass' being a favourite epithet.
[20] Such a recurring pattern is usually described as a 'motto'.

time to indulge in self-pity. The first woodwind phrase we hear, bars 14–16, does express anguish more openly—and is sternly reprimanded for so doing. (Note how the initial rhythmic unit is toughened as soon as it is concentrated on one note.) The opening theme comes a second time without waiting for the bassoons to finish their cadence; it then modulates, subtly moving from G minor to B flat major. An altogether bolder idea appears, striding proudly; but within seconds it too is put on the rack and the music seems positively to writhe in pain before breaking off into silence. With a soothing gesture the second subject eases the tension, though the way it is divided between strings and woodwind prevents it from being entirely bland. A chromatic descent pulls it away from its proper key (B flat) towards a rocking figure in A flat, a move which brings a disturbed reaction from flute and bassoons. With some effort the music is hoisted back to B flat, though a chromatic ascent and a sharply accented rhythm cause some commotion before the key is properly established.

It is at this point that Mozart's obsessional use of the initial falling semitone begins to prove its worth. Violins and cellos exchange long-drawn-out sighs (Bb–A or Eb–D), a classic example of what is known as augmentation, while at the same time clarinet and bassoon re-introduce the opening motif in its original form. Violins accept its validity with some passion; but then the same exchanges are repeated with violins and cellos reversing their roles until a brilliant descent in unison quavers sweeps away such open declarations of grief, bringing the exposition to an emphatic conclusion in which the 'motto' rhythm is hammered home forcibly by the full wind band.

The key so firmly established is the so-called 'relative major', B flat. A single chord like a sword-stroke switches us back towards G minor for the repeat that eighteenth century composers so valued, since it gave the listeners a better chance of absorbing unfamiliar material. The second time round the 'sword-stroke' is followed by two swifter blows leading us *away* from G minor. A slow, quiet descent in the woodwind leads us to the totally unexpected key of F sharp minor. (Notice again how the violins cannot wait for the woodwind to establish the key properly before they set off into the development.) The opening theme now appears three times in succession, each time with a downward turn. Just at the moment when the theme seems about to wilt it is grabbed roughly by the lower strings; a remarkable new treatment begins with a jagged counterpoint in staccato quavers effectively removing all trace of sentiment from the theme. It is a journey through turbulent waters until, after being tossed from side to side, the 'motto' rhythm settles on an alternation between B flat and A. There follows the most extraordinary passage in the whole movement; time and again the 'motto' theme is exchanged between strings and woodwind, now here now there, so that one can never predict where it will appear next nor on what pair of notes. At one point there is an angry outburst, as though frustration sets in, but for the most part the tone is forlorn. Saddest of all is a chromatic descent in the woodwind (still observing the all-pervading rhythm) which leads at last to the recapitulation.

A notable feature here is a far more extended and dramatic treatment of the boldly striding theme which made a brief appearance early in the exposition. Urged on by the horns, it develops into a fierce conflict between the lower strings and the first violins—while the 'seconds' run round in agitated circles. At its first appearance this theme lasts precisely six bars before it disintegrates; now it occupies Mozart's whole attention for twenty-six bars.

The second subject, again preceded by a silence, now appears in the minor, emphasising the tragic cast of the movement; indeed from here on there is not a single release from minor tonalities. One last point should be noted when, just near the end of the movement, the motto theme is momentarily treated as a tiny three-part fugue by the violins and violas over a sustained bass-line that gives it a feeling of weary resignation. Mozart is almost tempted to end the movement quietly, but no; self-indulgence is not permitted and the ending shows no pity.

The slow movement shows graphically just how far Mozart was able to develop a style intrinsically designed as entertainment, for much of it could legitimately be described as dance-music; yet it has a mysterious beauty that reveals a profound spirituality. The opening phrase is not so much a tune as a suggestion of a tune:[21]

Ex. 1

(Notice the extraordinary effect of the C flat on the fifth quaver of bar 2)

The music continues with two grave obeisances in the violin parts which

[21] There is a fascinating prophetic vision of this sequence in the slow movement of Mozart's very first symphony (K. 16, II, bars 14–17), written when he was eight. Furthermore the implied melodic outline E flat–F–A flat–G is fundamentally the same pattern that comes at the start of the finale to the 'Jupiter' Symphony—C–D–F–E. There is food for thought here for those who are interested in the relationships between key and mood; both the examples in E flat (K. 16 and 550) and darkly mysterious, whereas the C major version (K. 551) is clear sunlight.

receive equally courteous replies. (The elegant little flick of the lace cuff followed by the gracious bow must surely be a gesture taken straight from the aristocratic ballroom.) The introductory phrase reappears with a new sustained violin line above it and once again formalities are exchanged. Mozart now makes wonderfully resourceful use of what had seemed a triviality, the 'flick of the cuff'. This pattern of two demi-semi-quavers (♫) is transformed first into a continuing accompaniment and then into the main feature. When the opening music returns in the surprising key of D flat the 'flicks' continue in a descending scale pattern in the woodwind until a considerable climax is reached. (Did Wagner have a subconscious recollection of this in the very different circumstances of the *Tannhäuser* Overture?) The resolution is unexpected, a pleading phrase for the first violins falling from B flat to F four times in succession. A brief passage for full orchestra rises through rich chromatic harmonies, but again the little 'flicks' intervene and the exposition of this surprising sonata-form movement ends quietly.

The mysterious character of the opening of the movement gives no indication of the dramas that are now in store. Still preserving the calm rhythm of the first phrases, the strings shift to a unison C flat, a move that evokes a powerful reaction from the full orchestra. An extraordinary conflict follows between weighty repeated quavers and descending 'flicks', now raining down like blows. It is not too much to suggest that a similar passage would have served to illustrate the flagellation of Christ had Mozart ever written a setting of the Passion. Lamentation follows in a profoundly expressive passage, the woodwind taking the lead but the paired demi-semi-quavers continuing to fall, their anger now transformed to tears.

The start of the recapitulation is easily recognised though some changes soon occur; but Mozart's instinctive feeling for the proper proportions of a movement ensures that the remainder of the music provides a perfect balance to what has gone before.

The Menuetto shows little of the grace that the title implies. It has a rugged quality that is almost brutal at times as though Mozart bitterly resented the convention of providing a dance movement in a symphony so tinged with tragedy. The natural rhythmic pulse of a movement in 3/4 time is disrupted by syncopations and cross-accentuation, while the overlapping entries are deliberately designed to confuse the ear. A brief respite is afforded by a few bars for wind alone, but even here the chromatic harmonies give a feeling of anguish that has no place in the ballroom. By contrast the Trio is innocence itself, much of the time in two parallel parts with only the sketchiest bass. The horns are featured in the second section, lending a rustic air to the music. The delicacy of the scoring and the artless simplicity of the theme make the inevitable return to the opening Menuetto almost painful as though, granted a fleeting glimpse of Elysium, we are savagely dragged back to harsh reality. All the same, it prepares us admirably for the finale which has the same demonic force that we found in the last movement of the D minor Concerto.

The initial rising phrase is marked *piano* but its suppressed energy explodes into an angry *forte*, setting up a pattern of violent contrasts which continues for some time. Soon the violins begin a swiftly running passage that is urged on its way with stabbing thrusts from the bass before finding its way into the lower depths. The music continues with inexorable drive for seventy bars. Out of the turmoil emerges the solace of a second subject of marvellous grace, scored for violins and violas alone. The first clarinet finds it irresistible, adding his own embellishments and inducing still greater calm as the other wind instruments join in. An impression of a slower pace is given as all the instruments except the bass move in minims and semibreves.

A sudden flare of excitement in the violins rekindles the initial energy and the music rushes headlong towards the double-bar which marks the end of the exposition and the point of repetition.

The development begins with one of the most astonishing passages Mozart ever wrote, a stark unison whose angular intervals are made the more startling by the abrupt and irregularly spaced silences which break them up. Oboes and bassoons exert a calming influence which restores some sort of order. A dialogue concerning the opening theme begins between violins and woodwind, but the violas seem to resent this flighty treatment of so serious a matter and launch themselves into a vigorous fugue. At once the challenge is taken up and the music becomes a complex web of counterpoint which is given an awe-inspiring aspect by great striding semibreves in unison wind. The tonality is constantly shifting until frenzied G sharps in the violins establish the dominant of C sharp minor, a key that is totally alien to the 'home' key of the movement. Five abrupt chords break the continuity and for three bars there is a suggestion of calm. Then, like a fire caught by a gust of wind, the main subject flares up again with renewed violence. Suddenly the music stops in mid-flight. There is a dramatic silence as though Mozart himself feels that things have gone too far and must be put to rights. The recapitulation begins, following the original pattern until it reaches the second subject which is extended by some curiously wavering passages. They lead to a coda whose ferocious intensity could not be exceeded by Beethoven himself. Those who remember this symphony by its hauntingly poignant opening alone would do well to remember that its final movement shows Mozart at his wildest, a tormented soul driven by the Furies. To follow this emotional extreme with the classical perfection of the 'Jupiter' symphony is one of the most baffling juxtapositions in the history of music.

> I doubt if there exists in all music anything more deeply incisive, more cruelly anguished, more violently distracted, more agonisingly passionate than the second half of this finale . . . (Oulibicheff, Russian critic writing in 1843, sixteen years after Beethoven's death.)[22]

[22] G. de Saint-Foix. *The Symphonies of Mozart*, Dennis Dobson, 1947.

Symphony No. 41 in C Major (The 'Jupiter')
K.551

Mozart here returns to a favourite opening formula, a brisk 'masculine' phrase to establish the key followed by a tender 'feminine' response. The pattern is then duplicated on the dominant. A martial tutti follows, establishing beyond 'all possible probable shadow of doubt' that this is the key of C major. The music comes to rest on a portentous pause, as though, at the end of a miniature overture, we await the rising of the curtain. The opening dialogue of opposites begins again, but this time both elements are *piano* to allow a countertune on flute and oboe to make its full effect. The 'feminine' phrase is then extended—even more so once the music shifts to the dominant. Its gesture becomes less submissive, strengthened by military rhythms from horns, trumpets and timpani; there is a sense of straining at the leash as the intensity increases until the military element becomes all-pervasive.

After a momentary silence the second subject makes a discreet entry, its first phrase a mere three notes whose gentle rise is echoed by the cellos and violas as the remainder of the theme trips lightly onward. After the turbulence of the G minor symphony all seems crystal clear, though we should not miss the ingenious way in which the 'feminine' phrase insinuates itself into the second subject group. The section ends chirpily on a question-mark. Silence—in other words, 'Look out!' With a frightening impact the full orchestra crashes in on the 'wrong' chord of C minor, an error corrected two bars later but enough of a shock to make us concentrate the more. An ingenious extension of the 'feminine' phrase begins, its tail-piece twitching as the sequence rises. The passage builds to a climax out of which the violins emerge on their own with a descending arpeggio that leaves us hanging in suspense. A comically irreverent little tune appears on the scene, literally out of place since Mozart had originally written it to add a touch of class to another composer's opera.[23] It causes the exposition to end like comic opera, with the violins playing little flourishes that remind us of Papageno's pipes. (This very un-god-like tune makes the name 'Jupiter' quite unsuitable for this symphony, but no matter . . .)

The development begins with an artlessly simple switch to E flat major that hardly deserves to be called a modulation. Our cheerful little operatic interloper takes over as though there was nothing else available. Its final notes are soon subjected to some severely disciplinary counterpoint and a degree of symphonic respectability is regained. It is strange, though, that for the first

---

[23] Paisiello, but see D. F. Tovey, *Essays in Musical Analysis*: Vol. I, p. 196.

forty bars of the development there is not a single reference to either the first or second subjects. At last, over quietly sustained string chords, the violins come by a devious route to F major. Quietly the opening phrases make their long-delayed reappearance, complete with woodwind countertune. As if to compensate for his neglect of these basic materials, Mozart now subjects the opening group of notes (not even the whole phrase) to a violent and highly concentrated development punctuated by off-beat chords in the wind. Our operatic friend shows his tail briefly and then a downward scale of C major leads us safely back home to the recapitulation. This follows the usual precedents although we should savour the significant difference that changes of key make in music as formally constructed as this.

The second movement unusually requires muted strings. Its operatic lineage is very clear, the stressed chords on the second beat of bars 2 and 4 at once suggesting recitative. Soon the 'aria' develops in the first violins (with wind support) over a gently throbbing accompaniment. The lower strings duly echo the opening phrases, playing the baritone role and bringing a singularly tender response from the 'soprano' violins. Enter a distraught parent, or some equally disturbing character, for the entire mood changes abruptly with a plunge into C minor. Agitated arpeggios in the violins break into breathless sobs, even the rhythmic pulse is profoundly disturbed, giving the impression of 2/4 instead of 3/4 as the woodwind screw up the tension with a slow chromatic ascent.

Calm is restored with a benign theme in C major; but then a delicately fluttering figure in the violins touches our hearts as it descends through the most sensuous harmonies. Here surely is a heroine exercising all her feminine charms. Even the repeated notes on the horns suggest a quickening of the male pulse in response to her seductive powers. Sterner critics will dismiss this as pure fantasy on my part and I am not suggesting that Mozart consciously had any such scene in mind; but his music is so steeped in opera, especially in his slow movements, that the sound of voices is seldom far from his inner ear. The purely instrumental writing is easy to distinguish coming as it does at the very centre of the movement with dramatic and tortuous scales in the strings and aggressive rhythms in wind and brass. The storm is soon over and the 'benign' theme again restores calm. Towards the end of the movement some soft fanfares for horns take us into the woodlands before a reprise of the opening 'aria' brings this exquisite *scena* to a close.

It is hard to believe that the third movements of this and the preceding symphony share the same title, Menuetto. The rough and angular style of the G minor symphony is replaced by a suave smoothness that suggests gliding rather than dancing. There is hardly a moment where the music shows any real muscle. This is not to say that it lacks invention, the high spot being a sublime little passage for wind alone whose chromatic harmonies introduce a

note of poignancy that is quickly repressed. The Trio begins almost apo-
logetically but then, in a sudden and unexpected display of strength, introduces a stamping rhythm that takes us all by surprise. As if ashamed of such
ill-mannered behaviour the music retreats abashed and the 'apologetic'
phrase ends the Trio. A miracle awaits us, perhaps Mozart's supreme
achievement as a truly symphonic composer.

The finale is both simple and complex, simple because the essential materials
are so clearly defined, complex because of the amazingly varied ways in
which Mozart treats them. In an astonishing feat of ingenuity all five of the
main ideas are fitted together towards the end of the movement and since this
is a good way of making their acquaintance they can conveniently be shown
in full score.

Ex. 1

The movement begins with Theme 1 on violins with the simplest
accompaniment, but by bar 9 it is taken up at full strength with dramatic
'sword-thrusts' in the lower strings. Bar 19 sees the first appearance of
Theme 2 which is skilfully built up in layers, ending with a clear-cut cadence
on the dominant. It is a point where we might legitimately expect a second
subject to appear. Instead we find a beautifully contrived fugal treatment of
Theme 1 passing in sequence through the whole string section until the next
tutti. Theme 3 makes its presence felt as a dialogue between violins and basses

while brass and wind provide glorious sustained harmonies. A modulation into D major brings the return of Theme 2, now treated as a close-knit canon. After a momentary silence a true 'second subject' appears (Theme 4), while dancing in its wake comes a little four-note motif on the oboes (Theme 5); already Mozart is beginning to combine his themes as bassoons match '3' against the flutes' '2'. Flute and bassoon begin an overlapping duet around '3' while the violins embark on a brilliant run based on rising and falling scale passages.

We now find a sequence of great strength initially constructed from the first three notes of '4'; soon the whole theme is thrown into a maelstrom of counterpoint, overlapping at four different points a mere beat apart. As if to compensate for the complexity of this veritable maze there is now a tutti of a more chordal nature, hammering out rhythms with great insistence. Soon a new game begins in which '2' is matched against itself mirror-fashion— travelling in opposite directions. The exposition ends with a single oboe and bassoon in turn reminding us once more of '2'.

The development brings the first drift towards minor keys, the strings cloaking '1' in mysterious harmonies, oboe and bassoon offering a distortion of '2' which flute and bassoon neatly turn upside down. Mozart now concentrates his attention on '2', subjecting it to the same intensive contra-puntal treatment previously extended to '4'. The onward rush of this theme is occasionally interrupted by a wistful version of '1' in the woodwind and the contrast between the forward drive of '2' and the lingering sadness of '1' creates a new miniature drama.

The return to the recapitulation is accomplished with a wonderfully subtle modulation, mostly woodwind, but ending with a quiet C major version of '2' on violins, with a soft murmur from the timpani to confirm its importance. It is in the final section of the movement that Mozart produces the greatest marvels. Violins in thirds transform '1' by inverting it and giving it a tinge of sadness with chromatic harmonies whose effect is enhanced by overlapping imitations from the lower strings. (Notice also the special touch given by a slow chromatic descent in oboe and bassoon.) Then, like an assembled cast taking their bows at the final curtain the five themes shown in Ex. 1 are brilliantly combined. It is a tour-de-force that Bach himself would have been proud to have brought off so effortlessly. Small wonder that the movement ends with triumphant fanfares on horns and trumpets. It was to be Mozart's last foray into the symphonic field; *Così fan Tutte, Die Zauberflöte, La Clemenza di Tito* and the Requiem were enough to occupy him in the remaining three years of his tragically short life.

MUSORGSKY—RAVEL

Pictures from an Exhibition

This work, originally a suite for solo piano, is perhaps the most literally 'pictorial' piece ever written, for its inspiration was an exhibition of paintings by an artist called Hartmann, who had died in 1873. The next year this exhibition was held in Moscow, and Musorgsky, who had been a close friend of the painter, naturally went. He was deeply moved, so much so that he at once projected the work. He called it *Pictures from an Exhibition*, and named each piece with the title of one of the pictures. The sole unity is provided by a theme rather like a primitive Russian folk-song, which appears several times under the name of Promenade; in fact it enables us to walk to the art gallery, and from picture to picture. One can easily imagine the massive columns of some great public building housing the exhibition, with its broad stone steps and portico, and Musorgsky with a party of friends walking there one afternoon.

The first picture that catches their eye is called the 'Gnome', and shows a limping dwarf-life figure. Musorgsky aims at two things in this piece; fear, which he evokes by sudden sharp bursts of sound, and the grotesque angular gait of the gnome which he portrays with gawky octaves. At the end of the piece, the misshapen creature scuttles away.

Now when one hears this music in the original version it isn't surprising that one has the impression that Musorgsky was really sketching an orchestral work. His piano writing is very clumsy in places, and yet there is so much colour in its conception. Various musicians subsequently tried to orchestrate the 'Pictures', but it wasn't until 1929 that Ravel was commissioned to do it. He produced a version which shows the true imaginative worth of what up to then, had been an obscure and not very successful set of piano pieces. To coin a phrase Musorgsky was a genius without talent; in other words his mind teemed with wonderfully original ideas, but often his technique faltered. Present-day taste has now accepted the fact that Musorgsky's original score of *Boris Godunov* is much better than Rimsky-Korsakov's slicker and tidier version of it. But his piano writing lacks a real sense of the keyboard—it's the imagination behind it that we háve come to treasure. Ravel penetrated to the heart of this imagination and his scoring of this work is probably the most masterly example of one composer adapting another's work that has ever been known.

The opening 'Promenade' is straightforward enough, alternations between a solo trumpet and brass choir followed by an increasingly substantial use of the full orchestra; but as soon as we come to 'Gnomus' we find the first of a sequence of brilliant lessons in the art of orchestration. The piano version begins with the two hands in unison playing a swift but angular phrase that moves in fits and starts. Ravel adds not a note, but what he does give us is a striking tonal colour-scheme—dark strings, murky bass clarinets and double bassoon, sinister horns, sudden sharp percussion. At once the music takes on an infinitely more vivid life. So much for what I described as the 'fear' aspect. What of the 'limping'?

Musorgsky depicts this with high three-note chords in the right hand placed four, and then three, octaves above a deep bass. The passage descends by irregular steps, stamps to a halt and is then repeated. Ravel's treatment is vivid. He puts the top chords on woodwind, flutes and oboes; the bass notes are on a muted tuba, which is a rather grotesque sound, with a little splot of the bottom octave on the double bassoon, the deepest instrument in the wind family. In addition he etches in the top chords with plucked strings on the first beat of each phrase, and, most effectively of all, adds the dry chink of a xylophone as well. When it comes to the repeat the top chords go most unexpectedly on to the celesta, with harp harmonics to veil its glitter—just enough to take the sheen off; the bass is given to the oily-toned bass clarinet; but in addition something 'very nasty' happens in the strings, for they have an eerie sighing moan of a glissando. Is it the gnome sobbing? Is it the wind? Is it the creak of a door? Is it the prickle of fear on your spine? One cannot say precisely; maybe it's just a macabre sound. But Ravel saw it in the bare bones of Musorgsky's music, so he put it in. Further effective uses of glissandi come later in the movement but it is important to realise that Ravel did not alter harmonies or add new counterpoints; it is a literal transcription except for the enormously wider range of colour which the orchestra can bring.

Having seen the first picture, we go on a little promenade—not so imposing a version of the theme this time, and ending with two ravishing bars which in a wonderfully subtle way soften its harsh angularity into something much more tender, as though we stopped short at one picture and said, 'That's lovely'.

And what is this next picture? It's called 'The Old Castle', and it's an Italian landscape, at night, with a minstrel singing in the foreground. The colourings are obviously sombre.

Over a sad, monotonous drone we hear the doleful voice of the singer, with a suggestion of Italian rhythm, but the whole concept darkened by Hartmann's Russian melancholy. Ravel has a surprise for us here, for he gives the minstrel's song to a most unexpected instrument—the saxophone. One would imagine that it would strike an incongruously twentieth-century note but his ear is infallible and it seems not in the least out of place.

Another brief 'Promenade', each one differently scored, brings us to the third picture, a gay scene of children playing in the Tuileries Gardens in Paris, watched tolerantly by their nannies, who overlook the odd squabble and just enjoy the sunshine. To judge by the rhythm some rocking game is in progress, a see-saw perhaps, or a swing . . . Ravel exploits woodwind brilliantly here, the transparency of the scoring admirably conveying the impression of sunlight.

No intervening 'Promenade' takes us to the next painting; Musorgsky realised that the convention could easily become predictable and boring. Here then is a picture of a lumbering wagon, the lazy oxen reluctantly dragging it, leaning on each other the way they do, with the huge wheels screeching and groaning as it goes on its way. Musorgsky captures this image in terms of sound by giving the left hand stolid chords in the muddiest part of the piano, and a tired work-song above. This builds up to a tremendous climax and then dies away, like a long shot in a film, with the wagon drawing closer and closer, looming huge in front of us and then slowly receding into the distance.

Ravel divides his cellos and double-basses to give the thickest possible sound (though not loud) and puts the 'song' onto a solo tuba, an instrument that even suggests the lowing of oxen in its high register. As the wagon moves into 'close-up' he exploits the full orchestra for the first time, building to a huge climax which then recedes, dying away until nothing is left but almost inaudible pizzicato double basses.

A rather more ethereally scored 'Promenade' leads us to the next picture, strangely titled 'Ballet of chickens in their shells'. Hartmann's picture is indeed a sketch for some ballet costumes and Musorgsky provided music which would inspire even the most unimaginative choreographer. The piano writing is more truly pianistic except for a central 'Trio' which relies overmuch on trills. As though accepting the weakness of invention here, Ravel does, for once, add an additional element, though one that is totally derived from figures that occur in the first section. His 'cheeps' in flutes, oboe and clarinet are more ornithologically convincing than mere trills. As a further example of the additional interest the orchestral texture provides, notice how ascending chromatic scales in the piano left-hand part are split between bassoon and oboe reinforced by pizzicato strings to give a pecking sound.

The next picture is unpleasantly anti-semitic, a portrait of two Jews, rich, fat Samuel Goldenberg and the wretched snivelling Schmuyle with his endless complaints. Goldenberg's gestures are expansive and Hebraic, an opportunity for Ravel to exploit the G string of the violins. (Notice though that he makes no attempt to enrich Musorgsky's unison line with extra harmony.) The choice of a muted trumpet brilliantly conveys Schmuyle's nasal tones which grow increasingly strident. Goldenberg has the last word, dismissing his unfortunate companion with a derisive gesture.

'The Fishmarket at Limoges' is technically the hardest piano piece in the original version and its final toccata-like figuration taxed even Ravel's ingenuity—as did his own Toccata in *Le Tombeau de Couperin* which he found impossible to orchestrate. All the same, his kaleidoscopic orchestration suggests the bustle and clatter of the market, not to mention the noisy gossip of the fishwives. It is in the following piece, 'Catacombs' that we find the greatest gain of all. Musorgsky's piano writing is visionary but unrealistic—a single massive octave or chord to each bar which inevitably loses power on a piano since there is no way of truly sustaining the tone; nor can any pianist, however gifted, make a crescendo on a held note. Ravel's scoring is awe-inspiring, a thrilling demonstration of how to write for brass, while the contrasts between the loudest and softest sounds are inevitably more impressive than a pianist can make them.

The ensuing piece, 'Cum mortuis in lingua mortua', is suitably enough like an introduction to a Requiem. Musorgsky ingeniously works the 'Promenade' theme into the opening phrases, giving it a very different quality even on the piano. But the high tremolando octave is a weak device that is greatly enhanced by the transfer to violins, and the deeper-voiced instruments bring out the spectral quality of the music.

'The cabin on chicken-legs' is an example of Hartmann's fantasy, anticipating Surrealism by nearly half a century. It inspired some grotesque music from Musorgsky, much of it in unison octaves— potentially dull for an orchestra. Ravel's ingenuity in coping with this problem is remarkable, reinforcing notes with timpani in one bar, with horns in another but always remaining true to the original. He does allow himself one giant glissando which Musorgsky implied but could not bring off on the keyboard. It is well worth while to listen to the two versions closely and hear how a transcription that is scrupulously faithful to the original notes manages to give them a new significance.

The final picture, 'The Great Gate of Kiev', represents a design by Hartmann that was never actually built—*grace à Dieu* some would say since it is frankly hideous. Here again we find the pianist at a huge disadvantage, expected to produce ever more massive sounds from chords that by the nature of the instrument are doomed to die just when one wants them to grow louder still. The music is rather shallow in content, relying too much on descending scales to represent peals of bells, and every pianist must feel a certain impotence towards the end of the piece when the musical reward is scarcely commensurate with the physical effort involved. Ravel tries to find ways of making the music more genuinely orchestral in texture without departing at all far from the original, but even he cannot disguise the essential vulgarity of the piece. This criticism apart, it must be acknowledged that his orchestration has made a masterpiece from something that is less than satisfactory in its original form; that is not to belittle Musorgsky's composition, for without its intense imagination, its daring and its poetry Ravel could never have responded so brilliantly to the task he was given.

PROKOFIEV

1891–1953

Born into a comparatively wealthy family with a mother who was herself an able pianist, Prokofiev's precocious talent for music was given every chance to flower. When, in 1904, he was admitted to the Conservatory in St. Petersburg he had already written a remarkable amount of music for a young child, some of which even then gave premonitions of his distinctly unorthodox approach. The strict academic regime of a Russian conservatory was not at all to his liking and he proved to be a rebellious student whose individuality irked his professors. Nevertheless he made a memorable impression for when, in his last year as a student, he entered for the Rubinstein Prize (the highest award for pianists) he chose to create a daring precedent by playing his own First Concerto instead of the normal classical work. The music upset some of the more conservative members of the jury including Glazunov but there was no denying the brilliance of his playing and he was duly rewarded with the first prize, a grand piano.

As soon as he left the Conservatory Prokofiev was able to begin a successful career both as pianist and composer. He managed to avoid getting caught up in the turmoil of the Revolution of 1917 by moving to the country, where he could continue to compose, undisturbed by political upheavals. The *Classical Symphony* and the First Violin Concerto belong to this period, but in the following year he decided to emigrate to America where he scored an immediate success. Unfortunately he began to devote his energies to composing operas; funds ran out and performances were not forthcoming. Post–revolutionary Russia held little appeal for him so he moved to Paris, at that time the most musically sophisticated city in Europe. The opera *The Love for Three Oranges* had been completed and was due to have its premiere in Chicago, but meanwhile he was engaged on another opera of which he had high hopes, *The Fiery Angel*. The ballet *Chout* was produced in Paris in 1921 and caused a sensation there though it was too progressive for London audiences. Turning away from the theatre, Prokofiev began work on his Third Piano Concerto which was to prove to be one of his most popular works. The ties with America were by no means severed and he returned there late in 1921 for several months to conduct and to play. He was soon to grow used to the mixed reception given to musical pioneers, the critics often expressing diametrically opposed views. Nevertheless his reputation continued to grow, so much so that the Soviet authorities endeavoured to entice him back to his native country. For some time Prokofiev resisted; he had married and made a home in Paris. At last, after an absence of nine years, he agreed to make a three-month tour in Russia where, perhaps to his surprise, he was treated handsomely. It kindled a longing to return permanently and in 1936 he settled once more in Moscow.

It was a bad time to choose, for the politicians had taken over and composers were henceforth expected to write music for the people rather than the decadent intelligentsia. The music Prokofiev originally provided for the ballet *Romeo and Juliet* was rejected out of hand as 'unsuitable for dancing' and even his *Cantata for the Twentieth Anniversary of the October Revolution* was turned down. On the other hand *Peter and the Wolf* was immediately acceptable, as were some children's pieces and such film scores as *Alexander Nevsky*.

Ill-health prevented Prokofiev from taking any active part in the war against Nazi Germany nor can the removal of his Spanish-born wife to a labour-camp have made him feel inclined to fight to defend the New Russia. Yet the appalling devastation of so much Russian territory by the invading armies inspired him to begin work on his most ambitious opera, *War and Peace*. He completed the score in April, 1943, but in spite of many drastic revisions demanded by the Committee of the Arts the opera was not staged during his lifetime. More acceptable was the Fifth Symphony (1945), perhaps because it was less demanding than previous works in the same genre.

In 1948 Prokofiev incurred the wrath of the Soviet authorities—as did many of his colleagues—and much of his music was banned from performance. Unable as he was to leave the country, disillusionment set in, though, if only to avoid a worse fate, he accepted a number of official commissions—politically 'proper' works that were neither inspiring nor inspired. It was a sad end to a career that had begun so brilliantly; inevitably one cannot help speculating whether his output would have maintained a more consistently high standard had he decided to stay in the West. As it is he is mostly known by a relatively small proportion of his total number of compositions, the piano works, two or three out of nine ballets, some chamber music, two out of eight operas, several (but not all seven) of the symphonies, and the concertos for violin or piano. His music is often steely or ironic but he had a wonderful gift for melody when he chose, as well as a sense of humour all too rare in Russian music.

Classical Symphony
(1917)

Even though Prokofiev found his ten years at the Conservatory (1904–14) less than satisfying, he re-enrolled as a student when he found that by doing so he could avoid conscription into the Czar's army. Having gained the highest award for piano-playing and having proved his exceptional talent as a composer, he was scarcely eligible to continue his studies in either field; he therefore opted for the organ, an instrument which seems to have had little appeal since he subsequently wrote nothing for it.[1] In the summer vacation of 1917 he went to stay in the country and, as an exercise in composing away from the piano, wrote a symphony for small orchestra, using the same forces that were available in Haydn's day—double woodwind, a pair each of horns and trumpets, three timpani (one more than Haydn would have used) and strings. In no way is the music a deliberate copy of eighteenth-century style; it is the form that is 'Classical' as is the clarity of texture. Incidentally it is a virtuoso piece for orchestra in which the writing is cruelly exposed; every note counts and there can be no passengers in the ranks.

The work begins with a brilliant flourish in unashamed D major. It is over in a flash, immediately followed by a quiet bustling theme on the first violins with a chattering accompaniment from the second violins and violas. After a couple of elegant turns in the violins there is a sharp explosive chord of C major, after which the bustling phrase is repeated in the new key. (An old convention—repeating the initial phrase—given a new twist by the sudden jump into the 'wrong' key.) Two stamping chords bring us back to D and herald the arrival of a subsidiary theme which passes swiftly through the woodwind from flute to bassoon. This too is repeated and then briefly discussed by flutes and violins.

The second subject is unmistakable, an elegantly mincing phrase whose sole accompaniment comes from a pedantically inclined bassoon and a sketched-in bass, pizzicato. The tune itself is notable for its downward swoops of two octaves which are extremely awkward to play. Having begun this theme in the 'proper' key of A, Prokofiev again does a sudden switch to C major and as quickly contradicts it by cranking the music up a semitone into C sharp. 'That won't do!' says the full orchestra with three abrupt chords, and the second subject reappears as before. This time three dainty trills mark the conclusion of the theme and the exposition ends with a slightly extended version of the opening flourish, rounded off with some mischievously skidding scales. There is a momentary silence, enough to make us expect the

---

[1] He did make a piano transcription of an organ Prelude and Fugue by Buxtehude.

conventional repeat of classical usage. Prokofiev foils expectation by pitching into the development, the original bustling theme now in D *minor*. Flutes begin a dancing extension of the subsidiary theme which skips down through several keys. Suddenly the second subject appears transformed, no longer elegant but playing at giants. The violins tell the cellos and basses, 'Anything you can do we can do higher', and quite a trial of strength ensues, so much so that the violins become disoriented and lose touch with the beat. A solo trumpet tries to put them right and then, to the excitement of wind and strings, produces an 'augmented' version of the opening flourish (half-speed.) This establishes C major well and truly, and it is in that unconventional key that the recapitulation now begins. The subsidiary theme, led by the flute as before, restores the proper tonality of D major and it is in that key that the second subject duly appears. The movement ends with the augmented version of the opening flourish, three whiplash scales and finally the flourish 'as it was in the beginning'.

The slow movement is a grave dance that is sheer enchantment. After four 'till-ready' bars to set the tempo, the violins enter on a high A with a tune that is basically a descending scale with decorations. It breaks off in a most coquettish way, climbs back up again, and once more descends. The thematic interest moves into the lower strings while the coquettish figure flutters along, lending a special grace to the music. The style is eighteenth-century but the altitude of the violin part precludes any possibility of it being confused with the genuine article.

A new figure begins, all strings pizzicato with the bassoons giving a more positive outline to the important bass part. The delight of this is that it is 'fast' music played slowly, the continuous pattern of semi-quavers suggesting a rapid scherzo to the eye, but sounding positively cautious to the ear. A lengthy scale travelling outwards in opposite directions leads to a big C major climax where, for a moment the oboes and flutes exchange a phrase that sounds remarkably like Dvořák. (Notice how effective the sharp little comment from the violas and bassoons is.) Three downward scales seem to be heading with absolute certainty for F major. A delightful contest of wills creates a momentary clash, the lower strings settling happily into F major, the violins bringing back their opening tune in A. Differences are soon reconciled, though the return of the continuous semiquaver pattern comes as something of a surprise. Flutes have a tiny fanfare, as though on fairy trumpets, but soon the violin tune reappears for the last time, accompanied by two garrulous oboes whose incessant chatter disturbs the calm. The movement ends as it began, the quiet introductory bars fading away to nothing.

The third movement is a Gavotte that tries hard to stay in D major but keeps slipping into 'wrong' keys. It is the nearest thing to parody in the whole symphony, especially in the central section which jogs along over a drone bass in a way that Haydn would have accepted as perfectly normal. The devious modulations in the first and third sections are a different matter and would have seemed monstrously perverse to an eighteenth-century ear.

The finale is a whirlwind, not unlike the first movement but even more breathless. It's a classic example, in musical terms, of a puppy chasing its tail, for while one has an impression of frenzied activity, it doesn't really *get* anywhere. The ear is tantalised and bewitched by a quicksilver glitter of orchestral sounds—a flash of flutes, scurry of fiddles, rush of reeds, all tripping, tumbling over each other, as though Prokofiev had envisaged the Weelkes madrigal come to life: 'Nymphs begin to come in quickly thick and thréefold; / Now they dance, now they prance, / Present there to behold.'

What can one pick out in such a breathless rush? Nothing really, for what is important is not the detail, not the development of any particular idea but the headlong gallop of the whole movement. True, we do arrive at a recognisable second subject, but even that is only a snippet of a tune, given out by a solo flute.

In the development Prokofiev plays a game of hide-and-seek with this theme, tossing it from wind to strings and back again; but cold analysis serves little purpose in such a movement. We should enjoy its wit and marvel at the dexterity of the players. Prokofiev once said that he'd written it to 'tease the geese', referring no doubt to the stuffy academics who shuffled through the corridors of the Conservatory. Not surprisingly the work proved to be an instant success and was the first Prokofiev work to receive international acclaim.

Violin Concerto No. 1 in D Major
Op. 19 (1916–17)

This relatively early work admirably demonstrates the two musical faces of Prokofiev, the one tender and romantic, the other aggressive and unyielding. It begins with a gentle and lyrical tune for the soloist over the merest whisper of an accompaniment from divided violas. Although the tune is essentially in D major, it is given a tinge of sadness by occasional B flats which bring suggestions of the minor. Flutes and then clarinets link tunes with the violin until the thematic interest actually passes into the orchestra, first in the violas and then on a solo oboe; at this point the soloist seems to have lost interest in the theme, descending from the highest register in a wandering sequence of triplets. Briefly the first violins have their first taste of the melody, only to have it taken from them as the soloist once again ascends to the heights. Having attained a high C natural, the violin part begins to take wing with swooping phrases that cover its entire range—not in a particularly athletic fashion but enough to give notice that there could be fireworks ahead. Meanwhile something of interest is going on in the orchestra. The first two notes of the initial theme constituted a rising fourth (A–D), and it is this interval that now crops up with an almost desperate insistence in the orchestra as though the players were constantly reminding the soloist of the true theme. We hear the rising fourth (usually twice) in oboes, clarinets, bassoons, flutes, oboes again, then more urgently in clarinets and so on; and all the time the violin part is growing more capricious, circling wider as though running rings around its colleagues. Low trills strike a more ominous note, playful growls that could turn nasty. An agile ascending scale puts us at ease, leading into a distinctly different section.

The cellos try to initiate a rather old-fashioned idea, strictly C major and with a suggestion of a gavotte about it. (It is curious that Prokofiev, so much of an iconoclast by nature, should have preserved such affection for antique dance-forms.) Despite the cellists' persistence with this theme, the violinist will have nothing to do with it. It's a sort of symbol for musical common-sense, like a man trying to be rational with a girl determined to have her own way. It's a useless exercise, and it brings out an attack of capricious whimsy in which the violin mockingly imitates the antique style, either by playing slightly perverted scales or going off into a grotesque distortion of the 'gavotte'.

When the cellos and basses start trying to lay down the law in a more heavy-handed way with a rather lumpish theme, they elicit a nonstop flood of slightly acid comment for their pains. I'm not saying that this is what Prokofiev actually meant by the music, but looked at in this way, it becomes immediately comprehensible as a dialogue of opposites. Indeed it is quite helpful in this work to feel that the violin represents a woman, not a specific woman, but the archetypal female, alluring, capricious, at times irresistibly seductive, at others maddeningly impossible for a mere man to comprehend—the sort indeed of whom Rex Harrison said so feelingly, 'Why can't a woman be more like a man?' (The violin-to-woman equation is one that has often been made, as, for example, when Richard Strauss chose the violin to paint a somewhat unflattering portrait of his wife in his *Heldenleben*.) For while the seductive woman has extraordinary power over men, causing them to give up even the throne itself, let alone prestige, wealth, home and family, she can also, if she feels her hold weakening, turn into a fearful nagger. Once the tongue acquires an edge to it, she can show a side the poor fellow never dreamed of when first he fell for her undoubted charm. If a woman can be seductive and alluring but also extremely talkative and downright nagging, the same can be said of the solo violin part in this concerto; volatile too in the scherzo, but then we've known about that ever since *La donna è mobile* and earlier.

The end of the exposition is marked by a silence followed by a quiet sustained unison in the woodwind (note the fourths again) accompanied by sedate pizzicato notes from the soloist. The interval of a fourth dominates the orchestral part in the development, alluding continuously to the first subject without allowing it to extend to its full length. There are also quite extensive references to the cello theme—the heavy-handed one—which, however, makes little impression on the soloist who keeps up a virtually non-stop musical chatter above until at last, like a weary husband, the orchestra is reduced to silence. There is a short lyrical passage for solo violin and then, having got her way, our violinistic heroine becomes seductive again, for there is a recapitulation of sorts, exquisitely scored for the orchestra with flute, harp and tremolando strings, while the violin part is like gently teasing laughter, laughter that is accompanied by playful caresses. Certainly all argument ceases from here to the end of the movement; the reconciliation is complete.

The scherzo turns the violin from seductress to harridan, although here too there is also an element of playfulness. The sheer vitality of the music is breathtaking, and most of the time the orchestral contribution is fairly small, literally marking time. (The opening bars are like a metronome.) For the most part the orchestral texture is transparent, allowing us to focus our attention on the extremely athletic violin part. At one point we find a satirical march, Marlene Dietrich in jackboots and helmet, at another a daring clarinet enters a race with the violin. At the centre of the movement there is a torrential downward scale in wind and strings leading to a violently dissonant passage for full brass, almost as though the orchestra was turning on the soloist and saying 'Do shut up and let us get a word in.' It evokes an even more rapid-fire stream of notes, a waspish relative of Rimsky-Korsakov's famous bumble-bee. Again the brass raise their voices in protest but to little effect and the movement ends with the violinist's dancing harmonics goading the orchestra like a gadfly.

The last movement (there are only three) starts in a fairly brittle and heartless way, giving us little or no indication of the truly romantic ending that Prokofiev has in store for us. There seem to be two themes of importance, one allotted to the bassoons, the other to the soloist.

There is a third element, more lyrical in character, that first appears on the violas; it is disregarded by the violin, but is taken up by the other strings, its rising sevenths bringing a curious suggestion of Elgar into this very un-English score. The middle section of the movement becomes extremely lyrical, with some beautiful double-stopping effects (two notes at once) of the sort violinists revel in. In the closing pages of the concerto, which are scored with a marvellous luminosity, Prokofiev cleverly combines the main themes of the first and last movements. The first is slowed down, cherished one might say, while the second, so much more compact, just provides a commentary. Combine this with a glittering figure on the harp and a shimmer on the strings, and one has a positive sunset of a coda, an ending which avoids any concessions to the normal idea of a grand-slam finish. This is all the more remarkable in a youthful work written by a composer anxious to make his mark, a rebel by nature, and one with little respect for his elders.

In this final section, Prokofiev reveals not just a marvellous ear for orchestral colour, but a quality of tenderness that we don't usually associate with such a young firebrand. And contrary to reports from some quarters, he showed that D major was not dead, not for quite a while anyway.

Piano Concerto No. 3 in C major
Op. 26 (1917–21)

After the sensation caused by his First Piano Concerto it was not surprising that Prokofiev, with a parallel career as a concert pianist in view, should follow it up with a second. It proved to be so violent and dissonant that, to quote a contemporary critic, it left the audience 'frozen with fright, hair standing on end'. Although sketches for the Third Concerto were begun in 1917, Prokofiev's move to America and his growing involvement in opera caused the work to be put aside and it was not until the summer of 1921, while in Brittany, that he settled down to put the concerto into order. This was no spontaneous burst of inspiration for he drew upon materials that dated from 1911, 1913, 1916 and 1918, somehow overcoming the diversities of style that were inevitable in so significant a period of his development. The result was singularly successful, and to this day the Third remains justifiably the most popular of his five keyboard concertos.[2]

Piano concertos of the post-Beethoven period tend to be cast in the heroic mould, allowing the pianist to dominate the scene by literal 'feats of arms', and usually culminating in a romantic apotheosis. Prokofiev's approach is rather different, anti-romantic but combining a classical attitude with a modern idiom. He begins disarmingly with a simple tune for solo clarinet in the style of a folk-song; a second clarinet joins the first in an

---

[2]No. 4 is for left hand only, a commission from Paul Wittgenstein who had lost an arm in the war.

ascending scale in thirds leading to a reprise of the opening theme on soft violins with a silver lining from the flute. The music is unashamedly in C major, almost as though the notorious rebel was declaring, 'Look how good I'm being'. A sudden rush of semiquavers catches us unawares as it climbs through the string section, supported by a primitive pounding rhythm. Enter one soloist, not heroically, but with a joyfully clattering theme whose texture is crystal clear in comparison to that of the two earlier concertos. Choppy chords in the strings give a rhythmic bounce to the accompaniment; these are important, since they offer an idea soon to be exploited by the soloist. Before that happens the pianist's opening theme is twice elaborated by the flute, although the soloist takes a perverse delight in turning the theme on its head.

Suddenly the texture alters as the piano writing changes from agile brilliance to aggressive brutality, stamping chords that soon develop into a pitched battle with the orchestra. (It is a twentieth century version of the famous passage in Beethoven's 'Emperor' Concerto where the orchestra throws down the gauntlet with repeated chords of C flat major only to have them hurled back by the pianist. Here the conflict is less formal, no longer a duel but a hand-to-hand struggle.) Not surprisingly the pianist emerges as victor and celebrates with strutting chords and crows of triumph.

Oboe and pizzicato strings now introduce the second subject, a crisp gavotte with a perversely angular melody. The soloist produces an exaggerated parody before embarking on a nimble running passage that is purely decorative. (The oboe bravely persists with the 'gavotte' theme, only to be mocked once more.) With a change to a slightly quicker tempo the piano breaks into a tarantella-like rhythm whose melodic pattern is crisply outlined by the strings; the piano-writing here has a steely brilliance very typical of Prokofiev and it is a surprise when it comes to a sudden halt to allow the return of the very opening theme. Of necessity it is loud at first but gradually subsides until the soloist takes it over in the one 'romantic' passage in the movement. This meditation is shared by bassoon and clarinet in turn. The ascending thirds, originally on a pair of clarinets, appear clearly recognisable in the piano part in an extended version which dissolves into an exquisitely conceived passage of 'water-music', splashing fountains and trickling rivulets that ultimately descend chromatically in a way that would have rejoiced Liszt himself.

A vaguely sinister march begins in the orchestra, as though at a distance. Against it the pianist is given a long stream of semiquavers based on 'the sudden rush' that appeared in the strings before the soloist's first entry. The pounding rhythm of the march persists as the piano part grows even more brilliant; violins begin to compete as though in a race. At the climax the pianist's original theme reappears and we realise that we are witnessing a particularly ingenious recapitulation. Having given us just enough to make the structure clear Prokofiev takes a short-cut to the 'tarantella' section, though flute or clarinet make periodic if abortive attempts to reintroduce the pianist's original entry. By now, though, the piano part has become too frenzied to take notice of such subtle hints; with three wild glissandi it introduces a manic version of the 'gavotte' against a thumping orchestral accompaniment. At last, all energy spent, the music dies down to virtual silence. There is barely time to take a breath before the last headlong rush begins, still built on the same pattern that appeared so early in the movement but this time destined to drive to a sprint finish.

After the hectic pace of this movement we need some respite, and Prokofiev gives it to us in the shape of the Theme and Variations. The Theme is given to the orchestra, a grave dance whose measured steps again reveal the young rebel's enduring affection for fake antiques. The theme is of classical proportions, sixteen bars long with a little A-men cadence tacked on to the end. Variation I begins with an extensive piano solo whose initial trill and swift ascending scale are like a classical version of the famous clarinet glissando at the start of Gershwin's *Rhapsody in Blue*; indeed some of the harmonies we find here would have delighted Gershwin. Gradually the soloist wanders further from the theme until the orchestra gently reminds him of the closing phrase.

Variation II is a tempestuous *moto perpetuo* in which the trumpet has an aggressive treatment of the theme against ferocious repeated chords from the horns. Meanwhile the pianist is called upon to show dazzling agility until suddenly the movement splutters to a close, complete with the A-men.

Variation III is slightly slower, designed to give the impression that orchestra and soloist are never quite together since the pianist's accents are always displaced. There is something deliberately grotesque here, a gawky angularity that even affects the closing cadence—a sort of 'Arrgh-men'.

The contrast in Variation IV is extreme. It is a nocturne that makes a particular feature of the initial rising octave. For all the difference of idiom the ghost of Chopin walks here, especially in the filigree decoration in the central part, reminiscent of his famous *Berceuse*.

Variation V arouses us abruptly with a crisp dotted rhythm, peremptory as a side-drum. Its basic march step carries it on to an immensely energetic passage in which references to the theme can be detected in the orchestral part against a battery of double octaves from the pianist. Towards the end, the piano writing changes to sweeping arpeggios while the orchestral part breaks into a rising pattern of quaver chords which are neatly appropriated by the pianist in the reprise of the Theme which follows. After the heroics of the preceding pages this provides a beautiful contrast with the original tune (slightly modified) lightly sketched in by the orchestra while the staccato chords in the piano part are like the crystals of a chandelier set in motion by a summer breeze. The final orchestral A-men is repeated by the pianist with a very un-churchy harmonisation; divided strings give a farewell sigh and the piano closes the movement with a gong-like chord.

The third movement is ferociously difficult, with chunky chords, glittering scales, athletic leaps and a demand for unflagging energy. The first few bars for pizzicato lower strings and bassoons give no hint of the fireworks ahead, but the pianist establishes his authority from the eighth bar. Nevertheless those opening bars are important thematically and are treated as such in the piano part. A secondary idea is easily identified with its combination of a hopping step followed by swift scales, either descending or ascending. In due course this is combined with the initial theme which, after a diminuendo, is used by the pianist to initiate a slightly quicker section that soon builds to a barbaric climax.

Suddenly the music seems to disintegrate, breaking into two-note fragments divided between piano and orchestra. Like a glimpse of another world, an expressive theme appears in the orchestra, its lyrical phrases a total contrast to the previous savagery. Capriciously the pianist at first disregards this, preferring a curious little tune whose repeated notes suggest a child bouncing a ball; the ball then becomes a spinning top in a series of trills. At last the pianist surrenders to the lure of the orchestra's lyrical theme and, supported by the cellos, indulges in a romantic rhapsody that nearly rivals Rakhmaninov in sheer voluptuousness. A variation follows, brilliantly contrived for the keyboard so that a third hand seems to be providing feather-light decorations in the top register of the piano while the tune, well supported in the bass, continues in the middle. A second variation, full-blooded and passionate, seems to accept the challenge laid down by Tchaikovsky and Rakhmaninov; here, we think, is the Romantic apotheosis which will bring the work to a glorious and heart-warming conclusion. Prokofiev has other plans. The opening theme, crisp, dry and unemotional, struts in and is soon taken up by the pianist. Gradually accumulating in strength, it returns to the orchestra where it is provided with a quite remarkable accompaniment by the pianist who is expected to play two notes at once with individual fingers at great speed. To chronicle the remaining events would be insulting to the intelligence since the sheer physical excitement of the music sweeps the audience along as though on a tidal wave. The concerto serves as a vivid testimony to Prokofiev's own brilliance as a pianist since only a performer of the highest order could have devised music that was not only so challenging but so dazzlingly effective.

Violin Concerto No. 2 in G Minor
Op. 63 (1935)

By 1935 Prokofiev had returned to Russia after his long self-imposed period of exile, although he had not as yet made up his mind to settle there. His links with Europe were still strong and it was from a little group of French friends that the commission for a second violin concerto came. They were admirers of a French violinist named Soëtans and no doubt felt that to give the first performance of a new work by Prokofiev would substantially further his career. Prokofiev had spent much of his time in Paris and was a well-known figure in Parisian musical life. He possibly welcomed this reminder of his important emergent years as an international composer, and settled down willingly to the task. Ideas for a violin-work had been floating round in his head for some time, and the commission was just the stimulus that was needed.

The start is original in a subtle and unassuming way. Generally speaking, the introduction to violin concertos had tended to become shorter over the years. Brahms and Elgar had still clung to the classical exposition that Beethoven had canonised, a substantial chunk of orchestral music that presented all the main themes while the soloist stood silent and patient, waiting to make a carefully prepared entrance. Tchaikovsky shortened this considerably, Mendelssohn and Sibelius even more so. In this, his second concerto, Prokofiev takes the perfectly logical step of starting with the solo violin on its own, something which so far as I am aware had never been done before. For eight bars the violin presents a simple melody with all the characteristics of a folk-song about it. The tune is clearly in G minor though its final two notes, E flat falling to F sharp, might be construed as B major by changing the E flat to a D sharp. The point is worth making since Prokofiev makes a sort of musical pun, accepting the implication of B major and then bringing the orchestra in with a contradictory B *minor* statement of the same theme, somewhat abbreviated. After a brief spurt of energy from soloist and orchestra alike, they both settle down to a serious discussion of the initial theme. Cellos and basses lead off and the soloist follows a couple of beats later. Counterpoint is the order of the day, but Prokofiev soon tires of this—or so it seems as the woodwind introduce a cocky little tune to a busy accompaniment from the soloist. Yet although this appears to establish a break, the lower strings continue to dwell on the opening material in a quiet and unobtrusive way. A gently rocking figure in the clarinets has a calming effect and the tempo eases back considerably to prepare for the entrance of the second subject, a frankly romantic tune of the type that few composers in the thirties would have been willing to acknowledge lest they be condemned as *passé.* Prokofiev develops the tune at some length before giving his soloist some nimble passage-work over the very same rocking figure that had preceded the second subject. The tempo quickens briefly before a curious little dialogue between the soloist and his colleagues in the string section creates a feeling of indecision.

Pizzicato cellos and basses put the music firmly back on course with a reprise of the opening theme in the new key of F minor. The solo part flits elusively above but it cannot escape from the initial theme which continues to march through the lower regions of the orchestra. Flutes and bassoons in unison three octaves apart produce what seems like a new and strangely distorted theme but it is only a distraction; the original tune continues in the solo violin part, rough and choppy but still surviving.

Not for nothing is this called a concerto, and Prokofiev keeps a positively classical grip on the material, reintroducing the second subject at just the right psychological moment. The solo part still remains active, but responds in part to the seductive tones of the orchestral violins.

Back comes theme No. 1 once more, this time accompanied by shrill little flutterings from the upper strings and the soloist. It's a very characteristic Prokofiev sound this, a combination of Mendelssohn's fairies and Grieg's trolls—though both are seen in a more contemporary light.

The concentration on the first subject is exceptional in this work, considering Prokofiev's reputation as a rebel. In fact the form is almost glaringly traditional, complete with first subject, transition, second subject, development and a recapitulation that can scarcely be missed, coming as it does in unison cellos and basses without any additions. As for the ending, it is delightfully tongue-in-cheek, a witty send-up of the classical 'perfect cadence'.

The second movement is outstandingly beautiful. The soloist has a long sustained melody over an accompaniment of classic simplicity. Several original touches of orchestration combine to give this its special flavour. The pizzicato strings are doubled by a couple of clarinets, which gives a curious hollowness to the sound. The violin line stands out the more clearly because its string brethren are playing pizzicato. Once they take over the tune, the monotonously ticking rhythm continues in the lower reaches of the orchestra; the texture remains clear despite its greater depth. The music aims to be beautiful in the conventional sense without any of Rakhmaninov's concessions to sentimentality.

In the centre of the movement we find a miniature scherzo with will-o'-the-wisp figurations fluttering through the violin part. In the first of these mercurial sections the flute has an important role to play, but soon the lovely opening theme casts its spell once more, only slightly disturbed by a strangely grunting cello part. Once more the shrill flutterings begin, exploiting the upper register of the violin in a cruelly taxing way.

A clarinet leads us into an intermezzo of sorts, lyrical in character in spite of the self-important chatter from the violas. Their bustling semiquavers are taken over by the soloist and for a while there is a mild disagreement within the ranks, as the essentially lyrical theme is harrassed by darting semiquavers. Peace is restored with the return of the opening melody, so instantly appealing that it must remain the abiding memory from this concerto.

The finale might be described as a *Valse macabre* since it is a wild dance basically in 3/4 time. However it's a world away from Johann Strauss, and at times the rhythms grow increasingly irregular, sevens and fives predominating rather than the traditional 1–2–3. The youthful restlessness of the Prokofiev of the 1920s seems to be making a return, with the machine-like drive of the rhythm and its sharp spiky harmony. It's the only movement that could be said to make any obvious concessions to virtuosity, perhaps at the expense of some musical value. There is no cadenza, but the final section of the work begins with a virtuoso passage for the soloist with a rhythmically drumming accompaniment in which the bass drummer marks the time with an almost hypnotic effect. It is calculated to sweep the audience off its collective feet; indeed it is an admirable concerto to make converts to 'modern' music with its clearly defined first movement, the glorious tune in the Andante and the tingling excitement of the finale.

RAKHMANINOV
1873–1943

Although Rakhmaninov's father inherited a considerable fortune, his profligate ways soon reduced the family to relative poverty. By the time the young Rakhmaninov was nine years old several country estates had been sold to pay off mountainous debts and the parents and four children had to face the humiliation of moving to a small flat in St. Petersburg. Sergey, the second son, had already shown a natural gift for music and was able to gain a scholarship to the Conservatory. He was rather lazy as a student and managed to fail all his end-of-term exams in 1885. A stern hand was needed to counter his idleness; soon Rakhmaninov found himself as a lodger in the household of a famous piano teacher named Zverev. House rules were strict and piano practice began at six in the morning and continued under supervision for most of the day. The new regime brought about a spectacular improvement. Piano studies were given the first priority, but even during his adolescent years the boy revealed a natural flair for composition. Indeed it was composition that led to a breach with Zverev, for Rakhmaninov found it impossible to compose against a constant barrage of piano practice from other pupils. He transferred to the Moscow Conservatory where he soon became the star pupil. At his final examination in keyboard harmony he was given a unique mark; the maximum score possible was five, which, as an acknowledgement of exceptional ability, could be supplemented with a plus mark. Rakhmaninov earned a five with four pluses, one each side, one above and one below. They were put there by Tchaikovsky himself, who was on the board of examiners. Naturally such a pupil soon made a name for himself, and his First Piano Concerto and a one-act opera called *Aleko* were successfully performed when he was in his early twenties. When he was twenty-five, he wrote his First Symphony, but the performance of this work from which the young Rakhmaninov had such high expectations was to prove a nightmare. Glazunov conducted, not at all competently; Rimsky-Korsakov expressed a cold dislike for the music at rehearsal; the orchestra failed to respond to its challenge. It was an evening of total disaster, best described in Rakhmaninov's own words.

> There are serious illnesses and deadly blows from fate which entirely change a man's character. This was the effect of my own Symphony on myself. When the indescribable torture of this performance had at last come to an end, I was a different man.
>
> During the evening I could not go into the concert-hall. I left the artists' room and hid myself, sitting on an iron fire-escape staircase . . . There I spent the time, huddled on a step, while my Symphony, which had fanned in me such great expectations, was being played . . . It was the most agonizing hour of my life! Sometimes I stuck my fingers in my ears to prevent myself from hearing my own music, the discords of which absolutely tortured me . . . No sooner had the last chords died away than I fled, horrified, into the street, boarded one of the trams, and drove incessantly up and down through wind and mist, martyred by the thought of my failure. At last I calmed down so that I was able to face the supper which Belayev was giving in my honour that evening. But all my hopes, all belief in myself, had been destroyed.[1]

The effect on Rakhmaninov was catastrophic. He found himself unable to compose, and it wasn't until he had had a course of treatment (including hypnotism) that he was able once again to believe in himself. The result of that treatment, the Second Piano Concerto, was dedicated to Dr Dahl, the hypnotist who cured him, but the manuscript of the symphony was destroyed by the anguished composer. The ironic twist to the story came in 1945, when some Soviet musicians discovered a dusty set of parts from that original ill-begotten performance. For some years Rakhmaninov's music had been totally banned in Russia as decadent and bourgeois, 'class propaganda under the cover of music' as the authorities put it. Rakhmaninov was condemned as 'a tool of the worst enemies of the proletariat'. When in due course he came to be reinstated, the Russians sought for some gesture they could make as an act of restitution. What could be better than to reconstruct the score of the lost symphony? In 1945 the work was performed in Moscow and hailed as a significant landmark in Russian musical history; but the composer was no longer alive, and we shall never know if he would even have agreed to its performance, let alone have come to terms with the music that he had grown to hate. Since it is now regarded by some critics as the best of his three symphonies it would seem that his fears were groundless.

During the three-year period of depression that followed the failure of the First Symphony Rakhmaninov embarked on a new career as a conductor, mostly in the opera-house. Despite his youth—he was only in his mid-twenties—he immediately made a favourable impression and it was in this capacity that he made his début in London in 1899, conducting his own orchestral tone-poem, *The Rock*. In the following year he began work on his Second Concerto which was originally performed without its first move-

---

[1]*Rakhmaninov's Recollections, as told to Oscar von Riesemann*, George Allen & Unwin, 1934.

ment, about which the composer still had misgivings. The complete work was first performed in 1901 and its instant triumph put new heart into Rakhmaninov. It also established his definitive style, sumptuous melodies (sometimes over-dependent on sequences), rich harmonic textures and a tendency to indulge in long drawn-out cadences that are inclined to sink rather too predictably towards their ultimate destination. The writing for piano reflects not only his remarkable virtuosity but also the size of his hands. (Some of the chords in the Preludes are literally unplayable for most normal pianists.)

From 1902 to 1918 Rakhmaninov concentrated on composition and conducting, producing a number of major works including the Second Symphony and the Third Piano Concerto. The latter was composed with his first American tour in mind; since piano playing was at the time the least of his musical activities he took a dumb piano with him on the trans-Atlantic voyage and spent many an hour training his fingers to cope with the formidable difficulties this mammoth concerto poses. The first performance, conducted by Damrosch, was favourably received though some critics felt that the work was overlong.[2] The second performance was conducted by Mahler, who kept the orchestra long after the scheduled end of the rehearsal by insisting that the entire first movement should be played through again. A heavy programme of concerts exhausted even Rakhmaninov and he was thankful to return to Russia, little realising that America would ultimately become his home.

During 1912–13 composition took second place to conducting but he then travelled to Italy to work on his longest choral work *The Bells*, a colourful setting of Edgar Allan Poe's poem. An English premiere was promised for the autumn of 1914 but the outbreak of war caused it to be cancelled. For a time he was able to continue his career as a conductor and concert artist in Russia, but the events of 1917 augured ill for a descendant of a Russian noble family and he welcomed an invitation to give some concerts in Sweden as a valid excuse to gain visas for his family to leave Russia, never to return.

Deprived of the assets built up during half a lifetime, and homeless, Rakhmaninov faced a serious crisis; thus it was that at the late age of forty-four he decided to put his faith in his piano-playing. Although his technical facility had always been remarkable he had hardly any repertoire apart from his own compositions. Living in extremely frugal conditions in Copenhagen, he set about learning the standard concertos that most virtuosi have at their fingertips in their late 'teens; solo recitals presented a considerable problem as he had a pitifully small number of works to hand. With unhappy memories of his first American tour he at first refused offers to return; but after some thought, he reluctantly decided that his best chance of

[2] A few cuts are normally made even now.

supporting his wife and two daughters would come in the States. In November 1918 they set sail for New York to begin a new life. His first concert tour, nearly forty concerts in four months, established him as one of the greatest pianists of the age and he was soon able to buy a home.

Europe still beckoned and in 1923–4 he returned to ever greater triumphs. He even founded his own publishing firm, TAIR,[3] specialising in the works of Russian composers who shared his exile. He spent much time on his Fourth Concerto but though it has a characteristically stirring beginning it was never greatly liked, perhaps because the slow movement has an unfortunate if quite unintentional resemblance to 'Three Blind Mice'. Far more successful was the brilliant *Rhapsody on a Theme of Paganini*, an admirably concise set of variations that show him at his most skilful as a craftsman. Together with his revised version of the First Concerto (1917) it refutes all the criticisms so often levelled against his music, for not a note is wasted. A Third Symphony followed in the late thirties while his final work, the *Symphonic Dances*, was completed in the autumn of 1940.

It has been said that Rakhmaninov spent his life writing the same work over and over again and it is true that many works have much in common. For instance the Cello Sonata shares much of its material with the Second Piano Concerto, dating from the same period. Certain patterns crop up time after time, but the same could be said of other pianist-composers such as Chopin, Brahms or Liszt. His music does tend to be self-indulgent, although he himself was its least sentimental interpreter; moreover there is one recurring structural weakness which inevitably invites criticism—a tendency to be anchored to one note in the bass so that implied modulations fail to escape into genuinely new tonalities. Despite critical disdain and considerable over-exposure, such works as the Second Concerto have never lost their popularity with audiences, while in recent years the substantial number of songs have earned more acclaim than they were once granted. He could be described as a survivor from the nineteenth century, for his musical heritage stems from the great Russian school that flourished in his boyhood years; his essentially Romantic approach became outmoded in an era that saw Stravinsky and Schoenberg rise to the fore. But because his music supplies an emotional need that more revolutionary figures have failed to satisfy, his stock has remained high and will continue to do so as long as audiences sustain an appetite for nostalgia.

[3] The word was a fusion of TAtyana and IRina, the names of his two daughters.

Piano Concerto No. 2 in C Minor
Op. 18 (1900—1)

The genesis of this work would scarcely be credible in a Hollywood script—the young composer shattered by the failure of his first major work, the breakdown, the visits to a hypnotist, the spiritual resurrection leading to the triumphant achievement of a supremely successful concerto. It begins with what has become one of the most famous openings in the entire repertoire, those tolling bell-like chords (anchored to a low F despite the changing harmonies) that grow in intensity until they find their release in the most crucial pattern of the movement.

Ex. 1

(For purposes of identification I will call this the 'motto' theme.)

Two bars of surging arpeggios launch the majestic main theme on unison violins and violas. The first two broad phrases place much emphasis on the key-note C; a recession of tone leads to a significant continuation begun by the cellos—significant because it evolves from the 'motto', using G–A♭–F–G as a starting-point. Violins take over and extend the tune through a fine climax to its ultimate dying close, a remarkable forty-five bars in all. The piano has accompanied throughout, its first melodic phrase being a modified version of the 'motto' stolen from the cellos. A remarkable feature of the concerto is that at no point does the pianist have the main opening theme, an example of self-denial that Rakhmaninov improbably shares with Mozart in his concerto in the same key! It gives the soloist an air of independence that is confirmed by the fact that for more than three-quarters of the movement, the orchestra is never allowed a full statement of the glorious second subject. They allude to it lots of times; they also change its character, whipping it up into a faster tempo; but only once are they allowed to spell it out in full, and then it's as a horn solo, very simple and effective.

The transition to the second subject is very compact, a quickening of the tempo, some fluent passages from the soloist, a pounding reiteration of the first two notes of the opening theme, a rising crescendo and a final sigh from the violas—all this in the space of twenty-one bars. The change of mood brought about by the emergence of the second subject seems so sudden that few people take in its relationship to the exciting orchestral crescendo that precedes it. The climax of the crescendo is reached with these notes:

Ex. 2

Change the alien C flat to a conventional B flat and we find the second subject:

Ex. 3

This tune, so characteristic of Rakhmaninov at his most memorable, is beautifully extended with expressive comments from violas, cellos or wood-wind in turn. It ends with a slow ascent to the most ethereal register before suddenly breaking into a brisker tempo. Here we find an example of the composer's greatest weakness, for the music has remained almost entirely in E flat for more than sixty bars. One would think that the point hardly needs to be laboured, but having confirmed a very positive arrival at a key he had never really left, Rakhmaninov hammers the cadence home five more times. Some weighty brass chords then make a ponderous modulation to G major which also has to be underlined in a similarly repetitive way. Though the piano part has a glittering brilliance, it can scarcely disguise the poverty of harmonic invention.

A brief interlude for orchestra alone gives the violas a chance to brood over the first subject, but the attentive listener should also be aware of grumbling allusions to the 'motto' theme (now in quavers) in cello and bass, allusions which are also taken up by the flutes. With some impatience the piano snatches this idea away from the orchestra, and, pushing the tempo onward, begins an extensive development in which the five-note 'motto' is cleverly exploited. Gradually the orchestral part begins to assume greater importance as the violas introduce a lyrical extension of the second subject against which flutes and oboes fit a counterpoint neatly derived from the second main stanza of the first subject. As the tempo increases still more the pianist urges the orchestra on with martial chords although the strings continue to be preoccupied with their modified version of the second subject. Through the welter of sound a trumpet can be heard sounding an alarm based on the 'motto' theme which also spreads in a more expansive way to the strings. Massive chords for full orchestra lead to a majestic reprise of the first subject (*Alla marcia*) against which the soloist seems to hurl defiance with an ingeniously contrived version of the 'motto'.

The second limb of the theme, originally initiated by the cellos, is now taken over entirely by the pianist as a virtual rhapsody. Although it sounds like a free improvisation, it actually follows the exact course of the original theme until its final descent, which is extended in a series of 'dying falls'. In one of the most inspired moments a solo horn quietly plays the second subject at half-speed against a whispering accompaniment from the strings. As the piano re-enters, the wind instruments begin a rising sequence built entirely from repetitions of the 'motto' at constantly varying pitches. Their version is in crotchets which the pianist then doubles in length to minims. The ensuing sequence is one of Rakhmaninov's most gratifying inventions with the pianist musing on the 'motto' theme while the cellos offer nostalgic memories of the second subject's opening phrase. A twilight cadence leads to the final coda, an awakening from a dream whose initial restlessness grows increasingly agitated as the music leads to an exciting finish. (Note how the last three chords on the piano are derived from the main theme, though in a very compressed version.)

The slow movement begins with a gravely beautiful modulation from C minor to E major, a juxtaposition of keys which has a classic precedent (though without any transitional link) in Beethoven's Third Piano Concerto—also in C minor. The piano then begins a serene accompanying figure which has an intriguing ambiguity of rhythm. The basic pulse is four beats to the bar with a triplet on each beat; four times three equals twelve, but Rakhmaninov groups his twelve quavers so that they suggest three times four. The effect is one of languor so that when the flute enters with its haunting melody in 4/4 time the pianist appears to be playing at a slower pace in 3/4. Only when the clarinet takes over with the second phrase does the piano part fall into line. The long-drawn melody is centred on the third degree of the scale, to which it keeps returning as though unable to drag itself away. It is like a lingering and oft-repeated caress, a romantic gesture enhanced by sensuous sighs in the strings. Once the tune has run its course, roles are reversed, the accompaniment being given to pizzicato strings and oily-smooth clarinets, an intriguing combination, and the tune to single notes on the piano. Divided violas add an expressive new counterpoint; only at the last phrase are the violins allowed a first tantalising taste of the melody.

With a slight increase of tempo the piano begins a central development section taking a small fragment of the original tune and extending it in sequences. After a series of wave-like progressions, this fragment builds to a considerable climax, only to begin the whole process again. This time the 'waves' are somewhat more agitated and the climax even more impassioned.

The piano part now has a slow step-by-step ascent culminating in a huge chord of C sharp major which unleashes a torrent of notes. With a stroke of genius Rakhmaninov inserts a miniature scherzo into the movement, demanding extremely agile fingers and a sure rhythmic sense. Thundering trills in the bass and a scale that sweeps through four octaves terminate this section dramatically. A short cadenza leads to a reprise of the opening music in a somewhat shortened version. The final coda consists of bell-like chords in the piano giving sonorous support to a yearning new melody in the violins. Soft triplet chords in flutes and clarinet seem to float in an almost disembodied way and the whole passage perfectly exemplifies Rakhmaninov's enduring appeal.

The third movement breaks the spell with a distant suggestion of a brisk march. (Was Beethoven's Fourth Concerto the model here?) As the music grows louder the violins offer a snatch of the 'motto' theme from the first movement, leading to a typically explosive cadence for full orchestra. A rocket-like cadenza soars to the top of the keyboard and down again followed by climbing arpeggios whose bass notes are heavily emphasised. (A point often missed by pianists is that the last four of these before the orchestral entry are yet another reference to the 'motto' theme.) An exciting thrumming in pizzicato strings recalls the chord-sequence which came at the very beginning of the concerto, no longer a solemn bell but a pounding rhythm.

Caught in a tumult of notes the main theme of the movement appears on the piano:

Ex. 4

Shortly afterwards the music breaks into languid waltz-time, languid for the orchestra but continuously hectic for the soloist. Flying quavers lead to a vigorously stamping version of Ex. 4 over striking unisons in the orchestra. Left on his own, the pianist shows a more lyrical approach to Ex. 4, changing its rhythm and supporting it with widespread arpeggios in the left hand.

Comes a moment of glory for the violas as they reveal the beauties of the second subject, a theme that the soloist expands in a style that decades later was to be copied by unnumbered Hollywood composers. What they did not copy was the strange section that follows. Bass trombone, tuba, bottom strings and timpani sustain a long-held B flat above which woodwind, pizzicato strings and softly clashed cymbals play curiously isolated chords. Meanwhile the piano is given smoothly gliding triplets derived from Ex. 4 interspersed with mysterious trills. The entire passage, short though it is, is so unexpected in this context that I honestly believe it to reflect the experience of being hypnotised, an experience which had such profound significance for Rakhmaninov in relation to this work.

The emergence from the trance is sudden and violent with a swift octave ascent leading to an ingenious variation of Ex. 4. The tempo becomes more impetuous as Ex. 4 disintegrates in a rough-and-tumble squabble between piano and orchestra. After some restless fidgeting the violins begin a little fugue, a brilliant new treatment of Ex. 4 that spreads like wildfire through the orchestra. The final entry of the fugue subject comes on a trumpet, whipped on by flailing chords in the piano part. Wind and strings exchange blows with strident unisons before horns and woodwind give us a forceful reminder of the 'motto' theme. Ex. 4 appears yet again, first trickling down through the lower strings and then with extreme violence on the full orchestra.

It is time for a reprise of the second subject; it duly arrives in the new key of D flat, its tone-colour lightened by violins and flute in place of the more sombre violas. The pianist again rhapsodizes, the hypnotic section again casts its strange spell. Over a sustained low G, clarinets and bassoons begin a muttered exchange of fragments stolen from Ex. 4. This continues for a few moments until the pianist starts out on an exciting ascent that leads to three climactic chords. Against tumultuous arpeggios from the piano and swiftly darting chords in the woodwind the cellos launch a splendid new theme which the pianist is too impatient to allow full rein. Continually gathering pace the music once again builds to the same rocket-like cadenza with which the pianist had entered the fray at the start of the movement. With immense majesty and power the full orchestra proclaims the second subject, punctuated by massive chords from the piano. Having achieved the grandest climax of the whole work, Rakhmaninov wraps it up with a brilliant coda that might unkindly be described as first cousin to Tchaikovsky's comparable ending.

One point should be stressed before leaving this hackneyed but indestructible concerto. As this analysis should have revealed, it is actually constructed with remarkable economy; the first movement makes the most ingenious use of a five-note fragment that also appears in the finale; the third movement is based almost entirely on two themes, the first of which is treated in a great variety of ways. The broad sweep of the melodies misleads us into thinking that the concerto is a sprawling self-indulgent wallow in romantic nostalgia. The material itself may be open to criticism, but Rakhmaninov's craftsmanship is considerably better than critical opinion has allowed; moreover it is easy to forget that the work was written as long ago as 1901 at a time when Romanticism was not so suspect as it has become after two world wars. I was once amused by a huge graffito (in California of all places) that said 'Help stamp out Rachmaninoff' in letters three feet high; the writer's prayer has not been answered.

Piano Concerto No. 3 in D Minor
Op. 30 (1909)

Rakhmaninov is good at beginnings. The First Concerto begins with a blazing fanfare for brass followed by a torrent of double octaves from the soloist, an electrifying cadenza calculated to stir the most apathetic audience; the Second Concerto begins with softly tolling chords that lead to a majestic richly-scored orchestral theme; the Third begins with a murmured accompaniment above which the pianist plays a tune of the utmost simplicity, the two hands in unison without a single supporting chord. This theme is so seminal that it needs to be quoted:

Ex. 1

Though very different in character from the opening theme of the Second Concerto, it shares a characteristic reluctance to escape from the key-note (D). Without a trace of ostentation, it continues for twenty-four bars before breaking off into a Bach-like pattern of swiftly moving semiquavers that serve as a sparkling decoration to an orchestral reprise of the theme on violas and French horn. A transitional passage follows in which the soloist has a positive flood of notes whose perpetual scurry seems to leave the orchestra lagging behind, their syncopated entries frequently dragging after the beat. An arresting little fanfare from a trumpet causes a flurry of excitement in the woodwind before the soloist takes command with a short cadenza whose A major arpeggios[4] spread increasingly wide arcs across the keyboard only to die away to silence. Cellos and basses recall the pattern if not the exact contour of Ex. 1, but a sudden surge of ecstatic harmony counters their melancholy, leading us to expect the imminent arrival of the second subject.

Rakhmaninov has a nice surprise for us at this point; instead of the

[4]The so-called 'dominant' of D minor.

voluptuous tune we anticipate, he provides a crisp but subdued little march whose rhythm was cunningly planted in the trumpet fanfare mentioned above. The march fails to get under way owing to frequent interruptions from the soloist, who clearly has other plans. They are soon revealed as he transforms the dry and unemotional march into a gloriously lyrical tune.

Ex. 2

(a)   (b)

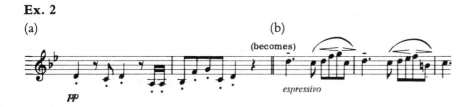

This melody is extended until a huge climax invites the participation of the strings and wind. A long descent follows, its devious chromaticisms assisted by oboe and clarinet in turn. The pace suddenly quickens and a brief display of agility from the soloist leads to a more thickly scored development of 2b which is sometimes cut.

The development begins with a masterstroke, a reprise of Ex. 1 with the C sharp in the fourth bar changed to a C natural. Step by step the tune moves down until it settles into the key of B flat. We now find what seems at first hearing an episode of little relevance. Two elements predominate, a gruff and limping ascent in the bass and flitting three-note figures in the woodwind. Both are actually derived from fragments of Ex. 1 and the two are interwoven in a long sequence before the pianist sets out boldly with a new figuration. On closer examination this too proves to be a variation on the opening theme. Climbing ever higher, it leads to an immensely exciting passage of pounding chords and stamping rhythms which few listeners appreciate as yet another variation of Ex. 1.

Martial trumpets signal an increase of speed, though the beat itself—two in a bar instead of four—may seem slower. A sudden recession of tone leads to a curiously bleak passage in which the piano part is reduced to two-part counterpoint covering a wide range of the keyboard while the violins have wailing semitones over a grinding bass. Divided strings have some strangely gasping chords as the tempo slackens; simple three-note chords sound bell-like in the piano; we are on the threshold of a substantial and thematically important cadenza.[5]

After an initial chromatic ascent the music evolves into a tumult of notes which can be discerned as a fleet variation on Ex. 1. The pattern persists for twenty-four bars of brilliantly conceived keyboard writing divided skilfully

[5] Rakhmaninov provided an even harder alternative but it is seldom played and leaves less room for development.

between the hands. A more recognisable variant of the opening tune then appears; the texture thickens, building to a dramatic climax that offers vivid evidence of the composer's technique, especially in the rapid execution of full-bodied chords. A series of climbing arpeggios in D major brings us to one of the most original passages in the whole concerto. The piano part becomes a series of delicate silvery ripples that gradually descend through various keys; meanwhile flute, oboe, clarinet and horn in turn play expressive derivations from Ex. 1. The pianist then begins a dreamy meditation on the second subject that merges into a quicksilver passage that flashes across the keyboard only to dissolve in a sequence of trills. A gentle rocking figure on horns leads us to a reprise of the opening tune in its original guise. A short coda consists of no fewer than ten references to that significant little trumpet fanfare while the pianist adds a glitter to the texture before making a final brief allusion to the 'march' which preceded the second subject. (Ex. 2a). The movement ends as quietly as it began.

The slow movement is called 'Intermezzo' and, following the pattern of the Second Concerto, includes a miniature scherzo. The orchestral introduction reveals the most criticised aspect of Rakhmaninov's work, over-indulgent in its expression of melancholy and with altogether too many cadences that seem to seek an ever softer bed to lie on. Once the soloist enters, the music becomes far more inventive, the conflicting rhythms of three against five, five against eight or four against three giving a wonderful impression of spontaneous improvisation. A richly contrived modulation from F sharp minor to D flat major brings us to the main theme for which the orchestra seemed to have been searching in vain. It begins and ends in D flat, a tonality that is confirmed no less than six times in a rising sequence of cadences culminating in a sustained trill. Such cadences are a hallmark of Rakhmaninov's style and must be considered a weakness since they too often mark the end of a journey which has not really taken us anywhere new: we start in D flat and finish in D flat and we do not need six announcements to tell us that we have merely changed platforms without quitting the station.

This criticism is made the more cogent by a passage that is usually cut in spite of its structural value. Against an impassioned rhapsody from the pianist, the first violins introduce a deeply expressive version of the opening theme from the first movement. Sadly, the root of the harmony remains firmly anchored to F for eighteen bars; the richness of the keyboard writing cannot disguise the poverty of the bass that lies beneath. As if by way of compensation the ensuing passage is one of Rakhmaninov's finest. Beginning with a passionate extension of the main theme, it gradually builds through a series of rising phrases to a noble climax in the unexpected key of D major. With a subtle change of direction the music shifts back to D flat, repeating the climax with orchestra and piano reversing their roles. The pianist is left on his own to bring the section to a close in a passage of exceptional richness, though the strings quietly join in the final affirmation of—yes, D flat major once again.

Suddenly the tempo changes as the piano begins a whirring figure like a spinning top. The strings softly insinuate a quick waltz rhythm against which the piano has patterns of mercurial brilliance. Clarinet and bassoon in unison begin a long tune which seems vaguely familiar. Closer acquaintance shows us that this is a brilliant transformation of the opening theme of the concerto (Ex. 1). Not only is its rhythm changed, but also its relative position within the scale so that it now begins on the second note; a comparison of even one phrase should be enough to establish how it is done.

Ex. 3

The very different key, F sharp minor, makes the disguise still more deceptive. The theme runs its full length in this transformed version surrounded by the glittering figuration from the piano. The firework display ends as the orchestra resumes the initial mood of the movement. Will there be a recapitulation to balance the lengthy first section? Just as we visualise the possibility the pianist interrupts with some abrupt octaves. We are suddenly engulfed in a tidal wave of sound from the full orchestra; two staccato chords launch us into the finale.

The woodwind set an energetic pace with a repetitive rhythm against which the pianist plays a fanfare-like motif which spills over into handfuls of notes that seem to tumble out of the keyboard. Soon a more clearly defined theme appears, a Russian dance whose rhythmic drive sets the audience's toes tapping. Horns take over the opening 'fanfare', inspiring the pianist to heroic feats, hurling thunderbolt chords at all and sundry. A sudden diminuendo creates a sense of expectancy; what will happen next?

It is an event of considerable importance, a theme beginning with four chords of C major before embarking on a strongly syncopated ascent and descent. The pattern is repeated twice more, the rhythm unchanging but the tune rising to greater heights. And now yet another theme appears in this richly endowed movement, soaring lyrically upwards in ecstatic flight. A brief orchestral interlude brings us down to earth again, its military tread gradually slowing with solemn brass chords. The music settles quietly into E flat major, a point the strings make abundantly clear by repeating the chord a number of times.

It is here that we find an extreme example of Rakhmaninov's ingenuity but also his strange ineptitude. The latter shows in the orchestral part which stays firmly rooted on an E flat bass for more than thirty bars. (There are a couple of minor diversions but they quickly return to base.) The ingenuity lies in the piano part in which the second subject from the first movement (Ex. 2b) appears in a delightfully capricious disguise. The strings provide a cushion of harmony above which the piano part swoops and darts in little flurries of notes; the suggestion of a brightly-coloured tropical fish disporting itself in clear waters is enhanced by a second variation whose silvery ripples are truly a *Jeu d'eau*. A third and substantially slower variation follows, but it is usually cut since it perpetuates the overdose of E flat.

This ingenious and subtle reminder of the first movement causes violas and cellos to muse on the opening theme which in turn brings a beautiful response from the soloist—a dreamy memory of the second subject in its original mood. A fine crescendo that only Rakhmaninov could have written leads to a final variation on Ex. 2b, showing exceptional brilliance, though once again rooted to the E flat bass. It is an Achilles heel that assumes the size of a calf-muscle, a notable weakness in what would otherwise be a conception of remarkable originality and ingenuity.

A recapitulation of sorts follows in which themes by now familiar are encountered again although with many differences of detail. Progress is halted by a series of abrupt disjointed phrases that sound remarkably like the noises made by steam engines of the old type making their way out of the station. The 'train' seems to gather speed as the piano sets up a persistent pattern of rapid paired chords. In the general excitement few people are aware of just how cunning a link this represents for the sequence of harmonies is stolen directly from the beginning of the first movement cadenza. The music drives on towards the sort of climax one expects from Rakhmaninov, releasing a short but extremely forceful cadenza. Massive chords seem to set the 'train' in motion again before strings and soloist combine in a great sweep of melody. It is a theme we have met before in a strongly syncopated version, what I described as 'an event of considerable importance'. Just how important we now realise as it provides a magnificent final climax to the fascinating design of this finale.

Rhapsody on a Theme of Paganini
Op. 43 (1934)

Of the twenty-four Caprices that Paganini wrote for solo violin it was the final one in A minor that proved to have a quite extraordinary 'after-life' in the hands of other composers (Ex. 1).

Ex. 1

At first glance it seems strange that this relatively obscure violin piece should have become the most fruitful source of variations of all time, having been used by Liszt, Brahms, Rakhmaninov, Boris Blacher, Lutoslawski and Andrew Lloyd Webber. But when one thinks about it, one can see that it has the most essential attributes you could wish for in a theme for variations. First, the basic framework is not only extremely clear, but is instantly recognisable. Its bare bones consist of alternations between the first and fifth notes of the scale followed by a series of descending steps from the top down. As to its flesh, it consists entirely of two patterns; the opening loop, which comes thirteen times in all, and a sort of upside-down version which comes four times. Rakhmaninov was at pains to emphasise the basic outline of the theme right from the start, apart from an opening orchestral flourish which is primarily concerned with the 'loop'. He then has what he calls Variation I which actually comes before the theme, and which is just about as stark as he can make it, an outline, no more.

The actual theme follows, very properly given to the violins. The piano simply sketches in the bare bones, giving little hint of the immense technical challenges that lie ahead. In Variation II—the first to follow the theme—the pianist has an opportunity to give his version of Paganini's 'Caprice', a word which gives a clue to the approach for he puts 'crushed' notes at the beginning of each phrase to add piquancy and introduces a quicksilver glitter to the repetition of the second part.

During the next two variations it's the 'loop' idea that takes precedence, first shaken briskly in the orchestral part and then given to the piano in a non-stop whirl of notes. Despite its pace the music is all very compact and stays closely linked to the theme. Inevitably, Rakhmaninov now begins to break away a little bit from the constraints of Paganini. The balance of phrases remains the same, but the harmony has a little more bite, and the extreme symmetry of the rhythm starts to break up in a crisp exchange between soloist and orchestra. In effect this fifth variation severs the cord that bound Rakhmaninov to Paganini's theme. In the next variation one can sense his need to break free, and he does it in two ways; partly by introducing little cadenzas which cut across the rather too predictable sequences of the original theme, and then by introducing ideas which are much less tied to the 'loop' pattern. All the same we get an occasional snatch of that too from a clarinet, a flute, or, more expressively, from a cor anglais, but the pianist begins to go his own way.

A short silence precedes Variation VII, one of the most memorable. The solemn chords on the piano spell out the 'Dies Irae' theme—that great medieval chant that has inspired many composers. Pizzicato cellos explore variants of the Paganini theme in slow motion while occasional reminders of the 'loop' flit past in the violins.

In Variation VIII the 'loop' theme comes back with a vengeance, fairly stamping across the score. But notice that it appears at two speeds, quavers in the piano and semiquavers in the orchestra. Rakhmaninov is writing for his own marvellous chord-playing technique here, and most pianists find the last phrases of this variation difficult.

Variation IX is notable for a feverish urgency with swiftly paired repetitions in the orchestra and panting off-beat syncopations from the piano. Occasionally these break into sudden showers of octaves which are extremely effective.

Variation X is a march which again draws on the 'Dies Irae'. At first it appears in stark octaves in the piano as the clarinet seems to be leading us into the fray; but full brass and percussion produce a jazzy version that shows that Rakhmaninov had not been totally uninfluenced by his American surroundings. The snatch of 'Ellingtonowsky' dies away as the pianist sets the 'loop' spinning again while the orchestra persists with the 'Dies Irae', either on glockenspiel and harp or trombones and tuba.

Variation XI is a dreamy meditation on the 'loop', clearly meant to sound like an improvisation. After three speculative phrases the pianist has some glittering chromatic runs against which flute and cor anglais offer a deeply expressive version of the rather neglected second portion of the theme. (Notice the oboist's preference for the first portion.) A cadenza for harp and piano leads to Variation XII, a dance for a haunted ballroom. Marked *Tempo di Menuetto*, it begins with pizzicato violins suggesting the 'bones' of the theme. Gradually, after several tentative false starts, the piano initiates a lilting rhythm which seems to lead the music into a different world. Sustained reminders of the basic harmonic shape of the theme appear in the orchestra as solos from clarinet, horn or cellos; violins whisper the 'loop' almost inaudibly from time to time; oboe and clarinet exchange a poignant reminiscence of the theme.

Such romantic nostalgia is summarily dismissed in Variation XIII in which unison strings treat the theme with immense vigour accompanied by violent stamping chords from the pianist.

Variation XIV brings a refreshing shift of key to F major—the first variation in the major. Although it is in 3/4 time it has the character of a march, especially when its rousing tune is taken over by trumpets and trombones. It is not (as many listeners believe) a new theme, but the first of several in which the original patterns are inverted. Here are three such inversions; for ease of comparison I have put them into the same key.

Ex. 2

Variation XV begins with a scintillating piano solo that makes great play with the fragment shown as 2b. With the entry of the orchestra the piano-part goes into free flight and Paganini is for the moment left behind. Towards the end of the variation members of the orchestra try to impose order by dropping in brief reminders of the trumpet theme from the previous variation but the soloist emphatically rejects them.

After such excitements Variation XVI is curiously woe-begone. The strings seem extremely hesitant to begin at all, but then the pianist sets a gently rocking figure in motion which sends shivers down the spines of the violin section. Meanwhile a solo oboe refers to the theme in touchingly expressive tones. A solo violin takes the hint and treats the second part of the theme in a similar way; a clarinet copies, making slight modifications. The pianist is content to go his own way before descending to the depths of the keyboard for the deep melancholy of Variation XVII. To very different effect Rakhmaninov here exploits the same rhythmic ambiguity that he uses in the slow movement of the Second Piano Concerto. Against the darkly brooding accompaniment the brass take a lingering look at the 'bones' of the theme, gradually widening the arc of the phrases in a passage of great individuality. Those gloomy phrases lead us through the dark wood to the release of the big D flat tune, a Sleeping Beauty surrounded by a forest where no bird sings. The discovery of this tune has been well-prepared as we have seen in Ex. 2c, but it's still a moment of revelation.

From here to the end of the work, the pace is piled on in six concluding variations, increasingly brilliant, yet always relevant to the matter in hand. The Day of Wrath theme makes a final appearance, but the very last notes are a surprise, quiet and a throwaway, a last touch of caprice that is a superbly calculated risk. The often repeated accusations of self-indulgence, too much repetition, dependence on nostalgia and so on simply do not apply here and the work must be regarded as flawless of its kind. It combines brilliance with economy, it avoids ostentation, it has memorable and ingenious moments and never loses its intellectual grasp.

Symphony No. 2 in E Minor
Op. 27 (1906—7)

It can be truly said of Rakhmaninov that he worked the same vein of musical ore rather too many times; the resemblances between various works cannot be denied. He never developed, in the way a composer of real stature develops. Instead, he went about a process of refining, of perfecting, rather as some painters have concentrated on one subject over a long period of time, painting nothing but circus pictures or street scenes or still lifes. In a sense, Rakhmaninov kept on writing the same piece of music, trying it out in different ways. Perhaps it is one of the reasons why his musical personality is so strong even though the material itself is sometimes shoddy. 'That phrase again—it hath a dying fall' might have been written about Rakhmaninov. His themes may soar into the sky, but the wings on which they climb belong to Icarus, and always they sink down again in a too final return to earth. Here in the Second Symphony, he builds a prototype which has later to emerge in the Third Piano Concerto, more compact, more disciplined, and consequently more satisfying; but the model is clear enough.

The work begins with a long and impressive introduction. The shadow of Tchaikovsky looms over the music; just as Brahms seemed to lean on Beethoven in some of his early works, so Rakhmaninov leans on his great predecessor. Tchaikovsky's Fifth Symphony begins with a darkly brooding theme in the lowest register of the clarinets; it serves as a 'motto', reappearing in various guises throughout the symphony. Rakhmaninov begins this mammoth fifty-minute symphony with a 'motto' in an even darker register—low cellos and double-basses. Two subsidiary themes immediately grow out of this, the first (scored for wind) echoing the falling semitone C–B, the second (on violins) elaborating the significant quaver figure in the 'motto' (Ex. 1).

It is the decorated version of 1c that will prove to be the most rewarding, a point that is underlined by the second violins as they immediately copy it an octave lower. The whole tripartite sequence is then repeated in a different key before a series of ascending passages leads to a complex interweaving of 1c which, with a gradual increase in tempo and texture

Ex. 1

brings us to the first major climax. The music unwinds in a typically drawn-out descent until only a solo cor anglais is left to bring the introduction to a close.

The first movement proper begins with a swaying accompaniment on divided violas and clarinets four times repeated. Violins in unison then introduce the main subject, a long, slightly restless melody whose closing bars echo the B–C–B relationship established in the first two bars of the symphony. (Though different in actual notes, the format is basically very similar to the opening of the Third Piano Concerto, a soft rotating accompaniment with a long unison tune extended above it.) The theme is developed spaciously until a livelier element intrudes, its frequent rising triplets giving the music greater energy. The excitement this generates soon dies down and a brief clarinet solo extends a courteous welcome to the second subject which alternates between oscillating chords in the wind and a decorated descent through four adjacent notes in the strings. It is an unpromising beginning but it soon develops into an unashamedly lyrical theme which rises step by step to a substantial climax from which Rakhmaninov extricates himself in a characteristically sequential manner. The tempo gradually eases back until, after a particularly lush cadence in G major, we hear once again the softly murmuring accompaniment that supported the first subject. (Rakhmaninov's feeling for tradition made him ask that the exposition should be repeated but in all truth it is not essential and few conductors observe the instruction.)

The development begins with a slightly more disturbed version of the initial rotating accompaniment over which a solo violin produces an expressive extension of 1c. It causes quite a strong reaction in woodwind and strings with rippling derivations of 1c spreading wide. The whole process is repeated with a clarinet replacing the solo violin. As the tempo quickens the first violins have a restless figure that rocks uneasily from G to A flat and back; it could charitably be described as a development of 1b though too much repetition weakens its effect; more interesting are the woodwind derivations from 1c which flit by and the limping scales which set up a wave motion in the lower strings. Impressive brass chords act as a check to the speed, releasing a new theme that descends through violas and cellos. A quick-fire salvo from the timpani, dramatically reinforced by violas and low horns, signals the beginning of a further section of the development in which a notable feature is a curiously Elgarian sequence with the violins reaching upwards in a pattern of sixths and fifths while the cellos seem set on 'rocking the boat'. Meanwhile the violas are totally preoccupied with the opening few notes of 1c. Gathering force, the music builds to an impassioned climax in which horns and woodwind turn the first three notes of the second subject into a persistent fanfare strongly reinforced by majestic passages for the heavy brass. The music tumbles down from its peak (E flat minor) leaving the strings in a deeply disturbed state. Stirring horn-calls 'set the wild echoes flying' in a magnificent passage which leads to a clearly recognisable recapitulation. The subsequent transition is made considerably more dramatic with cymbals and bass drum being called on for the first time to add their considerable weight. Gradually the tension eases even though the timpani continue with a martial rhythm for some time after the explosive climax. At last violins, violas and cor anglais are left on their own to muse quietly over an augmented version of 1c.

Flutes and clarinets begin a reprise of the second subject, almost forgotten in the main development. Rakhmaninov now allows it full rein in some richly scored passages. The long melodic lines ultimately disintegrate as bass clarinet and bassoon remind us of the 'motto' theme that came right at the start of the symphony. It sets the violins aflutter again with nervous fleeting references to 1c; the increasingly urgent rapping of the timpani leads us to a sudden but short-lived outburst for full orchestra. It dies away almost to nothing, but again the drum-beats goad the music onward. The first horn sounds an alarm as the violins begin a racing tarantella. It is the start of a precipitate rush towards the dramatic closing bars of the movement.

The ensuing Scherzo allows little respite to the players. The strings set up an exciting dactylic rhythm[6] against which the horns project the main theme; it begins with three dancing crotchets, an easily recognised feature in a number of derivations. An insistent little fanfare on flutes and clarinets also claims our attention—'too often' some might say, but it is a very typical gesture which reappears in much more significant form in the Paganini Rhapsody (Var. XIV). The strings show no interest in the horn theme, preferring a rather more capricious idea of their own which descends through two octaves by a slightly tortuous route. The horns offer their theme a second time but surprisingly it is the less positive string theme that takes hold, spreading through the woodwind with the bright tones of the glockenspiel adding a silvery glitter to some of the phrases. A full-bodied chord of E major (the

---

[6]The same pattern is used at the start of the finale of the Third Piano Concerto but at a slightly slower pace.

dominant of A minor) allows the trombones and trumpets to put in a strong plea for the horn theme but it is again rejected. Cellos and basses carry the violins' theme down into the depths against sustained brass chords and an insistent drum-beat. The music dies to near-silence, leaving a single clarinet to play a smoothed-out version of the little triplet fanfare that originally harassed the opening theme.

At a considerably slower tempo a broad tune appears in the strings with the modified fanfare providing a gently flowing accompaniment. The tune is extended at some length before crisp staccato chords on horns and woodwind create an impatient desire to get back to the opening tempo. For a time the violins refuse to take the hint, preferring to linger on a slow chromatic descent. Inevitably, though, a return to the initial theme comes, albeit in a considerably shortened version. After the obligatory climax it dies away to nothing—literally a silent bar with a pause.

And now comes the most surprising episode, a quick-moving fugue, which suddenly rears its academic head in the middle of the movement. Rakhmaninov must have been fully aware of his tendency to ramble, and may well have felt that the intellectual exercise involved in writing such a fugue would have a salutary effect. Although the conception is undoubtedly fugal the subject is not treated in the traditional way since the first three entries copy each other slavishly instead of appearing in the tonic, the dominant and then the tonic. Nor does the fugue continue along predictable lines since it soon breaks up into segments which then become the topic of heated discussion throughout the orchestra. Finally the violas are left virtually on their own, keeping up a continuous pattern of quavers which in due course is handed over to violins and woodwind as the brass begin a measured dance. The running counterpoint here is distinctly weak, too dependent on conventional scale-patterns; but the admirable brass writing offers compensations.

The return to the opening material is well managed and a full reprise follows, complete with the lyrical string tune. The coda is clearly marked by a timpani solo, quiet but persistent, over which the brass cast a sombre shadow. The movement ends quietly with a last flicker of life from the little triplet fanfare.

The growing popularity of this symphony must surely be attributed to the slow movement, a song for orchestra whose most notable phrases tread perilously close to the romantic ballads of the thirties. The very opening phrase with its lush harmony and predictable sequences sounds like the 'cue for song' introduction from many a Hollywood musical. (It is only fair to remember that it was written in 1907; one should not blame Rakhmaninov for creating something that would subsequently be debased by counterfeits.) Indeed the 'song' duly follows, a long sustained melody for solo clarinet with a softly murmuring accompaniment in the violins and expressive comments in violas or cellos. It continues for twenty-two leisurely bars before the violins take over with a new theme that rises step by step until it flowers gloriously with the very phrases which had come at the start of the movement, an alpha transformed into an omega.

A contrasting section follows with flowing semiquaver figures cooling the passion. Solo violins begin a close-knit dialogue[7] which is interrupted by a sequence of forlorn little phrases for cor anglais and oboe. The music grows increasingly restless as these two new ideas are developed at some length. A summons from the horns brings reinforcements from the trumpets; the texture thickens inexorably until a glorious climax is reached with the third appearance of the opening phrase. Exerting admirable control, Rakhmaninov refuses to indulge this tune, allowing it just one sweeping arc of melody before it is dispersed into thin air and silence.

A properly symphonic development now begins, intermingling the opening theme with the contrasting flowing semiquaver passage; but Rakhmaninov soon tires of this and reintroduces the long clarinet theme, now given to the violins and with snatches of the opening theme adding an unforseen counterpoint. The 'song' continues to its full length until, having reached its final and biggest climax, it gradually unwinds and brings the movement to a quiet conclusion.

The fourth movement (Allegro vivace) exploits the swift triplet figures much favoured by Rakhmaninov. Four introductory bars set the pace before the main theme appears, its opening notes unmistakably marked by blaring horns. Characteristically it tends to centre itself on one note, the dominant B, which, in a subsidiary passage, is replaced by an equally persistent A. This frenzied tarantella gallops on furiously until it is suddenly checked by the peremptory beat of a drum and a stabbing *sforzando* on horns. A march-like interlude follows, strangely muted, as though the army is still at a distance. Chattering triplets in the strings herald the reappearance of the first subject which continues its headlong rush for some time. A true second subject makes a striking entry with a downward plunge of an octave. Its lyrical phrases fail to seduce the flutes and clarinets who continue the tarantella rhythm; but as the tune develops still further, woodwind and horns acknowledge its superiority and begin a throbbing accompaniment which persists for fifteen pages of score. All passion spent, the music sinks down into the lowest depth of the cellos. Mysteriously and magically the theme from the slow movement makes a brief appearance, accompanied by a flowing figure in the woodwind which keen listeners will identify as 1c from the first movement. (It first appeared on page 1; we are now on page 260!)

This moment of nostalgia is abruptly terminated as the strings resume the original tempo and begin the development section. For several pages the

---

[7] Whether consciously or not, it is closely related to Ex. 1c.

music bustles along in suppressed tones without having much of significance to say. A solo flute then produces an almost perfect allusion to 1c which is taken up by several wind instruments in turn. A second march-like interlude follows, based entirely on descending scales. Considering the poverty of the material, it is remarkable how effectively Rakhmaninov uses it; one may resist intellectually, but the build-up is so thrillingly orchestrated that only the most strong-hearted can stay aloof. The accelerating tumult of scales rushes into the recapitulation which, though different in detail, follows a more or less familiar path. The broad span of the second subject carries us magisterially towards the final coda which ends the movement in hurricane fashion.

There is no doubt that the symphony is overlong for its content and the composer himself sanctioned a number of cuts. Yet a live performance by a virtuoso orchestra can be overwhelming in its impact. Those who criticise the work for its expansiveness should remember the period from which it comes, a period in which audiences had become accustomed to the concept that symphonies were large-scale affairs. Bruckner and Mahler had established the pattern which other composers were almost bound to follow. For English listeners the most apt comparison to make is with Elgar, whose symphonies are almost exactly contemporaneous with this work; indeed Rakhmaninov might be said to be a Russian Elgar since both composers shared a liking for sequences, for exploitation of small rhythmical units and for rich orchestral colour. Both have a tendency to ramble, both are intensely emotional and are unafraid of expressing emotion to the full. If their type of Romanticism fell out of fashion for a time, they cannot be blamed; in a computer-dominated age they offer an escape from present-day reality which grows increasingly welcome.

RAVEL
1875–1937

'He is not afraid of approaching the attractive realms of bad taste, that good bad taste which in fact is only a human weakness.' So wrote one of Ravel's biographers in a frank admission that there is an element of decadence in his music. The phrase 'good bad taste' is reminiscent of Richard Strauss's description of himself as 'perhaps not a first-class composer but a first-class second-class one'. It is probably true that despite the huge differences between them Ravel and Strauss both fall into this category. Ravel's musical inheritance consists of a strange and contradictory mixture of styles. On the one hand he was fascinated by the grand pianistic tradition of Liszt even though he was in love with the distant past, much drawn towards classical purity. These two inclinations are at odds with each other but there are further conflicting elements to be considered—a smart sophistication, brittle and witty, and a surrender to the exoticism of the East. A quick survey of some of his compositions reveals these varying facets of his art.

One of the commonest views holds that he is brittle, witty and sophisticated but without heart, the French *boulevardier*, a Maurice Chevalier of the concert world. The delightful dialogue between the cup and the teapot in *L'enfant et les Sortilèges* illustrates this admirably, as does the song of the clock or the remarkable chorus of mathematical numbers. This is the music of the twenties and it could only have been written by a city dweller. But what he wrote as burlesque in his opera *L'enfant et les Sortilèges* appears in the piano concerto as serious concert music, glittering, brilliant and again seeming to be quite without emotional involvement. Nor could there be a better example of classical restraint than the slow movement of the same concerto whose austere accompaniment in the left hand rejects every temptation to indulge in any of the conventions of Romantic pianism.

Yet if we turn to the song cycle *Shéhérazade*, we find a sheer sensuous beauty which is overwhelming. Debussy may have showed Ravel the way with *L'après-midi d'un faune* but Ravel goes far beyond him in the lush richness of sound that he produces. This is the last word in sensuality, and shows a mastery of orchestration that is virtually unrivalled. It is here that we find the exotic, Eastern element in Ravel's music, though to a lesser extent something of the sort can be heard in the famous Bolero as well as in the Princess's music in *L'enfant et les Sortilèges*.

If we look for the Ravel who was enamoured of the past there are a number of examples—the *Pavane pour une Infante défunte*, the whole of *Le Tombeau de Couperin* and perhaps most perfectly the second of three part-songs for unaccompanied choir, *Trois beaux oiseaux du Paradis*. Here is a simple heart-touching beauty quite different from the seductive sensuality of *Shéhérazade*. However, such works as *La Valse* and the *Valses nobles et sentimentales* show a nostalgia for a more recent past which Ravel himself must have known in his twenties even though he did not mix with high society.

If we turn now to the influence of Liszt, it is evident in such virtuoso piano pieces as *Gaspard de la nuit*, the *Alborada del gracioso* and *Jeux d'eau*. All show a phenomenal mastery of keyboard writing and to this day hold challenges for the most accomplished pianists. For pure beauty of sound *Ondine* can have few rivals and it is a delightful speculation to imagine how Liszt himself would have responded to it.

When one considers these contradictory aspects of Ravel's art one realises that there is some justification for them. Like the English, the French had no great musical tradition behind them to give assurance to a new generation of composers. Figures like Gounod, Saint-Saëns and Massenet can scarcely have held any great inspiration for the young Ravel, and Berlioz was still dishonoured in his own country. But Debussy had created an enormous stir, and the influence of the medievalism of *Pelléas et Mélisande* must have been enormously strong. This alone might account for Ravel's delight in antiquity, even if we don't allow for the historical splendours of French architecture and their inevitable effect on any young impressionable mind. Debussy too had succumbed to the spell of the East; as long ago as 1889 there had been an exhibition in Paris at which Debussy heard a Javanese orchestra; he was fascinated by the sound, and it's intriguing to follow the thread of Oriental influence through Debussy, Ravel and Roussel to the contemporary figures of Boulez and Messiaen.

Here, then, we have some explanation for Ravel's artistic personality, the medievalism and the oriental streak, while the derivations from Liszt can be ascribed to the lack of any solid French inheritance. Had Berlioz been a great writer for piano, Ravel might have written in a totally different style. As for the dry sardonic wit, that is a French trait shared with other composers such as Poulenc, Auric, or most directly in its influence on Ravel, the music of Satie which he much admired.

Ravel had a traumatic experience over the coveted Prix de Rome. Four times he entered for it and four times he was rejected; the last attempt was the most wounding for he did not even survive the preliminary trial. The jury solemnly pronounced that Monsieur Ravel's musicianship was not up to the required standard. At the time he had already written his String Quartet, the famous *Pavane, Jeux d'eau* and a number of other works. There was a major scandal and reaction was so strong that the Director of the Conservatoire, Theodore Dubois, resigned. But the wound bit deep, and when years later Ravel was offered the Légion d'Honneur, he refused it.

Now, however much a composer believes in himself, such treatment must lead to a certain lack of security and this may well be the explanation of one unique aspect of Ravel's music, and that is that he should so often have produced two versions of a composition, one for piano and one for orchestra. His piano writing is so masterly, so absolutely pianistic moreover, that it seems quite absurd that he should have squandered his energies orchestrating works that were already perfect in themselves. Even that absolute gem, the *Sonatine*, exists in an orchestral version, the other better known examples being the *Pavane, Le Tombeau de Couperin* and the *Valses nobles et sentimentales*. Ravel was very self-deprecatory, showing, at any rate to the world, a strange lack of interest in his own music. If a piece of his was being played at a concert, he would often walk outside and smoke a couple of cigarettes, more from an affectation of boredom it would seem than nervousness.

Perhaps in another sense he felt something of an outsider. His period coincides almost exactly with the stylistic disintegration that was so notable in European music during the second decade of the century. The language of music was changing so fast that many composers failed to keep up and were left to fade in their own Romantic twilight. For all his love of sensual beauty Ravel was able to avoid this fate; that edge of cynicism, the contact with the music-hall so characteristic of the French, and his ability to strip his music down to a monastic simplicity when he wished, all combined to save him from drowning in a welter of impressionism. To think of him as a pale reflection of Debussy is totally wrong; to call him merely brittle and sophisticated is misleading; like most great composers he has many facets and it is up to us to appreciate them all.

Shéhérazade
(1903)

The East has lost much of its glamour in the last fifty years or so. Twentieth-century progress—if that's the word—has many crimes to answer for, but few are worse than the universal use of concrete whereby the streets of

Teheran, Bangkok or Tokyo have been made to share a common factor of indescribable ugliness. Future generations will surely look back with disgust and disbelief at the architectural heritage we have left them which manages to combine shoddiness and indestructibility in the most depressing manner. Yet back at the start of the century the French poet Tristan Klingsor could write lyrically of an imagined Asia, a fabled ancient land he'd never seen, a land of fantasies learned from a nursemaid's tales.

> I long to take myself away to those flower-deck'd isles where I can hear the bewitching song of the sea; I long to see Damascus, and Persian cities whose delicate minarets touch the sky; I long to see fine silken turbans, velvet clothes and long-tasselled coats, to see Persia and India and then China, where there are fat mandarins beneath their parasols, princesses with fragile hands and scholars arguing about poetry and beauty.

Rimsky-Korsakov had been one of the first composers to exploit the exotic charms of the East in his orchestral suite *Schéhérazade*. He had actually travelled there as a naval officer before its beauties had been corrupted by commerce and destroyed by humanity's insatiable desire to breed and multiply. But in 1899 Ravel, then twenty-four years old, produced an overture called *Shéhérazade* as the first step towards writing an opera on that tempting subject. The overture was not a success and the operatic project never got under way. The fascination remained however and four years later Ravel decided to set three of Klingsor's poems for soprano and orchestra and call them *Shéhérazade*. The resulting songs, 'Asie', 'La flute enchantée' and 'L'Indifferent', are orchestrated with such absolute mastery that it's hard to believe that Ravel could have heard very little of his music actually performed at the time. Apart from the ill-fated overture and a relatively slight song-cycle called '*Sites auriculaires*', he had nothing behind him except two piano pieces and a string quartet. He had failed to win the coveted Prix de Rome three times and must have felt depression and disillusionment. Part of the appeal of Klingsor's poems may well have been their evocation of romantic and distant places, far removed from Paris and the musical establishment. All the same, the sureness of touch he brought to the orchestration of these songs indicates an uncanny ear that could dispense with practical experience and achieve instant perfection.

The first song, 'Asie', lasts some ten minutes and is as elaborate in conception as a major operatic aria, tempo and mood frequently changing, responding to the vivid imagery of the poem. Surprisingly, the work doesn't seem to have caused any great sensation when it was first performed the year after the score had been completed.

The cycle begins with a shimmering trill on violins, half the players trilling downwards, half trilling upwards. The effect is of sustained harmonies kept in a state of glittering motion, an aural equivalent to the glare that dazzles the eye when one gazes into the distance in bright sunlight. The solo line is given to an oboe, partly because its reedy tone does have a vaguely oriental tang, but also because Ravel wants to keep the flute in reserve for the second song, 'The enchanted flute'. There follows a sequence of descending harmonies so characteristic of Ravel that they virtually became his personal property. In themselves they don't sparkle enough for his purpose so he adds brightness with a nimble little phrase for the piccolo which is then passed on through flutes, oboes and clarinets. In six bars he has captured the heat and glare of the sun, the languor of the East, the sparkle of light, all in less time than it takes to develop a polaroid colour-film. Three times the singer declaims the magic word 'Asie', so much more poetic than our 'Asia', and all its haunting beauty is summed up by this master of orchestral colour. The pictorially descriptive quality of the music is constantly evident. The poet's first wish is to sail away in a schooner 'whose violet sails will unfurl like the wings of some immense night-bird in a golden sky'. Ravel suggests the gentle rocking of the boat with lazy arpeggios in the bass, but the merest mention of the word 'Asie' again brings an instant shimmer of light from the violins like a fleck of gold paint on a canvas.

Ravel achieves an extraordinary iridescence by his treatment of the single note 'A'. An obvious if trite approach would be to have it played at three different octaves, first violins at the top, second violins in the middle and violas beneath. Ask for a quiet tremolando from all three, and a shimmering effect would be easily obtained. Such a solution is far too ordinary for Ravel. He wants the music to dance and glitter like sunlight reflected from a thousand ripples on the surface of the water. To achieve this he arranges for half the first violins to play a figure that continually spans the whole two octaves; the other first violins have a similar figure but not exactly synchronised so that their highest note coincides with the top violins' middle note and vice versa. Meanwhile the second violins have a two-octave jump, the upper note being a harmonic, giving it an ethereal insubstantial quality. Against this delicate background the woodwind place paired harmonies. Not a note is miscalculated.

With each change of thought in the poem the music changes correspondingly, yet somehow Ravel manages to hold the song together. For instance the paired harmonies mentioned above serve as a link between two differing sections while in other cases a brief melodic pattern will be promoted from a mere suggestion in one passage to a dominant feature in the next. When the poet's vision changes—'I long to see eyes that are dark with love though their pupils shine with delight'—Ravel contrives yet another subtle link. A pattern that began in cellos and basses rises to the upper woodwind only to be reduced to four lazy notes on the harp. The texture, so vibrant previously, suddenly becomes almost immobile, languorous and sensual.

Towards the end of the song there is a huge climax. 'I yearn to see poor people and queens, roses and blood; I want to see those who can die for love or for hatred, and then return home to tell my adventures to those who are curious about my dreams. . . .' After the line about dying of love or hatred the orchestral wash of sound engulfs the solo voice, a moment that Richard Strauss himself never surpassed in an operatic score.

The two remaining songs that make up the cycle are less substantial, their combined length being less than the ten minutes of 'Asie'. The second, 'La flute enchantée' is sung presumably by a slave-girl who watches over her sleeping master while, from the courtyard outside, comes the sound of a flute, ravishingly played by her lover, each note flying to her through the sultry air like a mysterious kiss. Naturally it invites a musical setting, and Ravel had the problem of escaping from the influence of Debussy's faun, whose seductive flute had astonished and delighted audiences nearly ten years previously. He steps out of Debussy's shadow skilfully by introducing quite a lively dance rhythm as though the lover is eager to arrange a rendezvous with his enchantress.

The third song, 'L'Indifferent', shows Ravel in a far more restrained mood. There is no call for passion here for the poem tells of a mysterious youth 'with eyes like a girl's . . . who speaks an unknown and charming language like music out of tune'. As he passes down the street with his 'languid and feminine walk' the singer watches him from her window, too shy to call out or attract his attention. Inevitably after the opulence of 'Asie' the work seems to end on a note of anticlimax even though Ravel's setting of the third poem is entirely apposite; but apart from its beauty *Shéhérazade* has a special significance in Ravel's output for here for the first time we meet the sumptuous orchestrator whose mastery was so wonderfully demonstrated in *Daphnis et Chloé.*

Piano Concerto in G Major
(1929–31)

'They say my music has no melody' said Ravel plaintively, 'but it is *all* melody.' The concerto demonstrates the point well for it includes passages where the melody, while undeniably present, is obscured by the surrounding wash of sound. In particular the very opening pages alarm the conservative listener. There *is* a tune, a very conventional one that could be mistaken for a folk-song; but it is played by a single shrill piccolo set against a glittering background that creates a dazzling blur by fusing the contradictory keys of G and F sharp in a swift clatter of triplets (Ex. 1).

At the time that it was written Paris was still in the grip of the jazz fever of the twenties and to a certain extent this concerto reflects something of the

Ex. 1

age. One might almost say that it is the concerto Gershwin tried to write twice, and it's interesting that Gershwin actually went to Ravel, hoping to have some lessons, at about this time.[1]

In the first pages the piano serves a purely orchestral function as part of the colour, and in time it drops out leaving Ex. 1 triumphant on the orchestra. When the pianist reappears it is as a real soloist, introducing a new idea for the first time, and assuming, as Ravel so often does, a sort of Spanish mantle. The music is extraordinarily balletic in conception, and summons up vivid images of dancers in the listener's imagination. But where Ravel is so clever is when he really flirts with danger. His melodies at times seem about to cross the border into the world of popular music, and then with a deft flick of the wrist he just lifts them out of banality into something cynical, satirical or just distinguished. The true second subject offers a good example; the tune itself could well be mistaken for Gershwin:

Ex. 2

but the jerky little syncopations that interrupt its progress coupled with their acid harmony effectively counter the potentially saccharine quality of the melody. ('He is not afraid of approaching the attractive realms of bad taste, . . . good bad taste' . . . (see page 201).) The technique used here, prodding a slow melody into life with jabbing syncopations, is identical to Gershwin's in the 'Rhapsody in Blue', but Ravel's touch is far more subtle.

After the orchestra has been given a taste of Ex. 2 the soloist embarks on a brilliant passage whose figuration resembles that of the Toccata from *Le Tombeau de Couperin*. Every now and then a tune emerges out of the clattering chords, referring back to a 'blues' phrase that has appeared several times in the orchestra (Ex. 3).

Another jazz influence can clearly be heard as the pianist drums out

---

[1] An authentic story relates that Ravel asked Gershwin how much he earned in a year; on being told he said, 'It is I who should be taking lessons from you'.

Ex. 3

rhumba rhythms in the bass register. The focus is entirely on the piano part during this section, the orchestra merely giving support with sharp explosive chords. A brief cadenza consisting of a swift unison run that climbs through five octaves leads to a reprise of Ex. 1, briefly taken over by the soloist before being handed back to the orchestra.

The 'Spanish' theme reappears as a piano solo culminating in a dramatic gesture based on Ex. 3. It is a display of temperament that is magically checked by a sudden recession of tempo; mysteriously a harp produces a solemn little tune with a suggestion of plainchant. It is like an apparition, a ghost that halts the dancers in their tracks. The pianist resents the interruption, throwing a violent arpeggio from end to end of the keyboard as the orchestra blares out Ex. 3. Again the harp casts its strange spell. This time the soloist succumbs, accepting the change of mood. It is the cue to begin one of the most original cadenzas in the entire concerto repertoire.

Using Ex. 2 as the melodic basis, Ravel produces an illusion of a three-handed pianist, the left hand actually playing the tune *and* a wide-spanned rippling accompaniment while the right hand has a sequence of sustained trills far above. Now one thing that a piano cannot do is a portamento, the slide from one note to another that is easily accomplished on a string instrument by simply sliding the finger along the string. As if intrigued by the 'can't-do' challenge, Ravel creates another illusion unique in piano literature, a continuous trill that appears to slide from note to note much as the cinema organists of the twenties used to. The siren song lures the orchestra to join in and Ex. 2 rises to a rhapsodic climax.

The urgent toccata begins again, treating the piano like a set of pitched drums. It is the start of a non-stop drive towards the end of the movement in which the orchestra turns Ex. 1 into a brilliant moto perpetuo.

The slow movement is an extraordinary invention. On the whole, innocence is a virtue that composers have not exploited greatly in the twentieth century. This music seems to be completely innocent; the left hand accompaniment is simplicity itself, and the melody that lies above it, although sophisticated in the sense that it is far from obvious, has an indefinably touching quality. Here, one feels, is that same *Fille aux cheveux de lin* whom Debussy described; but now she is dancing a grave sarabande in some stone courtyard in an idyllic chateau. The soft light of an evening sun is on her fair hair, as alone she dances with that intense concentration that a child displays when caught up in some absorbing fantasy. For thirty-three bars the melody continues uninterrupted with the left hand never breaking its pattern save for one single crotchet where Ravel wants to emphasise the end of a phrase. When Ravel does bring in the orchestra it's a breathtaking moment, with a high clear solo flute taking over the melody, as though a watching shepherd-boy had found the urge to join in irresistible.

The middle of the movement consists for the greater part of elaborate decorations in the piano over the persistent rhythm in the left hand, enriched by sensuously beautiful harmonies in the orchestra. Then the whole of the long opening melody is repeated on the cor anglais with an almost Beethoven-like figuration high above in the piano part. And yet for all its classic simplicity there is a romantic heart to this music though the romance belongs not to the nineteenth century but to the distant times of Bayard or Roland.

The last movement is short, sharp and very much to the point. It has a positively chromium-plated glitter about it, but after such a display of heart as we have just experienced in the slow movement we can't complain if now Ravel rejoins the twentieth century. (The jazz influence is again evident here.) A few abrupt chords from the orchestra check the headlong flight of the piano part, whereupon the soloist introduces a country bumpkin of a tune:

Ex. 4

Perhaps it's a couple of knockabout comedians at a sleazy music-hall, the sort of thing that the cultured French so adore in their weaker moments. The orchestra takes it over, while the piano part skims through brilliant repeated notes that have all the sparkle of sequins on an acrobatic dancer's costume.

A change of rhythm suggests the arrival of an equestrienne on the scene and once more we are vividly aware of the balletic quality of the music. Ravel himself said that the music of a concerto should in the truest sense be light-hearted and brilliant, not aiming at profundity or especially dramatic effects. This is not to equate it with triviality, and in amongst the glitter there are some masterly flashes of orchestral invention including one of the most awe-inspiring bassoon parts that an unfortunate orchestral player is ever likely to encounter.

The music keeps up a virtually non-stop chatter right to the end, exuding enormous vitality and enjoyment. Certainly the concerto is a lightweight that scorns the heroic aspirations of Rakhmaninov or Tchaikovsky, nor does it even provide the rich textures that we find in some of Ravel's music for solo piano. Apart from a large percussion section, the orchestra is relatively small with only six wind players, four brass, a timpanist and harp to complement the usual strings. Clarity of texture seems to have been of fundamental importance and in this sense the work can be regarded as neo-classical. It is almost ironic that the concerto for left hand only should by contrast be dense in texture and romantic in conception.

Piano Concerto for Left Hand Alone in D Major (1933)

This work, in a single movement lasting some seventeen minutes, was commissioned by Paul Wittgenstein, an Austrian concert pianist who had lost his right arm during World War I. (Prokofiev's Fourth Concerto came to be written in the same way.) To a non-pianist it may seem strange that music for the left hand only is a much more practical proposition than music for the right. There are two reasons for this; first, that though we may tend to listen to top lines for melodies, the true foundations of music lie at the roots of the harmony, in the bass; second, that if a tune needs to be brought out strongly the thumb is better equipped to do it than the little finger of the right hand. In the event Ravel made the handicap a virtue since his writing is so spectacular that any performance that does justice to the work becomes a tour-de-force.[2]

In complete opposition to the glittering opening pages of the Piano Concerto in G this work begins in the darkest area of the orchestra with murmuring double-basses setting up a barely audible movement. Out of the murk emerges a solo for double-bassoon:

Ex. 1

Gradually, with a constant thickening of the texture, the music climbs towards the light until the full orchestra—the *very* full orchestra—is employed. Throughout this graduated ascent the dotted rhythm shown in Ex. 1 is a feature. It has an almost heraldic flavour like a very stately fanfare. After a tremendous preparation (not an orchestral 'tutti' in the historic or conven-

---

[2] Wittgenstein was compelled to make modifications that infuriated Ravel.

tional sense) the soloist makes his long-delayed entry. It is well worth waiting for, a majestic cadenza which makes no compromises. Perhaps because the very idea of a one-armed pianist implies a form of heroism, the music has precisely the heroic and romantic attitudes that Ravel conspicuously avoided in his other concerto. Listening to a broadcast or a record, it is virtually impossible to accept that these massive almost Brahmsian passages are being played by a single hand, and Ravel was determined to create the illusion of normality.

Once the pianist has shown that concessions are neither asked nor given, the full orchestra triumphantly affirms the theme of pageantry. In these opening pages Ravel keeps orchestra and soloist firmly apart, an unusual plan for a twentieth-century concerto, but one no doubt dictated by the special circumstances. The soloist is the first to present the second subject. It is a deeply expressive tune tinged with such sadness that one feels it could well be an expression of sympathy for Wittgenstein's plight. Certainly the emotion seems more personal than is usual in Ravel's music.

The reappearance of the opening theme in the orchestra disturbs this hauntingly beautiful meditation and now, for the first time, we find some integration of piano and orchestra as the soloist casts little webs of decoration over the strands of melody beneath. The ceremonial quality of the music is put aside for the time being, replaced by a sombre elegy with silvery ripples from the piano edging it with brightness. The mood changes as bravura octaves lead us towards a climax. Suddenly the brass introduce a jazzy element that is almost shocking in its effect. Although seemingly alien it is in fact a variation on the themes already presented. It evokes a furious reaction in the piano part which soon becomes a '*danse macabre*', offering a grotesque parody of the initial theme in the rapid 6/8 time which seems to be the accepted gait for witches and demons. This section is terminated by a fully orchestrated version of the main theme, decorated with sweeping arpeggios from the keyboard. There follows an astonishing cadenza in which the themes are reviewed, surrounded by glittering cascades of notes. Ravel's resourcefulness in writing for the one hand is extraordinary; he exploits every imaginable colour, using the extreme treble registers as a corrective to any tendency to be bass-heavy. And having done all this, he seems to say 'That's enough—' for with the briefest possible coda, a mere five bars, he brings the concerto to an abrupt end. It is unfortunate that performances are relatively infrequent for the concerto shows a profundity and depth of feeling that is comparatively rare in Ravel's music. It was the last work he was to write for the piano, an instrument whose repertoire he had enriched with a string of masterpieces. For the last five years of his life he suffered from a tragic mental illness that created a block between mind and hand. The last letter he ever wrote, in March 1934, took him eight days to get down on paper. It consisted of a mere fifty words, each one of which he had had to search for laboriously in a dictionary as he could not remember how to write even the individual letters. On one occasion during this nightmare period he was taken to a concert of his works. At the end he wept. 'It was lovely all the same,' he managed to say with difficulty. And then, 'I still had so much music in my head. Now it's finished for me'.

SCHOENBERG

1874–1951

The death of Schoenberg's father when the boy was only fifteen left the family in straitened circumstances. Although young Arnold had started to learn the violin at the age of eight—and later turned to the cello for preference—the expense of private lessons was out of the question and apart from occasional guidance from musical friends he remained largely self-taught. Music was the dominant art in Vienna and it was no problem for him to become involved with other students through a society called 'Poly-hymnia'. The leading light was Alexander von Zemlinsky, a talented composer, only two years Schoenberg's senior, who was to have a considerable influence on the young man's approach to music. At the time there was a marked divide between the followers of Wagner and the devotees of Brahms. Although Schoenberg was a great admirer of Wagner, later claiming to have heard each of the operas twenty or thirty times during these formative years, his musical instinct drew him more towards Brahms. However, without the benefit of a proper course at the Conservatory and the passport to respectability given by a diploma, he could scarcely contemplate a musical career. In 1891 he became a junior employee in a private bank, a safe path to the financial security he needed. Ironically the bank proved to be far from safe and four years later the owner declared himself bankrupt. Schoenberg must have regarded this as a heaven-sent sign and resolved that come what may he would now devote himself to music.

He began to scratch a precarious living, conducting a metal-workers' choir in nearby Stockerau and doing soul-destroying hackwork scoring popular song hits for café orchestras and even entire operettas by lesser composers. It was practical experience of a sort that partly compensated for his lack of academic training. Meanwhile he took lessons in counterpoint from Zemlinsky and composed some songs and two quartets. The second of these was written in 1897 when he was twenty-three. It is much influenced by Brahms but the string writing is accomplished, the form coherent and well planned, while some of the themes are quite memorable. Schoenberg himself felt that there was a real quality in the Quartet; it was the only substantial piece from this apprentice period that he allowed to survive, even though it was not to be published until 1966, 69 years after it had been written.

Despite his lack of prospects, Schoenberg married in 1901, thus becoming Zemlinsky's brother-in-law. He was fortunate to gain a post as conductor of a light opera in Berlin; it was only a temporary job but it brought in a small but much-needed income. It was through the influence of Richard Strauss that something much more to his liking then materialised—teacher of composition at the Stern Conservatoire. Strauss had been greatly impressed by a mammoth work that Schoenberg had been writing for over a year, a setting of some poems by the nineteenth-century Danish poet Jens Peter Jacobsen. The *Gurrelieder* was an insanely ambitious work for an unknown composer to begin since the immensity of its demands would scare off any impresario—8 flutes, 5 oboes, 7 clarinets, 3 bassoons, 2 contra-bassoons, 10 horns, 7 trumpets, 7 trombones and tuba, 4 harps, celesta, at least six percussion players, a huge complement of strings, three 4-part male-voice choirs and an 8-part mixed choir, plus 5 soloists and a narrator. To this day it seldom crops up in a live performance. Yet its very size gives us a clear indication of its place in musical history, for it represents the ultimate apotheosis of nineteenth-century Romanticism. Together with Mahler's 'Symphony of a Thousand' the *Gurrelieder* is the largest musical canvas ever painted; there are longer operas, but I am thinking of works designed for the concert hall.

It took him eleven years to orchestrate, eleven years in which his outlook as a composer went through a radical change. Now, it is impossible to deny that Schoenberg was a romantic at heart whose early works follow directly in line with the late nineteenth-century Germanic tradition. *Verklärte Nacht*, (1899) is a string sextet whose melodic beauty and harmonic richness create an emotional atmosphere akin to the 'Liebestod' from *Tristan und Isolde*. The subsequent version for full string orchestra that Schoenberg made in 1917 (further revised in 1943) makes the tonal palette even richer. Inevitably someone with an intellect as powerful as Schoenberg's realised that this was a path that could not be pursued much further. In a sense his lack of a long and formal musical training gave him an advantage for his thinking had not been moulded by others; on the other hand it gave him a sense of insecurity that made him feel dependent on classical models. The String Quartet Op. 7 (1904–5) is intensely romantic in idiom but is deeply indebted to Beethoven in its formal structure. It was at this time that the inner conflict began which was to take Schoenberg the best part of fifteen years to resolve. His intellect told him that to follow Mahler and Strauss in their pursuit of ever richer sounds was a *folie de grandeur*; nevertheless his temperament drew him towards music of the greatest emotional intensity. Such are the pressures that can work on a composer when he is torn between the dictates of the mind and the inclinations of the heart, and they are much more likely to influence his music than the stirring love affairs or romantic brushes with death in the sick-room that lady novelists dwell upon at such length when they write stories about imaginary composers.

One of the first and most significant attempts to resolve this conflict came with the Chamber Symphony No. 1 Op. 9 (1906). Scored for only fifteen instruments, it is a strong reaction against the musical elephantiasis of the *Gurrelieder* which he was still laboriously orchestrating. The music is turbulent, romantic, post-Wagnerian, but because of the small resources it employs it gives a feeling of extraordinary compression. There are times when the tension seems too great, when the ideas spill out too profusely. Written as one continuous movement, it could be described as a descendant of the Liszt Piano Sonata for the thematic materials of the whole appear early in the work to be developed later. We can trace a 'first movement' of sorts, an embryonic slow movement and a scherzo during the initial stages of the symphony; certain clearly defined landmarks such as harmonies built on fourths, a horn theme, or a 'Wagnerian turn' help us to find our bearings at later stages. In fact the symphony is susceptible to formal analysis of a virtually traditional kind though the rapid fluctuations of tonality can be disturbing to a listener brought up on more conventional fare.

The ensuing work, the Quartet Op. 10 (1907–8), stands on the critical border-line over which Schoenberg was going to step into an alien world. The first movement begins securely in the key of F sharp minor; it is Classical in form if Romantic in conception. It openly acknowledges a debt to Brahms; but halfway through the work there is a radical change, symbolised graphically by the addition of a soprano voice which appears on the scene most unexpectedly singing a children's nursery-rhyme—'Du lieber Augustin'. It may seem a moment of incongruity but the words of the song could hardly be more significant:

> Ach, du lieber Augustin, alles ist hin.
> (Ah, you dear Augustin, all is lost.)

What is lost? The answer lies all around for it is the old security of tonality and all that went with it. The first movement started clearly in F sharp minor; but in the last two movements the harmony often loses touch with conventional tonality and breaks new bounds in which we find wind-blown fragments of music that are in no identifiable key. Even so, Schoenberg is careful to integrate this new concept of quartet-writing with the more traditional opening movements by incorporating recognisable quotations from time to time.

The poems used in the last two movements are by Stefan George, 'Litany' and 'Transcendence'. 'Litany' is deeply sorrowful, a 'De profundis' cry of despair, and it is easy to share the intensity of emotion that Schoenberg brings to it, especially in its closing pages.

The last movement is the hardest in every sense, and the opening line of the poem which, being translated, reads 'I feel an air from other planets blowing' has been widely interpreted as a metaphor for Schoenberg's own impatience with traditional language and a longing to start his exploration into the uncharted areas of what was to become first atonality and then serialism. But this quartet makes one realise how strong the roots of tradition actually were in Schoenberg, and that his journey into the unknown was not the act of a madman but a calculated and deliberate attempt to discover a new world that would be valid and full of potential. His enormous influence on other composers proves that his musical space-probe was justified. In *Pierrot Lunaire* he was to make his journey to the moon; this quartet was like a first satellite. No one could doubt his integrity or his courage from this time onwards.

The quartet, first performed in December 1908, was received with hostility, derision and mirth, reactions Schoenberg was to become accustomed to as he pursued an ever more individual path. Busoni once said 'It is the task of the creator to establish laws rather than to follow them' and Schoenberg realised that if (as he felt to be essential) the traditional concepts of tonality were to be jettisoned, new laws would have to be laid down. So began the gradual formulation of a new musical 'grammar', Serialism, or the art of composition with twelve notes. I will not duplicate here the explanation given in Volume 1 pp. 105–7,[1] but whatever one's reactions to the theoretical basis, serialism was to prove one of the most profoundly significant influences on the course of twentieth-century music.

In 1912 Schoenberg wrote his Op. 21, 'Thrice seven poems from Albert Giraud's *Pierrot Lunaire*' for speaking voice and five instrumentalists who, by 'doubling', provide eight instruments. Instead of the vast span and the immense forces of the *Gurrelieder* we find twenty-one miniatures for a small chamber ensemble; but whereas the *Gurrelieder* stretch the idiom of the nineteenth-century to breaking-point, *Pierrot Lunaire* creates a new sound-world that severs all tonal connections with the past.[2] To Schoenberg's delight and surprise the work received an ovation and soon spread his name across Europe. In a previous cycle of piano pieces, Op. 19, he had fined down his compositions to the most concentrated brevity, as though his steps into the unknown must of necessity be tentative. (Two pieces are only nine bars long.) But a sigh can be as expressive as a flood of tears and it was the distillation of emotion that now fascinated Schoenberg. The brief poems of Giraud gave him a formal structure which suited his purpose admirably. Despite the bizarre nature of the poems the music is subjected to severe

---

[1] Or see my *Understanding Music*, pp. 48–53; J. M. Dent, 1979.

[2] The rejection of tonality, of traditional major or minor keys and their relationships, is known as atonality; it is not the same as Serialism which was a later development for Schoenberg. Serialism might be described as the harnessing of atonality.

contrapuntal disciplines; it was as though having discarded tonality, Schoenberg sought every other prop he could, variations, canons, passacaglia, mirror-images, fugue, and even dance-forms such as the waltz. The instrumental colours are sharply differentiated rather than blended, while the voice-part is scrupulously notated even though it is spoken, not sung.

Between 1915 and 1923 Schoenberg seemed to write almost nothing save sketches for *Jakobsleiter*, an oratorio that he never completed. Even allowing for the enormous upheaval of the War, in which he served humbly in the ranks, it was for him a period in the wilderness in which the formulation of serialism came into being. He had seen its possibilities as early as 1915 but to exploit those possibilities and discover a way of organising their potential took years of intellectual struggle. During this period he became renowned as a teacher, acquiring a small coterie of devoted disciples whose support was to prove invaluable during the trials that lay ahead. In 1925 Schoenberg took over the composition class at the Prussian State Academy of Arts in Berlin. Continuing to compose, he showed in such works as the Op. 29 Suite and the Third Quartet that though he had rejected the implications of tonality, classical forms still had a genuine validity for him. (He even extended an affectionate hand towards the past by orchestrating Bach's organ prelude and fugue in E flat.) In 1928 one of his most important works appeared, the Orchestral Variations, Op. 31; but he was beginning to move far beyond the comprehension of the ordinary public and even an attempt at a comic opera *Von heute auf morgen* (From one day to the next) failed to win him a more receptive audience. In the early 1930s he became absorbed in a giant task, the opera *Moses und Aron* for which he wrote his own libretto. He could scarcely have chosen a subject more likely to create trouble with the authorities. Hitler's accession to power in 1933 gave a warning that even the politically neutral composer could not disregard. In May of that year he was summarily dismissed from his post at the Academy.

His first thought was to go to France; it was essential that he should find work since all income from Germany was blocked. Paris offered him nothing, neither, to its shame, did London. A small music college in Boston, the Malkin Conservatory, offered him a professorship, and so it was to America that he and his family travelled to begin a new life, free from fear. Ironically within months he became so seriously ill that he was given only weeks to live. In search of a kinder climate he moved to Los Angeles in 1934 and remained there continuing to teach and compose until his death in 1951. They were fruitful years in which his enormous influence over the course of twentieth-century music came to be acknowledged. That is something to which a brief introductory essay such as this cannot do justice. If I give the last words to Schoenberg himself it is to show how aware he was of the antagonism he had aroused, but also of the relentless inner force that drove him to take such a lonely road to his deserved immortality.

That you should regard all I have tried to do in the last fifty years as an achievement strikes me as in some respects an overestimate. My own feeling was that I had fallen into an ocean of boiling water; and, as I couldn't swim and knew no other way out, I struggled with my arms and legs as best I could. I don't know what saved me, or why I wasn't drowned or boiled alive—perhaps my own merit was that I never gave in. Whether my movements were very economical or completely senseless, whether they helped or hindered my survival, there was no one willing to help me, and there were plenty who would gladly have seen me go under. I don't think it was envy—what was there to envy?—and I doubt whether it was lack of goodwill, or worse, positive ill-will on their part. Perhaps they just wanted to get rid of the nightmare, the agonising disharmony, the unintelligible thinking, the systematic lunacy that I represented, and I must admit that those who thought in that way were not bad men—though, of course, I could never understand what I had done to them to make them so malicious, so violent and so aggressive. I am still certain that I never took anything from them which was theirs. I never interfered with their rights and privileges, and never trespassed on their preserves. I didn't even know where these lay, or what was the line of demarcation that marked off their estate, or who gave them the right to ownership of the property. I am proud to accept this distinction, awarded on the assumption that I achieved something. Please don't call it false modesty if I say that perhaps something was achieved, but that it is not I who deserves the credit. The credit must go to my opponents. It was they who really helped me.[3]

Five Orchestral Pieces
Op. 16 (1909)

If one first approaches the music of Schoenberg through such immediately appealing works as the *Gurrelieder* and *Verklärte Nacht*, the Five Orchestral Pieces, Op. 16, provide the most suitable path to follow towards his more mature style. Originally he even planned to give them titles—'Premonitions', 'Yesteryears', 'Summer Morning by a Lake', 'Peripetia' (a high-flown word to describe the turning-point in a drama) and lastly and most enigmatically 'The Obbligato Recitative'. Before publication he withdrew these titles, replacing them with mere tempo indications. That Schoenberg had an affection for these relatively early pieces, written in his mid-thirties, is shown by his decision forty years later to return to them and rescore them for a normal orchestra rather than the vast and prohibitively expensive forces he'd origin-

---

[3] Schoenberg's letter of acceptance of a prize of $1,000 from the American Academy of Arts and Letters, May 1947. From H. H. Stuckenschmidt, *Arnold Schoenberg*, John Calder, 1959.

ally had in mind. He did this without changing their content, but simply as a practical gesture that would encourage performances at a time when, after all too long a wait, his music was beginning to be recognised as amongst the most significant of the century.

Since the first piece is the most demanding, it may be advisable to begin by listening to the second. Two points should be underlined strongly before hearing a note: one is the essentially romantic and expressive quality of the music which is far from the cerebral intellectual style so often associated (mistakenly) with Schoenberg; the other is the absolute mastery of orchestration he reveals. Despite the richness of orchestral sound at his disposal, the scoring is often delicate and subtle. For instance trumpets are virtually never given what might be described as martial music; much of the time they will be muted and playing brief expressive phrases. Harp and celesta contribute tellingly, solo string-players will be picked out of the orchestra to play a single chord or just a few notes. During the opening phrases of this piece notice the effectiveness of the solo cello at the start, the low muted trumpet, the dark threads of woodwind tone, the reiterated bell-like note on the celesta, the general air of restraint.

As the music moves forward a little we still find a solo viola and a pair of cellos as the sole contributors from the strings. The counterpoint is clear to follow; a phrase from that viola-player will be echoed in a slightly more elaborate version by a solo flute. In turn it will be taken up by a muted trumpet or horn or the second violins. Meanwhile, little dabs of sound on the celesta register their effect with the minimum of fuss. Soon Schoenberg sets up a series of recurring patterns almost as though he wants to hypnotise us. The most involved is to be found in the celesta part; one little shape is made to overlap itself at different levels; against these gentle undulations, two flutes reiterate a simple alternation of two chords. Only the bassoon shows a more adventurous spirit, but even his part is largely a permutation of one pattern of notes. However, it's one that soon spreads through a conglomeration of clarinets and bassoons, who seize on it avidly but quietly, like gossips whispering in a corner. These patterns suffice for the whole of the rest of the movement, the music being crystal clear once one realises its components.

Piece number three is strangely static; it originally had two titles. 'Summer Morning by a Lake', but more significantly, 'Colours'. In it Schoenberg explored a theory that had long fascinated him and that he'd discussed with Mahler on occasion. Just as an object can be made to seem to change by being subjected to changing and varying light, now bathed in crimson, then darkening to a deep purple and so on, Schoenberg felt that an effect of melody might be produced by changing the tone-colour of a single note or harmony. (Known as 'Klangfarbenmelodie', this theory was to have significant repercussions, especially in the music of Webern.) It was this idea that Schoenberg started to play with in the third of the five orchestral pieces. Initially he took a single harmony, this enigmatic chord:

Ex. 1

Having once established it by a number of repetitions, unusually but consistently scored, he then experimented with continually varying tone colours, while tiny fragments of sound flicker through the score like birds or insects by still water.

After such stillness one needs a dramatic contrast, and this Schoenberg provides with a vengeance in the next piece. Phrases rear upwards like stallions, yet the music does not stay violent and the initial gestures, heroic and romantic though they are, are quickly suppressed. Despite this suppression the aggressive urge of the opening phrases will not be denied and soon the angular shapes ring out stridently. Even so, the brass are for the most part muted, giving a sense of strain so that when at last in a final cataclysm the mutes come off, the effect is of a huge force unleashed.

Though Schoenberg's scores often look black to the eye, a closer examination reveals that much of the time he is beseeching the players to play as quietly as possible. Mutes are often called for, not only on brass but strings as well; the texture is sometimes so delicate that just a few notes on the harp can be marked 'solo', implying that it must be heard clearly against whatever else is playing at the time. All the same, there are big climaxes, though we shall find that the work ends quietly.

I have suggested postponing an approach to the first of these 'Five Pieces' until last since it is the only one that provides truly difficult listening. The discarded title 'Premonitions' raises the question 'Premonitions of what?' Perhaps of the course Schoenberg was destined to take, turbulent and storm-tossed.

It was not easy for him to choose the path he did; whether we like his music or not would have been a matter of complete indifference to him. It was Beethoven who said 'Muss es sein? Es muss sein!' 'Must it be? It must be!' It could as well have been Schoenberg's motto as, like that other great revolutionary, he accepted a destiny that was to change the world.

A Survivor from Warsaw
Op. 46 (1947)

The idea of the spoken word combined with music has tempted composers over a long period of time. There are classic instances such as *Lélio*, the melodrama which Berlioz planned to be a sequel to the *Fantastic Symphony*. Liszt wrote a fascinating piece for recitation accompanied by piano solo. In rather more recent times we have had Bliss's *Morning Heroes*, or the brief spoken passage that occurs near the end of Stravinsky's *Persephone*, with the melting flute solo that accompanies it. But somehow or other the combination of speech and music is always looked upon as something of a bastard art, even though experience has taught us that a subtle fusion of the two can be profoundly moving. It is a proposition that Hollywood took to its heart a little too dearly over the years, and our ears have become dulled by the constant reiteration of platitudes or hysterics over endless streams of rather meaningless music.

Perhaps because of the significant success of *Pierrot Lunaire* Schoenberg produced three other works for recitation with instrumental accompaniment, *Kol Nidre*, Op. 39, the *Ode to Napoleon Bonaparte*, Op. 41, and *A Survivor from Warsaw*, Op. 46. This compact work for narrator, male-voice chorus and orchestra was first performed at the University of New Mexico in the spring of 1948. Its impact was so overwhelming that it was received in shocked silence; it was played again and was given an ovation. It commemorates a brief episode in the savage destruction of the Jewish ghetto in Warsaw, an episode so horrifying that a quasi-operatic treatment with a sung narrative might seem to distance it from reality. It raises an aesthetic question that Schoenberg must have pondered deeply: can one translate human vileness into art? Is not the attempt to do so a sort of blasphemy in itself?

The truth is that the artist cannot escape the world that surrounds him. Picasso's picture of Guernica expresses a more powerful cry of anguish than a newspaper photograph can; it is an assault on the eye as well as on the conscience, and we have become too easily immune to everyday pictures of suffering. It needs an artist to make the shock go deeper. No Jew can escape the aftermath of the concentration camps, even if he was not there himself. In fact, if he wasn't there, his sense of guilt for having escaped the horror may cause it to prey on his mind more lastingly than on those who endured and survived. Their only wish must surely be to erase for ever the bitter scars of suffering; it's the ones whose relatives and friends went through the nightmare who must now be prone to morbid brooding.

A Jewish composer can be forgiven for wanting in some way to comment on the wholesale slaughter of his race. How clearly he must be able to share in his imagination just what his fellow-men went through. To sleep in hideous and crowded discomfort, and to be awoken in the cold dark morning by the shrill call of a trumpet, the harsh reveille that we hear at the beginning.

> *And then the feverish scramble for tattered clothes and belongings, the hands shaking with cold, jostled by neighbours, teeth chattering, one's whole existence a crazy dream in which it is impossible to believe. Dirt, hunger, misery, utter debasement, humans treated worse than animals.*

Anyone who can listen to this work and remain unmoved must have a heart of stone. Plaintive protests about dissonance are meaningless when the music describes a situation of such nightmare horror.

What could the composer do? Use harmonies from the comfortable cosy world of Parry and Stanford? There are frightening sounds in Wagner or Berlioz, but they are romantically conceived, and there was no romance in the Warsaw sewers. If ever there was a situation which demanded this sort of music, we find it here.

Time is confused; everything is confused, as one's recollections are. Schoenberg quotes the words of a young Pole who actually survived the massacre:

> *I cannot remember everything; I must have been unconscious most of the time; I remember only the grandiose moment when they all started to sing, as if pre-arranged, the old prayer they had neglected for so many years, the forgotten creed!*

This prayer, 'Scemah Israel', the final climax of this short and agonising work, is the musical culmination for which the composer is aiming. It is in the mind of the narrator as he tells the ghastly story, and so we hear an anticipation of it on a solo horn. The notes are identical to the final chant, but at this stage we can only guess at their purpose. Further musical links are forged between the very opening notes on the trumpet which are later identified as the dreaded reveille. Time after time we hear its insistent call, but transferred to cellos and basses and later in violins. In other words, the sharp memory of the trumpet call is echoed in the minds of the unfortunate wretches who are dragging themselves out of their half-sleep. And always the music has an awful twitching, nervous energy, the desperate energy of the hunted.

Comes the dreadful moment when the sergeant yells that in one minute he's going to pick out which ones are for the gas chamber. There begins the horrid scrambling stampede to fall in, anything to please this creature in whose hands one's destiny lies, and then, the moment when suddenly human dignity and courage assert themselves, when music, the singing of an ancient chant, turns frightened animals back into men, men who find in the singing of a traditional hymn a new spirit of resistance, new strength to defy the oppressor.

It was this legend from Warsaw that prompted Schoenberg to take this incident of all incidents and translate it into a musical experience. This piece is not about men being killed, not about persecution, not even really about Warsaw. It's about the power of music to refresh the broken spirit, it's about the immense strength that tradition and race can bring to man in time of desperation. These are subjects that are entirely the province of the artist, and it would be as stupid to accuse Schoenberg of pandering to sensationalism in this work as it would be to make all the usual dreary accusations about him being incapable of writing real music. The self-indulgent romantic warmth of *Verklärte Nacht* is here refined to a laser-like beam of searing intensity focussed on an episode that both indicts and exalts mankind.

SCHUBERT

1797–1828

While the child prodigy is not all that rare as a performer, the true prodigy in composition is something altogether exceptional. Mozart, Schubert and Mendelssohn all had the uncanny ability to produce music far beyond the normal capacity of even the most exceptionally talented boy. Such a gift (talent is too small a word), enables its possessor to take a staggering short cut that bypasses the experience and insight that lesser mortals can acquire only by long study and hard-won maturity. Imagine, then, what it must be like to come in contact with a boy of this type.

At the age of eight or nine, Schubert went to a teacher called Holzer for music lessons. He was the church organist at Liechtentahl, and in the presence of this astonishing pupil he was frankly nonplussed.

'If I wished to instruct him in anything fresh', he wrote, 'the boy already knew it. So I gave him no actual tuition but merely talked to him and watched him with silent astonishment.' Other teachers found the same thing; the violin teacher at the choir school where Schubert received his official education summed it up in the words, 'He has learnt it from God, that lad'. Every spare moment that Schubert had at the school seems to have been spent composing, and indeed this frenzied activity went on for the rest of his all too short life. One of the things he was doing at school was inventing a new art-form—what we now know as 'lieder'. This type of song—an intimate marriage of poetry and music in which the piano part clothes the poem in colours that are reflected from the words, was virtually unknown at the time. An eager schoolboy mapped out a new world of music, and he did so unaided, since there was nobody equipped to help him. Some of the greatest songs in the world, the 'Erl-King', 'Gretchen at the Spinning-wheel' and others were written by a bespectacled youth in his 'teens. His facility was truly astonishing; for instance, in his seventeenth year, when he was at a training college for teachers, he produced a full-length Mass, two string quartets, over a hundred songs, and a three-act opera running to 341 pages of full score. (This besides his normal studies, remember.) Composition was a natural function like eating or sleeping: the first movement of his quartet in B flat, Op. 168, was written in four and a half hours; leaving aside the actual composition, I doubt if a professional copyist could get it down on paper in the time. On the 19th October, 1815, he wrote no less than eight songs; feats like this border on fantasy. It was as though he had a never-ending flood of music bubbling up inside him; to check the flow by the application of intellectual disciplines was almost beyond him. The result was a short life in which an enormous quantity of music was written, all too much of it wasted, like the dozen or so operas that we never hear of.

One of music's great mysteries is why he never achieved wider popularity even in his all too short lifetime. If his compositions had been provocative, challenging or even extravagantly impractical, some excuse might be found for the relative indifference of the Viennese public; but few composers have endowed their music with such a wealth of melody. Nor was he above setting out to court popular favour by writing a great number of dances, marches and salon pieces that made no intellectual demands on performers or listeners. Certainly he had an audience, and those of the songs and chamber works which were performed in public were usually received enthusiastically. To be a Schubert enthusiast during his lifetime though was to be a member of a small but devoted clique, scarcely representative of the general climate of musical opinion. His works failed completely to cross national frontiers in the way that the music of Haydn, Mozart and Beethoven had done, and an English dictionary of music published in 1827, the year before his death, makes no mention of Schubert's name at all. The first performance of the 'Unfinished' Symphony was not given until 1865, forty-three years after its composition; even the great C major Symphony remained unperformed for eleven years. It seems inconceivable to us today that a composer of such unique qualities can have remained so undervalued for so long a period. Is there perhaps an explanation?

It was Schubert's misfortune to appear on the scene at a time when music was on the threshold of a great upheaval. Only a few years after his death, Romanticism transformed musical attitudes. In piano music, the sonata became almost obsolete, being replaced by ballades, rhapsodies, intermezzi, romances, pieces that often had a literary or descriptive content that a 'classical' composer would have considered unworthy. Schubert's choice of the word Impromptu to describe some of his most enchanting piano-pieces, written in the penultimate year of his life, was an indication that he was aware of the trend, and that had he lived longer, he might well have welcomed it. His superb gift for musical illustration is shown time after time in the accompaniments to the songs, and even some of the greatest of the sonata movements have a manifestly pictorial quality. Who can listen to the first movement of the great posthumous Sonata in B flat and not feel that those marvellously placed trills in the left hand suggest distant thunder? The whole movement is surely as descriptive of a serenely beautiful landscape as anything in Beethoven's *Pastoral* Symphony although Beethoven's own reservation, 'more an expression of feeling than a painting', is equally applicable. It is not wholly surprising, though, that audiences in the 1830s, intoxicated by the excitement of the new era and the heady fare being produced by Schumann, Chopin, Liszt, Berlioz and their many lesser contemporaries, should have failed to have been drawn retrospectively to a composer whose output consisted of nine symphonies, fifteen or more piano sonatas, fifteen string quartets, a number of other chamber works, seven masses and a series of disastrously unsuccessful operas. Of course, there were the songs; but songs can all too easily be regarded as miniatures, even when there are 600 of them. Since nobody had heard the symphonies and few knew the chamber works well, the almost total neglect of Schubert's music in the mid-nineteenth century becomes more understandable. Lacking the overwhelming personal impact that Beethoven made on all who met him, unable to dazzle audiences by performing his major keyboard works adequately, he failed to reach the larger musical public he deserved. Classical in his aspirations, but Romantic by inclination, his problem was to find the proper mould for his genius. He could not resist the challenge of the larger forms such as opera or the symphony and sonata, partly because he must have felt that only by accepting them would be himself be accepted as a serious composer. Yet one cannot help but wish that he had been born fifteen years later so that he could have entered a musical scene more suited to his exceptional qualities. Perhaps then he would not have squandered so much of his tragically short life on works which even today are virtually never performed.

Symphony No. 5 in B flat Major
(1816)

In the spring of 1816, when he was nineteen years old, Schubert wrote his Fourth Symphony. With a touch of ostentation not wholly in character he gave it a title—'Tragic Symphony'. While the music can hardly be said to live up to this description, it is uncannily well orchestrated; quite how Schubert acquired such sureness of touch remains a mystery for so far as we know none of his symphonies was publicly performed.[1] Certainly at the time of writing it he can have had no practical experience of the way his orchestral music might sound. The symphony shows the influence of Beethoven in a number

[1]The Fifth Symphony was played once, shortly after it was written, but it was at a domestic concert.

of places, most notably in the finale; but there are flashes of Haydn and Mozart as well, as might be expected of a boy who could only learn by example. It seems as though the young Schubert was quite well aware of the danger of losing his own individuality in the shadow of such giants for in the autumn of the same year he wrote his Fifth Symphony in which, despite its Mozartian scale, he found a voice that was unmistakably his own.

The symphony begins with four blissful bars of introduction in which the woodwind have a quiet but expansive phrase whose seriousness is undermined by a gurgle of delight from the first violins. The first subject (short phrases to begin with but then spreading its wings in melodic flight) elicits approving comments from the cellos and basses. The entry of the sole orchestral flute sets off a brief argument with the violins which is resolved when they repeat the theme with the addition of a flute descant. The first *forte* in the movement brings a tautening of the musical muscle so that the initial dotted-crotchet-quaver rhythm becomes quite aggressive, especially when a head-to-head conflict develops between violins and cellos. Agreement is reached on a repeated unison C, establishing the dominant key in preparation for the second subject. (The little silence that intervenes certainly follows one of Mozart's favourite patterns.)

The second subject first appears on strings alone, its suave opening phrase receiving a light-footed response. With some eagerness it is taken over by flute and bassoon, barely leaving the violins room to get a note in edgeways. A sudden shift to D flat provides a touch of Schubertian magic, its soft but contradictory tones soon countered by a forceful assertion of F major. A splendid passage follows with a dramatically striding bass climbing chromatically to an unforeseen destination—A flat major. Momentarily disoriented, the music dithers between F major and F minor; the climb is repeated even more emphatically but leads to the same confusion. 'This won't do', says Schubert, and brusquely establishes F major beyond any further doubt.

So ends the exposition. The development begins with a masterstroke. Flute and oboe in turn suggest a subtle variant of the first subject, superimposing it over the same harmonic sequence which began the symphony. It is now in D flat, the key Schubert has twice flirted with in the exposition, and brings the same enchanting reaction from the violins. The sequence is played out four times in all, each in a different key. (D flat, B flat minor, G flat, E flat minor.) Out of this delicate texture emerges a much more robust episode, the hard core of the development in which Schubert assumes a gravity beyond his years. Even so, it shows an honest confidence quite different from the storms of searching enquiry so often found in Beethoven's developments. Beethoven wrestles with his material; Schubert strides easily across it. A powerful descent down the scale of E flat minor leads to an 'after you, no, after you' exchange between strings and wind. A sustained chord on the strings and a woodwind phrase tinged with a note of sadness bring us to the recapitulation.

At this point we come across a deviation from the usual pattern of sonata-form movements, a short cut that Schubert often used; a brief excursion into technicalities is necessary fully to appreciate it. The established convention in the first movement was to have the First Subject group in the 'home' or Tonic key; a bridge passage would then modulate to the Dominant key a fifth higher and there we would find the 'home' of the Second Subject. Forgetting about the development for the moment and moving on to the Recapitulation, we find a significant alteration in the plan. The First Subject will be the same, establishing a return 'home' after the voyages into other (and probably distant) tonalities during the preceding passages. We then find a modified bridge which does *not* modulate but leads to the Second Subject now in the 'home' key. Schubert's 'invention' was to start his Recapitulation in what is called the Sub-dominant, the key a fifth lower than the Tonic. He could thus keep the bridge passage as it was since the same modulation up a fifth would bring him back 'home' for the Second Subject. Cynics have dismissed this as a variant dictated by laziness and Schubert has been much criticised for this innovation since it obviates the need for fresh ingenuity in altering the bridge passage. To him it must have seemed a happy discovery, its musical advantages being that it gives new colour to the First Subject as well as offering a greater variety of key in the Recapitulation.

The first movement of this symphony offers a perfect example of this technique for the Recapitulation begins not in B flat but in E flat, the Sub-dominant. From this point on it follows the original plan almost exactly until we reach an exhilarating coda easily recognised by the swift unison scale which sweeps upwards through nearly two octaves only to overshoot the mark and land on an unexpected B *natural*. The movement ends with a reference to the closing patterns of the exposition.

The slow movement begins with a theme that rivals Mozart in sheer perfection. The unaffected simplicity of the tune suggests that it is going to be a theme followed by a set of variations, but Schubert has other, more enterprising plans. The second part of the theme, from bar 9 onwards, introduces chromatic twists and turns that add poignancy; but these occasional brushes with minor keys are soothed away with a heart-warming return to the initial key of E flat. Having laid the music gently to rest in this key, Schubert has a wonderful surprise for us, an unexpected rise of a semitone that opens a magic door into a new world, B major. (Since the movement is in a 'flat' key he stays in flats for the moment so that the notes are written in the somewhat hypothetical key of C flat; however the subsequent drift into B minor defeats him and he has to change the notation to the conventional sharps. C flat minor would theoretically have nine flats in its key signature!)[2] Against a softly murmuring accompaniment from second

[2] C♭ D♭ E♭♭ F♭ G♭ A♭♭ B♭—rather more complex than B C♯ D E F♯ G A (♯)

violins and violas, the first violins begin a quasi-operatic duet with the woodwind. The concept is one we often find in Mozart, especially in the piano concertos, but there is something about the way the music modulates into different keys that gives it an unmistakably Schubertian flavour. Four stressed chords in the strings establish tension instead of tranquillity and for a moment or two its seems as though there may be a central storm such as Haydn sometimes incorporates in a slow movement. The chords quickly disperse and after some charming evasions the music arrives back at the first theme, now elegantly embellished.

The whole central section is repeated in suitably different keys (G flat instead of C flat) until a sublimely beautiful coda brings this singularly lovely movement to an end.

The next movement may bear the conventional title 'Menuetto' but the tempo indication 'Allegro molto' shows that all thoughts of aristocratic ballrooms have vanished. Schubert would have been tongue-tied in such company; instead we find ourselves in rustic surroundings, a country inn perhaps, with beer on the tables and the men in *lederhosen*. As for the girls—you can hear them in the soft answers that are given to the boisterous unison phrases. (One staccato chromatic descent suggests the sound of laughter of the formalised 'Ho-ho' kind demanded of the chorus in operettas.) The central Trio reflects its rural character in a gentler way with a disarmingly innocent tune poised over a discreet drone bass.

In the finale Schubert is not nineteen so much as about twelve. It has all the fun of a children's party game and its occasional storms are no more than the aping of grown-ups' rages. In structure it has an exemplary sonata form with a beguiling second subject and a compact and wholly relevant development. The whole symphony is a model of what a young composer's music should be; the music remains today what it has always seemed, fresh, boyish, unassuming and utterly captivating. One would have thought it deserved more than one amateurish performance in his lifetime.

Symphony No. 8 in B Minor
(The 'Unfinished')

It may seem ironic that what is probably the best-known symphony in the world after Beethoven's Fifth should be incomplete; however the absence of the two final movements normally required has proved no more of an obstacle to its general acceptance than has the lack of arms on the Venus de Milo. A masterpiece is clearly a masterpiece, truncated or not. From its very first notes, mysteriously outlined by cellos and basses on the threshold of audibility, the music casts its spell. If one were hearing the symphony for the first time, it would be tempting to regard the opening phrase as no more than an introduction since one waits in vain for it to reappear anywhere else in the exposition. Softly the violins begin a gently rustling accompaniment above which oboe and clarinet in unison have a song-like phrase whose tender melancholy is given a hint of unease by the rhythmic ambiguity that accompanies it. Is it in 3/4 (three pairs of two) or 6/8 (two pairs of three)? Characteristically Schubert extends the melody as though it were indeed a song rather than a symphony, building in intensity until at last the accompanying figures become too powerful for it; eight forceful repetitions of the dominant (7th) chord paired off in this rhythm: ♪|♩ ⅂♪|⅂♪ ♫| lead us back to a chord of B minor. In theory we are back at square one and this impressive build-up has led us nowhere. It is at such moments that genius can prove that theoretical considerations are vacuous. With a bold masterstroke, Schubert virtually dispenses with the usual bridge-passage; a single sustained note on horns opens the door to the key of G major, a typically unorthodox choice. (The 'proper' key would be what is known as the relative major, D, but propriety was not Schubert's concern.) Gentle syncopations on clarinets and violas provide the perfect accompaniment to the graceful second subject, the answer to any cellist's dream. The violins cannot resist the temptation to take the melody over; but then, as the phrases fall away in a dying sequence, there is a sudden silence. A shattering chord in the completely unexpected key of C minor shocks us like a clap of thunder on a summer day. Another chord, G minor, follows as dramatically, and we feel suddenly disoriented, all harmonic stability destroyed. The next chord, repeated emphatically no fewer than nine times, is equally disturbing, appearing as it does to be heading for the even more remote key of A flat, though whether major or minor we cannot be sure.

By shifting his bass-note up a semitone, Schubert reaches the traditional suspense chord known as a diminished seventh which hovers uneasily in the woodwind. The strings try to restore the limpid song of the second subject, but the drama of those thunderclaps precludes so easy a return and we are soon caught up in a fierce dialogue.

Ex. 1

Such a treatment of the second subject more properly belongs in the Development section, and it is another characteristic of Schubert's spontaneous approach to composition that he allows himself to be carried away prematurely, as though unable to suppress his excitement at discovering the music's potential. After several more forceful chords Schubert finds time to take another heart-touching look at the second subject, giving it an enchanting new twist before some mysterious pizzicato notes lead us tiptoeing back to the repeat of the exposition.

As I have suggested, it is easy to fall into the trap of imagining the opening theme to be no more than an introduction; but once we arrive at the Development, Schubert shows us that it is destined to occupy a very important place in the centre of the movement. The violins change its shape, turning it into an almost Tchaikovsky-like lament, giant tremors shake the earth, trombones turn the crepuscular opening into intimations of the Day of Judgement. This whole central section is one of the most magnificent passages Schubert ever wrote; nor is it just *Sturm und Drang*. Every now and then we find a brief moment of pathos in which he reminds us of the second subject in a manner whose subtlety could not be surpassed since we hear its syncopated accompaniment only, now in the woodwind. The gentle tune has fled before the storm and its absence is the harder to endure in the face of these poignant reminders of its existence.

The arrival of the recapitulation is magically contrived so that we are hardly aware of what has happened, since Schubert deprives us of the introductory phrase completely. That has dominated his thoughts long enough, and in doing so has changed its character so fundamentally that to present it once more in its original guise at this point would be a denial of the development's power. In other respects the recapitulation is a model, ending with a coda that flares up into a final dramatic gesture. The very last note of the movement presents a problem for the interpreter. The sign $>$ means an accent; the sign $\Longrightarrow$ means 'getting quieter'. Many conductors take the second meaning as proper for the final chord, but Schubert wrote at great speed and often scatters accents across the page with considerable abandon. If one examines the manuscript, it seems very probable that he intended an accent here rather than a *decrescendo*, which not only makes for a stronger ending but allows a more beautiful contrast to take place when we open the magic casement that leads into the second movement.

This is marked 'Andante con moto', an instruction frequently disregarded by conductors who wish to enfold the work in a romantic haze of sentiment tinged by morbid delusions of the composer falling lifeless as he penned its final note. Its pastoral beauties belong to the countryside, not to a cemetery, and the first phrase on the violins should warm us like the summer sun as we open the curtains on a perfect morning (Ex. 2).

The subtle transformations this theme undergoes in the course of the movement show Schubert's craftsmanship at its finest. At the first repetition

Ex. 2

of the phrase (directly after the opening statement) he changes its direction at the end, falling through D sharp, C sharp, C natural (surprise!) and then on to B. The harmony through which he pivots on that unexpected C natural is one of those delicious moments that we savour with renewed joy every time we hear it. Another delight is the elegantly compressed version of the opening theme which appears from time to time:

Ex. 3

original

later he toys with this in the most beguiling way:

Ex. 4

But perhaps the most surprising event in a movement that seems so idyllic in intention is the almost military character this theme is capable of assuming (Ex. 5).

Ex. 5

This, with its striding bass so obviously derived from the descending pizzicato scale which accompanies the opening horn chords, is a typical Schubert extension of a melody, not so much symphonic development as a further line in a song. By his gentle standards (and he never really bullies us as

Beethoven is inclined to do) this is a large-scale heroic treatment of the theme. Yet whenever he feels he has been taxing us a bit he's always ready to offer us tunes that are like a smile of apology. 'I *was* carrying on rather', he seems to say, 'do forgive me'. And he smiles enchantingly and hands us back the tune in its original form, newly scored for woodwind by way of a change.

A single strand on the first violins steps slowly and mysteriously into C sharp minor.

Ex. 6

Notice the syncopations in the fifth bar which set up an accompanying figure that may well be a reminder of the accompaniment to the memorable cello tune from the first movement. Here they support a long sustained theme for solo clarinet whose tender sadness is occasionally ameliorated by ravishing changes in harmony. There could be no better example of Schubert's genius in this respect, and anyone who wishes to discover his true quality is urged to listen to this passage again and again until it is etched on the memory. What cannot be foreseen at the time is the dramatic use to which this seemingly frail melodic line is to be subjected. At first it is truly a song without words:

Ex. 7

later it becomes the *bass* of a major symphonic storm.

Ex. 8

But where Beethoven would have developed this at considerable length,

Schubert, so often accused of longwindedness, quells the storm after less than a minute. Another transformation takes place and once more the frown becomes a smile.

Ex. 9

The rise to the C natural in the sixth bar is a stroke of invention that opens new possibilities and soon we find ourselves in the key of G major, alien territory insofar as it eliminates or contradicts all those notes which are most essential to E major, the key in which the movement had started. Such an adventure is needed if a reprise is to have its full effect; one cannot experience the joy of returning home if one has never been away, and Schubert is master enough to realise that the time to depart furthest from the original key is paradoxically just when it is approaching. A beckoning horn-call, a falling octave five times repeated, ushers in the return of the opening theme, as radiantly beautiful as before.

The reprise is surprisingly extensive, being virtually a repeat of all the varied events of the movement so far, albeit with suitable transpositions into different keys. The last touches of magic come in the coda where he uses Ex. 7 to wonderful effect, opening the door to the remote kingdom of A flat major before re-entering the home key of E by a secret passage known only to composers of genius. It is a fitting close to a movement that reveals not just beauty, but strength, not just a song-writer with aspirations to greater things, but a true master of symphonic concepts.

The work had to wait forty-three years to be performed, so Schubert himself never heard it except in his imagination. Various theories have been advanced as to why it was left incomplete, illness, pressure of work and so on; my own solution is simpler. It's my belief that having written two movements of such incomparable quality, he felt it impossible to cap them; one cannot improve on perfection, so he just left them as they were. He did start a third movement, and very promisingly too, but after ten bars his pen faltered. To come back to earth after such a journey into a celestial world was too much of a let-down; and so he left it as it was.

Symphony No. 9 in C Major (The 'Great')
(1828)

To begin a symphony is to put one's first step upon a mountainside; how inviting and yet challenging its peaks appear to be, and what a hard uphill slog is ahead before those peaks can be reached. Even a composer who wrote as effortlessly as Schubert knew only too well what it involved, yet like a great mountaineer welcoming a chance to tackle Everest, how gladly he must have put pen to paper when this noble theme came into his mind.

Ex. 1

Scored for solo horn, it provides a memorable opening to his largest orchestral work, certainly his greatest, even though it lacks something of the absolute perfection of the 'Unfinished'. By this I mean that there are moments when it is somewhat rough-hewn; there are occasional problems of orchestral balance that need a sympathetic and imaginative approach from the conductor. Indeed in the early stages the symphony was regarded as unplayable, and it wasn't until eleven years after it had been written that it was performed, and then it was in a shortened version. Several earlier attempts at performance had been foiled by the orchestral players, who had struck on being confronted with a work of such length and difficulty.

The initial theme develops as an orchestral song to begin with, first in the wind and then, extended, in the strings. But it isn't long before Schubert displays his full orchestral resources with trombones and strings declaiming the theme in an impressive unison, the third and sixth bars being allotted to the woodwind. As the music progresses, the trombones increasingly draw our attention to the second bar of the theme which is to prove the most important single element, both rhythmically and melodically.

This slow introduction is seventy-seven bars long, gradually gathering excitement until it explodes into the main part of the movement, a vigorous Allegro whose arrival is preceded by increasingly urgent fanfares on the horns. These anticipate the shape of the true first subject, especially in its original version which was a simple alternation of tonic and dominant.

Ex. 2

Now Beethoven would have spotted the weakness of this idea straight away and sent it back to the inner recesses of his mind for reappraisal. This is where the two different approaches of a quick and a slow worker become so intriguing, for Schubert also realised that the theme was too repetitive and simply wouldn't do. The point is that he didn't change it until he'd written the whole movement. The excitement of composition overcame all critical assessment and he just had to charge on until he got to the end. Presumably he then fingered through all the pages of the manuscript with that pride in a job-well-done which any composer must feel at the end of days (if not weeks) spent putting innumerable dots and lines on the score. Only then, when the creative fire had burned down a bit, did he realise that so many repetitions of this prosaic pattern could not remain. So out came a pocket knife and he settled down to the grisly job of excising and changing the fourth and eighth notes of that theme from C to D whenever they appeared—literally hundreds of times.

Even in this revised form, it can't really be described as a great tune, but at this point Schubert is more concerned with finding something capable of development than just a melody. He'd already given us a marvellous melody, that first theme on the horn, and this again provides us with an interesting comparison with Beethoven. Tunes, and by that I mean long, lyrical themes, flooded into Schubert's mind without effort, while Beethoven fussed over them for long periods. But development material, those immensely fertile seeds from which pages of Beethoven's symphonies derive, caused Beethoven much less of a problem, while Schubert is sometimes liable to pad. It's part of the difference between such an instinctive writer as Schubert and a more consciously intellectual one like Beethoven.

The dotted rhythm persists for several pages, whipped on by flailing triplets in the woodwind. The relentless insistence on just the two rhythms was surely an attempt to meet Beethoven on his own ground, and the arrival of the second subject comes as something of a release. It is typical of Schubert, an attractive tune that could easily find a place in a song-cycle. (He is particularly kind to the woodwind in this symphony, frequently giving them the real meat while the strings must be content with repetitive accompanying figures—it was this as much as anything that caused grumbles amongst the players at the earliest performances.) Schubert makes much of this tune, handling it delicately at first, but then changing its character with stamping hornpipe rhythms and some powerful passages for brass. After a substantial climax the music softens as an E flat arpeggio drifts upwards in the violins. There is an air of quiet expectancy as the violins pick out the 'hornpipe' rhythm pizzicato. With solemn and mysterious tones the trombones introduce a series of brief chorale-like phrases which are derived from bar 2 of Ex. 1. The ensuing development of this rising figure reveals a structural mastery that rivals Beethoven, and few could fail to thrill to the moment when, with ample reinforcement from the timpani, the woodwind extend the three rising notes into an exultant melody that soars to a high G before the exposition is allowed to end.

The development section begins with a sudden switch to A flat major; first and second subjects are brought into a much closer relationship, the rhythm of one providing encouraging support to the melody of the other. A long crescendo, urged on by repeated triplets in trumpets and horns, brings a number of shifts of tonality until a fine climax is reached with a return to A flat—this time in the minor. The moment can scarcely be missed as the trombones lend their full voice to the rising three-note theme. More modulations follow but again the music seems to be drawn compulsively towards A flat, a destination confirmed beyond doubt by pounding unisons in the strings topped by the full orchestra. Out of this tumultuous sound clarinets and bassoons emerge, then clarinets alone. It gives us warning that we are about to enter a very different world, perhaps the most inspired passage in the movement. The throbbing triplets pass from clarinets to violins. Time and again the rising three notes appear softly in the darker registers while flute, oboe and clarinet in turn offer a foil, a single held note followed by a swift descent like a falcon hovering and then dipping down. To a soft rumble from the timpani a solo horn sounds a summons in the familiar dotted rhythm, calling on the initial subject to reappear. And so it does, though its tone is now muted. This change of volume is maintained for fifty bars, giving the music the feel of a coiled spring. At last Schubert permits the crescendo which every player has been crying out for and for a few moments the orchestra can let fly. The appearance of the second subject (now in C minor) calls for renewed restraint, but the recapitulation follows a conventional course until the substantial coda. The increase of tempo gives us a clear indication that our ultimate destination is in sight though our arrival is postponed by a series of glorious fanfares in the brass, sometimes majestic, sometimes brilliant. Finally the long forgotten horn theme that began the movement (Ex. 1) makes a splendid reappearance, its single strand transformed into a massive statement of affirmation.

The slow movement is one of Schubert's greatest, even though nearly forty pages of Andante might seem rather too much to some impatient souls. But then there are some very big and dramatic moments in it so that at times it seems more like a first movement than a mere interlude of relaxation. Cellos and basses set the ball rolling before handing over to the oboe. As a foil to its rather forlorn little melody (which has a certain dogged perseverance about it despite its air of pathos) there is a wonderfully sweet tune in A major over a sustained bass. However, Schubert is very firm with himself, and seems determined not to get carried away into an over-sentimental or lyrical mood. It is only a matter of seconds before the first theme returns, this time in quite a tough guise. These contrasts between pathos and severity are maintained throughout the movement for the most part. There is one other idea of great importance, however, a truly gentle tune whose tenderness and beauty is made the more melting by its comparatively austere surroundings. Here it is as it first appears.

Ex. 3

pp

But even this tune is treated fairly toughly and those caressing opening notes are soon split up and translated into something altogether more dramatic. A little later in the movement something occurs which prompts a rather interesting comparison with a passage in Beethoven's Fifth Symphony. At one point Beethoven checks the insistent onward drive of quavers so that the movement becomes suddenly mysterious with block chords alternating between strings and wind and seeming to recede into the distance. Now while this is extraordinarily romantic in effect, the actual resources Beethoven uses are severely classical—in fact they are just blocks of sound either in strings or wind, each of which is a complete entity in itself. It is their juxtaposition that makes them so surprising and even magical. Schubert now achieves rather the same effect, but using a more romantic technique—keeping the harmonic changes in the strings, and repeating a bell-like horn note above the ever-changing chords. The contrast of colours is less direct than Beethoven's, lying as it does between the dark tones of cellos and basses as opposed to violins and violas. The passages are recognisably of a similar intention and yet surprisingly different in the end result. Immediately after these repeated horn-notes the oboe begins a reprise of the opening theme, now given a strange urgency by distant little fanfares on trumpet or horn that are duly passed over to the violins. Any thought that this is to be a conventional recapitulation is soon banished as Schubert introduces a number of changes. Not least is his treatment of Ex. 3, now provided with a flowing semiquaver accompaniment which in due time forsakes its subsidiary role, even intruding into the oasis of calm formerly provided by those repeated horn-notes. (They are now given to a clarinet and the strings are replaced by quiet trombones.)

The third movement is a wonderfully robust scherzo, packed with a prodigal wealth of tunes. The dance character of such movements always appealed to Schubert, and though he evidently took Beethoven as his model, the music is very much his own in its idiom. The countless delightful miniature dances he wrote for piano here attain a very different stature. An unusually interesting timpani part, canons between violins and cellos, interesting modulations and dramatic tone-contrasts all give evidence of his determination to produce a movement that would stand comparison with Beethoven at his most inventive.

 The central Trio is announced by twenty-four repetitions of the note E, as though the conductor must hold the band in check until every couple has taken to the dance-floor. Then, with a lovely bounce to the rhythm, we are away to strains that Johann Strauss himself might have penned—or so we may believe to begin with. However, Schubert develops his material at considerable length with characteristic excursions into foreign keys and the movement may be regarded as properly symphonic in scale.

The finale is wonderfully concentrated in its material, much of which is derived from two fragments that appear at the onset and are instantly repeated.

Ex. 4

It is from such fragments that symphonic movements are best built, a lesson that Schubert had learned from hard experience. Both rhythms are instantly recognisable and consequently can be turned to almost any purpose. For instance, a sustained tune that circles round less energetically in oboes and bassoons is decorated by triplets stolen from bar 3 and prodded forward by the rhythm from bar 1. At another point a unison rise and fall in the strings seems to be leading in a new direction; but bar 3 is promptly turned upside down while bar 1 proclaims its authority in wind and brass. Another 'new' theme is heralded by four notes on a solo horn but is immediately made relevant by a galloping accompaniment made up entirely of the inversion of bar 3.

 One important new theme does appear at a major climax, Schubert's answer to Beethoven's 'Ode to Joy'. In less exultant guise it is used to begin the development (soft clarinets in thirds) and continues to occupy the stage for some time. Its fusion with the four strident minims originally given to a solo horn is one of the most thrilling passages in the whole symphony.

The recapitulation, in the unorthodox key of E flat major,[3] is in no way shortened, and the movement is a gruelling test of stamina for the players. It is a savage irony of fate that Schubert never heard this, his symphonic masterpiece, for as was indicated earlier, the first performance was not given until eleven years after his death. Yet it is sometimes longer than that before an enduring monument is erected by a grateful people to some historic figure. Schubert built his own, for what more splendid memorial could one ask for than this?

SCHUMANN

1810–56

With the encouragement of his father, a publisher and bookseller by trade, the young Schumann developed a passion for literature which inevitably affected his attitude towards his other great love, music. A number of his works seem to have a literary basis and there can be no doubt that his songs rank among the greatest of all time. One book had a special appeal for him, Jean Paul's *Die Flegeljahre* ('Adolescence') in which the author admits to having two sides to his personality, *Walt* and *Vult*. It made Schumann aware of a similar split in himself, so much so that he gave them two names, 'Florestan' and 'Eusebius', the one extrovert and heroic, the other introvert and dreamy.

The death of his nineteen-year old sister and then, a few weeks later, his father was a profound shock for the sixteen-year old boy. His father had been the one who supported him in his musical aspirations; his mother, more cautious and looking to a future in which Robert would have to provide for her, insisted that he should train for a more respectable profession, and to this end he was duly enrolled in the law school at Leipzig (1828). It was not much to his taste and he soon moved on to Heidelberg where at least he found some congenial friends and a law professor he could admire. Even so the call of music was too strong and he wrote a passionate plea to his mother begging her to let him pursue his piano studies seriously under the guidance of Friedrich Wieck, a famous teacher whose daughter Clara (then eleven years old) was a child prodigy. Schumann's introduction into the Wieck household was to play a crucial part in his life for two reasons; the first was his growing affection for the abnormally gifted child whose pianistic prowess roused his admiration and envy; the second an injury to his right hand which effectively put a stop to any thoughts of a career as a virtuoso. (This has long been ascribed to a mechanical device designed to strengthen the weaker fingers, but a more recent and well-argued theory associates it with the effects of mercury on the nervous system—mercury being the standard treatment for syphilis, of which Schumann already showed the early symptoms and which ultimately was to destroy him.)[1]

Schumann, always susceptible to female charm, fell briefly in love with a fellow-pupil, Ernestine von Fricken, to whom he dedicated a fine and neglected piano work, the Allegro, Op. 8. They became engaged but agreed to break it off shortly after. Consolation came in an increasingly tender relationship with the child Clara; at first brotherly, it soon acquired a more intense significance for both. By the time she was sixteen they were ready openly to declare their love to her father with a view to marriage. He was appalled. How could a penniless failure scratching a living as a musical journalist, unable to play the piano properly, dare to presume that he would make an acceptable husband for a girl who had been acclaimed throughout Europe as a prodigious pianist? He made every effort to separate them, banning Schumann from all contact and virtually placing Clara under house-arrest. He was prepared to stop at nothing to protect Clara, whom he regarded as his own creation as much as a daughter. To Wieck's surprise Schumann turned out to be an obstinate adversary who after three acrimonious years resorted to the law to gain Clara. It was ironic that at this stage it was the father who seemed to be mentally deranged in his fanatical hatred of Schumann, whereas in later years it was Clara's husband who became insane.

The first year of the marriage (1840) released a flood of compositions from the jubilant composer including well over a hundred songs.

With the duality of his personality clearly established during his formative years, Schumann is particularly interesting to study with regard to what we call, rather confusingly, Classicism and Romanticism. A classical composer, using sonata form as his chosen medium, will exploit contrast; he too will have a Florestan and Eusebius. But one might almost say that the function of sonata form is to reconcile opposites. A sonata movement opposes its first and second subjects, but it also binds them together, making them accept their relationship in a way that gives us satisfaction. There is an innate rightness about their balance. The Romantic composers of the nineteenth century abandoned this concept of integration; emotional contrasts became more extreme, and inevitably, as a consequence, there was a tendency for the larger forms to break up into chunks of music. Berlioz and Liszt tried to cement these fissures by transferring themes from section to section, but that wasn't everyone's technique. For example in the B minor Sonata of Chopin we find a First Subject group that, for all its heroic stance, is cast in a classical mould, compact, taut and susceptible to development. But when he reaches his Second Subject he becomes transported by the sheer beauty of the material and embarks on a virtual rhapsody that is longer than the first subject and bridge passage put together. The classical proportions have been demolished, and with this significant change, the justification for writing works in sonata form has largely vanished. Now Schumann realised

---

[1] See Eric Sams, 'Schumann's hand injury', *The Musical Times*, Dec. 1971.

this by instinct. Because of the marked duality of his nature, he, perhaps more than any of his contemporaries, felt the need to split his emotions down the middle. His music rarely changes and develops in the classical sense; rather it consists of sections, complete in themselves, and often violently contrasted in emotional content. It isn't surprising that what most people regard as his most successful large-scale work, the piano concerto, was actually written as three separate compositions—the middle movement being a cleverly contrived graft to join together a Fantasia for piano and orchestra and a Rondo written four years later. It was not that he lacked the technique to handle large forms, but that his temperament was too divided to be able to encompass two conflicting moods at once and juggle with them, as a composer with the detachment of Mozart, Beethoven or Brahms could. 'Detachment' may seem an odd word to use, but to organise a large sonata or symphony movement one has to be capable of standing outside it.

The great dis-service that Clara did to Schumann was to divert his energies into forms for which he was basically unsuited. She was full of the Germanic tradition, obsessed with the need to write important works. For all her devotion to him, she could not see that he was far more inventive than she realised and that his method of unifying a composition (as he does so brilliantly in *Carnaval*) was far more original than adhering to a tradition could ever be. Schumann excelled as a miniaturist and it is interesting to note that even the songs tend to sustain one mood throughout, unlike many of Schubert's which cover a wider range.

Perhaps his supreme achievement in a larger form is the Piano Quintet which, though rich in melody, is constructed with exemplary control. The reconciliation of the demands of his dual personality is symbolised in the finale where he magnificently combines the very opening theme of the work with the main subject of the last movement. The symphonies cannot be regarded as equal in accomplishment for when he came to write them the shadows were already beginning to gather.

Once the euphoria of the hard-won victory over Clara's father had worn off Schumann found it a little difficult to live the life of a celebrity's husband for Clara continued to be much in demand as a pianist. Various tours were undertaken in which concessions to his growing stature as a composer were made by the performance of his orchestral works, but there was no doubt that Clara was the star. He was a poor conductor and found it onerous to mingle with high society. In 1844 a five-month tour of Russia caused his deep depression, partly due to the frustration brought about by being unable to compose. He began working on an operatic version of *Faust* which he was never to complete. The first signs of serious mental illness were becoming increasingly obvious, and even listening to music soon became a torture owing to the development of tinnitus. His preoccupation with large-scale projects such as *Faust* and the opera *Genoveva* seems to us now to have been a waste of time; he was clearly more at ease with songs and piano pieces.

The story of the remaining years makes sad reading for although he continued to compose prolifically, few of the works from this latter period have survived into the general repertoire. In February 1854 he began to suffer hallucinations and, on a sudden impulse, attempted suicide by throwing himself into the Rhine. He was rescued, but after a few days he was committed to an asylum from which he never returned although at times he had quite lucid periods. Communication with Clara was by letter only and for nearly two and a half years they did not see each other. In the final days she and Brahms were constantly at his bedside, but though Schumann appeared to recognise her, he was unable to speak intelligibly. Death was a welcome release both for him and those who waited on him, a tragic end to a life that only realised its full potential for two decades.

Piano Concerto in A Minor
Op. 54 (1841–5)

Schumann had set his heart on writing a concerto as early as 1833, and while they were still on speaking terms he wrote to Wieck saying that it would be in A minor. Years passed and the first movement did not materialise until 1841, the year after the marriage to Clara. It was called a 'Konzert-Fantasie'; for some reason Clara did not study it at once and the work is dedicated to a friend, Ferdinand Hiller. Perhaps because of the novelty of its single movement it was rejected by three publishers, lying dormant on the shelves for no less than four years. In 1845 Schumann composed a Concert-Rondo in A major, and it was then that Clara pointed out that the addition of a central movement would provide a full concerto. With great skill Schumann grafted in a delightful Intermezzo whose closing bars look back to the main theme of the first movement before looking forward towards the finale. Clara was delighted and took up the work, scoring an instant success with it in Dresden, Leipzig, Vienna and Prague. It has deservedly remained a popular favourite ever since.

The concerto begins with a single explosive unison from the full orchestra that has rather a similar effect to a starter's pistol. Like a sprinter galvanised into action, the soloist unleashes a flurry of chords in a strongly marked dotted rhythm. The gesture is enough to establish dominance and in bar 4 the woodwind alone introduce the main subject of the movement, an expressive tune which is at once copied by the pianist (see Ex. 1, p. 248). In a way, these opening phrases could be said to epitomise the first movement of the Concerto, in that so often aspirations towards virtuosity are defeated by

Schumann's preference for a lyrical style. It's the opposite way round from most concertos where lyricism so often gives way to exhibitionism, however skilfully disguised. There is little virtuosity as such in the Concerto, a fact that is all the more remarkable when we remember the sort of showy, empty fare that audiences of the time seem to have thrived on. Much of the mid-nineteenth century piano writing was unbelievably shallow, just bags of keyboard tricks, rattled off by pianists who were great showmen. Schumann's Concerto represents the extreme opposite pole, in which the scale of thought is nearer to chamber music. Much of the time the piano is given accompanying figures which might come from a violin and piano sonata.

So it is now, as the violins begin a subsidiary theme whose smooth contour is given a touch of urgency by the accompanying figuration in the piano part. A brief quaver phrase rises out of the shadows, its importance confirmed by the woodwind. It is soon elaborated by the soloist, though without any fuss so that a sudden break into commanding octaves takes us by surprise. The orchestra adopts the quaver phrase with enthusiasm leading us to expect a substantial tutti but they are interrupted by a similar octave passage from the pianist. There follows a cadenza of sorts based on expressive paired quavers and ending with a noble transformation of Theme I, now in C major instead of A minor. It descends through a sequence of sevenths, that could well have been written by Elgar, before racing off into a new development.

Against galloping triplets in the piano part a solo clarinet begins a beautiful extension of Theme I. After two such phrases the pianist takes over with a tune that is suggested rather than spelled out; the restless triplets continue but the top notes of the descending patterns form a melodic impression. A reminder of the little rising-quaver phrase from earlier on awakens a response from the soloist and a charming dialogue between oboe and piano ensues. There is a momentary slackening of the tempo and then the melodic line of the piano part is made more positive, building to a splendid octave climax.

And now we do find an orchestral tutti that triumphantly confirms our arrival at C major before gradually becoming more subdued and drifting from C minor to A flat major. There follows the famous nocturne-like middle section in which clarinet and piano muse together on the most expressive version of an already expressive tune. This, one feels, is where the true heart of the movement lies, and it shows considerable skill on Schumann's part that it doesn't seem like an intrusion. (The way he extricates himself from it is particularly brilliant, bringing the forgotten flourish from the opening bars right into the foreground in a dramatic dialogue between piano and orchestra.) In his original conception the 'nocturne' must have been intended to serve as a miniature slow movement but as it is we can regard it as a particularly beautiful variation on Theme I.

The ensuing clash between piano and orchestra awakens us cruelly from the dream. Two dashing octave passages, rivalling the Tchaikovsky concerto in virtuosity, lead to an impassioned extension of Theme I, now in G major, with a solo flute giving a silver edging to the pianist's melody. A long descending sequence, curiously prescient of Rakhmaninov in its use of chromatic intervals, gradually brings us to a reprise of the opening theme, scored as before for woodwind and again copied by the soloist. The recapitulation follows the same course as the exposition until some sudden and unforgettable shifts from A major to B flat and back again open the way for the cadenza. The material for this, seemingly new, is derived most ingeniously from a fragment of Theme I as a comparison of these examples show (Ex. 1a).

Ex. 1

Some exciting chord passages lead to a sustained trill beneath which the left hand reintroduces Theme I in more conventional guise.

The orchestral return sets a brisker tempo, converting the opening few notes of Theme I into a cavalry march. How well this theme has served Schumann, appearing as pensive, noble, nocturnal, impassioned, tragic or nimble, and what a satisfactory ending it provides to a perfectly proportioned movement.

The second movement is an Intermezzo of great charm. It begins with a little rising phrase of four notes which soloist and orchestra treat as a polite exchange of courtesies (see Ex. 2, p. 249). Although it cannot be proved, it is possible that the pattern is derived from the rising quavers in Ex. 1, bar 2 since Schumann was only persuaded to write the movement as a link between the already existing first and third movements. The piano phrases grow more expansive before the orchestra introduces a sustained phrase which still observes the pattern of four rising notes but in a very different style—lyrical instead of staccato and with the rhythm changed. For twenty-eight bars the exchanges between orchestra and piano continue, a plan which surely makes this movement unique among concertos. After the first section has been neatly tidied away, the cellos take charge with a broad and lyrical melody in C major. The pianist accompanies each phrase with triplet arpeggios and then adds an expressive comment of his own which integrates this new section with what had gone before. A touch of magic comes as the violins take over the cellists' tune when it soars beyond their reach.

Clarinets and bassoons extend this central melody still further, giving it a new slant by drifting into minor keys. At no point in the movement is there a hint of virtuosity and the central part can truly be described as a 'song without words'. Towards the end of the movement the music shows signs of disintegration as the violins almost come to a halt. Clarinets and bassoons offer a gentle reminder of Theme I from the first movement which the pianist promptly questions as though saying 'Did you really mean it?' Quietly they try the same phrase in the minor but the pianist remains unconvinced. A return to the major seems to be a better prospect and, sure enough, a swift rising scale on the strings sweeps us into the finale. (Schumann may have used Beethoven's 'Emperor' Concerto as a model for this link.)

The pianist launches the finale with a proud theme which clearly has trumpets and horns in mind. (For technical reasons the horns in Schumann's day could not have played this theme in A major though they are able to later when it comes in E major.) The rising quavers may again be a unifying link as this juxtaposition of the opening themes of all three movements reveals:

Ex. 2

It is probable that the relationship shown above is more of a family likeness than a contrived similarity, but it certainly contributes to the unity of the work—a consideration that must have been in the forefront of Schumann's mind when faced with the problem of marrying two works separated by a gap of four years.

The first theme bounces along with great vigour for thirty-nine bars before giving way to unbroken patterns of quavers which span the keyboard in the most exhilarating manner. Their headlong flight is checked by the appearance of the second main theme, a hushed tune whose syncopations have brought the downfall of many an amateur orchestra. It is important that the orchestral version should sound like a cheekily syncopated 3/4 rather than a prosaically boring 2/4; the soloist on the other hand has the fun of turning a tap-dance into a sanctimonious chant, a 'Pax vobiscum' which collapses into giggles as piano and orchestra join forces.

In analysing this movement one should remember that it was planned as a concert-rondo; we must therefore expect a number of 'episodes'. A new one is introduced with a strong unison phrase on the orchestra, immediately capped by the soloist with a dramatically leaping phrase. The exchange is repeated before dissolving into a continuous pattern of quavers which wittily refuses to comply with the natural stress of 3/4 time. A brilliant link with the slow movement usually passes unnoticed but is well worth pointing out. Here is a fragment from the last movement's 'moto perpetuo' while beneath is an oft-recurring pattern from the slow movement:

Ex. 3

Rhythmic ambiguities are exploited with great panache as the pianist's arpeggios become more emphatic, and the conductor needs an iron nerve to keep the orchestra on track. At last the opening theme returns, restoring an unequivocal 3/4 to everyone's relief. (The preceding passage is notorious not only for its rhythm but also because pianists can easily take a wrong turning thereby causing irremediable chaos.) A series of rising trills, with the left hand assuming the mantle of the horns and trumpets in turn, leads to the only substantial tutti in the whole concerto. Beginning with a triumphant version of Theme I (which the horns are now capable of playing), the music surprisingly develops into a fugue of Mendelssohnian delicacy using a *minor* version of Theme I as subject. Having given proof of academic respectability, Schumann tires of the game and introduces a further episode with a bell-chime of a tune on the oboe. It is at once taken up by the pianist and provides the material for the next few pages, though forceful paired chords and unison arpeggios seem to be trying to break away.

After considerable to-ing and fro-ing, including some flying waltz-passages for the pianist, Theme I returns in the new key of D major, the so-called sub-dominant. It is a trick learnt from Schubert though it again means that the horns cannot play a tune so suited to their character. A standard recapitulation follows, interrupted by a dancing coda whose circling theme perfectly describes the movements of a quick waltz. References to Theme I occasionally introduce a more martial note as though the male dancers are in their best regimental rig, but the abiding impression we take away with us is that the music is pure dance. How tragic that a mind capable of producing such completely happy music should have been engulfed by black depression and a loss of reason.

SHOSTAKOVICH
1906–75

'SOVIET ART CAN HAVE NO OTHER AIM THAN THE INTERESTS OF THE
PEOPLE AND THE STATE.'

Such was the resolution passed by the Plenary Congress of Composers in 1946, to little avail, it seems, since in 1948 an even more savage attack was launched against Russia's most distinguished composers, Prokofiev and Shostakovich among them.

> Shostakovich's Seventh, Eighth and Ninth symphonies are supposed to be considered as works of genius abroad. But who considers them as such? Who . . . apart from the reactionaries against whom we fight, apart from the bandits and imperialists? Do you think people in foreign countries like these works? I can say quite categorically, 'No; impossible.' Today the most popular composer in the world is our Tchaikovsky. His music is used in many foreign films.[1]

The speaker was Comrade Zakharov in a less than comradely mood. The injustice of this diatribe cannot have been lost on Shostakovich whose Seventh *Leningrad* Symphony had been acclaimed throughout the Western world as a testament to the courage of the Russian people and had been performed many times in the bastion of Capitalism, the U.S.A. The criticism must have seemed all the more wounding since it was not the first time that Shostakovich had incurred the displeasure of his political masters.

His First Symphony, written when he was only nineteen, had scored a sensational success that took it beyond the confines of Russia; it was even conducted by Toscanini in America. Meanwhile, in his twenties, Shostakovich continued to write with great fluency, such fluency that he was soon in trouble with the authorities. Three years after he'd produced the First Symphony he turned to opera, using a satirical short story by Gogol as plot.

[1] Norman Demuth, *Musical Trends in the Twentieth Century*, Rockliff, 1952.

The Nose, as the opera was called, was at first hailed enthusiastically by the Russian press, but later Shostakovich was compelled to withdraw it. In the late 1920s the first of Stalin's five-year plans was launched and the artistic climate of Soviet Russia settled into a winter of discontent. Shostakovich was only one of many composers to excite official disapproval, and his second opera, *Lady Macbeth of Mtsensk*, having been proclaimed an out-and-out masterpiece in 1934, was not long after damned as 'unhealthy, formalistic, bourgeois and unintelligible'. It was the first of several notable collisions Shostakovich was to have with the Soviet government.

To consider one's public is not necessarily the road to artistic disaster, as works such as the *Academic Festival Overture* of Brahms prove. But to make concessions by choice or by compulsion are two very different matters, and the composer who has to put up with political interference is in a difficult position. One of the most fascinating IF's in music is to consider what difference it might have made to Shostakovich if he had been born in the West. There is no question that his music was enormously affected by the political background in which he lived the greater part of his life. He suffered what would seem to us unwarrantable interferences with the artist's liberty; the result is a curiously patchy output, though there is no doubt that he genuinely developed as a composer, having written symphonies, concertos, quartets and the like which can rank with some of the finest music of our century.

Shostakovich's acute artistic crisis came with his Fourth Symphony. He listened to it at rehearsal and then withdrew it; in fact he not only withdrew it, he withdrew himself into a shell. Somehow he had to find a way of reconciling his creative self to the demands that communist society was making on him. Let me try to put the situation as fairly as I can, and by that I mean being fair to both sides.

It cannot be denied that the Russian state does a lot for its musicians. It pays them a very reasonable living, feeds and clothes them, provides them with a holiday centre in the Crimea where they have ideal conditions for composition and study; it provides well over 300 state schools of music plus nearly 100 music colleges and twenty or more higher music training institutions. From early childhood onwards through the rest of his days, the Soviet musician is nurtured by the State. In return, it expects unswerving devotion to the interests and will of the people as expressed through the official policy of the Communist Party. This seems a perfectly fair bargain. However there are a number of snags. When you have a country of over 180 million people speaking 108 different languages, it's hard to find a common musical denominator. Furthermore, great areas of this vast land have absolutely no cultivated musical tradition, and are inhabited by people who have only ever used folk-music as a means of expression and have had no contact with the sophistications of the symphony, the concerto or the fugue. It is therefore understandable, even praiseworthy that the Communist government should say to composers, 'write music that our nation can take to its heart and learn to feel pride in as its own'. If you are building a nation on a new basis, which is what they were trying to do, give that nation a musical heritage. The nonsense starts when this desirable maxim becomes more than just a request for the composer to repay his debt to society by writing music for the nation; the nonsense is compounded when this request becomes extended into a ban on the composer writing anything else. Because a musician is a specialist in a highly specialised language, he will inevitably have some element of the esoteric in what he says. If the taste of the masses is to be the sole criterion for judging merit, then all new procedures in harmony, melody and rhythm must either be severely restricted or abolished. In the past, folk-music has always co-existed with art-music as a sort of country cousin. Mozart will use an Austrian dance in the third movement of a symphony, but that won't stop him from writing a first movement of great intellectual power. But as soon as the hard-line party man hears a bit of music he can't understand he trots out the usual polemical cant about it being formalist and bourgeois, thereby showing merely that he is a staunch traditionalist—a die-hard conservative.

The answer Shostakovich came up with was his Fifth Symphony which he actually called *A Soviet Artist's Practical Creative Reply to Just Criticism*. It is a work of stature and authority apart from its bombastic finale; its points are made clearly so that an untrained ear can comprehend what is happening. The official decree was that 'all aspects of music should be subordinated to melody, and such melody must be clear, singable and organically linked with popular art because singing is the image of melody'. While it is doubtful that any member of the Politburo could actually sing the entire work, it must be acknowledged that Shostakovich managed remarkably well to reconcile the demands of officialdom with his musical conscience.

Further symphonies followed, including the famous Seventh written in Leningrad during the actual German assault and the contentious Ninth that supposedly celebrated the victorious end of the war, though not with the pomp and ceremony his masters would have liked. The vicious attack of 1948 forced him to make artistic concessions that he must have loathed. He wrote film music and patriotic cantatas; anything of more enduring worth he put aside, hoping for a more liberal climate to emerge. It came with Stalin's death in 1953, an event which Shostakovich could be said to have 'celebrated' in his own way with the Tenth Symphony, one of his finest, though needless to say it met with a mixed reception in Soviet circles. Surprisingly, the two symphonies that followed do commemorate Communism, though they are concerned with the revolutionary periods of 1905 and 1917 when idealism counted for more than party dogma.

Meanwhile Shostakovich was revealing a truer picture of his creative genius through the more intimate medium of the string quartet, and his contributions to that genre may ultimately be classed as his finest work. Inevitably, though, the pressures of such an enclosed society began to affect the composer more and more deeply and a note of bitterness became increasingly apparent.

The Thirteenth Symphony is a choral work based on poems by Yevtushenko. Once again Shostakovich was censured and he was forced to withdraw the work until the poet could remove and rewrite certain passages that offended the arbiters of taste. Driven into a mood of deepest pessimism Shostakovich devoted his next symphony to a contemplation of Death. One line in particular seems to hold a special significance: 'What comfort is there for talent among villains and fools?' The dedication to Benjamin Britten is surely like a hand stretched out asking for sympathy.

The final symphony, No. 15, is a curiosity, full of quotations not just from his own works but from Rossini and Wagner as well. The sudden eruption of the *William Tell* Overture caused much scratching of critical heads. For what it's worth I propose my own explanation.

Think for a moment of Shostakovich's situation. Twice in his life he had been in severe trouble with the artistic authorities; he was now reasonably secure in his acknowledged position as Russia's greatest living composer. But with that position came responsibilities, the strange Communist concept of making the artist the servant of the people, their voice rather than his own. He wrote this symphony in 1971, when he was in his mid-sixties. Is it cynical to suggest that at such an age, starting one's fifteenth symphony and one's 141st official composition, there could be at least an element of 'Here we go again'? Isn't it possible that the State's Orpheus found himself strumming an idle string without really being able to bring much enthusiasm to the task? In which case, what the hell—why not give them *William Tell* or anything else that came to mind? At least they would sit up and recognise it. Satire, though, is a risky form of humour in Russia and by this time Shostakovich knew all too well what it meant to be officially censured. If then, as I believe, this Rossini quotation was a gesture of disillusionment, let the message at least be delivered so as to retain its enigma; that way, nobody could take exception to it or regard it as a criticism of the all-perfect State.

The second movement, a profound adagio, is so different that it's hard to believe it comes from the same hand, let alone belongs in the same work. The only thing it has in common with the first is economy of scoring. There can be no doubt about the seriousness of purpose in this music and one is tempted to see the two movements as two faces of Shostakovich, as though in the second movement he says to authority, 'You ask me to write cheerful music to amuse the masses, but how can I do so convincingly when I bear this sorrow within me?' And, suddenly, we detect a note of deep sincerity that never appeared in the relatively trivial chatter of the first movement. In few other composers' works do we find triviality and profundity appearing so frequently within the same covers; it is an indictment of the system under which Shostakovich spent his whole life that triviality and banality were necessary for him to be able to survive.

Symphony No. 5
Op. 47 (1937)

The voluntary withdrawal of the over-inflated Fourth Symphony and the virulent official condemnation of his opera *Lady Macbeth of Mtsensk* caused Shostakovich to look inwards more deeply than he ever had before. In doing so he explored the very depths of the creative spring that lay within him. If he did indeed find a more potent source of inspiration there it was not by following the dictates of rigid and imperceptive bureaucrats but because the wounds inflicted by their mindless criticisms had cut him to the quick. The inner crisis bore fruit in the Fifth Symphony whose first two movements reveal a more profound quality than any of his previous works had shown.

The beginning is intensely serious, with cellos and basses leading off with a strongly marked rhythm that is at once copied by the violins. The alternate rise and fall of the phrases and the severe two-part counterpoint have more than a suggestion of Bach in the first few bars, but soon the opening phrase is reduced to a shadow of its former self, the measured rhythm providing an almost ritualistic setting for a sustained melody on the violins. (See Ex. 1, p. 258)

Cellos and basses drop out, leaving the violins (with occasional flutes) to wander round the fringes of D minor without committing themselves firmly to any key. Now if the standard classical symphony can be said to be concerned with the development of themes, this symphony is also concerned with Relationships. Nothing could be more solid and confident than the opening bars of the movement, while this subsidiary theme is vague and diffuse. Yet it is not long before a marriage is effected between these unlikely partners, the wandering theme now in the cellos, the confident Bach-like motif in the violins. A shrill climax is reached with the encouragement of horns and trumpets.

Suddenly the somewhat severe and forbidding character of the music is changed, and there emerges a long sustained tune on high violins, with a gently throbbing accompaniment beneath. This is the perfect answer to those people who are always saying that modern music is never 'beautiful'. Their conception of beauty is a limited one, based on the formula of tune and accompaniment, both clearly defined. Shostakovich is dangerously near to making too great a concession here, but the music's purity and indeed innocence save him, for even the most fastidious ear could not accuse this passage of vulgarity. The persistent accompanying rhythm dies to nothing, leaving the violins to fend briefly for themselves.

In a most beautifully scored section, tenuous lines of melody now drift across the page, as uncluttered as a sketch by Matisse. One seed, though, is planted here, a tiny three-note pattern (F–Ab–G), which seems to be no more than embroidery. Starting in violas and cellos, it flowers into a more extended melody in flute or clarinet. Quietly the lower strings bring back the throbbing accompaniment as the violas remind us of that high sustained violin tune.

The mood changes abruptly, and it's this three-note idea that now sprouts into life. The piano, seeming like the voice of materialism, and making an unexpected appearance in a symphonic score, whips up the tempo. Right near the start, the violins had suggested a falling melody with these few notes:

Ex. 1

The horns now proclaim it as threateningly as a war-cry. Excitement increases as the woodwind follow suit. Rushing scales give a new forward impetus while insistent clanging octaves on the piano seem to sound an alarm. Swiftly paired chords on horns suggest trotting horses; the trot becomes a canter in powerful unison strings.[2] The very opening phrase of a rising sixth makes a dramatic entrance in the lower strings hotly pursued by the horns; the gently throbbing accompaniment of the previous pages becomes a galloping rhythm on trumpets. Ex. 1 is transformed into a paean of triumph in the woodwind and is treated as a canon with the lower strings following a bar later. It is this theme, at the beginning so modest and unassuming, that now predominates in a march that might provoke critical sniffs from some. But if a march is permissible at all in a symphony, and Tchaikovsky has surely shown us that this is so, then this one has every right to existence since its derivation is unquestionably symphonic. It is not planted in the middle; it has truly grown.

Side-drum and timpani emphasise the war-like flavour of the music as trumpets turn the expressive phrase of Ex. 1 into a triumphal procession. At its climax, easily recognised by insistent repeated notes on violins, wind and xylophone, tuba and bass trombone reintroduce the opening 'Bach' phrase in magisterial augmentation. Having thus reminded us of this seminal theme, Shostakovich soon treats it as a tightly woven two-part canon scored for full wind and strings. Against this the brass are given the long lyrical melody that had so graced the early part of the symphony as a serenely floating violin line.

The immense tension created by this new relationship is sustained for

---

[2] The suggestion of a cavalry charge gradually increasing in pace is similar in technique to the Battle of Agincourt sequence in Walton's music to *Henry V*.

some time until it breaks off into a tremendous unison version of the vague and diffuse theme that originally appeared in the violins as early as the third page. The end of the movement is a quiet dissolution, in which several themes reappear in their earlier guise or in inversions, mirror-fashion. The scoring is again delicate and individual, with an especially lovely duet between flute and horn, some subtle passages for woodwind only, and a last touch of magic in the celesta scales which give a hint of D major against the prevailing D minor.

The second movement is a scherzo which I once described as 'a Russian peasant dressed up as Beethoven for a fancy dress party'. The powerful opening, scored for unison cellos and basses, clearly has its roots in Beethoven, while the grotesque woodwind response is as clearly derived from folk-music. After the woodwind have had something of a field-day, the horns produce a tune of such staggering banality that even the stoniest-faced commissar might allow himself a glimmer of approval; not so the violins who greet it with derisive glissandos. A little later a solo violinist produces a passage of pure café-music, and it is only charitable to assume that Shostakovich has his tongue lodged firmly in his cheek. 'You asked for simple music that everyone could understand', he seems to be saying, 'and by the beard of Karl Marx, here it is.' Whether one regards it as satire or parody, the music cannot be taken seriously—but does not the word scherzo mean a jest?

There is no doubt about the quality of the slow movement, which for my taste is the kernel of the work, lifting it far from the realms of the political manifesto into the loftier plane of genius. It is largely scored for divided strings. Its language is no less deeply felt for being simply expressed, and there is not a note of false rhetoric. A section for two flutes and harp is a masterly demonstration of economy in scoring, a transparent texture that serves as an admirable foil to the richness of the full strings. The central climax sounds a shriller note but the harmony is notably simple despite the emotional intensity. One strange effect that deserves comment is an extraordinary *tremolando* on two clarinets that provides an agitated accompaniment to some eloquent and tragic phrases in the lower strings. The final chord of the movement provides a sweet release from sorrow.

As much cannot be said for the finale which is at its worst at its climaxes. There's a great deal of sound and fury signifying not very much except the musical equivalent of all those glib phrases that politicians love to spout. Of course the end will always bring the house down; it's noisy and exciting, but it plays to the gallery blatantly, as any work designed to fulfil this particular function would have to do. Shostakovich could scarcely end on a note of pessimism. As the party spokesman Zhdanov said, 'Soviet music must faithfully reflect Soviet reality, especially the dynamic aspect'. Perhaps the symphony reflects more reality than he realised.

Symphony No. 10
Op. 93 (1953)

Conceived on a very large scale, the Tenth Symphony takes some fifty minutes to play, half of which is occupied by the first movement. It begins with a phrase so understated that we might be forgiven for thinking it unimportant, whereas the three rising notes are of fundamental significance.

Ex. 1

For some time, cellos and basses brood on this, while for the most part the upper strings hold long sustained notes as a quiet background. For the moment, the rest of the orchestra is silent. The first tempo change comes as the cellos and basses begin to give a sense of greater urgency to the same theme, now in G minor. A new strand of colour appears, a single clarinet presenting a long melody which also features the three-note pattern.

Ex. 2

The early stages of the symphony are notable for their restraint; Shostakovich has a huge orchestra available, but he's deliberately holding back, not out of some perverse desire to keep us waiting for the big bang, but because the span of his thought in this work in very large. Very gradually, the texture begins to thicken; horns creep in almost inaudibly, then the woodwind begin to reinforce the strings, though Shostakovich still refrains from putting them in opposition to each other. As yet, he wants to avoid strong contrasts of tone-colour; the music grows continuously in an impressive but deliberately unspectacular way.

The first climax is signalled by four explosive chords for trumpets, trombone and timpani; the three rising notes from Ex. 1 are doubled in speed before making a majestic return in which the horns offer three *descending* notes as a thrilling counterpoint. Within the span of the whole movement this brief *fortissimo* is a minor event, an initial ridge on the slopes of a great mountain. Beyond the ridge is a valley, a quieter section in which an unaccompanied clarinet winds its way back to a restatement of Ex. 2. Soon a solo flute introduces a note of contrast with a wistful little waltz in its lowest register. It is the third main theme of the movement, but need not be quoted since its gentle undulations make it easy to recognise in all its derivations. The mood continues to be restrained, even receding into the shadows as a bassoon reminds us of Ex. 2 while the even deeper contrabassoon muses on Ex. 1. The benefit of holding back for so long is that when at last Shostakovich unleashes the full strength of his orchestra it is that much more effective. The rising three-note pattern makes an awe-inspiring appearance in tuba and bass trombone as trumpets blare out the 'waltz' theme. At the peak of the movement exciting drum rhythms and skirling woodwind themes stimulate us to a degree that would be impossible if we had been subjected to numerous lesser climaxes on the way.

The central section, as befits music on this scale, sustains its force for some time with the brass and percussion adding their full weight.

The analogy of a mountain is a useful aid in following the course of this lengthy movement; the climb to the summit is long; it is there that the wind blows most fiercely, and it is once we begin to descend on the other side that we find immediate relief from the battering force of the gale. The music unwinds in an almost exact reversal of previous events. The only smile Shostakovich allows himself is when the initially rather wistful little waltz thaws out, becoming a lilting dance with two clarinets weaving seductive thirds over a gentle pizzicato accompaniment. It is a positive oasis in a movement that is for the most part bleak and forbidding; it comes just before the recapitulation, a clearly defined landmark, though the initial material is scored quite differently, being given entirely to the woodwind whereas originally it had been just for strings. (The woodwind sound is more penetrating but perhaps even more forlorn.) The proportions are distinctly unorthodox for despite the huge length of the movement its recapitulation takes less than two minutes out of a total of twenty-five. The ending is strange, almost eerie, with a couple of piccolos circling around above sombre string chords, a picture of desolation.

One might naturally expect the scherzo to be on a comparable scale, but Shostakovich defies expectation. The entire movement takes a mere four minutes, an extraordinary feat of compression after the expansiveness of the first movement. The strings set the tempo—extremely fast—before oboes and clarinets propose a theme which by coincidence or design is based on three rising notes, though their effect is very different from what it was in the previous movement. The rhythm grows more excitable with the addition of a side-drum. Although the idiom is certainly derived from folk-music, the writing demands a virtuoso orchestra, especially in the woodwind. Shostakovich has a habit of doubling up strings and wind in very fast passages, a feature that needs careful rehearsal if it is not to sound a blur. Two-thirds of the way through the movement the main theme appears in augmentation, its rhythm squared off into minims, one to each bar. The final build-up, starting quietly with strings alone, is brilliantly contrived to sweep through to a whirlwind finish.

The rising three-note motif that began the symphony persists into the next movement, an *allegretto* scored with great delicacy. (A true slow movement would be out of place after the largely contemplative mood of the lengthy first movement.) Variety is introduced by considerable fluctuations of tempo, metronome marks ranging from crotchet = 136 down to 72, while a quicker section with a strong dance rhythm goes into quite a quick one-in-a-bar. In a different context it could easily have been described as 'A day in the life of a Russian village', but since Shostakovich doesn't give us any programme, it's best to sit back and enjoy the music in its own right. The opening theme appears in many guises but the central section is dominated by a horn solo that is nearly a waltz. The heavy brass set up a bouncy rhythm of a more bucolic kind which encourages the strings to enter into the same spirit. (At one point they treat the delicate opening theme very roughly.) But however powerful the opposition, the horns insist that their theme is the most important and, once the tumult has subsided, its bell-like chime is repeated a number of times, alternating with a solo violin's efforts to persuade us that the opening tune is really the one we should pay attention to. The movement finishes quietly, fading to silence. Its final notes are on the flute and piccolo, and for all their quietness, accustom our ears to a sharp clear tone-colour. This makes the opening to the finale all the more effective, for once again, as at the start of the first movement, we are plunged into the dark world of cellos and basses. The slow introduction has a random improvisatory mood in which oboe, flute and bassoon are given opportunities to show their expressive capability. It is as though they are searching for the theme which ultimately materialises in the violins as the music breaks into its proper quick tempo. Here again we find the characteristic swift unison runs in the woodwind and more chunky peasant tunes in the horns. At one point horns and woodwind produce an unmistakable reference to the rising three-note pattern that has appeared in every movement. Soon it spreads to the strings as a strong unison, then even more powerfully to the brass.

A frenetic crescendo whipped on by the side-drum leads to a huge climax, a giant proclamation of the notes D–E♭–C–B. If we use German notation these would read D–(e)S–C–H, the musical signature of *D*mitri *Shostakovich*, one which he uses in several works such as the Eighth Quartet, the Symphony No. 15 and the Second Violin Concerto. Here it is followed by a lull in which, over a sustained timpani roll, the strings recall motifs from the introduction to the movement. An impatient bassoon banishes such nostalgic sentiments and soon the music is humming on its way again. As it races towards its conclusion the woodwind runs grow ever more brilliant; but beneath their glitter the musical 'signature' recurs time after time in the deepest register of the orchestra. Mightn't a psychologist explain Shostakovich's recurring obsession with this theme—based on his own name—as a passionate insistence on his right to be an individual in a society in which individuals are expected to conform by surrendering their individuality? How can a composer of Shostakovich's stature accept egalitarianism if it involves the suppression of all who fail to comply with the State's concept of order? Doesn't the end of the symphony proclaim in ever more vehement tones, 'Listen to me; I am Dmitri Shostakovich; I am Dmitri Shostakovich; I am Dmitri Shostakovich. . . .'?

Symphony No. 13 ('Babi Yar')
Op. 113 (1962)

This work, a setting of five poems by the contemporary Russian poet Yevtushenko, is direct and simple, moving in its compassion for humanity, deeply felt and for a time unacceptable in the composer's homeland. It was the first movement that caused outrage. Babi Yar was the site of a notorious Jewish massacre committed by the Nazis during the war. Yevtushenko's 'In Memoriam' of the event dared to suggest that anti-Semitism lived on in Russia. Even so popular an idol as the poet could not be allowed to cast such a slur on a nation where all men are known to be brothers living in an ideal society; he was compelled to revise the poem so that it was made clear that not only Jews were slaughtered but other races as well.

With so many bitter experiences behind him, Shostakovich surely didn't set out with any sense of mischief to bait the authorities by writing this work, and it's only fair to say that he was more criticised for using the suspect texts of Yevtushenko than for the actual music. All the same, there are several things about this symphony that must strike any Westerner as strange. First, the open propaganda content of some of the poems would be completely unacceptable to any Western composer. We just can't take seriously statements like '*He who gives them false change is a scoundrel*'—this of a queue of housewives in a shop—or '*He who gives them false weight is a swine*'. Can one imagine Britten or Walton setting such a text to music? Or what about '*The goodness of my land I never doubt; How vile then that the anti-semite rabble without a qualm should have called themselves "The Union of the Russian*

People!" ' Even allowing for translation, these are phrases which Western composers would find difficult to set to music convincingly. In this respect, the Thirteenth Symphony reflects the society from which it springs, a society where propagandist catch-phrases are normal currency. But this leads me to a second point, and that is that we must surely find it very difficult to comprehend why the work was banned. It is far from militant; in fact at times it falls over backwards to be patriotic in the deepest sense. Certainly it is thoughtful and self-searching; but if there is guilt, Yevtushenko and Shostakovich both give a sense of sharing it indirectly, as do we all. *'Which one among you shall cast the first stone?'*

Shostakovich uses a large orchestra, a male voice chorus and a bass soloist. The five poems are each allotted a complete symphonic movement. In 'Babi Yar' the poet (and therefore by implication the composer) identifies with the Jews, so often the victims of persecution. Yevtushenko is careful not to single out only those who died at Babi Yar; he tells of Ancient Egypt, of one who was spreadeagled on the cross, dying, of Dreyfus, of Anna Frank, of those who died in the camps. The music is weighed down with a burden of immense grief.

The orchestra begins with a dark unison phrase that is like some ancient chant against which muted horns and trumpets seem to have a cry of lamentation. As in the Tenth Symphony we find Shostakovich making much of the first three notes of a rising minor scale, sometimes in crotchets, sometimes in quavers. The basses of the chorus match the sombre mood as they begin the stark tale: 'There is no memorial at Babi Yar . . .' Against a minimal accompaniment the bass soloist outlines the history of Jewish persecution over the ages. One of the most notable aspects of Shostakovich's score is its avoidance of overstatement. He tells us of the horrors of massacres, but he doesn't indulge in sound orgies as he does so. There is an occasional suggestion of marching feet and a brief stabbing phrase that recurs on oboes and bassoons, but no orchestral excess. A few strident dissonances lead to a great cry from the chorus: *'Strike the Jews dead! Awake the Fatherland!'* But the hymn of hatred is soon suppressed and the dark opening phrases return. The bass soloist then has the presumably rewritten passage deploring the anti-Semitism that once—but no longer!—existed in Russia. Again we hear the marching footsteps, the stabbing phrases in wind and strings; but soon after comes the touching little reference to Anna Frank. With great sensitivity, using divided cellos and basses to suggest that dark attic in which she was secreted so long, Shostakovich sketches in a brief and tender episode.

'. . . *Even they cannot forbid us the delight of holding each other close in this dark room'.* But then again we hear the marching feet; the chorus, almost like the chorus in the *Matthew Passion* with their impotent cries of warning to Jesus, now try to warn Anna of the approach of the Gestapo. But she doesn't want her idyll to be destroyed and takes no notice. *'They're breaking the door down!'*

shout the chorus, but Anna dismisses the sound as the ice cracking in Spring. She is engulfed in a massive wave of sound, one of only three really big orchestral climaxes in the whole work.[3] It is a direct development of the very opening of the symphony, a solemn chant transformed into a frenzied battering at the door.

There is a brief silence before Shostakovich launches his own impassioned protest, a fresh working-out of the opening theme with woodwind and strings providing the musical equivalent of shrieks of anguish culminating in a huge chord reinforced with heavy percussion. Silence. The basses resume their sad chant; *'Over Babi Yar the wild grass rustles softly . . .'*

The rest of the movement is for the most part quiet and introspective, as the singer identifies himself with every man, woman and child that was killed at Babi Yar. 'No Jewish blood runs in my veins' he says, 'but like a Jew I arouse the hatred of all anti-semites; that is why I claim to be a true Russian.' And once again that huge sound beats about our ears like a universal cry of protest.

The second movement is called 'Humour', but there is a considerable undercurrent of bitterness, for it is more concerned with the indestructibility of humour under repression than it is with a merry laugh. Shostakovich uses a ballad-like approach, and indeed much of this symphony suggests a very similar style to Brecht's old partner, Kurt Weill. 'Tsars, kings and emperors may have ruled the earth from great palaces, but humour? No, they didn't have that.' We could well be in the middle of a rousing folk-opera put on by a collective community far from Moscow. Surely the most rigidly doctrinaire party member could not call this music revisionist, corrupt or decadent.

The music dances on in its brassy way, but memories of Babi Yar cannot be expunged, and quietly the orchestra reminds us that though it may be all right to laugh, some things are no laughing matter.

One can imagine a stage production of this symphony with immensely effective dances to match its changing moods. Later, the poem describes a political prisoner going to his death in a tattered coat suddenly giving a laugh and a wave; it makes an interesting comparison with the romantic hero of Berlioz' Fantastic Symphony on his march to the scaffold and his last vision of his beloved before the blade of the guillotine falls. The romance has gone out of death now and we have grown too hard and cynical to look on it as anything to glorify.

The third movement is perhaps the strangest to Western ears. It is a long eulogy of women, but not the woman that someone like Richard Strauss

---

[3]Having regard to the closing paragraph of the preceding essay, I find it significant that Shostakovich's most violent reaction is to the death of an *individual*, a child, rather than to a mass slaughter.

would have had in mind. These are the workers, backs bowed by toil, hands made rough by the harshness of life. In the dreary little village shop, they queue patiently, heads wrapped in shawls or scarves, carrying the empties back to the store. (Shostakovich makes a point of the sound of clinking bottles with a little rhythmic figure on castanets and wood block.) It does not present a very rosy view of life in Russia and the scoring is as dark as the icy dawn in which the workers' day begins. There is a notable horn solo against a soft background of strings and harp as the singer describes the women standing waiting to pay, their hard-earned money clutched in chilly hands. (It is truly ironic that after all the talk of 'Socialist Realism' a work that genuinely attempts to present a realistic view should be banned. This with deep feelings of tenderness and affection for the Russian people as the string writing in particular shows.)

It is followed by 'Fears', an extraordinary movement that looks back (again with remarkable understatement) at the Stalinist days when a man lived in constant dread of the knock at the door at night, when fear dictated silence, when a husband dared not speak openly even to his wife. One theme hangs over from the previous movement, for those women have lived through those dark ages themselves. With striking economy of means, Shostakovich suggests a sinister world, a Kafka-like nightmare in which every natural impulse is subdued.

Distant trumpets, echoed by flutes, herald a new era; '*All that has changed now*', says the text, '*today it seems distant*'. And again one asks why a work that makes such statements should cause such offence to authority. There's some superb writing for the brass a little later on, when the poet once more remembers those nights when marching feet and a peremptory knock at the door struck fear into the heart.

The chorus recalls days of comradeship in wartime, the courage of men who didn't flinch under bombardment. '*If there was a fear*', they sing, '*it was a fear of speaking honestly*'; and one remembers Solzhenitsyn who got eleven years for writing a letter to a friend in which he dared to criticise Stalin. Yet Shostakovich's love of Russia and the Russian people is totally sincere and indestructible.

The Fifth Movement, 'Careers', is the most immediately appealing, delicately scored, and beginning with a passage for two flutes that positively invites balletic interpretation. It has the longest instrumental introduction of the five and provides some relief from the generally rather grim content of the symphony. The text tells of such men as Galileo, men who had the courage to stand up for their own beliefs. '*That's what I mean by a career*', says Yevtushenko with considerable personal courage, and Shostakovich sugars the pill by setting the words to music that is without malice.

'*Shakespeare, Pasteur, Tolstoy, the astronauts, or doctors who cured cholera, these are the models for my career, I pin my faith on them.'* Unexceptionable sentiments one would think. Later, a rigidly academic fugue from Shostakovich's pen is presumably directed at the inflexible bureaucracy of the State. Then the happy little tune returns and the work ends with an enigmatic smile. It is clearly impossible to discuss this symphony without raising contemporary political issues. Neither the poet, the composer, nor the Russian authorities would complain at that, as it is an intensely political work. But unlike so many propagandist works written to celebrate the opening of a factory or the building of a dam, I have a feeling this one will not date; for it is deeply concerned with humanity, with problems of conscience, with freedom and with ideals. These are things that do not pass like changing fashions; they are always with us, as I suspect this symphony may well be.

Concerto for Violoncello and Orchestra Op. 107 (1959)

This concerto, written for Rostropovich, is scored for a relatively small orchestra—a pair each of flutes, oboes and clarinets, a bassoon and contrabassoon (doubling as a second bassoon where necessary), a single horn part calling for a virtuoso player, timpani, celesta and strings. The light instrumentation enables the cello part to be heard at all times, a technical problem which composers have always had to take into consideration in works of this kind.

The musical argument might be said to centre round the note G and three possible harmonisations, E minor, E flat major and C minor (Ex. 1).

Ex. 1

(The notation of the first three notes of Ex. 2 may not look like E minor but in effect that is what they are.)

The cello begins the movement with the diminutive fanfare shown in Ex. 2, to which the orchestra responds with a crisp rat-a-tat. The tone is brisk

Ex. 2

and unemotional. The cello part continues with unflagging energy; indeed a remarkable feature of this work is the virtually non-stop writing for the soloist. As the music presses on, two subsidiary themes may catch our attention, easily recognised since they both begin with repeated notes; but it's the very first four-note pattern (Ex. 2) that keeps returning, cropping up frequently in both the solo and orchestral parts.

Repeated notes seem to be something of an obsession, for the second main subjects has no fewer than ten Gs in the first fourteen notes.

Ex. 3

This theme exploits the third harmonisation of G, C minor, while the catchy rhythm of the accompaniment gives it a jaunty swagger.

The orchestral clarinet takes over this third theme while the cello grumbles away down on its lowest strings. Then suddenly there is a dramatic re-entry of Ex. 2. A french horn bursts in with it in a most exciting way. (The horn part is so important in this concerto that Rostropovich usually asks the horn player to stand and share in the inevitable ovation, and rightly so.)

Since Shostakovich has deliberately kept the horn in reserve up to this moment, it makes a marvellous impact when we hear these stirring tones for the first time.

The entry of the horn marks the beginning of the development section. For the time being the soloist remains preoccupied with some of the subsidiary themes we have already heard, but a second powerful reminder of the opening theme from the horn unleashes a rapid quaver pattern derived from the same four-note motif but elaborating it at length.

The woodwind in the orchestra become affected by all this bustle and join in with similar patterns while the solo cello snaps angrily at them with some pretty aggressive dissonances. This is the only part of the movement that sounds really 'modern' if we are to use the word in the way that most people do, as a synonym for ugly. But it's an ugliness that can be exhilarating and the outlines are so clear to follow that one shouldn't really complain; it's just a bit spiky, that's all.

Order is restored as the horn once again asserts the importance of the opening theme, a hint which is duly accepted by the soloist with reasonable good grace. There follows a passage for horn and cello only in which Ex. 3 does its best to maintain its dignity despite the irreverence of the cellist's bouncy accompaniment. Once the orchestra rejoins the fray the cello takes over the lead again, maintaining its dominance until the end of the movement.

The slow movement begins with strings alone; the rhythm suggests a sarabande, the mood a grave dance. The solo horn has three comments to make before the soloist enters with a simple tune, folk-inspired but with occasional chromatic twists to give it interest. The accompaniment is confined to the lower strings and is rather sparse. In due course a clarinet borrows the soloist's tune while the cello part wanders in a somewhat vague counterpoint. The comparative austerity of this section gives added radiance to the opening theme when it reappears on muted strings. They provide a soft bed of harmony for the solo part which occasionally takes wing with elegantly curved phrases that are for the most part unsupported.

A rustic accompaniment in the woodwind brings a change of mood even though the tempo remains the same. Soon oboes, clarinets and bassoons begin to create a stir with sinuous phrases that increasingly provoke the soloist. A considerable climax is reached, with restless triplets in the cello part and in the woodwind even though the strings are still marked *piano expressivo*. The growing rhetoric of the solo part finally conjures a strong reaction from the full orchestra which is quelled by the threefold comment from the horn which we heard near the beginning of the movement.

And now begins a strange epilogue in which the cellist reintroduces his first theme in ghostly harmonics; to each phrase the celesta gives a haunting reply. The orchestral part is reduced to a mere whisper from the violins; the effect is magical and is an outstanding example of Shostakovich's aural imagination.

The greatest formal innovation in this admirable concerto is the third movement which is entirely for solo cello. It is in fact a monumental cadenza in which the soloist muses on the material we have heard so far. There are no fireworks to begin with since the mood of the slow movement is sustained for some time. The thematic relationships should be quite easy to trace, that is until five pizzicato chords seem to sever the link with the preceding music. Quietly, but with accelerating pace, a triplet figure begins, imparting ever greater urgency to the music. As we might expect, the four-note theme from the first movement reappears later in the cadenza when the music becomes still more agitated. Tremendous paroxysms of chord playing and abrupt scales lead to the finale which is a garish brightly-coloured piece that suggests a fairground at times. The writing is almost frighteningly energetic, and will leave a permanent testament as to the quality of Rostropovich's playing. Historians of the future will be able to look back and say what a phenomenal cellist he must have been for the composer to write such passages for him—just as we do now about Mühlfeld, the clarinettist for whom Brahms wrote, or Leutgeb, Mozart's horn-player.

The finale cannot be said to contain the best music—the main theme depends too much on a rather banal figure of descending chromatic thirds; but the writing is spectacular enough to sustain our excitement, if not our interest, and there is a superb moment when the horn triumphantly produces the initial theme of the opening movement. It sets the orchestra agog and they can think of little else as the cellist performs ever greater feats of dexterity, bringing the work to a brilliant and irresistible conclusion.

SIBELIUS
1865–1957

The Symphonies

Although Sibelius lived on until 1957 his career as a composer effectively ended in 1926 with the orchestral tone-poem *Tapiola*. At that period and in the subsequent decade his standing was at its highest and he was often referred to as the greatest symphonist since Beethoven. The claim sounds loftier than it is since the symphony as a form had suffered a considerable decline in the latter part of the nineteenth century, but in the end it can have done him nothing but harm for the critical pendulum swung violently against him to reach probably its opposite pole in the late sixties. In recent years there has been a swing back to favour and a more balanced view. The pace of change has accelerated alarmingly in the last twenty years and the gulf between Sibelius and such of our contemporaries as Stockhausen and Boulez seems so great that it is hard to believe that they belong to the same century. It is for this reason that we should be reminded that Sibelius' composing life ended sixty years ago and that his first major works were written when Brahms was still alive.[1] Too old-fashioned to be 'Modern', too bleak and austere to be 'Romantic', Sibelius inhabits an artistic limbo. Such contemporaries as Strauss, Mahler, Stravinsky or Debussy all offer a more colourful appeal; compared to their sumptuous orchestration and exciting rhythms his music can easily seem drab to a listener unwilling to enter his private world, yet part of his individuality lies in his almost puritanical avoidance of the sensuous allure of virtuoso orchestral writing. (This is not true of the First Symphony where the Russian influence is so strong that it might be regarded as Tchaikovsky's Seventh . . .)

[1] A young singer named Ida Ekman sang one of Sibelius' songs (Op. 17 No. 1) to Brahms who was so delighted by it that he insisted on an encore, playing the piano accompaniment himself.

Perhaps a bigger obstacle is the very different time-scale to be found in all his larger works; we have grown accustomed to music in which violent and rapid change is the norm. His long paragraphs, in which he holds back from a climax, have grown wearisome, where once they were regarded with awe. His musical structures, which were once compared with Beethoven's last quartets, have now had their mysteries revealed by industrious commentators, whose well-meaning efforts have caused us to listen far too analytically. Pictures of the man, the totally bald head giving an intensely cerebral look, have coloured our response, so that we feel that the music is primarily intellectual.

One common misconception should be firmly squashed, and that is the assumption that all his music tends to sound alike. Each of the seven symphonies has a marked individuality, showing that although symphonic form best suited his genius, he never allowed it to become a mere formula. The First, dating from 1899, is an intensely romantic work conceived on a grand scale with a final Big Tune to rival Tchaikovsky, and a scherzo that marries Beethoven to Borodin. To learn by example is not only understandable but prudent, yet there are many passages that establish a completely personal style, not least the very opening with its long clarinet solo supported only by soft timpani. The true function of this introduction is not revealed until the fourth movement when the same theme reappears in glowing colours. It is like a mountain whose outline is at first perceived in the distance but which looms immense and imposing when, after a long and adventurous journey, we at last reach its foot. To link four movements with such simple ingenuity gives an early indication of Sibelius' concern for symphonic unity.

In the Second Symphony, written three years later, we find that the strong Russian influence has virtually been discarded. The form of the first movement is totally original even though the bare essentials of Exposition, Development and Recapitulation are preserved. What is different is the way the materials are assembled. The opening pages contain a number of seemingly unrelated ideas, divided from each other by silences. Gradually, as the music progresses, relationships are revealed that we did not suspect, priorities are established, the span of musical thought is extended. Continuity is provided by a characteristic 'spinning-top' figuration which was to become a hall-mark. The movement ends not with an apotheosis but a dissolution.

The slow movement is remarkably original, beginning with a quite extraordinary passage for pizzicato cellos or basses, (I say 'or' because they alternate), whose monotonous rhythm suggests the thud of a long-distance runner's feet upon the earth, keeping up a steady tireless gait through the deserted countryside. There is nothing comparable in the entire symphonic repertoire.

The big surprise in this movement is the sheer force that it ultimately generates after so insubstantial a beginning. Was the image in Sibelius's mind

Man dwarfed by Nature? Certainly there is something elemental about the massive brass chords, magnificent but forbidding.

As for the scherzo, it must surely have been inspired by the wind battering at the shutters and whistling round the housetops. Snatches of themes are blown hither and thither, but it is the continuous pace which sweeps us along in its wake. In the midst of the storm there is a period of intense calm with a theme of extraordinary expressive power that is theoretically a very poor tune. Students are not encouraged to write melodies beginning with nine repetitions of the same note, yet Sibelius gives the oboe such a theme and silences criticism with its magical effect. Who can ever hear the symphony for the first time and not cherish this inspired moment? Though it may be swept away by the force of the gale, it cannot be forgotten.

The transition to the finale is magnificently done, the processional music emerging with absolute logic from the preceding turmoil. The simplicity of the material is a notable feature of this movement. Most composers would disdain to use what is basically a five-finger exercise over and over again for nearly eighty bars, yet this figure is like a great engine that propels the final tune inexorably on its way. The sheer relentlessness of the repetition has an overwhelming effect, a sort of Finnish equivalent to Ravel's *Bolero*.

With the Third Symphony (1908) Sibelius turned in a completely new direction. When we talk of Neo-classicism we tend to think of Stravinsky's middle period, of the *Symphonies of Wind Instruments* (1920), the *Octet* (1923), *Dumbarton Oaks* or *The Rake's Progress* (1951); but Sibelius explored a different approach, less self-conscious in its attitudinizing than Stravinsky's. He returned to the pre-Beethoven three-movement structure and was not the least embarrassed to write music in pure C major. The textures are bright and clear, nor is the work potentially descriptive in the way that the first two symphonies are; it does not conjure up images of lakes and forests, of storms or snowscapes. The slow movement plumbs no great emotional depths and is simple in form, while the final triumphal march is as optimistic a passage as you will find anywhere in his works, splendidly scored for the brass, and establishing C major with a finality that would have satisfied Beethoven himself.

The Fourth Symphony (1911) is generally considered to be Sibelius' masterpiece even though it is the shortest. Here we no longer find the epic qualities of the first two symphonies nor the bright sunlit texture of the Third; the hues are dark, the mood sombre, the thought concentrated. Right from the start we must be impressed by its total individuality, utterly unlike anything that had ever been written before even though it uses a perfectly normal orchestra and still retains in part the conventions of symphonic form. Almost exactly contemporary with Stravinsky's *Firebird*, it contains not a suspicion of Stravinskyan glitter. Much of it consists of single lines unsupported by harmony, the music of the blind, groping their way through the first snowflakes of a cold winter evening.

Now Sibelius himself was fully aware of the risk he was running;[2] he knew that by denying himself bright pigments he was liable to be thought drab. But black and white photography is often more evocative than technicolour, the shadows more romantic than the sunlight. If colour is to be the sole criterion of musical worth then we shall be forced to admit that some of our way-out avant-gardists are greater than Beethoven, Bach and Mozart rolled together. Colour is only one aspect of music and it is my contention that even though he uses basically the same orchestra in all his symphonies, Sibelius still manages to give them an individual colour of their own. Other composers may use colour more, but he is still far from monochrome.

The Fourth Symphony represents an 'Ultima Thule' of compression in comparison to which the Fifth (1915–19) seems almost self-indulgent in the richness of its colouring. The opening horn-call is an unashamedly romantic gesture so often copied in film-scores that it has become a cliché. Interestingly enough Sibelius did not number the individual movements, thereby creating some argument—are there three or four? In the Second Symphony the finale emerges from the scherzo without a break but the material of the two movements is completely unrelated. In the Fifth Symphony the first movement consists of two parts different in time-signature, in tempo and in mood; but the initial horn-call is common to both and indicates that Sibelius' thoughts were turning towards a more unified conception of an entire symphony, a goal he achieved with the Seventh Symphony (1924) which is one giant movement.

Further evidence of the quest for unity appears in the last two movements of the Fifth Symphony. Ask anyone who has a reasonable acquaintance with the work to sing the 'big tune' in the finale and he will be sure to oblige with the swinging bell-like theme in thirds played first by horns and then by trumpets. It is simple, overwhelming and instantly memorable. Ironically, though, it is not really the theme but an accompaniment to a much longer and more essentially lyrical melody played by woodwind and cellos. What the hypothetical listener is less likely to recall is that the same tolling pattern has been brilliantly planted in the double-basses during the slow movement, establishing a strong link between two fundamentally different pieces of music.

If the Fourth Symphony is 'dark', the Sixth (1923) is 'light'. Although certain techniques are common to both, such as continuously rotating patterns in the strings and brief snatches of melody in the woodwind, the effect of each is entirely different. The Sixth begins with a passage for divided strings which has often been compared to Palestrina, so clear and pure is its texture. In an

[2]Let the others give them cocktails; I will give them pure water.'

age when most composers were writing music that was brittle and sophisticated, mechanistic or plain abstract, such a sound was completely original without resorting to shock tactics of any kind. The first theme of consequence is a rising scale of five notes in D minor on an oboe. Sibelius once said, 'What is written today is often no more than empty sound effects which are completely superfluous if the composer himself has anything to say . . . Personality can show itself in five notes. What is eternal sometimes lives in very modest form.'[3] Five-note patterns are very common in Sibelius's music whether as an integral part of a significant theme or as a repeated figure in the background.

The second movement of the Sixth Symphony is a rather bleak little dance that might even be thought of as a 'Valse Triste' were it not for the fact that Sibelius avoids anything so obvious as the traditional waltz rhythm. He begins with plangent chords on flutes and bassoons that obstinately refuse to establish three beats in a bar. When a tune does appear its dance character is discreetly veiled; soon the music drifts off into vague scale-patterns which in turn become a background for a restatement of the theme.

Passages based on scales are often dismissed as a weakness in Sibelius. He seems to be drawn compulsively to them; again, they are an aspect of music that ceased to be viable for most of his contemporaries, having too strong an association with outmoded concepts of tonality, of being in a key such as G minor or A major. Scales in Sibelius are not so much a means of establishing a key as being a way of progressing from one key to the other. If we can hear 'where' they are going rather than 'how' they are going, they become much more interesting. It may be tempting to regard them as so much note-spinning, but if instead we see them as a slow change of harmonic perspective, they become fascinating.

In the third movement of the Sixth Symphony we find frequent use of a galloping dotted rhythm of the sort that Schumann was particularly addicted to, but the sound is far from Schumannesque. The texture is too clear for that, the contrasting themes too fleeting. The full orchestra is hardly used at all save for the last few bars.

A folk-song element, whether authentic or not, becomes more apparent in the finale which uses the wind and violins as a bright contrast to a darker group composed of violas and cellos. The song-like phrases are soon replaced by a fluttering semiquaver motif which a keen ear will recognise as an elaboration of the viola theme in the opening bars. Relationships between a variety of thematic fragments show Sibelius's preoccupation with unity. As for the ending, it underlines his indifference to popularity for the music dies away to nothing, leaving the audience uncertain if there is more to come.

The Seventh Symphony (1924–5) is in one continuous movement within

[3] Santeri Levas, *Sibelius, a personal portrait*, J. M. Dent, 1972.

which four subdivisions can be detected. To begin with we find a slow introduction whose initial ascending scale leads to a surprise chord of A flat minor. The ensuing themes are presented in a curiously tentative manner, often beginning just after the beat. One fragment, A–G–F♯–G, seems little more than a conventional 'turn' in slow motion but it is a most important seed which flowers in a number of different ways. More obviously significant is a majestic trombone theme, a full realisation of an idea which a solo flute had shyly hinted at in the early stages.

The tempo moves forward as a transitional section begins which may loosely be compared to the traditional 'bridge passage'. It introduces a second group of themes whose origins can mostly be traced to the introductory Adagio. A substantial quickening of pace suggests a scherzo but links with earlier material are still maintained so that the section can be compared to a 'development', however unorthodox it may seem. A reversion to the original Adagio tempo confirms this judgement since it reveals further development of the trombone theme. A second scherzo follows, introducing some new ideas but again linked with past events. Thus the two scherzi with the intervening Adagio can be seen as an ingenious variant of the scherzo-trio-scherzo plan of the Beethoven period while at the same time comprising a Development section. A Presto link leads to a third and final Adagio which serves as both recapitulation and coda. In essence the whole work can be described as a classic sonata-form movement—Exposition, Development, Recapitulation—enormously expanded so that it assumes the dimensions of a full symphony. As a conception it is literally unique, showing a completely personal resolution of the problems of symphonic form.

In the strict sense of the word sterility means an inability to pass on one's seed to give birth to a new generation. By this definition Sibelius could be said to be sterile, for, unlike Debussy, Webern, Mahler or Schoenberg, he has had little influence on music of a subsequent era. Walton's First Symphony shows a marked Sibelius influence, which is hardly surprising when we consider how highly Sibelius was rated at the time Walton wrote it. Apart from that one work, he seems to have had little effect on the course of music, a fact which would have caused him neither surprise nor pain. He was content to pursue his very individual road. For years he grappled with an Eighth Symphony, ultimately getting a substantial part of it down on paper. Finding that it failed to meet his own high standards he destroyed it, not wanting to risk its discovery and resurrection by some well-meaning archivist after his death. He clearly felt that the music he had created was a worthy enough monument as it stood.

Concerto for Violin and Orchestra
Op. 47 (1903; revised 1905)

Sibelius' first musical ambition was to be a violin virtuoso and to this end he studied the instrument intensively, although a year in the law school of Helsinki University must have interfered with his progress. Like Schumann, he found the lure of music irresistible; like Schumann he gave up thoughts of being a concert-performer in favour of composition. The first substantial fruit of this decision was an epic symphonic poem called *Kullervo* which called for solo voices, male voice choir and a large orchestra. Based on the collection of Finnish mythology known as the *Kalevala*, it scored an instant and sensational success for the twenty-six-year-old composer. Literally overnight Sibelius found himself hailed as a national figure, an experience that could easily have turned the head of a lesser man. After only four performances he withdrew *Kullervo* and never allowed it to be performed again. (It was, in the year after his death, against his express wishes. It is now available on record!) However, his intensely nationalistic sentiments caused him to seek further inspiration in Finnish mythology and several works such as *En Saga* and the four 'Lemminkäinen' legends followed soon after. His spirit of self-criticism did not desert him as his reputation grew, and he frequently revised his scores after hearing them performed.

Despite his considerable success he went through a difficult period, living far beyond his means and succumbing to the temptations of alcohol. The small pension he received from the state was not enough to cater for his somewhat extravagant tastes and even the success of the first two symphonies failed to bring him happiness. With a young wife and two small daughters to provide for, as well as having to meet the demands that came with international recognition, he must have felt a huge burden of responsibility, a burden he would relieve by heavy bouts of drinking. A move to the country in 1904 did much to stabilise him and it was in the villa that was to become his lifelong home that he began to produce his most individual work, from the Third Symphony onwards. It was in the year before this crucial move that he wrote the first version of the Violin Concerto; it was in the year after he had settled there that he revised it extensively. It received its first performance in Berlin in October 1905; the conductor was Richard Strauss, who devoted three rehearsals to the orchestral accompaniment before combining orchestra and soloist for the first time.

Since the violin was the instrument to which Sibelius had devoted intensive study for a number of years it was only natural that his thoughts should turn towards a concerto. The writing shows a deep understanding of the violin's outstanding characteristics, first among which must come the ability to sustain a lyrical melodic line. A quiet shimmering figure in the orchestral violins forms a restful background (Ex. 1) to the long expressive tune which the soloist presents as the main theme, thirty bars in all.

Ex. 1

This great outpouring of melody is unusual at the start of a work, particularly a work by Sibelius. He tends to spend the first few pages of a composition gathering together various seemingly unrelated threads. The only clue he gives us as to the relative importance of the many phrases which make up this melody is that one, and one alone, is taken up by an orchestral instrument. The first three notes of the violin part are also to be found on a solo clarinet a few bars later.

Now Sibelius does in fact develop these three notes quite substantially but he does it in a very undercover way. Once the soloist has concluded the first rhapsodic theme we hear two sombre phrases, first on clarinets and then on bassoons. Both are derived from the first four bars of the violin part but they seem like a distorted shadow rather than a direct quotation. The first *two* notes are then emphasised by repetition in the dark-toned woodwind, a modification which soon takes the soloist's fancy.

Two staccato chords from the brass interrupt the flow and launch the violin into a Bach-like cadenza whose termination is marked by a much elongated version of those initial four bars, again in the clarinet part.

A complete change of style is now evident, a square-shouldered sort of tune, as plain as can be, so as to act as the best possible foil to the sinuous and elaborately decorated lines that the violin has been displaying. It is the first chance the orchestra has had of holding the stage, but it is noticable that Sibelius favours bassoons, cellos and basses so as to give the greatest contrast to the solo line. This new theme is based on scale-patterns but its most significant phrase comes last; it is given to the bassoons:

Ex. 2

Clarinets bring additional warmth to the second phrase by harmonising it in thirds as the soloist makes an undemonstrative entrance with a simple upward scale which has two hesitant steps in its ascent. Undemonstrative it may be, but it is destined to provide an important orchestral counterpoint as the soloist seizes on Ex. 2 and offers an impassioned version in sixths and octaves. A slow ascending arpeggio in D flat major then leads to a particularly beautiful moment, a variation on the second part of Ex. 2 in 'broken' octaves. Pizzicato cellos show that they feel this is too sentimental, and soon the music changes tempo as the orchestral violins present a stirring work-song. The second stanza of this, to which the flutes add a silver lining, becomes positively Tchaikovsky-like, and for the first time in the movement we see a glimpse of sunlight. A dramatic crescendo reinforced by timpani brings back the clouds; the heavy brass add to the threat of storms ahead but the thunder dies away leaving us in a state of expectancy, unsure of what lies ahead.

We have reached the halfway mark in this vast episodic movement and, suitably enough, the centrepoint is an elaborate cadenza for the soloist. A long looping thread of arpeggios leads us to a reminder of the opening theme, provoking a brief but violent reaction from the orchestra. For the second time the soloist launches a torrent of notes that lead into the cadenza proper, very much to the point despite the obligatory fireworks. At last the orchestra rejoins the fray and a recapitulation begins, now in G minor instead of D minor, and exploring the rich tones of the violin's lowest string. To anyone who has absorbed the material prior to the cadenza, the recapitulation should present no difficulties since there are no new themes, just new treatments of them. The final coda exploits the cheerful second stanza of the 'worksong' with Tchaikovsky's ghost dancing happily at Sibelius' shoulder.

The opening bars of the slow movement give little idea of the riches in store. Clarinets pose a brief question which is echoed by oboes; flutes seem about to do the same but no answer is forthcoming and the two clarinets have a descending phrase that ends with a shrug of resignation. Horns and bassoons provide a soft bed of harmony over which the violin spreads a wonderfully expansive tune, possibly the finest melody ever to come from Sibelius' pen. The scoring gives it the dark texture of a Rembrandt painting, while quiet pizzicato scales and gently throbbing syncopations prevent the emotion from spilling into sentimentality. Once the theme has run its full span, the orchestra introduces a sterner note, an impassioned exchange between strings and wind which is given added urgency by the timpani. Just as the music builds to a peak the soloist intervenes with one of the most fearsomely difficult passages in the repertoire. It consists of both theme and accompaniment, written as two parts, the upper line a syncopated four beats to the bar, the lower line a regular six beats (two triplets). Daunting though it may be to play, technically and mathematically, it is a passionate extension of the preceding orchestral material. From this point to the end of the movement there is not a single break in the continuity, for after a passage of considerable turbulence the great opening theme returns in the orchestra, freely decorated by the violinist. Sibelius, often accused of writing movements composed of fragments, here sustains one line of thought for an immense span. By any standards it is a remarkable feat of composition.

The last movement is in the tradition of the finales of many violin concertos insofar as it is a gipsy dance. Donald Tovey called it 'a polonaise for polar bears', an enchanting description but one which is a little misleading with regard to the actual sound. There is nothing gruff here. The initial pounding rhythm makes an exciting background to the soloist's theme. The element of virtuosity is more openly apparent here than it was in the preceding movements.

The first break in the rhythm brings a rather more sedate melody for orchestra alone—a dance for the older villagers perhaps. For a moment or two the soloist rests, but he can't resist this new theme for long and in due course makes an athletic entrance, jazzing it up with syncopations and glittering arpeggios. Difficult though it may be for the player, this movement presents few problems for the listener since one is swept along by the sheer exuberance of the music. Critical reactions to the concerto remain conflicting, but violinists will always find it a superb showpiece whose challenges bring a musical and emotional reward.

STRAUSS

1864–1949

As the son of one of the finest horn-players in Germany Richard Strauss had
some valuable advantages, and though he never went through a conventional
course at a conservatory or music academy, his father ensured that he had a
thorough musical education. Orchestral rehearsals gave him the opportunity
to gain a special insight into the art of orchestration so that by the time he was
sixteen he had gained sufficient assurance to write a symphony. Two years
later he was being acknowledged as a composer of outstanding talent. A
Serenade for thirteen wind instruments made a more than passing impression
while his father, not noted for graciousness of manner, must have been
delighted to receive a horn concerto from his gifted offspring. Considering
his lack of orthodox training, Strauss must have been overwhelmed to
become assistant to one of the greatest conductors of the day, Hans von
Bülow. After barely a month's apprenticeship the twenty-one-year-old
composer found himself taking over the Meiningen orchestra when von
Bülow impulsively resigned. It was an experience of immeasurable value,
giving him first-hand experience of working with one of the finest orchestras
in Europe. Unfortunately the Duke of Saxe-Meiningen, the orchestra's
patron, felt that so young a man, however talented, was a less than adequate
replacement for Hans von Bülow; he began to reduce the orchestra, causing
Strauss to accept (though with some reluctance) a post as assistant conductor
at the Munich Court Opera. Although he resented his junior position, this
too was to prove more valuable than he could have realised, since at the time
he could scarcely have known that his destiny was to lie in the opera-houses
of the world. His three years at Munich were far from taxing since he was
seldom allowed to conduct; he thus found ample time to continue with his
composition. A symphonic fantasy, *Aus Italien*, aroused a mixed reaction
which he took in a good spirit. 'My first work to have met with some
opposition from the mob, so it must have some importance', he wrote to one
of his female admirers.

Although Strauss had written two symphonies by the time he was twenty, he became convinced that it was an outmoded form and that the symphonic tone-poem following Liszt's model was the logical replacement. He began to work on a major orchestral piece based on *Macbeth*, and, once he had completed it (1888), sent it to von Bülow with high hopes. A lukewarm reaction was made more palatable by some constructive suggestions as to how it could be improved, suggestions which Strauss took due note of in subsequent revisions. Meanwhile there was no flagging of inspiration; fired by his love for a soprano named Pauline de Ahna, he wrote what was to be acknowledged as his first masterpiece, *Don Juan*, a tour-de-force of orchestral writing which offered a virtually unprecedented challenge to the virtuosity of an orchestra. It was an immediate triumph, causing him to be regarded as the rightful successor to Wagner even though as yet he had made no mark in the opera-house except as a highly regarded conductor. Another tone-poem, *Tod und Verklärung*, followed shortly after, but his hectic schedule weakened his health and during the period 1891–2 he suffered several serious illnesses which put a brake on his activities.

Marriage to Pauline seems to have restored his strength. Shortly beforehand he had conducted the premiere of his first opera, *Guntram*, though without any great success. It followed too closely in the wake of *Parsifal* and its religious connotations were not to the taste of Catholics or Protestants. He resolved that he might do better with a comedy and turned to the German folk-hero Till Eulenspiegel. His attempt to write a libretto convinced him that words were not his natural medium; perhaps the story could be told in music alone. And so it was that in 1894–5 he composed what was to become one of his best-loved works, *Till Eulenspiegels lustige Streiche*.

This witty and brilliant score was followed by an altogether more serious challenge, *Also sprach Zarathustra*, which, though inspired by Nietzsche's philosophical poem, resisted the temptation to use a chorus and soloists.[1] Scarcely had he finished it than he embarked on yet another contrasting work, *Don Quixote*, a set of variations for solo cello and orchestra of a quite unique kind. These four tone-poems, five if we include *Ein Heldenleben*, represent a remarkable achievement for they were composed between 1889 and 1898, together with a great number of lieder and the substantial (if unsuccessful) opera, *Guntram*. It should be remembered that during this period Strauss was extensively occupied as a conductor, not only in Germany but in a number of European countries and even in Russia.

Other orchestral works such as the *Domestic Symphony* and the *Alpine Symphony* were to appear in later years but it is true to say that from the turn of the century onwards Strauss was increasingly drawn to opera. With *Salome* (1905) and *Elektra* (1907–8) he won both fame and notoriety, since the subject matter of both was regarded as sensational and scandalous—a sure recipe for success. Nor should we forget that Strauss was regarded as a musical

---

[1] The same poem provided the text for Delius in his large-scale choral work *A Mass of Life*.

revolutionary of the most cacophonous kind, though the dramatic impact of these two operas made their dissonance acceptable to a sensation-hungry public. As if to prove that critics who condemned his music as 'abominably ugly' were wrong, Strauss proceeded to astonish in a different way with *Der Rosenkavalier*, a romantic glorification of eighteenth-century Vienna whose lush harmony and voluptuous melodies have conquered audiences ever since the premier in 1911.

It was a peak that could not be surpassed and subsequent operas were conceived on an altogether less lavish scale. Paradoxically, the young revolutionary became something of a conservative whose fancy was drawn to the classical purity of Ancient Greece—a conversion he shared with Stravinsky though they had little else in common. He was more concerned with refining art than expanding it, and the enclosed nature of the German community in the Hitler era may have intensified the process. Strauss was naively non-political and failed to realise the effects of Nazism until his collaboration with the Jewish writer Stefan Zweig got him into serious trouble. His resignation was called for and to try to protect his Jewish daughter-in-law and his grandchildren he acquiesced to whatever demands the authorities made. At the outbreak of war he was already seventy-five and could scarcely be expected to make a dramatic stand against the Nazis. He sought refuge in composition, writing several works of which the finest was the *Metamorphosen* for twenty-three strings, a profound elegy for a dying world based on the funeral march from Beethoven's *Eroica* Symphony. Two years after the war in Europe had ended he came to London for a Strauss festival organised by Sir Thomas Beecham. It was a reconciliation with the outside world that meant much to him. One masterpiece remained to be written, the *Four Last Songs* for soprano and orchestra; he did not live to hear them, but he could scarcely have written a more moving coda to his long and amazingly productive life.

Don Juan
(1888)

This brilliant orchestral showpiece gave convincing proof that Strauss had finished his apprentice years and become a full master. Although supposedly inspired by Lenau's poem of the same name, it makes no attempt to tell a story; it is a series of character studies depicting the passionate attributes of Don Juan and the contrasting attributes of his female conquests. The second part of the work describes a carnival procession, while the overall structure is that of a rondo, the Don Juan motifs serving as recurring themes.

The opening flourish is a notorious hazard for orchestra and conductor alike. (On being asked how he began *Don Juan*, André Previn wittily replied, 'Before the applause stops . . .') Within seconds the first of the hero's themes appears in unison violins against galloping triplets in the wind.

Ex. 1

This is developed at some length and at a driving pace until a sudden broadening of the phrase followed by a coquettish 'wink' from a solo flute signals the Don's first encounter with a female. His reaction is instant as the initial flourish returns, though there is a suggestion of laughter in the flutes that seems to indicate that she is not taking his amorous advances too seriously. The impetuous rush of the strings is checked by an expressive gesture from oboe and clarinet in unison; soon a solo violin seems to indicate that the lady is beginning to yield, and its elegantly turned phrases are extended into a quasi-operatic duet between clarinet and horn (the 'male' voice) and the violins (the female response). Although the melodic outline is quite expansive, the rapid murmurings in the viola part indicate the under-lying urgency of the Don's passion. This episode is developed at some length, richly orchestrated and building to a considerable climax after which the muted reappearance of the opening flourish on cellos alone and *senza espressione* suggests that the Don has his doubts about the lady in question, or at least that the conquest has not brought him the fulfilment he craved.

With renewed vigour Ex. 1 appears again as he sets out in pursuit of some new *amour*. This time he tries a different approach as the violas and cellos offer an impassioned serenade that tells of his 'breaking heart'. A solo flute gives a fluttering response, the dialogue between dark-toned strings and silvery flute continuing for several pages. There are occasional spurts of passion from the trumpets as the Don's fervour increases but then, as the tempo slackens, a solo oboe proffers a meltingly beautiful theme on the lady's behalf. It is a true song without words and reveals the young Strauss's potential as an operatic composer, The work was written when Strauss had just fallen in love with Pauline de Ahna and it may well be that he imagined her voice singing this exquisitely tender refrain. This whole episode is scored with great delicacy, the melodic interest being confined almost entirely to the woodwind. (The only significant entry for the violins is uncannily prophetic of the famous *Adagietto* from Mahler's Fifth Symphony.)

The Don's reply to these loving phrases is Romantic in the grand manner, a heroic theme declaimed by four horns in unison. It is a moment that anyone who knows the work looks forward to with mounting anticipation since its impact never diminishes. It causes some agitation in the female heart as a disturbed phrase on the oboe indicates; but her feeble protests are swept aside on the tide of his passion, the noble horn theme now combined with frequent references to the opening flourish. A sudden change of mood comes with a chuckling phrase for the woodwind suggesting the laughter of the masqueraders as they hurry along the streets to join the carnival. The glockenspiel irreverently quotes the grand horn theme as if to show that the Don too has put on a mask and joined the revellers. The chattering triplet figures spread through the score as the crowd grows in size and brilliant cascades of notes suggest the swirling movement of the mob spilling into some central square.

A quiet interlude enables Strauss to recall the 'feminine' themes in the work but a rising sequence based on the opening flourish tells us the hero is approaching once more and in due course Ex. 1 reappears in its fully glory, a glory that is enhanced by a reprise of the magnificent horn theme at a higher pitch than before. Its closing phrase is taken up by the strings, in a torrid sequence that Wagner himself could not have excelled, until a huge climax is reached. There is a long silence out of which emerges a quiet sustained chord of A minor whose peace is disturbed by a stabbing dissonance from the trumpets as the Don clutches his heart and sinks to his knees; he must pay the price for his licentious life-style and in death he is alone without the comfort of a woman's love. To end a virtuoso work in virtual silence was a brave risk for the young Strauss to take but the ending never fails to make a deep impression.

Till Eulenspiegel
(1894–5)

'Till Eulenspiegel's Merry Pranks', to give a translation of its full title, is, like *Don Juan*, an extended rondo with a number of contrasting episodes; but there the resemblance ends. The earlier work is heroic-romantic whereas *Till* is sardonic-humorous. The number of themes in *Till* is not excessive but Strauss treats them in such an ingenious way that they often seem like new inventions. The two principal themes appear on the very first page, one elegant and charming in a courtly way (Ex. 1), the other toying with a few notes in a rhythmically ambiguous way (Ex. 2). (No doubt Strauss had the sound of his father's horn-playing in his mind as he penned this famous solo.) The first statement of this theme sends a shiver of excitement through the strings. The theme is repeated before being taken up in distorted versions by

Ex. 1

Ex. 2

several different wind instruments in turn, then to spread through the whole orchestra in a frenzied ascent. A few startling chords hold us in suspense; a portentous pause on a unison C leads us to expect some important event. Instead, Till cocks an irreverent snook at us with an intriguing transformation of Ex. 1, whose first six notes appear in a very different guise:

Ex. 3

This is Till showing his true character and his appearance is hailed with an explosive chord for full orchestra. A rum-ti tum-ti tune sends him off on his mischievous wanderings, with Ex. 3 making frequent interpolations. A huge chord dissolves in a swift rising scale, leaving a solo flute to introduce a Maskerade in which Till can enjoy the benefits of his disguise to tease and torment without risk of discovery. The initial three-note figure of Ex. 3 dominates the score, becoming a helter-skelter flight in a breathless flute solo. (Notice the way Ex. 3 is broken into little two-note fragments by cellos and basses.)

A sweeping ascent through three clarinets leads to Till's wild gallop through the market-place, scattering the shoppers and overturning stalls. He vanishes into the distance leaving chaos in his wake, but the music is far from chaotic, treating the first three notes of Ex. 3 with ingenuity worthy of a symphony.

Violas and bassoons introduce a folk-like tune of a rather sober kind to reveal our hero dressed up as a priest, a disguise that hardly convinces as an impish smile keeps breaking through his solemn expression. Muted trumpets and horns sound a warning—'Your sins will find you out . . .' Till remains unimpressed, his cheeky little theme recurring on a solo violin like a bird-call. A skittering chromatic descent sees him sliding down a bank to chat up one of the village girls, the downward *glissandi* in the violins portraying his mock courtesy. He arouses the anger of the locals and is chased on his way. Trombones turn Ex. 3 into a boldly striding theme as Till vows to take vengeance; soon this new version is hammered out by the full orchestra until its awe-inspiring progress is halted with a peremptory phrase from the four horns. Is this a first brush with the Law? If so, Till responds with a characteristically impudent gesture (Ex. 3 on shrill clarinets) and goes on his way.

A further episode ensues which at one point has Till blowing a very obvious 'raspberry'—and another, even more grotesque, follows soon after. Not a whit put out by the angry reaction he produces, Till walks away to a jaunty little tune scored for violins and clarinets. But something stops him in his tracks and there is a strange little interlude that seems almost static, though bass-clarinet and contrabassoon present a much elongated version of Ex. 1. This becomes the basis for an extensive new episode in which flowing semiquaver figures seem to run rings around the elongated theme. Suddenly we hear Ex. 2 again in its original form, proof that Strauss has more concern for the balance of musical form than for mere narrative. He builds the music to a substantial climax, dominated by horns and trumpets, their triumphant march ingeniously derived from Ex. 2, its rhythmic caprice converted into a boldly striding two-in-a-bar. Particularly ingenious is the combination of Exx 1 and 2 that follows:

Ex. 4

The compressed version of Ex. 1 shown above becomes increasingly dominant until, in a tremendous conflation of sound, the 'priest' theme makes a spectacular reappearance in the full brass. A chord like a hammer-blow silences the whole orchestra except for an ominous sidedrum. Massive chords tell us that Till has been brought to the Court of Justice. Even the majesty of the Law cannot suppress Till's sense of mischief and his cocky impertinence brings a thunderous rebuke. He still maintains an air of indifference, but the sentence of Death does produce a shrill cry of protest. The prophecy of a bad end is confirmed by muted trumpets and horns; the axe falls with a thud, and Till's spirit wings its way upwards. It seems that he is refused admission for, after a pause, a descending sequence of chords appears to take him to an alternative destination.

The very opening phrase, traditionally interpreted as 'Once upon a time', tells us that the story is finished; but it is Till who has the last laugh as the work ends in a final raucous outburst of high spirits.

Don Quixote
(1896–7)

Strauss gave this unique work an explanatory sub-title, 'Fantastic variations on a theme of knightly character'. To represent the figure of Quixote he chose a solo cello, while the podgy figure of Sancho Panza is depicted by a viola. The structure is clear, a long introduction, possibly symbolising the length and complexity of Cervantes' rather rambling tale, ten variations, each describing a specific episode from the book, and finally an epilogue in which the hero dies, exhausted by the nightmare delusions of his madness. Three themes need to be borne in mind. The first is a miniature fanfare, its military pretensions softened by its initial presentation on flute and oboe rather than trumpet or horn.

Ex. 1

Second, symbolising the gracious and courtly manner of the ageing knight, we find an elegant phrase for violins:

Ex. 2

Thirdly we have a gesture rather than a theme, descending arpeggios on a clarinet, terminated by cadences that go slightly awry.

Ex. 3

These three motifs appear in the first seventeen bars of a composition lasting some forty minutes but each proves its value as the work progresses.

Taking a lyrical approach to Ex. 1, the orchestral violas begin a rather wayward meditation which may represent the slow-witted Sancho Panza's bewilderment as he follows his knightly master. Strauss then introduces a tender oboe solo that represents Quixote's ideal of Womanhood. These idyllic thoughts are interrupted by a martial passage for muted trumpets as Quixote in his imagination sees himself defending his Beloved Ideal from some fearsome monster—grotesque phrases for bass trombone and tuba. A curious dialogue ensues, the knight all twirling moustachios and braggadocio, the lady (solo violin) graciously condescending.

The texture grows increasingly complex as conflicting ideas crowd into the Don's befuddled mind, creating a *mélange* of themes that would need exhaustive analysis to disentangle. Strauss employs a huge orchestra but the addition of instruments is finely graded so that one only gradually becomes aware of the unusual density of the score. A final crisis is precipitated as the trumpets sound an alarum; there is a long pause sustained by deep trumpets and trombones. Quixote's entrance has been magnificently prepared.

After his long silence the solo cellist begins with a direct allusion to Ex. 1 which bassoons and cor anglais copy rather ineptly. (It is now in the minor key to convey the essential sadness of Quixote's plight.) Ex. 2 follows, with discreet comments by the solo violin, as does Ex. 3, subtly altered. Bass clarinet, bassoons and tuba introduce a waddling theme to portray Sancho Panza's girth, but the solo viola shows him to be garrulous and rather given to uttering platitudes as though they were gems of wisdom. He finishes with an apologetic squeak in the highest register, possibly nervous apprehension as he sees his master about to embark on the first of his ill-conceived adventures.

In Variation I they encounter the windmills. They set off together with an ambling gait, their minds filled with visions of the lovely Dulcinea (the oboe theme from the introduction). Suddenly Don Quixote catches sight of the 'Giants' and urges his steed into a gallop. The great arms of the windmills begin their slow rotation (clarinets, bassoon, trumpet and tuba in unison) while the Don launches a second attack which ends with the disastrous fall. Wincing with pain, he climbs back into the saddle and attempts to salvage his pride with a gracious gesture (Ex. 2).

Variation II deals with the battle with the sheep. Quixote's morale is restored and he feels three times the man he was—three cellos in unison in place of one. Charging across the arid plain he sees a great cloud of dust. It must be the armies of the legendary King of the Garmantas. He checks his horse to weigh up the odds. There follows a classic example of Strauss's descriptive skills as he uses muted brass to imitate the bleating sheep, while the woodwind play a pastoral theme for the shepherd boy; divided violas cast a dust haze over the scene. With ferocious determination Quixote launches himself into the fray, scattering all before him. Ex. 3 sounds a cry of triumph at the end.

Variation III is a conversation-piece for the knight and his faithful if talkative squire. A clear relationship to Exx. 1 and 2 is established right from the start as the Don discourses on chivalry. Sancho Panza's replies are on a less lofty plane and his verbal meandering ultimately provokes a furious outburst from the Don in which all the cellos join, not to mention horns and bassoons. In one of the most beautiful passages in the work Don Quixote then expounds his vision of knight-errantry; the Dulcinea theme is linked to Ex. 2 in an ecstatic rhapsody. Softly, trumpet and trombone spell out a much elongated version of Ex. 1 to conclude the dream. Tactlessly Sancho Panza asks a witless question (bass clarinet), causing the knight to curse him angrily.

Variation IV follows without a break as the Don gallops onward across the Sierra. A band of pilgrims approaches singing a woeful chant and carrying an image of the Virgin. Quixote believes they are abducting some unfortunate maiden and wheels in to attack. He takes a fearful tumble and is left lying inert as the procession disappears in the distance. Sancho Panza goes to weep over the prostrate knight; to his amazement the 'corpse' sits up abruptly, eliciting a gasp of surprise from his devoted square.

Variation V is a meditation for solo cello in which the Don keeps a midnight vigil in a 'chapel' (actually a farmyard) and dwells on the beauty of fair women. The Dulcinea theme is conspicuous and for the most part the orchestration is very spare. One gust of wind sweeps across the plain to extraordinary effect, but this variation is the emotional core of the work.

Variation VI sees our two heroes setting off in search of the beauteous Dulcinea, but all they find are three peasant girls trotting along on their donkeys. Victim of his own delusions Don Quixote imagines them to be grand ladies and bows ceremoniously to them, scaring them into flight.

Variation VII involves the sorry pair in a strange adventure in which, blindfolded on a 'magic' wooden horse, they believe themselves to be flying 9,681 leagues through the air to the aid of a bearded woman. Strauss depicts this fantasy with some brilliant orchestral effects including a wind-machine, but his masterstroke is the persistently held D in the bass which shows that 'take-off' is never achieved.

Variation VIII describes a boat journey that needless to say ends in disaster as they approach a water-mill. Pizzicato chords describe them shaking the water from their clothes, and the variation ends with Sancho's fervent prayer that he may be delivered from further mishaps.

Variation IX begins with energy restored, but its headlong rush is interrupted by a tortuous argument for two bassoons. It is two monks engaged in theological discussion; to the Don's crazed eyes they are wizards or evil spirits, and he charges them down, putting them to flight.

Variation X depicts a duel between Quixote and a well-meaning neighbour who, by defeating his misguided friend, extracts a promise that he will forgo knightly adventures for at least a year. The Don returns home in wounded dignity, the steady drum-beat marking his steps while Sancho Panza fusses round him. The shepherd's pipe from the third variation tells us that a peaceful life can be contemplated without too much loss of face but it is not to be. In a moving epilogue we sense that the old knight has driven himself too hard. As though remembering how it all began, the solo cellist recalls the three opening themes and then quietly, without dramatics, allows Don Quixote a final release from his tortured visions.

Strauss's music has such abundant vitality that it seems strange that in *Don Juan, Till Eulenspiegel* and *Don Quixote* the hero-figures should all die in the concluding bars; yet it is not their deaths that we remember but their passion, their prodigious energy and, in the last two works, their humour. Inevitably *Don Quixote* raises a problem. Unless one is aware of the significance of each variation the music can seem to lack coherence. One may legitimately ask whether music should be so literally descriptive; does not the need to follow the course of events distract the listener? A first hearing can be daunting; but once the music has been fully assimilated one can begin to appreciate the subtlety with which Strauss treats the material. It is truly a set of variations rather than a set of events; in the long run it is the music which counts.

STRAVINSKY

1882–1971

In any history of twentieth-century music two figures must stand out as being the most significant in their influence, Schoenberg and Stravinsky. Both inherited a Romantic tradition which, in their earlier works, they tried to extend; both sensed that a fundamental break with the past was essential; both made the break at almost exactly the same time, Schoenberg with *Pierrot Lunaire* in 1912, Stravinsky with *The Rite of Spring* in the period 1911–13.

When Stravinsky was twenty his father, a distinguished operatic bass, died after a long and painful illness. At the time Stravinsky was studying law at St. Petersburg University but his heart was not in it and he had already dabbled in composition quite extensively. By good fortune he was able to cultivate a friendship with the Rimsky-Korsakov family, so much so that for the next six years he became almost like a son to them. Rimsky-Korsakov supervised his studies and taught him the techniques of orchestration, something he was supremely well qualified to do. As a gesture of gratitude and respect Stravinsky dedicated his Symphony in E flat, Op. 1 (1906) to the master; it is a good student work very much in the tradition of nineteenth-century Russian music. However, it gives no intimation of the startling progress he was to make, and had he continued to write in this vein we would look on him as a very minor composer. Much more significant was a short orchestral work called *Feu d'artifice* (Fireworks, 1908) which Stravinsky composed to celebrate the wedding of Rimsky-Korsakov's daughter Nadia; he posted the score to his teacher's country-home to gain his approval but the old man never saw it; he died unexpectedly before it arrived. Now although Rimsky-Korsakov never heard *Fireworks* someone else who was ultimately to prove even more significant in Stravinsky's life did. Purely by chance, the Russian impresario Diaghilev was in the audience when it was first performed in the winter of 1909. Diaghilev himself was still quite a young man, only ten years Stravinsky's senior, but he was the sort of artistic all-rounder who had dabbled extensively in composition, in painting, in history, in opera and in theatre. By the happiest of coincidences he had just decided in that same year to form a ballet company and he was on the lookout for young composers of talent from whom he could commission new music. He was sufficiently impressed by *Fireworks* to contact Stravinsky, and, really as a try-out, offered him a rather hack job orchestrating a couple of Chopin piano pieces for *Les Sylphides*. Stravinsky did it, collected his modest fee, and then returned to an opera, *The Nightingale*, on which he had been working for some time. He had virtually finished Act I when a telegram arrived from Diaghilev asking him to write music for a new ballet to be performed in Paris the following year. It was a golden opportunity, and Stravinsky rightly decided to drop the opera for the time being and set to work on the ballet-score. Fokine, the choreographer, and Benois, the designer, both found Stravinsky a delight to work with, a delight shared by the composer, so gifted were his collaborators. The Russian fairy-story about the legendary Firebird offered wonderful scope for colourful music; indeed it would have been hard to find a more perfect subject for Stravinsky's particular genius.

It's an interesting speculation that had Stravinsky been asked to write music for such a ballet in his maturity he would almost certainly have refused. His musical progress through life was to move from a romantic descriptive style to an intellectual detachment. But in his late twenties he was still aware enough of the colourful tradition of Russian music, of Borodin, Tchaikovsky and Musorgsky to relish the opportunities *The Firebird* gave him to extend that tradition, preserving its colour but stretching its harmonic resources. Not surprisingly *The Firebird* scored an immediate success; overnight Stravinsky found himself fêted as the coming composer.

Later in that same summer of 1910 Diaghilev paid a call on Stravinsky in Lausanne, expecting to hear the first draft of a project they had already discussed, a work describing a pagan ceremony to welcome the arrival of Spring. To his surprise Diaghilev found that Stravinsky was engaged on something completely different, a concert-work for piano and orchestra in which the pianist would seem to play the part of a puppet miraculously brought to life, goading the orchestra with 'diabolical cascades of arpeggios'. Diaghilev managed to convince the composer that this was a truly balletic conception; thus was *Petrushka* born, and its triumphant success in the following summer confirmed Diaghilev's judgement.

Once the ballet season was over, Stravinsky returned to Russia to begin serious work on *The Rite of Spring*. Although its idiom was to be 'modern' in the most revolutionary sense, it also represented a foray into the distant past when, in primitive times, human sacrifice was deemed necessary to propitiate the gods of nature. The score severed all links with the nineteenth century, exploiting dissonance, asymmetrical rhythms, extreme colour contrasts and the dramatic use of percussion.[1] The music was still primarily descriptive but

---

[1] A photograph of Stravinsky taken in his Paris studio shows a whole shelf full of drums on which he used to try out various effects.

it was much less individualised, less detailed than *The Firebird* or *Petrushka*. Significant a landmark though it is, we should perhaps regard it as the destruction of the old world rather than the birth pangs of the new, for if it was indeed the start of a new era, Stravinsky would have continued to develop in the same direction, instead of which—whether by force of circumstance or by design—he was to turn his back on the luxury of a large orchestra and concentrate on much more restricted sounds.

The premiere of *The Rite of Spring* (May 1913) caused one of the most famous riots in theatrical history, and the unfortunate dancers had to battle on against a barrage of cat-calls and whistles; fighting broke out in the stalls and one elderly Countess was heard to shout 'This is the first time in sixty years that anyone has dared to make fun of me!' It was certainly no fun for Stravinsky, though a concert performance the following year was an over-whelming triumph. The ballet was not revived until 1921 when it was given a completely new choreographic interpretation by Massine, but it is generally felt that the work is more effective in the concert-hall than in the theatre.

The outbreak of World War I severely restricted the activities of the *Ballets Russes*; Stravinsky settled in neutral Switzerland where he worked on a number of projects of which the most important was another Russian ballet, *Les Noces* (The Wedding). His student years had brought him into contact with a wealth of Russian folk-song, of which Rimsky-Korsakov had made a notable collection. He resolved to make use of such material in a ballet describing a typical village wedding. (There are a number of folk-songs in *Petrushka*, but the glamour of the orchestration gives them an unnatural sophistication.) Deciding on the instrumentation took an unusually long time; it ultimately proved to be starkly original, four pianos and percussion, a strikingly different sound from the 150-strong orchestra which he had had in mind in the early stages. An interesting comparison can be made between the closing pages of *The Firebird* and *Les Noces*; in the earlier work a gloriously simple horn theme is developed into a simulation of bell sounds, ringing triumphantly in a peal of rejoicing. Turn to the end of *Les Noces* and we again find bell sounds, but stripped down to the barest components. It is the difference between a cathedral and a small village church, between richness and austerity.

A similar austerity is to be found in *The Soldier's Tale*, a work for narrator and seven instrumentalists which tells a legend of a soldier's encoun-ters with the devil. In this case the limitation of resources was dictated by the exigencies of wartime. The private income Stravinsky had enjoyed from Russia was cut off at source; no royalties were coming in and there was a genuine need for a work that could be put on without undue expense. The first performance in September 1918 must have shown Stravinsky that he could achieve artistic and financial success without calling on the lavish resources of a full orchestra.

With the end of the war the artistic life of Europe began to revive.

Diaghilev suggested a new project to Stravinsky that was to have more far-reaching consequences than either of them could have realised; it was to arrange and extend some fragments of music attributed to the eighteenth century Italian composer Pergolesi. The characters in the ballet would be drawn from the *commedia dell'arte* and would centre on Pulcinella, the Italian equivalent to Punch. Scored for a chamber orchestra and three singers, this delightful work inspired in Stravinsky an enduring fascination for the clear textures and formal rhythms of the baroque period. He was never again to write for the large orchestra required for *The Rite of Spring* or *Petrushka*. He embarked on a long period of 'neo-classicism'; the Russian heritage was largely dispensed with and replaced by an obsession with the values of abstract or absolute music. Divorced from the human associations implicit in the ballet scores, music should speak for itself alone. He even began to mistrust the expressive contribution of the performer and forbade all the subtle nuances of tone that a musician feels by instinct. In this respect he took a directly opposite stance to Schoenberg, whose music demands extreme variations of tone and emotional expression. Both composers felt the need to impose order on their music; Schoenberg found it in the serial techniques he devised as a rigid system, Stravinsky found it by resorting to classical disciplines, not only from the eighteenth century but even from the spirit of Ancient Greece.

There are a number of works that demonstrate these attitudes; among the best examples of neo-classicism are the Octet, the *Duo Concertante* for violin and piano, the *Symphony in C*, the *Concerto for Two Pianos* (without orchestra), the *Symphonies of Wind Instruments* and the opera, *The Rake's Progress*. The 'Grecian' works are *Oedipus Rex, Apollo Musagètes, Persephone, Orpheus* and the *Symphony of Psalms*.

Soviet Russia had no place for such an innovator as Stravinsky and he remained an exile from his native land, assuming French nationality in 1934 and becoming an American citizen in 1945. For financial reasons related to the expiry of copyrights he was forced to spend time revising and re-orchestrating works from an earlier period, as well as to accept commissions that were not truly worthy of him. (*Circus Polka* and *Ebony Concerto*!) However, the American period was by no means fallow, and he continued to compose despite his advancing years. Until he was seventy he had regarded serialism with some distaste, saying that composers who used the method were slaves to the number 12 while he felt more freedom with 7. It was his devoted disciple Robert Craft who directed his interest towards Schoenberg and Webern, and in his seventies Stravinsky began to adopt some, but not all, of the processes of serialism. Some of the resulting works are comparatively small in scale but the *Cantum Sacrum* is a notable achievement, as is the ballet *Agon*. It is perhaps a fitting comment on the immense range of his genius that his last two listed compositions should be *Requiem Canticles* and a setting of Edward Lear's 'The Owl and the Pussycat', both written when he was eighty-four. Without question he is one of the giants of music, a trail-blazer whose influence spread far and wide. The stylistic changes which so disturbed contemporary critics were a deliberate policy and he admitted that he liked to explore a problem and, having solved it, turn to something different. To some, his attitude to music may seem unduly cerebral and it is true that many of the late works are intellectually challenging; yet such is his variety that he provides for every taste, ascetic or voluptuary; the span from *The Firebird* to the *Mass* is surely wide enough to disarm criticism.

The Firebird
(1909–10)

Once upon a time there was a young Prince called Ivan. One day, on a hunting trip through a forest, he saw a bird whose brilliant plumage was like a flame. He followed it and it led him to a magic garden belonging to a wicked ogre called Kashchey, a green-taloned giant who could turn people into stone. Unaware of his danger, Ivan managed to capture the Firebird, but the poor creature was so distressed that he let it go in exchange for one of its feathers. Then a group of girls, all princesses needless to say, joins the young Prince in the garden, dancing a sad dance since they are all prisoners of Kashchey. Suddenly the ogre appears and captures Ivan; he too is about to be turned to stone when the Firebird flies to his aid; magically it hypnotises everyone with its song and Kashchey's attendants all fall into a deep sleep. Ivan destroys the huge egg which contains the soul of the wizard, and everything ends happily with him marrying the loveliest of the princesses.

This typical Russian fairy-tale forms the plot of the ballet. It would have been well known to Russian audiences and indeed had been treated as an opera by an obscure composer named Cavos as long ago as 1822. Before Diaghilev's first encounter with Stravinsky he had asked Lyadov to compose a suitable score; fortunately for posterity Lyadov was never one to do today what could be put off until tomorrow and he made so little progress that he raised no objection when the commission was transferred to Stravinsky.

The start of the ballet is marvellously atmospheric, misty and mysterious; bassoons grunt like bullfrogs, clarinets twitter like birds and the strings suggest the dark entangling undergrowth through which the Prince searches for his prey. A shimmering trill on violas tells us of the approaching flight of the Firebird; she appears in a dazzling coruscation of notes from woodwind and strings and begins a solo dance whose music is all brilliance, a striking contrast to the dark tones that precede it. The use of the piccolo is particularly effective while both harp and piano add splashes of iridescence.

The ensuing *pas-de-deux* for the Firebird and Ivan shows that Stravinsky had imbibed all the tricks of pseudo-orientalism from his teacher, Rimsky-Korsakov. (By a strange coincidence Diaghilev produced a balletic version of *Scheherazade* in the same season.) It was a style that Stravinsky was himself to parody in *Petrushka* when he wrote the music for the grotesque Moor. The music has a dream-like quality with a very slow pulse that leaves room for elaborate decoration.

A darting descent for solo clarinet leads into the Dance of the Princesses, a movement for which Stravinsky had to devise different tonal colours from those he had used for the Firebird. One theme is of particular importance:

Ex. 1

Numerous exciting variants of this appear in Kashchey's Infernal Dance later in the ballet.

Ivan, having observed the Princesses' dance from a place of concealment, joins them in a touchingly beautiful Rondo which is introduced by a simple two-part canon for flutes. The main theme is given to a solo oboe; it is a genuine Russian folk-song, 'In the Garden', taken from Rimsky-Korsakov's collection. The scoring is extremely delicate so that the violence of the Infernal Dance comes as a considerable shock. Here perhaps we have the first inkling of the primitive barbarity that was to explode so dramatically in *The Rite of Spring*, but at this stage the rhythms are not so irregular nor the dissonances as sharp.[2] The gradual acceleration towards the final climax is brilliantly contrived. At the end of the dance the members of Kashchey's retinue fall exhausted to the ground; soothing phrases from oboes, clarinets and violas in turn lead into the lullaby with which the Firebird puts them all into a deep sleep. The lugubrious bassoon melody is ingeniously related to the plangent oboe theme in the first *pas-de-deux*. A softly rustling descent for divided strings ushers in the most magical moment in the score, the entry of a solo horn with the final hymn. This too is an authentic folk-song, 'By the Gate', No. 21 in Rimsky-Korsakov's collection. The subsequent awakening with a slowly rising scale serving as a simple counterpoint is highly imaginative, as is the transformation of the hypnotic melody into a triumphant peal of wedding bells.

Stravinsky may have written more interesting, more challenging, more unified and more original works than *The Firebird*, but he never wrote

---

[2] An intriguing comparison may be made between Kashchey's theme and 'Jupiter' in Holst's *Planets*—almost identical patterns used to very different purpose.

anything more sheerly beautiful than the beginning of this final section. It is a moment to remember for always; let us at least be grateful to Rimsky-Korsakov for passing the tune on to his pupil; he certainly made good use of it.

(These notes refer to the Concert Suite; the stage version of the ballet contains considerably more music but it is seldom played in the concert hall.)

Petrushka (1910–11)

Petrushka—'Little Peter'—is the Russian equivalent to the Pierrot of France and Italy. His story is part of traditional Russian folk-lore, and travelling puppet-theatres had delighted children with it for a century or more before the ballet brought him a more international fame; indeed the ballet is supposed to be set in the year 1830 or thereabouts. The scene is the Easter Carnival in St. Petersburg. A bright and cheerful little tune on a flute tells us that the sun is shining on the gaily dressed crowd of peasants and merchants who have flocked to the fair; there are roundabouts, swings, a helter-skelter, sweet stalls, carts bringing in country produce and, dominating the scene, a puppet theatre, its curtains still closed. To convey the constant movement of the crowd, Stravinsky builds up a mosaic of repeated patterns, mostly composed of four notes. Against their constant rotation he puts irregular groups of seven or eight quavers to be played in the same time as six, or five in the time of four, so that we get a vivid impression of certain figures jostling their way through the crowd. Down in the bass we hear a gruff theme starting with nine repeated notes; it is a few drunks lurching into the square. (The music is an authentic folksong.) Soon their theme dominates the whole orchestra; the texture is rough, home-spun, without being violently discordant. Other figures emerge from the crowd to catch our eye. There's a little old man playing a hurdy-gurdy while a girl, his daughter perhaps, dances to his music. Somebody else has a tinkling musical-box, and they set up a musical conflict just as nowadays we might pass down a street and hear pop music drifting out from different shops. But interesting though it may be to pause for a moment to listen to hurdy-gurdy or music-box, we catch only fleeting glimpses of them as the crowd passes to and fro across the square.

The little dancer's tune has an interesting story attached to it. It seems that when Stravinsky was working on the ballet a man with a barrel-organ would arrive in the square nearby every day, always playing this tune, a music-hall song about a lady with a wooden leg. This maddened Stravinsky so much that he ended up paying the man handsomely to stay away out of earshot; but the tune found its way into the ballet all the same. The orchestral simulation of the musical box and the little pipe-organ is brilliantly contrived but soon their squeaky tones are drowned in the general hubbub. The drunks pass by again on their way to yet another tavern, but then suddenly everyone stops in their tracks as two drummers appear in front of the puppet-house and arrest everyone's attention with a stirring roll of drums. A thunderclap of a chord introduces the old Showman; he makes some strange magic passes which greatly impress his naive audience, and then, blowing on his little pipe, he conjures the three puppets to life; they are Petrushka, a doll-like Ballerina and a sinister Moor, the villain of the piece. Jerked into action by their master, they go into a wild dance—'to the great astonishment of the public' it says in the score. This vigorous dance alternates between the full orchestra with vibrant stamping rhythms and contrasting sections for solo violin with a light chamber orchestral accompaniment. Horns and woodwind provide suggestions of accordion music; there is an earthy tang that is quite different from the neurotic torment that we find in the music allotted to Petrushka himself.

The ballet uses that old device, the play within a play, for in the second scene we are taken into the puppets' world and there we find that both Petrushka and the Moor share an equally ardent passion for the Ballerina, while she scorns Petrushka, being more impressed by the virility and the obvious wealth of the Moor. Petrushka is heartbroken, and Stravinsky finds a touching way of expressing the little puppet's sorrow with a forlorn fanfare, the voice of someone who wants to be a hero but who just isn't cut out to be one. So the fanfare sounds more than a little sour with two clarinets playing in adjacent keys. A dazzling cadenza for piano reminds us of the origin of the work (a concert-piece for piano and orchestra) and then we hear an eloquent expression of Petrushka's rage and frustration with strangled fanfares for trumpets. A wistful little solo dance does nothing to comfort him, but the entrance of the Ballerina moves him to passionate protestations of love. She takes little notice; she wants a real man, the Moor. She goes off in search of him leaving Petrushka more desperate than ever. (A shrill clarinet solo leads to more convulsions and again the strangled voice of muted trumpets *in extremis*.) At the end of the scene the paired clarinets seem to weep before a last furious gesture brings down the curtain.

The third scene takes place in the Moor's 'quarters'; the initial chords are strident enough for the King of the Apes, but after their violent impact the tempo slows down substantially and clarinet and bass clarinet in unison have a lugubrious chant that admirably demonstrates Stravinsky's gift for humorous parody. Occasional savage outbursts show that, though brainless, the Moor is an adversary to be feared. A brisk rhythm on a side-drum and a trivial cornet solo serve as entrance music for the Ballerina; the Moor makes a clumsy grab for her but her response (on a solo flute) is prim.

A bassoon begins a stilted accompaniment over which cornet and flute have a brief duet of studied banality. There follows one of the most comical of pas-de-deux, with flutes and harps playing an inane waltz—one of the *Danses Styriennes* by Josef Lanner—while cellos and basses, cor anglais and contra-bassoon grope their way around in a different tempo as the oafish Moor tries vainly to stay in step with his flighty partner. This ill-coordinated dance is checked by the sound of Petrushka's 'voice' (muted trumpet) in the distance; in a fury of jealousy he bursts into the room and begins a desperate fight with the Moor, dashing round in circles while the Moor takes ferocious swipes at him with his sword. (The music is so vivid that one can imagine every move.)

With the conflict unresolved we are pitched into the fourth scene, back in the main square. The music hums with activity, much being made of the accordion effect. Out of all the bustle fragments of a tune emerge on an oboe, then on a horn. Soon, after a few preliminary scales and trills, it is taken up by the violins and flowers into a glorious theme, a favourite Russian folk-song called 'I was at a feast'. It is the dance of the nursemaids and is perhaps the most memorable tune in the whole ballet. Oboes introduce a contrasting, less lyrical melody, 'Oh my room, my little room' which would have been equally well known to Russian audiences of the time. It is taken up by a solo trumpet with a swaying accompaniment on a bassoon and pizzicato strings. Soon the two tunes are ingeniously combined, interleaved with cheerful scales that are like friendly waves.

Suddenly the crowd scatters in alarm as a peasant arrives with a performing bear. He is equipped with a particularly shrill pipe (clarinet top register) to whose crude strains the wretched animal howls a grotesque response (tuba). The diversion is quickly over but more excitement is caused when a merchant who has presumably been gambling with remarkable success begins to fling rouble-notes into the crowd. Unison strings play his happy tune while the circling figures in the woodwind depict the notes fluttering through the air. A perky theme on oboe and cor anglais is for two gipsy-girls who realise the merchant is worth cultivating and are rewarded with the scattering of more money. As they disappear into the distance (two muted trumpets over a rapid patter of notes from harps) a space is cleared for the dance of the coachmen. A suitably galloping rhythm is set up in clarinets with strongly marked accents in the full strings. Hidden in these virile chords is the suggestion of a tune which duly appears phrase by phrase in trumpets, pizzicato strings, trombones and horns. Again it is an authentic folksong, 'I was going up a hill', taken from a collection made by Tchaikovsky. The nursemaids, excited by this manly display, cannot resist joining in; their tune returns on clarinets and bassoons in unison, punctuated by little pouncing phrases on trombones and tuba which Stravinsky presumably visualised as the coachmen making a grab at the passing girls. The music grows more exuberant as the coachmen's song dominates the scene. A sudden break into a quicker tempo indicates the arrival of a group of masked revellers one of whom is dressed as the Devil (bold octaves in heavy brass). Two others, disguised as a pig and a goat, cause quite a stir, enticing the crowd to join them in a frenzied dance; the music builds to a powerful climax from which a single strident note emerges to arresting effect. It is a scream for help from Petrushka who dashes out of the theatre pursued by the Moor. At such points the change of idiom is striking; the music for the crowd is seldom chromatic and is made up of repetitive patterns of a very conventional kind and clearly outlined folk-tunes. The effect of brilliance is achieved by the mixture of various rhythms and by the glitter of the orchestration. The music of the puppets and their master is much more advanced harmonically, sometimes bi-tonal (two keys at once) sometimes atonal (no fixed key.)

The Moor chases after Petrushka and with a savage blow of his scimitar cuts him down. A muffled squeal from two clarinets signals his death agony, a graphic 'flop' from flute and piccolo his fall to the ground. To a soft *tremolando* from high strings, the crowd gathers round the pathetic body as the first snowflakes fall. A fussy bassoon tells us that the Showman is hurrying up to see what has happened. He picks up the broken body, sighing heavily as he does so (horns with an eloquent chromatic descent). Softly the 'accordion' theme is heard as the crowd disperses dumbstruck by the tragedy. Only the Showman is left in the square dragging Petrushka's body towards the theatre. Suddenly to his amazement he sees Petrushka's ghost sitting astride the theatre's roof, threatening and jeering, defiant to the last. The Showman drops the puppet and scuttles away nervously; the curtain falls.

With the score of *Petrushka* one can say that the end of a colourful and nationalist school of Russian music was reached. For all the originality of its scoring, its frequently daring harmony and its frequent asymmetrical rhythms it still derives from the traditions of Borodin and Rimsky-Korsakov. From now on Stravinsky was destined to sever such links with his cultural heritage. He was at the threshold of a truly revolutionary break with the past.

The Rite of Spring
(1912–13)

Stravinsky had his first intimation of this historic musical landmark whilst he was still at work on the closing scene of *The Firebird*. 'I had a fleeting vision which came as a complete surprise, my mind at the time being full of other things. I imagined a solemn pagan rite; wise elders, sitting in a circle, watched as a young girl danced to her death. She was being sacrificed to propitiate the god of spring.'

Pierre Monteux, who conducted the first performances of the ballet, gave a vivid description of his first impression of the work as played by Stravinsky on the piano. Admirer though he was of Stravinsky's music, before long he became convinced that the composer had gone mad as he literally jumped up and down from the stool to give even greater emphasis to the huge accents the primitive rhythms demanded. Gradually the sheer power of the work overwhelmed him and he realised he had been present at the birth of a masterpiece. The premiere, as we have seen (p. 295), was a disaster but the score is now established as one of the most crucial to the development of music in our century. The vision of spring may seem strange to those of us who live in more temperate climes but it should be remembered that in the greater part of Russia it is a huge convulsion in which a world imprisoned in the freezing grip of ice and snow bursts out of its straitjacket; rivers that were immobilised as if by some magic spell become raging torrents; the iron-hard earth yields flowers. To primitive man the emergence from the cold dark winter must have seemed a miracle which, if it failed to materialise, would mean the end of the world.

Stravinsky used a huge orchestra for these 'Pictures of Pagan Russia' as they are called in the subtitle. There are two main parts, 'The Adoration of the Earth' and 'The Sacrifice'. Both parts have an introduction followed by six and five sub-sections respectively.

The opening bassoon solo, exploring the very upper reaches of the instrument, is a Lithuanian song, the only borrowed theme in the whole work. There follows a much more elaborate version of dawn awakening than we found at the start of *The Firebird*. One hears similar animal and insect voices, but these are less identifiable. As the texture grows even more complex we feel we are in a tropical jungle rather than a Russian landscape still snowbound, but Stravinsky is describing life stirring restlessly, determined to break out from winter's grip. Sap rises in the tree even though the boughs may still glisten with icicles. The first suggestion of a tutti (almost entirely woodwind) gives us an indication of the technique Stravinsky uses most frequently in this score, a mosaic of repetitive patterns each of which has an independent life. The solo bassoon interrupts this first *mélange* of sounds with a variant of its opening theme. A soft trill from a clarinet seems to set wings a-quiver and then we hear a significant four-note figure from pizzicato strings; it is the first intimation of the arrival of Man on the scene; it leads into

'The Dance of the Adolescents'

The basic chord, repeated 212 times in all during the short first section of the movement, sustains our interest through the asymmetrical placing of strong accents. It combines two perfectly orthodox harmonies, E major (written as F flat) and the dominant seventh of A flat. (One of Stravinsky's most notable gifts is his ability to take familiar materials and shed new light on them so that we feel we have never heard them before.) The pounding rhythm of the strings is periodically interrupted by repetitive patterns on cor anglais and bassoons and a strident phrase (muted trumpet and oboe) beginning with four repeated notes and a chromatic descent. The second part of the dance becomes more complex, giving the impression of an increase of speed by packing more notes into the bar. The clarinets are particularly active, but the theme to bear in mind (Ex. 1) is played by four trumpets in closely bunched parallel harmonies, the top line reinforced by three cellos.

Ex. 1

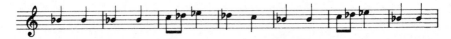

The mounting hysteria of the dance is brilliantly conveyed although it should be noted that the patterns in each instrumental part are not only repetitive but nearly always amazingly conventional. This immensely diffi- cult score is paradoxically made up from surprisingly simple components.

A break into a quicker tempo indicates our arrival at the next section, the 'Jeu du Rapt' (the Mock Abduction), whose brilliant woodwind flourish bears a fleeting resemblance to the prominent flute theme at the start of *Petrushka*. Horns sound the calls traditionally associated with the chase while pizzicato violins scamper through the component notes of the A flat domi- nant seventh that was so prominent in the preceding movement. We now encounter the first of the many musico-mathematical problems presented in this work, bars of 9/8 in which some instruments observe the conventional grouping of 3+3+3, while stronger emphasis is placed on 4+5 in one bar and 5+4 in the next.

The effect is of impetuosity as certain instruments break out of the normal restraint of a regular beat.

An exciting tutti in asymmetrical rhythms unleashes more hunting calls from the horns, while two tremendous thumps from the bass-drum seem to indicate historically inaccurate gunshots. The hunt ended, a quiet trill on flutes leads to the next section:

'Spring Rounds'

After a brief introduction the tempo slows considerably with heavy chords on strings interrupted by short curved phrases from unison wind. As the movement progresses Ex. 1 reappears, duly to be developed with awe-inspiring power and ear-tingling dissonance. An explosion of activity follows, quickly suppressed by a commanding flute trill and a return to the calm introductory music to the section.

'Games of the rival tribes' (Jeux des cités rivales)

This, one of the most brilliantly scored of all the thirteen sections of the ballet, has several clearly defined themes to represent the rival tribes, one choppy and aggressive, the other more lyrical.

Ex. 2

These two contrasting ideas are tightly interwoven against a restless undercurrent of stamping rhythms in percussion, deep brass and lower strings which ultimately turns into a continuous growl. The section ends with a simple five-note theme on high tubas, a long sustained note on horns and a curious clucking of bassoons. This leads us straight into

'The Procession of the Sage'

Horns and tubas dominate the scene while around their stately processional we sense the continuous excitement of the spectators. Abruptly the procession halts. With some considerable effort (groaning contrabassoon and thumping heart beats from timpani and pizzicato double-bass) the elderly Sage kneels to kiss the earth (muted string chord). It is the cue for a savage dance of exaltation,

'The Dance of the Earth'

Drums pound continuously, woodwinds squeal, brass bays; the tempo is breathtaking but again one must acknowledge the basic simplicity of the repetitive patterns which pervade the score. Taken at a suitably slow speed much of the music could be sight-read by a school orchestra of limited ability; but it is the speed which is the challenge, and virtuoso players are needed in every department.

The Second Part, 'The Sacrifice', begins with a slow introduction that shows Debussy's influence; it is the one passage in which the conventional conception of Beauty is allowed, an orchestral nocturne, though the night is cold, the moon reflected off ice rather than water. A rather mournful phrase for horns in three parallel parts leads into

'The Mystic Circle of the Adolescents'

a slow ritual dance; the theme is taken up by six solo violas divided into six parts with a hypnotically monotonous accompaniment. A slight increase in tempo brings a new theme, first on a solo flute, then on two clarinets a seventh apart. The music returns to the slower tempo suggesting a gently swaying movement from the dancers. A sudden ascent, a sort of orchestral shriek, sets a savage throbbing beat going (four timpani simultaneously and jabbing strings chords.) It is the cue for the

'Glorification of the Victim'

which Stravinsky originally imagined as a dance for a wild troop of Amazons. Here rhythm is all, barbaric and elemental with violent off-beat chords and sharp stabbing phrases from the horns that sound like an animal baying in fury. At times the drumming seems frenzied, while brilliant runs in the woodwind suggest light glinting on raised knives. A sudden pause on bass clarinet, cellos and basses (low D sharp) tells us we have reached the

'Evocation of the Ancestors'

After the pace and brilliance of the preceding section the music here is solid, foursquare, with strong inclinations towards C major ('ancestral' harmony?) contradicted by the D sharp (= E flat) rooted in the bass. The phrases circle round a very limited number of adjacent notes, punctuated by explosive accents from the strings and menacing rolls on timpani and bass drum. The ensuing

'Ritual of the Ancestors'

is at a much slower tempo, the harmony static and repetitive while sinuous coils of notes from cor anglais or alto flute give a pseudo-oriental flavour. An illusion of increased pace comes as the low flute murmurs a continuous pattern of semiquavers but trumpets add solemnity with yet another 'Russian' theme based on four notes. A sudden outburst for full orchestra adds an electric vibrance to the previously rather sluggish music, the swiftly flutter-ing notes on flute and violins adding a strange glitter to the sound. The texture then breaks into fragments, chopping from bassoons to oboes to clarinets and trombone and back again so that the ear is constantly teased with new tone-colours. Another outburst is dominated by unison horns, their bells held high to enhance their effect. The movement ends as it began with a hypnotic trudging beat and 'oriental' wails. There remains the final

'Sacrificial Dance'

the most brutal and primitive section of the whole ballet. It is a conductor's nightmare, with continuously changing beats which often fail to coincide with the orchestral accents. Nijinsky, who was entrusted with the choreogra-phy, was musically illiterate, and to present him with such a score was asking for disaster. The irregularity of the rhythms was a totally new problem for the dancers although in the end the sheer force of the music silenced the hecklers in the audience. There is virtually no melody save for a stuttering chromatic descent that occasionally cuts through the drumming harmonies. At one point the violins hammer away at a four-note tune beginning with five repetitions of the same note, but even they are harassed by stridently dissonant trumpets. The final gasp comes with a swift ascending scale on flutes as the sacrificial victim expires; there is a dramatic crash and this amazing score ends, crushing an entire tradition of music beneath its ruthless and unrelenting rhythmic drive.

Symphony of Psalms
(1930; revised 1948)

It was the conductor Koussevitsky who asked Stravinsky to write a work for the Boston Symphony Orchestra's fiftieth birthday. He probably hoped for an orchestral show-piece, perhaps something *à la Petrushka*. It must have come as a shock when the composer produced a work of great austerity in which the violins and violas weren't even used. History doesn't seem to record what the string section of the orchestra felt at being so scurvily treated. There are no clarinets either, and even the percussion is reduced to a timpani part. But Stravinsky showed how he regarded his values when on the title-page he wrote 'This work is composed to the glory of God, and for the Boston Symphony Orchestra'. A cynic might say that this is getting the best of both worlds, but there is no doubt that Stravinsky's religious involvement was completely sincere. As text he chose portions of Psalms 38 and 39 in the Latin Vulgate, and the whole of Psalm 150. He chose Latin for the same reason that he had in *Oedipus Rex*, to universalise, to go beyond national barriers, and to de-personalise. With his love of ritual, he wanted to strip off all the more recent accretions of religion and get back to a more primitive hieratic attitude.

Strangely enough the first idea that came into his mind was so simple that one would scarcely imagine it to be particularly fruitful. It was just a rhythm on one note (♩ ♫ ♬). Its machine-like quality, totally lacking in sentimentality, was just the thing for him. He wanted to escape completely from all the sentimental associations that had gradually swamped religious thought in the nineteenth century, to get back to the harsh core of Christianity as it once was, a religion that had to contend with persecution and hardship. After all, David was a warrior as well as a writer of Psalms.

There are three movements, the first a solemn chant with suggestions of a Bach toccata in the orchestral part; second is a double fugue, one for orchestra and one for the choir which are combined; lastly a 'Laudate Dominum' of grave beauty which incorporates an exciting Allegro in which the rhythm quoted above makes a number of appearances.

The work begins with a famous chord, unadultered E minor but spaced in such a way that it sounds completely new; it has a yawning space in the centre and close-knit triads at the outer edges. The chord appears several times, separated by toccata-like figures in the woodwind. The scoring, 5 flutes, 4 oboes, cor anglais, 3 bassoons, brass, harp, 2 pianos, cellos and basses, establishes a curiously austere sound at once.

The first choral entry is completely undemonstrative, a stark chanting of narrow intervals. I once saw a film about religious cults that still survive to this day in Russia against every sort of discouragement, and it showed old peasant-women parading on their knees around a statue till their flesh was cruelly bruised and broken. There's something of that harshness here, as though the body must be scourged. Even the orchestral accompaniment has a dogged pertinacity, eschewing any suggestion of sentimentality. There are scarcely any variations of tone indicated save for one *fortissimo* climax on 'Remitte mihi', while the final triumphant chord of G major is marked 'senza diminuendo'. It is the first major chord in the work and is like a sudden blaze of sunlight streaming into a dark church.

The second movement is extremely austere, a fugue for orchestra and a fugue for chorus, each having a separate identity, but able to be worked out together. The subject of the orchestral fugue is a strange one, so angular and twisted that it is not unlike those crucifixion themes in Bach or Handel in its exploitation of distorted intervals. Stravinsky's theme has a similar angularity, but is less fierce than Handel's 'And with His stripes' or Bach's 'Let Him be crucified'.

The counterpoint that develops with the four fugal entries is uncompromisingly severe, often producing dissonances that are the result of the conflict between horizontal lines that pursue their logical course regardless of harmonic consequence. By comparison the choral fugue is more lyrical, more readily comprehended. Some relaxation of the orchestral tension comes in a quiet passage after 'et direxit gressus, gressus meos'. There is a momentary silence followed by a dramatic outburst in G minor, the orchestral fugal subject now given renewed impact by a dotted rhythm whose traditional associations with Christ's passion should not be forgotten. The chorus ends with a serene unison E flat, the contrapuntal web untied.

The third movement is thought by some critics to be the most beautiful thing ever written by Stravinsky. Its sheer simplicity reminds one of one of those perfect churches in which there is no excess of ornamentation, just bare white stone. Stravinsky made an interesting remark about it. It took him some time to understand, he said, that God must not be praised in loud fast music. And so we find *quiet* Alleluias, and a sense of great stillness and peace. The voice parts now tend to move through adjacent notes, the widest interval being a falling fourth. The orchestral part is almost devoid of harmony save for occasional wide spaced chords of C major.

As a contrast to this monastic calm, the battering of the outside world comes as a rude shock. The appearance of the repeated quaver rhythm quoted above galvanises the orchestra into action as though the tribes of Israel were praising God even as they marched into battle. Stravinsky was fired by a vision of Elijah's chariot riding up to heaven, and as the horns soar athletically to the top of their compass, he indulges himself in a moment of pictorialism that is rare in this work. But whatever its symbolic significance, the music is immensely exciting, the staccato drumming of 'Laudate Dominum' in the chorus alternating with majestic steps in the bass part.

A return to the serene calm of the opening brings a gentle 'Alleluia' from the choir, but it is only a brief moment of repose. The driving rhythms begin again with the orchestral part dominant. After a considerable climax there is a sudden reversion to the slow tempo as the repeated quavers lose their sting. The music unwinds with a slow descent through a G flat major arpeggio in the bass as the quavers flicker and die on an F major chord. Sopranos introduce a new theme whose lilting rhythm is copied by the basses. Meanwhile the solemn minims in the orchestra set a pattern which in due course will evolve into the final hymn. The music here is founded on a constantly repeated pattern of four notes (E♭–B♭–F–B♭) though the melodic line is clearly three beats in a bar; the resulting rhythmic ambiguity is almost the only complexity in this astonishing passage, music that seems to be carved in marble rather than written on a page. The soprano part swings gently to and fro through three adjacent notes while the other voices hold an almost static line. The orchestral harmonies are occasionally dissonant yet there is a logic about them that is completely convincing.

These final pages are like a hymn of praise floating down from the skies, and the phrase is not mine but Stravinsky's. It has an extraordinary sense of timelessness, as though it was truly eternal. After the violence and complexity of a work like *The Rite of Spring* it would seem to be the opposite pole, a simple assertion of enduring faith, enduring because the music itself seems to be centuries old.

TCHAIKOVSKY
1840–93

Like so many other composers, Tchaikovsky was doomed to squander precious years preparing for a non-musical profession. Not until he was twenty-three was he able to desert the Civil Service for his musical studies. As a more than usually mature student he was able, on Anton Rubinstein's recommendation, to take up a teaching post at Moscow's new Conservatory of Music as soon as he had graduated. He remained there teaching harmony for twelve years, composing in his spare time. His ill-starred attempt at marriage and the subsequent near-suicidal breakdown are too well-known to be chronicled here except to stress his neurotic and unbalanced temperament. Human relationships were difficult for him but Providence brought a strangely satisfying solution in the shape of a wealthy patroness, Nadezhda von Meck, with whom he sustained a completely platonic but emotionally rewarding correspondence for fourteen years; he saw her only twice but no words were exchanged. He valued her not merely for her financial and moral support but also for the fact that she made no demands on him; she valued him because she felt great satisfaction in seeing his progress from relative anonymity to international recognition and acclaim, a progress that her aid undoubtedly facilitated.

During his mid-twenties Tchaikovsky wrote a number of fairly ambitious orchestral works most of which he was later to disown. Any criticism cut him to the quick and he suffered severe crises of self-confidence. His first opera, *The Voyevoda*, was actually very well received at its premiere, but the composer remained dissatisfied with it and subsequently destroyed the score. With considerable encouragement from Balakirev Tchaikovsky embarked on what was to prove to be his first masterpiece, the Overture-Fantasy *Romeo and Juliet* (1869). The original version was far from successful and Tchaikovsky humbly accepted Balakirev's numerous suggestions about improvements. (The overture as we know it was not completed until September 1880.)

His First Symphony, *Winter Dreams*, had already been performed in 1868 but it cannot be regarded as a truly characteristic work. Meantime the opera-house continued to exert an irresistible fascination and many months were wasted on *Undine*, an opera which shared the fate of its predecessor. A further opera, *The Oprichnik*, followed, but once again a successful first performance brought no satisfaction to the composer, who was confident that he could do better things. More significant was the Second Symphony, *The Little Russian* (1873). The use of Ukranian folk-tunes as thematic material helped him to shake off the inhibiting effect of his academic training and begin to develop an artistic personality that was more his own. The trend was even more evident in yet another opera, *Vakula the Smith*, one of the first works which Tchaikovsky did not turn against in disillusionment.

A significant commission came in 1875 when, at the instigation of the Imperial Theatres in Moscow, he began his first ballet score, *Swan Lake*, little realising that in the course of time his ballets would be more higly valued by the general public than the many operas which consumed so much of his energy. He had recently completed the First Piano Concerto which, to his despair and dismay, was witheringly criticised by Nikolay Rubinstein to whom he had dedicated it. Fortunately Hans von Bülow took a more favourable view and gave a first performance that brought much-needed balm to Tchaikovsky's severely wounded ego. Travel gave him stimulating contact with other composers, though at this stage in his life it was to hear other people's music rather than to conduct his own. (Conducting was not easy for him and for a time he suffered from the insane delusion that he had to support his head with his left hand in case it fell off!)

1877 was the year of his disastrous marriage; he found intimate contact with a female completely unbearable and within months attempted suicide to extricate himself from the situation. A less drastic solution was found in total separation, but he paid a heavy cost with a complete nervous breakdown. Despite these pressures he managed to write his Fourth Symphony and the greater part of the opera *Eugene Onegin*. In the following year, as the trauma of the marriage faded, he was able to sketch the whole of his violin concerto in eleven days and, even more remarkably, orchestrate the entire work in a fortnight. Another blow awaited him for Leopold Auer, to whom he had dedicated the concerto, rejected it as unplayable. The first performance was given three years later by Adolf Brodsky, but once again Tchaikovsky was castigated by the critics.

The ensuing years were relatively fallow; he continued to compose but the music was often fabricated rather than inspired. His opera *The Maid of Orleans* was unanimously condemned by the critics even though Tchaikovsky took twenty-four curtain calls at the end of the first perform-ance. The best works from this period are the delightful *Seranade for Strings* and the *Manfred* Symphony which would probably never have been written without the insistent encouragement of Balakirev. His morbidly introspective nature continued to bring acute bouts of depression and self-doubt but his periodic trips abroad brought him gratifying acclaim from the public and a better appreciation from the critics than he was given in his native Russia. It was after one such tour, taking him as far afield as Prague and London, that he settled in a new home in the country. He found great comfort in tending the small garden, and was able to start work on the Fifth Symphony. The first stages were laborious, but as the music began to take shape 'inspiration seemed to come' and within two months the score was completed.

His confidence restored, he was able to tackle the next ballet commission, *The Sleeping Beauty*, with some enthusiasm; the whole ballet, as long as a normal symphony, was sketched out between January 18th and 30th, 1889. The orchestration did not come as easily and he worked on it through most of the summer. A week after the first performance he set off again to Italy, thus avoiding the worst of the Russian winter. He took up lodgings in Florence and quickly began work on a new opera, *The Queen of Spades*. He wrote at a feverish pace and was able for once to look at the completed score with gratification. 'Unless I'm terribly mistaken' he wrote to his brother who had written the libretto, 'the opera is a masterpiece'. As if destined never to be able to enjoy happiness for any length of time he soon had to endure a bitter blow, the termination of his valued relationship with Nadezhda von Meck. She wrote to say she was nearly bankrupt and would no longer be able to provide him with the 'pension' which had made up a third of his annual income for a substantial period. It was a decision Tchaikovsky accepted with a good grace until he learned that her finances were still perfectly sound; her changed attitude was the result of a nervous illness which was slowly destroying her, but Tchaikovsky suddenly experienced the humiliation of having been 'a kept man'. 'I have never felt so lowered or my pride so deeply injured', he wrote. The wound never really healed. Further trips abroad became a nightmare and his arrival in New York after a miserable voyage caused him to weep like a child in his bedroom. The American audiences took to him warmly and he found some consolation in their kindness. On his way there he had passed through Paris where he was delighted to be shown a new instrument, the celesta; he determined to use it in the ballet he was working on. Curiously enough *The Nutcracker Suite* was first performed in the concert-hall where it proved to be triumphantly successful. The ballet was not so well received and the composer went through a further period of depression. He dismissed a Symphony in E flat as 'an empty pattern of sounds . . . written for the sake of writing'. He thought of destroying the score but, less drastically, converted the first movement into a concert work for piano and orchestra.

The composition of his Sixth Symphony was interrupted by a trip to England where he received an honorary Doctorate at Cambridge and earned an ovation in London with his Fourth Symphony. Whatever successes came with such journeys would be blighted by terrible homesickness; he was a prey to agonising headaches and weeping fits. In the late summer of 1893 he returned to Russia for the last time, finishing the score of the Sixth Symphony towards the end of August. The performance in October was coolly received.

Nine days later the composer died, poisoned by his own hand. The tale that his death was caused by drinking unboiled water during a cholera epidemic was circulated to protect his name. It seems that a scandal was about to break involving Tchaikovsky and the young nephew of a member of the aristocracy. A small group of one-time students at the School of Jurisprudence (where Tchaikovsky had studied in his early twenties) formed a Court of Honour to decide how the good name of the School could be safeguarded. Tchaikovsky was arraigned before this self-constituted tribunal, and after lengthy discussion told that suicide was the only answer. Rather than face further anguish, Tchaikovsky agreed to the verdict; it was sixteen years since he had attempted to kill himself, sixteen years in which he had written an enormous quantity of music despite perpetual doubts and destructive self-criticism. The last movement of his last work provides a perfect elegy, a profound lament for a life that was needlessly full of sorrow but which has brought joy to millions.

Symphony No. 4 in F Minor
Op. 36 (1877)

The dedication '*To my best friend*' tells us that this work was written with Nadezhda von Meck very much in mind. Their first letters had been exchanged in December 1866 and they had kept up a steady flow of correspondence since then. When Tchaikovsky expressed a wish to dedicate the symphony to her she said that she would rather remain anonymous but that the words 'to my friend' would be acceptable; Tchaikovsky appears to have felt that this was a little too cool and added the word 'best' without permission. He had begun the symphony in May, but progress was halted when he became engrossed in his opera *Eugene Onegin*. In July a drastically inhibiting event took place—his abortive marriage to an infatuated student. He fled to the country to escape from the unforseen horror that intimacy caused him and in August he resumed work on the symphony. Progress was slow as he was still in a state of shock, but in the following month the crisis was renewed when his conscience drove him to attempt a reconciliation with his wife. He found the situation intolerable and one bitterly cold night waded into the river up to his waist and stood there for some time, hoping to catch pneumonia and thereby die a 'natural' death that would not carry the stigma of suicide. He returned home soaked to the skin claiming he had fallen in by accident while fishing. The dramatic gesture proved futile and in despair he took the train to St. Petersburg and sought refuge with his brother Anatol. (As a final melodramatic twist to the tale, his unfortunate wife ended her days in a lunatic asylum.)

Not until December was he able to resume work on the symphony; he admitted in one of his letters that it was costing him immense labour but he believed that it contained the best music he had ever written: 'I am convinced that in technique and form it represents a step forward in my development, which has been proceeding extremely slowly.'

The first performance took place on 10th February 1878 in Moscow, a city that held such dread for Tchaikovsky that he stayed away in Florence. Inadequately rehearsed and poorly conducted, it failed to make a significant impression, though a later performance in St. Petersburg was a triumph.

Once the symphony had been completed, Tchaikovsky wrote a long and detailed analysis of it to Nadezhda; its flowery language reads strangely now but it does have some value, even substantially reduced:

> The introduction is the germ of the whole symphony, unquestionably its central idea. This is *Fate*, that fated force that prevents our search for happiness from succeeding . . . that hangs above like the Sword of Damocles constantly poisoning the soul. One can only submit to it and seek refuge in futile longings. Why not reject reality and plunge oneself into a dream world? . . . At last a sweet, tender dreams appears . . . How wonderful!   Little by little dreams completely envelop the soul. All gloom and sorrow is forgotten . . . But no! Happiness is only a dream and Fate awakes us . . . Life shifts constantly between grim reality and fleeting visions of joy . . .

He continued in a similar vein, only occasionally suggesting specific images such as a military procession passing in the distance during the third movement; such images 'have nothing in common with reality, they are strange, wild, incoherent.' In a postscript he added: 'I was in terribly low spirits last winter while I was writing this symphony and it truly reflects my feelings at the time. Much is already forgotten. Only a general impression of my intense and terrible experiences remains.'[1]

The symphony opens with a truly imposing fanfare, the 'Fate' motif, scored for four horns reinforced by bassoons (Ex. 1). The theme is repeated by trumpets and the upper woodwind with exciting new harmonies that suggest E major rather than F minor. A massive chord chops off the end of the phrase like a headsman's axe. The first bar is repeated but again the blade falls. The horns persist with the initial rhythm though now sustained string chords act like a brake, checking the forward impulse of the music until it dies away

---

[1]Quotations freely paraphrased from the preface to Eulenberg Score No. 430; translation by David Lloyd Jones.

Ex. 1

in a sequence of forlorn sighs. After a pause the last two notes become not an end but a beginning, for they are taken over by the strings to initiate the main theme of the first movement (*Moderato con anima: in movimento di Valse*).

The tempo of a waltz is not the same thing as a waltz and even to mention the word may give a misleading impression. The tortuous shape of the melody and the rhythmic ambiguity caused by the hesitant syncopations give the music an air of melancholy that would be out of place in any ballroom save a haunted one. The tune is taken up by the woodwind over an agitated accompaniment whose repeated notes briefly spill into the brass at the first climax. A long descent carries the theme down into the depths, whence it climbs again to a far more dramatic peak. Characteristically, Tchaikovsky extends the music by sequences and by repetition at different levels. Curt exchanges between strings and wind lead to a thunderous restatement of the main theme with rushing scales adding to the impact. A short dialogue between clarinet and bassoon is all that is needed as a bridge passage. The music slows considerably, setting a new tempo for the second subject. This is pure ballet music, a languorous dance whose melodic stanzas are interspersed with fluttering chromatic descents. Here surely is a *prima ballerina* who duly finds a male partner in an eloquent sustained counterpoint given to the cellos.[2]

Tentatively a choir of woodwind instruments offers reminders of the first subject though the violins still show a lingering affection for the languid second theme. A gradual acceleration of the tempo enables the first subject to gain ascendance, a victory that is saluted with stirring trumpet fanfares. Unison horns introduce a magnificent new subject that Richard Strauss himself would have been proud to have written. A tremendous tutti follows, exploiting the basic rhythm of the first subject. Its progress is interrupted by the 'Fate' motif from the Introduction, played with the utmost force by trumpets in unison. Horns take up the challenge in resplendent harmony, setting an agitated development of the main theme into motion. This continues for some time until again we hear the strident 'Fate' motif, though now surrounded by orchestral turmoil.

[2] In his 'analysis' Tchaikovsky wrote, 'Some blessed, luminous human form passes by and beckons . . .'

In the biggest climax yet, 'Fate' strikes again until exhaustion sets in. Despite the romantic programme suggested by Tchaikovsky, we begin to realise that this is a properly proportioned symphonic movement when the second subject reappears. The music follows a very similar course to that of the exposition until a notably quicker tempo tells us that the coda has been reached. Here the 'Fate' motif loses some of its dominance, unable to progress beyond its initial rhythm. The movement ends brilliantly even though the minor key prevails.

After the dramatic turbulence of the first movement the ensuing Andantino may seem a little too slight. 'In the style of a song' says Tchaikovsky, and the gently flowing oboe solo is supported by the most rudimentary accompaniment. The cellos take over the refrain with some added comments from clarinets or flutes. Soon they are joined by the violins who lead the tune in a new direction with a firmer tread. Even when the full orchestra is employed, the texture remains simple with block chords on wind and brass decorated with a chain of semiquavers in unison strings.

A charmingly decorated variation of the opening tune now appears with bright staccato passages in flute and clarinet adding a crystalline sparkle to the wistful theme. In the centre of the movement we find a surprising change of mood as clarinet and bassoon introduce a more virile tune that is surely folk-inspired even if not authentic. It has a strutting gait that conjures up visions of peasants dancing with growing exuberance, but it dies away to be replaced by the opening theme, now given to violins instead of an oboe. Fluttering descents in the woodwind remind us of the 'ballerina' in the first movement, but towards the end there is an interesting section in which the tune is broken up into fragments. We should also notice an eloquent passage for the cellos. The movement ends with several forlorn attempts to re-start the tune but each one is quietly checked by still chords from horns, wind and strings. The last phrase is given to the bassoon but it lingers in the air, unfinished.

The third movement is a brilliant invention that is almost a guide to the orchestra. For 132 bars the strings play pizzicato, something that certainly had no precedent in symphonic literature. It is music fit for the court of Titania and her fairies, but its light-footed progress is suddenly halted by a single held note on an oboe. Enter the rustics—Shakespeare's 'rude mechanicals'—scored entirely for woodwind. Tchaikovsky suggested that this might be a drunken peasant's song, but its suitability for *A Midsummer-Night's Dream* is remarkable for soon the brass are introduced with a brisk march, admirable music for Bottom to make a swaggering entrance. A clarinet solo offers a cheeky reminder of the peasant's song, like a street urchin darting between the ranks of soldiers; a piccolo is even more irreverent. Woodwind suggest to the strings that it's time they got back to work while pointing out to us that the march on the brass is taken directly from the string passage. The dancing pizzicato quavers begin again in a reprise of the first section until the woodwind can no longer resist joining in. So begins a gradual fusion of the different orchestral families. In the closing pages the march makes a brief return but quickly disappears in the distance. The movement ends not with a bang but a whisper.

The finale begins with two torrential cascades of notes. Having captured our attention so forcefully, Tchaikovsky gives the horns dronelike minims above which the woodwind play an authentic folk-tune, 'In the field there stands a birch-tree'. The strings find it boring and interject impatient little spurts of semiquavers between each phrase. These fragmentary scales develop into a spirited argument between wind and strings whose relevance is soon revealed as the opening cascade returns. This time it leads to a stirring quick march for full orchestra complete with cymbal clashes and thumping bass drum.

A variation on the 'birch-tree' follows, rather forlorn at first but growing in conviction as it passes to the horns and then the trombones. After a considerable climax the woodwind suggest a more tender approach which elicits polite applause from the strings. The gentler mood doesn't last long for soon the tune is given new vigour by doubling its speed. More tumbling scales lead to another reprise of the opening flourish, complete with its attendant march. It is now the violins' turn to offer a touching variation to the 'birch-tree', their melancholy unaffected by a solo flute's nimble interpolations. The double-speed variant drags us out of the doldrums until, amid mounting excitement, the brass treat the tune as a canon, horns and trumpets following in the wake of trombones and tuba. As the music reaches its climax it is violently interrupted by the 'Fate' motif that began the symphony. Spectre as the feast though it may be, it cannot dampen our spirits entirely, for after it has cast its shadow the timpani begin a quiet roll over which horns reintroduce the march. It is taken up with increasing enthusiasm until the whole orchestra is involved in a brilliant and joyous rush to the final cadence.

> Simple but strong joys exist. Take happiness from the joys of others. Life is tolerable after all.

For the time being at least Tchaikovsky had conquered the black dog Despair.

Symphony No. 5 in E Minor
Op. 64 (1888)

During the first months of 1888 Tchaikovsky was engaged on an extensive European tour conducting his own compositions. It met with heartening success but left him physically and emotionally exhausted. He returned to Russia to take up residence in a new home in the country. Perhaps it was the vivid memory of conducting the best orchestras in Europe that turned his thoughts towards a fifth symphony—the sixth if we include *Manfred*. To begin with he found it hard going, but as the work progressed the creative fire burned more brightly, quelling his usual doubts and self-questioning. Having penned the first tentative notes in May, he actually finished the full score on 14th August and was able to write, 'Heaven be praised, it isn't inferior to the earlier ones. It gives me great delight to be able to feel this.' The enthusiastic reaction of fellow-musicians to whom he showed the score gave him further encouragement, but despite a triumphant reception at the first performance the St. Petersburg critics were in a particularly venomous mood and the reviews were mostly scathing. The inevitable depression followed and shortly afterwards Tchaikovsky wrote to Nadezhda: 'I have become convinced that the symphony is unsuccessful. There is something repellant about it, a certain patchiness, insincerity and artifice . . . All this causes me a keen torment of discontent . . . it is all most distressing.'

Fortunately the verdict in Germany was more favourable and a few weeks later he was able to write to his brother that the symphony 'ceased to strike me as bad ˙. . . I have fallen in love with it again'.

The Symphony begins with a sombre statement of the 'motto' theme which is destined to appear in all four movements. Scored for clarinets in their darkest register and accompanied by the lower strings it seems to be enshrouded in gloom.

Ex. 1

The theme was borrowed from Glinka's opera *A Life for the Tsar*; Tchaikovsky felt that it expressed 'complete resignation to Fate' though his final treatment of it is far from resigned.

The heavy-hearted introduction dies away into silence. Very quietly the strings set a new tempo in motion, marking the time with two alternating chords. Clarinet and bassoon in unison introduce the first subject which shares something of the hesitancy we found in the Fourth Symphony. Violins and violas duly take over the theme, to which smooth-flowing scales in the woodwind add a new impetus. Gradually the theme gains in confidence, encouraged by increasing activity in the wind. The first climax is marked with the rhythm ♪♫ on the full orchestra, its several repetitions linked by swift ascending scales. Something of a battle develops between the strings and the rest of the orchestra; the first subject emerges in triumph with a magnificent striding bass. Suddenly all the strings converge on a single F sharp which introduces a passionate new theme that spreads outwards in contrary motion like arms outstretched to greet a lover (see Ex. 2a). We can be forgiven for assuming it to be the second subject since Tchaikovsky repeats it in the woodwind over a highly effective pizzicato accompaniment and then extends it through a long sequence of sighing phrases in the horns or violins. However, just as we feel the music is about to expire, an abrupt pizzicato chord from the strings breaks the mood and the woodwind (with clarinets at the top) have a brisk hunting-call, four times repeated, interspersed with a string phrase derived from the 'false' second subject. Out of this curious and unexpected dialogue emerges the true second subject, a yearning melody that lingers after the main beat in a most affecting way. Its essentially operatic nature is contradicted as it reaches a notable climax with trombones, horns and trumpets sounding a glorious fanfare based on the first subject. The 'hunting-call' provides an extended peroration, gradually descending from the heights until the horns are left on their own.

At this point the music seems to be going through a process of fragmentation, with the 'hunting' motif being used to open the way to new tonalities while brief unsupported scales in the strings follow their lead. The true development begins when the violas reintroduce the first subject. Counterpoint did not come easily to Tchaikovsky and he gives the material the superficial appearance of a fugue by passing it from one part to another without actually observing the contrapuntal implications of fugal composition. Meantime the 'hunting-calls' continue in woodwind or horns. Sustained chords like giant breaths build to a sudden climax on the rhythm quoted above, which then becomes an energetic accompanying figure in horns and woodwind. The violins now embark on a long sustained tune followed by violas and cellos in perfect imitation. It has the feel of a new theme but is actually a more lyrical version of the 'false' second subject. Skilfully Tchaikovsky reveals a subtle relationship between this and the first subject, here shown in the same key to simplify comparison (Ex. 2).

The 'hunting-calls' assume even greater importance as a conflict develops almost as dramatic as the ones in *Romeo and Juliet*. The horns gradually exert a calming influence, ironing out the rhythms until the music almost

Ex. 2

comes to a halt. A lone bassoon begins a clearly identifiable recapitulation. Allowing for the necessary transpositions, this pursues a remarkably orthodox course and all the main features should be easily recognised. The coda seems all set to go out in a blaze of triumph, but it is not to be, and the movement ends in a funereal mood, even darker in tone than the initial Introduction.

The second movement begins with solemn chords on the lower strings which may have provided Rakhmaninov with a model for the start of the slow movement of his Second Piano Concerto. Their rich harmonies are destined to provide a cushion for one of the most famous horn solos in the entire repertoire, one that has been debased by commercial pirates but which, in its proper context, always casts a spell. The gently supportive comments from a solo clarinet are a touch of genius. The essentially operatic conception is underlined with the entry of a new theme on a solo oboe, assuming the soprano role while the horn as willingly stands in for an absent tenor. Soon we find all the material for an operatic ensemble with the cellos (as 'chorus') singing the main theme while the 'tenor' and 'soprano' add appropriate descants. The melody takes a different course, rising in sequences to an impassioned climax. Two sustained chords for horns, clarinets and bassoons cool this display of fervour before Tchaikovsky produces a truly wonderful variant on the oboe ('soprano') theme. It must be counted as one of his finest melodies and only the most stony-hearted can fail to respond to the overwhelming effectiveness of its treatment.

All passion spent, the music dies down to give way to a new theme for solo clarinet. The tempo is slightly quicker and the syncopated cello part adds a touch of unease. The new theme creates waves which spread through the strings with growing intensity. A sudden entry of the timpani provokes an agitated response; a tumultuous crescendo engulfs us. With stunning effect trumpets proclaim the 'motto' theme from the Introduction to the First Movement (Ex. 1), now dragged from the shadows onto the field of battle. The impact is shattering, leaving an awed silence. The pizzicato chords which follow give a spectral quality as though Death himself was walking from the scene, his scythe stained with blood. Bearing much-needed comfort, the violins bring back the opening horn theme above which the oboe adds an individual lament. As the tune develops, unison woodwind supply a more elaborate counterpoint before themselves taking over the melody. A massive crescendo leads to a climactic statement of the 'soprano' theme whose final sighs are again interrupted by stentorian trombones and the 'motto'. Ten battering chords seem like a gesture of impotent fury against Fate's harsh blows; they are followed by a gesture of resignation and despair. Against a gently throbbing accompaniment from the horns, violins and violas tenderly remind us of the 'soprano' theme, no longer exultant but tinged with yearning. The movement ends as quietly as possible (*pppp*!)

The third movement is a waltz and has been harshly criticised for not being placed in a ballet, as though dance movements are unsuited to symphonies; yet the precedent of the Minuet was well established in the eighteenth century—Tchaikovsky simply brought the concept up to date. With great subtlety, first beats are omitted in the bass so that the tune seems to float in the air. The scoring is full of imaginative touches—changes of tone-colour, cunning breaks in the rhythm, varied accompaniments, even slightly sinister dabs of sound from muted horns. There is a delightfully humorous moment when a wilful bassoonist gets badly out of step, a disturbance of the natural flow of the dance which spreads to the other woodwind.

The equivalent of a central Trio is provided by a long sequence of agile semiquaver passages whose delicacy Mendelssohn himself could not have excelled. (One wonders if the basic pattern was inspired by the movement of ladies' fans in the heat of the ballroom.) The figuration continues as a neat counterpoint to the waltz theme. Near the end of the movement clarinet and bassoon offer a sombre reminder of the 'motto' theme. Knowing Tchaikovsky's temperament, its function is probably morbid, but it also serves a useful purpose, recalling the phrase to those of us with short memories so that we recognise its reappearance at the start of the finale.

In this last movement we find an imposing Introduction which treats the 'motto' theme (Ex. 1) majestically. Transposition into E major transforms its character, as does the rich tone of unison strings. The solemn processional continues for some time until horns and trumpets turn the initial rhythm into an expectant fanfare. A long-held timpani roll adds a touch of menace; strings stir impatiently, shifting from E to D sharp and back like sprinters waiting for the starter's signal. Without further warning we are pitched into the true finale, a wild Cossack dance beginning with those same three notes. A solo oboe introduces a more supple theme which is answered by the cellos but then one of Tchaikovsky's typical 'false' second subjects appears as a lyrical canon between violins and cellos. A fine climax is cut off at its peak by isolated off-beat chords and threatening snarls from deep trombones and tuba. Galloping triplets make an exciting accompaniment to the second subject which, apart from one group of four quavers, has an almost hymn-like quality.

Strings whip up the excitement in a rising sequence, preparing the way for a triumphant version of the 'motto' theme in the brass. The rushing scales that surround it are like great banners waving above a victory procession. Soon our attention is caught by majestic rising phrases in trombones, trumpets and horns, one of the finest passages Tchaikovsky ever wrote since it combines the regal splendour of the brass with the vigour of the Cossack dance. Some development of the second subject follows, growling basses alternating with shrill woodwind; but soon the forward impulse is checked. The woodwind are given sustained organ-like chords while the strings hover indecisively around the same E–D sharp-E figure which had ended the Introduction. For a moment or two we are held in suspense, then, with a rush, we are away into a more or less formal recapitulation. At one point its progress is suddenly slowed by powerful reminders of the 'motto' rhythm which then grow more urgent with a marked increase in tempo. A series of crashing dominant chords over a thunderous timpani roll is followed by a dramatic silence (sometimes filled with applause by impatient souls with no feeling for tonality!)

To a somewhat ponderous tread the Coda begins, with skirling triplets in the woodwind and the 'motto' theme in coronation garb in the strings. Pelion is piled upon Ossa as the theme is transferred to trumpets with surging counterpoints in the strings. The music builds to a climax of the utmost splendour, or vulgarity according to the taste of the listener, before breaking into a final Presto whose figuration seems literally breathless with excitement. In the closing bars trumpets and horns produce an inspired quotation taken from the main subject of the first movement.

> I'm terribly anxious to prove to others as well as myself that I'm not yet played out. I often have doubts . . . hasn't the time come to stop . . . hasn't the source dried up?

Audiences the world over have given repeated reassurance that Tchaikovsky's lack of belief in himself was in no way justified.

Symphony No. 6 in B Minor
(The 'Pathétique')
Op. 74

In December 1892, Tchaikovsky, a much-travelled composer in the last ten years of his life, was just starting out on a journey to Paris. For some time he had been working on a Sixth Symphony but he suddenly became disillusioned with it and gave it up; now at the start of this journey he felt revitalised and an exciting new idea came to him, a new symphony with a programme or story to it, but one that should remain a riddle in that it would never be stated openly. During the long hours of the train journey he worked at this new project in his mind to such good effect that when he got home he was able to get the whole of the first movement down on paper in four days. Progress was interrupted by a further trip, this time to England to receive an honorary degree at Cambridge; but by the autumn the new work was ready, and Tchaikovsky wrote to his publisher, 'I give you my word of honour that never in my life have I been so contented, so proud, so happy in the knowledge that I have written a good piece'. Little could he have known that it was to be his swan song, for a week after the first performance he met his tragic and unnecessary death (see p. 314). The coincidence of his death so soon after the production of this so-called *Pathetic* Symphony gave the work an almost supernatural reputation, and indeed its tragic finale and gloomy opening could be interpreted as some pre-vision of death.

The beginning of the symphony is unconventional in more ways than one; it is in the 'wrong' key, the sub-dominant E minor instead of the tonic B minor; it is scored with divided double basses, a truly sepulchral sound, with a solo bassoon playing not the theme but a sequence from which the main theme will be derived. Twice the bassoon gropes its way upwards before seeming to give up the ghost. Oboe and then clarinet confirm that three ascending notes are significant before violas lead us back into the shadows. There is a silence.

The first movement proper (*Allegro non troppo*) begins tentatively on divided violas and cellos with a phrase derived from the preceding bassoon solo.

Ex. 1

It is followed by a quietly bustling figure with a delicate off-beat accompaniment that lends it an air of agitation. Both phrases are repeated by divided flutes and clarinets, though the bustling phrase is instantly modified. The fluttering semiquavers descend into the cellos where they continue to mutter quietly while, for the first time, the violins are given Ex. 1. A swift chattering ascent in the violins is followed by a charming sequence of descending thirds bringing a notable change of mood. If, as some commentators believe, the programme of the symphony is the course of life itself, the opening is the darkness not of the tomb but of the womb, and this section must be accounted a happy childhood.

There is some justification for the theory that the symphony's concealed programme is Life itself, for after his death a memorandum was discovered among Tchaikovsky's papers which, however, bore no written reference to a specific work:

> The ultimate essence of the plan of the symphony is LIFE. First part—all impulsive passion, confidence, thirst for activity. Must be short. (Finale, DEATH—result of collapse.) Second part, love; third, disappointments; fourth ends dying away, (also short).

Almost certainly this brief note sums up his original intentions with regard to the Sixth Symphony. The scheme was changed in detail, but the idea remains; nevertheless it reveals a basic weakness in his conception. The Symphony is a pure musical form, having its own disciplines, its own structural laws. To superimpose a literary programme on top of these only weakens the structure, for the narrative will inevitably be at odds with the musical content. Tchaikovsky's introduction of the second subject is extraordinarily clumsy and obvious in comparison to the methods of Beethoven or Brahms. The music comes to a stop, there is quite a long silence, and then out comes this marvellous melody. As a handling of symphonic form it is frankly inept: as a musical expression of the impact of love, it's wonderful.

Ex. 2

This quintessentially romantic theme (Ex. 2) is followed by a more flowing dialogue between flute and bassoon with a quietly rhythmic accompaniment *à la Espagnole* in the strings. This material is extended at some length before Tchaikovsky yields to the irresistible appeal of Ex. 2 and allows its passion full rein. A long sequence of dying falls terminates the episode, sinking to the threshold of inaudibility. The last four notes demand an impossible *pppppp* from a solo bassoon and the phrase is normally played on a bass clarinet in present-day performances.

The spell is shattered with an explosive chord and a fine example of Tchaikovsky's 'battle' music; exciting though it is, it appears to be totally irrelevant until the violins begin a ferocious fugal treatment of Ex. 1 in D minor. The little group of semiquavers is extended upwards in a brilliant sequence while jabbing syncopations in the wind goad the strings to even greater exertions. Soon the semiquaver group becomes a positive whirlwind in strings and woodwind while trumpets declaim a powerful new theme which may have its genesis in the second subject, though that might be wishful thinking. The whirlwind dies down, reduced to a continuing rumble in cellos and basses above which the brass begin a solemn chorale. Any pretensions to solemnity are soon swept aside as the music builds in a characteristic crescendo with striding brass and lagging violins. After a stirring climax we are left with a quiet insistent rhythm on horns, the eye of the hurricane. In its unnatural calm we hear subdued references to Ex. 1, somewhat compressed. Tension mounts as the pitch rises and soon we are caught in another tempest in which Ex. 1 appears for the first time on the full brass section. The excitement is maintained at fever-pitch until there is a sudden broadening of the span. Over a continuously sustained pedal-point on a low F sharp, Tchaikovsky builds a magnificent passage that seems to be in a slower tempo since it is conceived in minims rather than crotchets. It is Mahlerian in intensity with the strings covering two-and-a-half octaves in a majestic but impassioned descent while trombones raise their voices in cries more eloquent of anguish than heroism. Two shattering chords bring this wonderful passage to an end. Silence follows.

The second subject (Ex. 2), now in B major, brings a marvellous release from tension even though traces of agitation still remain. It dies down to give way to a solemn coda, almost a funeral march, in which the timpani mutter the last word.

The second movement is a classic example of 5/4 time and audiences have tapped erratic toes to it ever since it first appeared. The trick is quite simple since the pulse is always divided into alternate groups of two and three. Neither a slow movement nor a scherzo, it belongs more to the world of the serenade than the symphony. Brahms wrote a comparably relaxed movement in his Third Symphony, but whereas he tends to have a web of interwoven ideas, Tchaikovsky adopts the simple technique of tune and accompaniment. As is so often the case one feels that the music has more of a leaning towards the theatre than the concert-hall, even though ballet-dancers of the day might have baulked at the asymmetrical rhythm.

There's a delightful story in Tchaikovsky's biography, the one written by his brother Modest, which tells how in 1875 Tchaikovsky met Saint-Saëns, the French composer, in Moscow. Both confessed to a secret and life-long yearning to have been ballet-dancers.

Solemnly the two men, Saint-Saëns aged forty and Tchaikovsky aged thirty-five, produced a little ballet on the stage of the Moscow Conservatoire. Tchaikovsky was Pygmalion, Saint-Saëns, Galatea, and both played their parts conscientiously, while Nicholas Rubinstein, I should think killing himself with laughter, provided the accompaniment.[3]

[3]A comparable incident occurred when Wagner improvised a balletic interpretation to Beethoven's Seventh Symphony to Liszt's piano accompaniment.

The 'Trio' section of this unusual movement is rooted to a drone bass which is maintained in one form or another for fifty-five bars. It then reappears throughout the coda for a further twenty-six bars, a procedure which would court disaster were it not for the sheer charm of the music above.

The third movement begins as though it were a Mendelssohnian scherzo with dancing triplets that give little indication of the splendidly martial music that lies ahead. Quite early on the oboes drop a hint that should not be disregarded. Softly the trombones acknowledge its worth, as do horns and trumpets; meanwhile the triplets scurry along with the utmost delicacy, blissfully unaware of the approach of the military. A bolder theme made from a simple descending scale adds strength to the texture, and though the triplets continue their dance we grow increasingly aware that something very different in mood is imminent. At last it comes into the open, a splendid march tune first presented in the distance by clarinets. Soon the violins cannot resist its swaggering gait. The horns give vent to an open call to arms which is soon capped by trumpets.

A short contrasting section follows with a proud ascending phrase on strings answered coquettishly by the woodwind—pure ballet music again! The clarinets proffer the marching song once more but Tchaikovsky keeps us in suspense with a return to the nimble triplets. A swift descending scale ending on a drum-roll tells us that this time the cavalry will appear, lance-tips sparkling in the sun, harnesses jingling. Fragments of the march tune are built up into glorious fanfares that set the blood tingling; a tremendous crescendo breaks off into swirling scales as the flags billow out in the wind. This is true pageantry which Elgar himself could not surpass. In its full splendour the march is irresistible, parade-ground music with not a hint of war to stain its glory. The ending is brilliant and overwhelming, courting applause; Tchaikovsky would have been devastated to know that at today's perform-ances it is greeted with a few subdued coughs as people shift in their seats.

The finale is unique in the symphonic repertoire, an *Adagio lamentoso* of profound sadness. The opening phrase sounds like a simple descent through five notes yet its underlying anguish is indicated by the tortuous violin parts which give this illusion (Ex. 3).

This grief-stricken phrase is extended at length through strings and wind until a solo bassoon drags us down into the depths of despair. Horns begin a softly throbbing accompaniment as the strings offer a gesture of comfort with a theme of the utmost simplicity. Gradually it grows in intensity as though all the choirs in Christendom are taking up the refrain. It is at such a moment that Tchaikovsky's demon is most likely to strike him, and at the very point where salvation seems assured a tumult of notes drags him into the abyss.

Ex. 3

There is a shocked silence followed by two vain attempts to start the hymn of comfort once more. It is to no avail and the tragic first phrase returns. One more huge build-up occurs with a relentless rising scale in trombones against which the wailing strings seem impotent. With searing intensity the opening phrase appears again four times before seeming to be buried in the depths of sombre brass harmonies. The hymn of comfort now brings nothing but torment and the music sinks at last into the darkness from which it first emerged at the very start of the symphony.

TIPPETT
1905–

If the early recognition shown to Walton and Britten is to be seen as the norm in a century as publicity-conscious as ours, Tippett must be regarded as an abnormally late starter. He scarcely knew that he wanted to be a composer until he was seventeen and he entered the Royal College of Music with an insecure piano technique and a very limited knowledge of the mainstream repertoire. As a student he was hungry to make up for lost time and listened to all the music he could, especially Beethoven; it was an influence that was to endure, as did his absorption in the English Madrigal School and its Italian counterpart. Like most would-be composers, he had to turn to teaching to earn some sort of a living and for a time he was on the staff of a preparatory school in Surrey. In the generous school holidays he was able to get on with composing but, feeling that his technique was inadequate for the expression of his ideas, he courageously embarked on an intensive course of study with R. O. Morris, a noted academic of the day. He later renounced all the music he had written prior to the age of thirty, feeling that his search for an individual style had failed. A string quartet and a piano sonata from the mid-1930s survived his ruthless self-criticism but were substantially revised some years later before he would allow them to be published.

The first work to make a deep impression was the Concerto for Double String Orchestra (1938–9). It is a totally English work, though in a strikingly different way from the Englishness of Delius or Elgar. It exploits a rhythmic flexibility that is derived from the Elizabethan madrigalists and a lyricism that stems from English folk-song. The first movement is restless and eager, even fidgety at times, but there is a sheer exuberance in the writing that manages to avoid all the clichés of string compositions. Despite the two opposed bodies of strings the texture is transparently clear and all the most significant points are made with great economy.

The slow movement begins with a favourite device, essentially two-part writing given greater depth by duplication at the octave. Thus Orchestra I has a phrase played in unison by all the strings, violins at one pitch, lower strings an octave below; Orchestra II has an even simpler phrase treated in the same manner. By this means the music has warmth without recourse to sensuous harmony. Out of this introduction emerges a tune of great beauty for solo violin with a softly murmuring accompaniment. The tune is halfway between a folk-song and a spiritual, but its span is wider than any normal voice could encompass. Even when taken up by the two orchestras it preserves a remarkable purity. The central section is fugal with a subject that seems to reach out towards the unattainable so that even when a climax is achieved it quickly melts away. The opening tune reappears as a cello solo but Tippett refuses to exploit it and the movement ends with allusions to it rather than a further statement.

The third movement is brisk and energetic with interesting contrasts between the two orchestras, whose occasional agreement provides sudden outbursts of rich harmony to complement the mostly contrapuntal texture. A memorable theme arrives in the cellos, its sole accompaniment a flowing figure in the first violins of Orchestra II. This theme is a prime example of Tippett's lyric gift, a soaring melody whose refusal to comply with a constant rhythmic pulse gives it a feeling of spontaneous invention. Towards the end of the movement a thrilling new tune appears in unashamed C major. Having reached a fine climax its opening phrase is treated as not-quite-a-fugue before returning in its full glory to end the work.

The next significant work could scarcely be more different, the oratorio *A Child of Our Time* (1939–41). Tippett prepared a draft libretto and submitted it to T. S. Eliot hoping for his collaboration; but Eliot convinced him that his own text was more than adequate. Tippett accepted his judgement, and began work two days after war was declared. In his slow and patient way, he worked on, sometimes composing *under* the piano, using it as a handy air-raid shelter. As model, he used the three-part structure of Handel's *Messiah*, in which Part 1 sets the scene, preparing us for the action in Part II, and the experience is meditated on in Part III. As subject-matter, he chose the true story of a young seventeen year-old Jew called Grynspan who, in 1938, shot a minor German diplomat in Paris, thereby causing one of the worst anti-Jewish pogroms in Nazi Germany; but the story is told in such general terms that it becomes universalised. An operatic treatment would have been entirely different; as it is the young man is just a figure, caught up in forces too powerful for him to control. Like so many in the world, he is lost; we are all carried 'like seed upon the wind' to the great slaughters of history, whether they be wars or massacres.

Although by nature Tippett's mind is a complex one, he was determined in this work to reach out to his audience in simple and direct terms. Thus the young man tells us of his plight in a popular dance rhythm of the thirties, a tango. When one remembers all those dance movements in the *Matthew Passion*, it seems logical; after all the subject here is a secular one. Having heard the young man's point of view, we hear his mother; but again, it is better to think of her as *a* mother, representative of all overworked, poverty-stricken, harrassed women. The sense of being crushed by the burden of life is subtly conveyed by chords in which major and minor elements clash, but the vocal line is tender and lyrical.

Out of this emerges the first of the Negro spirituals used by Tippett so imaginatively as the nearest equivalent to the Lutheran hymns which every member of Bach's congregation knew so well, and which Bach consequently used as chorales in the *St. Matthew Passion*. The audience at a performance of *A Child of Our Time* isn't expected to join in, but at least these great traditional tunes strike a special response, a response moreover which has very considerable overtones of conscience, conscience about slavery, oppression and the like. To integrate material like this into a twentieth century score was a stylistic problem, and some critics still find the transition difficult to accept. Yet any choir performing the work looks on the spirituals with the deepest affection.

In Part II, Tippett focusses on the actual tragedy. 'A star rises in midwinter. Behold the man, the scapegoat, the Child of Our Time.' There are obvious suggestions of the star of Bethlehem, of Christ as the scapegoat. But there is another, more pertinent reading. If being on the front-page of every newspaper in Europe means being a 'star', Grynspan was a star. He is the scapegoat, the 'child of our time', and Tippett's setting of those last words is one of the most lyrical and expressive passages in the whole work. It emerges like a blaze of light out of the darkness; indeed it is the passage which perhaps best illustrates the motto written at the top of the score, 'The darkness declares the glory of the light.'[1]

A chorus of the persecuted and a chorus of the self-righteous make their points graphically and economically. But 'the boy becomes desperate in his agony'; the dark forces of his soul take over, and he shoots the official who, in his eyes, stands for obdurate authority. This one act of violence, so small in comparison to the horrors that followed, causes scarcely a ripple on the score. The words 'He shoots the official' are almost concealed. 'But he shoots only his dark brother . . .' In other words, the act of violence has purged his own demonic self. The chorus of vengeance is a tartar to sing, but again, Tippett has deliberately mentioned a mediaeval torture—'Break them in pieces on the wheel', so as to indict cruelty in any period.

It is in the third part that Tippett expounds his belief that man must reconcile the light and shadow of his inner self, that the winter cold is the secret nursery of the seed of future hope. As he puts it, 'the garden lies beyond the desert'. And as the work began with the words 'It is winter', so, towards the end, we hear the same phrase inverted to the words 'It is Spring'. The final chorus leading into the last spiritual, 'Deep River', is unforgettable in its effect.

---

[1] From T. S. Eliot's *Murder in the Cathedral*.

In 1943 Tippett was given a short sentence in gaol as a conscientious objector, but once released from prison, where he mentally planned his First Symphony, he resumed his activities as Director of Music at Morley College. Composition, never an easy task for him, continued with the highly rated String Quartet No. 2 and a remarkable cantata for solo voice, 'Boyhood's End', written for Peter Pears and Benjamin Britten. It is an admirable example of his technique of word-setting, openly derived from Purcell, in which a single syllable may be extended over several bars whose music actually symbolises the content of the word. Soon after the war he embarked on a major project, the opera *The Midsummer Marriage*. It took him the best part of seven years to write but after an initially cool reception from the critics (more hostile to the plot and the text than the music) it has now been acknowledged as a true masterpiece. As a model he took Mozart's *Magic Flute*. That opera's principal characters Tamino and Pamina are re-created as Mark and Jenifer, Papageno and Papagena become Jack and Bella—the down-to-earth foils to the more ethereal central characters. Sarastro becomes Sosostris; the Queen of the Night (Pamina's mother) becomes King Fisher, Jenifer's father. The parallels are certainly there but the opera is a genuinely new creation, based on a model though it may be. Nevertheless it too is concerned with the quest for identity, for the reconciliation of opposites; like *The Magic Flute* it also delves into profound matters whilst giving an appearance of frivolity. Tippett's essentially visionary outlook is revealed throughout this wonderfully lyrical score as is his preoccupation with psychoanalytical theory and his deep awareness of myth.

The opera having occupied his mind for so long a period, it is not wholly surprising to find that several works, among them the Piano Concerto (1953–5) and the song-cycle *The Heart's Assurance* (1951), are what we would now call 'spin-offs', sharing the opera's lyrical flow but also the complexity of its accompanying textures. Perhaps more significant in his total output is the superb *Fantasia Concertante on a theme of Corelli*, a work of great individuality and beauty, and the Second Symphony (1956–7).

The initial inspiration for this major composition came from a chance hearing of a Vivaldi concerto in which the note C appeared prominently repeated in the bass. For some reason it touched off a particularly strong response, and Tippett stored it away for possible use in the future. Several years passed while this idea lay dormant in his mind. Now, Tippett likes to plan the overall shape of a work very clearly before he even begins to think about the actual notes or themes; in his own words: 'I prefer to invent the work's form in as great a detail as I can before I invent any sounds whatever. But as the formal invention proceeds, textures, speeds, dynamics become part of the formal process. So that one comes closer and closer to the sound itself until the moment when the dam breaks and the music of the opening bars spills out over the paper.'

The reiterated Cs in the bass which form the virile opening to the symphony act as a sort of anchor, a feature that is easily recognised but which is subjected to increasing stresses; the horns exert a pull towards G major, the strings take us further to A major and then to D—all traditional relationships.

The increasing brilliance of the string-writing ultimately induces the trumpets to join in, although they too are concerned to stick to rhythmic patterns which Vivaldi might well have used himself, even if the notes might have seemed a little foreign to him. Ultimately the activity is suddenly stilled by the arrival of what would traditionally be called the second subject. Its gentle rocking is almost a lullaby though the freedom of the counterpoint surrounding it prevents it from being entirely restful. It is tranquil in spirit, but the tranquillity is shared by several other wind instruments, each with something individual to add. Later in the movement the two main ideas, the stamping one and the lullaby, are brought much closer together, and this could be said to be like a classical recapitulation, somewhat condensed. The final coda gives a roll-call of the principle themes confirming the essentially classical structure of the work.

The slow movement properly inhabits a very different world; it's the sort of music that the American composer Charles Ives would have understood very well, for it contrasts visionary and atmospheric sounds with something much more human. The visionary element might almost be called 'Forest Murmurs', though Tippett's conception is not as openly descriptive as Wagner's. A single melodic strand on the trumpet, wide-spaced in its intervals, elusive as to key, is surrounded by little rustling whispers of sound mostly given to harp or piano. It has the same elemental magic that we find so often in *The Midsummer Marriage*. The trumpet suggests the ruined fragments of a castle, perhaps that same 'dark tower' to which Childe Harold came, with the forest and all its attendant sounds pressing close against its walls. This, then, is the magical element which occasionally is violently interrupted by a much more aggressive trumpet-call, as though for a moment we are transported back in time to the days when the castle was no crumbling ruin but a true fortress around whose walls battles were fought.

There follows a complete contrast, a passage of sustained lyrical writing in closely-knitted harmony, what one might call the 'human' element. Wilfred Mellers in a revealing criticism of the work says that this movement is a dialogue like the one in Beethoven's Fourth Piano Concerto between this human music and 'the magic arabesques of God and Nature'.

Dance has always been an important element in Tippett's music, even in so serious a work as *A Child of Our Time*. Obviously, then, the scherzo of the symphony will be nimble and athletic; but its rhythms are too fluid to be identifiable as any particular type of dance. Quite a test-piece for the conductor, it makes much play with irregular metres, so that the quavers are grouped 3|2+3|2|2+3|3|2+2 and so on. The central section again exploits solid repeated notes, perhaps a cross-reference to the first movement, while the writing for trumpets is particularly brilliant.

The opening bars of the finale show a strong Stravinsky influence unusual in Tippett but we soon find a set of variations over a ground bass, a form hallowed in Purcell's day. It is easily identified by the three sharply staccato notes with which each repetition begins. Later, an extraordinary shimmering effect on woodwind and piano serves as a glistening background to a long sustained tune on violins, beginning on a high A flat and gradually climbing down through more than five octaves to a low D flat. Quietly we are reminded of the low repeated Cs which began the symphony. The recollection provokes a brilliant and excited reaction in the upper strings. There is a silent pause. Again the repeated Cs knock at memory's door; the reaction is even more florid. For a third time the knock-and-answer pattern is repeated. The last two 'gestures of farewell' as Tippett calls them are given to a solo trumpet while the strings hold fast on a high chord that seems to shine like a bright ray.

The next major work, the opera *King Priam* (1958–61), shows a radical change of style almost as striking as the difference between *Petrushka* and *The Rite of Spring*. Based on Homer, it is a tragedy, for Tippett takes the side of the defeated Trojans in preference to the victorious Greeks. The treatment of the orchestra is almost stark in comparison to the luxuriance of *The Midsummer Marriage*; the harmony is strident and harsh, the melodies more angular. Like the earlier opera it bore other fruits, the *Songs for Achilles* for tenor and guitar and the Second Piano Sonata.

Deserting the opera-house for a time, Tippett turned his attention back to the orchestra in 1962–3 with the *Concerto for Orchestra*. Briefly, his purpose in this work was to split up the orchestra, not into the familiar families of wind-brass-strings as Tchaikovsky did in the scherzo of the Fourth Symphony, nor into the divisions of those families as Bartók did in the 'Joke with Couples' (second movement) in his *Concerto for Orchestra*; instead we find small mixed groups so that a more accurate title would be 'Concerto for Orchestral Groups'. These groups tend to have not only themes but types of themes specifically allotted to them. Tippett himself suggested words such as 'line and flow' to describe a family of musical ideas. The work begins with a section for flute and harp, delicate chamber music that does nothing to suggest the resources of a full symphony orchestra.

In *A Child of Our Time* one key phrase stands out in the text—'I would know my shadow and my light'. If the flute and harp can be equated with 'light' the tuba and piano (bass) might be said to represent 'shadow'; not surprisingly the first 'light' section is followed by its 'dark brother'—to use another Tippett phrase. As in fraternal relationships there can be a family resemblance but a complete difference of character.

A third group makes its presence felt, three horns. They can provide their own harmony and need neither harp nor piano to support them. Their first phrases are gentle, almost caressing, but soon their music grows agitated with vehement close-knit counterpoint. As if to soothe their protest, flute and harp return with the opening idea, quickly followed by tuba and piano. Three main contrasts of texture and material have been established. Tippett next turns his attention to other areas of the orchestra, the percussion, a group of woodwind, the trombones; but in each case the material allotted to the group remains its own property.

As well as different groups, he also has sections of differing speeds. For instance, he characterises the piano, xylophone, clarinet, bass clarinet and trumpets as being particularly nimble. Later, with each group still preserving both its character and its thematic identity, he starts to mix the various elements together. For the whole first movement, the strings sit as silent observers. Their time is to come in the second movement, where, in turn, there is no brass or wind. All of this has been meticulously planned; yet the music conforms to no previous plan. In other words, Tippett has invented a form, disowning both the fashionable lure of serialism and the more trad-itional moulds. But the form is remarkably lucid; and if the work is not traditional, it is at least in a tradition, a tradition that extends back as far as a Sonata for Five Orchestras by Gabrieli (?1557–1612).

Tippett followed the Concerto with one of his most challenging and ambitious works, *The Vision of St. Augustine* for baritone solo, chorus and orchestra (1963–5). (The Saint, searching for the meaning of Time, experi-enced a vision of Eternity which, if prolonged, would have literally given him eternal life.)

It's a work of quite exceptional difficulty, both for performers and listeners, for it deals with things that in a material age we find increasingly difficult to understand. It also flies in the face of all our traditional concepts of what 'visionary' music should sound like, which tends to be somewhere jointly inhabited by Palestrina and Vaughan Williams, with wordless choirs singing rather formless music. It's almost axiomatic that 'visionary' equals 'vague', precisely because our own ideas of visions are so ill-defined. A composer like Handel makes things easy for us by fulfilling expectation; his angelic choir obliges us by being high and distant; that's where angels belong.

But once we get to the shouts of Hallelujah the music, for all its exaltation, is earthbound in the sense that *we*, not they, sing it and we enjoy it the more for its sturdy rhythms and clearly defined melodic line. In this sense the music isn't visionary at all, but highly practical, an act of worship *shared*. The Alleluias that Tippett writes can't be sung by an audience, nor will many people even be able to comprehend them without making an effort to come to terms with an unfamiliar language. Yet the ecstatic nature of the music does reveal itself to a sympathetic ear; the sounds are not as chaotic as they may seem.

> Where wert thou when I laid the foundations of the earth? Where wert thou when the morning stars sang together and all the sons of God shouted for joy? Alleluia.

The text is almost Biblical and has implications too vast for the mind to comprehend; yet we cannot fail to respond to the beauty of the language and its imagery. Well, the imagery is to be found in the music too; the immensity of the concept of laying the foundations of the earth is expressed in giant steps whose dissonance is logical insofar as foundations are in the very nature of things incomplete. Above their measured paces we hear cries of 'Ubi eras?', 'Where wert thou?', and they have an urgency about them that is perfectly understandable.

The world was made out of chaos, as even Haydn realised in his overture to the Creation, and here there is a sense of chaos, but also a strange and overpowering glory, not the silent emptiness of space, but space teeming with a multitude of stars and the sounds of God beating upon his anvil, a vision such as Blake might have had, a vision that is literally awe-inspiring.

Gongs and drums frequently underline the primitive basis of this highly sophisticated score, of which the greatest climax comes near the end. The sopranos have a series of ecstatic alleluias, even in a clearly identifiable key. The lower voices span huge intervals giving an impression of sheer mass which is overwhelming. Biggest of all is the sound of 'Lift up your heads O ye gates and be ye lift up ye everlasting doors' in which the sheer immensity of huge bronze portals is conveyed more graphically than any Hollywood scene designer could envisage; but at the very end, after a huge silence, comes, first in Greek and then English,

'I count not myself to have apprehended'.

The vision of St. Augustine was literally blinding in that even his inner eye could not cope with its brilliance; the mind was stunned, as I believe Tippett meant us to be stunned by this kaleidoscope of sound.

The two subsequent operas *The Knot Garden* and *The Ice Break* are on a smaller scale but reveal Tippett's constant desire to experiment, to move in new directions. Between them came the Third Symphony (1972–3) which in the long run may well prove to be a more important and lasting work. In his own words this is how it began:

> I was listening to a concert of modern music, what I call a very 'motionless' modern music: it hadn't a harmonic or rhythmic or any other sort of drive that I could hear. Now I'm never very close to such music, and I kept saying to myself—as I've said it many times before—'I don't see how I could ever use this kind of thing for expressive purposes unless it were part of a piece based upon sharp contrasts'. And this suddenly clicked, and I knew that a symphonic work had begun and that divisions had already appeared between what I then started calling 'arrest' and 'movement'—terms which are actually in the score. 'Arrest', not so much in terms of 'motionless', as in the Stravinskian sense where the use of ostinati[2] precludes harmonic movement.'

[2] The same pattern of notes repeated many times.

However difficult the first movement may be to listen to, its structure is wonderfully clear; taking up the classical concept of first and second subjects, Tippett places them in brutal proximity to each other, harsh and brassy chords being alternated with extraordinarily vigorous passages for strings and wind. The only relaxation is provided by strange little mewing glissandi; otherwise the two identities are clearly differentiated for what is the equivalent of a classical exposition. Then there is a development of the brass material, a development of the string material until at last the two opposed ideas are brought into violent conjunction. The sheer pace of the music as it reaches its final climax is breathtaking.

Without warning Tippett carries us from the harsh chromium-plated neon-lit glare of the twentieth century into a sort of dream-world, a 'windless night sky' he calls it, but this is not pictorial music such as Delius or Vaughan Williams might write. It is extremely static harmonically, exploiting a combination of tonic and dominant familiar to Beethoven in the *Eroica* or the *Pastoral* symphonies but here expressed in linear form. This whole lengthy slow movement is built up from a relatively small number of decorative patterns, often divided one from the other by quite long silences. The only disturbing features are repeated notes on a trumpet (always alternating between two tones) and an occasional clash of bells.

As a sonic landscape it is completely individual, the only possible influence that one can detect being Charles Ives who, though he never wrote anything quite like this, would certainly have understood it and been fascinated by it, just as Debussy understood and was fascinated by *The Rite of Spring*.

The lengthy slow movement is followed by what Tippett calls Part Two, actually a scherzo and finale. The scherzo is a death-ride for orchestra, the violins having to play passages that would have daunted Paganini. But then, out of the hurly-burly there suddenly emerges an extraordinary surprise that must have made the players scratch their heads in bewildered disbelief when they first came across it. It is a direct quotation of the wild passage that begins the finale of Beethoven's Ninth Symphony, its violence being answered in the gentlest terms by a small group of six strings. Capricious though it may seem, the quotation has a double purpose. As in Beethoven it prepares the way for the human voice to intrude, not a chorus as it happens but a solo soprano; but also as in Beethoven it symbolises a break with the rest of the symphony, a rejection of past events. The question Tippett asks himself is whether Beethoven and Schiller's 'Ode to Joy' have any real validity for our time since all men are clearly not brothers however much we would like them to be. The last movement is a sequence of three 'blues', influenced by jazz though far removed from real jazz; the words, Tippett's own, emphasise the tragic dilemmas of our society whether in the quest for identity or in the need for compassion. For example the third poem reads:

I found the man grown to a dwarf.
After the circus, in his tent, he said:
So many take me for a doll.
    I gave him milk and kisses.

I found the girl born dumb and blind.
She stroked my hand and tap-wrote in the palm:
I feel but cannot see the sun.
    I gave her milk and kisses.

I found the beautiful moronic child.
His smiling eyes shone bright; he said:
Nothing; for his mind is lost.
    I gave him milk and kisses.

As I lay down beside my mate,
Body to body,
We did not heed the sorrow.

Ah, merciful God, if such there be,
Let him, let her, be born straight.
But if no answer to the prayer,
    We shall give milk
    We shall give kisses.[3]

As the music melts to nothing, the Beethoven quotation beats about our ears once more, reminding us that we are supposed to be thinking about Joy not Sorrow. In a sort of mad ecstacy the singer sings of the Goddess of Joy and how when she waved her wings she would make us one. But was that ever true?

As we have seen, the symphony has been much concerned with the contrast of opposites, brass to strings, quick to slow, loud to soft. Now Tippett turns his gaze on the opposites within human kind itself, that for one to be tortured there must also be a torturer. As he puts it elsewhere, 'The devil is always the wicked other man for you and me—but it is you and me of course for *them*'. And so he ends the work with the dream that

    my strong hand shall grip the cruel
That my strong mouth shall kiss the fearful
That my strong arms shall lift the lame
And on my giant legs we'll whirl our way
Over the visionary earth
In mutual celebration . . .'[3]

But the singer does not have the final notes, only the final word. The dream is not yet realised however tenderly she may sing of the redeeming power of love; only by repeatedly shaming anger with gentleness can the world come to its senses. If ever there was a musical symbol of the soft

[3]From the full score, Schott & Co.

answer turning away wrath it must surely be at the end of this symphony where the almost inaudible string chords soothe angry brass. Tippett is a pacifist and the ending is clearly an expression of pacifism. Thus it is that not just the whole symphony but the composer's whole philosophy is summed up in the closing bars.

The Fourth Symphony (1976–7) was commissioned for the Chicago Symphony Orchestra. It is a single-movement work lasting some thirty minutes and conceived for a very large orchestra. Described by the composer as his 'birth-to-death' piece it literally employs the sound of breathing to symbolise human life; life begins, life ends. There is no Mahlerian agony, but an acceptance of mortality. Yet much of the score teems with a vitality that is astonishing in a composer who was in his early seventies when he wrote it. The Triple Concerto for violin, viola and cello which followed (1978–9) shows in its central portion a return to the lyrical style that we associate with the works of the 1940s, though now tinged with Oriental colouring through the extensive use of tuned percussion. One interlude is scored almost entirely for percussion, something that Tippett would have found unthinkable in his early days.

To produce *The Mask of Time* (1982) as the culmination of a life's work is an amazing testament to the intellectual and spiritual vitality of the composer. To continue to develop throughout a long creative life is a hallmark of greatness, and it may well be that future generations will place Tippett among the greatest of twentieth-century composers.

VAUGHAN
WILLIAMS
1872–1958

A glance at the dates above is revealing, for to have been born when Brahms
was thirty-nine and to have died when Stockhausen was thirty indicates a
great deal more than simple longevity; it means living through a period of
violent change in music in which a composer would have to be towed along
in the wake of the *avant-garde* or decide to disregard its radical innovations.
Vaughan Williams definitely belongs to the latter category. He had taken too
long a time to discover a satisfactorily personal style wantonly to change it; as
a student at the Royal College of Music he was looked on as a hard worker
who lacked facility. His teachers expressed doubts about his talent and felt
that it was unlikely that he would ever make a mark as a composer. Like
Tippett, Vaughan Williams considered that his studies at the College had left
him with an inadequate technique. After acquiring a degree in history at
Cambridge he returned to the College to take a second course, but even this
left him dissatisfied and in 1897 he went to Berlin where for some months he
studied intensively with Max Bruch. A far more important influence than
any teacher was Holst, with whom he had struck up a warm friendship while
they were at the College. Both were intensely interested in English folk-song
and felt that it provided the most promising source of influence if a genuinely
English style of composition was to be developed. Together they would go
on walking tours in the depths of the country listening attentively to songs
that had been handed down through generations but never transcribed. In all
he took down over 800 songs; they were to form the basis of his personal
idiom from that time onwards.

In 1905, when he was thirty-three, he composed a short choral work,
Towards the Unknown Region to a text by Walt Whitman. Although the music
is austere it owes something to the Brahms Requiem. Hearing it at the Leeds
Festival in 1905 made him realise that he was not yet a master of orchestration; with characteristic humility he went to Paris in 1908 to study with Ravel
for three months. The two men were complete opposites in their approach to
music, but the arduous exercises Ravel gave him made Vaughan Williams

feel greater confidence in handling orchestral forces.

Not until he was thirty-nine did he produce a work that made a significant impression on public and critics alike. It was the *Fantasia on a Theme by Tallis*, played at the Three Choirs Festival in Gloucester. Scored for two string orchestras, one large, one small, its exploitation of string sonorities was impressive, especially when heard in a cathedral. Here at last he found an idiom that was uniquely his own, serious and meditative with a direct and simple approach that was far removed from the glittering sophistication of its exact contemporary, Stravinsky's *Firebird*, or the lush romanticism of Elgar's Violin Concerto, also from the same year (1910). Even so, Vaughan Williams realised that the work was too long and subsequently abridged it.

The *Sea Symphony*, again using Walt Whitman's words, was performed in the same year but despite inspired moments it is a less individual work, too frequently resorting to the predictable fugal entries in the choir that were the approved practice of late Victorian church composers. At the time Vaughan Williams had had a lot of experience with amateur choirs and it is possible that the standard repertoire of such bodies had affected him rather too deeply. Only in the slow movement, 'On the beach at night alone', do we find a consistently authentic voice.

Work on the *Sea Symphony* fired his ambition to write other large-scale compositions and he decided to expand a tone-poem about London into a four-movement symphony. The *London Symphony* was first performed in March, 1914. It takes into account the majesty of a great city but it also acknowledges the poverty and suffering of the workless poor. It begins with a vision of dawn on the river within range of Westminster for we hear the half-hour chime of Big Ben in the distance quite early in the first movement. As the morning mist clears and the fine buildings and monuments come into view, the brass build a sequence of fanfares suggesting imminent pageantry. There is a moment's silence followed by a considerable surprise, an outburst of some bitterness that suggests the squalor that lies beyond the splendour. The glimpse is only brief for Vaughan Williams had not yet reached the bitterness of the Fourth Symphony or the austere beauty of the G minor Mass. He was still in the stages of his love-affair with folk-song and time after time fine 'outdoor' tunes go striding across the pages of the score—not the most ideal material for a symphony, but as individual in their own homespun way as the more exotic wear of Stravinsky or Ravel. There is one notable passage scored for a small group of just eight strings, a lovely contrast to the full orchestral sound.

Such writing anticipates the slow movement which contains some of the best music in the symphony. It uses the sort of parallel harmonies that Debussy had exploited in much of his piano writing as well as in *Pelléas*, but the melodies that float above are essentially English. If Vaughan Williams's natural instincts drew him away from a truly metropolitan character, it is perhaps because one of the beauties of London is that its parks can often be like the deep countryside.

The scherzo is paradoxically called a Nocturne, a typical instance of Vaughan Williams's quirky humour, and a reminder that the night is not only for romance. It shows a night out 'on the town', but of a fairly unsophisticated nature. This was before the shallow glittering facade of the twenties which the young Walton was to capture so brilliantly a few years later. Vaughan Williams said something about seeing London as an observer, and perhaps he feels here like a country-man up for 'a special do'. The Trio suggests that someone is playing a mouth-organ while elsewhere we hear a cleverly contrived 'barrel-organ' effect.

The finale begins with a few anguished bars which show that the poor have not been forgotten, but soon we find a solemn march in C minor, less exuberant than those in Elgar's *Pomp and Circumstance*, but still eminently singable. It is swept aside by a boisterous Allegro which leads us to expect a brilliant coda. Instead there is a return to the opening theme of the symphony; is not the light at dusk similar to the light at dawn? Big Ben chimes again and the symphony recedes into the mist from which it emerged.

The outbreak of World War I put a stop to Vaughan Williams' composing for despite being in his early forties he felt he must join up. He served in the Royal Army Medical Corps and later in the artillery—an unwise choice one would think for a composer with the example of Beethoven's deafness behind him. He was not demobilized until 1919, but as soon as he was able he picked up the threads of his interrupted life. The very personal type of music festival he had founded at Leith Hill was organised anew, while conductorship of the Bach Choir kept him in touch with the amateur choral singing that he felt to be the backbone of English music-making. At first he seems to have been hesitant about actual composition, preferring to revise pre-war works such as the *London Symphony*, the lyrical *Lark Ascending* (for violin and small orchestra) and the opera *Hugh the Drover*. It was 1921 before he produced another symphony, the *Pastoral*, its gentle understatement perhaps a reaction from the horrors of war. At a time when music in Europe was going through a period of rapid experiment—atonality, serialism, neo-classicism, extreme chromaticism—the *Pastoral* symphony is a testament of belief in the common chord. The music tends to move in parallel blocks of harmony; modes are used in preference to conventional scales;[1] themes grow one from another rather than exploiting contrasts. Only in the third movement do we find large orchestral climaxes or robust rhythms. The last movement employs a wordless human voice (soprano or tenor) which recollects themes from the first two movements. The work ends quietly.

The Fourth Symphony (1931–4) is a very different matter. As though

---

[1]The effect of modes can easily be explored by playing scales on the white notes of the piano beginning with notes other than C.

accepting the challenge of the modernists Vaughan Williams seems to have set out to prove that he too could handle dissonance and tension. The material is much more concentrated, the contours bolder. The symphony ends with a taut fugue, a device which Walton may have copied in his First Symphony. Vaughan Williams, never one to be sentimental about his music, is reputed to have said of his Fourth Symphony 'I don't know whether I like it but it's what I meant!'

Four years passed before he attempted another symphony, years in which one notable favourite was produced, the *Serenade to Music*, commissioned by Sir Henry Wood to celebrate his golden jubilee as a conductor. It demanded sixteen singers, all of them well-known concert artists who had worked with Sir Henry on many occasions. The text was taken from Shakespeare's *The Merchant of Venice*, ideal for the purpose. Other choral works from the same period include the *Five Tudor Portraits* (1935), a racy work full of bawdy humour and, at the extreme opposite pole, *Dona Nobis Pacem* (1936). Meanwhile, over a number of years Vaughan Williams had been working at one of his most ambitious projects, a staged setting of Bunyan's *The Pilgrim's Progress* which he preferred to call a 'morality' rather than an opera. Doubting if he would ever complete the work, he used some of its material in the Fifth Symphony over which he laboured off and on from 1938 to 1943. Even then he was not satisfied and in 1951 he revised the score—a common practice with him and one that must have exasperated his publishers.

The Fifth Symphony begins magically with soft horn calls over a sustained bass. The ultimate aim of the work is to reach a pure D major but at this stage the consistent use of the flattened seventh (C Natural) gives a feeling of limbo. Tonality is an important element in Vaughan Williams's compositions since he makes such frequent use of the 'common' chords—major or minor triads which at any moment can be identified as traditional but which he uses in a curiously drifting manner so that in a single bar we may find consecutive chords such as A, G, F and E flat, all major triads.

The restraint in this symphony extends into the ghostly scherzo in which the strings are mostly muted; the rhythmic pulse varies more than is usual, giving great flexibility to the music. The slow movement, a *Romanza*, is regarded by some authorities as the most sublime piece to come from his pen; it has a huge span and contains some deeply expressive solos for oboe and solo violin in particular. Although the composer regarded himself as a cheerfully philosophical agnostic, there is an air of genuine devoutness in this movement stemming from its association with *The Pilgrim's Progress*. The mood even extends into the finale, a Passacaglia which refuses to flaunt the technical challenge the form presents. There is certainly an exalted climax but, as Vaughan Williams generally seems to have preferred, the work ends quietly with an affirmation of D major, the key that had seemed so elusive at the start of the first movement.

At the age of seventy-five Vaughan Williams produced his Sixth Symphony, a work which had occupied him for three years. Its effect was stunning, from the dramatic rhetoric of the opening to the frozen stillness of the eerie last movement. The initial flourish is as powerful a gesture as can be found in Tchaikovsky, placing the chords of F minor and E minor in conflict beneath a descending cascade. For a time F minor seems to prevail but this is a misapprehension since the symphony is avowedly in E minor. Syncopations abound, whether in a curiously choppy theme for brass or a wailing passage for strings. An abrupt staccato phrase for trumpets is placed above a lurching bass. A first and rare hint of tenderness comes with a rising theme for violins and violas, but even this betrays a loss of confidence in its uncertain shifts from major to minor. During the development this more sustained theme is constantly harassed by the more restless elements until for a time it is lost in the turmoil of a recapitulation. However, it survives to reappear in E major, the only true major section in the entire symphony. The movement finishes explosively, the tonal conflict sustained to the end.

A single held E in the bass links the first and second movements. Instead of the anticipated Lento or Adagio we find a rather strange Moderato whose music has an inherent restlessness which is kept on a tight leash of restraint. A gradual crescendo is quietly encouraged by subdued trumpets and drums until there is a sudden explosion, a jagged descending passage in the strings that offers a prophetic vision of the scherzo. A tremendous fanfare for brass speaks more of doom than glory and is followed by a recession of tone to *pianissimo*. After some time we become aware of a persistent rhythm derived from the opening phrases; it continues its nagging for over forty bars rising and falling in volume like waves approaching the shore. It takes a huge and angry climax to put a stop to it. The movement dies down to nothing only to be replaced without a break by the scherzo.

This movement is based almost entirely on the interval of an augmented fourth (D–G sharp), the 'Devil in Music' as it was called in the Middle Ages. Vaughan Williams had used it in Satan's dance in the ballet 'Job', and its function is clearly devilish in this context. The first striding notes seem to break into a run as they climb. At the summit we find (in the composer's own words) 'a trivial little tune, chiefly on the woodwind'. It mocks the attempt to establish any firm tonality, dodging between E and B flat. A loosely constructed fugue fails to restore respectability to this deliberately chaotic movement.

The symphony finishes with an Epilogue which makes subtle allusions to the preceding movements. It is virtually without contrast, *pianissimo* throughout, a lunar landscape devoid of humanity. Its eerie coldness attracted the makers of the film *Scott of the Antartic* and Vaughan Williams was asked to provide a score. It was not his first excursion into film music, but it was the most fruitful since he turned the material into the *Sinfonia Antartica*. The transformation was made not without difficulty but the effort was worthwhile since the score is very different in timbre from his other works. A solo soprano and a small women's chorus may seem to invite comparisons with the banalities of Hollywood, but Vaughan Williams' unerring taste evades the problem. It was completed when he was eighty but he could still enjoy experimenting with sound, not least the tuned percussion.

Remarkably he continued to compose; moreover his self-criticism remained as acute as ever and both the Eighth and Ninth symphonies were subjected to revision after he had heard them. The Eighth symphony has a notable first movement, a set of variations on an imagined theme, imagined because it is never actually revealed. The second movement is a wisp of a scherzo scored for wind alone, the third a Cavatina for strings. Such economies were not dictated by the indolence of great age but by the continuing desire to experiment. The finale is a rowdy Toccata in which the percussion have a field-day.

The Ninth symphony, revised in 1958 (fifty years after he had completed the *Sea Symphony*!) is a serious work which introduces new colours—flugelhorn and saxophone—into the conventional orchestra. It shows no sign of the fatigue we might justifiably expect and finds new things to say as well as new colours to express them with.

This brief survey has of necessity concentrated on the symphonies, but we cannot leave this composer without stressing the enormous range of his accomplishment considering his very late start. There is a huge amount of choral music, a great number of songs, operas, ballet, music for theatre and cinema, chamber music, concertos, music for brass band, hymn tunes, masques, organ music—the list shows amazing versatility, yet despite this he retained a self-depreciating humility to the end. The story goes that a rather sanctimonious composer described to Vaughan Williams how he had gone down on his knees in gratitude for divine inspiration when he had written a particularly jammy piece of sacred music. 'Hmmff' snorted 'V–W' as he was always known; 'I wrote the whole of my London Symphony on my bottom . . .'

WALTON

1902–83

Choir schools are admirable nurseries for musical talent and the young William Walton was fortunate to gain a place as a chorister at Christ Church Cathedral in Oxford when he was ten. Inspired by the music which consequently became his daily diet he soon began to compose and by the time he was in his mid-teens had produced some choral music which showed a precocious talent. It was while he was an undergraduate at the university that he became friendly with the influential Sitwell family. Impressed by his talent they took him under their collective wing during the first crucial period of his career as a composer, sparing him the more conventional path of school-mastering or the organ loft. It was in 1922 that he collaborated with Edith Sitwell in an 'entertainment' to be called *Façade* which consisted of the rhythmic recitation of some of her poems to music for flute, clarinet, saxophone, trumpet, cello and percussion. The first performance caused a famous scandal but the more perceptive members of the audience noted the wit and brilliance of the young composer's score. Feeling he must earn something towards his keep, Walton took on hack-work arranging fox-trots for the Savoy Orpheans, a fashionable dance-band of the time. Never a quick worker, he did not produce another significant composition until 1925 when the overture *Portsmouth Point* revealed a spiky and brittle idiom that was unlike any other English music. The rapid and frequent changes of the time-signature were comparable to those found in Stravinsky, though in a later revision Walton ironed out many of the conducting problems. On the other hand the thematic material has something in common with Gershwin and there is no doubt that Walton's close contact with jazz had a considerable influence on him. He was soon to show a very different aspect of his genius with a Viola Concerto (1928–9) for the great English violist Lionel Tertis. Ironically enough Tertis at first rejected it and the first performance was given at short notice by a fellow-composer, Hindemith. Here, for the first time, Walton revealed his innate romanticism, for the music expolits the dark tones of the viola in a profoundly expressive way. The work was rightly hailed as a masterpiece, the closing pages making a particularly deep impression.

With his name now well established it was no surprise that the B.B.C. offered Walton a commission to write a major choral work for the Leeds Festival of 1931. He turned to his friend and patron Sacheverell Sitwell for help in choosing a text; the subject was to be Belshazzar's Feast. The result of this collaboration is now well-known. The impact at the first performance was overwhelming. No English composer had written music with such rhythmic drive or with such barbaric splendour. It was as if Berlioz had been reincarnated as an Englishman for in addition to the virtuosity of the orchestration the choral writing, especially in the opening pages, showed that his years as a chorister had given Walton an infallible ear for vocal effect. The text gave him numerous opportunities for vividly descriptive music; for example the sequence of praise for the pagan gods specifies the deities of Gold, Silver, Iron, Wood, Stone and Brass. For each of these Walton finds apposite music though he claimed to have spent seven months searching for the right chord for 'Gold'. There could hardly have been a greater contrast to the Viola Concerto than this mammoth work with its huge orchestra augmented by two brass bands and its purposely garish colours. To this day it holds a unique position in the repertoire, unchallenged in its mastery of the largest resources.

Walton's next work, the First Symphony, gave him immense trouble and he laboured over it for over three years. The first performance set an unusual precedent for it consisted of three movements only, the finale still being incomplete. The work provides an orchestral parallel to *Belshazzar* in some ways but the prevailing influence in the first movement is Sibelius. By this time Walton had gained an international reputation granted to no other Englishman except possibly Elgar. Acknowledgement of his status came with a commission for a concerto from the world's greatest violinist, Heifetz, who must have been delighted with the tailor-made work which resulted. It is designed to show off all that the violin does best with soaring lyrical melodies and dazzling virtuoso passages.

The advent of war checked Walton's career as a composer of concert works; instead he turned his talent towards the cinema, writing brilliantly crafted scores for such propaganda films as *The First of the Few* and *Next of Kin*; somewhat later came Laurence Olivier's Shakespeare productions, *Henry V, Hamlet* and *Richard III*. His contribution to their success was notable and revealed an unsuspected gift for pastiche as opposed to parody.

Shortly after the war Walton married and settled on the small Mediterranean island of Ischia where he spent the remainder of his life in voluntary exile. He continued to compose in his leisurely but fastidious way though never again on the epic scale of the pre-war works. During the period 1945–50 he produced a fine string quartet (later transcribed for string orchestra) and a sonata for violin and piano. His most ambitious venture was the opera *Troilus and Cressida* which was produced at Covent Garden in 1954. Although the craftsmanship is impeccable, its adherence to the Romantic tradition made it seem dated, while the subject seemed to challenge Strauss's *Elektra* which had had a far more startling impact nearly half a century earlier. It may well be that *Troilus* will find a place in the standard repertoire at some future date when the transient phases of musical fashion carry less weight. Walton's other opera *The Bear* (1967), a one-act comedy based on Chekhov, resurrects the wit and parody he had shown so precociously in *Façade*. It has always caused delight but one-act operas are notoriously difficult to place and the rarity of performances is in no way an indictment.

As he approached his sixties Walton continued to accept commissions for important works such as the Cello Concerto and the Second Symphony, but his star had dimmed somewhat in the face of Britten's meteoric rise. Everything he wrote showed the same high quality of craftsmanship but music was moving in directions for which he had little sympathy. The accelerating pace of change and the incessant demand for novelty caused his considerable virtues to be devalued; once regarded as outstandingly Modern, he was in the end faintly praised as a dated Romantic, an irony he accepted with characteristic grace. Like Stravinsky, though for exactly opposite reasons, it seems that he will remain best loved for the works of his comparative youth.

Symphony No. 1 in B flat Minor (1932–5)

The first movement is notable for its sheer relentless drive, a sustained feat that belies the length of time it took to compose. After an initial timpani-roll and a soft suggestion of harmony from two horns the second violins begin an urgent rhythmic figure which continues for nearly thirty bars.[1] This memorable opening achieves a rather special effect, as though the music is being played at two speeds. The consistently reiterated rhythm is extremely fast, giving an impression even of breathlessness as it gallops on its way. But against its constant pulsation there are slow-moving chords, suggesting a huge machine, impressive in size, but within whose bulk wheels and pistons are in constant motion, whirring and spinning almost faster than the eye can see. The idea of symphonic themes seems to have been forgotten in the excitement of building up this great mosaic of sound, but in fact the

---

[1] The music is actually supported by the same note (B flat) in the bass for 63 bars.

movement is constructed with meticulous care and there is very little that isn't relevant. If the violins' pattern represents Rhythm and the slow-moving horn chords Harmony, an expressive oboe solo stands for Melody. It has a very Sibelian feature, a long sustained note followed by a brief but rapid figure, a flick of the tail. Notice also a terse pattern in the cellos, a mere five notes but destined to play an important role.

The violins' persistent rhythm shifts to the double basses as the texture begins to thicken. The cellos' five-note group starts to rotate like a giant wheel, setting up a circling motion which spreads to the woodwind, frayed by trills. At the first great climax a bass trombone sharply reminds us of the original five-note pattern of the cellos, in case we have failed to appreciate the massively augmented version the horns are playing. The first oboe theme reappears in unison woodwind, no longer forlorn but passionate.

A sudden outbreak of a dotted rhythm in the woodwind, quickly suppressed, provides a pattern for the accompaniment to the second subject, a sustained and brooding theme for the first violins which disregards the darting figures in second violins and violas. Inevitably the sustained line is broken up by the jagged phrases that increasingly attack it from all sides.

For a moment the tempo slackens, only to drive on even more fiercely than before. The music builds to a huge climax, though amazingly Walton has no need for cymbals or gongs or the conventional noise-making apparatus; even the timpani have surprisingly little to do considering the sheer intensity of this movement. The tempo continues relentlessly for more than thirty pages of score before letting up substantially. Even so, it's for little more than a breathing-space; when the violins do have a broad singing tune (showing what a romantic Walton is at heart) the lower strings still have an urgency that refuses to slacken; the patterns are less jagged than before but the nervous tension is still there.

One theme, so far unmentioned, draws our attention more forcibly during the development; it is easily recognised by the rising seventh with which it begins:

Ex. 1

It also appears regularly in augmented (half-speed) versions.

An especially massive climax with bell-chime thirds ringing through the brass is resolved by a repeated-note rhythm in the strings, vaguely reminiscent of Holst's 'Mars' in *The Planets*. Down in the depths the double-basses remind us of the first three notes of the five-note fragment originally played by the cellos on page 1. The tuba turns them into giant footsteps (quarter-speed) while the violins begin an impassioned restatement of the oboe's opening theme. Again we have the feeling of a huge machine throbbing with energy. The drive towards the final cadence becomes irresistible until the return of the restless opening rhythm in unison strings signals the arrival at the final page.

What follows is sheer cruelty to orchestral players, for instead of a nice restful slow movement, Walton drives them straight into a devilish scherzo in which, though the notes are not so difficult nor the volume so sustained, the rhythms are intricate enough to keep every soul counting. As though aware of the danger of piling Pelion upon Ossa, Walton does score some passages very transparently, even making effective use of silent bars in places to create a subtle tension.[2] Amid the flying scurry of notes occasional features catch our attention, an almost Spanish theme beginning with six repeated quavers followed by a syncopated stamping rhythm that suggests heels drumming on the floor, and a somewhat fruitless attempt by violins and cellos in unison to calm things down with a soft descending phrase through that familiar classical stand-by a 'diminished seventh' (E–C♯–A♯–G). Perhaps the most remarkable aspect of the movement is its unrelenting pace; few composers can write genuinely fast music—the listener's ear usually imposes a slower one-in-a-bar pulse. Walton's syncopated rhythms effectively prevent any such pedestrian imposition. For instance he will have one section of the orchestra playing in 3/4, another in 2/4, creating a conflict that teases the ear. The indication *Presto con malizia* (very fast with malice) is wittily ambiguous; is the malice directed by the players towards the audience or by the composer to the orchestra? A little of both is perhaps the answer.

The slow movement reveals a truly romantic streak in Walton's make-up which early works like *Façade* and *Portsmouth Point* hadn't called for. It had first developed in the Viola Concerto; a few years later the Symphony showed him willing to employ a positively voluptuous sense of orchestral colour.

To begin with he employs a single note as accompaniment to a mournful tune on a solo flute—a single note, but what artifice goes into it, muted horns taking turns, pizzicato violins, muted violas, and almost every bar with an expression mark. This tonal anchor affects the flight of the melodies above for one feels that they are chained to it. They reach up, stretching wings towards an unattainable freedom but, like the falcon tied to its master's wrist, are forced to return. Even when the anchor-note changes from C sharp to G sharp it still exerts the same influence. Oboes circle disconsolately; quite independently a single high clarinet toys with a new idea as though, looking down into a village square from a height you might see a couple walking hand in hand while diagonally across their path a single figure strolls casually on his

---

[2] On the last page of the movement, wishing to establish a dramatic pause, he specifies *five* silent bars!

way. The pizzicato chords in cellos give a suggestion of a guitar and one wonders if the movement contains a prophetic vision of Walton's Mediterranean future. Certainly a lyrical phrase for unison violins anticipates the character of the Violin Concerto, the rising octaves in particular bearing the seed of the later work. Only towards the end of the movement does Walton allow himself the luxury of the full orchestra and then for a mere three pages of score. He ends with the same soft repeated C sharps with which he began.

The symphony was first performed without a finale; yet curiously enough Walton had planned the very end of the work before anything else. There remained the tricky job of joining up a preconceived ending to three complete movements. His solution was typically ingenious. He began the finale with a preparation for the ending so that the movement has two solid chunks of majestic music like bookends supporting the central part. Now this music is very much concerned with harmony, vertical masses of sound of varying tensions. The best contrast to this would be counterpoint, horizontal lines that interweave; so a feature of the movement is a brilliant fugue.

The opening bars, slow and majestic, create a vision of splendour and pageantry, laying much stress on the falling tones D–C or G–F. It is such paired notes that spring into life in the brisk and vigorous movement that soon emerges. Notice again how Walton enjoys suggesting two speeds when the brass have a chorale-like theme against which the strings keep up rapid-fire semiquavers. The arrival of the fugue is unmistakable with nothing to obscure its bold outlines. It adheres to classical disciplines until, having reached a considerable climax, its course is checked by a calmer theme from the first oboe. As it progresses we hear occasional subtle reminders of the fugue subject, its ferocity much subdued. For a moment or two the music seems to hang fire; distant calls from horn and trumpet summon the fugue subject and it makes a hasty reappearance in the strings before the brass lay heavy hands on it. After a passage of great excitement the music is brought to a complete standstill by trumpets and trombones with an imposing three-note phrase.

At this point Walton inserts a miniature scherzo whose relevance is not immediately apparent until, out of its bustling figures, second violins and horn produce a bold theme derived from the 'calm' oboe tune that had emerged from the turmoil of the fugue. A quick ear will also spot wisps of the fugue subject in a compressed form. A brilliant *moto perpetuo* runs through the strings like a bush fire and proves on inspection to be directly derived from the fugue subject, a discovery that is greeted with a whoop of delight from the horns and woodwind. Shedding its disguise for one less obscure, the second part of the fugue subject now appears in triumph in a passage that rivals the final fugue in Bartók's *Concerto for Orchestra* in the brilliance of its execution. A huge climax is made doubly effective by the first use of cymbals and tam-tam (large gong)—this on page 183 of the score! Almost as though ashamed of such a vulgar concession to popular taste, Walton introduces a gradual *diminuendo*, holds us expectant and then, with a great sweep of sound, brings back the majestic opening, magnificently harmonised in brass or strings. A trumpet plays a Last Post for fallen heroes, and then the orchestra gathers itself into a final paean of victory. Again we find classical precedent enough for the last isolated chords: they are only the contemporary equivalent of the oft-repeated harmony with which Beethoven or Mozart so often confirm the end of a movement. At the close of so immense a score, such an absolute affirmation of finality is not out of place.

WEBERN

1883–1945

On 15th September, 1945, the little town of Mittersill in Austria was still occupied by American troops; the war had ended only five months earlier, and the whole of Europe was still uneasy, now that the first elation of victory and liberation was over. The town, no more than a village really, was under a curfew, patrolled by soldiers who despite the official peace were still a bit jumpy; there was always the chance of meeting the occasional desperate Nazi. One such soldier on patrol suddenly saw the glow of a cigarette in the darkness beneath a tree. What happened next has never been really solved, but it seems that he jumped to the conclusion that this could be an ambush; the quiet of the isolated village was rudely shattered by a quick spurt of gunfire, and a man, mortally wounded, staggered towards a nearby house. He died in a matter of minutes, an unnecessary sacrifice to the God of War if ever there was one. He was sixty-one years old, a gentle, shy intellectual, who hated violence and certainly presented no danger to an armed man. His name was Anton Webern, and he was one of the most extraordinary composers who ever lived; he raises a question that has troubled quite sincere music-lovers ever since. Why does a composer, who is a man of great musical talent, an excellent conductor, choir-trainer, scholar, why, with all these gifts, does he elect to write music which is virtually incomprehensible to any normal audience? Why does he deliberately jettison everything on which music had depended for centuries; why throw over melody, harmony, cadence, sequence, and to a certain extent the very props of form which had made a great musical enterprise such as a sonata or a symphony possible?

In attempting to answer this question I would like to make a comparison with the special breed of men who climb the most challenging mountains by the hardest possible routes. There are those to whom in its own way the music of Webern is as difficult to tackle as a hitherto unclimbed precipice, and it's certainly not for everybody. Most of us don't want to spend a night clinging to a tiny ledge by frozen finger-tips, our bodies nourished by some rather unpalatable food-concentrate, our heads aching from the day-long glare of sun on snow and ice. And most of us—with due respect to those who would have it otherwise—do not want to be bothered with music that is so difficult to come to terms with that we find no immediate pleasure in it. When there is so much music that we can enjoy at first hearing, is it worth while to plod on with something that sounds meaningless; is life long enough to make the effort?

Here we stand, then, at the great dividing line, the line that separates those for whom music is just a relaxation, and those to whom music is an adventure. The first essential difference between Webern and earlier composers is his time-scale. Wagner wrote operas lasting over five hours, great sprawling masterpieces that are like a range of hills seen from a fair distance. You see the majesty and the grandeur. But when you're clinging to a rock like a fly, all fingertips and toenails, you don't see a mountain; you see just that little crevice in the granite, a few inches long and half an inch wide, and it's so close to you that the surface of the rock has a dozen colours, the green of lichen, the red fleck of iron, the black stain of water, the sudden minute sparkle of a tiny grain of quartz. In the same way, Webern is concerned with the individual colours of sound. A note on the violin, probably plucked to isolate it, a note on the trumpet, probably muted to remove its military blatancy, two notes on the oboe, a sigh on the harp, a tiny glitter on the celesta. This is sound, pure sound, treated as an abstraction. To demonstrate his approach to sound he even orchestrated a Bach fugue giving each individual note of the theme to a different instrument, forcing the ear to accept the individual components of the line rather than the line itself.

Webern's first published composition was a Passacaglia for orchestra, one of the very few occasions in which he used a large orchestra. (Usually he preferred the more subtle colouring of a small group of players.) A passacaglia is a piece in which the same theme is repeated over and over again, but always with different decorations around it. In this early work, Webern's theme is simplicity itself (Ex. 1), and there's only one note which is different from what Bach or Handel might have used.

Ex. 1

(Change the fourth bar from A flat to A natural and you have a totally 'classical' theme.)

He presents this much with just the strings playing pizzicato. Then the trumpet, muted as it so often is in Webern's music, takes over the theme, while a flute provides a sadly musing counter-melody and the lower strings put in highly imaginative harmonies. Next the clarinet launches into a freer, more rhapsodic type of melody while the basic theme recedes into the background. It's still there for honour's sake, but it's now stated on off-beat notes on the harp, almost inaudible. The music continues, growing more positive in its outlines, and sometimes indulging in quite dramatic gestures but always you can feel the same skeleton, the bone-structure of the passacaglia theme, continuing through the rapidly shifting moods of the music. In the fifth variation we find the first inklings of the real Webern style, the quietness, the strange little ghost-like phrases that flitter across the score, and a feeling that despite the severity of the form, the music is on the verge of disintegration. And in a way, this is true, for Webern was on the brink of an extraordinary new world. No man has ever cut himself off so completely from the language of his predecessors, and it's this fact in particular that makes me want to underline the loneliness of all great innovators. When Beethoven pushed the boundaries of music back further than anyone had imagined, he set himself apart, and his deafness might be taken as a symbol of his withdrawal from the rest of the world. I'm not suggesting for a moment that Webern in the long run will ever be considered as great as Beethoven, but he had the courage of Beethoven, he had the same single-minded devotion to what he believed to be true and right, and so he shared with Beethoven the isolation of genius. Now this sense of isolation is reflected in much of his music; it's the music of loneliness. Even the notes themselves are alone, for often a player finds that the part in front of him is no more than a series of isolated dots with great chasms of silence between each one.

The second of his *Five pieces for string quartet* (Op. 5) is a mere fourteen bars long, lasting barely a minute; but one cannot dismiss it as purely cerebral. It has the most intense emotional quality and its yearning is eloquently conveyed in the sad groping phrases of the viola at the start.

It must be admitted that his music seldom concerns itself with the normal. There is always a certain neurotic quality, whether the sudden frenzy of hysteria or the brooding melancholy of the introvert. We find this even in one of his most approachable works, the *Six pieces for orchestra* (Op. 6)— twenty-nine pages in all! The music is extremely imaginative, full of nightmare images and fantasy. Each piece is extremely short by the usual standards of orchestral composition and it may be helpful to regard them as dreams. For instance the third piece inhabits a strange world of silence in which it is easy to imagine we are exploring the deserted colonnades of a crumbling underwater city while the ocean moves above us, cutting off the inhabited world. The fourth piece starts with some extraordinary distant clanking sounds which continue throughout; then sudden stabs of horror, like a hand clamped over your mouth while you're asleep; a mocking dance on a flute; a funeral procession, punctuated by the heavy beat of a drum; lastly a relentless grinding dissonance, ending with the swift blade of the guillotine. It is a vision as strange as those we find in the Berlioz *Symphonie Fantastique* translated into twentieth–century terms.

As he developed an ever more personal style Webern carried concentration to an extreme. It may be helpful to make an unexpected comparison. The first composer to attempt to condense a really profound emotional content into a single page was Chopin. In his preludes Chopin distils emotions, reducing them to their very essence. Each prelude tends to be a single emotional entity, even using one type of figure throughout. In this respect he was flying in the face of all his contemporaries who were tending to move to ever larger forms with ever increasing extremes of emotional contrast. Compare a Chopin prelude with Liszt's *Damnation of Faust*, Berlioz's *Romeo and Juliet*, or the late Tchaikovsky symphonies and you will see what I mean about operating on a different time-scale. A Chopin prelude is like an emotion put under a sort of microscope, examined in such close detail that to extend the view would overwhelm one. In his very different language, Webern does the same thing. Apart from the language, though, the other important difference is that even within his very brief time-scale Webern will introduce a much wider variety of subject-matter and of tempo than Chopin allows. A variation of speed and mood acceptable within the large framework of a movement from a Mahler symphony becomes almost unbearable when the piece only lasts a minute or so. The lack of emotional preparation for the changes of mood leaves us bewildered unless we allow ourselves to be manipulated very rapidly.

The greatest fallacy in approaching his music is to regard it as primarily intellectual. It is truer to say that its emotional content is so intense that it had to be subjected to the most severe restraint to be at all acceptable. This restraint he found in the ruthless application of 'serial' techniques even though he must have been well aware that he was alienating the vast majority of ordinary concertgoers. Even he could not have guessed how enormously influential his music was to become in the post-war years; but then, as he said at the conclusion of one of his lectures, 'There is no other way'.

ACKNOWLEDGMENTS

In the course of preparing a book of this nature it is obviously wise to check facts as thoroughly as possible. Opinions remain my own and I hope that I have made clear the difference between speculation and verifiable fact. Needless to say, *The New Grove* has been a valuable source in general terms, as have the admirable *Pelican* books on symphonies and concertos, both edited by Ralph Hill; but the short bibliography below lists some other *aides-mémoire* that I have consulted.

BACH
Malcolm Boyd. (Master Musicians, J. M. Dent, 1983.) Schweitzer. (A & C Black)

BEETHOVEN
Essays in Musical Analysis: D. F. Tovey. (O.U.P., 1935.) *The Nine Symphonies of Beethoven*: A. Hopkins. (Heinemann, 1981.)

BERG
The Second Viennese School: Rognoni. (John Calder, 1977.)

BRAHMS
His life and work: Geiringer. (Allen and Unwin, 1948.)

BRITTEN
Michael Kennedy. (Master Musicians, J. M. Dent, 1981.)

CHOPIN
A Biography; Adam Zamoyski. (Collins, 1979.)

DEBUSSY
Edward Lockspeiser. (Master Musicians, J. M. Dent, 1936.)

DVOŘÁK
Alec Robertson. (Master Musicians, J. M. Dent, 1945.)

ELGAR
An Elgar Companion ed. Redwood. (Sequoia, 1982.) *Life and Works*: Basil Maine (Bell, 1933.)

FRANCK
Five Great French Composers: Donald Brook (Rockliff, 1946.)

HAYDN	H. C. Robbins Landon. (Thames and Hudson, 1976–81.)
HOLST	*Gustav Holst*: Imogen Holst. (O.U.P., 1938.) *The Music of Gustav Holst*: Imogen Holst. (O.U.P., 1951.)
IVES	*Charles Ives and his Music*: Henry and Sidney Cowell. (O.U.P., 1955.) *Charles Ives and his America*: Frank R. Rossiter. (Gollancz, 1976.)
KODÁLY	*The Selected Writings of Zoltán Kodály*: ed. F. Bónis. (Eng. trans. Boosey & Hawkes, 1974.)
MAHLER	*Mahler*: Kurt Blaukopf. (Allen Lane, 1973.) *Gustav Mahler*: Neville Cardus. (Gollancz, 1972.) *Mahler*: Michael Kennedy. (Master Musicians, Dent, 1974.) *Gustav Mahler* (2 vols): Donald Mitchell. (Faber, 1958 and 1975.)
MENDELSSOHN	*Selected Letters*: ed. G. Selden-Goth. (Paul Elek, 1946.)
PROKOFIEV	*Prokofiev by Prokofiev*. (Macdonald, 1979.)
RAKHMANINOV	*Rakhmaninov*: Geoffrey Norris. (Master Musicians, Dent, 1976.) *Rachmaninoff's Recollections*: O. von Riesemann. (Allen & Unwin, 1934.)
RAVEL	*Ravel*: Norman Demuth. (Master Musicians, Dent, 1947.) *Ravel*: Vladimir Jankelevitch. (John Calder, 1959.) *Ravel. Life and Works*: Rollo H. Myers. (Duckworth, 1960.)
SCHOENBERG	*Schoenberg*: Anthony Payne. (O.U.P., 1968.) *Arnold Schoenberg*: H. H. Stuckenschmidt. (John Calder, 1959.)
SIBELIUS	*Jean Sibelius*: Karl Ekman. (Holger, Schildt, 1935.) *Sibelius*: Cecil Gray. (O.U.P., 1931.) *Sibelius, a personal portrait*: Santeri Levas. (Dent, 1972.)
SHOSTAKOVICH	*Shostakovich, the man and his music*: ed. Christopher Norris. (Lawrence & Wishart, 1982.) *Shostakovich*: Norman Kay. (O.U.P., 1971.)
STRAUSS	*Strauss*: Michael Kennedy. (Master Musicians, Dent, 1976.)
STRAVINSKY	*Stravinsky*: Roman Vlad. (O.U.P., 1960.)

	Stravinsky: Eric Walter White. (John Lehmann, 1947.)
TCHAIKOVSKY	*Tchaikovsky*: John Warrack. (Hamish Hamilton, 1973.)
TIPPETT	*Tippett*: Ian Kemp. (Eulenberg, 1984.)
	Michael Tippett: David Matthews. (Faber, 1980.)
	Music of the Angels: Tippett. (Eulenberg, 1980.)
VAUGHAN WILLIAMS	*Vaughan Williams*: James Day. (Master Musicians, Dent, 1961.)
	Musical trends in the Twentieth century: Norman Demuth. (Rockliff, 1952.)

I have also made use of selected passages from my broadcast series 'Talking about Music'.

I should like to thank Beatrix Taylor for her great help in producing an exemplary typescript, and Tabitha Collingbourne for her preparation of the music examples.